U.S. REAL GDP AND ITS COMPONENTS

Year	GDP	Personal Consumption Expenditures	Gross Private Domestic Investment	Government Consumption and Gross Investment	Net Exports
			(billions of 1992 dollars)		
1959	2,210.2	1,394.6	271.7	618.5	-34.7
1960	2,262.9	1,432.6	270.5	617.2	-21.3
1961	2,314.3	1,461.5	267.6	647.2	-19.0
1962	2,454.8	1,533.8	302.1	686.0	-26.5
1963	2,559.4	1,596.6	321.6	701.9	-22.7
1964	2,708.4	1,692.3	348.3	715.9	-15.9
1965	2,881.1	1,799.1	397.2	737.6	-27.4
1966	3,069.2	1,902.0	430.6	804.6	-40.8
1967	3,147.2	1,958.6	411.8	865.6	-50.1
1968	3,293.9	2,070.2	433.3	892.4	-67.2
1969	3,393.6	2,147.5	458.3	887.5	-71.3
1970	3,397.6	2,197.8	426.1	866.8	-65.0
1971	3,510.0	2,279.5	474.9	851.0	-75.8
1972	3,702.3	2,415.9	531.8	854.1	-89.0
1973	3,916.3	2,532.6	595.5	848.4	-63.0
1974	3,891.2	2,514.7	546.5	862.9	-35.5
1975	3,873.9	2,570.0	446.6	876.3	-7.2
1976	4,082.9	2,714.3	537.4	876.8	-39.9
1977	4,273.6	2,829.8	622.1	884.7	-64.2
1978	4,503.0	2,951.6	693.4	910.6	-65.5
1979	4,630.6	3,020.2	709.7	924.9	-45.3
1980	4,615.0	3,009.7	628.3	941.4	10.1
1981	4,720.7	3,046.4	686.0	947.7	5.6
1982	4,620.3	3,081.5	587.2	960.1	-14.1
1983	4,803.7	3,240.6	642.1	987.3	-63.3
1984	5,140.1	3,407.6	833.4	1,018.4	-127.3
1985	5,323.5	3,566.5	823.8	1,080.1	-147.9
1986	5,487.7	3,708.7	811.8	1,135.0	-163.9
1987	5,649.5	3,822.3	821.5	1,165.9	-156.2
1988	5,865.2	3,972.7	828.2	1,180.9	-114.4
1989	6,062.0	4,064.6	863.5	1,213.9	-82.7
1990	6,136.3	4,132.2	815.0	1,250.4	-61.9
1991	6,079.4	4,105.8	738.1	1,258.0	-22.3
1992	6,244.4	4,219.8	790.4	1,263.8	-29.5
1993	6,389.6	4,343.6	863.6	1,252.1	-70.2
1994	6,610.7	4,486.0	975.7	1,252.3	-104.6
1995	6,742.1	4,595.3	991.5	1,251.9	-98.8
1996	6,928.4	4,714.1	1,069.1	1,257.9	-114.4
1997	7,191.4	4,869.7	1,192.2	1,270.6	-142.1

U.S. NOMINAL GDP AND ITS COMPONENTS

Year	GDP	Personal Consumption Expenditures	Gross Private Domestic Investment	Government Purchases	Net Exports
		(billions of dollars)			
1959	507.2	318.1	78.8	112.0	-1.7
1960	526.6	332.2	78.8	113.2	2.4
1961	544.8	342.6	77.9	120.9	3.4
1962	585.2	363.4	87.9	131.4	2.4
1963	617.4	383.0	93.4	137.7	3.3
1964	663.0	411.4	101.7	144.4	5.5
1965	719.1	444.3	118.0	153.0	3.9
1966	787.8	481.9	130.4	173.6	1.9
1967	833.6	509.5	128.0	194.6	1.4
1968	910.6	559.8	139.9	212.1	-1.3
1969	982.2	604.7	155.0	223.8	-1.2
1970	1,035.6	648.1	150.2	236.1	1.2
1971	1,125.4	702.5	176.0	249.9	-3.0
1972	1,237.3	770.7	205.6	268.9	-8.0
1973	1,382.6	851.6	242.9	287.6	.6
1974	1,496.9	931.2	245.6	323.2	-3.1
1975	1,630.6	1,029.1	225.4	362.6	13.6
1976	1,819.0	1,148.8	286.6	385.9	-2.3
1977	2,026.9	1,277.1	356.6	416.9	-23.7
1978	2,291.4	1,428.8	430.8	457.9	-26.1
1979	2,557.5	1,593.5	480.9	507.1	-24.0
1980	2,784.2	1,760.4	465.9	572.8	-14.9
1981	3,115.9	1,941.3	556.2	633.4	-15.0
1982	3,242.1	2,076.8	501.1	684.8	-20.5
1983	3,514.5	2,283.4	547.1	735.7	-51.7
1984	3,902.4	2,492.3	715.6	796.6	-102.0
1985	4,180.7	2,704.8	715.1	875.0	-114.2
1986	4,422.2	2,892.7	722.5	938.5	-131.5
1987	4,692.3	3,094.5	747.2	992.8	-142.1
1988	5,049.6	3,349.7	773.9	1,032.0	-106.1
1989	5,438.7	3,594.8	829.2	1,095.1	-80.4
1990	5,743.8	3,839.3	799.7	1,176.1	-71.3
1991	5,916.7	3,975.1	736.2	1,225.9	-20.5
1992	6,244.4	4,219.8	790.4	1,263.8	-29.5
1993	6,558.1	4,459.2	876.2	1,283.4	-60.7
1994	6,947.0	4,717.0	1,007.9	1,313.0	-90.9
1995	7,265.4	4,957.7	1,038.2	1,355.5	-86.0
1996	7,636.0	5,207.6	1,116.5	1,406.7	-94.8
1997	8,083.4	5,488.6	1,237.6	1,453.9	-96.7

MACROECONOMICS

MACROECONOMICS

AN INTEGRATED APPROACH

SECOND EDITION

ALAN J. AUERBACH AND LAURENCE J. KOTLIKOFF

THE MIT PRESS • CAMBRIDGE, MASSACHUSETTS • LONDON, ENGLAND

©1998 Massachusetts Institute of Technology

This book was set in Melior on the Monotype "Prism Plus" PostScript Imagesetter by Asco Trade Typesetting Ltd., Hong Kong, and was printed and bound in the United States of America.

Library of Congress Cataloging-in-Publication Data

Auerbach, Alan J.
   Macroeconomics : an integrated approach / Alan J. Auerbach and
Laurence J. Kotlikoff. — 2nd ed.
     p.   cm.
   Includes bibliographical references and index.
   ISBN 0-262-01170-0 (alk. paper)
   1. Macroeconomics. I. Kotlikoff, Laurence J. II. Title.
HB172.5.A85   1998
   339—dc21   98-6765
                                                  CIP

For Alex, Andy, David, and Ethan

Alan J. Auerbach is Robert D. Burch Professor of Economics and Law and Director of the Burch Center for Tax Policy and Public Finance at the University of California, Berkeley. He is also a Research Associate of the National Bureau of Economic Research. He received his B.A. from Yale University and his Ph.D. from Harvard University, where his dissertation won the Wells Prize. His teaching career includes stints at Harvard University and the University of Pennsylvania.

Auerbach has served as Deputy Chief of Staff (Chief Economist) for the Joint Committee of the U.S. Congress. He has testified frequently before congressional committees on a variety of topics including tax reform, national saving and investment, international competitiveness, mergers and acquisitions, and budget policy. He is a Fellow of the Econometric Society and a past member of the Executive Committee of the American Economic Association.

Professor Auerbach's numerous papers on investment, taxation, finance, social security, saving, and fiscal policy have appeared in a wide variety of top journals and several books. He is a past Editor of the *Journal of Economic Perspectives*, and currently serves on the editorial boards of several other journals.

Laurence J. Kotlikoff is Professor of Economics at Boston University, Research Associate of the National Bureau of Economic Research, Fellow of the Econometric Society, and a member of the Executive Committee of the American Economic Association. He received his B.A. from the University of Pennsylvania in 1973 and his Ph.D. in Economics from Harvard University in 1977. Before joining Boston University, Kotlikoff taught at the University of California, Los Angeles and Yale University. In 1981–82 Professor Kotlikoff was a Senior Economist with the President's Council of Economic Advisers.

Professor Kotlikoff has served as a consultant to the U.S. and other governments, international financial institutions, and private corporations. He has provided expert testimony on numerous occasions to committees of Congress, including the Senate Finance Committee, the House Ways and Means Committee, and the Joint Economic Committee.

Professor Kotlikoff is author or coauthor of five books and numerous journal articles. He also contributes to the policy debate through editorials and radio and television appearances. A former Associate Editor of the *American Economic Review*, Kotlikoff is currently an Associate Editor of the *Japanese Economic Review*.

Contents

LIST OF FIGURES … xi
LIST OF TABLES … xiii
PROLOGUE: THE QUESTIONS OF MACROECONOMICS … xv

PART ONE FROM MICRO TO MACRO:
MODELING INCOME DETERMINATION AND GROWTH … 1

CHAPTER 1 OUTPUT, INPUTS, AND GROWTH … 3

2 THE DYNAMIC SUPPLY OF INPUTS … 29

3 THE DYNAMIC DEMAND FOR INPUTS AND THE EVOLUTION
OF OUTPUT … 53

4 ECONOMIC FLUCTUATIONS … 85

5 THE MEASUREMENT OF OUTPUT AND PRICES … 111

TWO FISCAL AND MONETARY POLICY … 139

6 FISCAL POLICY, SAVING, AND GROWTH … 141

7 MONEY AND PRICES IN THE CLOSED ECONOMY … 169

THREE ECONOMIC FLUCTUATIONS … 199

8 THE KEYNESIAN MODEL OF PRICE AND WAGE RIGIDITY … 201

9 UNDERSTANDING RECESSIONS … 229

10 THE NATURE AND COSTS OF UNEMPLOYMENT … 265

11 COUNTERCYCLICAL POLICY … 295

FOUR THE INTERNATIONAL ECONOMY … 321

12 SAVING AND GROWTH IN THE INTERNATIONAL ECONOMY … 323

13 MONEY, EXCHANGE RATES, AND POLICY IN THE
OPEN ECONOMY … 347

FIVE ENRICHING THE MODEL … 377

14 THE BANKING SYSTEM, THE FEDERAL RESERVE, AND THE
MONEY SUPPLY … 379

15 SAVING BEHAVIOR AND CREDIT MARKETS … 411

16 FINANCIAL MARKETS AND THE INVESTMENT DECISION … 433

INDEX … 457

FIGURES

1.1   U.S. Real GDP, 1929–1996
1.2   U.S. Real GDP per Capita, 1929–1996
1.3   U.S. Private Business Capital Stock, 1950 and 1994
1.4   U.S. Adult Population and Employment, 1950–1996
1.5   Sources of U.S. Business Sector GDP Growth, 1948–1994
1.6   Capital-Labor Ratio and Technology Determine Output per Worker
1.7   U.S. Real Output and Real Labor Compensation per Hour, 1960–1996
1.8   Growth in Labor Productivity, Multifactor Productivity, and the Capital-Labor Ratio, 1948–1994
1.9   Average Annual Growth Rates of per Capita GDP, 1960–1994
1.10   Real GDP per Capita in Five Developing Countries, 1960–1992
1.11   Per Capita GDP: Growth Versus Level, 1960–1992
2.1   The Two-Period Model's Time Line
2.2   1990 Distributions of U.S. Wealth and Population by Age
2.3   Distribution of Hours Worked per Week. March 1993
2.4   Lifetime Budget Constraint
2.5   Indifference Curves
2.6   Utility Maximization
2.7   U.S. Rates of National Saving and Domestic Investment, 1959–1996
2.8   Share of Population Age 65 and Over in the United States, Germany, and Japan
2.9   Projected Growth in the U.S. Capital-Labor Ratio Due to Population Aging
3.1   Shares of Employment and Establishments by Number of Employees, 1994
3.2   Dependence of the Wage and Rate on Capital-Labor Ratio
3.3   Dependence of the Interest Rate on the Capital-Labor Ratio
3.4   Budget Constraints of Successive Generations
3.5   Living Standards in Japan and Germany Relative to that of the United States, 1950–1992
3.6   U.S., Japanese, and German National Saving Rates, 1960–1997
3.7   Transition Diagram
3.8   Adding the 45° Line to the Transition Diagram
3.9   Using the Transition Diagram: A Shortcut
3.10   Transition Following an Epidemic
3.11   Transition Following an Increase in the Propensity to Consume
3.12   Refresher
4.1   Real GDP Since 1960
4.2   Volatility of Real GNP
4.3   Growth in Real Personal Income, United States and California
4.4   Index of Leading Indicators, 1948–1996
4.5   Overtime Hours and Capacity Utilization in Manufacturing
4.6   Consumption and Investment Growth Rates
4.7   Growth Rates of Real GDP: United States, Europe and Japan, 1988–1996
4.8   Nominal GDP, 1982–1992
4.9   Business Cycles or Random Walks? A Comparison
4.10   An Increase in the Level of Technology
4.11   The Accelerator
5.1   The Circular Flow of Income and Output
5.2   Saving, Investment, and the Trade Balance, 1980–1996
5.3   Inflation Rates Since 1960
5.4   Real GDP Growth Rates: The Impact of Chain Weighting
5.5   Nominal and Real Interest Rates, 1970–1996
6.1   Expenditures and Receipts, All U.S. Governments, 1996
6.2   Federal Receipts and Expenditures, 1959–1997
6.3   Components of Generational Accounts
6.4   Lifetime Net Tax Rates of Living and Future Generations
6.5   Transition Equation with Fiscal Policy
6.6   Government Purchases Financed by the Young
6.7   Percentage Increase in Average Consumption by Age Group, 1960–1961 to 1987–1990
6.8   U.S. Private and Government Gross Investment Rates, 1959–1996
7.1   Money Stock (M1) and Price Level, 1959–1996
7.2   Inflation and Real Money Balances During the German Hyperinflation
7.3   Annual Rate of Growth of the Price Level, 1870–1996
7.4   Impact on the Capital-Labor Ratio of Printing Money to Make Transfers to the Young at Time 0
8.1   Distribution of Nominal Wage Growth
8.2   LM Curve
8.3   IS Curve
8.4   Equilibrium with Rigid Prices
8.5   Monetary Policy with Rigid Prices
8.6   Fiscal Policy with Rigid Prices
8.7   Nominal Wage Rigidity and Unemployment
8.8   Aggregate Supply Curve
8.9   Monetary Policy with Rigid Nominal Wages
8.10   Fiscal Policy with Rigid Nominal Wages
8.11   Aggregate Demand Curve and Impact of Policy
9.1   U.S. Phillips Curve, 1950–1969
9.2   Output Determination in the Keynesian Model
9.3   Keynesians' Permanent Inflation-Unemployment Trade-off
9.4   Shifting U.S. Phillips Curve, 1950–1996
9.5   A Shifting Phillips Curve Nullifies the Inflation-Unemployment Trade-off
9.6   Misperception Theory's Explanation of Employment Increases in Response to a Monetary Expansion
9.7   Oil Price Shocks and Postwar Recessions, 1947–1991
9.8   Output Shocks and Anticipated and Unanticipated Changes in the Money Supply
9.9   Illustrating Multiple Equilibria in the Two-Period Model
9.10   Index of Consumer Confidence in Recent Recessions
10.1   Unemployment and Labor Force Participation Rates Since 1950
10.2   Labor Market Dynamics

10.3   Types of Unemployment Since 1970
10.4   Long-Term Unemployment and the Unemployment Rate
10.5   Efficiency Wages and Unemployment
10.6   Unemployment Rates, by Sex, Since 1970
10.7   Percentage of Female Employees, by Industry, February 1996
10.8   Unemployment Rates, by Age and Race, Since 1972
10.9   Cost of Voluntary Unemployment
10.10   Cost of Involuntary Unemployment
10.11   Unemployment and Crime
10.12   GDP Growth and the Unemployment Rate, 1960–1996
10.13   Unemployment in the United States and Europe, 1970–1996
11.1   Real GDP During the Depression
11.2   Growth Rates of Real GDP and M1
11.3   Causes of Declining Output
11.4   Velocity and Real Output
11.5   Fiscal Policy During the Depression
11.6   Dating the 1990–1991 Recession
11.7   Stagflation, 1973–1975
11.8   Productivity Shocks, Output, and Unemployment
11.9   Problem of Dynamic Inconsistency
12.1   Exports, Imports, and Net Exports, 1960–1996
12.2   Equilibrium in Autarky
12.3   Factor-Price Equalization
12.4   Real Interest Rates for the G-5 Nations, 1980–1996
12.5   Two-Country Equilibrium
12.6   Increase in U.S. Consumption
12.7   U.S. Net Foreign Asset Position, 1982–1996
12.8   Recovery from War: Closed Versus Open Economy
12.9   Japan's Trade Balance, 1960–1997
12.10   Net U.S. International Investment, Percentage of GNP, 1873–1931
13.1   U.S. Nominal Exchange Rates, 1951–1996
13.2   Index of U.S. Monthly Nominal and Real Exchange Rates with Japan, January 1973–August 1997
13.3   Percentage Change in Foreign-U.S. Exchange Rates Less Difference Between Foreign and U.S. Inflation Rates
13.4   Open Economy IS Curve
13.5   Why Monetary Policy Is More Effective in an Open Economy

13.6   Monetary Expansion in a Small, Open Economy
13.7   Impact of an Increase in Liquidity Preference
14.1   Size and Composition of U.S. Monetary Aggregates, 1997
14.2   U.S. M1 Money Multiplier Since 1959
14.3   Transactions Associated with Printing Money to Buy *Air Force 2*
14.4   Federal Reserve Discount Rate and Federal Funds Rate, 1955–1996
14.5   Growth Rates of U.S. Monetary Aggregates, 1980–1996
14.6   Variability of Growth Rates of U.S. Monetary Aggregates and the Monetary Base, 1980–1996
14.7   U.S. Currency Holdings, Monetary Base, and M1, January 1929–December 1933
14.8   Money Supply Targeting in the Face of Nominal Shocks
14.9   Interest Rate Targeting in the Face of Real Shocks
14.10   Growth Rates of M1 and Real GDP, the Inflation Rate, and the Federal Funds Rate, October 1979–October 1982
14.11   Is Monetary Policy Endogenous?
15.1   Franco's Budget Constraint with Certain Second-Period Income
15.2   Franco's Precautionary Saving
15.3   Income Uncertainty and the Capital-Labor Transition Curve
15.4   Bequests and the Capital-Labor Transition Curve
15.5   Annuitized and Nonannuitized Resources of the U.S. Elderly, 1962 and 1983
15.6   Budget Constraint of a Type B Individual
15.7   Borrowing and the Capital-Labor Transition Curve
16.1   Components of Fixed Investment, 1960 and 1996
16.2   Capital Stock Determination: The Corporate Tax
16.3   Housing Construction in the 1980s
16.4   Bond Yield Spread, 1970–1996
16.5   U.S. Corporate Finance Since 1980
16.6   Output Versus Profits, 1960–1996
16.7   Investment-GDP Ratios, by Type of Investment, 1960–1996
16.8   Office Vacancy Rates in U.S. Downtowns, April 1982–October 1992
16.9   Investment and the Value of U.S. Nonfinancial Corporations, 1987–1996

TABLES

2.1   U.S. Private Domestic Net Worth, 1994

3A.1   Complete Model for Any Time t

3.1   Illustrative Transition Path

3.2   Transition Path Following an Epidemic

4.1   Economic Fluctuations Since 1854

4.2   Real GDP Growth Rates, by Industry

4.3   Components of the Index of Leading Indicators

4.4   Response to a Technology Shock

5.1   National Income Accounting: An Example

5.2   GDP, NDP, and National Income, 1996

5.3   From National Income to Personal Income, 1996

5.4   Components of GDP: Types of Output and Uses of Income, 1996

6.1   Requiring the Young to Pay for Government Purchases

7.1   An Illustrative Transition Path: The Two-Period Model with Money

8.1   Impact of Monetary and Fiscal Policy with Rigid Prices: A Summary

9.1   Illustrating a Real Business Cycle

9.2   Comparing the Predictions of the Kydland-Prescott Real Business Cycle Model with the U.S. Data

9.3   Alternative Explanations of Recessions and Their Policy Implications

10.1   Theories of Unemployment: Causes, Evidence, Costs, and Policy Responses

12.1   Transition Arising from Increased U.S. Consumption

12.2   The Transition Following a War: Closed Versus Open Economies

14.1   July 16, 1997, Balance Sheet of U.S. Commercial Banks

16.1   Private Investment in the United States, 1996

PROLOGUE
THE QUESTIONS OF MACROECONOMICS

Macroeconomics is the study of the economy's performance and the government's role in altering that performance. Macroeconomics departs from microeconomics in focusing on the whole economy rather than its constituent parts. Looking at the big picture requires asking big questions.

Why do economies grow at different rates? The answer is important, particularly to developing countries. In recent decades some developing countries have grown rapidly enough to join the developed world. Others have stagnated, leaving their populations in extreme poverty.

Does it matter that certain economies save and invest more than others? People who don't save end up poor. The same is true for countries. In recent years, the United States has saved a much lower fraction of its national income than other leading developed countries.

How do foreign trade and investment affect the domestic economy? This question has never been more important. International economies have become increasingly linked through the expansion of foreign trade and investment. Take the United States in the second half of the 1980s. During these years, foreigners were responsible for almost as much net investment in the United States as were United States citizens.

What causes recessions and their attendant high unemployment? This is the most intriguing and controversial issue in macroeconomics. It's also extremely important. Learning the cause of recessions could offer the key to their prevention and save jobs. During the Great Depression of the 1930s, one-quarter of all United States workers were unemployed. Since then, we've been spared depressions but not recessions, with unemployment rates reaching as high as 10 percent.

What is money and its economic function? At one level, the answer is trivial: money is simply the cash or checks we use to make purchases. But money plays a special role in influencing the level and growth of prices and output, leading governments to try to control its supply.

How do monetary and fiscal policies affect the economy in the short and long runs? Governments use their ability to control the money supply and to tax, borrow, and spend as a means of influencing economic growth and fluctuations. Understanding these policy tools and how well they operate is critical to reaching an informed judgment about macroeconomic policy.

What causes inflation? How does it relate to unemployment? Inflation—the rate at which prices rise over time—varies tremendously across countries. Some countries have nearly stable prices; others have inflation rates reaching 500 percent per month. Even in the United States, the inflation rate has varied over time, frequently rising as

Macroeconomics
The study of the economy's overall performance

unemployment falls. Macroeconomic policy is generally targeted to achieve particular inflation and unemployment rates.

What role do banks play in the economy? Anyone wishing to understand monetary aspects of the macroeconomy must consider the role of the banking system. As one of many financial institutions that intermediate between suppliers and demanders of funds, banks take deposits and make loans. They also play a special role in determining the size of the money supply, which places them in a position to facilitate or impede the conduct of monetary policy.

What is the exchange rate, and how is it determined? An exchange rate determines the amount of foreign money that can be acquired in exchange for one unit of domestic money. Exchange rates are generally set in foreign exchange markets. Governments often intervene in these markets, buying or selling money in order to change the exchange rate. Since this intervention changes the money supply, exchange rate and monetary policies are interdependent. Learning about one necessitates learning about the other.

How do credit and insurance markets operate and alter macroeconomic outcomes? The public's ability to borrow through credit markets and to hedge risks by buying insurance influences a range of microeconomic decisions with potentially major macroeconomic implications. Understanding these markets is essential to grasping the way economies grow and fluctuate.

AN INTEGRATED APPROACH TO MACROECONOMICS

The seemingly unrelated questions listed above are, in fact, closely connected. The ability to borrow through credit markets, for example, influences how much a society saves, which in turn governs how much it invests and how fast it grows. Economic growth alters the public's demand for money and the rate of price inflation. And the inflation rate influences the choice of monetary and fiscal policies, which have their own independent effects on the economy's saving, investment, and growth.

Because these questions are connected, studying them requires a theoretical framework, or model, capable of linking the answers to each question to those of the others. Such an integrative approach is the hallmark of this textbook. It uses a single model—the life-cycle model—to explore and connect all of the central issues of macroeconomics.

The life-cycle model provides a set of building blocks that can be used to form a great variety of structures. These building blocks are the microeconomic behavior of households and firms. In building its macroeconomic structures on microeconomic foundations, the life-cycle model recognizes a fundamental fact of macroeconomic life: the macroeconomy must reflect the sum of its parts—the collective microeconomic behavior of households and firms.

The life-cycle model's linkage of macro- and microeconomics is one reason this book represents an integrated approach. But the text is integrated along other dimensions. It shows how short-run decisions and policies affect the economy's long-run growth path and how that long-run growth path constrains what short-run decisions are possible. It explores the links between foreign trade and domestic investment, between fiscal and monetary policies, and between goods and financial markets. It considers the economy's potential to sustain full employment as well as experience unemployment. Finally, it compares theoretical predictions with actual outcomes in order to test macroeconomic theory against macroeconomic fact.

MODELING MACROECONOMIC BEHAVIOR

Economists simplify reality to understand it.[1] This is particularly important in macroeconomics, a subject concerned with hundreds of national economies, thousands of markets, millions of firms, and hundreds of millions of workers. Anyone trying to understand all this complexity at once is likely to end up missing the forest for the trees. Accordingly, economists focus on the most important factors influencing economic outcomes, while ignoring what they believe to be minor details. Economists' models are thus simplified descriptions of reality. Good **economic models** capture key relationships.

    One approach to the complexity of the macroeconomy is to develop a separate and simple model for each economic issue. This approach, adopted in many other textbooks, fails to draw connections between key issues, such as the way an economy's openness to international trade alters its growth path. In contrast, our simple life-cycle model provides a unified framework for studying all the key issues of macroeconomics. The framework is very flexible. Indeed, most macroeconomic schools of thought can be illustrated in the life-cycle model simply by altering particular assumptions. For example, in studying what determines economic fluctuations, we can illustrate different explanations by assuming that some prices adjust slowly, as we do in Chapter 8, or that technology changes over time, as we do in Chapter 4. It's the same model, implemented with different assumptions.

Economic model
A simplified description of key aspects of a real economic issue

1 *Economists' tendency to make overly simplifying assumptions is captured by a familiar fable. A physicist, an engineer, and an economist are stranded on a desert island with lots of canned food but no can opener. First, the physicist tries to open a can by heating it, but it explodes. Next, the engineer climbs a tree and drops a rock on a can, but it splatters far and wide. Finally the economist offers the solution: "Assume we have a can opener."*

THE LIFE-CYCLE MODEL

Our life-cycle model is dynamic. It describes the evolution of the economy over time in terms of the behavior of overlapping generations of individuals, each of whom lives for two periods: youth and old age. Mastering our model—its basic graphs and equations—is straightforward, requiring only a modicum of high school algebra. As with any other economic model, do not take ours too literally. Remember that we're trying

"SURE, WE'RE DEALING WITH TINY PARTICLES, BUT YOUR FORMULA IS JUST A SYMBOLIC REPRESENTATION."

©1994 by Sidney Harris

to capture essential relationships without too much confusing detail. We don't really think there are only two types of individuals in society (the young and the old), or that individuals differ only with respect to their age. But studying these two types of individuals is the simplest way to recognize the important differences between those who work and those who are retired, and between those who save and those who spend.

EVALUATING ECONOMIC THEORIES

Macroeconomics is a controversial discipline. In particular, economists differ sharply about the causes, severity, and cure for economic downturns. Choosing the right theory matters; theories come packaged with policy prescriptions, and the choice of a particular policy (including taking no action) can influence the incomes, employment, and welfare of millions of citizens.

Which theory best fits the facts? Unfortunately, economists usually can't conduct controlled experiments to compare their theoretical predictions with actual outcomes. Instead, they must rely on **natural experiments**—variations in actual economic conditions or policies—that help them judge alternative macroeconomic points of view. This book is full of U.S. and international case studies based on natural experiments. These case studies illustrate macroeconomic concepts and test alternative hypotheses.

Natural experiment
A naturally occurring variation in economic conditions or policies

For example, Chapter 9 evaluates different theories about the macroeconomic importance of the price of oil by considering what happened to the U.S. economy in periods when oil prices rose or fell sharply. Chapter 11 evaluates the effectiveness of monetary and fiscal policy in reducing economic fluctuations by comparing the relative stability of the economy during periods when the degree of government activism differed. And Chapter 16 evaluates how the banking system influences investment by comparing investment in Japan and the United States, whose banking institutions are quite different.

SUMMARY

Macroeconomics is a fascinating and challenging subject. This book provides a systematic way to interpret macroeconomic outcomes, understand various policy proposals, and appreciate how individuals and firms fit into the big picture. We have endeavored to make the story as clear as possible so that, in combination with your own hard work, it can make mastering macroeconomics not just possible but also enjoyable.

FROM MICRO TO MACRO: MODELING INCOME DETERMINATION AND GROWTH

OUTPUT, INPUTS, AND GROWTH

INTRODUCTION

Advanced economies produce a multitude of goods and services ranging from pencils and haircuts to supercomputers and organ transplants. The means used to produce these commodities are as varied as the commodities themselves, but certain features are common to all production processes. All production processes use basic *inputs*, such as workers, managers, machines, and factories, to generate final products—the *outputs*. They all also use a method—a **technology**—for combining inputs to make outputs.

Macroeconomists are concerned with a country's total production of final goods and services—its **gross domestic product**, or **GDP**. When a nation's output grows faster than its population, its standard of living rises. There is more output and, on average, more output per person. Why does output grow? Why does it grow faster in some countries than others? Answering these questions is a key goal of macroeconomics and one we begin to address in this chapter. The answers depend, in part, on the availability and quality of inputs, the efficiency with which inputs are combined to produce output, and scientific and engineering advances that permit producing more output from given amounts of inputs.

The answers also depend on the state of the economy. As the Great Depression of the 1930s made painfully clear, there is no guarantee that available inputs will be utilized, let alone utilized efficiently, or that very much production will actually take place. Between August 1929, the month the Great Depression began in the United States, and March 1933, when it reached its depth, U.S. GDP declined in *real terms* (after adjusting for changes in the prices of the various commodities included in GDP) by 27 percent. Since there was very little change in available inputs and technology over this period, the decline in *real GDP* represented a failure of the economy to produce with the resources it had on hand. Understanding why slowdowns in production occur and how to prevent them is another important goal of macroeconomics. So is understanding how real output evolves during more normal economic times.

Technology
Methods of combining inputs to produce output

Gross domestic product (GDP)
The total value of all final goods and services produced in an economy during a given year

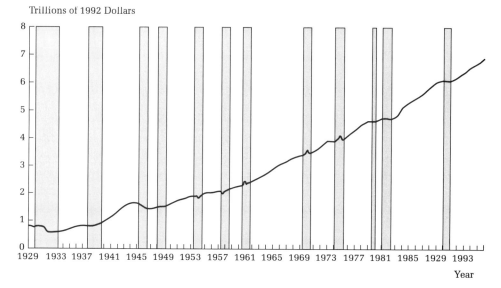

FIGURE 1.1 U.S. REAL GDP, 1929–1996
Since the early 1930s, U.S. real gross domestic product has risen in most years. The main exceptions, called recessions, are indicated by the shaded areas in the figure. Despite these recessions, real GDP in 1996 was nine times larger than in 1929.

Source: Bureau of Economic Analysis.

Figure 1.1 graphs U.S. real GDP in the years since 1929. The values of real GDP are expressed in "1992 dollars." This means the various goods and services entering the calculation of real GDP in particular years are valued using the prices for those commodities that prevailed in 1992. Hence, a "1992 dollar" refers to the amount of goods and services a dollar could purchase at 1992 prices.

The figure shows that real GDP has risen steadily since the Great Depression, with the exception of a number of short-lived declines, the sharpest of which occurred in the aftermath of World War II. Periods of declining output, which are shaded in the figure, are called *recessions*. Notwithstanding the Great Depression and subsequent recessions, U.S. real GDP was six times larger in 1993 than in 1929. This remarkable increase in output was certainly not due to changes in the utilization of a fixed amount of inputs with a given technology, but rather to an increased availability of inputs and improvements in technology.

Economists refer to increases over time in real GDP as *economic growth*. This chapter describes how more inputs and improvements in their productivity produce economic growth. Future chapters explain how input availability changes through time and how recessions and *expansions*—periods of positive growth—affect the utilization of available inputs.

Spelling out how more inputs and better technology translate into more output requires describing the production process. After doing so, we'll explore the implications of economic growth for countries' living standards and ask whether economic growth is leading to more or less equality in living standards between developed and developing countries. We'll also present a case study on the sources of U.S. economic growth and consider why the productivity of U.S. workers has grown so slowly in recent years. Finally, we'll consider whether the U.S. standard of living is falling behind those of other industrialized countries.

Here are some specific questions we'll address:

- How do economists conceptualize the production process?

- What are the key inputs in production?

- Why do small differences in growth rates lead to large differences in living standards?

- What is growth accounting, and what are its lessons for postwar U.S. economic growth?

- How do economists measure workers' productivity?

- What explains the recent slow growth in the productivity of U.S. workers?

- Is economic growth widening the gap between developed and developing nations?

HOW ECONOMIC GROWTH AFFECTS LIVING STANDARDS

The most familiar measure of a country's living standard is its *per capita GDP*—its output per person. According to Figure 1.2, U.S. per capita GDP rose from $6,495 in 1929 to $26,019 in 1996. To adjust for inflation, each of these dollar amounts is expressed in terms of the amount of real goods and services they could have purchased in 1992. Thus, on a per person basis, America's standard of living has quadrupled since 1929.

On the average, per capita GDP grew 2.2 percent per year between 1929 and 1996. Had this growth rate been twice as large, U.S. per capita output would have risen to $97,884 by 1996, leaving Americans with a living standard almost four times larger than they actually enjoyed. Raising a country's growth rate by just a few percentage points can make a substantial difference to its living standard over time. Long-run living standards are so sensitive to growth rates because growth differences *compound*; an extra bit of output this period means more than just this extra bit of output in future years because this extra bit will itself grow.

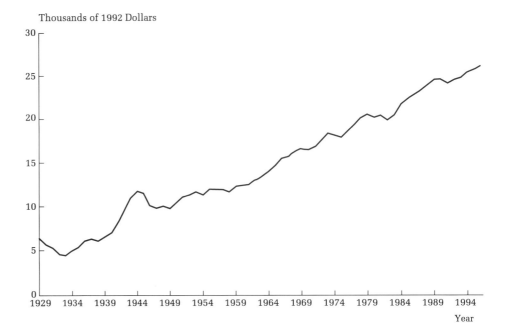

Thousands of 1992 Dollars

F<small>IGURE</small> 1.2 U.S. R<small>EAL</small> GDP P<small>ER</small> C<small>APITA</small>, 1929–1996
Measured on a per person basis, the U.S. standard of living has quadrupled since 1929.

Source: Bureau of Economic Analysis.

Consider what happens if $100 grows for two years at 10 percent per year. After the first year, the $100 has grown by $10 to $110. After the second, the $110 has grown by $11 to $121 (which equals $100 times 1.10 times 1.10). Growth is larger in the second year because the extra $10 accumulated after the first year also grows by 10 percent. If we extend this example and let $100 grow at 10 percent for ten years, we don't end up with 100 percent more money (which is 10 percent times 10), but rather 159 percent more. Because of compounding, we end up with $259 rather than $200.

MODELING PRODUCTION

To begin explaining the dynamic process by which output grows, we need to describe how economists conceptualize, or "model," production. Accordingly, we present a simple relationship known as the **Cobb-Douglas production function**, in which output depends on the amounts of two inputs employed, capital and labor, and on the efficiency with which they are used. **Labor** refers to the efforts supplied by workers, managers, and owners of business enterprises. Over time, population growth ensures that the amount of available labor will grow. At the same time, better training and education make the available labor more productive. **Capital** refers to the nonhuman

Cobb-Douglas production function
A mathematical relationship indicating how much output can be obtained from particular amounts of capital and labor, given a particular level of technology

Labor
The effort supplied by workers, managers, and owners of business enterprises

Capital
Buildings, equipment, inventories, residential structures, consumer durables, and other nonhuman inputs used to produce goods and services

inputs employed in production: buildings, machinery; business *inventories* of raw materials, parts, and finished goods; residential structures such as houses and apartment buildings; and *consumer durables*, such as refrigerators, televisions, and furniture. Another category of capital is land, an important input to agricultural production.

The Cobb-Douglas function describes the production of *final* goods, those that will not undergo further processing. It doesn't describe the production of intermediate inputs (such as wing assemblies for jet aircraft or integrated circuits for computers). As their names suggest, such inputs represent an intermediate stage of production that can safely be skipped for purposes of understanding growth in GDP, which, again, only measures the output of final goods and services.

THE COBB-DOUGLAS PRODUCTION FUNCTION

The Cobb-Douglas production function was named after Paul Douglas and Charles Cobb. Douglas was an economics professor who gave up academics to become U.S. senator from Illinois. In 1927, before running for office, he became intrigued by an empirical regularity in U.S. macroeconomic data: that the shares of output paid out as income to capital and labor appeared to be stable through time. Douglas realized that not all production functions, in the presence of competitive labor markets, would produce this result. So he asked his friend Charles Cobb, a mathematician, to help him derive a production function that did.

The result was a simple algebraic expression relating the amount of output produced during a particular time period to the contemporaneous inputs of capital and labor, as well as the prevailing level of technology. The function can be used to explain production over any time period. For example, in the two-period life-cycle model we will develop beginning in the next chapter, a period represents roughly 30 years, corresponding to the division of an adult's life into two 30-year periods of youth and old age.

What does the Cobb-Douglas function look like? Let Y stand for the amount of output produced, and let K and L be the amounts of capital and labor used in production. Finally, let A stand for the level of **multifactor productivity**, or simply productivity. As we will see, A measures how efficiently capital and labor are used together to produce output.

With these definitions, we can write the Cobb-Douglas function as

$$Y = AK^{\beta}L^{1-\beta}.$$

The exponent β (beta) is called a *parameter* of the production function. It is a fixed value that helps determine the function's characteristics. As shown in chapter 3, in a competitive economy operating with a Cobb-Douglas production function, the share of output paid by firms to the suppliers of capital turns out to equal β. It follows that $1 - \beta$ is the share of output paid to suppliers of labor (workers and managers). If β remains constant through time, the output shares of capital and labor will also remain constant, which is exactly the situation Cobb and Douglas were trying to explain.

Historically, capital's share of U.S. GDP has been remarkably close to 30 percent. Consequently, in using the Cobb-Douglas function, we'll assume that β equals .30.

Multifactor productivity
A measure of the ability of capital and labor to produce output

GETTING ACQUAINTED WITH THE COBB-DOUGLAS PRODUCTION FUNCTION

To get a feeling for the Cobb-Douglas function, let's try a few values for A, K, and L. First, set A equal to 10, K equal to 300, and L equal to 100.[1] Then

$$Y = 10 \times 300^{.30} \times 100^{.70} = 1{,}390.$$

Next, double the capital and labor inputs, leaving the level of productivity unchanged. Output doubles, since

$$Y = 10 \times (2 \times 300)^{.30} \times (2 \times 100)^{.70}$$
$$= 2 \times 10 \times 300^{.30} \times 100^{.70} = 2 \times 1{,}390.$$

This property of the Cobb-Douglas function—that a doubling of inputs leads to a doubling of outputs—is called *constant returns to scale*. In everyday language, constant returns means that increasing both inputs by a given percentage (in this case, 100 percent) leads to an equal percentage increase in output.

The Cobb-Douglas function also exhibits *diminishing returns* to each of the inputs, holding the other input fixed. For example, increase the capital input from 300 to 400, holding labor input constant at 100. Output will increase by 126 units, to a total of 1,516. Now increase capital by another 100 units; output will increase again, but this time by only 105 units. Add yet another 100 units of capital, and output will rise by 91 units. The fact that successive increments to output (126 followed by 105 followed by 91) diminish in size in response to equal 100-unit increments to capital is due to diminishing returns.

As more capital is added to a given amount of labor, output increases by smaller amounts. The same holds true for adding more labor to a fixed amount of capital. In either case, the input becomes less productive (produces smaller increases in output) the more of it we use. Note that we avoid diminishing returns and have constant returns if we increase both capital and labor by the same percentage.

MEASURING CAPITAL

In any modern economy, a wide variety of capital goods are used to help produce output. One category, called equipment, includes the metal-forming tools used in producing jet engines, the vans used to deliver pizza, and the printing presses that produced this book. Another category is business structures, which includes primarily office buildings, factories, and retail spaces. Land, inventories, and residential structures are also considered types of capital.

How can such an assortment of goods be combined into a single measure of capital? The usual approach is to convert them to constant dollar terms. In this case, we measure the real capital stock in 1987 dollars. Each different type of capital good in use in a particular year—each United Van Lines truck, each Chrysler Corporation

1 We can measure inputs and outputs in whatever units we'd like. For example, we can measure labor in number of workers, number of hours worked, or number of minutes worked by the workers. Changing the units or outputs changes the units of the technology coefficient, A. The adjustment of the units of A explains why we can relate output measured in units of, say, 1992 dollars to the inputs of capital and labor, measured in units of, say, 1992 dollars and hours worked, respectively.

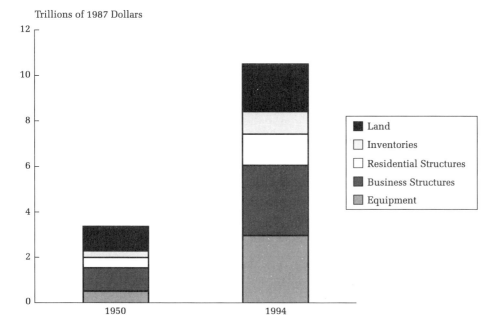

Trillions of 1987 Dollars

FIGURE 1.3 U.S. PRIVATE BUSINESS CAPITAL STOCK, 1950 and 1994
Between 1950 and 1994, the U.S. private business capital stock more than tripled and became more heavily weighted toward equipment.

Source: Bureau of Economic Analysis.

paint sprayer, each Holiday Inn hotel—is valued using its price in 1987. The idea is that changes in the constant dollar value of the capital stock fully reflect changes in the physical quantity of capital available.

Figure 1.3 shows how the U.S. business capital stock grew and changed in composition between 1950 and 1994. Measured in 1987 dollars, it more than tripled, rising from $3.3 trillion to over $10 trillion. This growth in the overall capital stock was far from uniform across different types of capital. For example, equipment's share of capital grew significantly over the four decades.

The data presented in Figure 1.3 take account of the fact that capital depreciates (wears out) over time. Each year, business firms undertake **investment**, the acquisition of new capital goods. Some of this investment goes to replace older, worn-out capital; the rest represents net additions to the capital stock. The capital stock data we use are *net of accumulated depreciation*; they reflect the productive capital actually available to firms. The formula determining the change between two time periods in the capital stock, ΔK, is given by

$$\Delta K = I - D.$$

In this formula I stands for new purchases of capital between the two time periods, which we call *gross investment*. The term D stands for the depreciation of the capital

Investment
The acquisition of new capital goods

stock that occurs between the time periods. The difference between I and D represents the increase in the economy's productive capital, which we call *net investment*. So the capital stock next period will be this period's stock plus net investment.

The rate at which capital depreciates depends on the type of capital in question. Some equipment loses as much as one-third of its value each year, whereas business structures lose only 2 to 3 percent of their value annually. Given the current mix of U.S. capital, the depreciation rate of the entire capital stock is about 5 percent per year.

AN ASIDE: THE RELATIONSHIP OF STOCKS TO FLOWS

Our equation relating the capital stock to investment and depreciation highlights an important distinction among macroeconomic variables. Quantities, such as investment, depreciation, and GDP, that arise between two points in time are called **flow variables**. Flows are distinguished from **stock variables**, such as the stock of capital, whose values are defined at a single point in time. We talk of investment *during* 1998 but of the capital stock *on* December 31.

Flow variables relate to *changes* in stock variables between periods. For example, the flows of gross investment and depreciation account for the change in the stock of capital between any two periods. Consider the analogy between the capital stock and a pot of water. Suppose that over a period of 10 minutes, you add 5 quarts of water to a pot that initially holds 3 quarts. We can say the *initial stock* of water was 3 quarts, the *flow* of water over the 10 minutes was 5 quarts, and the *final* stock is 8 quarts.

MEASURING LABOR

Economists typically measure labor input by the number of hours worked. Hours worked is the product of three terms: (1) the number of potential workers, given by the size of the adult population; (2) the fraction of the adult population that is employed, known as the *employment-population ratio*; (3) and the number of hours worked by those employed. In words,

Hours worked = Population × employment/population × hours/employment.

Each factor on the right side of this equation can have an important impact on total hours worked. To illustrate, let's examine changes in these factors in the United States since 1950. Figure 1.4 considers the first two factors: the size of the adult population and the fraction of the adult population that is employed. The numbers shown are quite remarkable in many ways. In just 46 years the U.S. civilian adult population increased by 96 million individuals to the 1996 total of 201 million. To put this in perspective, the increase exceeds the current population of Germany. It also exceeds the combined populations of Austria, Belgium, the Netherlands, Sweden, Finland, Denmark, Norway, Ireland, Portugal, and Switzerland. Over the same period, the number of employed adults increased by 68 million.

Flow variable
A variable defined over an interval of time

Stock variable
A variable defined at a particular point in time

Thousands of Persons 16 Years and Over

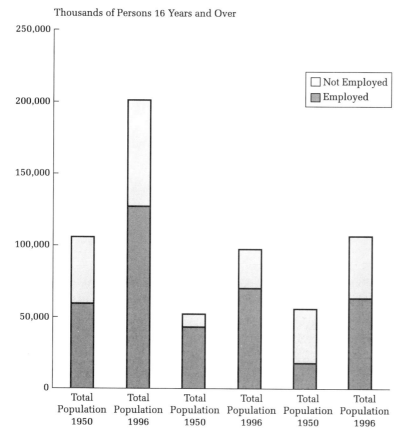

FIGURE 1.4 U.S. ADULT POPULATION AND EMPLOYMENT, 1950–1996

Source: U.S. Bureau of Labor Statistics.

Absorbing 68 million additional workers was no small feat, but the economy managed to do so without a long-term decline in the fraction of U.S. adults who were employed. In fact, because of changes in female employment, this fraction actually rose over the period, from 56 percent to 63 percent. In 1950 only one in three adult women was employed, compared with more than one in two in 1996. Consequently, women represented less than a third of total U.S. employment in 1950 but almost half in 1995. Over the same interval, the employed fraction of adult males declined. In 1996, 71 percent of adult males were employed, compared with 82 percent in 1950.

Although total U.S. civilian employment more than doubled between 1950 and 1996 (reflecting both population growth and an increase in the employment-population ratio), total hours worked by all persons in the U.S. business sector rose by only 54 percent. Part of the reason was a decline in average hours worked per week (from

40 hours in 1950 to 34 hours in 1996). The rest of the discrepancy reflects the trend toward working fewer weeks per year.

THE ROLE OF MULTIFACTOR PRODUCTIVITY

The term *A* in the Cobb-Douglas production function plays a special role in determining the economy's capacity to produce. It measures productivity, or the efficiency with which capital and labor are used to generate output. Over time, improvements in productivity make it possible to produce more output without additional inputs. Since 1950, the level of productivity has increased by over 70 percent. With only the inputs available in 1950, America can now produce 70 percent more output.

What causes productivity to change? A variety of factors are important, and we can classify them as either improvements *embodied* in the capital and labor inputs or *disembodied* changes that boost productivity in a more general way.

Embodied productivity improvements increase the *quality* of labor and capital. Better education, increased training, and improved health all mean that a labor hour in 1997 is more productive than an hour in, say, 1950. Since labor is generally measured in terms of hours worked, and the measurement is not adjusted for changes in the quality of labor, such changes in effective labor input will be captured in *A*. In a similar way, a unit of capital is better—more productive—today than in the past. Computers today are faster and more powerful; automobiles are more fuel efficient; lasers make surgery safer, quicker, and less painful. Better design helps speed the flow of work through factories. All of these changes help to squeeze more production from a given number of labor hours, machines, and buildings.

Disembodied productivity changes are a little harder to grasp, though no less important. They include better production processes, substitution of cheaper materials for more expensive ones, quicker transfers of knowledge from the laboratory to the production line, and reorganizations of production and distribution. Many of these disembodied productivity changes typify the idea of "working smarter, not harder." Disembodied productivity also reflects the presence of any productive factors not measured as capital or labor inputs. For example, if the measured input of capital includes only capital in the private sector, disembodied productivity growth will reflect the presence of government capital, or infrastructure, which makes production more efficient. Examples of infrastructure are interstate highways, the Internet, and airports, all of which help reduce the transportation and communication costs facing business.

CASE STUDY
HOW DOES PRODUCTIVITY GROW?

Over the long term, productivity improvements have permitted astounding changes in incomes and the quality of life. Some of the most obvious examples come from the transportation sector. Since the 1920s, the automobile has radically transformed life. People no longer need to cluster in urban centers, living and shopping within walking distance of their workplaces. Refrigerator cars on trains, and later refrigerated trucks, permitted shipment of perishable food items across the country and around the world. And the jet airplane has saved billions of hours of time for business and recreational travelers.

Many other examples are less obvious. In just the past decade, the introduction of quality circles has provided a forum for workers to suggest productivity-enhancing improvements to their supervisors. The Japanese-inspired "just-in-time" method of production reduces the amounts of resources firms have tied up in inventory. Once retailers and producers were able to settle on a standard system, bar coding was introduced very rapidly and has helped speed up checkout lines at retail stores.

Students of technology claim that small but continuous incremental changes probably do more to boost the economy's level of productivity than bigger, discrete changes do. A good example is the phenomenon called "learning by doing." The phenomenon was first identified before World War II when aircraft manufacturers noticed how the cost of assembling a plane decreased steadily and predictably over time. The cost reductions were closely tied to the total number of aircraft assembled at a plant or by a company. Since then, the same effects have been found in a variety of production environments. As the cumulative number of units produced increases, the average cost of production falls, probably because workers learn from their mistakes and find better ways of doing things.

Another example of the importance of small changes comes from Boston University economist Andrew Weiss. Weiss studied the electronics industry by visiting production plants in the United States and Japan. His conclusions were quite surprising. For example, he found no differences in absenteeism, no differences in labor turnover, and no evidence that the Japanese work harder than Americans. In fact, the pace of production in Japanese electronics plants was slower than in comparable plants located in the United States. In spite of these similarities, the Japanese plants were more productive. Why? One reason is that the Japanese support their workers with a high ratio of engineers to production workers. By investing heavily in engineering and by locating engineers on the shop floor, Mitsubishi Electric, Hitachi, and NEC were able to achieve almost continuous improvement in their production processes. In the United States, by contrast, there is much more emphasis on marketing than on manufacturing. Engineers tend to be segregated in design facilities far from the production line.

ACCOUNTING FOR GROWTH

According to the Cobb-Douglas function, increases in output over time reflect either growth in inputs (K and L) or improvements in productivity (through A). With a little manipulation, we can use the Cobb-Douglas function to write the percentage change in output between any two time periods in terms of the growth *rates* of capital, labor, and productivity. Let's denote the change in any variable X between two points in time as ΔX. Then the growth rate of X over that period is the change in X divided by the original level of X : $\Delta X / X$. For example, the growth rate of productivity is $\Delta A / A$. The relationship among our four growth rates is[2]

$$\frac{\Delta Y}{Y} = \frac{\Delta A}{A} + \beta \, \frac{\Delta K}{K} + (1 - \beta) \frac{\Delta L}{L}.$$

In words, the formula says the growth rate of output is approximately equal to the sum of (1) the rate of productivity improvement, (2) capital's share of output (β) multiplied by the growth rate of capital, and (3) labor's share of output $(1 - \beta)$ multiplied by the growth rate of labor.

We have relatively good data on output and hours worked and fairly good data on capital. What about multifactor productivity, A? Because it reflects the influence of a variety of factors, including improvements in the quality of the capital and labor inputs and advances in technology, productivity is hard to measure directly. Therefore it is usually estimated by finding the value of A that makes the Cobb-Douglas production function fit the available data on output, labor, and capital. Robert Solow, who won a Nobel Prize for his work on economic growth, devised this "residual" method of determining the growth rate of productivity.[3] Solow plugged known values of $\Delta Y / Y$, $\Delta L / L$, $\Delta K / K$, and β into the above equation and estimated $\Delta A / A$ as the value that made the two sides of the equation equal. This so-called Solow residual reflects the amount of output growth that cannot be explained by (or that's left over after) growth in the quantities of capital and labor. The residual is also known as the *rate of technological progress*.

As an example, suppose we know that the growth rates of output, capital, and labor between periods 0 and 1 are 3.0 percent, 2.0 percent, and 1.0 percent, respectively. Then the estimated rate of technological progress at time 0 is 1.70 percent (3.0 percent − .30 × 2.0 percent − .70 × 1.0 percent). We can use these estimated growth rates to do **growth accounting** by decomposing the overall growth rate of output into components that reflect the contributions of labor, capital, and productivity. In our example, the increase in the capital stock accounted for 0.60 percentage points of the total 3.00 percent growth in output. Growth in the labor input accounted for another 0.70 percentage point. We then attribute the remainder of the total growth rate—1.70 points—to improvements in productivity.

Growth accounting
The tracing of output growth to growth in inputs and multifactor productivity

2 *This relationship is derived by taking natural logarithms of both sides of the Cobb-Douglas relationship:* $\ln Y = \ln A + \beta \ln K + (1 - \beta) \ln L$. *Hence, the difference in the logarithm of output between two periods is given by* $\Delta \ln Y = \Delta \ln A + \beta \Delta \ln K + (1 - \beta) \Delta \ln L$. *Since the difference of logarithms of a variable approximately equals its percentage change, we obtain the approximation in the text.*

3 *Robert M. Solow, "A Contribution to the Theory of Economic Growth,"* Quarterly Journal of Economics *(February 1956): 65–94.*

CASE STUDY
SOURCES OF U.S. GROWTH SINCE 1948

Growth accounting is a handy tool for understanding why economies grow. It tells us what is important and what is not. Let's apply the growth accounting framework to

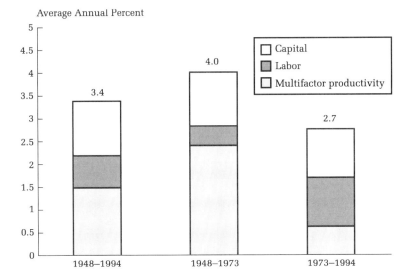

Average Annual Percent

FIGURE 1.5 SOURCES OF U.S. BUSINESS SECTOR GDP GROWTH, 1948–1994
Between 1948 and 1994, U.S. real output increased at an average annual rate of 3.4 percent. About two-fifths of that growth was attributable to productivity improvements. One-third was explained by increases in the capital stock, and the rest was due to growth in labor hours. Between 1948 and 1973, real output grew very fast due to rapid techno-logical progress. Since 1973, productivity growth has slowed dramatically and with it, output growth.

Source: Bureau of Labor Statistics.

understand the sources of the 3.4 percent annual growth rate of real output in the U.S. private business sector between 1948 and 1994. Figure 1.5 shows the shares of this average growth rate due to growth in productivity, capital, and labor. *About two-fifths of the economic growth over the period is explained by productivity improvements. One-third is explained by growth in the capital stock, and the rest is due to growth in labor hours.*

The sources of economic growth have changed over time. Annual growth in U.S. private business real GDP averaged 4.0 percent from 1948 to 1973, but only 2.7 percent from 1973 to 1994. Labor's contribution to growth was more important in the latter period than in the former. In the latter period, growth in hours accounted for about two-fifths of total growth, compared with about one-fifth in the former period. Whereas capital's contribution was roughly constant, productivity's contribution declined from more than half in the earlier period to only one-fifth in the latter.

Growth accounting is only as good as the raw data employed. Because produc-tivity is computed as a residual, it's hard to say exactly what fraction of productivity growth is attributable to improvements in input quality (and therefore should be added to capital's and labor's contribution to growth), what fraction represents disembodied technological change, and what fraction is just measurement error.

Independent studies by Harvard University economist Dale Jorgenson and University of Gröningen economist Angus Maddison suggest that most of measured productivity change takes the form of embodied quality improvements, particularly in capital.[4] Maddison estimates that embodied and disembodied changes in capital input explain over half the growth in U.S. output between 1973 and 1984. In the period 1950 to 1973, disembodied changes played a more important role, but capital was still the most important source of growth. The model we develop in later chapters highlights the importance of capital accumulation in generating economic growth.

LABOR PRODUCTIVITY

So far we've used the Cobb-Douglas function to discuss the level and growth rate of total output. Now let's use it to consider the amount of output per unit of labor input, which is called **labor productivity**. To define labor productivity, divide the Cobb-Douglas formula for output by the amount of labor input. The result is a formula for output per unit of labor input, also referred to as the Cobb-Douglas function in *intensive form*:

$$\frac{Y}{L} = \frac{AK^\beta L^{1-\beta}}{L} = A\left(\frac{K}{L}\right)^\beta.$$

In this textbook, lowercase letters are often used to denote variables measured on a per capita basis. So if we let y stand for output per unit of labor input (labor productivity) and k stand for the ratio of capital to labor, we can write this equation compactly as

$$y = Ak^\beta.$$

Thus, we see that labor productivity depends on two factors: the level of multifactor productivity and the ratio of capital to labor. Not surprisingly, the more efficiently that inputs are used (the larger the value of A), the more productive labor will be. Labor will also be more productive if it has more capital to work with—that is, if the capital-labor ratio is larger. This is just another implication of diminishing returns. As we increase the amount of capital relative to labor, capital becomes more abundant and less productive. Labor, on the other hand, becomes relatively scarce and more productive.

Figure 1.6 graphs labor productivity against the capital-labor ratio for two different values of A. Consider the lower curve, along which A equals 10. For capital-labor ratios of 3, 4, and 5, labor productivity is 13.9, 15.2, and 16.2, respectively. These values reflect two things. First, the higher the capital-labor ratio is, the higher labor productivity is. Second, because of diminishing returns, successive equal increments to the capital-labor ratio lead to smaller increments in labor productivity (16.2 − 15.2 is less than 15.2 − 13.9). Now compare the higher ($A = 15$) and lower curves. The clear message is that given the ratio of capital to labor, labor productivity is higher the higher the level of multifactor productivity.

Labor productivity
The amount of output produced per unit of labor input

4 See Dale W. Jorgenson, "Investing in Productivity Growth," in Technology and Economics *(Washington, DC: National Academy Press, 1991), pp. 57–63, and Angus Maddison, "Growth and Slowdown in Advanced Capitalist Economies,"* Journal of Economic Literature *(June 1987). 649–698.*

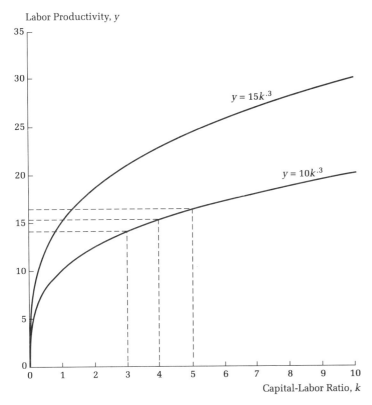

FIGURE 1.6 CAPITAL-LABOR RATIO AND TECHNOLOGY DETERMINE OUTPUT PER WORKER
Output per worker—labor productivity—increases as the ratio of capital to labor increases. As capital per worker increases, capital becomes more abundant and less productive. These diminishing returns explain why the curves become flatter as the capital-labor ratio increases. Labor productivity also depends on technology. The lower curve is drawn assuming the technology coefficient, A, equals 10. If A is higher, say 15, the higher curve prevails.

DOES LABOR PRODUCTIVITY INFLUENCE WORKERS' PAY?

Labor productivity is closely related to labor's *marginal product*—the additional output that can be produced by holding technology and capital fixed and increasing labor by one unit. In the case of the Cobb-Douglas function, labor's marginal product is simply $(1 - \beta)y$, the quantity $(1 - \beta)$ multiplied by labor productivity. As we'll describe in chapter 3, competitive firms pay workers a wage equal to their marginal product. Hence, if the Cobb-Douglas function provides a good description of production and firms hire workers competitively, workers' compensation should be closely related to labor productivity. This is indeed the case. Figure 1.7 shows that real compensation per hour in the United States closely tracks output per hour.

The tie to workers' compensation is one of the main reasons we are interested in studying labor productivity. Another is that, other things equal, a higher level of labor productivity means more output per person, which is economists' measure of an economy's standard of living.

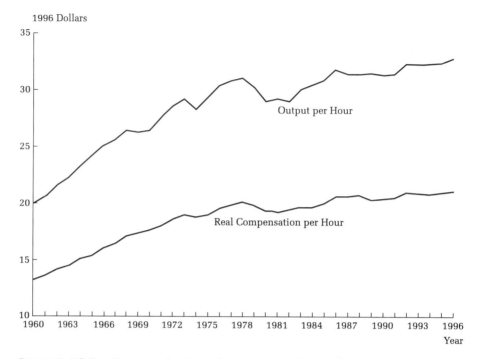

FIGURE 1.7   U.S. REAL OUTPUT AND REAL LABOR COMPENSATION PER HOUR, 1960–1996
Real compensation per worker-hour is closely tied to labor productivity. The post-1973 slowdown in labor productivity growth has meant slower growth of real compensation per hour.

Source: U.S. Bureau of Labor Statistics.

WHAT EXPLAINS THE U.S. LABOR PRODUCTIVITY SLOWDOWN?

We've seen that the United States has been experiencing a slowdown in the rate of growth of GDP. What is the connection, if any, between labor productivity growth and output growth? Recall that labor productivity is defined as the ratio of output to labor. This means that output equals labor productivity multiplied by labor itself. It also implies that the growth rate of output approximately equals the growth rate of labor productivity plus the growth rate of labor. Thus, it is certainly possible for labor productivity to speed up even as output growth slows, because output growth depends not only on the growth of labor productivity but also on the growth in the absolute amount of labor. Unfortunately, the slowdown in U.S. output growth has been associated with a slowdown in labor productivity growth. Figure 1.8 shows that since 1973, labor productivity has been growing at roughly a third the rate observed between 1948 and 1973. The labor productivity slowdown has contributed to the slow growth since 1973 in real compensation per hour. Had labor productivity grown as fast

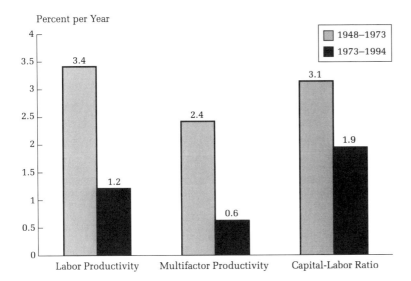

FIGURE 1.8 GROWTH IN LABOR PRODUCTIVITY, MULTIFACTOR PRODUCTIVITY, AND THE CAPITAL-LABOR RATIO, 1948–1994

Labor productivity grew much more slowly in the period 1973 through 1994 than between 1948 and 1973. Much of this change can be traced to slower improvement in multifactor productivity. However, a slower rate of capital deepening also contributed to slower labor productivity growth.

Source: Bureau of Labor Statistics.

between 1973 and 1994 as it did between 1948 and 1973, real compensation per hour would have been almost 60 percent larger in 1994!

About a quarter of the decline in labor productivity growth can be traced to slower *capital deepening*—growth in the amount of capital per worker. The rest of the decline results from slower growth in multifactor productivity. Let's consider each in turn.

THE ROLE OF CAPITAL DEEPENING

Since 1973, labor force growth has accelerated. Changes in labor force participation, which we've already documented, have combined with the large number of births during the postwar baby boom to produce sizable increases in the working-age population. Over the same period, the rate of investment has slowed. The capital stock is still growing, but its growth has slowed relative to that of employment. If the capital-labor ratio of the U.S. private business sector had grown as fast between 1973 and 1994 as it did between 1948 and 1973, the capital-labor ratio would now be a fourth larger.

Why has net investment—the growth in the capital stock net of depreciation—lagged? As we'll discuss in the next chapter, investment is financed by saving—output not consumed. A decline in the rate of investment ultimately must be explained by a decline in the rate of saving. Over the past two decades, the United States has saved and invested very little. Many economists believe the government's fiscal policy is largely to blame for this failure to save and invest. Others point to a change in the saving behavior of Americans, particularly the young and middle aged. Whatever the explanation, it's clear that the capital-labor ratio cannot be expected to grow faster unless and until Americans begin to save at a higher rate.[5]

OTHER CAUSES OF THE PRODUCTIVITY SLOWDOWN

Figure 1.8 shows that the average annual growth rate of A slowed from 2.4 percent during the period 1948–1973 to 0.6 percent during the period 1973–1994. Economists have investigated a number of possible causes of this slowdown. Although no single explanation is entirely satisfactory, each has some merit. Let's consider four of the most frequently mentioned.

A Changing Production Mix

Early in the twentieth century, the United States made the transition from an agrarian to an industrial economy. More recently, the trend has been away from the production of goods toward the production of services. Manufacturing's share of GDP fell from 29 percent in 1950 to only 18 percent in 1994. By contrast, the share of GDP produced in finance, insurance, real estate, and other services rose from 20 percent in 1950 to 37 percent by 1994. This shift of production to sectors where the scope for productivity improvement is limited can help explain the overall slowdown in labor productivity growth.

Many people think productivity growth occurs mainly in the industrialized sectors of the economy, as new production methods and inventions are applied to make goods more efficiently and cheaply. In fact, primarily thanks to advances in the computer industry, labor productivity growth in manufacturing has outpaced that in services. For the period 1973–1987, growth in output per worker-hour in manufacturing was 2.6 percent annually. Over this period, the same measure of labor productivity grew at an annual 0.4 percent rate for the service sector in general and fell at an annual 0.5 percent rate in the finance, insurance, and real estate component of the service sector. The shift in production away from manufacturing to services certainly lowered overall U.S. labor productivity growth, but other changes in the production mix had the opposite effect. Specifically, the shift away from mining and construction raised overall productivity growth because labor productivity growth in these industries was quite weak.[6]

Changes in the Quality of Capital and Labor

The slower growth in the U.S. capital stock has meant a slower rate of improvement in the quality of the capital stock. Jorgenson's and Maddison's research suggests that as much as one-third of the decline in multifactor productivity growth might be due to this factor. Slower growth in the quality of labor is another potential culprit. As mentioned, the U.S. **labor force**—those employed or seeking employment—has been changing in recent years as a greater percentage of women have entered the labor

5 As we'll see in the next chapter, foreign saving has also financed investment in the United States, but not enough to offset the effect on U.S. investment of a decline in U.S. saving.

Labor force
All noninstitutionalized individuals, 16 years of age and older, who are either working or actively looking for work

6 See Martin N. Baily and Robert J. Gordon, "The Productivity Slowdown, Measurement Issues, and the Explosion of Computer Power," Brookings Papers on Economic Activity (1988): 2, table 4.

Reprinted with special permission of Gary Brookins and North America Syndicate, Inc.

force. The labor force also swelled, beginning around 1970, as the large postwar baby boom generation began seeking employment.

This increase in the proportion of relatively inexperienced workers is often cited as a cause of the labor productivity slowdown. So is the slower rate of improvement in the education of the U.S. workforce. Indeed, average scores on the college entrance exam—the SAT—suggest that the level of education may actually be declining. Other measures are even more troubling. A 1993 study by the U.S. Department of Education found that nearly half of all adult Americans read and write so poorly that they can't hold a decent job and that almost four-fifths have math skills that are insufficient to perform simple calculations, such as determining the correct change from a restaurant meal.

In terms of our formula for labor productivity, the argument here is that labor input is being incorrectly measured, having suffered a reduction in quality during the period. However, adjusting the measured labor input for changes in the age-sex mix and educational attainment can, it appears, explain only a small fraction of the post-1970 decline in labor productivity.

Declining Research and Development

Economists who study the question have found that research and development (R&D) spending contributes to technological progress, providing new, more efficient production methods. The lack of adequate R&D has often been cited as a cause of the recent slowdown in labor productivity growth. Indeed, U.S. research and development spending did slow beginning in the mid-1960s, from just over 4 percent of industry sales to just under 3 percent in the late 1970s. However, the evidence indicates that this shift had only a small effect on technological change, accounting for perhaps 10 to 15 percent of the overall slowdown in labor productivity growth.[7]

7 See Zvi Griliches, "Productivity Puzzles and R&D: Another Nonexplanation," Journal of Economic Perspectives (Fall 1988): 9–21. Economists estimate the productivity of R&D spending using a production function approach like the one we have outlined in this chapter, adding the stock of research knowledge to capital and labor as inputs in the production process.

Government Regulation

Since the mid-1960s, governmental health, safety, and environmental regulations have proliferated. These regulations have had many beneficial effects in improving the quality of life in the United States, but they have also contributed to the slowdown in productivity growth. The effects of regulation have been felt in a variety of ways. For example, more resources are now dedicated to simply complying with regulations—undergoing more inspections, completing paperwork, and planning. Edward Denison, a leading productivity researcher, estimated that about 1 percent of resources have been diverted to pollution abatement, where they do not contribute to measured GDP. The same sort of phenomenon results from health and safety regulations: measured output falls as resources are shifted from producing GDP to improving the quality of life. Pollution control devices themselves may render capital less efficient in producing measured output. Finally, regulations create uncertainty and as a result make businesses think twice about the wisdom of installing new, expensive capital. These effects are all quite difficult to measure, but a reasonable estimate is that they explain about 15 percent of the productivity problem.

SUMMARY: WHY HAS GROWTH IN U.S. LABOR PRODUCTIVITY SLOWED?

About one-quarter of the post-1973 slowdown in labor productivity growth is due to slower growth of capital relative to labor. The remainder is due to a decline in multifactor productivity growth. Slower growth in the quality of capital may explain as much as one-third of this decline. Another third appears to be due to the changing production mix, a decline in labor quality, and a reduction in R&D spending. Explaining the rest of the decline in multifactor productivity is not easy. Part may be due to a slower growth rate in government infrastructure, which we'll document in chapter 6. Part may be due to measurement errors. And part may be due to other factors not yet fully understood.

IS THE UNITED STATES BECOMING THE POOR KID ON THE BLOCK?

Like the United States, other advanced countries have experienced slower growth in recent years. Nevertheless, per capita output is growing at a higher rate in almost all these countries than it is in the United States. Figure 1.9 displays average annual growth rates between 1960 and 1994 of real GDP per capita for the United States and other members of the Organization for Economic Cooperation and Development (OECD). The OECD is an association of major industrialized nations. With the exception of Switzerland, Mexico, and New Zealand, the U.S. per capita growth rate of 1.9 percent ranks lowest. Japan's rate was over twice the U.S. rate, and Germany's rate was almost one and one-third times the U.S. rate.

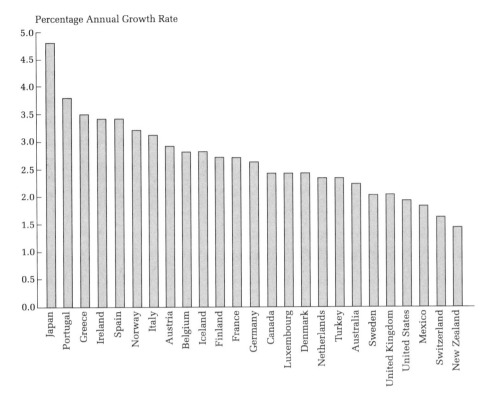

Percentage Annual Growth Rate

FIGURE 1.9 AVERAGE ANNUAL GROWTH RATES OF PER CAPITA GDP, 1960–1994
Output per hour has grown more slowly in the United States than in most other OECD countries. This reflects generally slower rates of U.S. capital deepening and technological progress.

Source: OECD.

Suppose these growth differences persist for the next 50 years. What will this mean for the future living standards of Americans relative to, say, Japanese? By the late 2040s, the Japanese standard of living, now about four-fifths of the U.S. level, will be more than three times as high! Such a rapid decline in the relative economic position of Americans may seem hard to imagine, but history is replete with examples of the toppling of economic giants. Remember the relative decline in the British standard of living. In the late nineteenth century, British per capita GDP was second to none. Today the British living standard is roughly 30 percent less than the American standard and among the lowest in Western Europe.

What explains the relatively weak growth performance of the United States? One part of the answer is America's slower rate of capital accumulation. Although other OECD countries have invested less of their output in recent decades, almost all of these countries have still invested a far larger share of their output than the United States has. The other part of the answer is that other developed countries have been experiencing more rapid technological progress.

These differences between the United States and other developed countries with respect to their rates of growth in capital per worker and their rates of technological progress are not immutable. In fact, these differences have gotten smaller in recent decades and could well decline further over time. The reason is that other developed countries are still catching up with the United States following the destruction of their economies in World War II. As we'll discuss in chapter 3, the growth path a country follows over time depends on the position it is in when it starts to grow. Countries devastated by war, such as Germany and Japan, can be expected to grow more quickly in the aftermath of war than those, like the United States, that were not hit so hard. Part of this process involves the restoration of these countries' capital stocks, and part involves the acquisition by these countries of technology already being used in countries with higher per capita incomes.

IS THE GAP BETWEEN RICH AND POOR COUNTRIES WIDENING?

The problems of developing countries are in some ways quite different from those of developed countries. The issue of growth and its determinants is probably more important for countries that have yet to achieve the relatively high living standards enjoyed in the developed world. There are two central questions concerning growth and development: Why do living standards vary so much across countries? Why are some countries more successful than others at making the jump from "developing" to "developed"?

After World War II, the devastated economies of Germany and Japan were essentially in the "developing" category in terms of living standards. Yet both countries grew rapidly during the postwar years, closing the gap with the developed world. The experience of other, truly developing countries has been more mixed. Some, like South Korea and Hong Kong, have rapidly approached the living standards of the developed world; others have fallen further behind.

Figure 1.10 shows real GDP per capita for South Korea, Hong Kong (during its colonial period, prior to its absorption by China), the Ivory Coast, Peru, and China. In 1960, the Ivory Coast and South Korea each had real per capita GDP of about $1,000. Hong Kong and Peru each had per capita GDP of just over $2,000 (compared to the U.S. figure of about $10,000). Over the period 1960 through 1992, per capita real GDP in South Korea and Hong Kong grew at average annual rates of 6.4 percent and 7.0 percent, respectively, far outstripping the corresponding U.S. rate of 1.9 percent and even surpassing Japan's rate of 5.2 percent. But Peru's per capita GDP didn't grow at all over this period, nor did that of the Ivory Coast. These different growth records had dramatic effects on the countries' relative living standards. Hong Kong, which started in 1960 with roughly the same level as Peru, had eight times Peru's per capita real GDP by 1992. And South Korea, which started 1960 at less than half of Peru's living stan-

FIGURE 1.10 REAL GDP PER CAPITA IN FIVE DEVELOPING COUNTRIES, 1960–1992
Since 1960, some developing economies have experienced dramatic growth, while others have stagnated. Hong Kong and Peru each had roughly the same living standard in 1960, but by 1992, Hong Kong's living standard was almost eight times that of Peru.

Source: Penn World Trade.

dard, had almost four times the Peruvian standard by 1992. Thus, the evidence shows the clear possibility for developing countries to approach the high standards of living enjoyed in developed countries. However, there has not been a significant increase in the share of world output going to the poorest countries. Some developing countries have grown even less rapidly than the developed economies that suffered the productivity slowdown of recent decades.

For students of development, China represents a particularly interesting country to keep an eye on. Because of its recent economic liberalization, China is starting to emulate Korea's and Hong Kong's extraordinary growth performances. Imagine the impact on the world's distribution of income if China, with more than a quarter of the world's population, moved from having one of the world's lowest living standards to having one of the highest.

Given the varying performance of the developing world, it is natural to ask which is the norm. Should we expect countries' per capita outputs to converge or to diverge? Figure 1.11 provides some intriguing evidence on this question. It shows growth rates of per capita GDP for different countries and regions for the period 1960 through 1992 plotted against their level of per capita GDP in 1960. If we look at the pattern established by the newly industrialized countries (NICs) of Asia—Korea,

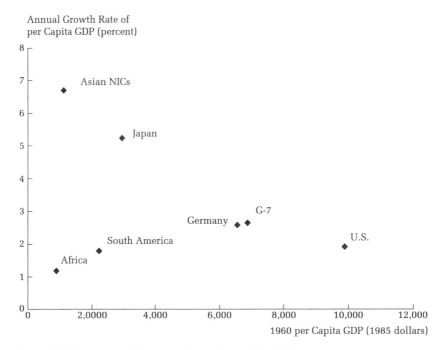

FIGURE 1.11 PER CAPITA GDP: GROWTH VERSUS LEVEL, 1960–1992

If poorer economies grow faster than richer ones, nations' per capita outputs will eventually converge. Japan and the newly industrialized countries of Asia had small per capita GDPs in 1960 but grew at high rates thereafter. The United States, Germany, and the G-7 industrialized nations had large per capita GDPs in 1960, but their growth has been modest since then. Apart from Africa and Latin America, these data support convergence.

Source: Penn World Trade.

8 The G-7 are the developed economies of Japan, Germany, Canada, France, Italy, the United Kingdom, and the United States.

9 See Robert E. Lucas, Jr., "On the Mechanics of Economic Development," Journal of Monetary Economics 22 (1988): 3–42, and Paul M. Romer, "Capital Accumulation in the Theory of Long Run Growth," in Robert J, Barro, ed., Modern Business Cycle Theory (Cambridge, MA: Harvard University Press, 1989).

Singapore, Hong Kong, and Taiwan—as well as Japan, Germany, the United States, and the Group of Seven (G-7) as a whole,[8] there is a clear negative relationship between growth in per capita output and the initial level of per capita output. This is strong evidence for convergence. However, this pattern is broken by the unfortunate experiences of Africa and Latin America over the period.

The basic economic model we will develop in the chapters to come does predict the type of convergence observed among the Asian NICs, Japan, Germany, and the United States. But there is more to the world than the basic model captures, including certain aspects of government performance or nonperformance. Many countries of Africa and Latin America have not been blessed with stable, efficient governments.

Furthermore, with some modifications of our basic model, we can generate a process of self-propelled technological change. In this modified model, there is no necessary requirement that growth rates and living standards of different countries converge. Models exhibiting self-propelled growth are called *endogenous growth* models and are at the forefront of modern research on the economics of growth. We'll discuss endogenous growth briefly in chapter 3.[9]

CHAPTER SUMMARY

1. Measured in 1992 dollars, the U.S. economy in 1996 produced almost $7 trillion of output (gross domestic product)—nine times the output produced in 1929. Economic growth is highly dependent on the state of the economy, with recessions marked by negative growth and expansions by positive growth. The most severe recession on record, the Great Depression, is a case in point. During its first four years, U.S. output fell by 27 percent.

2. Economists measure a country's standard of living in terms of per capita real GDP. The U.S. level of real per capita GDP has grown at an average rate of 2.2 percent per year since 1929. Consequently, the U.S. standard of living is now four times its 1929 level.

3. Growth rates compound, meaning that small differences in growth rates translate into large differences over time in living standards. Had the post-1929 U.S. growth rate of per capita output been twice as high, America's standard of living would be almost four times larger than its current value.

4. The Cobb-Douglas production function is a simple and empirically sensible way to model output. It relates output to inputs of capital and labor and the level of multifactor productivity and provides a basis for growth accounting.

5. Capital is measured as the value of business and residential structures, equipment, land, and inventories, expressed in prices from a particular year (e.g., 1992). Labor is typically measured as total hours worked, which is the product of three factors: the adult population, the fraction of that population employed, and hours worked per employed person.

6. Growth of real output in the U.S. private business sector has slowed in recent decades. The relative contributions of technological progress and capital accumulation declined, while the relative contribution of labor input growth increased.

7. According to the Cobb-Douglas production function, labor productivity depends on the level of multifactor productivity, A, and the capital-labor ratio. Since 1973, U.S. labor productivity in the private business sector has grown at roughly one-third the rate observed between 1948 and 1973. About three-quarters of this decline can be traced to a slower growth in multifactor productivity; the rest is due to slower growth in capital per unit of labor.

8. Although many phenomena may have contributed to the labor productivity slowdown, including a change in the composition of production, a decline in quality of the workforce, a reduction in research and development spending, a slower rate of net investment, government regulation, and slower growth of government infrastructure, much of the decline remains unexplained. Whatever the explanation, the slowdown has meant slower growth in the real hourly wages of American workers.

9. Other developed countries are also experiencing growth slowdowns. Still, the U.S. rate of per capita output growth is lower than those of almost all other developed countries. Among developing countries—those with a substantially lower standard of living than countries like the United States, Japan, and Germany—there has been a divergence of growth rates. Some developing economies, notably the newly industrialized countries of Asia, have grown quite rapidly—indeed, even more rapidly than countries in the developed world. Other countries, many of which are in Africa and Latin America, have grown at very slow rates. This suggests that rapid development is possible, but by no means assured.

CHAPTER **2**

THE DYNAMIC SUPPLY OF INPUTS

INTRODUCTION

Economic growth is caused by two things: technological progress and the use of more productive inputs. We've discussed technological progress. We now present a simple **life-cycle model** to explain changes over time in the inputs of capital and labor.

Developed in the early 1950s by Nobel laureate Franco Modigliani and University of Pennsylvania economist Albert Ando, the life-cycle model traces the supplies of capital and labor to household saving and work decisions.[1] This supply-side behavior is our current focus. The next chapter describes the demand for inputs and the way the economy grows in equilibrium—when input supplies equal input demands. Subsequent chapters use the life-cycle growth model to understand recessions and unemployment, fiscal and monetary policies, international trade and finance, and a host of other issues.

The life-cycle model's microeconomic underpinning is valuable. It reminds us that macroeconomic outcomes ultimately reflect the collective behavior of millions of individual households and firms. It also lets us trace out the macroconsequences of government policies by asking how they alter the work and saving decisions of individual households and the hiring and investment decisions of individual firms.

Understanding these decisions requires an understanding of **present value discounting**, a key topic of this chapter. Present value discounting tells us how to compare the value of money in the future with the value of money today. For instance, it shows whether paying $100 today is more or less expensive than paying $150 eight years from now. At a personal level, present value discounting may be the most important concept you'll learn in economics. It's absolutely critical for making an array of financial decisions, like buying a house, selecting a career, saving for college—even, as we'll learn in a case study, purchasing a lottery ticket.

This chapter begins at the beginning—by pointing out that households are the ultimate owners and suppliers of capital and labor. It then uses the life-cycle model, in conjunction with present value discounting, to show how households make saving

Life-cycle model
A framework that explains an individual's decision about how much to consume and save in each period of his or her life

Present value discounting
Determining the present value of a sum of money to be received or paid in the future

1 Albert Ando and Franco Modigliani, "The 'Life Cycle Hypothesis' of Saving: Aggregate Implications and Tests," American Economic Review 53 *(1963).*

and work decisions. Next, it combines these individual decisions to determine a country's aggregate or national saving and labor supply. Finally, it derives a fundamental macroeconomic identity: that **national saving** equals **national investment**.

National investment is the additional amount of capital accumulated at home or abroad by a country's citizens in a given period of time. Since the early 1980s, the United States has experienced a dramatic decline in its rate of national saving. Given the saving-equals-investment identity, this reduction in national saving has meant less national investment. This has taken the form of not only less *domestic investment* (investment in the United States), but also less *net foreign investment* (investment by Americans abroad less the amount invested in the United States by foreigners).

The low rate of U.S. saving threatens to persist. If it does, it will limit growth in the U.S. capital stock and, as a consequence, growth in U.S. output. So too will projected slower growth in U.S. labor supply. Recent growth in U.S. labor supply has been driven by the substantial rise in female labor force participation coupled with the large baby boom's entry into the labor market. These factors have now largely run their course.

If supply-side factors are slowing growth in both capital and labor, what will happen to the ratio of capital to labor, on which labor productivity depends? The answer, presented in a case study, is that it will rise, albeit gradually. Furthermore, since Japan and most Western European countries are experiencing similar demographic changes, capital deepening (a rise in the capital-labor ratio) will occur in other developed countries as well.

Before proceeding, consider this chapter's key questions:

- How does saving (acquiring more assets) relate to investment (acquiring more capital)?

- How do people decide how much to save?

- How do people value income they'll receive and purchases they'll make in the future?

- Has the U.S. saving rate declined in recent years?

- Will the aging of America, Germany, and Japan alter their capital and labor supplies?

National saving
Gross national product minus consumer spending by households minus government spending on consumer goods and services

National investment
The amount of capital accumulated by a nation, either at home or abroad, during a given period of time

WHO OWNS AND SUPPLIES INPUTS?

Who owns and brings productive inputs to the market? In the case of labor services, it's simply individuals with a capacity to work in some productive enterprise. Their total number and the number of hours they each wish to work influences total labor supply. But there is also a quality dimension to labor supply. The supply of **human capital**—the supply of labor adjusted for quality—reflects workers' training and education, as well as their raw talents. Finally, there is a dynamic element to labor supply: individuals make retirement and related plans that will affect their future as well as current labor supplies. They also decide how many children to parent, and thereby determine the future supply of workers.

The ultimate owners of physical capital are also individuals, although their ownership is often indirect. Consider the plants and machinery that General Motors uses to produce automobiles. General Motors Corporation, as a legal entity, holds the titles (bills of purchase) to these **real assets**. But General Motors is itself owned by the million or so households that hold shares of GM stock.

Financial assets and liabilities arise as a way of recognizing indirect ownership. For General Motors's shareholders, GM stock represents a **financial asset** rather than a real asset. The stock gives them legal claim to the income generated by GM's real assets rather than a direct legal claim to the assets themselves. Other examples of financial assets are bonds, saving and checking accounts, certificates of deposit, money market funds, accounts receivable, and stock options, each of which gives its owner a claim to income in the future.

For each financial asset, there is an offsetting *financial liability* of equal value. In the case of GM stock, the shares represent a financial asset of the shareholders but a financial liability of the corporation. The owner of an AT&T bond has a financial asset. But AT&T, as issuer of the bond, has a financial liability: to make the principal and interest payments specified on the bond. From an economy-wide perspective, financial assets and liabilities cancel. If we add up the values of all a country's real and financial assets and then subtract the values of all its financial liabilities, we are left with just the value of its real assets, which is called its *domestic net worth*. This makes sense; *ultimately a country's domestic net worth equals the value of the physical capital within its borders.*

Human capital
Labor input adjusted for skills, training, and on-the-job experience

Real assets
Capital goods, such as plants and machinery, used in conjunction with labor to produce output

Financial asset
A legal claim to the income generated by real assets (rather than a claim to the real assets themselves)

2 We'll have much more to say about the ownership of corporations in chapter 16, where we discuss corporate finance.

CASE STUDY
WHO "OWNS" THE U.S. PRIVATE CAPITAL STOCK?

At the end of 1994 the U.S. private sector capital stock totaled $20 trillion, which was a bit less than three times 1994 GDP. Table 2.1 indicates that about half this capital was directly owned by households. The rest was directly owned by businesses and, consequently, indirectly owned by households. Unincorporated businesses directly owned about a quarter of so-called business capital, but this capital really belonged to the proprietors and partners who ran these firms. The remaining business capital was legally owned by corporations, but was really owned by the individual stockholders who own these companies.[2]

TABLE 2.1 U.S. PRIVATE DOMESTIC NET WORTH, 1994 (TRILLIONS OF DOLLARS)

Real Assets	Sector with Direct Ownership		
	Household[a]	Business	Total
Residential structures	4.518	1.338	5.856
Plant and equipment	.520	5.541	6.061
Inventories	0	1.221	1.221
Consumer durables	2.491	0	2.491
Land	3.015	1.349	4.364
Total real assets	10.544	9.449	19.993

Source: Board of Governors of the Federal Reserve System.

[a] Includes nonprofit institutions.

Table 2.1 also shows the different types of real assets "owned" by each sector. Household real assets consist primarily of owner-occupied homes, the land beneath them, and consumer durables. Business real assets include plant and equipment, inventories, and land. They also include some residential structures, primarily apartment buildings and other rental units, owned by private and corporate landlords.

In addition to the $20 trillion of U.S. private capital in 1994, about $3 trillion in land, buildings, equipment, bridges, roads, and other capital was "owned" by the government. Like private capital, government capital is fundamentally owned by people, since the government is ultimately under society's control.

THE TWO-PERIOD LIFE-CYCLE MODEL

Saving means refraining from consuming all of current output now in order to produce and consume more in the future. But there is another meaning attached to the word *saving*: the acquisition of additional real assets. These two meanings are consistent. Whether the newly produced capital good is a Boeing 777 or inventoried rice, it is output that isn't consumed at the time it's produced; instead, it is available to help produce output in the future. It is also output whose titles of ownership are acquired by savers either directly or indirectly. Understanding capital accumulation thus requires linking the acquisition of claims to new capital and to the sacrifice of current consumption.

Our life-cycle model provides that link. As we'll see, the model is very simple and for that reason may seem implausible. Be assured that much more elaborate and realistic versions of this simple model have been constructed.[3] We develop this simple

3 For example, in Alan J. Auerbach and Laurence J. Kotlikoff, Dynamic Fiscal Policy (New York: Cambridge University Press, 1987).

model not because it provides highly accurate quantitative predictions (it doesn't) but because it provides the same *qualitative* predictions and economic insights as more detailed models.

THE MODEL'S BASIC STRUCTURE

Our model features a single country, which, for the moment, has no government. Inhabitants of this country live for just two time periods. In their first period, they are young and go to work. In their second, they are old and retired. At the end of their second period, they pass away. All individuals born at the same time are identical.

Although each generation dies after two periods, the economy is ongoing. At the beginning of each period, a new generation is born, and the previous young generation passes from youth into old age. Hence, in each period, there is always a set of young people and a set of old people.

A "period of time" in our model refers, in real time, to roughly 30 years of adulthood. You should think of each generation's "youth" as corresponding to the 30 years between ages 20 and 50 and its old age as corresponding to the 30 years between ages 50 and 80. Admittedly, it would be more realistic to have 60 or so periods of life— one for each year of adulthood—but this would overly complicate the model without altering its basic insights.

There is only one commodity in our model, which we'll sometimes call corn. This commodity is both a consumption good and a capital good. It can be consumed (eaten) or invested (planted) to produce additional output (corn). At the end of their first period, young people are paid in corn for their work effort. They consume some of these labor earnings and put aside, or save, the rest so they can provide for their retirements. Since there are no inheritances (until chapter 15), this saving by the young constitutes the assets they bring into their old age.

At the beginning of their old age, people invest their assets. For simplicity, we'll assume that old people invest their accumulated assets in their own firms. The assets of the old thus represent their stock of capital. To get labor to work with their capital, the elderly hire the new batch of young people. At the end of their old age, the output of the firms emerges.

The old people give part of the output to their young workers as wage payments. They keep the rest as a return on the capital they invested. We refer to this income as *capital income*. The elderly consume this capital income plus the amount they originally invested (their principal). In effect, we assume that the capital the elderly invest (the corn they plant) at the beginning of their old age does not depreciate and can be fully recovered (dug up) and consumed. Since the assets of the old are positive at the beginning of their last period but zero at the end, the old eat up all their assets (they dissave) during their second period of life. The time line in Figure 2.1 describes the order of events in our model for periods of time, beginning in period 1.

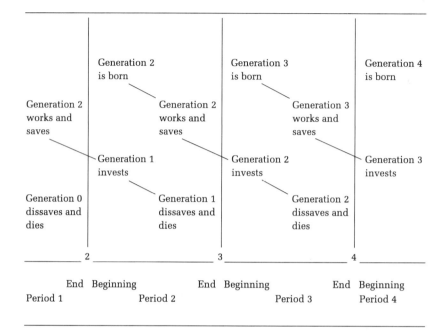

FIGURE 2.1 THE TWO-PERIOD MODEL'S TIME LINE
In the life-cycle model, each generation lives for two periods. For example, generation 2 is born at the beginning of time period 2. It earns wages, consumes, and saves at the end of period 2. It invests its assets at the beginning of period 3, consumes, and saves at the end of period 3, and then dies. The same life-cycle pattern is experienced by every other generation. Each earns wages and saves when young. Each invests and consumes principal and interest when old.

DYNAMIC INPUT SUPPLIES

Some simple equations help describe the supplies of capital and labor. Let's focus first on generation t, which is born at the beginning of time period t. This generation receives its wages, consumes, and saves at the end of period t. It then invests its assets at the beginning of period $t + 1$, consumes the principal plus interest on its assets at the end of that period, and then immediately dies.

Let c_{yt} denote consumption when young by a member of generation t (hence the subscript t). In addition, we'll use w_t to denote the wage earnings of each young person in generation t. Then $w_t - c_{yt}$ equals the amount each member of generation t saves when young. This is also the amount of assets, denoted by a_{t+1}, each member of generation t brings into period $t + 1$. In symbols,

$$a_{t+1} = w_t - c_{yt}.$$

If each member of generation t brings a_{t+1} units of capital into old age, how large is the economy's total capital stock at the beginning of time $t + 1$? The answer depends on the size of generation t. To keep things simple, suppose that there are N members of generation t, and of every other generation as well. In other words, there is no popu-

Percentage of Total Wealth

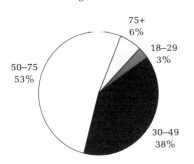

Percentage of Population

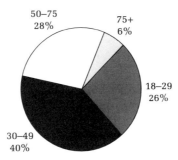

FIGURE 2.2 1990 DISTRIBUTIONS OF U.S. WEALTH AND POPULATION BY AGE
Our model assumes that the elderly, those in the second period of their lives, own all the economy's capital. This is a rough approximation to the U.S. experience. In the United States, individuals over the age of 50 represent about one-third of the population but own almost 60 percent of private sector net assets.

Source: Board of Governors of the Federal Reserve System.

lation growth; at any given time, there are N young people and N old people alive, making the total population equal to $2N$. If we let K_{t+1} stand for the economy's total capital stock at the beginning of period $t + 1$, we have

$$K_{t+1} = Na_{t+1} = N(w_t - c_{yt}).$$

Thus, the total capital stock at $t + 1$ is simply the number of old people around at that time multiplied by the amount each old person saved when she was young. Intuitively, the supply of capital at any time equals the total assets held by all generations alive at that point. In our model, only the old have assets, so total assets held by members of all generations is just the total held by the elderly.

The notion that the elderly hold claims to all the economy's capital is actually not far from the truth, especially if we are willing to stretch the definition of elderly a bit. In the United States, individuals over age 50 own 59 percent of total private sector net assets despite making up only 34 percent of the population. Figure 2.2 shows the shares of the 1990 private U.S. wealth owned by different adult age groups. It also shows the percentages of the population represented by those groups.

Since young people work full time (there is no unemployment), the total labor supply during period $t(L_t)$ can be measured simply by the number of young workers at time t, which is N; thus,

$$L_t = N.$$

In chapter 1 we measured labor in number of hours. Here we are measuring labor in number of workers. Since each young person works one period and there are N young people, total labor supply is N. The assumption that when people work, they work full time is fairly close to the mark, at least in the United States Figure 2.3 shows the

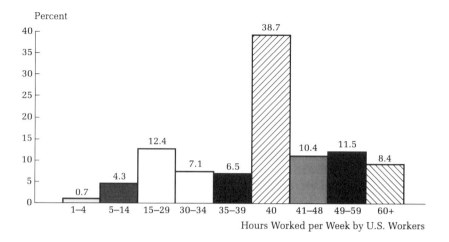

FIGURE 2.3 DISTRIBUTION OF HOURS WORKED PER WEEK, MARCH 1993
Our model assumes that when people work, they work full time. This is a reasonable approximation to the U.S. situation. Over three-quarters of U.S. workers spend more than 35 hours per week on the job.

distribution of weekly hours worked in March 1993 by U.S. workers. In that month, over three-quarters of all workers spent more than 35 hours per week on the job.

In our two formulas for the supplies of capital and labor, time t can stand for any time period: period 0, period 1, period 37, period 3421, or any other period. For example, if we set t equal to 7, our labor supply formula tells us that the economy's total labor supply at time 7 is N. If we set t equal to 6, our capital supply formula tells us that the economy's total capital stock at time 7 equals the collective asset holdings of the elderly at time 7. The assets of the elderly at time 7, in turn, reflect the saving they did out of their wages when they were young at time 6.

The formula for labor supply in this model is very simple. It says that the amount supplied is the same every period. The formula for the supply of capital, on the other hand, says that the capital supplied by each member of generation t depends on the wages the person earns and the amount the person consumes when young. Recall that the wage, w_t, is the price paid to labor at the end of period t—the amount that must be paid for the services of a young worker for that period. As we'll learn, the size of the wage is the outcome of a market equilibrium in which input supply equals input demand. The wage, then, is determined by market forces and is outside the control of any particular individual. The same is true of the interest rate, r_t, the amount paid to use a unit of capital for one period, which we'll discuss momentarily.

The point at which a typical member of generation t, let's call him Franco, can really exercise control over his saving is in deciding how much to consume when young. Franco makes this decision at the beginning of period t. Given his labor earnings, w_t, this consumption decision also determines how much he saves, $w_t - c_{yt}$, and therefore the amount of assets he carries into old age, a_{t+1}. Given the interest rate, it also determines his old-age consumption, which is $a_{t+1}(1 + r_{t+1})$. So a *decision about how much to consume when young is simultaneously a decision about how much to save when young and how much to consume when old*. To understand this consumption decision and its implications, let's consider how much Franco can afford to consume in both periods of his life.

THE LIFETIME BUDGET CONSTRAINT

If Franco earns w_t when young, consumes c_{yt}, and saves a_{t+1}, how much can he consume when old? Since he is retired in period $t + 1$, he must rely on the assets he accumulated when young. The maximum amount he can, and will, consume is the principal amount he saved when young, a_{t+1}, plus his total capital (or interest) income earned on that investment, $a_{t+1}r_{t+1}$. Putting this all together, we can determine his consumption when old, c_{ot+1}. The subscript $t + 1$ reminds us that individuals born at time t are old in period $t + 1$. In symbols,

$$c_{ot+1} = a_{t+1}(1 + r_{t+1}).$$

Let's combine this formula with the one relating assets when old to the amount of saving when young. Specifically, let's substitute $w_t - c_{yt}$ for a_{t+1} in the above equation, and rearrange it:

$$c_{yt} + \frac{c_{ot+1}}{1 + r_{t+1}} = w_t$$

This expression, called the **lifetime budget constraint**, connects consumption when young, consumption when old, and the wage and interest rates. It determines all the different combinations of consumption when young and old that a member of generation t can purchase based on his wages and the rate of return he can earn on his saving. One affordable combination is to consume as much as possible when young and nothing when old. This amounts to setting c_{yt} equal to w_t so that c_{ot+1} equals zero. At the opposite extreme, Franco could save all his wages when young (set c_{yt} equal to zero) and consume $w_t(1 + r_{t+1})$ when old. Of course, there are many intermediate possibilities. We'll see soon which one is chosen.

Figure 2.4 plots Franco's lifetime budget constraint. To graph the constraint, we use the familiar idea that two points determine a straight line. That is, if we can find two points that satisfy the budget constraint, we can connect them to form a line showing all other points that satisfy it. As we've seen, one combination is point A, at which Franco consumes all his wages when young and, since he saves nothing, ends up with zero consumption when old. Another point is B, at which Franco consumes nothing when young, saves all his wages, and consumes these savings plus interest earned on them when old. Connecting A and B gives us the lifetime budget constraint shown in Figure 2.4. Notice that all points lying on or southwest of the budget constraint are affordable.

Lifetime budget constraint
An algebraic description of all combinations of consumption when young and old an individual can purchase, given the wage rate and the rate of return on saving

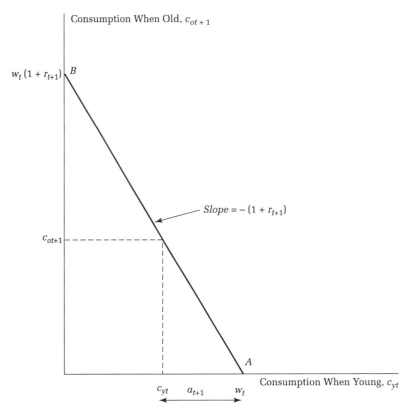

FIGURE 2.4   LIFETIME BUDGET CONSTRAINT
The lifetime budget constraint depicts all combinations of consumption when young and when old that an individual can afford over her lifetime. It is drawn for given values of the wage and interest rate. The constraint slopes downward, indicating that increased consumption when young comes at the cost of reduced consumption when old. The slope of the constraint reflects the amount of consumption an old person must sacrifice in order to consume one more unit when young.

The slope of this budget line is the "rise" divided by the "run." As consumption when young increases from 0 to w_t, consumption when old falls from $w_t(1 + r_{t+1})$ to 0. So the slope is $-w_t(1 + r_{t+1})/w_t$, which equals $-(1 + r_{t+1})$. It indicates the rate at which a young individual can trade consumption when old for consumption when young. A slope of -1.5, for instance, means that each extra unit of consumption when young requires giving up 1.5 units of consumption when old.

A higher interest rate will shift the vertical axis intercept upward, causing the budget line to rotate in a northeasterly direction around w_t and expanding the affordable combinations of consumption available when young and when old. A higher wage rate will also expand consumption opportunities; it will produce an equal percentage increase in both intercepts and shift the budget constraint outward to a position parallel to its original position. Consequently, the lifetime budget constraints for members of other generations will differ if either the wage they earn when young or the rate of return they earn on their assets when old differs from those available to members of generation t.

Although it may seem a bit strange at first, the lifetime budget constraint is exactly analogous to a budget constraint in a static setting faced by a consumer who spends his income Y on, say, apples and bananas. If A and B stand for the amounts of apples and bananas purchased and P_A and P_B are their respective prices, the static budget constraint is

$$P_A A + P_B B = Y.$$

In the lifetime budget constraint, lifetime labor income, w_t, takes the place of current income, and the quantities of consumption when young and old, c_{yt} and c_{ot+1}, take the place of the quantities of apples and bananas consumed. But what are the analogues of the prices P_A and P_B?

From the perspective of a young person, the price of anything is the amount (of corn) she must give up today, at time t, to get it. The price of a unit of consumption when young is just 1. Why? Because consuming one kernel of corn at time t costs just one kernel of the total kernels earned at time t. The price of one unit of consumption (say, one kernel of corn) when old is $1/(1 + r_{t+1})$. Why? Well, to consume one kernel of corn when old at time $t + 1$, a young person needs to put aside $1/(1 + r_{t+1})$ kernels of wage earnings at time t. When invested, this amount will yield, in principal and interest, $1/(1 + r_{t+1})$ kernels times $(1 + r_{t+1})$, or exactly one kernel in the future. So the price, evaluated at time t, of consuming one unit of corn in the future equals (involves giving up) $1/(1 + r_{t+1})$ units of corn at time t.

PRESENT VALUES

For a member of generation t, the price $1/(1 + r_{t+1})$ converts quantities of consumption goods tomorrow into their value in the present (which is time t). A shorter way to say "value in the present" is "present value." Learning how to compute present values is extremely important in everyday economic life. Take the case of choosing between two careers. One career, call it A, pays very little early in life, but a lot later on; the other career, B, pays a constant amount each year. Suppose the constant amount paid by career B exceeds the payments in the early years in career A. In later years, A pays more. How do we figure out which career is more lucrative? The answer is to form the present values (the values in the present) of the future payments in both careers and then compare them.

As another example, suppose you need to borrow a fixed sum of money to buy a house, and two different banks have offered to lend you the money, but on different terms. First National Bank offers a mortgage with low annual payments, but a large initial fee (referred to as "points"). Second National Bank offers a mortgage with higher annual payments but no points. Which mortgage is cheaper? Finding the answer requires comparing the present value of all the payments under each mortgage.

To make the concept more concrete, let's assume the annual interest rate is 10 percent and ask what is the present value of $100 to be received a year from now. The answer is $100/(1 + .10) = 100/(1.1) = 90.91$. The amount $90.91 is the value today of $100 received a year from now because we can take $90.91 today, invest it at 10 percent, and end up with $100 in one year. Therefore, having $90.91 today has the same value as having $100 a year from now.

Dividing $100 by one plus the interest rate is known as *discounting*. To find its present value, we discount (reduce in size) the $100 because it will not be received for a year. Indeed, if we had $100 in the present, we could invest it at 10 percent and end up with $110 a year from now. Thus, the present value of having $100 a year from now is not the same as the value of having $100 today (it's not $100).

If the present value of $100 received a year from now is $90.91, how much is the present value of $100 received, say, in three years? To make the problem a bit more interesting, suppose the annual interest rate will be 10 percent for the next two years and 8 percent in the third year. Computing this present value requires a little algebra. Denote the present value of $100 to be received three years from now as the amount D. Then we know that investing D, as well as accrued interest earned on the investment, for two years at 10 percent and then one year at 8 percent will yield a total amount of $100 in three years. After one year, the original amount D invested will have grown to $D \times 1.10$; after two years, the amount will be $(D \times 1.10) \times 1.10$; after three years, the amount will be $(D \times 1.10 \times 1.10) \times 1.08 = 100$. We can use this simple equation to solve for D, the present value of $100 received in three years: $D = 100/(1.10 \times 1.10 \times 1.08)$. This value is $76.52.

Notice that the investment of $76.52 grows by 30.68 percent to equal $100 in three years. The 30.68 percent increase is larger than 28.00 percent, the sum of the three annual interest rates. This reflects **compound interest**—the fact that interest is earned on previously accrued interest. Algebraically, compounding refers to the fact that the three interest rates (.10, .10, and .08) are not summed to form a total discount factor of 1.28. Instead, the three discount factors (1.10, 1.10, and 1.08) are multiplied together to form a total discount factor of 1.3068.

Cᴀꜱᴇ Sᴛᴜᴅʏ
Yᴏᴜ Cᴀɴ'ᴛ "Wɪɴ" ɪꜰ Yᴏᴜ Dᴏɴ'ᴛ Pʟᴀʏ

An increasing share of state government revenues in the United States comes from the proceeds of state lotteries. One lottery offering the potential for very large payoffs is the Powerball lottery, operated by the Multistate Lottery Association. In 1993, a winning Powerball player in Wisconsin won a prize of $111.2 million, the largest single lottery payoff on record.

Compound interest
Interest earned on interest

How can lotteries offer such large prizes and still have money left over from ticket sales to finance government programs? One part of the answer is that the odds of winning are extremely small. In addition, the lottery prizes aren't really as large as they are reported to be. Typically, large lottery payoffs are made in equal installments over a period of twenty years. Here's how the lottery association puts it: "When we advertise a prize of $20 million paid over 20 years, we actually have about $12 million in cash... We take the $12 million in cash and buy government-backed securities to fund these payments. We buy bonds which will mature in one year at $1 million, then bonds which will mature in two years at $1 million, etc." In other words, the lottery doesn't pay the winner of a "$20 million prize" $20 million the day the prize is won. Instead, it pays $1 million in the first year, $1 million in the second year, and so on for 20 years. If we discount these payments at a 6.18 percent annual interest rate (the rate the lottery association earned on its bonds), we find that the so-called $20 million prize turns out actually to be worth (have a present value of) just $12 million.

THE SAVING DECISION

The lifetime budget constraint indicates all the affordable combinations of consumption when young and old. But which combination will a member of generation t choose? That choice depends on the consumer's desires or preferences. We describe preferences about consumption when young versus consumption when old in terms of a *utility function*. A utility function is a happiness meter; the larger a person's utility, the happier he or she is.

Economists sometimes speak of utility being measured in abstract units called *utils*. They might just as well measure it in number of smiles. Why not? Utility can be measured in any units we choose—in utils, smiles, good vibes, or warm glows. Happiness is a relative concept. It's hard—apparently impossible—for anyone to know precisely how happy anyone else really is. Fortunately, what matters for economic choice is not the absolute level of happiness, but the relative happiness provided by different economic alternatives. Thus, we can think of a utility function as ranking different combinations of consumption when young and old, with a combination that produces more smiles ranked above a combination producing fewer smiles.

The utility function we'll use to consider the saving decision has the same Cobb-Douglas form as the production function introduced in chapter 1:

$$u_t = c_{yt}^{\alpha} c_{ot+1}^{1-\alpha}.$$

In this equation u_t stands for the utility of a typical member of generation t like Franco. (Recall that all members of a generation are identical, and so all have the same utility function.) Franco's utility level (his happiness) depends on the amounts he consumes when young and old and the preference parameter, α. The more he consumes when young or when old, the happier he is. The parameter α determines how Franco feels about consuming when young versus consuming when old. The larger α is, the more important consumption when young is to Franco's utility and the less important is consumption when old. Thus, α determines Franco's time preference—how much he prefers consuming when young to consuming when old. Moreover, for the utility function to make sense, more consumption in either his youth or his old age must make Franco better off. Accordingly, α must lie between zero and one. Otherwise, the exponent on either c_{yt} or c_{ot+1} would be negative, meaning that either more consumption when young or more consumption when old would result in lower utility. In future chapters we generally consider a value of α equal to .5.

Given his utility function, Franco's saving decision amounts to choosing a consumption combination—a particular amount of consumption when young and a particular amount when old. Specifically, Franco considers consumption combinations that satisfy his lifetime budget constraint until he finds the combination that gives him the most utility. As we'll show very shortly, Franco's search for the best affordable combination always leads to choices of consumption when young and old that satisfy the following two formulas:

$$c_{yt} = \alpha w_t$$

$$c_{ot+1} = (1 - \alpha) w_t (1 + r_{t+1}).$$

According to these formulas, Franco chooses to consume when young the fraction α of his lifetime labor income (w_t in this case). Since he earns w_t when young and consumes αw_t, Franco saves $w_t - \alpha w_t = (1 - \alpha) w_t$. This saving is the amount of assets he brings into his old age: $a_{t+1} = (1 - \alpha) w_t$. When Franco is old at time $t + 1$, he consumes his assets plus the interest earned on them, just as the formula for c_{ot+1} says. Note that although Franco's old-age consumption depends on the interest rate he receives when old, his saving and consumption when young do not. (In a more general model, saving would also depend on the interest rate.)

A CLOSER LOOK AT THE CONSUMPTION AND SAVING DECISION

One way Franco could choose the affordable consumption combination that makes him happiest is by mental trial and error, but this is quite tedious and ultimately unnecessary. Instead, he can simply use the two formulas for consumption when young and old to tell him exactly how much to consume in those two periods, given specific values of the wage and interest rate.

To understand these two formulas, consider Figure 2.5, which shows Franco's **indifference curves**. The curves are based on his utility function. Each curve refers to a particular level of utility and shows all consumption combinations that produce that level.

Although we don't show them, there is an indifference curve running through every combination of c_{yt} and c_{ot+1}. Indifference curves lying farther to the northeast correspond to higher levels of utility. The reason is that Franco prefers more con-

Indifference curve
A curve that shows all combinations of two commodities that yield the same level of utility

sumption to less, and as we move from one indifference curve to another in a north-easterly direction, we are increasing the amounts of both consumption when young and consumption when old, thus raising utility.

The slope of Franco's indifference curve at a particular point is called the **marginal rate of substitution (MRS)**, because it tells us the rate at which he is willing to substitute consumption when young for consumption when old. To see this, consider point A, where the slope of the indifference curve equals -1.5. Starting from point A, the MRS of -1.5 means that Franco is willing to give up 1.5 units of consumption when old in order to get an additional unit when young, as he will remain equally happy. Stated differently, the rate at which Franco is willing to exchange consumption when old for consumption when young is 1.5 to 1.

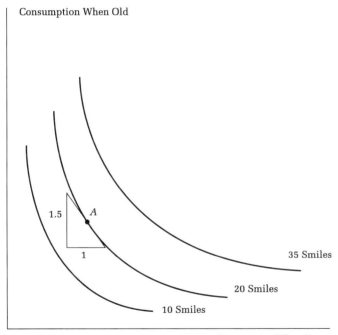

Consumption When Old

Consumption When Young

FIGURE 2.5 INDIFFERENCE CURVES
An indifference curve shows all combinations of consumption when young and when old that give a person a particular amount of utility. There is an indifference curve running through each possible consumption combination; three typical examples are shown here. Curves farther to the northeast indicate higher levels of utility.

The slope, or steepness, of an indifference curve at a particular point is called the *marginal rate of substitution* (MRS). It indicates the rate at which the individual is willing to substitute consumption when young for consumption when old while maintaining the same level of happiness. At point A, the MRS of -1.5 indicates that the individual can give up 1.5 units of consumption when old in return for 1 unit when young and remain equally happy.

Marginal rate of substitution (MRS)

The rate at which an individual is willing to substitute one good for another while maintaining utility at a constant level; the slope of an indifference curve at a particular point

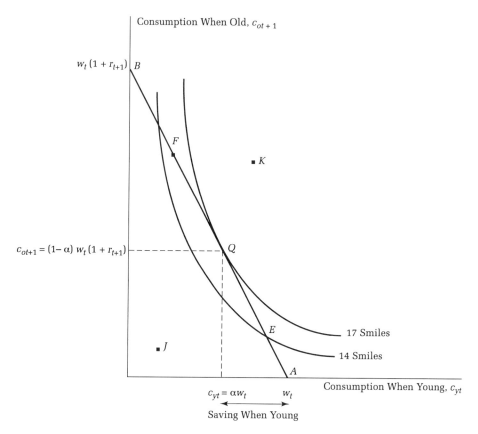

FIGURE 2.6 UTILITY MAXIMIZATION

An individual maximizes utility by choosing the consumption combination on the budget constraint yielding the highest level of utility (i.e., on the highest attainable indifference curve). In this figure, the utility-maximizing combination is c_{yt} and c_{ot+1}, as shown at point Q. At Q, the indifference curve for 17 smiles is tangent to (just touches) the budget constraint. The choice of point Q also determines saving when young, the difference between the wage earned when young, w_t, and first-period consumption, c_{yt}.

A GRAPHICAL DEPICTION OF FRANCO'S CONSUMPTION AND SAVING DECISION

Let's now combine Franco's indifference curves and his lifetime budget constraint in Figure 2.6 to consider his life-cycle consumption and saving decision. In looking at this diagram, Franco first realizes that he wants to choose a combination of c_{yt} and c_{ot+1} that is on his budget constraint, AB. A combination such as point K, which lies above the constraint, is not affordable. An affordable combination such as J, which lies below the constraint, will not be chosen either. Even though J is affordable, there are other affordable points on the constraint, such as E or F, that include more consumption when young *and* more when old. Since he prefers more consumption to less, Franco will always select a point on his lifetime budget constraint.

Franco will choose a point on his budget line, but which point will it be? We assume that his goal is to maximize his happiness, so it will be a point on his highest attainable indifference curve. The optimal point is Q, where the indifference curve of 17 smiles is tangent to (just touches and has the same slope as) the budget constraint. Note that all other points on the lifetime budget constraint, such as E and F, lie on lower indifference curves and reflect lower levels of happiness. The values of c_{yt} and c_{ot+1} corresponding to point Q determine the optimal consumption combination for Franco and other members of generation t. These values are the ones dictated by our two equations, indicating that Franco will spend a fraction α of his wages on first-period consumption. They also determine his *first-period saving*—the difference between wage income and consumption when young. This saving is shown as the distance $w_t - c_{yt}$, measured along the horizontal axis. In choosing to consume when young and old at point Q rather than point A (which indicates Franco's wage earnings when young and old), he smooths his consumption over his lifetime. He consumes less than his income when young and more than his income when old.

NATIONAL SAVING EQUALS NATIONAL INVESTMENT

We have analyzed the consumption and saving behavior of a particular generation over its lifetime. Let's now consider consumption and saving by both the young and the old at the same point in time and show that their combined saving equals the economy's total investment. In other words, we will show that the economy's national saving equals its national investment. This equality simply reflects the fact that the real assets saved by individuals in our model are made available to firms in the form of additional capital. Additions to the capital stock, as we've seen, are called *investment*.

We can always determine a country's national saving by subtracting its total consumption from its total output, Y_t. In our model, total consumption during a period of time is just the sum of consumption expenditures by the young and the old. Since there are N young people who each consume c_{yt} and N old people who each consume c_{ot}, total consumption expenditures at time t equals N times c_{yt} plus N times c_{ot}.

Let's use S_t to indicate total national saving. Then the formula for national saving is just

$$S_t = Y_t - Nc_{yt} - Nc_{ot}.$$

Our goal is to show that S_t equals national investment at time t, I_t. By definition, investment equals the change in the capital stock, $K_{t+1} - K_t$,[4] so we really need to show that $S_t = K_{t+1} - K_t$. This is easy. First, as we'll explain in the next chapter, total output is fully paid out to the young in the form of wage payments and to the old in the form of capital (or interest) income:

$$Y_t = Nw_t + r_t K_t.$$

4 *Recall that we've assumed that capital does not depreciate. Otherwise, as we learned in chapter 1, $I_t = K_{t+1} - K_t + D_t$. The equality of saving and investment also holds if D_t is positive.*

In words, output equals the total number of workers, N, times the wage payment to each worker plus the total amount of capital times the interest payment to each unit of capital. Substituting this expression for output into our previous formula for national saving and rearranging leads to

$$S_t = N(w_t - c_{yt}) + (r_t K_t - N c_{ot}).$$

This equation says that total national saving is the sum of the saving by the young plus the saving by the old. Next, recall that $w_t - c_{yt}$ equals a_{t+1}, the assets the young at time t bring into their old age, and c_{ot} equals $a_t(1 + r_t)$, the principal plus interest earned by the old at time t on their assets, a_t. Because $K_t = N a_t$, we can see that the saving by the old, $r_t K_t - N c_{ot}$, equals $N a_t r_t - N a_t(1 + r_t)$, which simplifies to $-N a_t$, a negative number. The old dissave because they consume more than their (interest) income.

Returning to the expression for national saving and recalling that $K_{t+1} = N a_{t+1}$, we end up with

$$S_t = N a_{t+1} - N a_t = K_{t+1} - K_t = I_t.$$

So we've shown that national saving does indeed equal national investment. We've also shown that national saving equals the economy's net asset accumulation between times t and $t + 1$; specifically, national saving equals the accumulation of assets (the saving) by the young, $N a_{t+1}$, less the decumulation of assets (the dissaving) by the old, $N a_t$. The young start at time t with zero assets and end up at time $t + 1$ with total assets of $N a_{t+1}$. The old start at time t with total assets of $N a_t$ and end up at time $t + 1$ with zero assets.

CASE STUDY
THE DECLINE IN U.S. SAVING AND ITS IMPACT ON DOMESTIC INVESTMENT

A country's rate of saving—its national saving as a fraction of its gross domestic product (GDP)—provides a comprehensive measure of its saving behavior. Since assets are held in the form of capital and since saving is the change in assets, understanding saving is central to understanding changes over time in the supply of capital. In the United States the national saving rate has declined considerably since 1980. Between 1959 and 1979 the rate averaged 21 percent per year. During the 1980s it averaged 18 percent per year, and since 1990 it has averaged only 15 percent per year. What explains this decline of over one-quarter in the rate of saving? As we'll discuss in chapter 6, a primary explanation appears to be the government's social security and Medicare programs, which have been taxing young savers at ever higher rates to make transfers payments to old spenders.

What are the implications of lower saving for investment? As we've seen, national saving equals national investment. In a *closed economy* (one not open to international trade and investment), all of a country's saving is invested at home, so national invest-

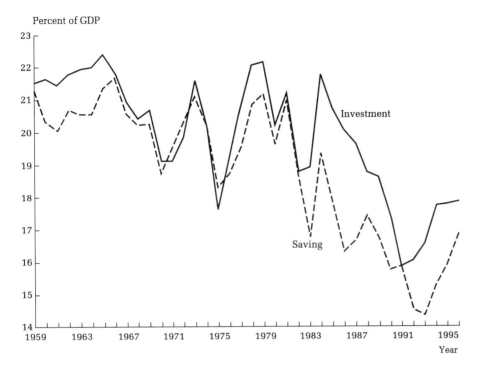

FIGURE 2.7 U.S. RATES OF NATIONAL SAVING AND DOMESTIC INVESTMENT, 1959–1996
National saving must equal national investment. Since the early 1980s, there has been a significant decline in national saving and, thus, in national investment. National investment is the sum of domestic investment and net foreign investment. U.S. net foreign investment, the vertical distance between national saving and domestic investment, has been negative in recent years; foreigners have been investing more in the United States than Americans have been investing abroad.

Source: National Income and Product Accounts.

ment equals domestic investment—the increase in the domestic capital stock. As we'll clarify in chapters 5 and 12, in an *open economy* some of the country's saving may be invested abroad. In this case national investment still refers to the increase in capital, but now it refers to the increase in the domestic capital stock plus the increase in a country's net ownership of foreign capital. Thus, in the case of an open economy, national investment is the sum of domestic investment (e.g., investment in the United States) plus net foreign investment (U.S. investment abroad minus foreign investment in the United States). *Since national saving equals national investment, which in turn equals the sum of domestic investment plus net foreign investment, lower national saving doesn't necessarily mean lower domestic investment. It could simply mean lower net foreign investment.*

Figure 2.7 graphs U.S. national saving and U.S. domestic investment, each expressed as a percentage of U.S. GDP, for the years from 1959 through 1996. Note that although U.S. national saving and domestic investment *have* moved roughly in tandem over time, they have rarely been equal. The difference between the two is the net foreign investment, just mentioned.

Since the early 1980s, U.S. net foreign investment has been negative—meaning that foreigners have been investing more in the United States than Americans have been investing abroad. Indeed, in the years 1985 through 1987, foreigners were responsible for financing almost one-sixth of all the new capital acquired in the United States by private firms and the government.

EXPANDING THE MODEL TO INCLUDE VARIATIONS IN LABOR SUPPLY

Up to this point, our model has not incorporated any explanation for changes in labor supply. However, it is possible to include variable labor supply as arising from two distinct factors: changes in the amount of labor supplied by the existing population and changes in the population.

Instead of assuming that each individual works a fixed amount when young and is retired when old, we could let households choose how much to work when young and old. For example, we could add leisure time when young and old to our Cobb-Douglas utility function. In this case, households would balance the benefits of additional income (and consumption) against the costs of reduced leisure time in deciding how much time to spend working. We will discuss the potential relevance of labor supply variations when considering the causes of unemployment and output fluctuations.

Another way to introduce variation in labor supply is to allow the population sizes of generations to differ. In the real world, neither the relative sizes of different generations nor the absolute sizes of countries' populations remain constant.

CASE STUDY
THE WORLDWIDE DEMOGRAPHIC TRANSITION AND THE RELATIVE SUPPLIES OF CAPITAL AND LABOR

There is a remarkable demographic transition currently underway in which the average ages of the populations in the leading industrialized countries are slowly but steadily rising. This reflects the very large increase in the number of children born in the United States, Western Europe, and Japan in the 20 or so years after World War II and the equally large decline thereafter in the number of births.

In the United States the *fertility rate* (the number of births a woman could expect based on prevailing age-specific births per female) increased from 2.9 in 1946, the first year of the baby boom, to 3.8 in 1957. Between 1957 and 1965, the U.S. fertility rate fell from 3.8 back down to 2.9. Since the 1960s, fertility has fallen even further, and

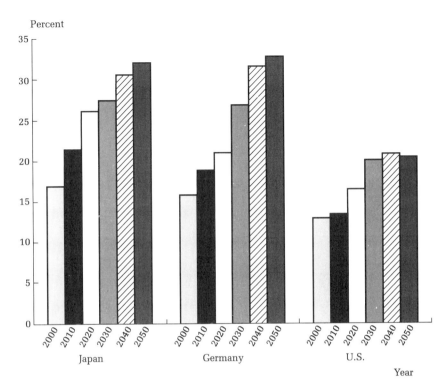

Percent

Year

Japan   Germany   U.S.

FIGURE 2.8 SHARE OF POPULATION AGE 65 AND OVER IN THE UNITED STATES, GERMANY, AND JAPAN
The leading industrialized countries are getting older. High birthrates in the two decades after World War II were followed by low ones, and people have been living longer. In the United States, there will be a large increase in the share of the population age 65 and over. Population aging will be even more dramatic in Germany and Japan.

Source: U.S. Census Bureau, International Data Base.

now averages only about 1.8 births per woman. Because there are so many American baby boomers and because they have relatively few children, baby boomers will continue to make big waves in the U.S. age distribution. In 1990, only 12 percent of Americans were 65 and older. In 2040, well after the baby boomers have retired, over a fifth of Americans will be 65 or older, and about a third will be 55 or older—roughly the same age makeup as in present-day Florida!

As Figure 2.8 makes clear, the "graying" of the populace will be even more pronounced in Japan and Germany. The bulk of Japan's aging will occur between 2000 and 2020, compared to the subsequent 20 years for Germany and the period from 2010 to 2030 for the United States. But by 2040, roughly one in three Germans and Japanese will be over age 65.

The low fertility rates of recent decades will also greatly affect population growth in these and other industrialized nations. Between 2000 and 2040 the total U.S. population is expected to grow by 95.3 million—only a 34 percent total increase.

This compares with a 64 percent increase between 1950 and 1990. Although U.S. population growth over the next 40 years is projected to be relatively small, it will nonetheless be positive. In both Germany and Japan, by contrast, the populations are expected to fall during this period, by 5 percent and 13 percent, respectively!

Projections are projections, and a lot can change in 40 years. Still, it is worth asking how these demographic changes may change the relative supplies of capital and labor in the future. Recall that labor productivity depends on the capital-labor ratio. Demographic change that raises this ratio will raise labor productivity and improve living standards. In our model the capital-labor ratio at any given time equals the assets per old person multiplied by the number of old people, divided by the number of young people (who are also the workers). That is, the capital-labor ratio equals the amount of assets per old person times the ratio of the old to the young. So far we've assumed that the ratio of the old to the young is one. But if this ratio rises, it will raise the economy's capital-labor ratio, ignoring any associated changes that might arise in assets per old person.[5]

Figure 2.9 shows how the impending changes in the U.S. age distribution will alter the ratio of U.S. household wealth relative to labor over the next decades, ignoring any changes over time in net asset holdings by age. According to the figure, the U.S. capital-labor ratio will increase by almost 30 percent of its 1990 value by the year 2030 simply as a result of demographic change.

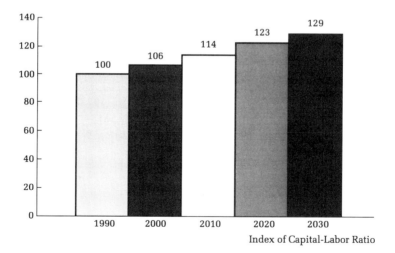

Index of Capital-Labor Ratio

FIGURE 2.9 PROJECTED GROWTH IN THE U.S. CAPITAL-LABOR RATIO DUE TO POPULATION AGING
The capital-labor ratio will rise as the U.S. population ages. The reason is that there will be more old people (who own capital) relative to young people (who supply labor).

Source: Board of Governors of the Federal Reserve System and Bureau of Labor Statistics.

5 As we'll see in chapter 3, the aging of society is likely to be associated with higher wages and, thus, higher assets per old person, which equal $(1 - \alpha)$ times wages.

CHAPTER SUMMARY

1. This chapter examined the supply of inputs. Households are the ultimate owners and suppliers of labor and capital inputs. They control the quantity and quality of labor they supply to the marketplace. They also decide how much of their income to save—that is, how much of their income to spend acquiring assets.

2. For the economy as a whole, the capital stock is the total of its real assets, directly owned by either households or businesses. Households own business capital directly through their roles as proprietors and partners in unincorporated businesses and indirectly as stockholders of incorporated businesses. In the United States about half of the capital stock is directly owned by households.

3. In our simple two-period life-cycle model, individuals work full time when young and are retired when old. Hence, the supply of labor depends on the number of young workers at a point in time. The supply of capital is determined by the amount of assets the elderly accumulated in the previous period, when they were young.

4. The lifetime budget constraint indicates all the combinations of consumption when young and old that are affordable given the individual's earnings when young and old. The lifetime budget constraint relies on present value discounting.

5. Individuals decide how much to consume when young and old by choosing the combination of consumption when young and old that is both affordable and most preferred (maximizes their utility). This combination occurs at a point of tangency between one of their indifference curves and their budget constraint. Given the wages workers earn when young, their decision about how much to consume when young determines how much they save when young. This, in turn, determines the assets they accumulate for old age.

6. The young consume a fraction α of their wages when young. They save the rest, so they bring $(1 - \alpha)$ of their wages into the beginning of their old age as assets. At the end of their old age, they consume this principal plus interest earned on it.

7. National saving is the sum of the saving of the young and the old. The saving of the young is positive; that of the old is negative—they dissave. National saving equals national investment. In recent years, the U.S. saving rate has been about three-quarters of the average annual rate observed between 1959 and 1980. The decline in U.S. national saving has meant both less national investment and less domestic investment.

8. Demographics play an important role in determining an economy's supply of capital and the ratio of its capital stock to its labor force. A decline in the number of young people relative to the number of old people raises the capital-labor ratio. Because of postwar baby booms, a decline in the working share of the population is underway in the United States, Japan, and Western Europe. This demographic transition could raise capital-labor ratios in these countries in the decades ahead.

CHAPTER 3

THE DYNAMIC DEMAND FOR INPUTS AND THE EVOLUTION OF OUTPUT

INTRODUCTION

Aggregate supplies of capital and labor reflect individual household saving and labor supply decisions. These decisions depend on the wages that households earn from working and the interest rate they earn on their savings. That's the supply side of our model. It's now time to consider the demand side—the decisions by firms to hire (to demand) the capital and labor supplied by the household sector. As we'll see, these decisions also depend on wage and interest rates, which represent the costs of hiring these inputs.

As prelude to modeling the demand side, we'll examine the size and financial structure of U.S. firms. We'll also point out some of the challenges firms face in hiring, retaining, and motivating workers. Once we've described the demand side, we'll combine it with the supply side to determine the wage and interest rates that equate supplies of labor and capital to their respective demands at each point in time. Thus, we'll describe the **general equilibrium** determination, through time, of wages and interest rates. The term *equilibrium* refers to the situation in which there is no upward or downward pressure on the wage or interest rate because the supplies of capital and labor equal the demands for these inputs. The adjective "general" refers to the simultaneous equilibration of all of the economy's markets. Knowing how the economy's wage and interest rates evolve over time tells us how the equilibrium amounts of capital and labor evolve and how the economy grows.

Our goal is thus to produce a complete model, albeit a very simple one, of economic growth. Though simple, the model is highly instructive. It allows us to answer the following types of questions:

- Do economies grow forever, or do they settle down into a permanent (or steady) state?

- How does a country's saving behavior influence its wage and interest rates?

General equilibrium
A situation in which supply equals demand in all markets simultaneously

- How does our two-period life-cycle model explain economic growth?

- How are different generations affected by the growth process?

- Does the extraordinary postwar growth of Japan and Germany simply reflect their catching up with the United States?

- How does a baby boom affect the economy over time?

- Why did real wages rise during the Middle Ages following the Black Death?

This chapter assumes that the economy is closed to international trade and investment. Chapter 12, in contrast, allows residents of one country to invest their savings in another. It shows that economic development can be much more rapid when developing countries are able to import capital from abroad.

ADDING FIRMS TO OUR MODEL

So far we've assumed that the elderly—the owners of capital—invest their capital in their own firms and hire labor to work with that capital. However, the model is unaffected if we assume instead that some of the elderly combine their savings and invest them in bigger firms. We require only that there be a large number of firms that compete with one another in hiring capital and labor. That is, we need perfect competition.

In the United States, the number of firms depends on how we count them. If we count all the proprietorships, partnerships, and corporations, including those with no employees except the owners, the number is 6.5 million—roughly one firm for every 15 adults. Figure 3.1 points out that most U.S. business establishments—87 percent—are small, with fewer than 20 employees. But it also shows that most U.S. workers—74 percent—work for medium and large establishments, those with 20 or more employees.

General Motors is the U.S. firm with the most workers—almost three-quarters of a million. That's more people than reside in Alaska, Vermont, North Dakota, South Dakota, Delaware, or Wyoming. But GM's workforce represents less than 1 percent of total U.S. employment. Indeed, total employment of the Fortune 500 largest U.S. companies accounts for only a tenth of U.S. employment. The very large number of U.S. firms hiring labor and capital make input markets in the U.S. highly competitive.

Capital structure
The division of a firm's liabilities between funds raised by borrowing and funds raised by issuing equity and retaining earnings

THE CAPITAL STRUCTURE OF FIRMS

Whatever their number, the firms in our model need capital to operate. We can think of these firms as either borrowing capital from the elderly or selling shares of stock (issuing ownership rights to the firm) to the elderly in exchange for the use of their capital. Selling stock is also referred to as issuing *equity*. Those elderly who own and operate their own firms can be thought of as borrowing from themselves or issuing equity to themselves.

In the case of borrowing, the elderly receive back, at the end of their old age, their initial capital (their principal) plus interest due on the borrowing. In the case of the sale of stock, the elderly can recover their initial capital plus the return on that capital through the receipt of *dividends* paid out by the firms. Alternatively, they can sell their shares of stock back to the firms or to the young, who are interested in acquiring assets.[1] Regardless of which method of finance firms use, the underlying outcome is the same: each firm gets to use some capital for one period but must return it, along with the income earned on that capital, at the end of the period. Hence, in our model, the method of finance has no impact. This discussion ties in with the point made in the previous chapter that no matter what form financial assets and liabilities take, the net wealth of a country boils down to the value of its real capital assets.

In the real world, the important difference between borrowing and selling shares of stock turns on the likelihood that the firm will make good on its commitment. Firms that suffer losses and can't repay their debts may go bankrupt, and the bankruptcy process can often tie up the use of the physical capital for long periods of time. In contrast, equity-financed firms with losses will see the market value of their stock fall but will not necessarily have to close down operations.

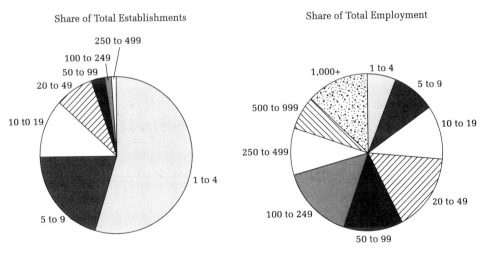

FIGURE 3.1 SHARES OF EMPLOYMENT AND ESTABLISHMENTS BY NUMBER OF EMPLOYEES, 1994

1 Firms that do not pay out the return on capital as a dividend but instead retain these earnings will raise the value of their stock. That is because the stock represents a claim, not only on the original capital invested in the firm, but also on the additional earnings retained by the firm. Stockholders who sell their stock will thus recover their return on capital in the form of a capital gain.

THE HUMAN CAPITAL STRUCTURE OF FIRMS

To keep things simple, we assume that firms hire labor—demand human capital—but do not improve its quality through on-the-job training. We also ignore improvements in workers' skills through the accumulation of job experience. These omissions don't distort the main message of our model. Still, it's important to keep in mind that hiring (demanding) labor in the real world is more complex than simply signing up people to work on a moment's notice and letting them go the next day. Actually, with the exception of longshoremen and certain farm and construction workers, it's hard to think of workers who are hired on a daily basis. On-the-job training, the accumulation of experience, and the process of learning by doing all require a long-term relationship between workers and firms. Indeed, many firms structure their compensation packages to encourage workers to stay with them for many years. They do so by providing higher wages at the end of the worker's career than at the beginning. This wage structure also stimulates workers to work hard to ensure keeping their jobs through the lucrative end stages of their careers.

In the United States, about half of workers find jobs that last 20 years or more.[2] However, making these successful long-term matches between employers and employees requires lots of searching by both parties. As a result, most jobs are of short duration, (8 years or less) though most workers spend a large part of their careers in a single job.

In addition to determining when and how much to train and compensate their workers during normal times, firms must decide how to handle their workforces during recessions. Because of the costs of training new recruits once a recession is over, many firms are loath to lay off long-term employees when the economy turns down.

PROFIT MAXIMIZATION

Financing decisions, incentive structures, layoff policy, and a number of other factors make employing capital and labor more complicated than it may appear. For now, we'll sweep aside these complexities and consider the simplest setting in which firms choose just the amounts of labor and capital to *maximize profit* (revenue minus cost).

Consider the collective profit of all firms in deriving their total input demands. These demands result from adding up the separate input demands of each of the economy's firms. The collective profit at any given time is:

Profit $= Y - rK - wL.$

The first term on the right-hand side of this expression is Y, which continues to stand for the quantity of total output. Since we take the price of output to equal 1, Y also stands for total revenue. As in chapter 2, r is the interest rate, and K is the total amount

2 Robert E. Hall, "The Importance of Lifetime Jobs in the U.S. Economy," American Economic Review (September 1982): 716–724.

of capital demanded by the firms. Capital doesn't depreciate. Consequently, there's no adjustment for depreciation in our expression for profit.

The interest rate is the cost to the firm of using a unit of capital for one period. The product rK stands for the total costs to all firms in the economy of using capital. The last term in the expression for profit represents the total costs of hiring labor; here, w still stands for the wage and L for the total amount of labor demanded by firms.

Profit is thus the income left over after paying the costs of hiring capital and labor. Economists often refer to this as *pure profit*. They do so to distinguish what they mean by profit from the everyday use of the term. In everyday parlance the term "profit" refers to the normal income earned by owners of capital, rK, as well as any additional pure profit. For example, "corporate profits" refers to all the capital income earned by corporations, most of which simply represents a normal return on their investment.

In deciding how much capital and labor to hire, firms take the interest rate and wage as given. Each firm correctly assumes that its decisions as to how much capital and labor to hire have no appreciable influence on the interest and wage rates. This reflects our assumption of competitive input markets; there are a very large number of firms, each of which is too small significantly to shift the aggregate demands for inputs.

THE DEMAND FOR CAPITAL AND LABOR

Suppose firms have chosen quantities of capital and labor that yield the largest profit. Then it must be the case that adding or subtracting a small amount of either capital or labor will leave profit unchanged. If adding or subtracting either a bit of capital or a bit of labor resulted in higher profit, it could not be the case that the firms had chosen the profit-maximizing combination of inputs in the first place.

Profit is defined as revenue minus cost, so the condition that changing either capital or labor leaves profit unchanged means that the change in revenue (the marginal revenue) from such adjustments must equal the change in cost (the marginal cost). With the output price fixed at 1, marginal revenue from changing either input simply equals marginal output. The extra output from increasing capital is called the **marginal product of capital**, and the extra output from increasing labor is called the **marginal product of labor**. Competitive firms take the interest rate and wage as given. So increasing capital by one unit raises total costs by r, and increasing labor by one unit increases total costs by w. Hence, the interest rate is the **marginal cost of capital**, and the wage is the **marginal cost of labor**. Profit maximization requires that the marginal product of capital equals the interest rate and that the marginal product of labor equals the wage.

COBB-DOUGLAS INPUT DEMANDS

For our Cobb-Douglas production function, the formulas for the marginal product of capital and labor are extremely simple. In the case of capital, the marginal product is $\beta Y/K$—the capital coefficient multiplied by output per unit of capital.[3] Hence, the condition that the marginal product of capital equals the interest rate can be written as

Marginal product of capital
The change in total output arising from a one-unit increase in usage of capital, holding labor fixed

Marginal product of labor
The change in total output arising from a one-unit increase in usage of labor, holding capital fixed

Marginal cost of capital
The change in the total cost of production when usage of capital increases by one unit

Marginal cost of labor
The change in the total cost of production when usage of labor increases by one unit

3 If you are familiar with calculus, the marginal products of capital and labor are the partial derivatives of the production function with respect to these inputs.

$$\beta \frac{Y}{K} = r.$$

If we solve this equation for β, we find that it equals the ratio of total capital income, rK, to output, Y, which also equals the nation's income; β is capital's share of income.

In the case of labor, the marginal product is $(1 - \beta)Y/L$. This is the labor co-efficient multiplied by the amount of output per unit of labor. The condition that the marginal product of labor equals the wage rate is expressed as

$$(1 - \beta)\frac{Y}{L} = w.$$

Solving this expression for $(1 - \beta)$ shows that $(1 - \beta)$ equals labor's share of income, wL/Y.

If firms hire capital and labor according to these formulas, what will their total profit be? The answer is zero, as can be verified by substituting for rK and wL from the above two equations into the expression for profit. This yields: Profit $= Y - \beta Y - (1 - \beta)Y = 0$. Since the owners of capital (the elderly) receive a share β of output, and since young workers receive a share $(1 - \beta)$ of output, all output is paid out to the two productive inputs, and nothing is left over as profit. Again, by saying that profit equals zero, we mean that pure profit equals zero, not that the income earned by capital is zero.

This zero-profit condition is the result of perfect competition. If profits were positive, additional firms would enter the market, and existing firms would expand their production. These actions would raise the demands for labor and capital, bidding up the wage and the interest rate until profits were zero. If profits were negative, existing firms would either leave the market or reduce their production. This would depress demands for labor and capital, driving down the wage and the interest rate until profits were zero.

THE RELATIONSHIP OF THE CAPITAL-LABOR RATIO TO THE WAGE AND THE INTEREST RATE

Let's substitute the Cobb-Douglas formula for Y, $AK^\beta L^{1-\beta}$, in the equation relating the marginal product of capital to the interest rate. The result is

$$\beta A \left(\frac{L}{K}\right)^{1-\beta} = r.$$

If the interest rate is high, then the demand for labor will be high relative to the demand for capital. Because capital is relatively costly, firms will require that an additional unit of capital be very productive in increasing output. By contrast, if the interest rate is low, then the demand for labor relative to capital will be low, because it is acceptable for an additional unit of capital to be less productive.

Now substitute the formula for output into the equation relating the marginal product of labor to the wage rate to get:

$$(1 - \beta)A\left(\frac{K}{L}\right)^{\beta} = w.$$

Thus, the larger is the ratio of capital to labor (the more scare is labor), the larger is labor's marginal product and the higher is the wage firms will be willing to pay.

THE EQUILIBRIUM VALUES OF THE WAGE AND THE INTEREST RATE

The last two equations tell us firms' demands for capital and labor when the interest rate equals r and the wage rate equals w. But they can also be used to determine what interest and wage rates must prevail if the firms are to demand the available amounts of capital and labor. This way of viewing these equations clarifies how the interest rate and the wage rate are determined at any given time. In equilibrium, the supplies of capital and labor must equal the demands. If we know the supplies of these inputs, we can substitute those values into the above equations to determine the interest and wage rates at which firms' demands for capital and labor equal the available supplies.

Do we know the available supplies of capital and labor at any given time? Yes. Total labor supply is simply N, the number of young people. Hence, in the above two equations, we can set the firms' collective demand for labor, L, equal to the collective supply of labor, N. The capital stock equals the assets of the elderly, Na, where a still stands for "assets per old person." Hence, in the above two equations we can set the firms' total demand for capital, K, equal to the elderly's collective supply of capital, Na.

Let's denote the equilibrium ratio of capital to labor by k. Because the demands for inputs equal their supplies, k equals K/L, which equals Na/N. By substituting k for the capital-labor ratio in the last two equations, we can write the equilibrium wage and interest rates prevailing at any given time more compactly[4]

$$r = \beta Ak^{\beta-1}$$

$$w = (1 - \beta)Ak^{\beta}.$$

A higher capital-labor ratio means a lower equilibrium interest rate and a higher equilibrium wage rate. Intuitively, larger supplies of capital relative to labor make capital more abundant relative to labor. This drives down the market price of using capital—the interest rate—and drives up the market price of using labor—the wage rate.

Are these formulas for the wage and interest rate consistent with the data? The answer appears to be yes. U.S. real wage growth has slowed in the past two decades. And this slowdown coincided with slower growth in U.S. productivity and capital intensity—precisely the elements that determine wage growth according to the above formula for the wage.

4 In generating the first equation, we use the facts that $L/K = 1/k$ and that $(1/k)^{1-\beta} = k^{\beta-1}$. If you are rusty or unfamiliar with the manipulating of exponents, consult the refresher on exponents at the end of this chapter.

DIAGRAMMING FACTOR MARKET EQUILIBRIUM

Figures 3.2 and 3.3 show the demand curves relating the capital-labor ratio to the wage and interest rates. Firms demand more capital relative to labor the higher the wage and less capital relative to labor the higher the interest rate. In equilibrium, the wage and interest rate are jointly determined so we can use either demand curve to consider the demand for capital relative to labor and end up with the same answer.

To determine the equilibrium wage and interest rates, we need the supply curve of capital relative to labor. Since all the capital and all the labor available are brought to market, the supply curve of capital relative to labor is simply a vertical line in Figures 3.2 and 3.3. For example, if the supply of capital relative to labor equals 3.8, the supply curve is a vertical line emanating from the value of 3.8 on the horizontal axis. The intersections of the supply and demand curves indicate the equilibrium wage rate (10.4) and the interest rate (1.178). You can use our formulas to confirm these values, assuming that A equals 10 and β equals .3.

MODELING GROWTH

We've just shown that the capital-labor ratio this period determines the wage this period. But from a supply-side perspective, the wage rate this period also determines next period's supply of capital, as well as next period's capital-labor ratio, since the supply of labor is fixed each period at N.[5] Hence, if we know the capital-labor ratio this period, we know the wage this period and can use it to figure out the capital-labor ratio next period.

To see this, let this period be time t, and start with the fact that $k_{t+1} = a_{t+1}$ (capital per worker at time $t + 1$ equals assets per old person). Next replace a_{t+1} with $(1 - \alpha)w_t$ (assets per old person equals the saving they did when young). This leaves $k_{t+1} = (1 - \alpha)w_t$. Finally, replace w_t by the marginal product of labor at time t, $(1 - \beta)A_t k_t^{\beta}$. The result is

$$k_{t+1} = (1 - \alpha)(1 - \beta)A_t k_t^{\beta}.$$

We call this the **transition equation** because it tells us how the economy's capital-labor ratio changes (transits) from one time period to the next. Since t can stand for any time period, we can use the transition equation to determine how the capital-labor ratio changes between any two consecutive time periods. For example, for t equals 3, the transition equation tells us that k_4 depends on k_3 according to $k_4 = (1 - \alpha)(1 - \beta)A_3 k_3^{\beta}$.

Transition equation

An algebraic equation relating the economy's capital-labor ratio in two successive periods

5 *Recall that the assets owned by the old at time $t + 1$ equal the saving they did when young, $a_{t+1} = (1 - \alpha)w_t$, and that the total capital stock at time $t + 1$ equals Na_{t+1}.*

USING THE TRANSITION EQUATION TO TRACK THE ECONOMY'S GROWTH PATH

Suppose it's time 0, and you're observing our economy. How do you determine the value of k_0? The answer is easy. Just add up the total assets of the elderly and divide by N, the supply of labor. Given k_0, you can use the transition equation to figure out k_1.

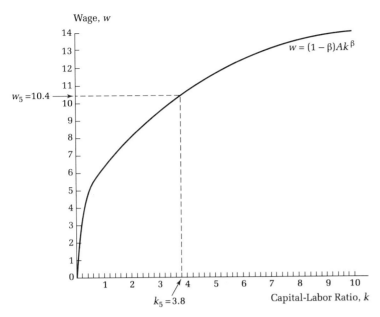

FIGURE 3.2 DEPENDENCE OF THE WAGE RATE ON THE CAPITAL-LABOR RATIO
In equilibrium, a larger supply of capital makes labor scarcer (relative to capital) and raises the price of labor—the wage rate.

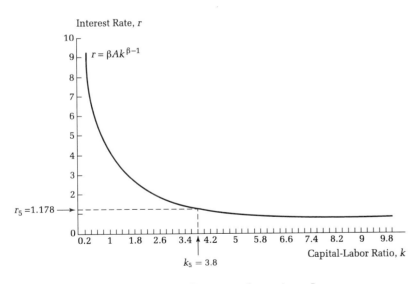

FIGURE 3.3 DEPENDENCE OF THE INTEREST RATE ON THE CAPITAL-LABOR RATIO
In equilibrium, a larger supply of labor makes capital scarcer (relative to labor) and raises the price of capital—the interest rate.

Then, given k_1, you can use the transition equation again (after setting t equal to 1) to determine k_2, and given k_2 you can use it (after setting t equal to 2) to determine k_3, and so on.

The transition equation and knowledge of the level of technology for all future time periods tell you everything you need to know about how our simple economy evolves over time. Once you know the value of the capital-labor ratio in each period in the future, you can figure out the absolute amount of capital in the economy in each period by simply multiplying each period's capital-labor ratio by N, the amount of labor available. Then, since you know each period's total capital and labor supplies, you can use the production function to determine the economy's output in each period. Knowing the path through time of the capital-labor ratio also lets you determine wage and interest rates at each future date. How? By applying the equations linking these factor prices to their marginal products, which depend, of course, on the prevailing capital-labor ratios.

From knowledge of the wage and the interest rate in each period, you can also determine consumption by the young and the old in each period and, thus, aggregate consumption. Recall that total consumption by the young in any period equals α times the prevailing wage times the number of young people. Consumption by the old in any period equals principal plus interest on the economy's assets—the capital stock multiplied by one plus the interest rate. Finally, by subtracting each period's total consumption from that period's output, you can calculate the economy's total saving, which, of course, also equals its total investment.

TRACKING THE ECONOMY'S GROWTH PATH: A NUMERICAL EXAMPLE

A numerical example is worth lots of words. Let's start at time $t = 0$, insert values of 0.5 for α, 0.3 for β, and 10 for A in the transition equation, and see how the economy evolves. By keeping the technology coefficient fixed at 10 for all time periods, we'll be able to concentrate solely on the process of capital accumulation. Since $(1 - \alpha)(1 - \beta)A$ equals $0.5 \times 0.7 \times 10 = 3.5$, the general form of our transition equation is $k_{t+1} = 3.5k_t^{.3}$. Finally, let's assume the population size of each generation (N) equals 100 and that the supply of capital at time 0, when we begin looking at our economy, equals 150. Hence, k_0 is 1.5 (1.5 units of capital for every worker). Application of our transition equation for periods $t = 1$ through $t = 5$ yields the following:

$k_1 = 3.5 \times 1.500^{.3} = 3.953$.

$k_2 = 3.5 \times 3.953^{.3} = 5.286$.

$k_3 = 3.5 \times 5.286^{.3} = 5.768$.

$k_4 = 3.5 \times 5.768^{.3} = 5.921$.

TABLE 3.1 ILLUSTRATIVE TRANSITION PATH

Period	k_t	K_t	Y_t	w_t	r_t	c_{yt}	c_{ot}	S_t	I_t
0	1.500	150.0	1129.3	7.905	2.259	3.953	4.888	245.27	245.27
1	3.593	395.3	1510.3	10.572	1.146	5.286	8.484	133.34	133.34
2	5.286	528.6	1647.9	11.535	.935	5.768	10.230	48.17	48.17
3	5.768	576.8	1691.6	11.841	.880	5.921	10.843	15.29	15.29
4	5.921	592.1	1704.9	11.934	.864	5.967	11.035	4.66	4.66
5	5.967	596.7	1709.0	11.963	.859	5.981	11.094	1.41	1.41
6	5.981	598.1	1710.2	11.971	.858	5.986	11.112	0.42	0.42
7	5.985	598.5	1710.5	11.974	.857	5.987	11.117	0.13	0.13
$\vdots$	$\vdots$	$\vdots$	$\vdots$	$\vdots$	$\vdots$	$\vdots$	$\vdots$	$\vdots$	$\vdots$
∞	5.987	598.7	1710.6	11.975	.857	5.987	11.119	0.00	0.00

Assumptions: $k_0 = 1.500$; $\alpha = .5$; $\beta = .3$; $A = 10$; $N = 100$

$$k_5 = 3.5 \times 5.921^{.3} = 5.967.$$

$$k_6 = 3.5 \times 5.967^{.3} = 5.981.$$

$$k_7 = 3.5 \times 5.981^{.3} = 5.985.$$

We can use these results on the capital-labor ratio plus other equations from our model to determine the time paths of all of the other variables. Appendix table 3A.1 lists the equations of our model. Table 3.1 uses these equations and the assumed values of A, N, α, and β to track all of the economy's economic variables for the periods 0 through 7. It also indicates the long-run (time $t = \infty$) values of our economy, which we'll explain later.

Examine the results in Table 3.1, starting with the values of the economy's variables at time 0. Plugging 150 for K_0 and 100 for N into the production function, we find that total output at time 0 equals 1,129.3. If we measure output in bushels of corn, we can say that the economy produces 1,129.3 bushels at time 0. As discussed above, knowledge of the capital-labor ratio is crucial for determining the values of the wage and interest rate. Using our formulas for the marginal products of labor and capital, we find w_0 equals 7.905 (bushels of corn per worker) and r_0 equals 2.259 (bushels of corn per unit of capital).

Since we measure output and capital in the same units (here, bushels of corn), r_0 is a unit-free number (its units are bushels of corn per bushel of corn). By a unit-free number, we mean that r_0 is a percentage rate of return—an interest rate. In the real world we are used to annual interest rates in the single digits, such as 3 percent or 8 percent. So, at first glance, a value of 2.259 (225.9 percent) for r_0 seems very high. But although r_0 is an interest rate, it is not an annual interest rate.

Recall that each period in our model corresponds to roughly 30 years, so r_0 is roughly a 30-year interest rate. The corresponding annual interest rate is 4.017

percent. Here's why. With an annual interest rate of 4.017 percent, the 30-year interest rate is calculated by determining how much $1.00 invested at 4.017 percent each year would yield at the end of 30 years. The answer is found by multiplying $1.00 by 1.04017 30 times (multiplying $1.00 by 1.04017 raised to the power 30). The resulting amount is $3.259, which equals the initial $1.00 invested plus $2.259 in interest.

The remaining variables in the first row of Table 3.1 are consumption by the young, c_{y0}; consumption by the old, c_{o0}; the economy's aggregate saving, S_0; and the economy's aggregate investment, I_0, all measured at time 0. With $\alpha = 0.5$, the young always consume half their wages, so $c_{o0} = .5 \times w_0 = 3.953$. The old consume their capital plus interest on that capital. We've already determined that each old person at time 0 has 1.5 units of capital. At the end of the period, the elderly each consume $1.5(1 + r_0) = 1.5 \times 3.259 = 4.888$ units of output (their original capital plus interest earned on it). If we add together the consumption by all the young and all the old and subtract this value of aggregate consumption from the economy's output, we arrive at the economy's total saving at time 0. The value given in the table is 245.27 units of output. This is the same value as the economy's total investment at time 0, where I_0 is calculated as $K_1 - K_0$. Indeed, our economy's saving equals its investment in each period. This should come as no surprise since national saving (the nation's acquisition of additional real assets) equals national investment (the addition to its stock of real assets used in production).

WHERE DOES THE ECONOMY GO, AND WHEN DOES IT GET THERE?

Now that you understand our simple economy at time 0, let's ask what happens to it over time. The short answer is that the economy grows. It enjoys an increasing stock of capital, which helps produce higher levels of output. Since the labor supply is fixed, the increase in capital also means an increase in the capital-labor ratio. This process of capital deepening raises the marginal product of labor and lowers the marginal product of capital, meaning higher wage rates and lower interest rates.

Each of the variables listed in Table 3.1 converges to specific long-run (time $t = \infty$) values. For example, the long-run value of output is 1,710.6, and the level of output gets closer and closer to this value through time. This long-run level of output is 51 percent larger than its initial level of 1,129.3 at time 0. Over time, the economy's output grows in total by 51 percent.

Most of the growth in output occurs in the first few periods of the transition. Indeed, measured in terms of the number of periods, all of the economic variables of our economy converge quite rapidly to their long-run values. In the case of output, the absolute growth between times 0 and 1 is 381.0 units, which is 65 percent of the 581.3 units (1,710.6 units $-1,129.3$ units) by which output ultimately grows. The growth in output between time 0 and time 2 is 89 percent of ultimate output growth.

Although convergence in terms of number of periods is quick, convergence in terms of years is rather slow. Again, each period corresponds to 30 years. So even after 30 years—the amount of real-world time between periods 0 and 1—completed output growth falls short—in this case, 35 percent short—of ultimate output growth.[6]

6 Fairly slow transitions are not simply an artifact of the current model. More realistic models in which each period corresponds to a year and people live for 75 or so periods also produce slow transitions.

GROWTH IN THE SHORT AND LONG RUNS

Another way of saying that output converges through time to a fixed (unchanging) value is to say that growth in our model slows down and ultimately ceases; growth is a temporary phenomenon. Should we be surprised by this convergence of the economy's capital stock and the eventual cessation of growth? Maybe, and maybe not. First, by keeping the population size of each generation constant at $N = 100$ and keeping technology fixed at the value $A = 10$, we've eliminated two mechanisms—population growth and technological change—that could keep the economy's output growing forever.

The only other source of output growth is an increasing capital stock. But for the economy to continue to grow at a rate that does not diminish through time, the capital stock would have to grow larger and larger. The explanation for why the capital stock does not continually increase, but instead converges to a fixed value, runs like this. The capital stock in period 0 is small. As a consequence, the wage in period 0 is low, so saving by the young in that period is limited. But even this limited amount of saving is sufficient to make the capital stock at time 1 larger than the capital stock at time 0. This makes the wage at time 1 larger, facilitating even more saving by the young at time 1. But as each period passes, the amount by which the wage rises becomes smaller. The reason has to do with diminishing returns to additional capital. When capital is very scarce, adding one more unit has a big impact on increasing the wage. But when capital is very abundant, adding another unit has only a negligible effect on the wage. Hence, along the transition path, the growth rate of the wage gets smaller and smaller, until eventually the wage doesn't change at all. At that point, with the wage constant, every generation saves the same amount when young and brings the same amount of capital into old age. As a result, the capital stock, as well as the wage, remains constant from one period to the next.

THE STEADY STATE

The long-run position, or state to which the economy converges, is called its **steady state**. As we've seen, our economy's growth rate in the long run is steady, albeit steady at the value of zero. Not only does output remain constant through time in our economy's steady state, but so do all other economic variables. We can find the long-run values of economic variables—the economy's steady state—by repeated use of the transition equation. This method of determining where the economy is ultimately headed works fine, but it is tedious. There is a quicker method that also uses the transition equation. It exploits the fact that if the economy is in its steady state in period t, the economy's capital-labor ratio a period later, at time $t + 1$, will be the same as at time t. Let's call the steady-state value of the capital-labor ratio $\bar{k}$. Then if the economy is in its steady state at time t, $k_t = \bar{k}$ and $k_{t+1} = \bar{k}$. Since our transition equation relating the capital-labor ratios in two adjacent periods holds whether or not we are in the steady state, we can replace k_{t+1} and k_t in the transition equation by $\bar{k}$ and write

Steady state
The long-run position toward which the economy converges; a situation in which all economic variables grow at the same rate (which may be zero)

$$\bar{k} = (1 - \alpha)(1 - \beta)A\bar{k}^{\beta}.$$

The final step in deriving the steady-state value of the capital-labor ratio is to solve this equation for $\bar{k}$.[7] The solution is given by

$$\bar{k} = [(1 - \alpha)(1 - \beta)A]^{1/(1-\beta)}.$$

To illustrate the use of this equation, assume $\alpha = .5$, $\beta = .3$, and $A = 10$. This gives

$$\bar{k} = 3.5^{1.42857} = 5.987,$$

which is the same value we eventually find by repeated use of the transition equation.

We can use the value of the steady-state capital-labor ratio to calculate directly the steady-state values of all the other economic variables. Specifically, we multiply $\bar{k}$ by N to calculate the steady-state capital stock, $\bar{K}$. Inserting the steady-state values of capital and labor into the production function determines the steady-state level of output, $\bar{Y}$. We can also use the steady-state capital-labor ratio to determine the marginal products of labor and capital that prevail in the steady state; they will equal the steady-state values of the wage and interest rate, $\bar{w}$ and $\bar{r}$, respectively. Finally, the steady-state values of consumption when young, $\bar{c}_y$, and consumption when old, $\bar{c}_o$, are calculated as $\alpha\bar{w}$ and $\bar{k}(1 + \bar{r})$, respectively.

STEADY-STATE SAVING AND INVESTMENT

Since the capital stock is fixed in the steady state—it's the same period after period—the change in the capital stock between any two time periods when the economy is in its steady state is zero. Since national investment is defined as the change over time in the economy's capital stock, the steady-state value of national investment is zero. So too is the steady-state value of national saving.[8]

A steady-state level of saving of zero may seem strange at first. After all, even when the economy is in its steady state, there are still new generations coming along each period who save for their old age. True, but in the steady state, the positive saving by the young just offsets the negative saving (the dissaving) by the old, leaving total saving equal to zero. In each period in the steady state, each old person receives income of $\bar{r}\bar{k}$, but consumes $\bar{k}(1 + \bar{r})$. Hence, each old person's saving is $\bar{r}\bar{k} - \bar{k}(1 + \bar{r}) = -\bar{k}$. But $\bar{k}$ not only equals the steady-state dissaving of each old person; it also equals the amount of capital being accumulated by each young person, that is, the amount of saving by each young person. Hence, the steady-state saving of the young is exactly offset by the steady-state dissaving of the old, and aggregate saving equals zero.

HOW GROWTH AFFECTS THE WELFARE OF DIFFERENT GENERATIONS

The fact that the wage rate rises and the interest rate falls in our transition has important implications for the welfare of each generation. The rising wage shifts the budget

7 We do so by dividing each side of the equation by $\bar{k}^{\beta}$, so that $\bar{k}/\bar{k}^{\beta} = (1 - \alpha)(1 - \beta)A$, or $\bar{k}^{1-\beta} = (1 - \alpha)(1 - \beta)A$. Next, we raise each side of this equation to the power $1/(1 - \beta)$.

8 If we were to include depreciation of the capital stock in our model, the steady state would feature positive gross investment, with the level of gross investment each period just sufficient to make up for the depreciation of capital in that period. Although gross investment would be positive, net investment—gross investment less depreciation—would be zero, as would net national saving, defined as total output minus depreciation minus total consumption.

constraints of successive generations outward; the lower interest rate rotates the budget constraints inward and away from consumption when old. The net impact of these changes on successive generations is indicated in Table 3.1. Compare, for example, the consumption levels when young and when old of the generations born at times 0 and 1. In reading the consumption values of these and other generations, keep in mind that a generation is old a period later than when it is young. Hence, the value of each generation's old-age consumption can be found in the row below the value of its consumption when young. In the case of generation 0, consumption when young is 3.953, and consumption when old is 8.484. For generation 1, consumption when young is 5.286, and consumption when old is 10.230. Thus, generation 1 consumes 33.7 percent more when young and 20.6 percent more when old than generation 0.[9]

Let's make one more comparison of consumption levels: between generations born in the long-run steady state and the generation born at time 0. The generations born in the steady state enjoy 51.4 percent more consumption when young and 31.1 percent more consumption when old, as shown by point B in Figure 3.4. Thus, the process of economic growth described by this particular illustration of our model has a very powerful effect in raising the living standards of successive generations. Of course, the extent of improvement in economic welfare during the transition to the steady state depends on how far from steady state the transition begins. In our illustration, the economy was rather far from the steady state. Its capital-labor ratio at time 0 was only 25 percent of the steady-state capital-labor ratio.

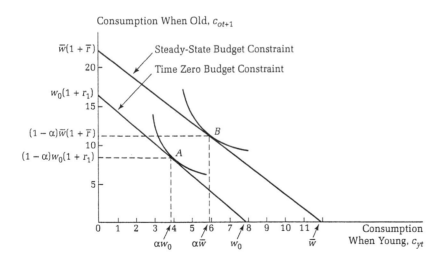

FIGURE 3.4 BUDGET CONSTRAINTS OF SUCCESSIVE GENERATIONS
During the transition in which k rises to a higher steady-state value, the wage rate rises, and the interest rate falls. That means that budget constraints shift outward and become flatter over time. Each successive generation is able to consume on a higher indifference curve, so that each is better off than its predecessor. The figure shows that generations born in the steady state, consuming at point B, enjoy more consumption when young and more when old than do those born at time 0 (point A).

9 The bigger percentage increase in consumption when young than when old across the two generations reflects generation 1's response to the lower interest rate. As discussed in chapter 2, a fall in the interest rate effectively raises the price of second-period consumption, leading households to increase first-period consumption proportionately more.

CASE STUDY

POST–WORLD WAR II JAPANESE AND GERMAN CAPITAL DEEPENING

One question left unanswered about our illustrative transition (Table 3.1) is how it started. How did the capital stock at time 0 come to equal 150 units? If the capital stock at time 0 had instead been 598.7 units—the steady-state value—the capital stock at time 1 and all future dates would also have equaled 598.7 units. This is what the term "steady-state value of the capital stock" means.

One way the transition may have gotten started is through a war. Suppose the economy had been in its steady state, but that at the beginning of period 0 (before production occurs), a war destroyed almost three-quarters of the capital stock, leaving only 150 units of capital for production at the end of period 0. For purposes of discussion, also suppose there was no loss in life in the war, so the postwar labor force always equals N. Then the postwar (period 0 and beyond) growth of the economy would be exactly as shown by the transition in Table 3.1.

Let's further suppose the war was fought against another country with the same economic structure, but which suffered no damage to its capital stock or to its labor force and, in that sense, was victorious. (By the "same economic structure" we mean the same values of A, α, and β, and, thus, the same form of the transition equation.) Finally, let's assume the victorious country was also in a steady state prior to the war. Since the victor lost none of its inputs at time 0, it remains in its steady state in time 0 and thereafter. The victorious country thus experiences zero growth and has a zero saving rate in the postwar period. The losing country, whose economy is described in Table 3.1, experiences rapid growth and exhibits a high saving rate for several periods. The postwar growth and saving rates of the losing country always exceed those of the winning country. However, the catching-up process slows over time, in the sense that the losing country's growth and saving rates are initially very high and then decline through time.

Citizens of the winning country may be distressed to observe that it is neither growing nor saving in the postwar period, while the losing country is doing a lot of both as it catches up. The winner can take solace from the fact that during the catching-up period, its per capita income remains above the losing country's. How long does the catching up process take? Quite a while, according to Table 3.1. Even after two periods—60 years in real time—the losing country's per capita income is still less than the winning country's.

This discussion has some strong parallels to the post–World War II performances of the Japanese and German economies compared with that of the United States. Intense Allied bombing during World War II destroyed a large portion of the Japanese and German capital stocks. In contrast, the U.S. nonmilitary capital stock survived the war entirely undamaged. As a consequence, Japan and Germany started the postwar era with much smaller capital-labor ratios than the United States.[10] To a certain extent, the remarkable postwar growth and saving rates of the Japanese and German econ-

10 Postwar Japanese, German, and American capital-labor ratios depended not just on the amount of capital that survived the war but also on the number of Japanese, German, and American workers who survived. Although a very large number of workers—or potential workers—in each of these countries were killed in the hostilities, there was a larger proportionate destruction of capital than of workers in Japan and Germany than in the United States.

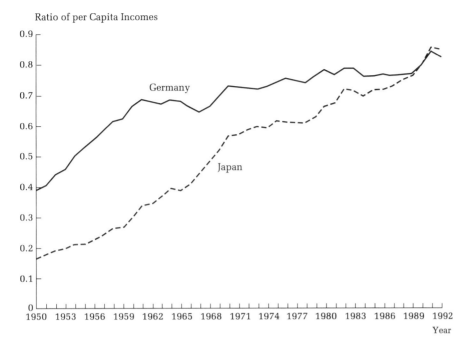

FIGURE 3.5 LIVING STANDARDS IN JAPAN AND GERMANY RELATIVE TO THAT OF THE UNITED STATES, 1950–1992
Japan and Germany started the postwar period with much smaller capital-labor ratios and much smaller living standards than the United States. Since then, both countries have restored their capital-labor ratios. Their living standards are now more than 80 percent of the U.S. living standard.

Source: R. Summers and A. Heston, The Penn World Table, *Department of Economics, University of Pennsylvania 1996.*

omies can be understood as a process of catching up with the United States through restoration of their steady-state capital-labor ratios. Figure 3.5 shows the post-1950 convergence of the Japanese and German living standards to that in the United States (measured by per capita income). The figure indicates that Japanese and German per capita incomes were only 16 percent and 39 percent of the U.S. level in 1950, respectively. By 1992, Japan and Germany had reached 84 and 82 percent of U.S. per capita income, respectively.

Figure 3.6 compares saving rates in the three economies between 1960 and 1997. Over this period, the annual Japanese saving rate averaged 1.8 times the U.S. rate, and the German saving rate averaged 1.3 times the U.S. rate. The Japanese and German saving rates declined over time in accordance with the prediction of our simple model. But the U.S. rate has declined as well, so huge differences remain between the saving rates of Japan and Germany, on the one hand, and the United States, on the other.

To summarize these postwar comparisons, the Japanese and German economies have been catching up to the American economy over the past several decades. But the American economy has not been a stationary target. Rather, its saving and growth rates

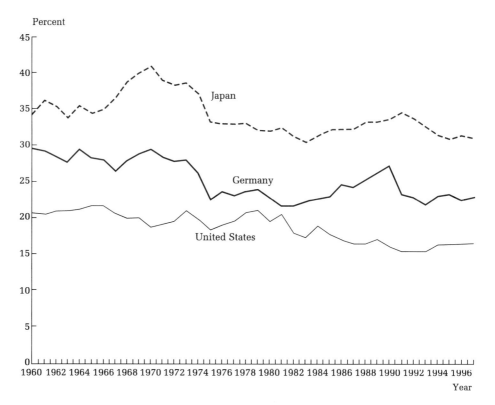

FIGURE 3.6 U.S., JAPANESE, AND GERMAN NATIONAL SAVING RATES, 1960–1997

Source: OECD.

have declined, thus causing the United States to play a form of "catch-down" with the Japanese and German economies.

CASE STUDY
THE BLACK PLAGUE

If wars can produce a sudden decline in a country's capital-labor ratio, is there anything that can produce a sudden increase? One such mechanism is an epidemic that wipes out a large fraction of the labor force. Unfortunately, the world has experienced such epidemics off and on throughout recorded history. The current AIDS epidemic is projected to kill 30 million primarily prime-age adults by the turn of the century.

The most notorious epidemic in history was the Black Death—the scourge of bubonic and pneumonic plague that killed about one-third of Europe's population between 1348 and 1351. The plague's intensity differed across regions; in some areas

TABLE 3.2 TRANSITION PATH FOLLOWING AN EPIDEMIC

Period	k_t	K_t	Y_t	w_t	r_t	c_{yt}	c_{ot}	S_t	I_t
Pre-plague	5.987	598.7	1710.6	11.975	.857	5.987	11.119	0.00	0.00
0	8.936	598.7	1292.5	13.503	.648	6.752	9.864	−146.36[a]	−146.36
1	6.752	452.4	1188.2	12.414	.788	6.207	12.072	−36.48	−36.48
2	6.207	415.9	1158.6	12.105	.836	6.052	11.395	−10.36	−10.36
3	6.052	405.5	1149.9	12.014	.851	6.007	11.201	−3.06	−3.06
4	6.007	402.5	1147.3	11.986	.855	5.993	11.144	−0.91	−0.91
5	5.993	401.5	1146.5	11.978	.856	5.989	11.127	−0.27	−0.27
6	5.989	401.3	1146.3	11.976	.857	5.988	11.122	−0.08	−0.08
7	5.988	401.2	1146.2	11.975	.857	5.987	11.120	−0.02	−0.02
⋮	⋮	⋮	⋮	⋮	⋮	⋮	⋮	⋮	⋮
∞	5.987	401.2	1146.2	11.975	.857	5.987	11.119	0.00	0.00

[a] Note that in subtracting aggregate consumption from output to form aggregate saving in period t, we need to multiply the consumption of the old by 100 (the number of elderly at time t), whereas we need to multiply the consumption of the young by only 67 (the number of young survivors of the time t epidemic). At any point from time 1 onward, there are always 67 old and 67 young people.

Assumptions: $k_0 = 8.936$; $\alpha = .5$; $\beta = .3$; $A = 10$; $N = 67$

almost half the population was wiped out. In England the plague returned in 1368, 1374, and 20 more times in the fifteenth century. The Black Death, combined with recurring wars, reduced England's population from 3.7 million in 1348 to 2.1 million in 1430.[11] The dramatic population declines in England and other regions were associated with equally dramatic increases in capital-labor ratios, since the principal form of capital—agricultural land—remained intact. Economic historians, studying commercial records of the period, report substantial increases in real wages in the aftermath of the plague. In England, real wages rose by over one-quarter in the years after the Black Death.[12]

An increase in real wages as a consequence of a sudden rise in the capital-labor ratio is exactly what our model predicts. Table 3.2 illustrates the case of an epidemic that strikes our economy at time 0, when it is in its steady state with a capital stock of 598.7 units and a workforce of 100 young people. When the epidemic hits, it wipes out a third of young workers, reducing their total to 67. The size of each generation born after the epidemic is also 67. This reflects our assumption that at the end of each period, the generation that is young gives birth to an equal number of children, who constitute the young workers of the following period.

The epidemic kills people, not capital. So at time 0 there are still 598.7 units of capital on hand to be used by the 67 surviving workers. Thus, the capital-labor ratio at time 0 no longer equals the steady-state value of 5.987—598.7 units of capital divided by 100 workers. Instead it equals 8.936—598.7 units of capital divided by 67 workers. At time 0, the higher capital-labor ratio drives up the wage and drives down the interest

11 Robert Paul Thomas and Douglass North, The Rise of the Western World (New York: Cambridge University Press, 1973).

12 B. H. Slicher Van Bath, The Agrarian History of Western Europe, A.D. 500–1850 (London: Edward Arnold, 1963), pp. 326–327.

rate. This makes the young survivors of the epidemic better off, at least on economic grounds, but makes the elderly survivors worse off; they have the same amount of capital but earn less interest on it.

The wage at time 0 is driven up to 13.503—13 percent larger than the pre-epidemic steady-state wage. The interest rate is driven down to 0.648, about a quarter smaller than its pre-epidemic value. As the economy evolves, the capital-labor ratio falls back to its pre-epidemic, steady-state value. This produces a decline over time in the wage and an increase over time in the interest rate. Since the wage remains above its pre-epidemic value until the economy returns to its former steady-state capital-labor ratio, all generations born in the interim end up better off as a result of the epidemic.

The explanation for why the capital-labor ratio falls during the transition runs like this. The increase in the capital-labor ratio produced by the epidemic raises the wage of the generation that is young at time 0. This leads them to accumulate more capital for period 1 than would otherwise have been the case. But because of diminishing returns, the wage at time 0 increases by a smaller percentage than the capital-labor ratio. This means that the capital-labor ratio at time 1, which depends on the wage at time 0, increases by a smaller percentage than does the capital-labor ratio at time 0. So there is more capital relative to labor at time 1 than there would have been without the epidemic, but not as much as at time 0, immediately following the epidemic. Over time, the capital-labor ratio gets smaller each period, but the reductions in the capital-labor ratio between successive periods also get smaller, so the ratio ends up stabilizing at the steady-state value.

During the transition back to the steady state, the national economy illustrated in Table 3.2 dissaves. The positive saving done by the young in each period is more than outweighed by the dissaving of the old in the period. Again, this makes sense, because the old people alive in, say, period 5 are dissaving based on the saving they did out of the wages they earned when young—w_4. But since wages are falling over the transition, w_4 exceeds w_5—the wage out of which the young in period 5 save. So the wage underlying the dissaving of the old (last period's wage) exceeds the wage underlying the saving of the young (this period's wage).

The epidemic does not change the form of the transition equation for the capital-labor ratio, and that is why the economy ultimately ends up with the same steady-state capital-labor ratio, wage and interest rates, levels of consumption when young and old, and level of output per worker. But in permanently reducing the population size—the number of young suppliers of labor and the number of old suppliers of capital—the epidemic permanently reduces the total supplies of both capital and labor as well as the level of output. In Table 3.2 the steady-state levels of capital and output are precisely one-third less than their pre-epidemic steady-state values. The one-third reduction in capital and output is the same as that in the workforce. That is what we expect, since the transition equation tells us that capital per worker and output per worker are the same as in the pre-epidemic steady state. In other words, the population size of each generation, N, ultimately determines the absolute scale of the economy, but not the level of capital per worker or any of the variables that depend on capital per worker.

THE TRANSITION PATH DIAGRAM

Now that we've described our simple economy algebraically and numerically, let's describe it graphically. The diagram we'll now develop shows the transition path for the capital-labor ratio as well as its steady-state value. It can be used to understand what happens in the aftermath of wars, epidemics, baby booms, and baby busts (sudden and dramatic reductions in the fertility rate). It can also be used to understand the economy's response to changes in saving preferences (changes in α), changes in the form of the production function (changes in β), and changes in the level of technology (changes in A). Finally, as we'll explore in detail in chapters 6 and 7, it can be used to understand the saving and growth effects of fiscal and monetary policy.

The diagram is simply a plot of the capital-labor ratio at one point in time, say time $t + 1$, against the capital-labor ratio the period before, at time t. According to our transition equation and our assumed values for α, β, and A, we know that $k_{t+1} = 3.5k_t^{.3}$. Figure 3.7 plots this relationship. Specifically, we measure k_t on the horizontal axis and its associated value of k_{t+1}, given by $3.5k_t^{.3}$, on the vertical axis. For example, for k_t equal to 1.50, the value of k_{t+1} is 3.953 ($3.5 \times 1.50^{.3}$), so the height of the curve above the value of 1.50 is 3.953. For k_t equal to 4.00, $k_{t+1} = 3.5 \times 4.00^{.3} = 5.305$, and

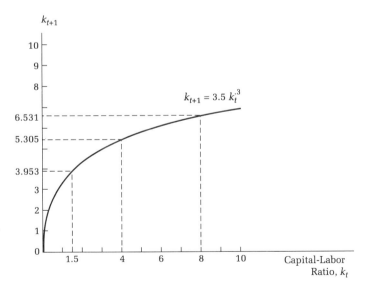

FIGURE 3.7 TRANSITION DIAGRAM
The transition curve depicted here relates the capital-labor ratio in any period, t, to the ratio in the next period, $t + 1$. For any value of the current ratio, k_t, measured on the horizontal axis, the height of the curve measures next period's ratio, k_{t+1}.

the height of the curve above the value of 4.00 is 5.305. And if k_t is 8.00, then k_{t+1} is $3.5 \times 8.00^{.3} = 6.531$, which is the height of the curve above 8.00.

The concave shape of the transition curve reflects the fact that the value of β, which determines the exponent of k_t, is a number less than 1. The larger the value of β, the less concave the shape of the curve. The curve passes through the origin, since when k_t equals zero, k_{t+1} also equals zero. Finally, the height of the curve for values of k_t greater than zero depends on the values of A, α, and β. For example, if we set A equal to 20 rather than 10, the transition equation becomes $k_{t+1} = 7.0k_t^{.3}$, and the graph of the k_{t+1} curve lies above the one shown in Figure 3.7.

USING THE TRANSITION CURVE TO TRACK THE TIME PATH OF THE CAPITAL-LABOR RATIO

Since the transition equation holds for any two successive periods, the transition diagram holds as well. Figure 3.8 shows how we can use the transition diagram over and over again to determine the time path of the capital-labor ratio. This figure is identical to Figure 3.7 except that it includes a straight line extending from the origin at a 45-degree angle. This 45-degree line will help us reuse the transition curve to follow the economy over time.

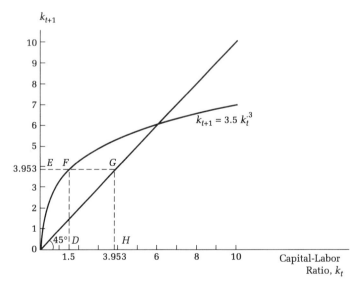

FIGURE 3.8 ADDING THE 45° LINE TO THE TRANSITION DIAGRAM
Adding a 45° line to the transition diagram makes determination of the time path of the capital-labor ratio easy. At any point along the 45° line, the horizontal distance from the origin equals the vertical distance from the origin. Starting at time 0 with a capital-labor ratio of 1.5 at point D, we see from this transition curve that the time 1 ratio is 3.953 at points F and E. By projecting this height over to the 45° line and then downward, we can find the value 3.953 on the horizontal axis. The properties of the 45° line ensure that distance OH equals distance OE. Thus, k_1 equals 3.953 at point H on the horizontal axis.

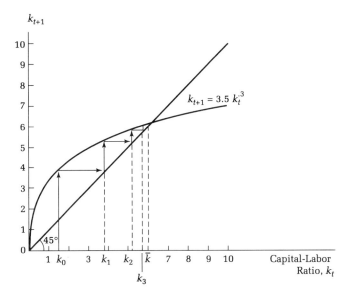

FIGURE 3.9 USING THE TRANSITION DIAGRAM: A SHORTCUT
The transition diagram with a 45° line can be used to trace the movement of the capital-labor ratio from any initial value to its ultimate steady-state value. Beginning at k_0, we read up to the transition curve to find k_1. We then move from that point over to the 45° line and downward, to locate k_1 on the horizontal axis. From that point, we read up to the curve line to determine k_2. The arrows indicate a shortcut way of determining the capital-labor ratio in any period and its ultimate steady-state value.

To see how this works, let's use the curve to plot the transition calculated in Table 3.1. Specifically, let's start at time 0 with a value of k_0 equal to 1.500. This value is marked on the horizontal axis in Figure 3.8. Given this value, we go up to the curve to find the value for k_1, which, as measured by the length of the segment DF, is 3.953. Now if we want to reuse the transition curve to find the value of k_2 given the value of k_1 of 3.953, we need to measure 3.953 along the horizontal axis. The 45-degree line helps us do that. We start at the value of 3.953 on the vertical axis (point E), then draw a horizontal line over to the 45-degree line at point G, and then draw a vertical from point G down to point H. The horizontal distance from the origin to point H is 3.953— the distance we wanted to measure on the horizontal axis. How do we know the distance from the origin to point H is 3.953? Because of the symmetry of the triangles $0EG$ and $0HG$. A shortcut in getting from point D to point H is simply to start at D, go up to the curve to point F, across to G, and back down to point H.

Figure 3.9 shows the repeated use of this technique. Starting at $k_0 = 1.500$, we go up to the curve, over to the 45-degree line, and then down to find k_1. We do the same to find k_2, k_3, and so on. To shorten our steps even further, we can skip the going down, and simply go up to the curve, over to the 45-degree line, up to the curve, over to the 45-degree line, and so on. The process of going up and over repeatedly is indicated by the arrows in the figure.

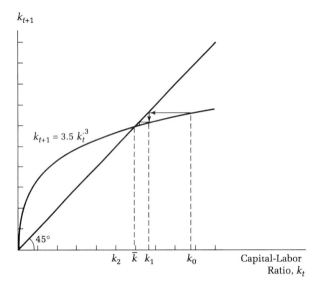

FIGURE 3.10 TRANSITION FOLLOWING AN EPIDEMIC
An epidemic that killed many young workers would initially raise the capital-labor ratio. Starting from this higher value of k_0, forces would be set in motion that would restore the capital-labor ratio to its steady-state value of k. The arrows in the figure trace the transition.

As Figure 3.9 makes clear, following the capital-labor ratio in this manner leads to convergence at the point where the curve intersects the 45-degree line. This intersection occurs at $\bar{k}$—the steady-state value of the capital-labor ratio. At the value of $\bar{k}$, going up to the curve, across to the 45-degree line, and then down puts us back at $\bar{k}$. So when k_t equals $\bar{k}$, k_{t+1} equals $\bar{k}$ as well, which is the definition of the steady-state capital-labor ratio.

The transition just described could well have been initiated at time 0 by a war that reduced the economy's capital-labor ratio from its steady-state value of 5.987 to a value of 1.500. Alternatively, it could have been initiated by a one-time baby boom occurring at time 0 that raised the value of N, the population size of each new generation, from 100 to 399. If the economy had previously been in its steady state, its capital stock would have equaled 598.7, and the higher value of N would have lowered the time 0 value of the capital-labor ratio to 1.500.

We can also use the diagram to describe the transition following the epidemic illustrated in Table 3.2. We do so in Figure 3.10 by starting with $k_0 = 8.936$, which is to the right of the steady-state capital-labor ratio of 5.987. To determine the value of k_1, we again go up to the curve. And to measure k_1 along the horizontal axis, we again go across to the 45-degree line and back down. The arrows in the figure show how we can trace the transition to the steady state by going over and down repeatedly. Whether we measure the capital-labor ratio each period on the vertical or horizontal axis, it is clear that Figure 3.9 shows a transition in which the capital-labor ratio rises through time to

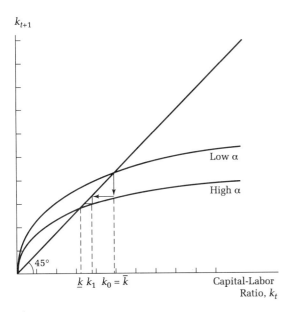

FIGURE 3.11 TRANSITION FOLLOWING AN INCREASE IN THE PROPENSITY TO CONSUME
The transition curve is drawn for given values of A, the technology coefficient; β, capital's share of output; and α, the propensity to donsume. Changes in any of these values will affect the transition curve. In the diagram, an increase in α has the effect of rotating the transition curve downward, triggering a transition to a new, lower steady state. Beginning at $k_0 = \bar{k}$, the capital-labor ratio falls over time until it reaches the new steady-state value $\underline{k}$ where the lower transition curve intersects the 45° line.

$\bar{k}$, and Figure 3.10 shows a transition in which the capital-labor ratio declines through time to $\bar{k}$.

USING THE TRANSITION DIAGRAM TO STUDY CHANGES IN SAVING PREFERENCES

In our model, saving preferences are governed by the value of α, the propensity to consume when young. The larger the value of α, the smaller the fraction of wages that each young person saves for old age. A decline in α has no permanent impact on saving in our model (steady-state saving is, as before, zero), but it does alter the steady state toward which the economy moves and lowers saving during the transition to this new steady state.

Figure 3.11 shows the transition curve before and after a rise in α. Unlike the war and epidemic examined in Figures 3.9 and 3.10, a rise in α does not involve moving along the historic transition curve. Rather, it causes a shift to a new transition curve, followed by a movement along that new curve. The reason we need to deal with a new transition curve is that the formula for the transition curve, $k_{t+1} = A(1 - \alpha)(1 - \beta)k_t^{\beta}$, clearly depends on α. Hence, our plot of values of k_{t+1} for different values of k_t will depend on the value we choose for α. Larger values of α shift the curve downward.

Suppose the economy of Figure 3.11 is in its steady state with capital-labor ratio $\bar{k}$ at time 0, when the first generation to have a larger α appears. The transition path of the capital-labor ratio will be as indicated by the arrows. To find the capital-labor ratio prevailing at time 1, we start with the value of k_0 which, by assumption, equals $\bar{k}$, and go down to the new transition curve. Then we follow this new transition curve by going across and down, across and down, until we reach $\underline{k}$, the new steady-state capital-labor ratio.

Since $\underline{k}$ lies to the left of $\bar{k}$, we see that the increase in α causes a reduction over time in the capital-labor ratio. With the labor supply fixed each period, the decline in the capital-labor ratio means a decline over time in the absolute amount of capital. And since investment is the change over time in capital, national investment must be negative during the transition, as is national saving. Thus, an increased preference for consumption when young produces a temporary decline in national saving, but a permanent reduction in the capital stock.

ADDING POPULATION AND TECHNOLOGICAL CHANGE TO OUR MODEL

With population growth or technological change, the capital accumulation process described above remains basically the same. In particular, each period's capital stock continues to reflect the saving done by the young in the previous period. And if population growth or technological change proceeds at a constant rate, the economy eventually converges to a steady state, albeit not one in which all variables remain constant through time. Instead, some variables remain constant, and others grow at a constant rate.

Consider first population growth, holding the level of technology fixed. Population growth means there are more young people saving each period than there were in the previous period. Consequently, were the amount of saving per young person to remain constant through time, the total capital stock would nonetheless grow simply because there are more young savers around each period. This is precisely what happens in our model in the steady state, assuming a constant rate of population growth. The amount of saving per young person remains the same through time, but the absolute size of the capital stock grows at the same rate as the number of young savers grows. Since young savers are also the economy's young workers, this means the capital stock and the labor supply both grow at the same rate in the steady state. Consequently, the capital-labor ratio in the steady state is constant, just as in the case of no population growth.

So, in the steady state with population growth, we find that all variables that depend on the capital-labor ratio, such as the wage, the interest rate, and output per worker, remain constant. All aggregate variables, such as output, the capital stock, and the workforce, grow at the rate of growth of the population. Thus, the absolute size of the economy grows through time, but in per capita terms it remains constant.

Next, consider technological progress, holding the population fixed. With technological progress, even if the capital-labor ratio were to remain unchanged through time (it doesn't), the wage would grow because the technology coefficient (A), which enters the formula for the marginal product of labor, would be larger each period. But a higher wage each period means that the capital-labor ratio will increase each period as well. The reason is that each generation will save more (accumulate more capital) than the previous generation. Since we are assuming no growth in the workforce, this means a higher capital-labor ratio through time. So technological progress, by raising the level of the wage each period, raises the capital-labor ratio each period.

If the rate of technological progress is constant, the economy will eventually converge to a steady state. This steady state features growth, at a constant rate, in both aggregate variables, such as output and the capital stock, and per capita variables, such as capital per worker, output per worker, and the wage paid per worker. Thus, unlike the steady state with constant population growth, a steady state with constant technological progress means rising living standards through time.

With both technological change and population growth, the economy will reflect the combination of the effects just described, with aggregates growing at the sum of the rates of growth of population and technology, and per capital values growing at the rate of technological change.

TECHNOLOGICAL CHANGE: THE STUDY OF ENDOGENOUS GROWTH

As shown in chapter 1, technological change "explains" a significant share of overall economic growth as well as growth in labor productivity. But there is considerable debate over its source. Some economists believe that what we measure as technological change is largely improvements in the quality of capital and labor; in other words, technological change is mostly embodied in inputs. Others believe that measured technological change primarily reflects pure technological breakthroughs—the discovery of ways to produce more products, better products, and new products with the same inputs.

The importance of technological change and the fact that its precise determinants are poorly understood has made its study a hot topic. Some economists have focused on the role of research and development, as influenced by government patent protection, in producing new technological breakthroughs. Others have studied learning by doing and the diffusion of production know-how among workers, industries, and countries, and even across generations. Still others have considered how better education becomes embodied in human capital and how better technology becomes embodied in physical capital.

What all of this new research has in common is that it makes technological change endogenous to (caused or produced by, and thus, responsive to) economic decisions. For this reason, the growth processes under study are referred to as **endogenous growth**. Endogenous growth models typically predict that the economy

Endogenous Growth
A growth process in which the long-run rate of growth is determined by economic decisions, such as how much to invest in R&D or how much schooling to provide children

will experience a constant rate of technological progress, at least in the long run. But these growth models also show that the particular rate of technological progress the economy ends up with is not immutable. Instead, it reflects economic decisions, such as how much to invest in research and development or how much schooling to provide children.

Another feature common to all endogenous growth models is that the process producing technological change does not peter out over time. To sustain growth through the indefinite future, it is not enough for technology to improve by a fixed amount and then stay fixed. Instead, technology must continually improve. For this to happen, the forces generating technological progress cannot be subject to diminishing returns. For example, if research and development is the critical input in technological progress, one must assume that regardless of the amount of R&D done in the past, an additional dollar spent on R&D will generate as much additional technological progress now as it did in the past.

We do not have space to extend our life-cycle model to include endogenous growth, but be assured that such extensions can be made. Consequently, think of endogenous growth as providing an economic explanation for changes through time in *A* that, for convenience, we take in this book to be exogenous.

CHAPTER SUMMARY

1. This chapter developed the demand side of our life-cycle model and combined it with the supply side to produce a simple model of economic growth.

2. Firms' demands for capital and labor result from their maximization of profit. Firms hire these inputs up to the point at which their marginal revenues equal their marginal costs. The marginal cost of capital is the interest rate, and the marginal cost of labor is the wage.

3. Marginal products of capital and labor depend on the capital-labor ratio. If the capital-labor ratio is high, capital is relatively abundant, and labor is relatively scarce. This makes the marginal product of capital low and the marginal product of labor high.

4. The values of capital and labor entering the marginal product formulas represent the demands by firms for these inputs. But in equilibrium, the total demands by firms for capital and labor must equal the total supplies of these inputs by the household sector. At any one time the supply of capital is given by the past asset accumulation of those who are currently old. And the labor supply is given by the number of young people. Equating each period's input supplies and demands determines the period's equilibrium wage and interest rate.

5. This period's wage determines next period's capital-labor ratio. But this period's wage depends on this period's capital-labor ratio, so there is a relationship (the transition equation) between this period's and next period's capital-labor ratio.

6. Given the value of the capital-labor ratio at some point, say time 0, we can use the transition equation to calculate the capital-labor ratio in all subsequent periods. And the time path of the capital-labor ratio is all we need to compute the time paths of all of the economy's other variables. In the absence of population growth or technological change, growth as well as saving are temporary, or transitional, phenomena.

7. The fact that country A is growing faster and saving more than country B does not necessarily mean that country B will be left in the dust. Country A may simply be catching up with country B. According to our model, the catching-up process can take many years.

8. The process of transitional growth may be triggered by shocks to the economy's capital-labor ratio such as wars, epidemics, baby booms, and baby busts. Transitional growth may also be triggered by factors that alter the transition equation. These factors include changes in the propensity of the young to consume (α), in the level of technology (A), and in capital's coefficient in the production function (β). Once the transition curve shifts, the economy's transition is determined by that new curve.

9. If either the population growth rate or the productivity growth rate is constant, the economy will converge to a steady state, but one in which certain variables grow at a constant rate through time.

10. Economists are trying to understand the forces behind technological progress through their research on endogenous growth. Endogenous growth models assume that an economy's rate of technological progress is determined by economic factors, such as the extent of research and development.

APPENDIX 3A.1
REFRESHER ON EXPONENTS

In stating the properties of exponents we let z, a, and b stand for three numbers. In our examples we let z equal 2, a equal 4, and b equal 3. Raising a number to the power zero gives 1.

General From
$z^0 = 1$

Example
$2^0 = 1$

Raising a number to the power 1 gives the number.

General Form
$z^1 = z$

Example
$2^1 = 2$

Negative Exponents

General Form
$z^{-a} = \dfrac{1}{z^a}$

Example
$2^{-4} = \dfrac{1}{2^4} = \dfrac{1}{16} = .0625$

Addition of Exponents

General Form
$z^a \times z^b = z^{a+b}$

Example
$2^2 \times 2^3 = 2^5 = 2 \times 2 \times 2 \times 2 \times 2 = 32$

Subtraction of Exponents

General Form
$\dfrac{z^a}{z^b} = z^a \times z^{-b} = z^{a-b}$

Example
$\dfrac{2^4}{2^3} = 2^4 \times 2^{-3} = 2^1 = 2 = \dfrac{16}{8}$

Multiplication of Exponents

General Form
$(z^a)^b = z^{a \times b}$

Example
$(2^4)^3 = 2^{4 \times 3} = 2^{12} = 4{,}096$

Division of Exponents

General Form
$(z^a)^{1/b} = z^{a/b}$

Example
$(2^4)^{1/3} = 2^{4/3} = 2^{1.333} = 2.519$

"THIS IS THE PART I ALWAYS HATE."

©1994 by Sidney Harris

TABLE 3A.1 COMPLETE MODEL FOR ANY TIME t

Labor supply equals the number of young	$L_t = N$
Capital supply equals assets of the elderly	$K_t = Na_t$
Assets of the elderly equal their savings when young	$a_{t+1} = (1 - \alpha)w_t$
Capital per worker is denoted by k	$k_t = K_t/L_t$
Output	$Y_t = A_t K_t^{\beta} L_t^{1-\beta}$
Marginal product of labor equals the wage	$w_t = (1 - \beta)A_t k_t^{\beta}$
Marginal product of capital equals the interest rate	$r_t = \beta A_t k_t^{\beta-1}$
Transition equation	$k_{t+1} = (1 - \alpha)(1 - \beta)A_t k_t^{\beta}$
The young consume α of their wages	$c_{yt} = \alpha w_t$
The old consume their assets plus interest	$c_{ot} = a_t(1 + r_t)$
National saving equals output less aggregate consumption	$S_t = Y_t - Nc_{yt} - Nc_{ot}$
National investment equals the increase in the capital stock	$I_t = K_{t+1} - K_t$

ECONOMIC FLUCTUATIONS

INTRODUCTION

In July 1990 the U.S. economy entered its ninth postwar **recession**—a period of negative economic growth. The recession, which lasted eight months, interrupted an eight-year period of positive growth—the second longest **expansion** in this century. How did the 1990 recession begin, and how did it end? Why was the previous recession more severe, and why did it last longer?

Understanding the cause of and cure for recessions is perhaps the most interesting and intriguing aspect of macroeconomics. There are a number of suspects, but no clear culprit for this economic crime. And there are lots of proposed remedies, but none that is foolproof. This chapter describes key features of economic booms and busts. It then uses our model to introduce the *real business cycle theory*—one of many explanations of **business cycles**. This theory traces economic fluctuations to shocks to production and utility functions.

The real business cycle theory is controversial. We present it here not because it's necessarily a more convincing explanation than others we'll describe starting in chapter 8, but because it's so easy to exhibit with our model. Indeed, just letting the multifactor productivity coefficient A in the Cobb-Douglas production function change through time transforms our model of smooth growth into one of fluctuating growth.

Before plunging ahead, take a look at the following key questions:

- How do we know whether an economy is in a recession or an expansion?

- How is unemployment defined, and how does it vary over the business cycle?

- How does labor productivity behave over the cycle?

- Which is more volatile: consumption or investment? And why?

Recession
A period of declining output and employment in many sectors of the economy, usually lasting from six months to a year

Expansion
A period between recessions characterized by economic growth

Business cycles
Periodic increases and decreases in output and employment around the economy's long-run growth path

- Are business cycles correlated across countries?

- How do seasonal fluctuations compare with business cycle fluctuations?

- Can our model help explain economic fluctuations?

WHAT ARE ECONOMIC FLUCTUATIONS?

Real gross domestic product normally grows from one year to the next. So does output per capita. But there are periods when growth does not occur, and these periods are generally classified as recessions. Figure 4.1 shows the quarterly performance of real GDP since 1960, with the shaded areas indicating periods of recession. The heavier line shows the level of real GDP, and the lighter line presents the corresponding percentage change in real GDP from its value in the previous quarter.[1]

The figure confirms that recessions are periods of negative and, at times, quite negative, growth. Recessions normally begin with two quarters of consecutive decline in real GDP and end when output stops falling. However, there is no precise rule for determining when a recession begins and when it ends. The formal dating of recessions is done by the Business Cycle Dating Group of the National Bureau of Economic Research (NBER). The NBER announces the beginning date well *after* a recession has begun and the ending date well after the recession has ended. The beginning date of a recession is called the business cycle *peak*; the end is called the *trough. The NBER defines a recession as "a recurring period of decline in total output, income, employment, and trade, usually lasting from six months to a year, and marked by widespread contractions in many sectors of the economy."*

Note that NBER's activity is dating business cycles, *not* predicting them. Its pronouncements are more useful to those wishing to understand how the economy functions than to employers, investors, workers, and others interested in knowing what's ahead. *Forecasting* business cycles is an entirely different activity, one we discuss below.

THE FREQUENCY, DURATION, AND VOLATILITY OF BUSINESS CYCLES

As Figure 4.1 suggests, expansions typically last much longer than recessions. Since 1960, full business cycles, measured from trough to through, have averaged about six years, with recessions averaging about 11 months and expansions just over five years. Interestingly, this pattern has changed over time. Table 4.1 presents data on all business cycles since 1854, divided into three subperiods of about equal length. During the 11 cycles between 1854 and 1900, expansions averaged 27 months, recessions over 23 months, and full cycles about 50 months. From 1900 to 1945, the 11 expansions averaged about 31 months and recessions about 18 months. Since 1945, expansions have been more than twice as long and recessions less than half as long as those before 1900. Indeed, the two longest expansions since 1854 occurred after 1960.

---

1 As is customary, the percentage changes are expressed in annual terms. For example, a 4 percent rate of change from one quarter to the next indicates that if real GDP grew at its current rate for a full year (rather than just one quarter), it would rise by 4 percent.

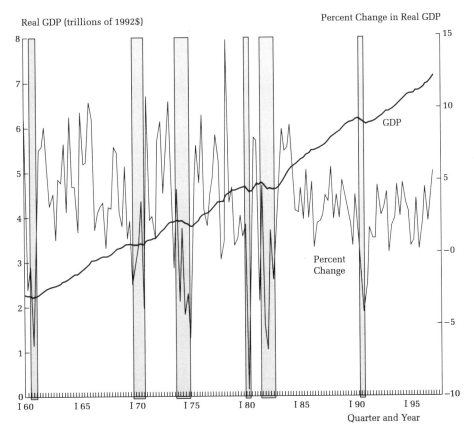

FIGURE 4.1 REAL GDP SINCE 1960
The heavier, smooth line in the figure shows quarterly real GDP since 1960, with shaded areas indicating recessions. The other line shows the corresponding percent changes (at annual rates) from one quarter to the next. It confirms that recessions are indeed periods of negative growth and that most quarters during which real output falls occur in recessions.

Source: National Income and Product Accounts.

Business cycle *volatility*, measured by the magnitude of swings in the growth rate of output, has also changed over time; it has declined. Between 1900 and the beginning of the Great Depression in 1929, output fell by at least 6 percent in four separate years. On six occasions, it rose by at least 10 percent in a single year. Nothing like this has occurred since the early 1950s.[2]

Many macroeconomists attribute the reduced frequency and severity of recessions in the post-Depression era to more active monetary and fiscal policy. There has certainly been no prolonged depression since the 1930s. But the general trend toward shorter recessions predated the 1930s and extended into the 1980s, during the administrations of presidents who seemed to oppose monetary and fiscal activism. Moreover, the apparent volatility of prewar cycles may be partially attributable to the poor quality of prewar data.

2 See R. J. Gordon, ed., The American Business Cycle *(Chicago: University of Chicago Press, 1986), appendix B. Gordon measures output in terms of gross national product (GNP), a statistic closely related to GDP. Many historical studies refer to GNP rather than GDP.*

TABLE 4.1 ECONOMIC FLUCTUATIONS SINCE 1854

Business Cycle		Length (months)	
Peak	Trough	Expansion	Recession
	December 1854		
June 1857	December 1858	30	18
October 1860	June 1861	22	8
April 1865	December 1867	46	32
June 1869	December 1870	18	18
October 1873	March 1879	34	65
March 1882	May 1885	36	38
March 1887	April 1888	22	13
July 1890	May 1891	27	10
January 1893	June 1894	20	17
December 1895	June 1897	18	18
June 1899	December 1900	24	18
September 1902	August 1904	21	23
May 1907	June 1908	33	13
January 1910	January 1912	19	24
January 1913	December 1914	12	23
August 1918	March 1919	44	7
January 1920	July 1921	10	18
May 1923	July 1924	22	14
October 1926	November 1927	27	13
August 1929	March 1933	21	43
May 1937	June 1938	50	13
February 1945	October 1945	80	8
November 1948	October 1949	37	11
July 1953	May 1954	45	10
August 1957	April 1958	39	8
April 1960	February 1961	24	10
December 1969	November 1970	106	11
November 1973	March 1975	36	16
January 1980	July 1980	58	6
July 1981	November 1982	12	16
July 1990	March 1991	92	8

Average Length		Expansion	Recession	Entire Cycle
	1854–1900	27.0	23.2	50.2
	1900–1945	30.8	18.1	48.9
	1945–1991	49.9	10.7	60.6

CASE STUDY
HAS U.S. BUSINESS CYCLE VOLATILITY REALLY DECLINED?

Before World War II, the collection of macroeconomic data was relatively haphazard. Since the war, the U.S. Department of Commerce has been responsible for producing standard output measures such as GDP. The Commerce Department's annual series extend back to 1929. Until recently, the most widely accepted output series for years before 1929 was that produced by Simon Kuznets, who won a Nobel Prize for his efforts. This series forms the basis for our conclusions about pre-1929 GNP volatility.

Because of data limitations, Kuznets had to make a variety of assumptions to arrive at his GNP estimates. For example, lacking information about production in some sectors of the economy, Kuznets assumed a constant relationship between the output in these sectors and output in the sectors for which data were available. In a challenge to Kuznets's approach, Christina Romer of the University of California at

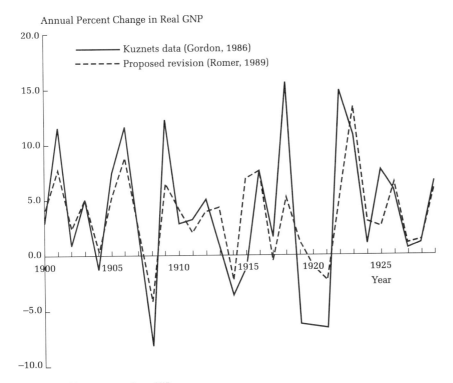

FIGURE 4.2 VOLATILITY OF REAL GNP
The Romer and Kuznets estimates of prewar real GNP differ markedly. In particular, Romer's estimates suggest considerably less volatility.

Source: R. J. Gordon, ed., The American Business Cycle *(Chicago: University of Chicago Press, 1986); Christina D. Romer, ''The Prewar Business Cycle Reconsidered.''* Journal of Political Economy *97 (February 1989): 1–37.*

Berkeley pointed out that during the postwar years, for which better data are available, the composition of output has varied over the business cycle.[3] She argued that output in the sectors not measured by Kuznets was less volatile than he assumed. Using postwar cyclical patterns in output composition and other information, Romer constructed an alternative series for real GNP. Her series, presented in Figure 4.2, is considerably less volatile than Kuznets's.

According to Romer's data, real GNP growth exceeded 10 percent in just one year—not six years—during the period 1900–1929, and never fell by more than 5 percent in a given year. However, her conclusions—that output fluctuations were only moderately more volatile before 1929 than after World War II—have themselves been challenged. Nathan Balke and Robert Gordon of Northwestern University used data from other sources to broaden the industrial coverage of the original Kuznets data. They constructed their own measure of real GNP for the years before 1929 that turned out to be just as volatile as the original Kuznets series.[4]

THE ANATOMY OF BUSINESS CYCLES

What do business cycles look like? Are any two the same? Are all industries and regions equally affected? Let's take a look.

SECTORAL VERSUS GENERAL EFFECTS

Modern economies constantly change the types of goods they make and where they make them. The U.S. economy shifted from farming to manufacturing early in this century. More recently, it shifted from manufacturing to services. These shifts have been accompanied by major population changes. Take agricultural South Dakota. Its population rose by just 7 percent between 1950 and 1990, compared to 64 percent nationwide. And manufacturing Detroit has lost almost half its population since 1950.

Such permanent and long-term industrial and regional declines should not be confused with recessions. Economists distinguish recessions—temporary, but widespread, output declines—from longer-term declines in particular industries because the two phenomena have different causes. Longer-term declines usually reflect fundamental shifts in household tastes and production costs. Short-term cycles ordinarily stem from shocks to the economy or inherent macroeconomic instability. Distinguishing recessions from longer-term economic processes isn't always easy. There are always significant differences in the severity of recessions across different regions and sectors of the economy, which raise the question of whether the underlying economic problems are really nationwide and industry-wide.

From the perspective of government intervention, there is little to be gained by attempting to stem the tide of changing tastes and technology. *The distinction between broad, brief recessions and localized, long-term downturns is important. Longer-term*

3 Christina D. Romer, "The Prewar Business Cycle Reconsidered: New Estimates of Gross National Product, 1869–1908," Journal of Political Economy 97 (February 1989): 1–37.

4 Nathan S. Balke and Robert J. Gordon, "The Estimation of Prewar Gross National Product: Methodology and New Evidence," Journal of Political Economy 97 (February 1989): 38–92.

TABLE 4.2 REAL GDP GROWTH RATES, BY INDUSTRY

	Percentage of 1994 GDP	1988	1989	1990	1991	1992	1993	1994
Total	100.0	5.1	−2.4	1.0	−0.6	2.3	1.9	4.2
Agriculture	1.8	−7.9	9.3	15.1	−0.6	11.4	−8.1	12.0
Mining	1.5	20.8	−11.1	4.4	0.6	−5.4	−1.6	6.6
Construction	3.8	3.8	1.2	−1.7	−7.5	0.3	2.8	7.2
Manufacturing	17.7	6.7	−0.4	−1.4	−3.6	1.3	3.0	6.6
Transportation and utilities	8.9	3.1	1.5	3.1	4.0	2.7	5.1	5.3
Trade	15.9	5.9	4.3	−1.4	0.9	3.9	3.3	6.5
Finance, insurance, and real estate	18.1	5.3	3.0	0.7	−0.3	3.8	1.0	2.8
Services	19.0	5.5	4.6	2.8	−0.6	2.3	1.8	2.3
Government	13.3	2.3	2.3	2.3	0.8	0.0	0.2	0.1

Source: *Survey of Current Business* (August 1996).

adjustments, as painful as they may be, do not present a case for short-run macro-economic policy intervention.

THE CYCLICAL VOLATILITY OF MAJOR INDUSTRIES

Table 4.2 presents real annual GDP growth rates for the economy as a whole and the major industries into which it is divided, for the period 1988 through 1994. The first column shows each industry's share of total GDP in 1994. The recession years of this period, 1990 and 1991, were characterized not only by slow growth in aggregate output, but also by declines in several industries: construction, manufacturing, and trade in 1990 and five separate industries in 1991. In each nonrecession year except 1994, at least one industry experienced a decline in output (for example, agriculture in 1993). But in those years the declines were not sufficiently widespread to qualify as a recession. The data also indicate long-term relative declines in certain industries. Over the period, mining grew by only 12 percent compared to a 17 percent growth in overall output.

A final point is the varying degree of volatility across industries. Mining experienced the widest swings in output growth during this period (with growth rates ranging from −11 percent to +21 percent). Production in agriculture and construction has also been quite volatile. At the other end of the spectrum, growth rates in finance, insurance, and real estate, and services have fluctuated in much narrower bands (each between −1 and 6 percent). Government activity has experienced even smoother growth, with growth rates fluctuating within a band of just 2.3 percentage points. As we know, the U.S. business cycle has changed over time, with recessions becoming shorter and expansions longer. Part of this change is due to the shift in production from volatile industries, like agriculture and mining, to stable industries, like finance, services, and government. These shifts in turn mean that different regions and industries may experience a particular recession in different ways.

CASE STUDY
CALIFORNIA'S ENDLESS RECESSION

California calls itself the Golden State, and as the second presidential term of its adopted son, Ronald Reagan, drew to a close in 1988, California's economy was indeed golden. A key reason was Reagan's defense buildup coupled with California's substantial role in the defense industry. When the rest of the country went into recession in 1990, the California economy continued to grow. But the recession eventually hit California, and its effects were powerful and long-lasting. These effects were exacerbated by the sharp defense cuts accompanying the demise of the Soviet Union, which Reagan had called the "Evil Empire."

A good measure of the well-being of a state's economy is the growth rate of its real personal income, an income concept closely related to GDP. Figure 4.3 compares

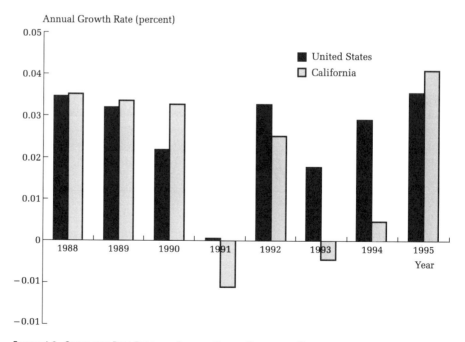

FIGURE 4.3 GROWTH IN REAL PERSONAL INCOME, UNITED STATES AND CALIFORNIA
Real personal income in California grew faster than U.S. income in each of the years from 1988 to 1990. After the 1990–1991 recession took hold and for several years after, however, income grew more slowly in California.

Source: Survey of Current Business, *various issues.*

real personal income in California and the United States as a whole during the late 1980s and early 1990s. It shows that income in California grew slightly faster than the national average in 1988 and 1989, and showed little sign in 1990 of the recession-induced national slowdown in income growth.

But by 1991, the recession had become much deeper in California than in the nation as a whole. Real personal income grew slightly in the United States, but it dropped by over 1 percent in California. And though California rebounded with the rest of the country in 1992, its growth was again slower than for the country as a whole. This was followed by negative income growth in 1993 and positive but below-average growth in 1994. Over the entire four-year period 1991 through 1994, California's real personal income grew by just 1.4 percent compared to 8.2 percent for the country as a whole.

California finally began catching up in 1995. But after so many years of relatively slow growth, it had lots of catching up to do. By the end of 1995, the California unemployment rate stood at 7.8 percent, still well above the national rate of 5.6 percent.

TIMING OF TURNING POINTS: THE INDEX OF LEADING INDICATORS

The beginnings and ends of recessions are referred to as turning points in the business cycle. They mark the points at which growth shifts from positive to negative or from negative to positive. Table 4.2 and Figure 4.3 indicate that turning points differ across regions and industries. For example, in the 1990–1991 recession, wholesale and retail trade fell only in 1990, whereas construction experienced its biggest drop in 1991. Similarly, California moved into the 1990 recession after the rest of the economy.

The trade industry's decline in 1990 did not necessarily presage a recession, since past declines in trade had not always been associated with widespread economic decline. However, there are some industries and types of activity whose business cycle patterns do normally foreshadow the overall business cycle. Because they *lead* the business cycle, we call them **leading indicators**. A decline in a leading indicator suggests that a recession is on the way.

Leading indicators were first developed in 1937. The Composite Index of Leading Indicators—the index periodically reported by the press—is constructed by combining the eleven monthly macroeconomic time series listed in Table 4.3. Some of these eleven series lead the business cycle because they are closely related to subsequent production activities. For example, building permits for housing must be obtained before housing construction occurs. New orders for plant and equipment and consumer goods and materials lead to the production and delivery of such goods. Unfilled orders and slow vendor performance indicate that producers face high demand that they eventually will meet.

The inclusion of the index of consumer expectations reflects the fact that consumers are forward looking. Their anticipations of changes in economic conditions are useful in predicting what actually will occur. As we'll see in chapter 16, stock prices act as a leading indicator for much the same reason: they indicate investors' optimism

Misleading Economic Indicators

Birdhouse starts are up.

Double yolk!

Fiver found in wash.

Puppies!

Danny Shanahan ©1992 from The New Yorker Collection. All Rights Reserved.

Leading indicator
An economic statistic whose movements foreshadow future changes in economic activity

TABLE 4.3 COMPONENTS OF THE INDEX OF LEADING INDICATORS

Average weekly hours of production workers in manufacturing

Average weekly initial claims for unemployment insurance

New orders for consumer goods and materials (in 1987 dollars)

Vendor performance index: Percentage of companies reporting slower deliveries

Contracts and orders, plant and equipment (1987 dollars)

Building permits index, new private housing units

Change in manufacturers' unfilled orders (1987 dollars)

Percentage change in sensitive materials prices

Stock price index (Standard and Poor's 500)

Money supply, M2 (1987 dollars)

Index of consumer expectations (from the University of Michigan)

or pessimism about the prospects of those firms whose stock prices are included in the index. The four remaining series in the index relate to employment, whose connection to the business cycle we will discuss shortly, and to money and prices, which we will discuss beginning in chapter 7.

Figure 4.4 graphs the Index of Leading Indicators for the period since 1948, with recession periods shaded. Each recession was preceded by a decline in the index. Even so, there are at least three problems with using declines in the index to predict recessions.

1. *How long?* The index often drops for a month or more. But how many successive monthly declines presage a recession? The customary rule of thumb is three.

2. *How soon?* Three successive declines in the index tell us a recession's likely, but not when it will hit. The index doesn't always lead the business cycle by the same number of months. It led the January 1980 downturn by 15 months but the July 1981 downturn by just 2 months.

3. *Whoops!* Regardless of the rule used, the index predicts some recessions that never materialize. For example, the index's 1984 sustained decline was a false alarm.

UNEMPLOYMENT

The unemployment rate rises during recessions. For example, near the trough of the 1981–1982 recession, the U.S. unemployment rate soared to over 9 percent. This explains why new claims for unemployment insurance, a program that pays benefits to

Index of Leading Indicators (1987=100)

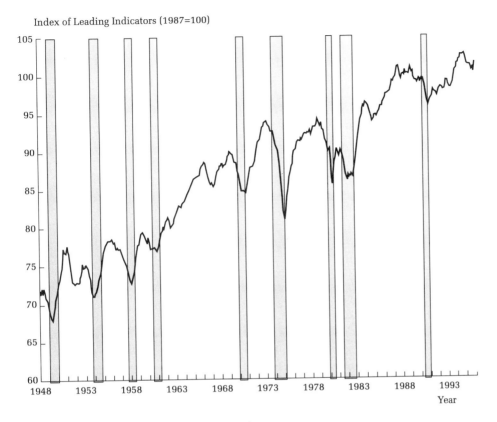

FIGURE 4.4 INDEX OF LEADING INDICATORS, 1948–1996
The Index of Leading Indicators is designed to forecast the future behavior of the national economy. The figure shows that the index started turning downward before each of the nine recessions of the postwar period. It also shows that some declines in the index were not followed by recessions.

Source: The Conference Board.

unemployed workers, appears in the index of leading indicators. But what exactly is **unemployment**? It's quite different from simply not being employed. In 1996, nearly 74 million U.S. adults (persons over age 16) were not employed. Of these, only 7.2 million, or less than 10 percent, were classified as unemployed. The remainder were considered neither employed nor unemployed.

THE HOUSEHOLD SURVEY

How is unemployment defined? The United States and most other countries define unemployment as the condition of actively seeking work but not having a job. In the United States, the tool used to measure the unemployment rate is the Current Population Survey, conducted by the Census Bureau. Each month, a sample of about 60,000 households is surveyed, and adult members are asked about their employment

Unemployment
The state of seeking work but not having a job

status. There is a three-way classification: employed, unemployed, and not in the labor force. The precise definitions are as follows:

- *Employed:* All persons who, during the past week,
    - — Did any work for pay or profit;
    - — Did at least 15 hours of unpaid work in a family-operated enterprise; or
    - — Were temporarily absent from a job for reason of illness, vacation, bad weather, strikes, etc.

- *Unemployed:* All persons who were not employed during the past week, but
    - — Had looked for work in the past 4 weeks and were available for work (unless temporarily ill); or
    - — Were awaiting recall from a job from which they had been temporarily laid off.

The sum of employed and unemployed individuals is the labor force. It includes about two-thirds of the adult population. All other adults, including students, retired persons, and those doing housework, are "out of the labor force."

At first blush it may seem natural to define unemployment in this way—as a state of seeking work but not having a job. But in practice, many cases are difficult to classify. For example, should an aerospace engineer who had previously worked for $30 an hour be considered available for work if she declines a job paying $8 an hour? (She is.) Should a college basketball player eager to drop out of college for the right professional contract be considered unavailable for work? (He is.)

Unemployment, as we define it, suggests the lack of a job at an individual's "normal" wage rate and working circumstances, but these are not precisely defined concepts. Their meaning has a tendency to shift over the business cycle as workers' perceptions of employment prospects change. Some so-called discouraged workers eventually abandon their job search and shift from the category "unemployed" to "not in the labor force." As a result, the fraction of the adult population in the labor force— the **labor force participation rate**—tends to decline slightly during recessions.

To keep up with changing times and labor market patterns (such as the increasing participation of women in the labor force), the Census Bureau periodically revises the questions on the Current Population Survey, most recently in January 1994. However, *there is no exact way of measuring unemployment.*

EMPLOYMENT AND HOURS

Recessions affect average hours worked by employed workers as well as the fraction of the labor force that is employed. The Index of Leading Indicators also includes the average weekly hours of manufacturing workers (see Table 4.3).

One of the categories of work most sensitive to the business cycle is overtime hours: the hours employees work beyond their normal weekly hours. Figure 4.5, which covers the period since 1970, plots the average number of overtime hours per

Labor force participation rate
The fraction of the adult population that is either employed or unemployed

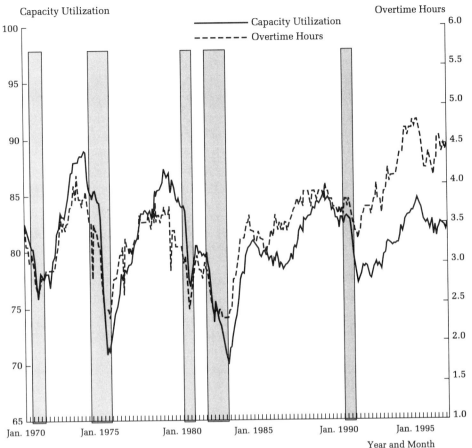

FIGURE 4.5 OVERTIME HOURS AND CAPACITY UTILIZATION IN MANUFACTURING
Immediately before and during recessions, firms reduce the amount of labor they employ. One way of doing this is to reduce the average number of hours each employee works. As a result, overtime hours in manufacturing fall during recessions; average overtime hours is a procyclical variable. Capital utilization falls too. When businesses operate with fewer workers than normal, they tend to use their plant and equipment less intensively.

Source: Economic Report of the President, *1997*.

week for manufacturing workers. The series moves with the business cycle, dipping during each shaded recession period.

In addition to employing fewer workers and reducing the hours of employed workers, firms appear to use their workforces less intensively during recessions. This phenomenon is called *labor hoarding* because it suggests that firms have more labor on hand than is needed to produce current output levels. Labor hoarding appears to help explain why labor productivity is **procyclical**—the fact that output per worker-hour declines (or at least grows more slowly) during recessions. The argument is that firms use their workforces less intensively during recessions, thus reducing output but not measured labor input, so that measured labor productivity declines.

Procyclical behavior
The behavior of any economic variable that increases when GDP increases and falls when GDP falls

CAPITAL BECOMES UNEMPLOYED, TOO

Firms also respond to recessions by changing their utilization of capital. The Federal Reserve System ("the Fed") measures capital's utilization. It does so by comparing an industry's current production with its capacity to produce, which it determines based on past production levels. Like unemployment, capacity utilization does not have a clear, unambiguous definition. For example, it might be possible, in wartime or other periods of extreme demand, for industries to exceed measured capacity by running machines for longer periods each day than would be the normal maximum.

Figure 4.5 also graphs the Fed's **capacity utilization** measure for U.S. manufacturing since 1970. Like overtime hours, capacity utilization is procyclical, falling during recessions and rising during expansions. Indeed, the two series have strikingly similar patterns.

UNDERSTANDING ECONOMIC FLUCTUATIONS

Describing patterns of output and employment changes over the business cycle is one thing. But what explains them? To gain some insight, we'll consider three issues: the uses of output over the business cycle, the relationships among different countries' business cycles, and the relationship of the business cycle to other dynamic behavior, including seasonal shifts in production.

USES OF OUTPUT OVER THE CYCLE

Why does the output of some industries fluctuate so severely? Much of the answer lies in how their output is used. There are four principal uses of output: consumption by households, investment by private businesses, exports to foreigners, and government purchases. Consumption and investment are familiar concepts. Exports are those goods produced domestically but sold abroad, and government purchases are goods and services bought by the government.

Not surprisingly, the business cycle fluctuations of various industries mirror fluctuations in the use of (demand for) their outputs. Goods purchased for investment consist of machinery and equipment, which are produced by the manufacturing industry, and structures (factories, office buildings, and so forth), which are produced by the construction industry. In contrast to this industrial concentration of the production of investment goods, goods purchased for consumption (which account for about two-thirds of GDP) are produced in a number of industries. Because investment demand is more volatile than consumption, the construction and manufacturing sectors are more volatile than most other industries.

Figure 4.6 shows the annual percentage changes in consumption and private investment since 1960. Although both series exhibit procyclical behavior, consumption has been much less volatile. Consumption grew at annual rates ranging from −2 percent to +6 percent. Investment declined by nearly 20 percent in 1975 and grew by nearly 30

Capacity utilization
The ratio of current production in an industry to that industry's measured capacity to produce

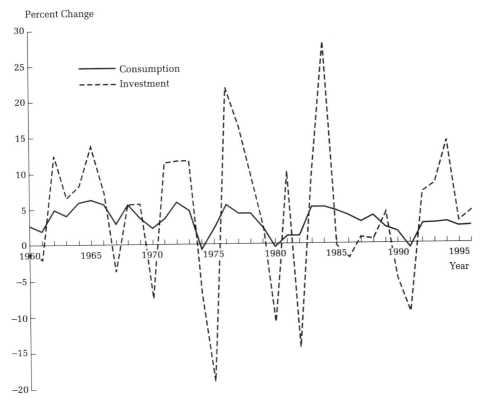

FIGURE 4.6 CONSUMPTION AND INVESTMENT GROWTH RATES

Both consumption and investment spending are procyclical variables. However, consumption spending tends to be much smoother and less volatile than investment spending.

Source: National Income and Product Accounts.

percent in 1984. Note also the connection between these investment fluctuations and the output fluctuations in industries that produce investment goods—for example, the negative investment growth in 1990–1991 and the output declines in manufacturing and construction over the same period shown in Table 4.2.

Why do the patterns differ so much? We'll return to this question, as we begin to relate business cycle behavior to the life-cycle model developed in chapters 2 and 3. Like consumption, exports and government spending are far less volatile than investment. Thus, *we can trace an important part of the industrial variation in output over the business cycle to fluctuations in investment.*

INTERNATIONAL SPILLOVERS

Fluctuations in investment, as well as in other uses of outpt, have many causes. One way of narrowing the list of suspects is to look at contemporaneous business cycle behavior in other countries. If a recession occurs in the United States but not in Japan,

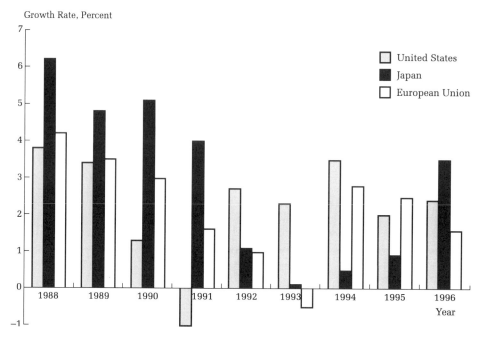

Growth Rate, Percent

FIGURE 4.7 GROWTH RATES OF REAL GDP: UNITED STATES, EUROPE, AND JAPAN, 1988–1996
Patterns in business cycle behavior among industrialized countries provide clues about the causes of business cycles.

Source: Economic Report of the President, *1997.*

that may rule out certain causes, such as a sharp increase in oil prices that affects all oil-importing countries. If a U.S. recession begins just after the outbreak of a worldwide recession, other causes, such as monetary and fiscal policy mismanagement in the United States, may be ruled out.

Figure 4.7 considers the correlation across countries in business cycle fluctuations. It presents the annual growth rates of real GDP for the United States, Japan, and the European Union. From the figure, it is easy to pick out 1988 as a boom year worldwide and 1993 as a year of generally subpar growth. However, this latter correspondence is a bit misleading, for the experiences of the different countries diverge in the years around 1993. While the United States was climbing out of its recession, Europe was in the midst of one, and Japan, which had grown quite rapidly earlier in the period, was just entering its most serious postwar slowdown. Thus, *although the experiences of the different countries are related, they are not always in sync.*

To what extent does the cross-country correlation of business cycles indicate a common source of economic fluctuations? And to what extent do cross-country business cycle differences suggest the importance of independent domestic factors? In chapter 12 we will consider how the existence of international trade and investment might help explain these patterns.

THE BUSINESS CYCLE AND THE SEASONAL CYCLE

We began this chapter by distinguishing business cycles, which typically last six years, from long-run growth. The argument for doing so was that the factors influencing business cycles may differ from those influencing longer-term dynamic transitions and that there may be more scope for government intervention in the case of business cycles. A similar distinction is normally made with respect to economic fluctuations of an even shorter duration: the seasonal cycle.

It is easy to identify the factors causing seasonal output fluctuations and hard to argue that government policy should be used to offset these fluctuations. People spend more in December because of Christmas, and produce less in August in order to take vacations. The seasonal fluctuations these phenomena induce are desirable; they reflect households' tastes.

Some seasonal fluctuations are associated with the nature of technology. For example, there is more construction activity in the fall than in winter, and more agricultural production in the summer. These seasonal fluctuations reflect a desirable allocation of social resources. There is nothing to be gained, and clearly something to be lost, in inducing people to shop for Christmas in July or to harvest their crops in January.

Because seasonal cycles are easier to understand than business cycles, and of less concern from a policy perspective, it is common to subject data to **seasonal adjustment**—the elimination from those data of seasonal fluctuations. (This technique is not necessary for use with annual series—only for those with a higher frequency, such as quarterly or monthly.) The quarterly GDP series shown in Figure 4.1 are seasonally adjusted, as are most quarterly data provided by the Commerce Department. Eliminating seasonal variation lets us study the business cycle properties of a macroeconomic time series. If we did not perform a seasonal adjustment, the seasonal variation in some series would swamp the variation associated with the business cycle.

Figure 4.8 shows the effect of seasonal adjustment on GDP for a recent period. The dashed line shows the quarterly values of nominal GDP. This series has been seasonally adjusted. The second series (the solid line) is also quarterly GDP, but it is not seasonally adjusted.[5] As the figure shows, seasonal fluctuations are much more regular than business cycle fluctuations, consistent with the view that they are more predictable and are part of an equilibrium path. Still, these seasonal fluctuations are large. With nominal output typically falling at an annual rate of about 16 percent from the peak of one year (the fourth quarter, October through December) to the trough of the next (the first quarter, January through March), and real output, after adjustment for price increases, presumably falling even more, the seasonal drop in output during the normal year far exceeds the drop in seasonally adjusted output of any recession quarter shown in Figure 4.1.

Economists study seasonal cycles to gain insights about business cycles. They've found that countries with large seasonal cycles also have large business cycles.[6] They've also found a strong, positive correlation between the seasonal and business

Seasonal adjustment
An attempt to isolate and remove seasonal movements from economic time series

5 We present measures of nominal GDP because no series on real, seasonally unadjusted quarterly GDP is readily available.

6 This evidence is presented in J. Joseph Beaulieu, Jeffrey K. MacKie-Mason, and Jeffrey A. Miron, "Why Do Countries and Industries with Large Seasonal Cycles Also Have Large Business Cycles?" Quarterly Journal of Economics 107 (May 1992): 621–656.

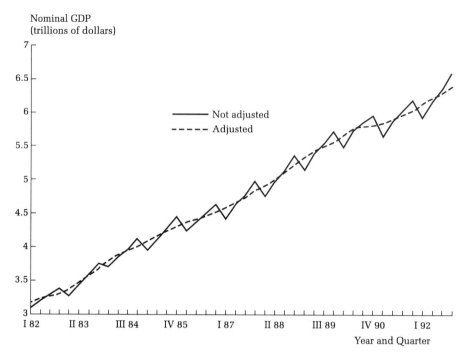

FIGURE 4.8 NOMINAL GDP, 1982–1992

The solid line depicts raw data on GDP; the dashed line depicts seasonally adjusted data. Comparing the two shows that seasonal fluctuations are quite predictable and large.

Source: National Income and Product Accounts.

cycles of most industries within a country. These findings suggest that similar factors cause both types of cycles. They also suggest the need to study factors that influence both types of cycles, such as the economy's production structure, rather than factors, such as changes in government policy associated with presidential elections, that occur over a period of years and hence influence only one type of cycle (in this case, the business cycle).

To understand why seasonal and business cycles might be correlated, suppose one industry can easily adjust its production level, whereas another cannot. Then, in response to variations in product demand, whether seasonal or not, the first industry will alter its level of production more sharply than the second. As a result, the first industry will exhibit larger seasonal and business cycle variations in production than the second.

ARE BUSINESS CYCLES ACTUALLY CYCLES?

The business cycle is an important phenomenon across industries and countries. Or is it? One line of research argues that the fluctuations we call business cycles aren't actually cycles at all.[7]

7 See Charles R. Nelson and Charles Plosser, "Trends and Random Walks in Economic Time Series," Journal of Monetary Economics *10 (1982): 139–162,* and John Campbell and N. Gregory Mankiw, "Are Output Fluctuations Transitory?" Quarterly Journal of Economics *103 (November 1987).*

Consider two alternative economies. In the first, the economy's long-run dynamic path is perturbed by temporary cyclical fluctuations in which periods of greater-than-average output growth tend to be followed by periods of less-than-average growth. In the second, the economy follows a **random walk**; it experiences permanent shocks to its long-run dynamic path, some of them positive and some negative In this case, there is no underlying cycle. Output is no more likely to fall after a period of positive growth than after a period of negative growth. However, by chance, runs of negative or positive shocks will give the appearance of cycles.

Take the following analogy. Imagine that output changes are determined by flipping a coin. If you flip a head, output rises one unit. If you flip a tail, it falls one unit. Each coin flip is independent of the others, with equal probability of being a head or a tail. Yet, by chance, you are likely to get some runs of successive heads followed by runs of successive tails among your flips. These runs of heads and tails will provide an up-and-down pattern of output fluctuations that resembles a cycle, even though no cycle exists. Now suppose instead that output rises by a bit more than one unit when a head occurs, and falls by a little less than one unit when a tail occurs. Then, in addition to the apparently cyclical behavior in output produced by your coin flips, there will also be a tendency for output to grow over time. Thus, through independent flips of this coin, you can generate a pattern of output that appears to exhibit cyclical behavior around a growing trend.

Figure 4.9 illustrates the results of such an experiment. The graph shows three curves. One, labeled "Trend," depicts smooth growth at a rate of 4 percent per period. The second curve, labeled "Cycle," is the result of adding a cycle to the first curve. The cycle has two components: a sine wave that causes output to oscillate smoothly, plus an annual random shock that is purely transitory, in that each year's random shock to output lasts for just that year.[8] This curve represents the business cycle as we've described it: fluctuations around a long-run trend.

The third curve, labeled "Random Walk," starts in year 0 at the same income level as the other curves and grows each year at a rate that is random, but on average equals 2 percent. In this case random shocks to the level of output are permanent in the sense that they influence output in all subsequent years. Unlike the case of the cycle, there is no tendency for output to return to the original trend line.[9] However, as the coin flip example suggested, this curve exhibits the two central characteristics of the business cycle curve: a tendency toward increasing output and apparent cycles around a smooth trend.

This experiment indicates why it is difficult to distinguish between the business-cycle-around-trend and the random walk hypotheses. But does it matter which hypothesis is true, if the time series behavior looks so similar under each view? Yes, because knowing which story is correct reveals something about the costs of economic disturbances. If a recession is not really a temporary phenomenon but actually a permanent downward movement of the economy's long-run path, its social costs may be considerably greater. Unfortunately, many more data are needed in order to

Random walk theory
The view that economic fluctuations result from permanent shocks to the economy's growth path, rather than temporary cycles around a long-run path

8 The curve's formula is $y_t = (1.04)^t + .4\sin(.1\pi t) + .15x_t$, where x_t is drawn randomly from a uniform distribution between -1 and 1. That is, the likelihood of year t's shock, x_t, taking any particular value between -1 and 1 is the same as that for every other value in the range.

9 This curve's formula for output is $y_t = y_{t-1}(1.02 + .2x_t)$, where x_t is the same random variable used to construct the "cycle" curve. Here, though, the value of x_t affects not only the current value of output, y_t, but every subsequent value of output $(y_{t+1}, y_{t+2}, \ldots)$ as well.

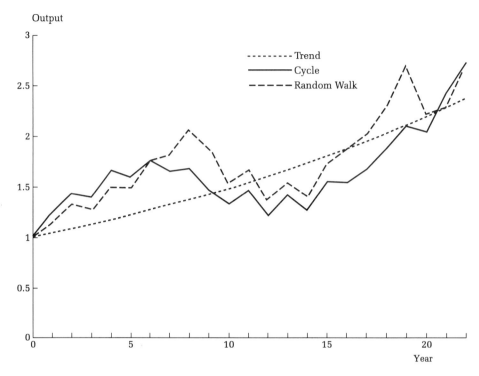

Figure 4.9 Business Cycles or Random Walks? A Comparison
The dashed line shows the simulated behavior of output assuming that it follows a random walk—that is, assuming that random shocks to GDP are permanent in the sense that they influence output in all subsequent years. The solid line labeled "Cycle" shows the simulated behavior of output as fluctuations around a long-term trend. Notice that the behavior of the two series appears to be quite similar, making it difficult to know which theory best describes the facts.

distinguish between these two statistical hypotheses. We return to this problem in chapter 11, when we discuss the costs of recession.

HOW DO ECONOMIC FLUCTUATIONS FIT INTO OUR MODEL?

Real business cycle theory
A macroeconomic theory that traces economic fluctuations to shocks to the level of technology

10 A good introduction to real business cycle theory is Charles I. Plosser, "Understanding Real Business Cycles," Journal of Economic Perspectives 3 (Summer 1989): 51–78.

Now that we know what business cycles (or what appear to be business cycles) look like, let's use our model to describe a prominent explanation of business cycles, the **real business cycle theory**.

According to this theory, business cycles are caused by shocks to technology and household preferences and are therefore simply part of the economy's equilibrium path.[10] To see the argument, consider what happens if our model's technology coefficient A temporarily increases, perhaps because of a reduction in oil prices, a good

TABLE 4.4 RESPONSE TO A TECHNOLOGY SHOCK

Period	A	k	y	i	c
0	10	5.987	17.107	0.000	17.107
1	10	5.987	17.107	0.000	17.107
2	12	5.987	20.528	1.197	19.331
3	10	7.185	18.069	−0.861	18.930
4	10	6.324	17.390	−0.238	17.628
5	10	6.086	17.191	−0.070	17.261
⋮	⋮	⋮	⋮	⋮	⋮
∞	10	5.987	17.107	0.000	17.107

Note: Lowercase variables are expressed per young person; $c = c_y + c_o$ (consumption of the young plus consumption of the old). Parameter values: $\alpha = .5$, $\beta = .3$.

harvest, or a new scientific breakthrough. This increases both output and labor productivity (output per worker), since the ratio of output to labor equals

$$y_t = Ak_t^\beta,$$

where β is the production function parameter, y is output per worker, and k is capital per worker. Moreover, the increase in A also leads to an increase in capital accumulation between period t and period $t + 1$. As we found in chapter 3, $k_{t+1} = (1 - \alpha)w_t$. That is, the economy's capital-labor ratio next period equals the amount saved by each young person this period, which is a fraction $(1 - \alpha)$ of that young person's wage. Since the wage equals the worker's marginal product, $(1 - \beta)A_t k_t^\beta$, the capital-labor ratio evolves according to the transition equation,

$$k_{t+1} = (1 - \alpha)(1 - \beta)A_t k_t^\beta = (1 - \alpha)(1 - \beta)y_t,$$

where α is the share of labor income young people consume and, in the case of the second equality, we have replaced $A_t k_t^\beta$ by y_t. If technology improves in period t, the capital-labor ratio will be larger in the following period. This will influence the level of output in that period and subsequent periods.

Take a concrete example, with $\alpha = .5$, $\beta = .3$, A initially equal to its long-run value of 10, and the economy at its steady-state value of output per worker and capital per worker.[11] Suppose A rises temporarily by 20 percent—to a value of 12—in period 2, and then falls back to 10 in period 3. The response of output to this one-period shock to A is presented in the column labeled y in Table 4.4 and shown by the curve labeled "Output" in Figure 4.10.

As indicated in the table, output increases by 20 percent in the period of the shock, from 17.107 to 20.528. This makes sense because existing resources initially are simply 20 percent more productive than in the previous period. In periods 3, 4, and thereafter, output per worker drops back toward its original level. Output temporarily

11 We can calculate this steady-state value of k using the following formula, which was derived in chapter 3: $\bar{k} = [(1 - \alpha)(1 - \beta)A]^{1/(1-\beta)}$. Given the values of α, β, and A chosen here, the solution is $\bar{k} = 5.987$.

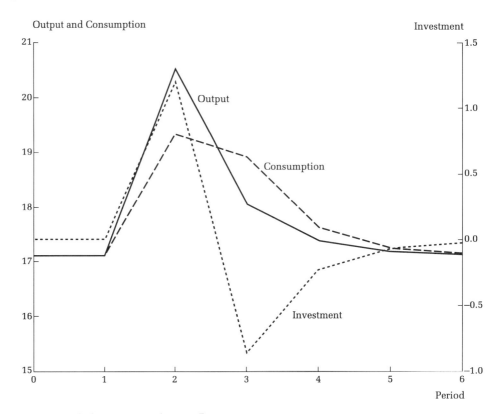

Output and Consumption   Investment

Figure 4.10 **An Increase in the Level of Technology**
According to the real business cycle theory, business cycle fluctuations result from shocks to the economy's technology. This figure depicts the responses of output, consumption, and investment to a temporary improvement in technology, assuming the real business cycle theory is valid. Output remains above its long-run level for some time after the technology shock abates. Consumption follows the pattern of output but is less volatile. Investment is more volatile than output, jumping immediately after the shock and then turning negative.

12 Recall from chapter 3 that, according to the Cobb-Douglas model, wages are a fixed share, $(1 − \beta)$, of output. Hence, workers receive the same share of any increase in output caused by the productivity shock, and owners of capital receive the rest.

remains above its long-run level even after the technology shock abates because the shock raises wages in period 2.[12] This leads workers in period 2 to save more than they otherwise would have saved. This increased saving by the young in period 2 means that they bring more capital into period 3, which causes output in period 3 to be higher than its long-run level even though $A = 10$. That is, output is higher in period 2 as a direct result of the technology shock, and in period 3, as well as subsequent periods, as an indirect result of the shock, through the increase in capital. Eventually the economy moves back to its steady state, following the process described in chapter 3. However, this transition is just one of a multitude we can generate by making alternative assumptions about the time path of technology shocks. By making the right assumptions about technology shocks, it's clearly possible to produce a pattern of output fluctuations similar to those observed in the actual economy.

THE RESPONSE OF CONSUMPTION AND INVESTMENT TO A TECHNOLOGY SHOCK

In addition to per capita output, Figure 4.10 and Table 4.4 also show investment and consumption during the transition. The two variables behave quite differently. Consumption rises by a smaller percentage than output in period 2 and falls by a smaller percentage than output in period 3. In contrast, investment jumps immediately from its initial value of zero and then falls quickly back, becoming negative as output falls in subsequent periods. Fully 35 percent of the initial increase in output is accounted for by increased investment, despite the fact that in the steady state, investment accounts for literally none of output. Thus, the simulation reproduces the volatility of actual investment relative to actual consumption documented in Figure 4.6.

Let's see why the model produces this pattern of investment and consumption, looking first at investment. Table 4.4 shows that investment equals 35 percent of the corresponding output *change* in each succeeding period. This is no coincidence. Consider the expression relating the next period's capital-labor ratio, k_{t+1}, to this period's output per worker, y_t. This relationship holds for every period t, so we can subtract the expression for k_t from that for k_{t+1} to obtain an expression for $k_{t+1} - k_t$, which equals investment per worker, i_t:

$$i_t = (1 - \alpha)(1 - \beta)(y_t - y_{t-1}).$$

In the simulation, $\alpha = .5$ and $\beta = .3$. Therefore, investment equals exactly $(1 - .5)(1 - .3) = .35$ times the change in output, for every period t. This change in output may be large, small, or even negative, so we can readily see why the model predicts wide swings in the level of investment.

This important proportional relationship—between the level of investment and the change in the level of output—is known as the **accelerator**.[13] How well does the accelerator theory explain movements in investment? Figure 4.11 plots annual U.S. net investment against changes in GDP and shows that the two series move closely together, as predicted. As we'll see in chapter 16, a variety of additional factors influence the pattern of investment over the business cycle. However, this basic accelerator relationship is very useful in helping us understand the volatility of investment.

The model predicts that investment will be more volatile than output and that consumption will be less volatile. Consumption rises by less than output in the period of the shock and falls less rapidly thereafter. This is a result of the life-cycle model of consumption. When income rises initially in period 2, the old consume all the additional income they receive in the form of higher returns to capital. However, the young consume only a fraction, α, of their increase in income and save the rest. This explains not only why consumption rises by less than output initially, but also why it falls by less in period 3. The increase in saving by the young in period 2 provides them with additional consumption in period 3, regardless of the level of income in that period, because they consume not only their income when old, but also the amount they originally saved. We refer to this behavior as **consumption smoothing**, because it spreads the impact of single-period shocks to income over more than one period's consumption.

Accelerator
The relationship whereby the level of investment is determined by the change in output

Consumption smoothing
The tendency of consumption spending to be less volatile than output

13 What explains the name? In physics, the rate of change of an object's position is called its velocity, and the rate of change of this rate of change is the object's acceleration. Here, the level of investment depends on the change in the level of output—output's velocity. That means a change in the level of investment will be caused by a change in output's velocity—its acceleration.

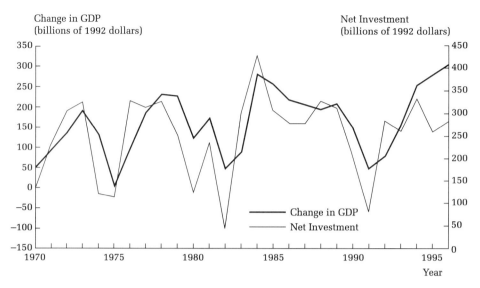

FIGURE 4.11 THE ACCELERATOR

The accelerator is a relationship between the level of investment and the change in output. When output increases at a fast rate, investment is high; when output increases at a slow rate, investment is low. This pattern is quite evident in the data presented in this figure.

Source: National Income and Product Accounts.

DOES THE REAL BUSINESS CYCLE MODEL EXPLAIN ECONOMIC FLUCTUATIONS?

Our simple real business cycle model is limited. It produces output fluctuations, but not the labor supply fluctuations that are a key part of actual business cycles. But labor supply fluctuations would arise in our model in response to technology shocks were we to expand the Cobb-Douglas utility function to include utility for leisure when young and old. In this case, our life-cycle agents would take advantage of periods of high wages to work harder and longer and take more leisure during periods when wages are depressed. Our model is also limited by the fact that each period corresponds to roughly 30 years rather than a single year. But this too could be remedied by constructing a multiperiod version of the model. The resulting model would be able to explain most of the short-run fluctuations in employment and hours observed in real business cycles.

Still, there is considerable dispute about the importance of technology shocks in causing fluctuations. Do the increase in unemployment and the drop in hours worked observed during recessions really reflect voluntary choices by workers to supply less labor? Undoubtedly, technology shocks and voluntary variations in labor supply over the business cycle are part of the story. But many economists find it implausible that the Great Depression could have been caused by a negative technology shock, or that voluntary withdrawals from employment explain the 25 percent unemployment rates during that period. As late as 1939, fully ten years after the Depression began, the civilian unemployment rate exceeded 17 percent, a level that has not even been approached during the postwar period. Could so many workers have been so patiently awaiting a return to "normal" productivity levels? Even in the more normal recessions that have occurred in recent decades, much unemployment is difficult to characterize in terms of optimal responses to wage variations over time.

In any event, the real business cycle theory is certainly a useful first step to understanding how economic fluctuations may arise in the model we have developed. Moreover, although economic fluctuations may be more than equilibrium responses to technology shocks, certain aspects of the model we have just discussed, such as consumption smoothing and the accelerator, are consistent with other theories of economic fluctuations as well.

CHAPTER SUMMARY

1. Aggregate output, measured by real GDP, normally grows over time, but there are recurring periods of negative growth, called recessions. Since World War II, recessions have, on average, lasted less than one year. Recessions combined with expansions (periods of growth, which typically last about four years) are called business cycles. Since the end of World War II, there have been nine full cycles. The frequency and severity of recessions have declined since the prewar years. Some economists see this as the result of a more active government economic policy. Others focus on changes in the composition of output and potential measurement errors.

2. Economic fluctuations affect different regions and industries differently, but still have a widespread impact. Though each business cycle is different, it is still possible to use certain recurring relationships in the timing of macroeconomic variables to form the Composite Index of Leading Indicators. This index normally declines several months before a recession begins. U.S. business cycle fluctuations are correlated with those in Europe and Japan, but certainly not perfectly.

3. The breadth and brevity of recessions distinguish them from longer-run shifts in regional and industrial development, which reflect changing consumer tastes and production methods. Business cycles differ from the shorter, more volatile, but also more predictable seasonal variations in production.

4. When recessions hit, firms use less labor and capital. The reduction in labor input occurs through reductions in the number of workers employed, the average

number of hours worked, and the intensity of work. The reduction in capital input is measured as a lower rate of capacity utilization. Some industries, such as construction, experience more volatile swings in output over the business cycle than do others, such as services. Part of the explanation lies in the relative volatility of the uses to which different industries' products are put. In particular, private investment is subject to much sharper swings than is consumption.

5. Economic fluctuations may not be cycles at all, but simply the reflection of negative and positive permanent shocks that randomly alter the economy's level of output. In this case, the drop in output during recessions has a permanent impact on the economy: there is no tendency for the economy to get back on its previous growth path. Under this hypothesis, stabilization policy becomes even more important, for such policy may provide permanent benefits.

6. Great controversy surrounds the cause of economic fluctuations. One theory explains fluctuations in output and employment as equilibrium phenomena by subjecting a model like our own to recurring shocks to the economy's technology coefficient. The resulting real business cycle model predicts some of what we observe: highly volatile investment and consumption smoothing over the business cycle. However, it is not the only approach capable of explaining consumption and investment behavior. It also characterizes unemployment as voluntary, a conclusion difficult for some economists to accept.

CHAPTER 5

THE MEASUREMENT OF OUTPUT AND PRICES

INTRODUCTION

Correctly measuring a country's production of goods and services—its gross domestic product—is very important. The level of GDP tells us the size of the country's economy. Per capita GDP measures its living standard. Changes over time in GDP indicate if the country is growing, and fluctuations in GDP tell us about business cycles. The measurement of GDP, its components, and related definitions of output is called *national income accounting.*

The process of measuring (accounting for) national income clarifies how different macroeconomic variables are related. For example, there are several ways to measure GDP. However, the *national income identity* tells us that these different ways must yield the same result. This requirement provides a check on the national income accountants' GDP estimates. It also shows that the output that a country produces is paid out to the factors of production as factor incomes.

National income accounting can be tricky in practice. How do we account for the output of homemakers? What should we do about pollution? Is the purchase of a house consumption or saving? Are illegal drug sales part of GDP? Does GDP measure a country's income when its citizens earn money abroad?

By far, the biggest measurement problem in national income accounting is distinguishing real from nominal increases in economic variables. Take the exploding growth in expenditures on personal computers. How much of this growth reflects the purchase of additional computing power, and how much reflects changes in the price of computing power? The answer depends on how we measure the price of a CPU (central processing unit). We know that the price of CPUs has fallen through time, but exactly how fast? If we overstate this decline, we'll understate the economy's rate of *inflation* (growth in the overall price level) and overstate its rate of growth.

We begin this chapter by explaining the three ways to measure GDP. Then we discuss related output measures, including gross national product (GNP), and the difficulties of distinguishing among the components of output, notably consumption and investment. After that, we use the national income identity to study the relationship between net foreign investment and the trade deficit. Next, we show how to measure inflation and real GDP. Finally, we turn to set of thorny GDP measurement problems.

As you read, keep these key questions in mind:

- How do we measure real GDP?

- How do we measure inflation?

- Which measurement problems lead to under- or overstatements of GDP?

- How should we assess the consumption services provided by houses, refrigerators, and other durable goods?

- How is net foreign investment—the difference between national saving and domestic investment—related to the trade deficit—the difference between imports and exports?

MEASURING GROSS DOMESTIC PRODUCT

Gross domestic product is the total market value of the *final goods and services* produced in a country in a particular year, no matter who owns the capital and labor used to produce them. The term "final" means that the commodities are not resold to other producers during the year.

GDP includes only domestic output. Output produced abroad, even if that output is produced with inputs owned by domestic citizens, is not part of GDP. The services provided by American baseball manager Bobby Valentine, after he left the Texas Rangers to run Japan's Chiba Lotte Marines, contributed to Japanese, but not U.S., GDP. On the other hand, U.S. GDP includes goods and services produced with the help of foreign-owned inputs working in the United States. Thus, the services provided to the Philadelphia Flyers by Canadian hockey star Eric Lindross contribute to U.S. rather than Canadian GDP.

There is a fundamental relationship between the value of a country's output and the income this production generates. Each dollar of output generated by firms provides a dollar of income for some input supplied by households. This income, in turn, is spent on output. Hence, income must equal output. The circular flow of income, depicted in Figure 5.1, clarifies this process. Dollars flow from households to firms to purchase output and from firms back to households to pay for inputs. Flowing in the opposite direction are the goods and inputs associated with these payments: goods flow from firms to households and inputs from households to firms. It might seem natural to think of production as occurring first in this circular flow, followed by the

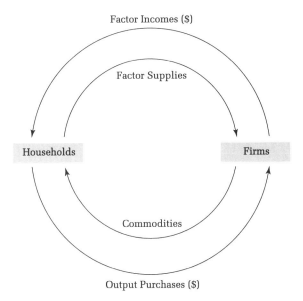

FIGURE 5.1 CIRCULAR FLOW OF INCOME AND OUTPUT
One of the most fundamental relationships in economics is the national income identity: the equality between income and output. This relationship is depicted graphically in the circular flow, which shows that factor supplies flow from households to firms and that output flows from firms to households. Household spending on output equals the national income paid as factor incomes to households.

payment of income. However, we actually measure the income as soon as it is earned, which is precisely when the production occurs. Thus, all happens simultaneously. There is no place where the circular flow "starts."

The equality between income and output is called the **national income identity**. Although output and income are certainly different concepts, we can think of GDP as a measure of domestic output or domestic income, since the two are always equal. We can measure GDP by adding up all incomes earned or by adding up the value of all final production. Indeed, these are two of the three distinct methods used to calculate GDP. They are called the *final sales method* and the *factor incomes method*.[1]

The third method is the *value-added method*. It differs from the final sales method in cases where production occurs in several stages, with one firm selling intermediate goods to another before the final product is sold. Examples of intermediate goods are the steel purchased by car manufacturers to make automobiles and the fertilizer used by farmers to stimulate crop growth. When a firm uses intermediate goods, the value of its output exceeds its payments to capital and labor by the amount it pays for the intermediate goods. We define **value added** as sales minus payments for intermediate goods; it also equals payments to the primary inputs of capital and labor.

When some firms produce intermediate goods and services and other firms produce final goods and services, we cannot simply add together the sales of all firms to obtain a measure of GDP. The problem encountered in doing so is called "double

National income identity
The logical requirement that the value of national output equals the value of factor incomes, as well as the sum of values added

Value added
The difference at a stage of production between the sales of a product and the value of intermediate inputs used to produce it

1 The word "factor" here reminds us that "factor of production" is a commonly used synonym for what we have called "inputs."

TABLE 5.1 NATIONAL INCOME ACCOUNTING: AN EXAMPLE

	Farmer	Manufacturer	Retailer	
(1) Sales	100	150	170	
(2) (For final use)	0	0	170	
Less:				
(3) Materials used	0	100	150	
(4) Wages	20	25	10	
(5) Rent	0	10	5	
(6) Interest	30	0	0	
Equals:				
(7) Business income	50	15	5	
(Proprietors' income)	50	0	5	
(Corporate profits)	0	15	0	
GDP				Total
Factor payments $(4 + 5 + 6 + 7)$	100	50	20	170
Value added $(1 - 3)$	100	50	20	170
Final sales (2)	0	0	170	170

counting": the sum of outputs exceeds GDP because some production is counted more than once. Steel would be counted when sold by the steel company and again as part of the automobile sold to consumers. The final sales method and the value-added method deal with this problem in different ways. The final sales method counts only the last sale during the period, whereas the value-added method subtracts each firm's payments for intermediate inputs. Both approaches ensure that every dollar of production is counted exactly once, so that the resulting total equals GDP. Since value-added equals factor income for each firm, the sum of values added must equal the sum of factor incomes, or GDP. And final sales by firms to purchasers must equal the income that such purchasers spend—once again, GDP.

Table 5.1 illustrates the three methods of calculating GDP. It considers the production and sale of popcorn by a farmer, a popcorn manufacturer, and a retail convenience store. The production process begins with a farmer, who harvests corn using a tractor he owns and a worker he has hired. The farmer sells the crop for $100 to a popcorn manufacturer, pays his employee $20, and pays the bank $30 as mortgage interest on his farm. This leaves $50 of income for the farmer. The farmer's value added is $100: he has produced $100 worth of corn without using (in this simple example) any intermediate goods. His final sales are zero, since the manufacturer is not the ultimate user of the corn; it will be turned into popcorn for resale. His factor payments equal total payments to labor and capital. Payments to labor equal $20. Payments to capital equal all payments to owners of real or financial assets. This includes not only the $30 of interest the farmer pays to the bank, but also the $50 of profit he clears in the transaction. We classify this profit according to whether the business is a corporation. In the case of a corporation, the profits are called *corporate profits*. In the case of proprietorships, such as the farmer's, profits are classified as *proprietors' income*.[2]

At the second stage of production, the popcorn manufacturer owns a popping machine and rents a factory building for his operations. After buying the farmer's corn for $100, he hires a master popcorn popper to pop it. Selling the popcorn to the retailer, the manufacturer receives $150, of which $25 goes for the popper's wages and $10 for the building rental, a category of capital income that is classified, not surprisingly, as *rental income*. This leaves $15, after the cost of the corn itself. The manufacturer is a corporation, and so this income is counted as corporate profits. Since the manufacturer's sales of popcorn are not to the ultimate user, final sales are zero. Value added equals sales less the cost of materials, or $50. Factor income to labor and capital is also $50.

The retail store owner rents space for $5, employs a store clerk for $10, and, after buying the popcorn for $150, sells it to her customers for $170. This leaves the owner, who is not a corporation, with $5 of proprietors' income. Final sales are $170, value added $20, and factor income $20.

Note that all three methods of calculating GDP give the same result. The factor income method adds the $100 of factor income paid by the farmer to the $50 paid by the manufacturer and the $20 paid by the retailer to obtain a GDP of $170. The values added at these three stages of production also sum to $170, which equals final sales at the last stage of production.

This example also shows why we do not wish to count the sales of all three businesses in calculating GDP. The retailer does not produce the popcorn she sells but does create additional output by providing the service of distributing the finished product. If we count the entire value of the popcorn when the retailer sells it, we cannot count it when the manufacturer sells it to the retailer, for the popcorn itself is produced only once, not twice. Another way to see this point is to consider the case in which the retailer and the manufacturer merge. The combined entity would buy the raw corn for $100 and sell popcorn to consumers for $170. This merger has no effect on GDP. The final sales approach still yields $170 for GDP; so does the value-added method ($100 + $70 = $170). However, adding all sales together produces a smaller measure than before ($100 + $170 = $270 versus $100 + $150 + $170 = $420), a nonsensical result, since there has been no change whatsoever in production.

CASE STUDY
HOW NOT TO IMPOSE A SALES TAX

The difference between total sales on the one hand and final sales and value added on the other has an important application for fiscal policy. In recent years, many U.S. politicians have proposed replacing or supplementing the federal income tax with a

2 Actually, a portion of proprietors' income is really labor income. In this case, the farmer's "profit" is partially a return to his farm's assets, but also a return to his own labor. The national income accounts do not separate proprietors' income into these two components.

national retail sales tax or a national value-added tax. National income accounting says these last two methods should be equivalent, and they are generally recognized to be so.

In contrast, taxes on all sales (including intermediate purchases), called *turnover taxes*, apply to more than total output. They are especially hard on production processes involving several stages of production, because the same output is taxed several times. In our popcorn example, a turnover tax on all sales at the rate of 5 percent would generate $21 in revenue on total sales of $420, equivalent to a tax rate of over 12 percent on GDP. For this reason, turnover taxes have generally been abandoned as a tool of fiscal policy.

RELATED MEASURES OF PRODUCTION AND INCOME

Let's now consider some related measures of output and income.

GNP VERSUS GDP

Gross national product (GNP) is closely related to GDP. The two differ in their treatment of national boundaries. U.S. GNP counts all output produced by U.S.-owned inputs, no matter where those inputs are situated in the world. GDP counts all output produced in the United States regardless of who owns the inputs involved. Thus, GNP includes the output of U.S.-owned inputs located in foreign countries and excludes the output produced in the United States by foreign-owned inputs. For example, if a U.S. business invests in France, the corporate profits it earns there are included in U.S. GNP but not U.S. GDP. If a French business invests in the United States, its U.S. earnings count in U.S. GDP but not U.S. GNP. Similar conclusions apply to wages earned by Americans working in France and by French men and women working in the United States.

The relationship between GNP and GDP is written as

$$GNP = GDP + Y^f$$

3 We measure depreciation by asking how much less an asset produces than a comparable new one. In the case of computers, for example, machines that are several years old may be just as productive as they were when originally produced. However, relative to the current state of technology, these machines have very low productivity and are viewed as having depreciated

where Y^f equals net factor income earned abroad: the income of U.S. inputs abroad minus the income of foreign inputs earned in the United States. In 1996, U.S. inputs earned $228.4 billion abroad, but foreign inputs earned $237.3 billion in the United States. To go from GDP to GNP, we add the first number and subtract the second. Hence, GNP fell short of GDP by $8.9 billion—roughly 0.1 percent of GDP.

NET DOMESTIC PRODUCT AND NATIONAL INCOME

Most physical assets depreciate. Some assets, such as buildings, depreciate slowly; others, like computers, depreciate quite rapidly.[3] Depreciation represents a decline in the value of existing capital. Part of GDP must be used to offset depreciation if the

TABLE 5.2 GDP, NDP, AND NATIONAL INCOME, 1996 (BILLION OF DOLLARS)

Gross domestic product		7,576.1
Less depreciation	845.5	
Equals		
Net domestic product		6,730.6
Plus		
Net receipt of foreign factor income	−8.9	
Less		
Indirect business taxes	617.9	
Business transfer payments	32.2	
Surplus of government enterprises	−17.5	
Statistical discrepancy	−75.1	
Equals		
National income		6,164.2
Wages and salaries	4,448.5	
Proprietors' income	527.3	
Rent	115.0	
Corporate profits	670.2	
Interest	403.3	

Source: *Survey of Current Business* (June 1997).

nation is to maintain its productive capacity. *Net domestic product* (NDP)—GDP minus depreciation—measures what's left over. In 1996, depreciation equaled 11.1 percent of GDP. This share has grown over time because of the increasing share of computers and other short-lived equipment in the capital stock.

National income (NI) goes beyond NDP in considering the income available to the economy. It differs from NDP primarily by subtracting *indirect taxes*, such as retail sales taxes, paid on business transactions and adding in income that U.S. inputs earn abroad, net of income earned in the United States by foreign-owned inputs. In 1996, NI was 81.4 percent of GDP. Table 5.2 presents 1996 figures for GDP, NDP, and NI, as well as the breakdown of NI into the various types of factor income: wages and salaries, rent, interest, corporate profits, and proprietors' income. The table also indicates three minor, additional adjustments made in computing national income.[4]

NATIONAL INCOME VERSUS PERSONAL INCOME

Different measures of income have different uses. GDP measures total domestic production, whereas NDP tells how much output we have left after subtracting depreciation. GNP measures total production by domestic-owned inputs. NI measures the income earned by capital and labor, excluding components of NDP not received as factor incomes and including factor incomes earned abroad that NDP omits.

National income
GNP less the sum of depreciation and indirect business taxes

4 The first two adjustments exclude net operating profits of government enterprises (because such profits are never received by any individual or business) and transfer payments, such as charitable contributions, made by businesses to households (since these reduce business profits without increasing any other form of factor income). The last adjustment is called the statistical discrepancy, which reconciles the final sales and factor income approaches to computing GDP.

TABLE 5.3 FROM NATIONAL INCOME TO PERSONAL INCOME, 1996 (BILLION OF DOLLARS)

National income		6,164.2
Less		
Retained earnings	439.6	
Plus		
Net government transfer payments	367.0	
Interest not in GDP	334.9	
Business transfer payments	23.0	
Wage payments less accruals	0	
Equals		
Personal income		6,449.5
Less		
Individual income taxes	863.8	
Equals		
Disposable Income		5,585.7

Source: *Survey of Current Business* (June 1997).

Personal income
The amount of before-tax income received by households; national income minus income earned but not received, plus income received but not earned

5 *Why exclude retained earnings? The notion is that households don't respond to income not actually received in cash. However, this is not as logical as it may seem. When corporations retain earnings, these earnings still belong to households, through their ownership of corporations, and they are reflected in higher stock values. If households consider the value of the firms they own, retained earnings should be included in an accurate measure of purchasing power.*

6 *Personal income also includes transfer payments made to households by businesses and an adjustment for the fact that the wages households actually receive in a year may differ slightly from those earned during that year. (In 1996, there was no difference.)*

Personal income includes those components of national income that households directly *receive*. It also includes certain household receipts that are *not* components of national income. As a result, personal income may sometimes exceed national income, as it did in 1996. Table 5.3 shows the differences between national income and personal income for that year. The primary exclusion from national income is *retained earnings*, those corporate earnings not actually distributed in cash as *dividends* to the owners, or shareholders, of corporations.[5] The primary additions made in going from national income to personal income are *transfer payments* from the government to households. Unlike other components of national income, transfer payments are not compensation for supplying inputs to the production process. The first category of transfer payments includes payments made under programs like social security and unemployment compensation, net of social security taxes paid by households. The second category consists primarily of the interest paid by the government on the national debt. This interest is classified in the national income accounts as a government transfer to households, since it does not arise from the production of output.[6]

Subtracting individual income taxes from personal income leaves *disposable income*, the income households receive and have available to them after they pay income taxes. That is,

Disposable income = Personal income − individual income taxes.

In 1996 disposable income was $5,585.7 billion, or 86.6 percent of personal income and 73.7 percent of GDP. Disposable income is often cited in the press as an indicator of household purchasing power.

Drawing by S. Gross; ©1997 The New Yorker *Magazine, Inc.*

COMPONENTS OF GDP

The goods and services that comprise GDP are used either to satisfy domestic demand for private consumption (C), private investment (I), and government spending (G), or shipped abroad as exports, X. Of course, domestic demand for $C + G + I$ can also be met through imports, M. Hence, we have

$$GDP + M = C + I + G + X$$

or,

$$GDP = C + I + G + X - M.$$

In words, this expression says that U.S. domestic product equals the sum of domestic U.S. consumption, private investment, and government purchases, plus net sales to foreign purchasers. The upper panel of Table 5.4 gives a breakdown of 1996 GDP into its output components, with some further divisions of the components themselves.

CONSUMPTION VERSUS INVESTMENT

In our two-period model, it is easy to distinguish consumption from investment. Consumption is the output consumed by the household this period; investment is the output carried into the next period to use in production. Making the distinction in the real world is more difficult. Businesses may unintentionally carry over some output into the future, and certain household purchases labeled as consumption may actually constitute investment.

The national income accounts treat business purchases carried into the next year as investment. This includes not only durable goods—equipment and structures (photocopiers, office buildings, factories, buses, etc.)—but also inventories—goods that eventually will be sold. Although inventory accumulation is always classified as investment, it is not necessarily intentional. Some firms may plan to accumulate inventories of goods they wish to resell. Others may find themselves in possession of unwanted inventories if current sales fall short of expectations during a particular year.

Refer again to the popcorn example given in Table 5.1. Here, all output is consumption—the $170 worth of popcorn bought by consumers. Suppose, however, that video stores were closed and the demand for popcorn dropped suddenly, so there was $50 worth of popcorn left in the convenience store at the end of the year. The national accounts would record this as a $50 investment in popcorn inventories by the retailer. This makes sense, because the $50 must be accounted for as output in the year it was produced. Still, if the retailer has trouble selling the popcorn, this particular investment may prove to be quite unproductive.

THE TREATMENT OF HOUSING

As Table 5.4 confirms, construction of residential structures is an important component of U.S. investment. In 1996, the majority of structures built were residential structures—both multifamily units (apartment buildings, condominiums, and cooperatives) and single-family houses. About two-thirds of this housing investment was made by households, through the purchase of owner-occupied housing; households, as well as businesses, can invest. But what does investment in owner-occupied housing produce in the future? It produces the shelter and other services the owner enjoys by living in her own home and not having to rent from someone else. In a sense, the owner rents the housing from herself, so we call the income **imputed rent**.

Since there is no market transaction to use in measuring imputed rent, it must be estimated by national income accountants. Their estimate of imputed rent is included in the rent component of factor income and in the consumption of services. As derived in chapter 16, the formula for imputed rent assumes that the value of the housing services compensates the home owner for the loss of interest income she could have earned by investing the funds used to purchase the house and the depreciation in the house's value while she's living in it.

Housing is not the only durable commodity households purchase. As Table 5.4 shows, the national accounts divide consumption into three categories: services, nondurable goods, and durable goods. The distinction between goods and services separates commodities into those that are tangible (e.g., potato chips) and those that are not (e.g., medical treatment). Durable goods are items that last for several years, like automobiles and washing machines. In principle, they should be treated just like owner-

Imputed rent
An estimate of the value of housing services enjoyed by home owners in a given year

TABLE 5.4 COMPONENTS OF GDP: TYPES OF OUTPUT AND USES OF INCOME, 1996 (BILLIONS OF DOLLARS)

Output			
GDP	7,576.1		
Private consumption (C)		5,151.4	
Durable goods			632.1
Nondurable goods			1,545.1
Services			2,974.3
Private investment (I)		1,117.0	
Nonresidential equipment			576.8
Nonresidential structures			214.3
Inventory accumulation			15.4
Residential structures			310.5
Government purchases (G)		1,406.4	
Consumption			1,173.1
Investment			233.3
Net exports (net foreign investment)		−98.7	
Exports (X)			855.2
Imports (M)			953.9
Income			
GDP	7,576.1		
Plus net foreign factor income (Y^f)	−8.9		
Equals GNP	7,567.1		
Consumption (C)		5,151.4	
Government consumption purchases (GC)		1,173.1	
National saving (S)		1,275.9	
Net transfers abroad		41.9	
Statistical discrepancy		−75.1	

Source: *Survey of Current Business* (June 1997).
Note: Net foreign investment (I^f) = −149.5.

occupied housing—as an investment by households. The services produced by these durables should be treated as consumption and measured as the imputed rent on the durables. Although this is possible, it isn't done in the official national income accounts. *The effect of omitting this correction is to misstate consumption, investment, and saving.*

CONSUMPTION OF THE SERVICES OF GOVERNMENT CAPITAL

Calculating the consumption of owner-occupied housing requires imputing its rental value. The same is true of services from government-owned capital goods, such as highways, parks, school buildings, prisons, and military aircraft. These capital goods provide a flow of consumption services whose value must be imputed and then added to other consumption expenditures, such as payments for police protection and garbage collection, to arrive at a measure of total government consumption. In 1996, imputed rent on government capital equaled \$149.1 billion—12.7 percent of total government consumption. We add government investment to total government consumption to arrive at the overall measure of government purchases,

$$G = GC + GI.$$

USING THE NATIONAL INCOME IDENTITY

There has been much concern in recent years about the size of the U.S. **trade deficit**—the difference between imports and exports. The national income identity can help us understand the connection between the trade deficit, national saving, and domestic investment.

NATIONAL SAVING AND THE TRADE DEFICIT

Recall that GDP is either consumed, purchased by the government, invested at home, or sent abroad as net exports. Hence,

$$GDP = C + I + G + X - M.$$

Now add net foreign income, Y^f, to both sides of this identity and note that GDP plus net foreign income equals gross national product, GNP:

$$GNP = C + I + G + X - M + Y^f.$$

Next, subtract private consumption and government consumption purchases from both sides of this formula for GNP:

$$GNP - C - GC = I + GI + X - M + Y^f.$$

National saving, S, equals that part of GNP that is not consumed during the period by either households or the government, $S = GNP - C - GC$, so we have:[7]

$$S - I - GI = X - M + Y^f.$$

Finally, note that the difference between national saving and domestic investment, $S - I - GI$, is simply the amount of saving invested abroad, which we call *net foreign investment*, I^f. Hence, replacing $S - I - GI$ by I^f gives[8]

$$I^f = X - M + Y^f.$$

It may seem strange that a country's net exports and its net foreign investment are so closely linked. But the relationship is easy to understand from the perspective of our simple two-period model in which a single good, say corn, serves as both a con-

Trade deficit
The difference between the values of imports and exports in a given year

7 In the actual national income accounts, there is an additional item subtracted in computing national saving: net transfers abroad (i.e., foreign aid), amounts that are used for neither domestic consumption nor national saving. We ignore this small and usually stable component in the derivation here.

8 In the presentation of international accounts, the right-hand side of this expression is called the current account. *Minus the left-hand side is called the* capital account. *Note that the current and capital accounts sum to zero.*

sumption and an investment good. The home country invests abroad when it plants some of its corn in the foreign country. Net foreign investment—the change in the amount of corn the home country has planted abroad—equals the net flow of corn to the foreign country—the net export of corn—plus the amount of corn earned by the home country and kept abroad—the net factor income earned abroad. Intuitively, investing abroad (planting corn in the foreign country's soil) requires either bringing corn from home to plant abroad (exporting some of a country's domestic output) or planting the corn one receives abroad as income earned on past investments (re-investing foreign earnings abroad). This intuition also holds in the real world in which there are many different kinds of investment and consumption goods. When a country exports goods, for example, it can be thought of either as placing some of its own capital goods in the foreign country—in which case the exports translate directly into the foreign investment—or as selling some of its consumption goods and services in the foreign country and using the proceeds to buy capital goods in the foreign country which it leaves (invests) there. Table 5.4 indicates that U.S. net foreign investment was −149.5 billion in 1996, which means that foreigners' investment in the United States exceeded U.S. investment abroad.

CASE STUDY
THE TRADE DEFICIT SINCE 1980

The *trade surplus*, $X - M$, also called the **trade balance**, and net foreign investment, I^f, generally move quite closely together. For given levels of Y^f, reductions in the trade surplus—or increases in the trade deficit—will also reduce net foreign investment, meaning that U.S. residents will be investing less abroad, foreigners will be investing more in the United States, or both.

Is it a bad thing to run a trade deficit and have foreigners adding to the capital stock in this country? Quite the contrary. As we saw in chapter 1, having more capital per worker raises labor productivity and real wages. If having foreigners invest in this country is a good thing, why is there so much concern about trade deficits? The answer can be understood by recalling that national saving, S, equals the sum of domestic investment, $I + GI$, and net foreign investment, I^f. When a country's saving falls, either its domestic investment or its net foreign investment must also fall. As we will see in chapter 12, when capital is internationally mobile, net foreign investment will fall (be **crowded out**) when saving declines. Hence, one reason we ought to be concerned about an increase in inbound foreign investment, and the associated increase in the trade deficit, is that they may reflect a decline in the nation's saving. We can, of course, look directly at the nation's saving behavior, but the trade deficit appears to attract more media attention than the national saving rate.

Figure 5.2 plots the ratios to GDP of national saving (S), domestic investment (I), and the trade balance ($X - M$) since 1980. As the figure shows, national saving

Trade balance
The difference between a country's exports and imports in a given period; a synonym for net exports

Crowding out
A reduction in investment as a result of a decrease in national saving

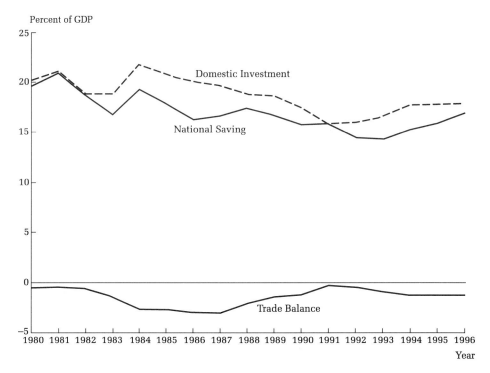

FIGURE 5.2 SAVING, INVESTMENT, AND THE TRADE BALANCE, 1980–1996
Since 1980, U.S. national saving has declined from about 20 percent of GDP to about 17 percent. Initially, much of this decline was absorbed by a decline in the trade balance. Toward the late 1980s, the trade balance improved as domestic investment fell. More recently, the trade balance has worsened with a rebound in domestic investment, despite a slight increase in the national saving rate.

Source: National Income and Product Accounts.

declined from around 20 percent of GDP in 1980 to 17 percent in 1996. During the early part of this decline in saving, most of the crowding out caused by the decline in national saving involved net exports. Indeed, domestic investment actually *rose* as a share of GDP into the mid-1980s. By the late 1980s, however, the pattern of crowding out had shifted. The rate of domestic investment declined, and net exports began to improve. By 1991, the trade deficit had fallen below 1 percent of GDP, from its peak of over 3 percent in the mid-1980s. But the deficit increased thereafter, as investment growth more than offset a slight increase in the national saving rate.

Explaining why national saving fell and the precise response of net exports is beyond the realm of national income accounting. Still, *national income accounting tells us it's impossible, in the short run when Y^f is given, to reduce a trade deficit without increasing national saving or decreasing domestic investment*—a lesson of considerable value when considering government policy toward international trade.

DISTINGUISHING REAL FROM NOMINAL MAGNITUDES

How do we combine information on the vast array of goods and services produced by modern economies into a single measure of real output? The answer quite literally requires combining apples with oranges, but in a sensible way. To lay the groundwork, we first describe how economists measure the level of prices—the **price level**—and the rate of change over time in the price level—the **rate of inflation**.

MEASURING INFLATION

Over time, expenditures increase for two reasons: because prices rise and because larger quantities of goods and services are purchased. Economists measure inflation—the rate of increase in prices—by determining how much a given bundle of goods—the goods purchased in a particular *base year*—would cost at different times. The ratio of the cost of a given bundle of goods at different points in time is called a *price index*. A price index holds quantities fixed at base-year values and lets prices vary. For example, if the base year is 1980, the price index for 1990 is

$$1990 \text{ value of price index} = \frac{\sum_{i=1}^{M} p_{1990}^{i} \times q_{1980}^{i}}{\sum_{i=1}^{M} p_{1980}^{i} \times q_{1980}^{i}}.$$

In this equation, the symbol $\sum$ means "summation." The term p_{1980}^{i} stands for the price of commodity i in 1980, p_{1990}^{i} for its price in 1990, and q_{1980}^{i} stands for the quantity of commodity i sold in 1980. The denominator of this equation is simply the sum of all expenditures (prices times quantities) actually needed to purchase a basket of goods and services in 1980. The numerator is the sum of all expenditures needed to purchase the same basket of commodities in 1990. To calculate the price index for another year, say 2000, we would substitute that year's prices in the numerator of the expression.

Perhaps the most frequently used price index in the United States is the **Consumer Price Index** (CPI), which has a base year (or to be more exact, base period) of 1982–1984; it holds quantities fixed at the bundle of final goods and services sold to consumers during the period 1982 through 1984. The CPI is useful because it provides an indication of the price changes households face in their daily lives. The CPI is basically computed as just indicated, and multiplied by 100 when reported (so that its value in the base period is 100, rather than 1). For example, for 1997, the CPI is:

$$1997 \text{ value of CPI} = \frac{\sum_{i=1}^{M} p_{1997}^{i} \times q_{1982-84}^{i}}{\sum_{i=1}^{M} p_{1982-84}^{i} \times q_{1982-84}^{i}} \times 100.$$

Price level
A weighted index of prices of individual goods and services at a particular point in time

Inflation rate
The percentage increase in the price level from one period to the next

Consumer Price Index
A measure of the price of a fixed market basket of consumer goods and services

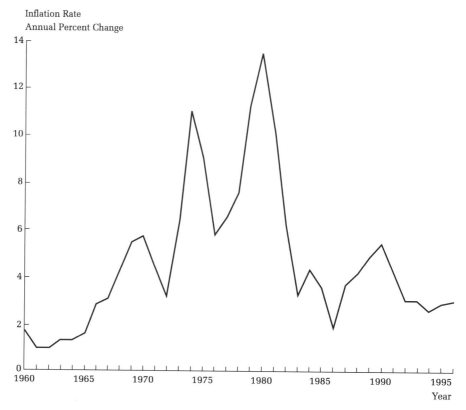

Inflation Rate
Annual Percent Change

FIGURE 5.3 INFLATION RATES SINCE 1960
The inflation rate, measured by annual changes in the Consumer Price Index, has varied markedly since 1960. Over the entire period, the price level increased by an average of about 4.7 percent per year. However, the average rate was 2.7 percent during the 1960s, 7.8 percent during the 1970s, 4.7 percent during the 1980s, and 3.1 percent in the 1990s. The lowest inflation rate, 1 percent, occurred in 1962; the highest rate, 13.5 percent, in 1980.

Source: Economic Report of the President, *1997.*

We can use the CPI to calculate the inflation rate, equal to the rate of increase in prices between two successive years. For example, if we wish to know the inflation rate of consumer prices in 1998, we take the ratio of the 1998 CPI to the 1997 CPI,

$$\frac{1998 \text{ value of CPI}}{1997 \text{ value of CPI}} = \frac{\sum_{i=1}^{M} p_{1998}^{i} \times q_{1982-84}^{i}}{\sum_{i=1}^{M} p_{1997}^{i} \times q_{1982-84}^{i}},$$

and subtract 1 from this ratio.

Figure 5.3 shows the annual rates of inflation since 1960, derived by taking the rate of change of the CPI in each year. How much did consumer prices increase between 1960 and 1996? Since the respective values of the CPI in 1960 and 1996 were 29.6 and 156.9, the consumer price level rose by a factor of 5.30 (156.9 divided by 29.6). However, this 430 percent increase in the price level between 1960 and 1996, an average of 4.7 percent a year, did not occur smoothly over the period. The average annual rate of inflation was only 2.7 percent in the 1960s. It was 7.8 percent in the 1970s, 4.7 percent in the 1980s, and 3.1 percent during the 1990s. During the entire period, 1962 had the lowest inflation rate, just 1.0 percent, and 1980 had the highest, registering 13.5 percent.

USING THE CPI

The CPI is often used to adjust nominal sums of money for the price changes that occur between two periods of time. Take, for example, the $297 billion and $345 billion of compensation paid to employees in 1960 and 1963, respectively. The nominal amount paid to employees rose by 16.2 percent during this period, but how much did the real purchasing power of employee compensation increase?

One way to answer this question is to convert the 1960 nominal amount of $297 into 1963 dollars and then compare the converted amount with $345 billion. We do this by first dividing the $297 billion by the price level, the CPI, for 1960. This neutralizes the price units of 1960. Then we multiply by the CPI for 1963 to express this price-free magnitude in terms of 1963 dollars. Since the CPI for 1960 was 29.6 and the CPI for 1963 was 30.6, the value of 1960 compensation expressed in 1963 dollars is $307 billion ($297 divided by 29.6, then multiplied by 30.6). That amount can now be compared with $345 billion, since both are expressed in 1963 dollars. The 12.4 percent difference reflects only the increase in real compensation. An alternative to converting the 1960 nominal sum into 1963 dollars is to convert the 1963 sum into 1960 dollars. In this case, we multiply $345 billion by the ratio of the CPI in 1960 divided by the CPI in 1963. The resulting amount of $334 billion is the same 12.4 percent greater than $297 billion.

BIASES IN THE CPI

The CPI tells us how much a bundle of consumer items from 1982 to 1984 would cost, now or in any other year; comparing the CPI at different dates provides a measure of the inflation rate of consumer prices. But there are several sources of bias that have led economists to conclude that the CPI overstates the annual inflation rate by perhaps 1 percentage point, or even more.[9] Three important biases arise from commodity substitution, the introduction of new goods, and changes in the quality of goods.

Commodity Substitution

Not all prices rise at the same rate. Over time, goods whose prices rise less quickly become less expensive, relative to other goods, than they were in the base period. Consider, for example, the components of the CPI apparel and housing. Both started at

9 See Brent R. Moulton, "Bias in the Consumer Price Index: What Is the Evidence?" Journal of Economic Perspectives (Fall 1996): 159–177.

100 during the period 1982–1984. By 1996, the price of apparel had grown to 131.7, but the price of housing had jumped to 171.0.

As households face changes in relative prices, they tend to reduce purchases of goods whose prices are rising more rapidly and increase purchases of goods whose prices are rising less rapidly (or falling). The CPI fails to account for this, for it assumes an unchanging market basket. This bias tends to become worse over time, as relative price differences widen and substitution increases. Hence, the inflation rate between any two of these years will be overstated.

New Goods and Quality Change

Because of technological progress, the price changes of many commodities are difficult to measure. A perfect example is computers. We encounter two related problems in trying to incorporate computer price changes in the CPI. First, some models have only recently been invented or introduced. What price should be used for these goods in the base year? For example, if a certain type of computer was invented in 1985, what was its price in 1982? One answer might be "infinity," since it was not available at any price. However, this overstates the price in that year if some substitute goods, however inferior, were available. Over time, the CPI does add new goods by substituting them in the index for comparable old goods, but this still overstates the increase in prices to the extent that the new goods are an improvement over the old.

The second problem involves changes in quality. The best personal computers commonly available in 1982 took much longer to perform calculations than their counterparts in 1998. In a sense, the 1998 models were new goods: the versions available in 1982 were inferior substitutes. The CPI deals with this problem by attempting to measure quality changes directly, by converting the 1982 and 1998 computers into comparable units. This is done by measuring not the quantity of computers produced, but the quantity of computing power. Although the 1982 computer may have borne a superficial resemblance to the 1998 computer, we might say it contained only a small fraction of its 1998 counterpart. Using computing power as a measure of output overcomes the problem of quality change. However, there are many goods—medical care, for example—for which it is more difficult to measure quality change. Economists generally believe that the CPI overstates price increases because of inadequate adjustments for quality improvements.

REFORM OF THE CPI

Overstating the CPI has significant effects on the economy, ranging from adjustments in labor contracts to the government's conduct of monetary and fiscal policy. For example, the federal government uses the CPI to adjust the federal income taxes it collects and the social security benefits it pays. An increase in the CPI leads to lower taxes and higher benefits. Thus, overstatement of the CPI leads to an excessive reduction in taxes and an excessive increase in benefits, both of which increase the government's *budget deficit*.

Part of the solution to the biases in the CPI is to change the base year frequently, to reduce the number of cases of new products and significant changes in technology that must be dealt with. For example, in 1998, the CPI is scheduled to move from a base period of 1982–1984 to one of 1993–1995. However, base-year changes only reduce the problem, because quality changes and product innovation occur continuously.

Why not simply change the weights each year? That is, rather than using weights from a prior year, producing what is called a *Laspeyres index*, why not use current year quantities to estimate the price level for the current year and all past years, producing what is known as a *Paasche index*? Unfortunately, this approach has all the biases of using fixed quantities from an earlier year, only in the opposite direction. For example, it would understate past purchases of goods that consumers had switched away from in response to rapid price increases; its inclusion of newer and higher-quality goods in the index would overstate the purchases of these goods in the past. Both biases would overstate prices increasingly more in earlier and earlier years, and hence understate the inflation rate between any two of these years.

In summary, *the CPI probably overstates the increase in prices that consumers face. Its accuracy can be improved through better accounting for new goods and changes in quality and periodic changes in the base year, but it is impossible to derive a measure of inflation that is exactly correct.*

MEASURING REAL GDP

To measure the change in prices over time, we use a price index like the CPI. To measure changes in quantities over time, we use a *quantity index*. A quantity index is like a price index, except that rather than holding quantities fixed at base-year values and letting prices vary, we hold prices fixed at base-year values and let quantities vary. We use quantity indexes to measure changes in real output—changes in the value of production not attributable to price increases. For example, to measure the rate of growth in real output from 1997 to 1998, with a base year of 1987, we take the ratio of the quantity index in 1998 to that in 1997,

$$\frac{\text{1998 value of quantity index}}{\text{1997 value of quantity index}} = \frac{\sum\limits_{i=1}^{M} p_{1987}^i \times q_{1998}^i}{\sum\limits_{i=1}^{M} p_{1987}^i \times q_{1997}^i},$$

and subtract 1 from this ratio.

The best-known quantity index is real GDP, which measures the quantity of all output produced in the United States. To understand the calculation of real GDP, let's first think about *nominal GDP*—GDP not adjusted for changes in prices. To determine nominal GDP in, say, 1998, we just add together the values of the sales (prices times quantities) of all final goods and services produced in 1998. Thus,

$$1998 \text{ nominal GDP} = \sum_{i=1}^{M} p_{1998}^i \times q_{1998}^i.$$

Until recently, real GDP was measured as a quantity index using fixed 1987 price weights, in which the prices used in the expression for nominal GDP were replaced by those from 1987. However, the use of fixed price weights from an earlier year leads to a substitution bias that overstates output growth, because it gives too much weight to the goods experiencing particularly strong output growth as a result of relatively slow growth in prices. Using current-year weights leads to an opposite bias: understating the importance of goods with declining prices and hence underestimating the growth in output. A compromise solution, now used to measure real GDP, is to use an average of prior-year weights and current-year weights, and to let the average base year change over time, following a procedure known as *chain weighting.*

Under chain weighting, the change in real GDP from one year to the next is the geometric mean (the square root of the product) of the ratio based on the use of weights from the two years. For example, the change in real GDP from 1997 to 1998 is:

$$\frac{1998 \text{ real GDP}}{1997 \text{ real GDP}} = \sqrt{\frac{\sum p_{1997}^i \times q_{1998}^i}{\sum p_{1997}^i \times q_{1997}^i} \times \frac{\sum p_{1998}^i \times q_{1998}^i}{\sum p_{1998}^i \times q_{1997}^i}}.$$

This procedure defines rates of change in real GDP but not its level. To fix the levels, we set the level of real GDP for 1992 equal to that year's nominal GDP,

$$1992 \text{ real GDP} = \sum_{i=1}^{M} p_{1992}^i \times q_{1992}^i.$$

Then, to calculate real GDP for years before or after 1992, we start with this 1992 value and apply the expression for year-to-year changes in real GDP. For example, we would calculate the value of 1998 real GDP as the value of 1992 real GDP, multiplied by the ratio of 1993 real GDP to 1992 real GDP, multiplied by the ratio of 1994 real GDP to 1993 real GDP, and so on, until we reached 1998. In this procedure, we use ratios based on prices from the years 1992 and 1993, 1993 and 1994, and so on—hence the term *chain weighting.*

CASE STUDY
BIASES IN THE MEASUREMENT OF REAL GDP

How important are the biases of using a fixed-weight quantity index? Figure 5.4 shows the impact of the change from fixed-weight measurement of real GDP to chain-weighted measurement. As the figure shows, the shift to chain weighting adopted in 1996 reduced measured growth rates of real GDP substantially in the mid-1990s. For example, in 1994, real GDP grew by 4.0 percent according to the fixed-weight calculation but just 3.5 percent according to the chain-weight calculation. Why? Because the use of 1987 price weights overstated the importance of items, such as computers,

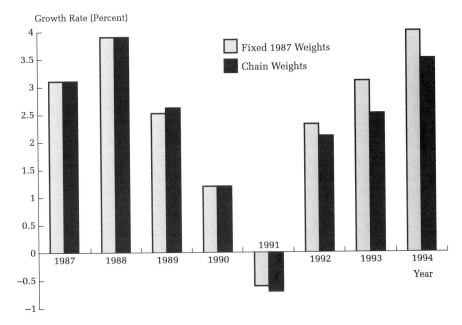

Growth Rate (Percent)

FIGURE 5.4 REAL GDP GROWTH RATES: THE IMPACT OF CHAIN WEIGHTING
In 1996, the United States changed its method of measuring real GDP from a quantity index based on fixed 1987 price weights to one based on chain weights. The impact was to reduce considerably the estimated growth rates of real GDP during the period 1992–1994.

Source: Economic Report of the President, *1995.*

that had experienced significant price declines between 1987 and the mid-1990s while at the same time experiencing explosive output growth.

AN ALTERNATIVE MEASURE OF INFLATION

The CPI measures the price level of goods purchased by consumers. Another measure of the price level and inflation is provided by the **GDP deflator**. It uses as its quantities the entire bundle of commodities comprising GDP rather than just those purchased by typical households. Unlike the CPI, the GDP deflator is defined implicitly, by dividing nominal GDP by real GDP and multiplying by 100. Thus, multiplying the GDP deflator for the current year by the current year's measure of real GDP yields the current year's measure of nominal GDP, multiplied by 100. Drawing an analogy to a household's expenditure decision, we may think of nominal GDP as the total amount spent, real GDP as the quantity purchased, and the GDP deflator as the price of real GDP. For example, in 1996, nominal GDP was $7,576.1 trillion, which equals the product of that year's GDP deflator, 109.7, and its real GDP, $6,906.8 trillion, divided by 100. Since the GDP deflator had a value of 100.0 in 1992, we see that prices rose by 9.7 percent between 1992 and 1996—an average annual rate of inflation of 2.3 percent.

GDP deflator
An index used to correct GDP for price changes, defined implicitly as the ratio of nominal GDP to real GDP

ADDING NOMINAL QUANTITIES TO OUR MODEL

The model developed in chapters 1 through 4 is expressed in real terms—in units of output. However, it is easy to express the same model in nominal terms (in units of money, such as dollars) by accounting for differences in the price level over time. We simply multiply each period's real quantities by the price level that prevails in that period.

Recall that the young household in period t earns a wage w_t, consumes c_{yt}, and saves a_{t+1}. We write this relationship in nominal terms by multiplying both sides by the year t price level, p_t:

$$p_t a_{t+1} = p_t w_t - p_t c_{yt}.$$

($p_t w_t$ stands for the *nominal* wage rate.) The expression relating the same person's consumption and assets one period later (when the person is old, and receives interest income) is recast in nominal terms by multiplying it by the current price level, p_{t+1}:

$$p_{t+1} c_{ot+1} = p_{t+1} a_{t+1}(1 + r_{t+1}),$$

where c_{ot+1} is consumption when old and r_{t+1} is the **real interest rate**, the rate of return earned on assets after inflation. Note that on the right-hand side of this expression, the assets acquired in year t are now multiplied by p_{t+1} rather than p_t. If we wish to express the nominal amount spent in period $t + 1$ in terms of the nominal amount saved in period t, $p_t a_{t+1}$, we rewrite the second-period budget constraint as follows:

$$p_{t+1} c_{ot+1} = p_t a_{t+1}(1 + i_{t+1}),$$

where i_{t+1} stands for the **nominal interest rate** at time $t + 1$, the percentage return in dollars the household earns on its assets. Comparing these two expressions relating old-age consumption to assets, we can see that $1 + i_{t+1}$ equals $1 + r_{t+1}$ multiplied by the price ratio, p_{t+1}/p_t. From this relationship, we derive the following one relating the two interest rates and the inflation rate, $\pi_{t+1} = (p_{t+1} - p_t)/p_t$:

$$i_{t+1} = r_{t+1} + \pi_{t+1} + r_{t+1}\pi_{t+1}.$$

As this expression shows, the nominal interest rate equals the real interest rate, r_{t+1}, plus the inflation rate, π_{t+1}, plus the product of the real interest rate and the inflation rate. Over relatively short periods of time (such as one year), the third term will be quite small compared to the other terms, and can be ignored. Thus, the nominal interest rate exceeds the real interest rate by approximately the rate of price inflation:

$$i_{t+1} = r_{t+1} + \pi_{t+1}.$$

This is the **Fisher equation**, which was derived by Irving Fisher of Yale, one of the world's leading economists during the years leading up to World War II.

Economists call the difference between the nominal and real interest rates the *inflation premium*. To understand why the nominal interest rate incorporates an

Real interest rate
The nominal interest rate adjusted for inflation; approximately the nominal interest rate minus the expected rate of inflation

Nominal interest rate
The interest rate paid on financial assets

Fisher equation
The proposition that the nominal interest rate (i) approximately equals the sum of the real interest rate (r) plus the expected rate of price inflation (π)

inflation premium, consider the return received in our model by a young person who saves by purchasing a financial instrument that pays off in a nominal amount of dollars rather than directly in the form of commodities, such as corn. Specifically, assume that rather than use their dollar savings to purchase real assets (corn) and invest (plant) their capital directly, young people at the end of their youth lend their dollar savings to firms and receive in exchange a bond. The bond promises to pay, in dollars, principal plus nominal interest on the loan at the end of the period. What do the firms do with the dollars they receive in exchange for their bonds? They use them to purchase corn, which they plant. At the end of the period, the firms sell off the crop for dollars and use the dollar proceeds to pay nominal wages to their young workers and to pay principal plus interest on the bonds.

Since people have the option of using their savings to purchase and plant corn themselves, the real return they receive from lending their savings to firms can't be any lower than what they can earn investing on their own. In calculating their real return from buying a bond, young workers will take into account that when they are repaid in dollars at the end of their old age, the real value of their principal will have declined if prices have risen during the period. Thus, in order to protect the real principal of young people's financial investments, firms will have to promise to pay a premium to take account of the inflation over the period. This is why the nominal interest rate equals the real interest rate plus the rate of inflation. How do firms get the extra dollars to pay a nominal interest rate in excess of the real interest rate? They sell their output at the end of each period at the prevailing price of output. If the price of output has risen, firms will earn more dollars, some of which they will use to pay the inflation component of their interest obligations.

MEASURING THE REAL INTEREST RATE

In most financial markets, transactions are in nominal terms; we observe the nominal interest rate and must compute the real interest rate by subtracting the inflation rate from the nominal interest rate. Figure 5.5 shows the nominal and real interest rates on U.S. government Treasury bills since 1970, with the inflation rate calculated based on the GDP deflator. To measure the real interest rate, we subtract the inflation rate that actually prevailed (rather than the rate that was expected to prevail) from the nominal interest rate. The figure shows that nominal interest rates peaked in 1981 at around 14 percent. Real interest rates, on the other hand, were highest in 1984, at nearly 6 percent, and were actually negative at times during the 1970s.

Some of the fluctuations in real interest rates shown in Figure 5.5 may be due to the fact that we are using the ex-post actual, rather than the ex-ante expected inflation rate. Presumably the nominal interest rate is set in accordance with the expected inflation rate, to deliver an appropriate real interest rate, should that expected inflation rate actually prevail. However, if inflation turns out to be higher (or lower) than expected in one year, the corresponding real interest rate, which we graph in Figure 5.5, will be lower (or higher).

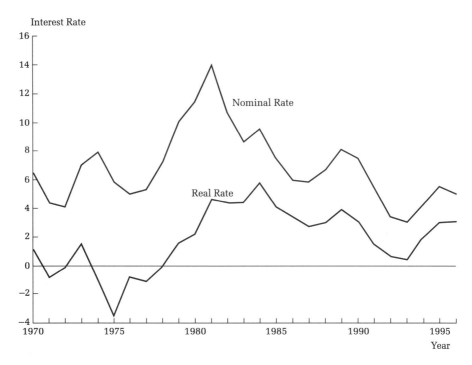

Interest Rate

FIGURE 5.5 NOMINAL AND REAL INTEREST RATES, 1970–1996
According to the Fisher equation, the nominal interest rate is approximately equal to the real interest rate plus the expected rate of inflation. In this figure, the real interest rate is estimated by subtracting the known rate of inflation from the known nominal interest rate. The graph shows that the estimated real interest rate was negative during the mid-1970s. Some of the fluctuations exhibited here may be due to errors in forecasting the rate of inflation.

Source: Economic Report of the President, *1997*.

Suppose the expected inflation rate is 5 percent and that financial markets set the nominal interest rate at 8 percent to provide an expected real interest rate of 3 percent. If the inflation rate turns out to be 9 percent, the observed real interest rate will be −1 percent; if the inflation rate is 2 percent, the observed real interest rate will be 6 percent. Thus, some of the variation in observed real interest rates over time is due to unfulfilled expectations with respect to inflation rather than changes in *expected* real interest rates. The distinction between expected and actual real interest rates may help explain why real interest rates were negative in the 1970s, when inflation was unexpectedly high, and why real interest rates rose in the early 1980s, as the inflation rate fell.

Can interest rates be set in real terms rather than nominal ones? In principle, the answer is yes. Rather than agreeing to pay a set nominal interest rate, the borrower could agree to pay a set real interest rate plus the inflation rate. For example, if the borrower agreed to pay a real interest rate of 3 percent, then the actual nominal interest rate paid would equal 8 percent if the inflation rate turned out to be 5 percent, but only

4 percent if the inflation rate turned out to be 1 percent. Because their nominal return depends on movements in a price index, such bonds are called **indexed bonds**. Because they offer savers a real interest rate protected from unexpected fluctuations in the inflation rate, economists have longed urged governments to issue them. Some governments, notably the United Kingdom, have begun doing so, and in late 1996 the U.S. Treasury followed suit.

Issuing indexed bonds has another benefit. Because the interest rates on regular nominal bonds should exceed that on indexed bonds by the expected inflation rate, comparing the interest rates on indexed and nominal bonds issued at the same time provides a measure of the expected inflation rate. For example, on July 2, 1997, the interest rate on regular 10-year U.S. Treasury notes was 6.40 percent per year, and the rate on indexed notes was 3.62 percent per year, suggesting that investors expected an average inflation rate of 2.78 (6.40 − 3.62) percent over the next 10 years.

ADDITIONAL PROBLEMS IN MEASURING GDP

The factor income and output measures of GDP differ by a very small statistical discrepancy, because of problems of measurement. Beyond that statistical discrepancy are more fundamental problems that national income accountants face in measuring GDP. These include some issues discussed above, such as distinguishing consumption from investment and accounting for changes in quality when estimating price changes. In measuring GDP, we rely heavily on our ability to value production by observing prices paid in market transactions. The absence of markets presents additional challenges to measuring and comparing GDP across countries.

NONMARKET ACTIVITIES

The labor force participation rate of women has increased dramatically in the postwar period. The effect was to increase measured GDP. However, this increase overstates the true increase in output, because it has been coupled with a decline in nonmarket activity—production that occurs outside formal markets and is therefore omitted from GDP calculations.

As women left the home for formal employment, families needed to rely more on others to provide services, such as day care, that previously might have been provided by a mother. When a mother leaves the home to accept formal employment, our measure of GDP includes not only her labor income, but also the income earned by the day care provider she uses. In the past, however, if a mother provided day care directly for her own children, this failed to show up in GDP. Hence, the shift of day care from the nonmarket sector to the market sector raises the share of day care provision included in GDP.

Another problem resulting from the lack of markets is the difficulty of valuing government expenditures. Much government spending is on police and fire protection,

Indexed bonds
Bonds that offer a fixed real interest rate by paying a nominal interest rate that varies with the inflation rate

education, garbage collection, and other services to the public. If these services were provided by the private sector, we could measure GDP using the final sales method based on sales prices. However, governments typically do not sell these services, so we have no market measure of their value. Instead, we value the production at the cost of inputs, for example, we measure the police payroll instead of the value of police services.[10]

UNREPORTED INCOME

Not all unmeasured income is nonmarket income. Some income is earned in markets but simply not reported to the government, for tax and other reasons. Waiters who don't report their tips, baby sitters who don't report their fees, and gardeners who don't report their wages are examples. Some of this unreported income shows up in GDP because it can be measured indirectly, but not all does. Such income—generated in what is commonly referred to as the *underground economy*—comes from engaging in legal activities, although evading income taxes on the income is illegal. In contrast, there are individuals who earn their livelihood in illegal ways, such as by selling illegal drugs. The income generated by drug sales and other illegal activities—as distinguished from the income generated in the underground economy—is intentionally excluded from GDP. In some countries, this leads to a considerable understatement of economic activity.

DISTORTED MARKETS

Another problem arises when markets are distorted. The formerly planned economies of Eastern Europe set many of their prices by decree. As a result, the prices of different goods and services often varied considerably from the values that households placed on these commodities. In their recent transition to capitalism, these economies have experienced significant shifts in prices and resource allocation. How should we account for the sharp reductions in the production of certain industries?

Consider the case of the Trabant, once a mainstay of East German driving. The undependable "Trabi," with its antiquated two-stroke engine and plastic body, was forced on East German consumers for a price far in excess of its value on the world market. As soon as German unification occurred and East Germans could purchase other cars, the long backlog of orders for Trabants disappeared and production ceased. Consumers placed such a low value on them that they were not worth producing. How much output was lost when the Trabant factories closed? Based on the prices for which Trabants had been sold, a lot. Based on the value of Trabants in the world market, far less.

POLLUTION AND OTHER ENVIRONMENTAL DAMAGE

Quality of life is affected by more than the amount of commodities produced in markets or in the home. Air and water quality, for example, are important determinants of health and life expectancy. However, the maintenance of a good environment or, conversely, the destruction of the environment, do not enter into GDP calculations.

10 Isn't this just the factor incomes approach, which should yield the same answer as the final sales approach? Not exactly. If a government service is more or less highly valued than the sum of associated factor payments, we ought to include an additional term to account for the "profit" the service generates for the economy (which is negative when factor payments exceed the value of the service).

This omission has two effects. First, it makes GDP an inadequate measure of national well-being. Second, and perhaps more important, it makes the evaluation of the benefits of environmental programs more difficult. For example, in the 1970s, U.S. companies devoted a considerable share of their investment expenditures to pollution control, in order to meet standards imposed by the U.S. government for clean air and water. Based on national income accounting measures, these expenditures were entirely unproductive; the cleaner air and water they produced did not show up in GDP. But it is clearly a mistake to view pollution abatement expenditures as unproductive. They may very well have been of great social value, but we lack a precise measure of their contribution to national welfare. This bears keeping in mind when comparing U.S. GDP with those of other countries with more severe pollution problems.

CHAPTER SUMMARY

1. National income accounting calculates the economy's GDP and related output and income measures. There are three ways to measure GDP: final sales, value added, and factor incomes. According to the national income identity, these three approaches must produce the same measure of GDP.

2. Other measures of aggregate production include net domestic product, which excludes depreciation; national income, which measures income directly earned by suppliers of labor and capital; and personal income, which distinguishes receipts of households from those of corporations. A common alternative to GDP is gross national product (GNP), which adds to GDP the foreign earnings of domestically owned inputs, but excludes the domestic earnings of foreign-owned inputs.

3. To divide GDP properly between consumption and investment, one includes in consumption the imputed rent on owner-occupied housing, government capital, and consumer durables. The U.S. national income accounts fail to impute rent on consumer durables and instead simply treat purchases of durables as consumption.

4. The national income identity has several applications. For example, it helps us understand why a turnover tax is undesirable and the relationship among national saving, domestic investment, and the trade deficit.

5. Economists construct quantity and price indexes to distinguish changes in the real quantity of goods and services produced, real GDP, from those changes in nominal GDP that are due to changes in the price level. Real GDP, currently

measured in 1992 dollars, is an example of a quantity index. It measures the increase in output over time. The GDP deflator is the corresponding price index that measures the change in the aggregate price level. Another price index is the Consumer Price Index (CPI).

6. The nominal interest rate less the inflation rate provides a measure of the real interest rate.

7. Measuring GDP presents several problems, including how to account for technological innovation and new commodities and how to value production that occurs in distorted markets or markets for which sales are neither measured nor reported. These omissions are especially important for economies in transition, whether away from distorted markets, toward a cleaner environment, or toward a higher labor force participation rate.

PART TWO

FISCAL AND MONETARY POLICY

CHAPTER 6

FISCAL POLICY, SAVING, AND GROWTH

INTRODUCTION

The government plays a major role in all modern economies. In the United States, government (at the state, local, and federal levels) purchases almost a fifth of output in the course of providing public goods and services ranging from education to national defense. It also redistributes large amounts of income across and within generations. **Fiscal policy** encompasses these functions, but it's also a tool for affecting macroeconomic performance. Many economists believe fiscal policy can and should be used to lessen the severity of short-term business cycles. Others are primarily concerned with its effects on long-term economic growth.

This chapter shows how fiscal policy affects growth. Subsequent chapters consider the role of fiscal policy in dampening the business cycle. Our main focus here is on government spending on consumption and investment goods and on **generational policy**—the government's allocation across generations of the burden of paying for its spending. As we'll see, these actions can have dramatic implications for both the macroeconomy and the well-being of current and future generations. We'll also briefly consider how a generation's fiscal burden is distributed among its members and the impact on private sector incentives, such as the incentive to save, of taxes and transfer payments.

The chapter's key questions are:

- What are the main features of U.S. fiscal policy?

- How does fiscal policy influence household behavior?

- What is the relationship between current and future fiscal decisions?

- How does generational policy work, and what are its macroeconomic effects?

Fiscal policy
The use of government purchases, taxes, transfers, and borrowing to influence aggregate economic activity

Generational policy
Shifting of fiscal burdens among different generations

- Is the government budget deficit a clear measure of generational policy?

- Is current U.S. fiscal policy sustainable?

- Can privatizing Social Security resolve its long-term funding crisis?

We begin with an overview of U.S. government expenditures, receipts, and budget deficits. Next, we describe the government's *intertemporal budget constraint*—the fundamental constraint a government faces in setting fiscal policy through time. Then we examine the macroeconomic effects of government consumption expenditures and the distribution across generations of the burden of paying for them. Specifically, we revise the transition equation to incorporate these policies. We also use the revised transition equation to study the growth effects of deficit finance, expanding social security, and increasing government investment. Along the way, we present five case studies covering budget deficits, *generational accounting*, the postwar decline in U.S. saving, privatizing social security, and government investment.

GOVERNMENT EXPENDITURES AND FINANCE

Transfer payments
Cash or in-kind benefits given to individuals by the government

Budget deficit
The difference between government expenditures and tax revenues in a particular period

1 *The government's budget, as defined by the U.S. National Income and Product Accounts, does not include government investment. On the other hand, as discussed in chapter 5, it does include in the measure of government consumption the imputed rent on government capital.*

2 *The small amount of revenue the government directly produces by printing money is included in corporate income taxes, because the Federal Reserve System that prints the money is formally included in the corporate sector.*

In 1996 consumption by federal, state, and local U.S. governments totaled $1.2 trillion and accounted for 15 percent of GDP. That's a lot of spending, but it represented only about half of total government expenditures. An additional $165 billion was spent to meet interest payments on borrowed funds, and $1.1 trillion more was spent on subsidies to firms and **transfer payments** to households, such as unemployment, welfare, and social security benefits. The sum of government consumption, interest payments, transfer payments, and subsidies of government enterprises is the government's annual budget.[1] In 1996, governments in the United States had an aggregate budget of $2.4 trillion—almost one-third the size of GDP. Figure 6.1 shows the division of this budget among expenditure categories.

How do governments raise the funds to make these expenditures? One method, which we'll discuss in the next chapter, is simply to print money. A second is to borrow from the private sector—to issue (sell) bonds. This gives the government funds today, but obligates it to repay the amount borrowed, with interest, in the future.

The third and primary way the government finances its expenditures is by collecting taxes from households and businesses. Figure 6.1 also breaks down 1996 tax revenues by type of tax. Individual income tax revenues is the largest revenue source, followed closely by social insurance contributions (payroll tax contributions) and indirect business taxes (primarily excise and sales taxes).[2]

In 1996 tax revenues were $5 billion less than expenditures. This difference, which is called the **budget deficit**, is the additional liabilities the government acquired by borrowing (by selling government bonds) less the additional amount of assets it

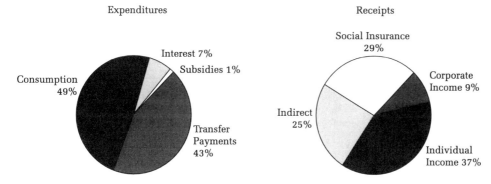

FIGURE 6.1 EXPENDITURES AND RECEIPTS, ALL U.S. GOVERNMENTS, 1996
In 1996 the consolidated budgets of all governments—federal, state, and local—in the United States equaled $2,418 billion. Its breakdown into expenditure categories is shown here. In the same year, these governments collected $2,413 billion in taxes, leaving a deficit of $5 billion.

Source: Bureau of Economic Analaysis.

acquired by investing. Since the government's budget deficit adds to the government's net liabilities (liabilities minus assets), which we call the **net national debt**, the budget deficit represents the increase in the net national debt, B, from one year to the next. Letting D stand for the budget deficit, we have:

$$B_{t+1} = B_t + D_t.$$

CASE STUDY
POSTWAR U.S. BUDGET DEFICITS

How have U.S. budget deficits changed in recent decades? Figure 6.2 gives the answer. It graphs the ratios of federal receipts, expenditures, and the budget deficit to GDP on a quarterly basis for the period since 1959.[3] Shaded areas indicate periods of recession. In most recessions, federal expenditures rise relative to GDP as the government spends more on unemployment and welfare benefits. Taxes, in contrast, generally fall relative to GDP, often because the government cuts taxes to try to stimulate the economy. These patterns mean the budget deficit generally rises during recessions.

    After hovering around zero through the 1960s, the deficit averaged 1.9 percent of GDP in the 1970s, 3.2 percent of GDP in the 1980s, and 3.5 percent of GDP from 1990 through early 1997. This secular growth in the deficit reflects faster growth over the years in federal expenditures than in federal revenues. However, the deficit has declined in recent years as a share of GDP and, at least temporarily become negative (producing a budget surplus), as a result of strong economic growth and government legislation.

Net national debt
The value of the government's financial liabilities minus its financial assets

3 *The federal budget accounts for only about two-thirds of total government budgets in the United States, but macroeconomists typically focus on federal fiscal policy. Why? Because there are too many separate decision makers and competing interests at the state and local levels for these governments to coordinate macroeconomic policies.*

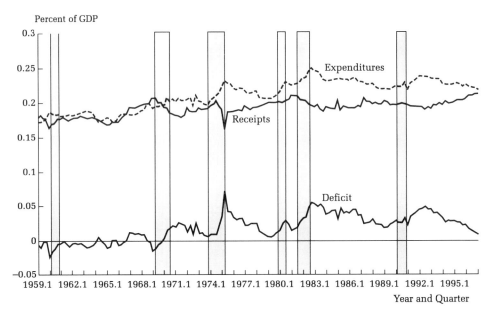

FIGURE 6.2 FEDERAL RECEIPTS AND EXPENDITURES, 1959–1997
The ratio of federal expenditures to GDP typically rises during recessions (marked by the shaded rectangles), whereas the ratio of tax receipts to GDP falls. As the result, the budget deficit rises.

Source: Bureau of Economic Analysis.

THE DYNAMICS OF FISCAL POLICY

U.S. budget deficits have received enormous public attention in recent years. To understand their possible economic impact, we need a framework for understanding the dynamics of fiscal policy.

THE GOVERNMENT'S INTERTEMPORAL BUDGET CONSTRAINT

The government may finance its budget using a mixture of taxes and deficits, with deficits increasing the size of the net national debt. Does this mean that the government can permanently avoid levying taxes, simply by borrowing more to pay for all its expenditures, including interest payments on past borrowing? The answer is no. As the net national debt grows, so do the interest payments that the government must make on this debt. If the government were to keep borrowing larger and larger amounts to make ever larger interest payments, the amount of new government borrowing eventually would exceed all the real wealth in the economy, which is all that possibly could be lent! The bottom line is that governments, like households, must eventually pay their bills. Governments, like households, face a budget constraint that limits the amount that they can consume over time.

To derive the government's budget constraint, let's rewrite the expression that relates the deficit to the change in government debt by breaking the deficit into its component parts. The deficit equals government expenditures less tax receipts. Expenditures, in turn, include purchases (denoted as G), transfer payments, and interest on the government debt. If we define Z to be net tax receipts (tax receipts less transfer payments), then the deficit equals $G - Z$ plus interest payments, which are equal to the interest rate, r, times the stock of outstanding government debt, B. Thus, in period $t + 1$, the stock of government debt equals

$$B_{t+1} \quad = \quad B_t \quad + G_t - Z_t + r_t B_t$$

New debt = Initial debt +   deficit

Suppose we write this equation for successive periods, make some substitutions among the resulting equations, and assume that the government's debt never explodes. The result is the **government intertemporal budget constraint** (GIBC):[4]

$$B_t \quad + \quad \frac{G_t}{R_t} + \frac{G_{t+1}}{R_t R_{t+1}} + \ldots \quad = \quad \frac{Z_t}{R_t} + \frac{Z_{t+1}}{R_t R_{t+1}} + \ldots$$

$$\text{Debt} + \frac{\text{Present value of}}{\text{government purchases}} = \frac{\text{Present value of}}{\text{net taxes}}$$

where R_t equals $(1 + r_t)$, $R_{t+1} = (1 + r_{t+1})$, and so on. The discount factors R are used to convert future consumption and net taxes into their present values. The GIBC dictates that the government pay its bills. Specifically, it requires the government to collect, over time, net taxes that are large enough, in present value, to cover the present value of its consumption as well as its initial debt.[5] This budget constraint is like the household's intertemporal budget constraint, but with the net tax payments, Z_t, in place of wages and government purchases, G_t, in place of household consumption expenditures. The analogue to B_t is the household's initial debt, which we've assumed in our model is zero. Unlike the household, which has a finite lifetime, the government's budget constraint takes account of government purchases and net tax payments into the distant future.

Households that consume more now are forced to consume less later. The same is true of governments. If the government purchases more now without raising current net tax payments, it must either reduce its future purchases or increase its future net tax payments by an amount that has an equal present value. This is the key message of the GIBC: fiscal policy consists of a series of interdependent decisions made over time. When the government takes actions today, it commits itself, explicitly or implicitly, to take compensating actions in the future. As long as the government makes these compensating changes, its intertemporal budget is balanced. But intertemporal balance can be achieved in a variety of ways, with very different implications for macroeconomic performance. To see why, let's consider how fiscal policy affects the economy.

Government intertemporal budget constraint (GIBC)
The requirement that the current value of net national debt plus the present value of future government consumption equal the present value of the government's net tax receipts

4 This expression is derived by substituting the equation for B_{t+1} into that for B_{t+2}, the resulting equation for B_{t+2} into that for B_{t+3}, and so on, each time dividing by the period's discount factor, R_t. For example, we divide the expression for B_{t+1} by R_t to obtain $B_{t+1}/R_t = (G_t - Z_t)/R_t + B_t$, and then substitute this into the expression for B_{t+2} divided by R_{t+1}, $B_{t+2}/R_{t+1} = (G_{t+1} - Z_{t+1})/R_{t+1} + B_{t+1}$, to obtain $B_{t+2}/R_t R_{t+1} = (G_{t+1} - Z_{t+1})/R_t R_{t+1} + (G_t - Z_t)/R_t + B_t$. As we continue this procedure, the left-hand side of the expression is the limit of the ratio $B_{t+T}/R_t R_{t+1}, \ldots, R_{t+T-1}$ as T increases. That limit is equal to zero because debt must grow at a rate below the interest rate to prevent it from exploding relative to the size of the economy. Writing the GIBC this way leads to another interpretation of the equation: that the present value of primary surpluses (the differences between Z and G) is large enough to cover the initial debt.

5 The GIBC does not require that the government ever fully pay off the national debt. For example, one way the government could satisfy the constraint is to make zero purchases through time and simply collect net taxes each period to cover interest payments on the debt. This policy leaves the stock of debt unchanged through time, but satisfies the GIBC since, in present value, paying interest forever is equivalent to paying off the debt immediately.

FISCAL POLICY AND HOUSEHOLD BEHAVIOR

Many macroeconomic effects of fiscal policy turn on the difference in spending propensities between old and young—the fact that the old tend to consume a greater fraction of the resources available to them than the young do. To sharpen conclusions and simplify exposition, we will highlight these differences using a simplified version of our model. Rather than have households consume when young and old, we'll assume that households consume only when old. That is, we'll set the parameter α, which determines first-period consumption, equal to zero. This means that the elderly have a propensity to consume of 1 (they consume every additional dollar received), as before, but that the young have a propensity to consume of 0 (they save every dollar received). The analysis would be more complicated using our more general model, but the same sorts of conclusions would follow.

Since c_{yt} equals zero in the simplified model, the lifetime budget constraint for the generation born in period t becomes

$$c_{ot+1} = w_t(1 + r_{t+1}).$$

Because households save all their wages when young, their consumption when old equals their wages plus interest earned on this saving.

Let's now add government fiscal policy to the picture, in the form of government spending and net tax payments. Fiscal policy affects a household's behavior through the net tax payments it has to pay when young and old. To determine these amounts, we need to know how each period's total net tax payments are split between the young and the old. Let each of the N members of the younger generation in period t make net tax payments of z_{yt}, and each of the N old people in period t make net tax payments of z_{ot}. Aggregate net tax payments in period t are then

$$Z_t = Nz_{yt} + Nz_{ot}.$$

In period t, the young generation's net tax payment will reduce its saving dollar for dollar; each young household will acquire assets equal to its wages less its net taxes when young, $a_{t+1} = w_t - z_{yt}$. When this same generation is old, in period $t+1$, the amount each member can consume, c_{ot+1}, equals the income and principal from her assets less the payment she must make when old: $(1 + r_{t+1})a_{t+1} - z_{ot+1}$. Combining these expressions yields the household budget constraint for a member of generation t,

$$c_{ot+1}/(1 + r_{t+1}) = w_t - z_{yt} - z_{ot+1}/(1 + r_{t+1}) = w_t - \hat{z}_t,$$

where $\hat{z}_t$ is the present value of the individual's lifetime net tax payments: $\hat{z}_t = z_{yt} + z_{ot+1}/(1 + r_{t+1})$. Thus, the consumption behavior of households does not depend on the timing of net tax payments made when young or old, but simply on their combined present value.[6] This fact is key to the analysis presented elsewhere in this chapter. As we will see, two seemingly different policies that imply the same present value of net tax payments will have the same impact on household behavior.

We refer to this present value $\hat{z}_t$ as a **generational account**. It represents, so to speak, the "fiscal price of admission" that each member of generation t must pay.[7] The

Generational account
The present value of net tax payments made by a particular individual over his or her lifetime

6 This result is straightforward in this case, in which households save everything for consumption when old. More generally, if households wish to consume more than $w_t - z_{yt}$ when young, our conclusion about only $\hat{z}_t$ being relevant (rather than its breakdown between z_{yt} and z_{ot+1}) rests on the assumption that households can borrow the additional money desired for consumption when young (to be repaid when old). If households cannot borrow, they are said to face liquidity constraints. We discuss this further in chapter 15.

7 The concept of generational accounting is developed in Alan J. Auerbach, Jagadeesh Gokhale, and Laurence J. Kotlikoff, "Generational Accounting: A Meaningful Alternative to Deficit Accounting," in David Bradford, ed., Tax Policy and the Economy, vol. 5 (Cambridge, MA: MIT Press, 1991), and Laurence J. Kotlikoff, Generational Accounting (New York: Free Press, 1992).

generational account has an important impact on different fiscal policies, because it determines how these policies affect household decisions. Moreover, it's a simple matter to rewrite the government's intertemporal budget constraint in terms of these accounts, rather than in terms of each period's aggregate net tax payments, Z_t. That is, the present value of all future net tax payments (the right-hand side of the GIBC as written above) can be rewritten in terms of the net tax payments by the old in period t plus the present value at time t of the future generational accounts (lifetime net tax payments) for all individuals born in or after period t. Written in this way, the GIBC tells us that, generationally speaking, fiscal policy is a zero-sum game.[8] Given the government's bills (the present value of its consumption and its current debt), reducing the generational accounts of some generations requires raising the generational accounts of others.

CASE STUDY
U.S. GENERATIONAL ACCOUNTS

How large are the generational accounts faced by young Americans? Without knowing the future, we can't be sure. However, we can make projections based on the assumption that current tax rules and transfer programs will be maintained. A recent

"I'll have someone from my generation get in touch with someone from your generation."

8 This statement abstracts from pure efficiency improvements associated with fiscal policy changes.

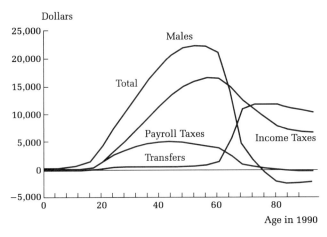

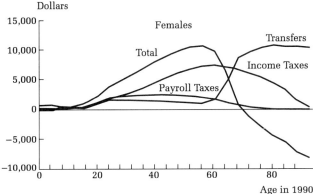

FIGURE 6.3 COMPONENTS OF GENERATIONAL ACCOUNTS

A generational account is the present value of remaining lifetime net tax payments (taxes paid minus transfers received) made by a member of a particular generation. This figure presents components of generational accounts for males and females, arranged by their age in 1990.

Source: Budget of the United States Government, *Fiscal Year 1993.*

9 See Alan J. Auerbach, Jagadeesh Gokhale, and Laurence J. Kotlikoff, "Restoring Generational Balance to U.S. Fiscal Policy: What Will It Take?" Economic Review Federal Reserve Bank of Cleveland 31 (1995).

generational accounting for the United States suggests that a typical male born in 1990 faces a net lifetime present value tax burden of $87,000; a typical female born in that year has a burden of $53,000.[9] These differences are due primarily to differences in life expectancy and labor force participation.

The figures underlying these accounts come from tax and transfer components with very different age patterns. Figure 6.3 shows the patterns of the different tax and transfer components over the lifetimes of the typical male and female. For each age in 1990, the figure shows the taxes each individual paid, the transfers he or she received, and the difference—the net tax payment—at that age. The generational account equals the present value of a generation's remaining lifetime net tax payments. The figure also shows the lifetime pattern of two important components of net tax payments: income and payroll taxes. Evidently a greater fraction of payroll taxes (which apply only to labor income) are paid earlier in life than is the case for income taxes (which apply to both labor and capital income). This is what we would expect from our life-cycle model in which individuals work when young and receive income both when young and when old. Thus, raising current net tax payments, Z_t, through the payroll tax hits younger generations harder than raising the same amount through the income tax. In terms of our model, the relative values of z_{yt} and z_{ot} would differ under the two types of tax increase, with z_{yt} being higher for the payroll tax.

Transfer payments typically occur later in life than taxes do. In fact, once males reach age 76 (and females age 70), transfer payments exceed taxes. We describe this in our model by making z_{yt} positive and z_{ot} negative. This difference in net tax payments reflects public provision of health and retirement benefits for older individuals. These different patterns of taxes and transfers suggest that raising Z_t through higher taxes will likely hit a younger population by more than raising Z_t through lower transfers. That is, raising taxes will increase z_{yt} relative to z_{ot}, whereas reducing transfers will do the opposite.

What will generational accounts look like for future generations? It is hard to know exactly. However, the future streams of government purchases, G_t, and net tax payments, Z_t, projected on the basis of the continuation of current fiscal policy, do *not* satisfy the government's intertemporal budget constraint. If current policy is maintained, the present value of net tax payments will fall short of the present value of government purchases plus the current national debt. By how much? You may find the answer may be hard to believe. To make up the difference from future generations alone would require their generational accounts to be roughly twice those of present generations. The accounts would rise from roughly a third of the present value of their lifetime labor income to three-fifths!

Figure 6.4 shows this. It plots lifetime generational accounts for generations born in this century as a percentage of their lifetime labor earnings. Note that the generation born at the turn of the twentieth century paid about a quarter of its labor income to governments in taxes net of transfers received. This lifetime net tax rate has risen for subsequent generations. For example, those born during the two decades after World War II are slated, under current policy, to pay about a third of their lifetime labor earnings in net taxes. The 60 percent column at the far right of the figure is the lifetime net tax rate future generations collectively will face given current projections of government purchases and the net tax payments of generations now alive.

This enormous tax bill facing future generations primarily reflects the fantastic postwar growth in social security (including health care) benefits paid to the elderly coupled with the baby boomers' enormous numbers. The not-so-distant retirement of the baby boomers together with the high and growing level of social security benefits they are being promised means these generations will shortly be contributing very low levels of net taxes to help balance the government's intertemporal budget constraint.

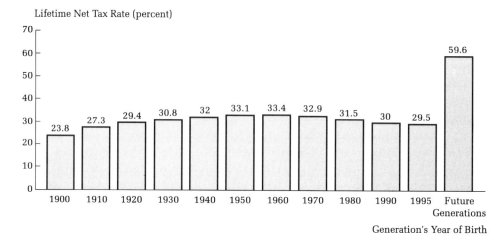

Lifetime Net Tax Rate (percent)

FIGURE 6.4 LIFETIME NET TAX RATES OF LIVING AND FUTURE GENERATIONS

Source: Calculations by Jagadeesh Gokhale of the Federal Reserve Bank of Cleveland and John Sturrock of the Congressional Budget Office.

"What's this I hear about you adults mortgaging my future?"

By permission of the cartoonist, Dave Carpenter.

Burdening future generations with such astronomical net tax rates is clearly infeasible, so what this generational accounting is really telling us is that the current course of U.S. fiscal policy is unsustainable. The current elderly as well as baby boomers will have to shoulder a much bigger share of America's fiscal burdens to avert a fiscal and economic disaster for the next generation. This is true despite the 1997 budget agreement that has produced a budget surplus. This and other policies have lessened the burden facing future generations, but generational accounting still indicates a dramatic rise in the net tax rates facing future Americans.

FISCAL POLICY AND ECONOMIC TRANSITIONS

A fiscal policy consists of a time pattern of government spending, net tax payments, and the breakdown of net tax payments in each period into payments by the young and the old. For a given time path of government consumption, the government must choose a corresponding time pattern of net tax payments that satisfy the GIBC. Simultaneously, it must determine how much of each period's net tax payments will be borne by young and old generations. Both decisions (each period's Z and its division between z_y and z_o) affect consumption by households and, hence, national saving, investment, and growth.

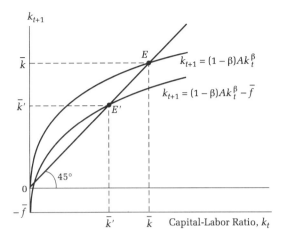

FIGURE 6.5 TRANSITION EQUATION WITH FISCAL POLICY
The transition curve without fiscal policy is shown as the upper curve in the diagram. In the presence of fiscal policy, some of what each worker earns goes to the government in the form of net tax payments or bond purchases and is not available to purchase capital. The sum of these two payments is $\bar{f}$ for a member of generation t. The introduction of fiscal policy shifts the transition curve downward.

THE TRANSITION EQUATION WITH FISCAL POLICY

Let's first consider the transition equation with no government, under our assumption that $\alpha = 0$. As before, we consider the acquisition of assets by each generation. Since $\alpha = 0$, each member of generation t wishes to save all of his wages. These savings, in turn, are used to purchase capital. Thus, we have:[10]

$$k_{t+1} = w_t = A(1 - \beta)k_t^{\beta}.$$

Figure 6.5 graphs this transition curve, showing its associated steady-state capital-labor ratio, $\bar{k}$, at E.

We derived this transition equation by setting capital purchased equal to wages earned. But in the presence of fiscal policy, some of what each worker earns will go to the government in the form of net tax payments, z_{yt}, and some will be spent on purchases of government bonds, which we denote as b_{t+1}.[11] Either way, workers have less left over to invest in (bring into their old age as) capital. Letting the term f_t (for fiscal) stand for $z_{yt} + b_{t+1}$, the sum of all payments the worker makes to the government in net taxes and bond purchases, our revised formula for k_{t+1} is[12]

$$k_{t+1} = A(1 - \beta)k_t^{\beta} - f_t.$$

In graphical terms this is simply the basic transition curve shifted downward by a distance f_t. The lower curve in Figure 6.5 provides one example, for the case in which f_t equals some constant positive value, $\bar{f}$. As the figure indicates, a positive value of $\bar{f}$ implies a lower steady-state capital-labor ratio—in this case, $\bar{k}'$.

The general form of the transition equation applies to every fiscal policy we will consider and leads to the following important observation: it is the *sum* of $z_{yt} + b_{t+1}$,

10 Throughout this chapter, the level of technology, A, is assumed to be constant over time.

11 Even though the net payment, z_{yt}, and the debt purchase, b_{t+1}, occur at precisely the same time—the end of period t—the debt has the time subscript $t + 1$ because it is the debt that will be held at the beginning of period $t + 1$.

12 This expression assumes that all of the government's purchases are for government consumption. We consider the case of government investment below.

and not their individual values, that determines the effect of fiscal policy. This sum indicates the extent to which the current elderly are relieved of paying for current government consumption. Moreover, whether the young acquire debt or pay taxes, they are left with less income with which to acquire capital. A policy that changes a single component of this sum will start a transition. Policies that imply offsetting changes in the two components will have no effect. As we'll discuss, the fact that the level, but not the composition, of f_t matters means that neither the government's official debt nor the change in the debt over time (the budget deficit) provides a clear or useful description of the government's *generational policy* (its fiscal treatment of different generations).

Let's now use the modified transition equation to study government spending and generational policies.

FINANCING GOVERNMENT CONSUMPTION

Suppose the economy is initially in a long-run steady state in which there is no government activity. The government now wishes to spend a constant amount, say $\bar{G}$, each period on consumption. But how will it finance this spending? How will it satisfy its intertemporal budget constraint? One way is to require that in each period the older generation make net tax payments to the government to cover that period's government consumption.[13] How would the government target the elderly for taxation? In terms of our model, a tax on consumption would suffice, since only the old consume. Even in the real world, consumption taxes tend to fall more heavily on the elderly than, say, payroll taxes do. Increasing the taxation of social security benefits, as the government did in 1993, would also do the trick.

The required payment from each old person would be $z_{ot} = \bar{g} = \bar{G}/N$, beginning in the first period that the government consumes. Clearly this policy satisfies the government budget constraint: the government has no initial debt, and government consumption equals net tax payments in each period and, hence, in present value as well.

Despite the change in government consumption, this policy has no impact on the level or path of aggregate output. To see this, check the formula for the transition equation and note that setting $f_t = 0$, as this policy does (the young pay nothing to the government), leaves us with the same transition equation that prevails in the absence of fiscal policy. Because it has no effect on the capital-labor ratio, this fiscal policy causes no change in output, investment, or any other macroeconomic variable.

Why is there no change in investment in this example? Beginning in period 0, consumption by elderly individuals will fall, since each must now make a net tax payment of $\bar{g}$ before consuming. But the aggregate decline in consumption by the elderly ($N\bar{g}$) exactly equals the increase in government consumption. Hence, aggregate consumption remains unchanged, and so does national saving, which is the difference between output and total (government plus household) consumption. Since national saving equals national investment and national investment equals domestic investment in our closed economy, there is no change in domestic investment either.

13 *What matters in our model is the* net *tax payment each generation makes. For example, a positive value of $z_{ot} = 10$ might be the difference between income taxes of 12 and social security benefits of 2.*

This exercise illustrates that increased *government consumption won't affect national saving and investment if it is financed in a way that leads to an exactly offsetting decline in private consumption.* As now shown, this condition is violated if the young, rather than the old, are forced to pay for each period's government spending.

GENERATIONAL POLICY

Starting with the fiscal policy just discussed, suppose the government decides to shift the burden of paying for its consumption to later generations. Specifically, suppose that the government begins charging each young person, rather than each old person, $\bar{g}$ in net taxes. The previous policy set $z_{ot} = \bar{g}$ and $z_{yt} = 0$. The new policy sets $z_{yt} = \bar{g}$ and $z_{ot} = 0$, but still satisfies the government intertemporal budget constraint since Z_t equals $\bar{G}$ in each period. However, the burden on each generation changes. If the shift occurs in period 1, then the generation that is old in period 1 bears no burden at all, since it paid no tax when young and, as a result of this shift, none when old either. The generation that is young at time 1 and subsequent generations have to pay a tax of $\bar{g}$ when young rather than when old. Having to pay the tax one period earlier raises the present value of their lifetime net tax payments from $\bar{g}/(1 + r_{t+1})$ to $\bar{g}$. Hence, one generation gains, and all subsequent generations lose.

The shift from taxing the old to taxing the young also has macroeconomic effects. Setting $z_{yt} = \bar{g}$ and $b_{t+1} = 0$ (there is still no government debt) yields a value of $f_t = \bar{g}$. Inserting this value in the general transition equation yields

$$k_{t+1} = A(1 - \beta)k_t^\beta - \bar{g}.$$

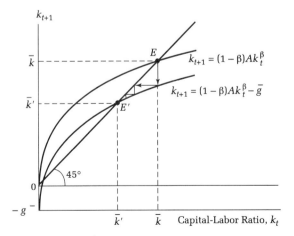

FIGURE 6.6 GOVERNMENT PURCHASES FINANCED BY THE YOUNG
Beginning in the steady state at point E, the introduction of government purchases ($\bar{g}$) financed by taxing the young shifts the transition curve downward by the distance $\bar{g}$. The transition to the new steady state at point E' is governed by the new, lower transition curve. The result is a lower capital-labor ratio, $\bar{k}'$.

TABLE 6.1 REQUIRING THE YOUNG TO PAY FOR GOVERNMENT PURCHASES

Period	k	y	c_o	b	z_y	z_o	$\hat{z}$	w	r
Tax Finance									
0	7.77	11.10	9.10	0.00	0.00	2.00	1.40	7.77	0.43
1	7.77	11.10	11.10	0.00	2.00	0.00	0.00	7.77	0.43
2	5.77	10.15	8.81	0.00	2.00	0.00	2.00	7.11	0.53
3	5.11	9.78	8.04	0.00	2.00	0.00	2.00	6.85	0.57
4	4.85	9.64	7.74	0.00	2.00	0.00	2.00	6.74	0.60
5	4.74	9.57	7.62	0.00	2.00	0.00	2.00	6.70	0.61
6	4.70	9.55	7.56	0.00	2.00	0.00	2.00	6.68	0.61
⋮	⋮	⋮	⋮	⋮	⋮	⋮	⋮	⋮	⋮
∞	4.67	9.53	7.53	0.00	2.00	0.00	2.00	6.67	0.61
Debt Finance									
0	7.77	11.10	9.10	0.00	0.00	2.00	1.40	7.77	0.43
1	7.77	11.10	11.10	0.00	0.00	0.00	0.00	7.77	0.43
2	5.77	10.15	8.81	2.00	0.00	3.06	2.00	7.11	0.53
3	5.11	9.78	8.04	2.00	0.00	3.15	2.00	6.85	0.57
4	4.85	9.64	7.74	2.00	0.00	3.19	2.00	6.74	0.60
5	4.74	9.57	7.62	2.00	0.00	3.21	2.00	6.70	0.61
6	4.70	9.55	7.56	2.00	0.00	3.22	2.00	6.68	0.61
⋮	⋮	⋮	⋮	⋮	⋮	⋮	⋮	⋮	⋮
∞	4.67	9.53	7.53	2.00	0.00	3.22	2.00	6.67	0.61

Note: Values of $\hat{z}$ correspond to those of the elderly in each respective period. Parameter values assumed: $\alpha = 0$, $\beta = .3$, $A = 6$, $\bar{g} = 2$

All variables are expressed in per worker terms.

The equation tells us that for any given value of the current capital-labor ratio, the next period's capital-labor ratio is now lower by the amount $\bar{g}$. Why? Because the young use some of their wages—wages that otherwise would be saved and invested in capital—to pay taxes.

As shown in Figure 6.6, this shift in the transition equation moves the economy from its initial capital-labor ratio at point E to its new capital-labor ratio at point E'. Of course, as the capital-labor ratio falls, so does the level of output and the real wage. At the same time, the relative scarcity of capital causes the real interest rate to rise.

The top panel of Table 6.1 illustrates this transition based on values of $\beta = .3$, $A = 6$, and $\bar{g} = 2$. In the initial steady state, in period 0, output per worker is 11.10. There is no net investment, and consumption by the elderly is 9.10. The remaining output is absorbed by government consumption ($\bar{g} = 2$) and paid for by taxes on the elderly, whose generational account has a value 1.40—the discounted value of the tax paid when old. In period 1, the next generation of elderly are relieved of the need to pay taxes, and can now consume an extra 2 units per person. But government consumption doesn't change. Hence, consumption by households *and* government rises in the aggregate. The savings of each young person, equal to the next period's capital-labor ratio, is reduced by the taxes they must now pay, again 2 units per person. (Their generational account rises to 2 because the tax now must be paid in the first period of life.) As a result, there is an immediate drop in period 2 in the capital-labor ratio. This drop leads to lower wages and still lower savings of the young. The process continues until a new steady-state capital-labor ratio is reached. The transition equation is

$$k_{t+1} = 4.2k_t^\beta - 2.$$

Requiring the young to finance government consumption leads to a decline in investment and the capital-labor ratio because it is the young who save and provide funds for investment. Indeed, in our simplified model, the young save everything they have, whereas the old consume everything they have. Shifting the tax burden from the old to the young redistributes from those who save to those who consume, producing a rise in national consumption and a decline in national saving and investment.

Let's summarize what we've learned. *First, government consumption, by itself, need not affect the economy's capital stock. Second, taking from savers and giving to spenders reduces national saving and investment and sends the economy to a steady state with less capital per worker and less output.*

CASE STUDY
EXPLAINING THE POSTWAR DECLINE IN U.S. SAVING

Chapter 2 discussed the postwar decline in U.S. saving but didn't explain its cause. One recent study lays the blame for the postwar decline in U.S. saving on government intergenerational redistribution, primarily that associated with the expansion of social security (including health care) benefits.[14] The study considers the *net national saving rate*, defined as national saving minus depreciation divided by net national product (GNP less depreciation).[15] This saving rate declined from 9 percent in the 1950s to less than 3 percent in the first half of the 1990s. The counterpart of a lower saving rate is a higher consumption rate—the ratio of consumption to output. The rise in the U.S. consumption rate turns out to be due entirely to an increase in the rate of private consumption, from 69 percent of NNP to 77 percent. Government consumption as a share of NNP was 21 percent in both the 1950s and the first half of the 1990s.

Whose consumption rose so rapidly over this period? The answer is the elderly's. Based on demographics alone, the elderly's share of private consumption should have increased by 16 percent between the early 1960s and the late 1980s; instead, it rose by 68 percent. Figure 6.7 compares consumption growth of different age groups over this period. The average value of the consumption of men aged 70 to 79 rose, in real terms, by 148 percent. In contrast, the average consumption of men aged 40 to 49 rose by only 63 percent.

14 Jagadeesh Gokhale, Laurence J. Kotlikoff, and John Sabelhaus, "Understanding the Postwar Decline in U.S. Saving: A Cohort Analysis," Brookings Papers on Economic Activity, no. 2 (1996).

15 Ibid. uses the pre-1996 National Income and Product Accounts, which treat government investment as consumption.

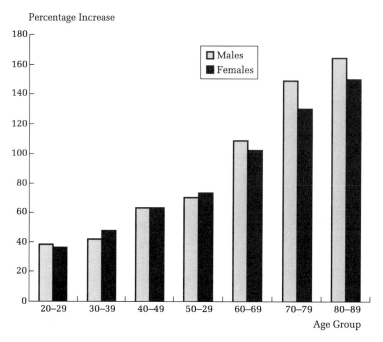

Percentage Increase

FIGURE 6.7 PERCENTAGE INCREASE IN AVERAGE CONSUMPTION BY AGE GROUP, 1960–1961 TO 1987–1990

Source: Jagadeesh Gokhale, Laurence, J. Kotlikoff, and John Sabelhaus, "Understanding the Postwar Decline in U.S. Saving: A Cohort Analysis," Brookings Papers on Economic Activity, *no 2, (1996).*

The striking increase in the relative consumption of the elderly coincided with an equally remarkable increase in their relative economic resources. For example, the remaining lifetime incomes of 70-year-olds was only 55 percent of that of 30-year-olds in the early 1960s, but 81 percent in the late 1980s. Remaining lifetime income includes social security retirement and health care benefits. The growth in these benefits is the principal cause for the rapid growth in the income and consumption of the elderly.

DEFICIT FINANCE

So far we've considered taxing either the old or the young to pay for government spending. Let's now consider government borrowing, which is also referred to as *deficit finance*. Specifically, assume that starting in period 1, the government borrows $\bar{g}$ from each young person to pay for that period's consumption. It does so by selling $\bar{g}$ worth of bonds to each young person—bonds that promise to repay the amount borrowed with interest in the following period. Hence, beginning in period 2 and continuing in every period thereafter, the government needs to repay principal and interest on the debt issued in the previous period.

Let's consider the case in which the funds needed to repay the debt in each period come from the old—the same group receiving the principal and interest. In this case, the young in period 1 lend $\bar{g}$ to the government, are repaid $\bar{g}(1 + r_2)$ in period 2, but must also pay taxes of $\bar{g}(1 + r_2)$ in period 2. Similarly, the young in period 2 lend $\bar{g}$, are repaid $\bar{g}(1 + r_3)$ in period 3, and pay taxes of $\bar{g}(1 + r_3)$ in period 3, and so on for all subsequent generations. Discounted to their period of birth, the present value of tax payments for the generation born at time 1 equals $\bar{g}(1 + r_2)/(1 + r_2) = \bar{g}$. The same is true for the generation born at time 2 since $\bar{g}(1 + r_3)/(1 + r_3) = \bar{g}$, and for all subsequent generations. Hence, this policy produces the same generational accounts as in the case of taxing the young to pay for government spending.

This fiscal policy satisfies the government intertemporal budget constraint. There is no debt outstanding at the beginning of period 1 and no net tax payments in period 1. We can pair government consumption in period 1 with taxes in period 2, government consumption in period 2 with taxes in period 3, and so forth, to see that for each period's government consumption, there are corresponding tax payments that occur one period later but have the same present value. This guarantees that the present value of government consumption will equal the present value of tax payments.

The economy's transition equation (and therefore its transition path) under this policy is also identical to that resulting from taxing the young. Why? Because f_t, the amount the government takes from the young (and, therefore, keeps them from saving in the form of capital), is exactly the same. In the previous case, in which the young paid taxes, $z_{yt} = \bar{g}$ and $b_{t+1} = 0$. In the case in which the young pay no taxes, but purchase government debt, $z_{yt} = 0$ and $b_{t+1} = \bar{g}$. In each case f_t, the sum of z_{yt} and b_{t+1}, equals $\bar{g}$. The bottom panel of Table 6.1 shows that, indeed, nothing is different about the transition except the fiscal variables b_t, z_{yt}, and z_{ot}.

Why do the two policies (taxing the young and deficit finance) lead to the same economic outcomes? Although the timing of tax payments is different for each generation after period 1, there is no difference between the two policies in the time path of generational accounts. For each policy, the generation born in period 0 pays no taxes and each subsequent generational account equals 2, regardless of whether the generation's taxes occur when it is old or young. Because the generational account governs household consumption, there is no difference in consumption in the two cases. Since government consumption is also the same in the two cases, there is no difference in national saving, which is equal to income less consumption and government spending, or in national investment, which equals national saving.

At first glance, we might have expected investment to differ in the two cases. When government taxes the young, each young person saves $\bar{g}$ less and buys that much less capital. In contrast, with deficit finance, the young pay no taxes and have more of their wages left over to purchase assets. But they spend all this extra income on government bonds, so they end up purchasing the same amount of capital.

Another way to see the equivalence of the two policies is to think about the net flows between each generation and the government. Under both policies, the government takes $\bar{g}$ from each person when young and gives her back, on balance, nothing when old. Indeed, the only difference between the two policies is the words the government uses to describe them. In one case, the government labels the policy as "taxing the young." In the other case, it labels the policy as "borrowing from the young, paying them principal plus interest when they are old, and then taxing them an amount equal to principal plus interest when they are old." Although one policy involves a permanently higher reported government debt than the other, both policies entail the same fiscal treatment of alternative generations.

What should one make of this? Three things: *First, government debt alone is not an indicator of the generational stance of fiscal policy. Second, governments have considerable leeway in the way they report their fiscal actions. Third, to understand generational policy, one needs to do generational accounting.*

The need to look through potentially misleading government accounting practices is nowhere more important than in considering the impact of so-called pay-as-you-go social security, the subject to which we now turn.

SOCIAL SECURITY

A century has passed since Bismarck instituted the first social security system in Germany. Since then, government provision of retirement income has spread around the globe. Were Bismarck alive today, he could point with pride to a policy that has alleviated poverty among the elderly, provided disability and health insurance, and forced people individually to save. But Bismarck would be surprised to learn that social security appears to have severely limited the investment, growth, and national saving of some of the world's leading nations.

It is the pay-as-you-go method of financing social security that lies at the heart of social security's problem. Under it, social security contributions of young workers are not saved and invested, but rather are given directly to the contemporaneous elderly as social security benefit payments that help finance their consumption. As we have learned, taking income from savers and giving it to spenders reduces national saving. An ongoing program promising such transfers—like pay-as-you-go social security—saddles each successive generation with the obligation—the implicit debt—to meet these promises. The size of this implicit debt and the burden on the next generation of repaying it will be much greater for countries that are rapidly aging, one of which is the United States.

THE U.S. SOCIAL SECURITY SYSTEM

The Social Security system is far and away the most important transfer program in the United States. It encompasses three major programs: Old Age and Survivors' Insurance, Disability Insurance, and Medicare (health insurance for the elderly). The acronym OASDI is used to refer to the first two of these programs. In recent years, Social Security has accounted for nearly half of all federal, state, and local government transfer payments.

Enacted in 1935, OASDI in 1994 paid $312 billion to retired and disabled workers and their surviving spouses and dependent children. The fastest-growing component of Social Security is Medicare, introduced in 1965. Since 1980, Medicare payments have almost doubled as a share of GDP. In recent years, they have been growing three times faster than the economy.

Social Security transfer payments are financed through payroll taxes assessed on wages and salaries. The payroll tax rate, which was 3.0 percent in 1950, now stands at 15.3 percent. The system works primarily on a pay-as-you-go basis in which the payroll taxes of workers are given to the elderly as Social Security benefits. Americans who retired in the 1940s, 1950s, 1960s, and 1970s enjoyed huge windfalls as a result of this method of finance. They received benefits they did not fully pay for, at least in terms of their own past Social Security contributions.

In contrast, current young and middle-aged workers are likely to lose, in present value, considerable sums of money through their mandatory contributions to the system. The reason, in part, is that their future benefits will depend on the payroll tax contributions of future generations. Unfortunately, those contributions are projected to be relatively small because of the slowdown in real wage growth and the post-1964 decline in U.S. fertility rates. U.S. real wage growth is running at about a third of the value observed in the 1950s and 1960s. In 1960, there were five workers contributing to Social Security for each beneficiary compared with three today and a projected two when the baby boomers retire. If payroll tax rates are raised at that time to pay for projected benefits, they could more than double.

Thus, even though the U.S. Social Security system has basically been financed on a balanced budget basis, in which current taxes equal current expenditures, leaving the government's official debt unchanged, the program has been and continues to be the major element in postwar U.S. generational policy. To understand precisely how Social Security redistributes across generations, let's consult our model.

ADDING SOCIAL SECURITY TO THE MODEL

Suppose the government at time 1 initiates a pay-as-you-go Social Security system. Each period the system taxes each young person an amount s and gives each old person the same amount s in Social Security benefits. Since there are N young taxpayers and N old beneficiaries, this is a "balanced budget" policy: taxes equal spending, so the policy has no effect on the budget deficit.

Who wins and who loses? The time 1 elderly are clear winners. They receive a windfall of s when old without having had to pay s when young. But what about the generation that is young at time 1 and subsequent generations? The answer is they are all made worse off. Each member of these generations pays s when young and receives back s when old. But the present value of the s received as a Social Security benefit when old is less than the present value of the s paid in Social Security taxes when young; their generational account is

$$\hat{z}_t = s - s/(1 + r_{t+1}) = r_{t+1}s/(1 + r_{t+1}).$$

The account equals the interest that each young person loses by having to pay the amount s when young before getting it back when old. For example, a payroll tax of $s = 3,000$ today, even if offset by Social Security benefits of \$3,000 in old age, still deprives the individual of the opportunity to earn interest on that \$3,000. The present value of this loss is the interest on \$3,000, discounted because the loss occurs in old age.

We saw earlier that shifting the burden of paying for government spending from old spenders to the young savers reduces national saving. This is also the case here since pay-as-you-go Social Security directly transfers resources from young and future generations to the initial old. The transition equation confirms this. For this policy, $b_{t+1} = 0$ and $z_{yt} = s$, so $f_t = s$ and

$$k_{t+1} = A(1 - \beta)k_t^{\beta} - s.$$

The government has a lot of flexibility in how it describes its policies. Governments generally label their social security policies in the manner described above, which keeps them from having to report larger budget deficits. But the same fundamental fiscal policy could be described in terms of deficit finance. Specifically, the government, in period 1, could have sold an amount s worth of debt to each young person rather than levying taxes immediately. It would then require those born in period 1 to pay taxes when old in period 2 to meet the principal and interest on that debt, $s(1 + r_2)$ per person. Then, in period 2, the transfers to this old generation of s per individual would be financed by debt sold to the young in period 2, to be repaid with interest using taxes on the same generation when old, in period 3. The same pattern would be followed in subsequent periods. The net fiscal burden (the generational accounts) on each generation would be the same as with direct tax finance (since a tax of s in the first period of life has the same present value as a tax of $s(1 + r_{t+1})$ in the second period) and each generation still receives a transfer payment of s when old. But this way of running (really, reporting) the policy would result in the creation of government debt.

Note that the actual cash flows to each person in each period are unchanged. The initial elderly still receive s; generations born at time 1 and thereafter still hand the government s when young and receive back, on balance, s when old. The s these generations hand the government when young is now called a "loan," and the s these generations get back when old is now described as "a social security benefit of s plus repayment of principal plus interest on the loan made when young less a tax equal to principal plus interest on the loan made when young."

Because it would shift resources from the young to the old, such debt creation would be associated with a decline in national saving. However, as in the previous case of financing government consumption, *it is the underlying shift in the fiscal burden across generations, and not the presence or absence of national debt, that causes the decline in saving.* Indeed, in the case of Social Security, economists have long emphasized the equivalence between the actual policy of tax-financed transfers and a hypothetical one using debt, by constructing a measure of the unfunded liability of the Social Security system, indicating how large the debt would be under the equivalent debt-finance policy. In the United States, the unfunded liabilities of the OASDI program exceed $8 trillion, roughly twice the amount of official U.S. government debt.[16]

CASE STUDY
SHOULD THE UNITED STATES PRIVATIZE SOCIAL SECURITY?

Chile, Argentina, Peru, Columbia, the United Kingdom, and several other countries have privatized their social security systems. They've done so by allowing their workers to make their contributions to private pension funds rather than to their social security systems. Does privatization offer the United States a way out of social security's long-term financial problems? The answer is maybe.

The basic question raised by privatization is where the government will get the funds to make benefit payments to existing social security recipients as well as to compensate current workers for their past contributions to the system. One response is for the government to borrow the funds and, over time, raise taxes to cover interest payments on this additional official government debt. Such a scheme changes the form, but not the substance, of generational policy. Workers send their contributions to

By Mike Keefe, The Denver Post, *for USA Today*

16 *The concept and measurement of this liability was first described by Martin Feldstein in "Social Security, Induced Retirement and Aggregate Capital Accumulation,"* Journal of Political Economy *82 (1974): 905–926.*

private pensions, which hand these contributions right back to the government in exchange for government bonds. Although workers now receive a market rate of return on their pension contributions, rather than a below-market rate of return on their Social Security contributions, they will be forced to pay higher taxes to cover the interest payments on the government's additional official debt. The net impact of such financial machinations is just a relabeling of existing generational policy.

Given the reality of its intertemporal budget constraint, the only way that government can make young and future generations benefit simply from privatization of the existing system[17] is to make current older generations worse off; reducing the net tax levied on young and future generations means raising the net taxes paid by current older generations. One privatization scheme, advanced by one of us, would pay for existing Social Security benefits as well as the accrued benefits of current workers by levying a consumption tax.[18] Such a tax would fall on all segments of society, including the current elderly. Simulations of the postprivatization transition path of the economy using a more realistic version of our life-cycle model indicate that privatization financed with a consumption tax could significantly improve the economic prospects of young and future Americans.

A CAVEAT: RICARDIAN EQUIVALENCE

This chapter has emphasized how a shift in the fiscal burden among generations alters capital accumulation and output. But what if those who must pay more are related to those who pay less? How, for example, will parents behave knowing that increased Social Security benefits for their own generation mean higher payroll taxes on their children?

In our model, parents consume all of the added Social Security benefits in old age, despite the greater fiscal burden imposed on their children. In reality, though, parents who care about the well-being of their children might react differently to such a windfall. Observing the increase in their own standard of living and the decline in that of their children, they might increase their gifts or bequests. One rather extreme view, known as the Ricardian equivalence proposition, holds that they would precisely offset the Social Security transfers. Parents would save the entire increase in their Social Security benefits and leave it to their children, allowing the children to pay their payroll tax increase without having to reduce their own consumption. The Ricardian equivalence proposition implies that intergenerational fiscal policy has no macroeconomic effects, for it is simply offset by the gift and bequest behavior of individuals.

As discussed in chapter 15, there is strong empirical evidence against this proposition. Still, the possibility that older generations may offset some portion of fiscal policy's intergenerational transfers through their own gifts and bequests is worth keeping in mind.

17 We say simply here because we are not considering more fundamental changes in the structure of the social security system. There are myriad changes in the underlying structure of the social security system, relating to work and retirement incentives, that might improve its functioning and the welfare of current and future generations, whether under a public or private structure. Our focus here is exclusively on shifts in the generational burden of social security.

18 Laurence J. Kotlikoff, "Privatizing Social Security: How It Works and Why It Matters," in James Poterba, ed., Tax Policy and the Economy, (Cambridge, MA: MIT Press, 1996).

GOVERNMENT CAPITAL FORMATION

To this point, we have examined how governments raise money to pay for government consumption or transfer programs to the elderly. Whatever the use of the funds raised, the distinction on the expenditure side between government consumption and transfers has not appeared particularly important. This is largely due to our assumption that government expenditures, whether for direct consumption or transfers to the elderly, do not contribute to capital accumulation. We have assumed that elderly households consume all resources at their disposal and that all government purchases are for consumption rather than for investment. In reality, governments do invest. They purchase capital goods, such as roads, buildings, and aircraft carriers. Government capital goods, like those purchased by households or firms, add to the nation's productive capacity.

How does government capital enter our model? The nation's capital stock includes government-owned capital as well as that owned by households. We simply need to add government capital per worker at the beginning of period $t+1, k_{t+1}^g$, to privately owned capital per worker to determine the total capital stock at time $t+1$:

$$k_{t+1} = A(1-\beta)k_t^\beta - f_t + k_{t+1}^g$$

Total capital = Private capital + Government capital

Using this transition equation, let's return to the case in which government purchases an amount $N\bar{g}$ in each period, financed by the young. Now suppose that these government purchases are capital goods added to the economy's overall productive capital stock. Since the purchases of capital are financed by the young, both f_t and k_{t+1}^g equal $\bar{g}$. Hence, all the fiscal terms in the transition equation disappear, leaving us with our basic no-fiscal-policy transition equation. This result makes sense: taking resources from the young causes them to purchase less capital, but the government exactly offsets this reduction through its own capital purchases.

Next suppose the government finances its purchases of capital goods by taxing the elderly each period rather than the young. In this case, $f_t = 0$ and $k_{t+1}^g = \bar{g}$, shifting the transition curve upward relative to what it would be in the absence of any government policy.

To summarize, *holding constant the method of financing government expenditures, investment expenditures will lead to more capital accumulation than consumption expenditures or transfer payments. Depending on its method of finance, government investment can increase an economy's overall capital accumulation.*

CASE STUDY
GOVERNMENT INVESTMENT IN THE UNITED STATES

In recent decades, U.S. government gross investment has declined dramatically relative to GDP, from almost 6 percent in 1959 to only 3 percent in 1996. As Figure 6.8

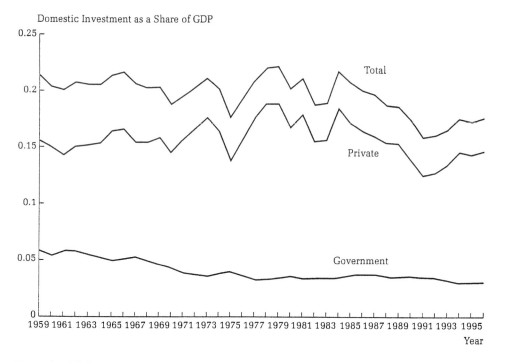

FIGURE 6.8 U.S. PRIVATE AND GOVERNMENT GROSS DOMESTIC INVESTMENT RATES, 1959–1996

Source: Bureau of Economic Analysis.

shows, this decline has coincided with an overall decline in the rate of U.S. gross domestic investment. Indeed, since there is very little secular decline in private domestic investment, it's tempting to attribute the overall decline in U.S. domestic investment to the decline in government investment. However, this conclusion must be tempered by the fact that government and private investment are interdependent. The financing of government investment can have important effects on private saving and capital formation. Had government investment been higher, private investment might have been lower.

INTRAGENERATIONAL TRANSFERS AND DISTORTIONS

This section considers two additional channels through which fiscal policy affects saving: intragenerational transfers—the redistribution of income among members of the same generation—and distortionary fiscal policy.

INTRAGENERATIONAL REDISTRIBUTION: THE SAFETY NET AND ITS EFFECTS

Government transfer programs transfer resources not only among different generations but also among members of given generations. Such **intragenerational redistribution** is typically designed to provide a safety net for the less fortunate members of each generation. Even though the transfers occur within a single generation, they can still influence overall saving.

There are two ways this can occur. First, transfers will increase consumption and reduce saving if those who receive the transfers consume a higher fraction of their resources than do those who pay for the transfers. Indeed, there is evidence that some poorer households consume whatever resources are available to them rather than saving for the future, as our two-period life-cycle model would suggest.

Second, the presence of a social safety net may reduce *precautionary saving*, a topic also taken up in chapter 15. Precautionary saving is saving for the "rainy day"—adverse and uncertain outcomes, like unemployment, large uninsured medical expenses, a pay cut, or big losses in the stock market. Protecting the public from these outcomes is one of the main rationales for having a social safety net. But this increased government protection may have contributed to the decline in U.S. saving during the past three decades.

In our general two-period life-cycle model (with consumption when young as well as when old), reductions in the propensity to save because of the presence of the government's social safety net increase the amount that the average individual consumes when young; it effectively produces a rise in the parameter α. As discussed in chapter 3, such a change lowers the transition curve and leads to a lower steady-state capital stock.

DISTORTIONARY FISCAL POLICY

To this point, we have analyzed government taxes as if they were lump-sum taxes—immutable assessments on individuals requiring them to pay a certain amount to the government. We have treated transfers in the same way, as fixed sums given to individuals. Some taxes and transfers are lump sum, but most are not. Instead, they are tied to some aspect of the individual's (or firm's) economic behavior. For example, a sales tax is tied to purchases of goods and services; an income tax is based on the amount of income earned. In most cases, taxing a particular activity distorts behavior. Taxpayers will tend to reduce activities subject at the margin to tax and expand activities subsidized at the margin to transfers. Consequently, **distortionary fiscal policy** can alter individual behavior and, it turns out, macroeconomic outcomes.

A tax on capital income can distort and discourage household saving behavior. The impact is similar to an increase in the parameter α that determines how much households consume when young and how much they save. The result is a lower transition curve and a lower steady-state capital stock. Other taxes distort other household decisions. Taxes on labor income—both the income tax and the payroll tax used to finance the social security system—distort the household's decision about how

Intragenerational redistribution
Government redistribution among members of a particular generation

Distortionary fiscal policy
Government policies that alter individuals' economic incentives to work, save, and consume particular goods and services

much to work and when to retire. Taxes on individual commodities, such as liquor, gasoline, tobacco, or telephone calls, discourage the purchase of these commodities. These *supply-side* effects received lots of attention during the 1980s. Interpretations of this doctrine range from the generally accepted view that non-lump-sum taxes and transfers distort behavior, sometimes in important ways, to the much more extreme view that reductions in distortionary taxation actually raise revenue by bringing forth more of the taxed activity, be it work effort or saving.

CHAPTER SUMMARY

1. This chapter discussed fiscal policy: how government borrowing and taxation are used to raise resources and how these resources are spent on government consumption, investment, and transfer payments. Fiscal policy is dynamic because current and future decisions are linked through the government intertemporal budget constraint, which requires the present value of net tax payments (taxes less transfers) to equal the current level of government debt plus the present value of government purchases.

2. How government expenditures affect national saving and the economy depend on (1) the nature of these expenditures (whether they are for consumption, investment, or transfer payments), (2) which generations and which members of those generations pay for what the government spends, and (3) the distortions associated with the collection of government revenue.

3. Redistribution from savers to spenders, as under an expansion of pay-as-you-go social security, raises aggregate consumption and lowers national saving.

4. Although the effects of fiscal policy are often framed in terms of the national debt, shifts in the generational burden of fiscal policy that influence saving may occur with or without a change in government debt. The burden of paying for government consumption can shift from old to young, and the size of the old-age pension system can increase, without any increase in the size of the national debt. Indeed, the government's reported debt is a reflection of its fiscal vocabulary, not of its economic policy. Generational accounting, rather than deficit accounting, provides a well-defined measure of generational policy.

5. Holding constant the method of financing government expenditures, the larger the investment share is of these expenditures, the larger will be the nation's capital stock.

6. Safety net programs may reduce saving by lessening households' perceptions of risk and by transferring resources to those who are not in a position to save very much.

7. Capital income taxes reduce the incentive for households to save, just as other taxes discourage the activities they tax and most transfers encourage the activities they subsidize.

CHAPTER 7

MONEY AND PRICES IN THE CLOSED ECONOMY

INTRODUCTION

Previous chapters focused on the real side of the economy: how real wages and interest rates are determined, how capital is accumulated, how output grows, and so forth. This chapter examines the economy's nominal side. It shows how the demand for and supply of money jointly determine the *price level*—the value of output measured in units of money. It also shows how the government can affect nominal and, potentially, real variables by changing the money supply.

What is money? The answer is less obvious than one might think. Money is a commonly used means of payment, but what constitutes money has varied enormously across different societies. Even within a particular society, it's often hard to say exactly what is and is not money. The reason is that the basic properties of money are consistent with narrow as well as broad definitions.

In the United States, pieces of paper printed in green and black serve as money, as do copper, nickel, and copper-steel coins. But this official currency is not the only commonly used means of payment. Personal checks are also accepted in most transactions. Indeed, most checking accounts are technically referred to as **demand deposits**, because deposited funds can be accessed immediately (upon demand) simply by writing a check. The value of all circulating currency plus the value of all demand deposits, called M1, is the measure of money most frequently cited by the Federal Reserve, the government agency responsible for determining the U.S. money supply.[1] But this is just one of the Federal Reserve's measures. In addition to M1, the Fed (short for Federal Reserve) keeps track of two other definitions of money, M2 and M3. M2 equals M1 plus, primarily, savings accounts, small time deposits, and money market mutual funds. M3 equals M2 plus, primarily, large time deposits.

Beyond the question of how to define money is the issue of its impact on prices. Figure 7.1 shows post-1960 growth in M1 together with the growth over the same period in the price level, measured by the *GDP deflator*—the price index for all final

Demand deposits
Accounts at financial institutions that pay little or no interest and against which depositors can write checks to obtain their deposits at any time

1 Chapter 14 discusses the Federal Reserve and its role in changing the U.S. money supply.

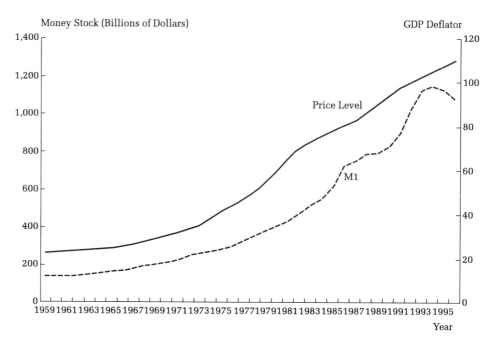

FIGURE 7.1 MONEY STOCK (M1) AND PRICE LEVEL, 1959–1996
Since 1959, growth in the price level has generally coincided with growth in the M1 money stock.

Source: Economic Report of the President, *1997.*

goods and services. Both the M1 money stock and the price level have grown dramatically over the period.

The proposition that increases in the money supply raise prices is an old one in economics. Indeed, the nineteenth-century classical economists believed in the **neutrality of money**—that a given percentage increase in the supply of money produces an equal percentage increase in the price level, with no impact on the economy's level of output or other real variables. As this chapter unfolds, we'll use the life-cycle model to understand when money is and is not neutral.

As we'll show, increases in the supply of money represent a means by which the government can finance its transfer payments and its spending on goods and services. Such **monetary policy** effectively imposes a tax on the holders of money and other nominal government liabilities, such as government bonds. In this respect, monetary policy, which involves the creation and spending of money by the government, is closely akin to fiscal policy. Just as we don't, in general, expect fiscal policy to be neutral, we shouldn't, in general, expect monetary policy to be neutral.

The close connection between monetary and fiscal policy identified in this chapter hinges on the assumption that nominal prices and wages adjust instantaneously to their market-clearing values (the values at which supplies equal their respective demands). As chapter 8 will clarify, if nominal prices or wages are either

Neutrality of money
The proposition that a one-time change in the money supply has no effect on any real variable and leads to a proportional change in the level of prices

Monetary policy
The creation and spending of money by the government

fixed or *sticky* (slow to adjust), then monetary and fiscal policies can play special, but distinct, roles in helping markets *equilibrate* (achieve prices at which supplies equal demands) and in moving the economy toward *full employment*, where all those seeking employment at the going wage have jobs.

Here are some of this chapter's key questions:

- What is money?

- What determines the demand for money?

- How do money supply and demand jointly determine the time path of the price level?

- When are money supply changes neutral?

- What is the relationship between inflation and the growth of the money supply?

- How are fiscal policy and monetary policy related?

- What are the costs of inflation?

WHAT IS MONEY?

Economists traditionally define money as those objects, whether rectangular pieces of paper, round pieces of metal, cigarettes, or animal pelts, that are generally accepted in payment for goods and services. Without money, goods would have to be exchanged through **barter**, the direct exchange of one good for another. This would be very inefficient, because barter requires a double coincidence of wants.

To see this, consider Milton, a barber, who wants to take juggling lessons; Paul, a juggler, who wants to hire a gardener; and James, a gardener, who needs a haircut. In a barter economy, Milton, James, and Paul won't be able to trade with each other. Instead, Milton will be forced to find a juggler who needs a haircut, James will need to find a barber who needs gardening, and Paul will have to find a gardener who wants to learn how to juggle—potentially, three very hard things for them to do. In contrast, with money, Milton can give James a haircut in exchange for money and use the money to pay Paul for juggling lessons, and Paul can use the money to hire James to work on his garden.

Although money makes an economy more efficient by reducing the time and other transactions costs of exchange, it can't work its magic unless participants in the economy are willing to accept it. That willingness, in turn, depends on a number of

Barter
The direct exchange of one commodity for another without the use of money

Source: B.C. by Johnny Hart. By permission of Johnny Hart and Creators Syndicate.

factors, including the physical properties of money and faith in the regulation of its supply.

PROPERTIES OF MONEY

Most monies perform three crucial functions. First, they are used as *means of payment*, or *media of exchange*. In the United States, currency, coins, and checks can be used to pay for the immediate purchase of goods and services. Second, they represent *stores of value* that can be used to maintain purchasing power over time. Dollar bills, for example, can be kept in your pocket or under the mattress and used later to purchase goods and services of intrinsic value. Third, they are *units of account*, meaning that they are the units in which the prices of goods and services are quoted.

The reason that certain objects, like dollar bills, are considered money whereas other objects, like pizza, are not is that dollar bills are generally acceptable in exchange; they are a highly **liquid** means of payment. Liquidity refers to the ease and speed with which an object can serve as a medium of exchange. Some of the liquidity properties of dollar bills stem from their physical characteristics; they are light and easy to carry, whereas cold pizza is smelly and pretty messy to carry. Some stem from their divisibility; money comes in large and small denominations, so there's no problem in providing change in transactions. Cutting pizza into identical slices is a challenge. And still others stem from their homogeneity; one dollar bill is like any other, so

Liquidity
A measure of the ease with which an object can be converted into money without significant loss of its value

everyone knows what he is getting when he accepts one. Pizza with anchovies is not pizza with artichokes. To appreciate the importance of liquidity, imagine the time and effort it would take to purchase a shirt or blouse by offering pizza in exchange.

To summarize, it's pretty easy to include dollars and exclude pizza in defining money. But in considering why we want to exclude pizza, we also learn that defining money is not so easy. Besides dollars, there are demand deposits, savings accounts, money market funds, and other stores of value that are highly liquid means of payment and that we might want to include in our definition of money. This helps explain why the Federal Reserve tracks three definitions of money, whose differences we'll discuss in chapter 14.

THE IMPORTANCE OF BELIEFS AND INSTITUTIONS TO THE DEFINITION OF MONEY

The intrinsic value of money is less than its value when used in exchange. For example, the intrinsic value of the colored piece of paper called a dollar bill is close to zero, since it can't be used for much besides lighting a fire or making confetti. The reason a dollar bill is worth more than its intrinsic value is that the holder of a dollar believes it's a store of value—something she'll be able to swap for goods and services of real value.

To maintain the *real value of money*, measured by the ratio of the money supply to the price level (the amount of goods that can be purchased with the money supply), it is critical that this belief be commonly held. To see this, suppose that most people suddenly came to doubt that they would be able to swap U.S. currency for real commodities. How would they react? Most likely they would refuse to accept payment in dollars. This would lead other individuals to question whether they too would be able to swap dollars for real commodities. If enough people came to believe that U.S. currency was worthless, the commonly held belief would turn into a self-fulfilling prophecy: no one would agree to accept the currency because no one would want to end up stuck with useless pieces of paper and metal that could not be swapped for goods or services. Money would become a hot potato (something no one wants to touch), and the price level—the amount of money one would need to purchase a market basket of goods—would be infinite.

What could trigger such a radical change in beliefs? One possibility is a suspicion that the government is printing, or is about to print, huge quantities of money that will dramatically raise the price level and lower the real value of money. Unrestrained printing of money is well within the realm of historical experience. After World War I the governments of Germany, Hungary, Austria, and Poland each began printing enormous quantities of money to pay their bills. More recent examples include Israel, Argentina, and Bolivia in the mid-1980s, and Russia and Brazil in the early 1990s. In each case the result of extraordinary growth in the money supply was **hyperinflation**, in which prices rise at incredible rates.

During Germany's hyperinflation, from 1921 through 1923, prices increased by a factor of 30 billion! Prices increased so fast that workers were paid in wheel-

Hyperinflation
An extremely high rate of inflation

"I PAID MY GARAGE WITH THIS CHECK, THEY ENDORSED IT OVER TO THE ELECTRICIAN, HE PAID THE HARDWARE STORE WITH IT, AND THEY HAVE PAID THEIR BILL TO ME WITH IT."

©1994 by Sidney Harris

barrows full of currency, which they pushed straight to the store because prices were literally rising by the minute. If they waited too long to spend their money, an entire wheelbarrow-full would be worthless. Eventually the German public resorted to barter exchange, with its attendant transactions costs. They also started using foreign currencies, in a practice called *currency substitution*. The German hyperinflation ended when a new government was formed, a new currency was issued, and, most important, growth in the supply of money was tightly controlled. The new currency was accepted because Germans believed it would have value and because they had faith that the new institutional arrangements would limit its supply.

2 For an excellent U.S. monetary history, see Milton Friedman and Anna Schwartz, A Monetary History of the United States, 1867–1960 (Princeton, NJ: Princeton University Press, 1963).

CASE STUDY
DIFFERENT MONIES IN U.S. HISTORY

One way to appreciate the importance of beliefs and institutions is to consider the different types of money that have been used throughout U.S. history.[2] During the

American Revolution, the Continental Congress printed *continentals* to help finance the war. The continentals were an example of *fiat money*—something declared to be money by the government but which has no intrinsic value. Because it did not offer to redeem continentals for gold or anything else of value, the Congress was free to print as many of them as it wanted. In fact, it printed so many that prices of commodities in terms of continentals skyrocketed. By the end of the Revolution, the real value of a continental—the amount of goods and services it could purchase—was essentially zero.

By 1788, when the Constitution was ratified, two other types of money had also appeared on the scene: *bills of exchange* and *bank notes*. Bills of exchange were IOUs written by prominent individuals thought to be able to repay their debts. For example, Paul Revere might pay for a horse by handing over an IOU. The horse seller might pay for an addition to his barn by endorsing Paul Revere's IOU over to a carpenter. The carpenter might further endorse the IOU to a woodsman in exchange for a large delivery of wood. In this way, the bill of exchange circulated as paper money. Bills of exchange were used for large transactions rather than everyday purchases.

Bank notes were pieces of paper redeemable for gold at the bank that issued them. The First Bank of the United States, established in 1790 and abolished in 1811, was a quasi-governmental agency that made loans to the private sector in the form of its bank notes. Borrowers could use First Bank notes in making purchases because other individuals believed the notes could be readily redeemed for gold and so were willing to accept them. The First Bank did not have a monopoly on issuing bank notes. During this period, state-chartered private banks also issued notes.

All the bank notes were claimed to be redeemable in gold, but the public's confidence in the ability to redeem a given note varied depending on the financial condition of the bank that issued it. When the public became sufficiently concerned about a bank's ability to redeem its notes, a **bank run**—a demand that the bank hand over gold in exchange for the notes—would ensue. These runs forced many banks with insufficient gold reserves to close.

During the Civil War, the North and the South maintained separate currencies. The Confederate dollar was freely accepted in the South at the beginning of the war when Southerners were confident of victory, but was worthless by war's end. The North's currency was called the greenback, because it was green on one side. Although the federal government promised to redeem greenbacks in gold, it waited until 1879 to do so. Hence, the period between the end of the Civil War and 1879 was very much like modern times. There was a paper currency, issued by the federal government, which was not convertible into gold. But unlike today, gold and silver coins as well as gold and silver certificates—pieces of paper guaranteeing payment in gold and silver—also circulated as money. So too did national bank notes—bank notes issued by federally chartered national banks.

In 1914 the Federal Reserve System was established with a mandate to produce a uniform national currency. In the years since, the Fed has been essentially the sole supplier of U.S. paper currency in the form of Federal Reserve notes: the one dollar,

Bank runs
Situations in which many depositors attempt simultaneously to withdraw funds from their accounts

five dollar, and higher denomination bills we use every day. Notwithstanding its interest in a uniform currency, the federal government permitted the use of gold coins through 1934, the year it effectively abandoned the gold standard (a topic we'll discuss in chapter 13).

To summarize, U.S. history has seen a great range of different types of money: continentals, bills of exchange, bank notes, gold and silver coins, gold and silver certificates, Confederate dollars, greenbanks, national bank notes, and modern Federal Reserve notes and coinage. The advent and demise of these different forms of money reflect changes in institutional arrangements and changing beliefs about the real value of these monies. They also reflect changes in the U.S. government's proclivity to print money and use it to purchase real goods and services from the private sector.

CASE STUDY
"HOLEY MONEY" IS A STAPLE OF INDIA'S PAPER CURRENCY

The following abridged article written by Miriam Jordan in the August 28, 1996 edition of *The Wall Street Journal* illustrates the importance of beliefs to the acceptability of money:

When Karen Grogg arrived in India, she was prepared for the red tape, searing summer heat and general discomforts of the developing world. Nothing, however, prepared her for "holey money."

On her first trip to the local market, a vegetable vendor refused to take her cash. "Exchange, madam," he said, pointing to a hole in the 50-rupee bill. "I got it from the bank," she protested. But he wouldn't take it—nor would anyone else.

You might say holey money is a staple of India's financial system. Ever since British colonial authorities started printing money in India in 1928, Indian banks have routinely used staples, rather than rubber bands or paper, to bundle bills. A few times through the system, and the bills start to tear. . . .

Everyone, from cashiers at luxury hotels to rickshaw-pullers, seems to reject the holey money. While notes aren't considered defaced if the denomination remains visible, commercial banks often refuse to exchange them—even though they are legally obligated to do so.

Consumer complaints have reached as high as Finance Minister P. Chidambaram who vows: "I'll take action against any bank that rejects" holey money.

Ms. Grogg is already taking action of her own. Each time she withdraws money, she asks the bank teller to remove the staples. Then she inspects every bill, demanding that the bank exchange any with holes. Ms. Grogg says this helps her "stay sane," though it does try the patience of the customers waiting behind her.

©1996 Dow Jones & Co.

THE CLASSICAL VIEW OF MONEY

The classical economists argued that money is neutral: changes in its supply have no influence on output or other real variables. They reasoned that the amounts of goods and services produced by the economy should not depend on the amount of money in circulation but rather on the economy's productive capacity and that the price level will adjust to changes in the supply of money. Thus, if there is an increase in the amount of money in the economy, there will be "more money chasing the same amount of real goods and services," and prices of goods and services will simply be bid up. Conversely, if the money supply decreases, there will be less money chasing those goods and services, and prices will be bid down. According to this view, the **real stock of money**—the amount of money divided by the price level—is independent of the nominal money supply.

The real money stock has fluctuated considerably in recent decades. It rose by 12 percent between 1960 and 1970, fell by 7 percent between 1970 and 1980, and rose by 45 percent between 1980 and 1996. Do these fluctuations in the real stock of money disprove the proposition that money is neutral? Not necessarily. The classical economists didn't deny that the real money supply could vary; they simply ruled out the possibility that such changes depended on the nominal quantity of money in circulation. As we'll see, the real quantity of money, like other real variables in the economy, is jointly determined by consumer preferences, technology, demographics, and other factors. As these factors change through time, we expect all real variables, including the real quantity of money, to change.

THE QUANTITY EQUATION AND VELOCITY

The classical view that money is neutral can be understood in terms of the **quantity equation**, which connects the level of nominal GDP, denoted by PY (the price level, P, multiplied by real GDP) to the product of the money supply, M, and the **velocity of money**, v. We can write the quantity equation as

$$Mv = PY.$$

Rearranging this equation so that velocity is by itself on the left-hand side, let's write velocity as the flow of nominal GDP divided by the stock of money: $v = PY/M$. Thus, velocity measures how many times the money supply turns over each year in helping to determine the nominal value of GDP.[3]

The quantity equation defines what we call velocity. By itself it has no theoretical content. However, if we assume that velocity is a constant $\bar{v}$ through time, we arrive at the **quantity theory of money**, which is a special case of the classical view. With this assumption, we can rewrite the quantity equation as

$$PY = \bar{v}M.$$

Since the term $\bar{v}$ is fixed, this formula indicates that increases in the supply of money, M, lead to equal proportionate increases in nominal GDP, PY. If we further assume, as

Real stock of money
The nominal amount of money in circulation divided by the price level

Quantity equation
Nominal GDP—the price level (P) multiplied by real output (Y)—is equal to the nominal money supply (M) multiplied by velocity (v): $Mv = PY$

Velocity of money
The ratio of nominal GDP to the nominal money supply

Quantity theory of money
The proposition that the velocity of money is fixed, so that changes in the money supply have proportionate effects on nominal income

3 We use the word "helping" here because a given form of money is not used in all transactions that are counted in nominal GDP and because many transactions, such as sales of existing assets, are not included in GDP.

the classical economists did, that Y, as well as all other real variables, is independent of the nominal variables (M and P), we arrive at the classical view that increases in M lead to equal proportionate increases in P; in other words, money is neutral.

IS VELOCITY CONSTANT?

Unfortunately for the quantity theory, the velocity of money has been anything but constant. Based on the M1 definition of money, the 1996 velocity was 7.1 because 1996 nominal GDP was $7.636 trillion and M1 was $1.077 trillion. In 1960, nominal GDP was $513 billion and M1 was $141 billion, so velocity that year was only 3.6.

The increase in velocity over this 36-year period was partly due to technological improvements in the way money is used to conduct transactions. The invention of automatic teller machines (ATMs) is a good example. ATMs reduce the amount of cash individuals need to have on hand to make purchases; they can quickly obtain additional cash at the nearest machine. Because of ATMs, a given amount of cash can circulate more quickly (not spend so much time sitting idly in peoples' pockets) and support a larger nominal value of transactions.

A second reason that velocity rose is the development of substitutes for M1 in making transactions. An example is credit cards. Since 1980 credit card use has more than quadrupled. Obviously, the more transactions that are made without cash or personal checks, the greater the total volume of transactions that can be supported by a given amount of M1, and the greater the measured velocity of M1.

A third reason that velocity has risen has to do with higher nominal interest rates that have led Americans to economize on their cash balances.[4] When individuals or firms hold money in cash or non-interest- or low-interest-paying checking accounts, they are sacrificing interest income. Rather than hold their money in this form, they could use the funds to purchase interest-bearing assets. As we'll describe shortly, higher interest rates lead people to lower their demand for real money balances (M/P). What does this have to do with velocity? Note that given the level of output, velocity is inversely related to real money balances. So if the public lowers its demand for real money balances because the interest rate has risen and if output is not thereby altered (or not altered very much), velocity will have to increase to make the smaller amount of real money balances circulate more rapidly in supporting an unchanged level of real output.

The data rule out the simple quantity theory in which velocity is constant. But the classical view does not hinge on velocity's being an absolutely rigid constant. It only requires that changes in real variables not be the result of changes in the money supply. Thus, the classical view requires that output, real money balances, and velocity (which, according to the quantity equation, is the ratio of output to real money balances) be constant with respect to changes in the money supply, but not necessarily constant with respect to changes in other economic factors.

We can easily reject the quantity theory, but is the broader, classical view consistent with our life-cycle model once we've added money? As we'll see shortly, the

4 *The classic articles on this topic are William Baumol's "The Transactions Demand for Cash: An Inventory Theoretic Approach,"* Quarterly Journal of Economics *(November 1952), and James Tobin, "The Interest Elasticity of the Transactions Demand for Cash,"* Review of Economics and Statistics *(August 1956).*

general answer is no. In our model, increases in the money supply, depending on how they come about, may affect real variables and consequently not be neutral.

ADDING MONEY TO OUR MODEL

Including money in our model requires describing both its supply and its demand. Our formulation of the supply of money could not be simpler. We just assume that there is an existing quantity (supply) of money circulating in the economy and that government has complete freedom to increase or decrease that total money supply. Our formulation of the demand for money is also simple. We assume that people care about how much time they spend obtaining money to make purchases. The larger their real money balances, the less time they need to spend going to the bank. One way to add the desire for leisure (time not spent going to the bank) to our model is to assume that leisure enters the Cobb-Douglas utility function. But since the amount of leisure depends on real money balances, we can replace leisure in the Cobb-Douglas function by its dependence on real money balances. Before doing so, let's consider how the demand for money fits into individuals' lifetime budget constraints and influences their real asset accumulation.

THE LIFETIME BUDGET CONSTRAINT WITH MONEY

To keep things simple, we'll temporarily ignore fiscal policy. We'll also retain the assumption that individuals consume only when old. But although each individual abstains from consumption when young, she doesn't save and invest all her wages in capital. Instead, she holds some aside in the form of money. When old, she uses this money, along with the principal and interest on her capital assets, to pay for her old-age consumption.

The following equation restates these points algebraically. It indicates that an individual who is young at time t allocates her real wages, w_t, to two things: real assets, a_{t+1}, and real money balances, m_{t+1}/P_t, where m_{t+1} is the nominal money balances (e.g., the number of dollars) she will take into old age, and P_t is the price level at time t:[5]

$$a_{t+1} + \frac{m_{t+1}}{P_t} = w_t.$$

When the individual reaches old age, her consumption is financed by her real assets, the interest on those assets, and her real money balances, which are her nominal money holdings divided by the price level at time $t + 1$. Thus,

$$c_{ot+1} = a_{t+1}(1 + r_{t+1}) + \frac{m_{t+1}}{P_{t+1}}$$

In a moment we'll substitute the level of assets out of these two equations to form the individual's lifetime budget constraint. Before we do, let's develop some intuition

5 The reason nominal money balances has a time $t + 1$ subscript rather than a time t subscript is the same reason that real assets, a, has a time $t + 1$ subscript. Both m_{t+1} and a_{t+1} are stocks (in one case, the stock of money, in the other case, the stock of real assets) the individual will have at the beginning of period $t + 1$.

about this constraint. First, suppose there is neither inflation nor **deflation** (a decline over time in prices), so $P_{t+1} = P_t$ and $m_{t+1}/P_t = m_{t+1}/P_{t+1}$. Now consider the first equation. It tells us that, given the individual's wage, there is a one-for-one trade-off between bringing real assets and bringing real money balances into old age. For every additional unit of real money balances brought into old age, the individual will bring one unit less of real assets. But according to the second equation, bringing a unit more of real money balances and a unit less of real assets into old age means a reduction in old age consumption by r_{t+1}. This reflects the fact that real assets pay interest, whereas money balances do not. So the higher the interest rate, the higher the cost, in forgone consumption, of holding money balances. Stated differently, this thought experiment tells us that the opportunity cost of holding money, measured in terms of forgone consumption, involves the interest rate.

Next let's consider how an increase in P_{t+1} affects the individual's consumption when old, holding all other variables (including P_t) fixed. According to the last equation, the higher P_{t+1} is (and therefore the higher the inflation rate between the two periods), the smaller consumption when old will be. Intuitively, higher inflation dilutes the real value of the individual's money holdings, meaning that she can buy fewer real goods for consumption in old age with her nominal money balances. In this sense, inflation represents a tax on money. The cost of holding money involves not only the real interest rate but also the inflation rate. Indeed, the lifetime budget constraint, which we now derive, indicates that the opportunity cost of holding money involves the nominal interest rate, i_{t+1}, which depends on both the real interest rate, r_{t+1}, and the inflation rate, π_{t+1}.

The lifetime budget constraint given below results from substituting a_{t+1} out of the last two equations and rearranging terms,

$$\frac{c_{ot+1}}{(1 + r_{t+1})} + \frac{i_{t+1}}{(1 + i_{t+1})} \frac{m_{t+1}}{P_t} = w_t,$$

where $i_{t+1} = r_{t+1} + \pi_{t+1} + r_{t+1}\pi_{t+1}$. Recall that the inflation rate π_{t+1} is just the percentage increase in prices between periods t and $t + 1$: $\pi_{t+1} = (P_{t+1} - P_t)/P_t$. We see that the nominal interest rate equals the real interest rate plus the rate of inflation plus the product of these two rates, the same definition presented in chapter 5. There we learned that the nominal interest rate adjusts for the fact that inflation reduces the real value of nominal assets, such as government bonds, whose principal plus interest payments are made in the form of money.

The lifetime budget constraint tells us that the present value of the individual's lifetime income (w_t) equals the sum of the present value of her consumption when old plus the present value of her acquisition of real money balances. Just as $1/(1 + r_{t+1})$ represents the price at time t of consuming when old at time $t + 1$, the term $i_{t+1}/(1 + i_{t+1})$ represents the price at time t of holding real money balances. The numerator in this ratio, i_{t+1}, measures the nominal interest income the individual forgoes as a result of holding \$1 in non-interest-paying money balances. The denominator in the ratio,

Deflation
A decrease in the price level over time

$(1 + i_{t+1})$, simply discounts, at the nominal interest rate, the nominal interest income sacrificed by holding each dollar.

THE DEMAND FOR MONEY

We'll derive our demand for money by assuming that real money balances enter the Cobb-Douglas utility function along with consumption when old (recall that we are leaving out consumption when young to keep things simple). The utility function in this case can be written as

$$u_t = [m_{t+1}/P_t]^\theta c_{ot+1}^{1-\theta}.$$

This looks the same as our previous utility function except that consumption when young is replaced by real money balances, and the parameter α is replaced by θ.

"This year, I'm putting all my money into money."

Recall that in deciding how much to consume when young and old, each individual chooses the combination given by the point where an indifference curve is just tangent to his budget constraint. The same decision process occurs here. Each individual finds the point at which an indifference curve between real money balances and consumption when old is just tangent to the lifetime budget constraint. And just as the choice of (the demand for) consumption when young equals a fraction (in that case α) of the wage, the demand for real money balances equals a fraction of the wage. We can write the demand for real money balances as

$$\frac{m_{t+1}}{P_t} = \gamma[i_{t+1}]w_t.$$

Note that the fraction γ of their wages that young individuals wish to spend on real money balances depends on (is a function of) the nominal interest rate. Indeed, it is easy to show that γ depends negatively on the nominal interest rate.[6] Thus, the higher the nominal interest rate, the smaller the demand for real money balances. Intuitively, a higher nominal interest rate means a higher opportunity cost of holding real money balances and a smaller demand for real balances.

CASE STUDY
REAL MONEY BALANCES DURING THE GERMAN HYPERINFLATION

If money demand is inversely related to the nominal interest rate, that fact should be evident in the data on countries undergoing hyperinflation. In a period of hyperinflation, nominal interest rates are driven sky-high. The German hyperinflation, which lasted from 1921 to 1923, produced astronomically high inflation rates and nominal interest rates (as our formula for the nominal interest rate suggests).[7] In response to these nominal interest rates, the public went to great lengths to economize on its money holdings. Figure 7.2 shows, on a monthly basis, the German inflation rate and the level of real money balances during the hyperinflation and immediately after prices stabilized at the end of 1923. Note that higher and higher values of the inflation rate (and thus, of the nominal interest rate) between 1921 and 1923 led to smaller and smaller holdings of real balances. However, once prices stabilized, the nominal interest rate dropped precipitously, and real balances began to grow.

Let's also consider the German hyperinflation in terms of the *quantity equation*, $Mv = PY$. Ignoring changes in output, velocity is inversely related to real money balances; given Y, the lower M/P is, the higher v is. During the hyperinflation, the velocity of money, v, more than quadrupled as Germans played hot potato with their currency, trying to lower their real money balances, M/P.[8] This increase in velocity explains why the price level rose much faster than the money supply did. Prices rose in part because of the increase in the money supply, but they rose even faster because each German mark was circulating at such a rapid rate. The increase in velocity was

6 The formula is $\gamma[i_{t+1}] = \theta(1 + i_{t+1})/i_{t+1}$.

7 See Thomas Sargent's study, "The Ends of Four Big Inflations," in Inflation—Causes and Effects (Chicago: University of Chicago Press, 1982), for an excellent analysis of Germany's hyperinflation.

8 In our model, velocity equals $1/\gamma[i_{t+1}](1 - \beta)$. A higher value of i_{t+1} means a lower γ and higher velocity.

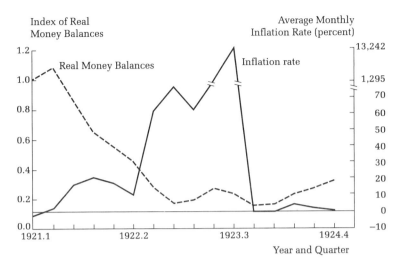

Index of Real Money Balances

Average Monthly Inflation Rate (percent)

FIGURE 7.2   INFLATION AND REAL MONEY BALANCES DURING THE GERMAN HYPERINFLATION

During hyperinflations, the nominal interest rate—equal to the real interest rate plus the rate of inflation—is driven sky-high. During the German hyperinflation of the 1920s, astronomically high nominal interest rates led to smaller and smaller holdings of real money balances. Once prices stabilized at the end of 1923, the nominal interest rate dropped, and real balances began to grow.

equivalent, in terms of its impact on prices, to having more German marks in circulation. Similar increases in velocity and declines in real money demand have been observed in every hyperinflation on record.

CAPITAL ACCUMULATION IN THE MONETARY ECONOMY

We next integrate the demand for money into our economy's capital-labor ratio transition equation. It turns out that our transition equation for the capital-labor ratio is simply

$$k_{t+1} = (1 - \gamma[i_{t+1}])A(1 - \beta)k_t^\beta - f_t.$$

To understand why, recall that the amount of capital per worker at time $t + 1$, k_{t+1}, equals the amount of capital assets per old person at that same time. But the assets of the old are those they acquired when young. In this case, they equal the real wage earned when young, w_t, less the amount held aside in real money balances when young, $\gamma[i_{t+1}]w_t$, less the amount handed over to the government in either net taxes (taxes net of transfers) or purchases of bonds, f_t, when young.[9] Hence, $k_{t+1} =$

9 We assume that a generation's demand for real money balances equals $\gamma[i_{t+1}]$ times the wage it earns when young, rather than $\gamma[i_{t+1}]$ times the present value of the generation's lifetime income. In so doing, we ignore the fact that under certain fiscal policies, the present value of a generation's lifetime income will differ from the wage it earns when young.

$(1 - \gamma[i_{t+1}])w_t - f_t$. Our transition equation is derived by replacing the real wage by the formula for the marginal product of labor at time t.

To keep things simple, we'll assume for most of what follows that in the money demand formula, the function $\gamma[\ ]$ is a constant equal to $\bar{\gamma}$, regardless of the value of i_{t+1}. That is, we'll consider the simple money demand formula $m_{t+1}/P_t = \bar{\gamma}w_t$. Leaving out the nominal interest rate greatly simplifies our analysis of the transition equation, without materially affecting the conclusions we draw. After presenting the results based on this simplified money demand formula, we'll mention how they would be modified by letting money demand be interest sensitive.

With this simplifying assumption, the capital-labor transition equation becomes $k_{t+1} = A(1 - \bar{\gamma})(1 - \beta)k_t^\beta - f_t$. Thus, given the value of the capital-labor ratio at some initial time 0 and knowledge of f_0 and subsequent values of f_t, we can use the transition equation over and over again to determine the economy's capital-labor ratio at time $1, 2, 3, \ldots, \infty$—at each date in the future. Armed with this information, we can solve for the time paths of all the other real variables in the economy, including the real wage.

DETERMINATION OF THE PRICE LEVEL THROUGH TIME

Now that we've seen how the economy's real variables are determined, let's consider how the price level evolves through time. To do so, we need to combine the demand for money with the supply of money. We've talked about the demand side—the fact that young people in each period wish to receive some of their real wage in the form of real money balances. Actually, we've also talked about the supply side—the fact that in each period, the old people, who hold the money, wish to supply it to the market by spending it to help pay for their old-age consumption. Since we are assuming for the moment that the aggregate supply of money in circulation is fixed at $\bar{M}$, this is the total amount of money supplied to the market in each period. In equilibrium, it must also be the amount of money the young collectively end up demanding.

To equate the demand for money by the young to the supply of money by the old, we must write our simplified money demand equation, $m_{t+1}/P_t = \bar{\gamma}w_t$, in terms of the total demand for money at time t, M_{t+1}. But the amount of money demanded by each young person is just the total demand for money divided by N, the number of young people. Thus, we can replace m_{t+1} by M_{t+1}/N in our money demand equation, which leads to $M_{t+1}/P_t = \bar{\gamma}w_t N$. The final step is to equate the total demand for money, M_{t+1}, to the supply of money, $\bar{M}$. Replacing the demand for money by the aggregate supply in our money demand equation and solving for the price level implies

$$P_t = \frac{\bar{M}}{\bar{\gamma}w_t N}.$$

This equation is an equilibrium relationship. It indicates how the price level at time t relates to the fixed supply of money, the money demand preference parameter, the real wage, and the population size of each generation.

Now we can determine the time path of the real wage from the time path of the capital-labor ratio, the calculation of which we discussed above. Inserting this time path of the real wage into the above equation yields the time path of the price level. For example, at time 0 we can plug w_0 into the above equation together with values of the three parameters $\bar{y}$, N, and $\bar{M}$ to get P_0. At time 1 we can plug w_1 into the equation together with the same values of these three parameters to get P_1, and so on, until the economy reaches its steady state.[10] When the economy reaches its steady state, the real wage remains fixed, implying that the price level remains fixed as well. Hence, we see immediately that when the money supply is fixed, changes in the price level are temporary; eventually the price level converges to its long-run steady-state value.

The price level equation tells us that there is an inverse relationship between the price level and the real wage. The larger the real wage at a point in time, the lower the price level. Why? Recall that the demand for real balances at time t equals $\bar{y}w_tN$. So the bigger w_t is, the greater the demand for real balances is at time t. But the nominal money supply is fixed, so the only way the real money supply at time t can adjust to satisfy a higher demand is for the price level at time t to fall. Intuitively, then, the bigger is the real wage (the real output received by the young), the more real output the young are willing to exchange for the money held by the old. This situation raises the amount of output that is swapped for each unit of money. Equivalently, it lowers the number of units of money that are swapped for each unit of output. But the number of units of money swapped for each unit of output is precisely the price level. So the real wage and the price level are indeed inversely related.

A NUMERICAL EXAMPLE OF A TRANSITION WITH MONEY

Let's use the price level equation in conjunction with the capital-labor ratio transition equation to illustrate how the price level adjusts through time to ensure that the real supply of money equals the real demand for money. To do so, let's assume the economy at time 0 has not yet reached its steady state. Specifically, let's suppose that at time 0, the capital-labor ratio is 3. Let's also assume that $\bar{y}$ equals .10, β equals .30, A equals 10, N equals 100, and $\bar{M}$ equals 10,000. Further assume that there is no fiscal policy, so f_t equals 0. Then, as you can readily confirm, the transition equation for the capital-labor ratio is

$$k_{t+1} = 6.30\,k_t^{.3},$$

and the equation for the price level is

$$P_t = \frac{1{,}000}{w_t}.$$

Table 7.1 presents the values for the capital-labor ratio, the real wage, and the price level for the first seven periods of this economy's transition. It also indicates the steady-state values of these variables. Since the economy's steady-state capital-labor ratio is 13.865 and its time 0 ratio is only 3, the transition path involves an increase over time in the capital-labor ratio. As more capital becomes available per worker, the

10 For the economy to reach a steady state, f_t must eventually become constant, which is something we assume.

TABLE 7.1 AN ILLUSTRATIVE TRANSITION PATH: THE TWO-PERIOD MODEL WITH MONEY

Period	k_t	w_t	P_t
0	3.000	9.733	102.746
1	8.759	13.423	74.500
2	12.080	14.782	67.651
3	13.303	15.215	65.722
4	13.694	15.348	65.154
5	13.813	15.388	64.985
6	13.849	15.400	64.934
7	13.860	15.404	64.919
⋮	⋮	⋮	⋮
∞	13.865	15.405	65.912

Assumptions: $k_0 = 3$, $\gamma = .10$, $\beta = .30$, $A = 10$, $N = 100$, $\bar{M} = 10,000$. Equations underlying the table: $k_{t+1} = (1 - \bar{\gamma})w_t$, $w_t = A(1 - \beta)k_t^\beta$, $P_t = \bar{M}/(N\bar{\gamma}w_t)$

real wage rises to its steady-state value. The figures in the second column show this: the real wage at time 0 is 9.733; at time 1 it is 13.423; by time 3 it is 15.215; and it eventually reaches 15.405.

The price level is inversely related to the real wage, so the increase in the real wage during the transition implies a decrease in the price level. Had the time 0 capital-labor ratio exceeded the long-run steady-state value, the transition would have involved a falling real wage and a rising price level over time. Hence, we see again that during a transition, the price level can fall or rise even if the money supply is constant.

In the case of the transition shown in Table 7.1, the price level falls by more than one-quarter between period 0 and period 1. Ultimately it converges to a value 37 percent smaller than it was initially (at time 0). Remember that a period corresponds to roughly 30 years, so the 27 percent decline in the price level between periods 0 and 1 corresponds to roughly a 1 percent annual rate of deflation.

Although we don't mean our example to represent any particular economy at any particular point in time, it is worth noting that a 1 percent annual rate of deflation is well within the historical record of U.S. price changes. Figure 7.3 plots the annual rate of change in the U.S. price level, as measured by the GNP implicit price deflator for the years 1870 through 1996. The United States experienced deflation in more than half the years between 1870 and 1899. In this century, deflationary episodes were concentrated in the early 1920s and early 1930s. The largest deflation in a single year occurred in 1921, when prices fell by 15 percent. The largest inflation in a single year occurred in 1946, when World War II price controls were lifted, and prices rose by 24 percent. Since 1983 the U.S. inflation rate has been quite low, running at less than 5 percent per year, after reaching 12 percent in the early 1980s.

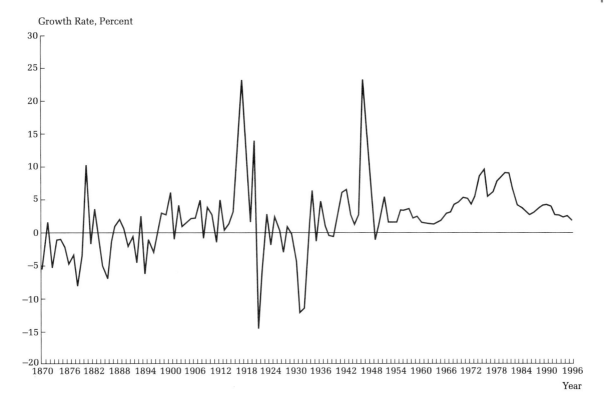

Growth Rate, Percent

FIGURE 7.3 ANNUAL RATE OF GROWTH OF THE PRICE LEVEL, 1870–1996
Between 1870 and 1899, there were more years of deflation (a fall in the price level) than inflation. Since World War II, the price level has risen in every year but one.

Sources: Milton Friedman and Anna Schwartz, A Monetary History of the United States, 1867–1960 *(Princeton, NJ: Princeton University Press, 1963) and* The Economic Report of the President, *various issues.*

CASE STUDY
THE U.S. DEFLATION OF 1865–1879

The fourteen years between 1865 and 1879 represent the longest sustained deflation in U.S. economic history. During these years, wholesale prices, on which there are good data, fell at an average annual rate of over 6 percent. The same item that cost $1.00 in 1865 cost only $0.42 in 1879. This deflation wasn't caused by a decline in the money stock. On the contrary, the nominal money stock rose by about 15 percent between 1865 and 1879. The cause was the substantial growth over this period in U.S. real GDP, which drove up the demand for money. Between 1865 and 1879, the U.S. population rose by almost one-third and per capita real GDP rose at roughly 4 percent per year. The increase in the nominal supply of money was insufficient to accommodate the increase in demand, so the price level had to fall in order to raise the effective (real) supply of money.

In the price level formula, the wage rate and the cohort population size capture the dependence of the price level on the economy's level of real income. Indeed, since $w_t N$ equals the share $(1 - \beta)$ of output, we can write our formula for the price level as $P_t = \bar{M}/\bar{\gamma}(1 - \beta)Y_t$. The larger that real output is, the lower is the price level needed to equate the demand for real money balances with the supply.

WHEN IS MONEY NEUTRAL?

Now that we have a model relating the price level to the money supply, we can use it to examine the neutrality of money—the proposition that a one-time increase in the money supply has no effect on any real variable and simply leads to a proportionate increase in the time path of prices. We'll consider three different ways in which the government might increase the money supply: (1) printing money to make transfer payments to the elderly, (2) printing money to finance government consumption, and (3) printing money to make transfer payments to the young. Only the first of these three policies is neutral, leading to the conclusion that the manner in which the money supply is changed determines whether it's neutral.

In considering these cases, it's useful to keep two questions in mind. First, does the way the additional money is injected into the economy affect the saving behavior of the young? If it does, the paths of all real variables will be altered. Second, are the elderly compensated for the decline in the real value of their money holdings resulting from the government's increase in the money supply and its associated increase in the price level?

CASE 1: PRINTING MONEY TO MAKE TRANSFERS TO THE ELDERLY

Suppose that at the beginning of period 0, the government prints money in the amount ΔM and hands it to the elderly, perhaps in the form of an increase in social security payments. This increases the money holdings of the elderly at time 0 from $\bar{M} + \Delta M$. At the end of period 0, the elderly supply their now-higher amount of money to the young in exchange for output. When the young of period 0 are old in period 1, they will hold the total money supply and will, in turn, supply it to the next generation of young people. This situation holds true for subsequent generations as well; each generation, when it is old, will supply the total stock of money to the young in exchange for output (that is, they'll use their money to purchase corn from the young).

Does this policy affect the real side of the economy, specifically the capital-labor transition equation, in either period 0 or subsequent periods? No. The policy doesn't involve the sale of bonds to the young or any net taxation of the young, so f_t is zero.

Hence, the saving behavior of the young at time 0 and in all subsequent periods is unchanged. Because the transition equation remains the same, the policy has no effect on capital accumulation, output, the real interest rate, or the real wage. The fact that the time paths of these real variables are unaffected by the government's printing money and handing it to the old at time 0 satisfies one requirement for money neutrality.

Neutrality also requires the time path of the price level to rise in proportion to the increase in the money supply. This requirement is also satisfied. To see why, note that the formula for the price level is the same as before, except that the money supply from period 0 onward is $\bar{M} + \Delta M$ rather than simply $\bar{M}$. The modified price level formula is

$$P_t = \frac{\bar{M} + \Delta M}{\bar{\gamma} w_t N}.$$

Since the time path of the real wage is not altered by the monetary policy we're considering, our formula indicates that the price level at each point in time will be proportional to the total money supply. Stated differently, the time path of the price level will rise by whatever percentage increase occurs in the money supply.

Finally, let's ask how the elderly at time 0 fare as a result of the money supply policy. In particular, does transferring money to the elderly make them better off? The answer is no. It's true that the elderly at time 0 end up with more money after the transfer, but the resulting increase in the price level dilutes the real value of their initial as well as their additional money. In the end, their nominal money holdings are larger, but their real money balances are just the same as in the absence of the government's transfer payment. We can verify this by examining the equation for consumption by an elderly individual at time 0:

$$c_{o0} = a_0(1 + r_0) + \frac{(\bar{M} + \Delta M)/N}{P_0}.$$

Clearly, consumption by the elderly at time 0 depends partly on the ratio of nominal money holdings to the price level (the real money balances). But a given percentage increase in the nominal money holdings of each elderly person at time 0, matched by an equal percentage increase in the price level, leaves the real money balances of the elderly unchanged. So consumption by the elderly will be unchanged. In reducing the real value of money, the increase in the price level in effect taxes the money holdings of the elderly. This implicit tax exactly offsets the extra money they receive, leaving them in the same real position.

The young are also left in the same real position. They receive the same real wage, and since they initially hold no money balances, the price rise does not affect them. Of course, when they sell their output to the elderly, the young will receive more money. But because of the price increase, the real value of the money received will be the same as in the absence of the government policy.

Now we've shown that both requirements for the neutrality of money are satisfied. The neutrality with respect to this particular type of one-time increase in the money supply does not depend on the specific parameter values we assumed. It follows immediately from the fact that the capital-labor transition equation doesn't depend on the money supply and that the price level rises in proportion to the increase in the money supply.

CASE 2: PRINTING MONEY TO FINANCE GOVERNMENT CONSUMPTION

Next suppose the government prints additional money in the amount ΔM and uses it to purchase output, which it consumes at time 0. In succeeding periods, the government prints no additional money and purchases no additional goods and services. The government policy is a one-time event, but the money supply is permanently increased. As in case 1, this policy leaves f_t equal to zero and therefore has no effect on saving by the young at time 0 or in any subsequent time period. They continue to retain the same portion of their real wages in the form of real money balances and save the rest. Hence, the capital-labor transition equation is not altered by the policy. Since the initial capital-labor ratio is unchanged, this transition equation grinds out the same time paths of the capital-labor ratio, output, the real interest rate, and the real wage as in the absence of the government policy. From the perspective of these real variables, the government's printing of money to purchase goods and services at time 0 has no effect.

Turning to the price level, the formula for the price level at time 0 and in all subsequent periods is the same as in case 1. This equation says that the entire time path of the price level rises in proportion to the increase in the money supply, an additional requirement for the neutrality of money.

So far, then, we haven't detected any difference between this policy of spending newly printed money on goods and services and the policy of transferring it to the elderly. But there is a difference, and it is precisely with respect to the elderly at time 0. They experience a tax on their nominal money holdings as a result of the increase in the price level at time 0, which is *not* offset by the transfer of money from the government. Indeed, the old at time 0 end up paying entirely for the government spending at time 0 through a decline in their real money balances. Why? Because the real money balances of the elderly at time 0 in this case are only $\overline{M}/NP_0$. So the total supply of money swapped by the elderly at time 0 for real goods and services is not the total money supply at time 0, $\overline{M} + \Delta M$, but only the amount $\overline{M}$. The rest of the money supply, ΔM, being supplied to the young (swapped for goods from the young), is supplied directly by the government. In exchange for this money, the government is able to obtain real output from the young equal to $\Delta M/P_0$, which is precisely the amount lost by each old person at time 0 multiplied by the number of elderly. In periods after time 0, the entire money supply will be held by the elderly because they will have acquired the entire money supply when young. So the consumption by the elderly in periods after time 0 will be unaffected by the policy.

To summarize, printing money to finance government consumption is not neutral because it reduces the welfare of those who are elderly and already hold money when the new money is introduced. We also learned that the government was able to get that generation of elderly people to pay for its consumption without explicitly taxing them. The reduction at time 0 in consumption by the elderly precisely equals the increased consumption by the government, so aggregate consumption at time 0 is unaffected. That explains why there is no policy-induced change in aggregate saving at time 0 and therefore no change in the capital-labor transition equation. This is analogous to our result in chapter 6 that taxing the old to pay for government purchases has no effect on the macroeconomy.

CASE 3: PRINTING MONEY TO FINANCE TRANSFERS TO THE YOUNG

Finally, let's have the government print ΔM of additional money and use it to make transfer payments to the young at time 0. These payments might take the form of educational grants, child care tax credits paid to young and middle-aged working parents, or welfare benefits to the young and middle aged. This policy alters the welfare of the initial elderly, as in case 2, but unlike case 2, it's not neutral with respect to the path of output and the real money supply. The rise in the price level associated with the increased money supply hurts the elderly at time 0 by diluting the real value of their nominal money holdings. This loss to the elderly means a gain to the young at time 0. Those young people are each handed $\Delta M/N$ in transfer payments, the real value of which ends up equaling $\Delta M/NP_0$ (whatever P_0 turns out to be). But unlike the other two policies, in this case f_0 is not zero, but equals minus this real transfer. Hence, the saving behavior of the young at time 0 is altered by the transfer payment. Specifically, the transition curve for k_1 is shifted up at time 0 but then returns to its original position in subsequent periods. This one-time shift in the transition curve means that the time paths of all the economy's real variables are changed.

Figure 7.4 shows this. It depicts the transition curve for k_1 as well as the original, no-policy transition curve, which is also the relevant curve after period 1 when no further monetary policy is being conducted and f_t is zero. To trace the economy's transition, start with k_0 and use the k_1 curve to find the capital-labor ratio at time 1. Then use this value and the original transition curve to find all subsequent capital-labor ratios.

Under this policy, the formula for the price level is the same as in cases 1 and 2. As before, the price level initially increases in proportion to the money stock in period 0, when the wage rate is already determined. But unlike those other two cases, the time path of the wage rate (which enters in the denominator of the price level formula) after period 0 is now altered. As Figure 7.4 implies, the policy produces a temporary rise in the wage rate. As a result, the percentage increase in the price level is smaller than the percentage increase in the money supply until the economy returns to its steady state.

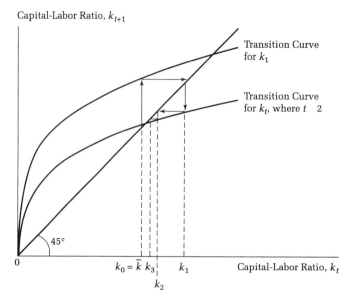

FIGURE 7.4 IMPACT ON THE CAPITAL-LABOR RATIO OF PRINTING MONEY TO MAKE TRANSFERS TO THE YOUNG AT TIME 0

At time 0, with the economy in steady state at the capital-labor ratio $k_0 = \bar{k}$, the government prints new money and transfers it to the young. This policy lowers f_0, net payments to government by the young, and shifts the k_1 transition curve upward. Therefore, the capital-labor ratio at time 1, k_1, is determined by the higher transition curve. After time 1, f_t is again zero, so the transition curve returns to its original (lower) position. Subsequent capital-labor ratios are determined along that lower curve as the economy moves back to its original steady state. Because real variables are altered during the transition, this policy is not neutral.

HOW ONGOING INCREASES IN THE MONEY SUPPLY CAUSE INFLATION

In each of the three examples, we assumed a one-time increase in the money supply. What happens if instead the government continues to engage in one or more of these policies period after period? The answer is inflation. Suppose the government prints money each period to finance transfers to the old. Then the price level each period will rise by an amount above and beyond what it would otherwise have risen, equal to the percentage increase in the money supply. Thus, if the government prints 10 percent more money each period to pay for its transfers, the price level will rise by 10 percent more each period than it would otherwise have gone up. In the economy's steady state, prices will continue rising period after period by 10 percent. Given our formulation of the demand for money and the fact that f_t equals zero, this will leave unchanged the capital-labor transition equation, but will hit each successive set of old people with an implicit tax on their real money holdings equal to the concomitant transfers they receive from the government.

In the case of an ongoing policy of paying for government purchases by printing money, each period's inflation rate is also dictated by the growth rate of the money supply in that period. But assuming, as we have, a fixed value of γ, this inflationary finance has no impact on capital accumulation.

Finally, in the case in which the government prints money each period to finance transfers to the young, the capital-labor transition curve will be permanently shifted upward, reflecting the ongoing government redistribution from the old to the young (f_t will be positive each period). The resulting change in the time path of the real wage will influence the rate at which the price level changes through time. In the steady state, however, both the real wage and f_t will be constant, so the inflation rate will not be influenced by feedback effects on the demand for money. Consequently, the steady-state inflation rate will simply equal the growth rate in the money supply.

THE INFLATION PROCESS UNDER A MORE REALISTIC FORMULATION OF MONEY DEMAND

The conclusion that the steady-state inflation rate is determined by the growth rate of the money supply holds equally well if we assume that the demand for money depends on the nominal interest rate. In this case, the function $\gamma[i_{t+1}]$, rather than the constant $\bar{\gamma}$, enters the expression for money demand. With this formulation, the transition path to the steady state as well as the particular steady state toward which the economy moves would both differ. When the nominal interest rate, and thus the inflation rate, influences the demand for real money balances, ongoing inflation will affect real money demand and the capital-labor transition equation. This is true even in case 1, in which the government prints money each period to transfer to the elderly and f_t equals zero, and case 2, in which the government prints money each period to finance its purchases. The reason is that now $\gamma[i_{t+1}]$, rather than $\bar{\gamma}$, enters the capital-labor ratio transition equation.

We know that inflation raises nominal interest rates. With money demand inversely related to the nominal interest rate, inflation reduces young people's demand for real money balances. Consequently, the young set aside less of their wages in the form of real money balances and invest more of their wages in capital. This shifts the capital-labor transition curve upward, leading to an increase in capital accumulation in cases 1 and 2. In case 3, in which the government prints money to make transfers to the young, including the nominal interest rate in the money demand would lead to more of an upward shift in the transition curve than would otherwise occur.

SEIGNIORAGE — "THE INFLATION TAX"

The money that the government creates directly is called the monetary base. The increase in the monetary base divided by the price level is referred to as **seigniorage**. Seigniorage is often referred to as "the inflation tax." It measures the real resources the government acquires by printing money and using it to make transfer payments or to purchase goods and services.[11] In our model, seigniorage at time t equals

Seigniorage
The real resources the government acquires by printing money

11 The word "seigniorage" can be traced to the Middle Ages, when coins were exclusively minted by the sovereign, or seignior, and the difference between the face value of coins and their cost of minting was called seigniorage.

$\Delta M_t/P_t$—the change in the supply of money between periods t and $t+1$ divided by the price level.

The inflation tax accounts for a very small fraction of the real resources collected by the U.S. government because the U.S. inflation rate is very low. But seigniorage can be a significant source of government finance. Take Israel's 300 percent annual rate of inflation during the mid-1980s. Producing this inflation required printing lots of Israeli shekels—enough shekels to finance 12 percent of total Israeli government outlays.

USING SURPRISE INFLATION TO REDUCE THE REAL VALUE OF GOVERNMENT DEBT

Seigniorage is not the only way governments use monetary policy to acquire real resources. Another way is to use inflation to dilute the real value of their nominal debt. Take the case of Alex, who purchases a 30-year U.S. Treasury bond for $10,000. The bond promises to pay interest of $1,000 per year for 30 years and then return the $10,000 principal. Both principal and interest are fixed in nominal terms. Now suppose that immediately after selling this bond, the government doubles the money supply, which leads to a doubling of current and future prices. (This is an extreme case, but it clearly illustrates the point.) What happens to the real value of Alex's bond? The answer is that it falls by half; the stream of nominal interest and principal payments can now buy only half the amount of real goods and services. Since the real value of government debt falls by half, the real taxes needed to meet these interest and principal payments fall by half as well. The government will experience this reduction in the real value of its outstanding debt in the form of a doubling of its nominal tax revenues as a result of the doubling of all commodity and factor prices. Its nominal revenues will double, but the nominal time path of its interest and principal payments will remain unchanged.

This example makes sense as far as it goes. But it neglects the possibility that the nominal interest and principal payments on the $10,000 bond were bigger to begin with in anticipation of the increase in prices. Indeed, our formula for the nominal interest rate tells us that the nominal interest rate will incorporate the anticipated (expected) inflation rate. Stated differently, the nominal interest rate will adjust in response to the expected rate of inflation to make savers indifferent between investing in real capital or in nominal government bonds.

In our model so far, we have assumed that whatever inflation is expected actually occurs. But if inflation turns out to be higher (lower) than was expected, the nominal interest rate will undercompensate (overcompensate) government bondholders for the reduction (increase) in the real value of their principal and interest receipts. This *unexpected inflation*—the difference between actual and expected inflation—represents the true degree to which the government acquires real resources by printing money and diluting the real value of its nominal debt.

CASE STUDY
HAS THE U.S. DILUTED ITS DEBT THROUGH UNEXPECTED INFLATION?

If we can measure the ex ante ("before the fact") expected rate of inflation and compare it with the ex post ("after the fact") rate, we can estimate the amount of unexpected inflation. One way to do this is simply to ask people in advance what they expect inflation to be. The Livingston Survey of business leaders' inflation expectations does this. It indicates that America's top executives have both under- and overpredicted inflation in recent years. In 1974, for example, the expected inflation rate of 5.4 percent fell far short of the actual 11.0 percent inflation rate. In 1986, expected inflation was 4.1 percent, but ended up at only 1.9 percent. In years when inflation was underpredicted the government raised real revenues by diluting its debt. But in years when inflation was overpredicted, the government ended up paying (in terms of nominal interest on its bonds) a higher inflation premium than proved, ex post, to have been warranted. In those years, the real value of the debt was raised, rather than lowered, because of unexpected inflation.

The sums involved in altering the real value of government debt can be substantial. In 1980, unexpected inflation cut real U.S. government debt by $60.3 billion, far exceeding the $17.5 billion raised in real seigniorage. Had this gain to the government been recorded as a source of revenue (it wasn't), it would have essentially eliminated the 1980 federal deficit of $61.3 billion! The federal government's failure to include these real revenue gains and losses in computing the deficit is another reason, in addition to those given in the previous chapter, to question the usefulness of the deficit as a measure of fiscal policy.

INFLATION IN THE PRESENCE OF NONINDEXED GOVERNMENT TAXATION AND SPENDING

The third way governments use inflation to garner real resources from the private sector is by failing to index their taxes for inflation. A prime example here is progressive income taxation. Most developed countries tax nominal income on a progressive basis, meaning that the higher the nominal income is, the higher the marginal tax rate is. In causing inflation, governments raise the nominal incomes of individuals and firms and push them into higher tax brackets. As a result, their real taxes rise even if their real incomes remain unchanged.[12] Since 1985, however, the U.S. tax code has included a provision to adjust tax brackets annually for inflation, to offset this effect.

A fourth way inflation has real fiscal effects involves the nonindexation of government expenditures. In the United States, Social Security benefits are indexed for inflation, but other transfer payments and purchases, such as wages paid to government workers, are not. As the price level rises, the real value of welfare benefits, unemployment insurance, and food stamps falls unless the government explicitly legislates nominal benefit increases.

12 Take the case of a 20 percent tax on income in excess of $20,000. Someone earning $30,000 pays $2,000—20 percent of the $10,000 excess of total income over $20,000. Now suppose inflation doubles all prices and nominal incomes, so that a person who previously earned $30,000 now earns $60,000. The taxes due would now be 20 percent of $60,000 minus $20,000, or $8,000. Even though the person's real income doesn't change, his tax rate doubles from 6.7 percent ($2,000/$30,000) to 13.3 percent ($8,000/$60,000).

CHAPTER SUMMARY

1. Money is a highly liquid means of exchange, a store of value, and a unit of account. What constitutes money in any particular society depends on institutional arrangements, beliefs, and transactions technologies. Historically, money in the United States has ranged from continentals to bills of exchange, to bank notes, to greenbacks, to modern Federal Reserve notes.

2. Classical economists argued that money is neutral—that increases in the money supply simply lead to equal proportionate increases in the price level, with no effect on real variables. Their view can be understood using the quantity equation, $Mv = PY$. Assuming that output, Y, is always at its full employment level and that velocity, v, is constant, an increase in the money supply, M, will simply lead to an equal proportionate increase in the price level.

3. In our model money is supplied by the elderly and by the government. It is demanded by the young based on their preferences and their lifetime budget constraints. The demand for money depends positively on the wage rate and negatively on the nominal interest rate, which is the opportunity cost of holding money. A striking illustration of the inverse relationship between the demand for real money balances and the nominal interest rate is provided by the behavior of real money balances during the German hyperinflation.

4. Our model with money reduces to two interrelated equations: the capital-labor ratio transition equation and the price level equation. One lesson from the study of this interrelationship is that transitions involving increases in the economy's real income, captured in our model by the real wage, raise the demand for real money balances. Given a fixed money supply, the increased demand can be satisfied only by a decline in the price level.

5. The model shows that the way the government injects money into the economy determines whether the injection is neutral. If the government increases the money supply by making a one-time transfer to the elderly, monetary policy will be neutral. In this case the value of the transfer to the elderly is offset by their loss in real money balances due to the rise in prices; prices rise in proportion to the increase in the money supply. In contrast, a one-time increase in the money supply that is spent on government consumption is not neutral. Prices rise in proportion to the money supply, and the elderly at the time of the policy change pay for the additional government consumption through a price-induced decline in their real money balances. Finally, a one-time increase in the money supply that is handed to the young as transfer payments stimulates their saving and thereby affects the time path of the capital-labor ratio. Ultimately the economy

ends up at the same steady-state capital-labor ratio to which it was headed, and the price level ends up, in the long run, rising in proportion to the money supply. However, since the economy's real variables are affected during the transition, this policy is not neutral.

6. Ongoing increases in the money supply, regardless of how they are spent, will produce inflation. The long-run inflation rate is determined by the long-run growth rate of the money supply. If the demand for money is sensitive to the nominal interest rate, ongoing increases in the money supply will be nonneutral even if each period's increase in the money supply is spent on transfers to the elderly.

7. Because the impact of money supply increases depends on how the new money is spent and because increases in the money supply raise prices and implicitly tax existing money holdings and nominal government bonds, monetary policy can be viewed as a form of fiscal policy. The relationship of monetary policy to fiscal policy is even tighter if the tax system and government expenditures are not indexed for inflation.

PART THREE

ECONOMIC FLUCTUATIONS

CHAPTER 8

THE KEYNESIAN MODEL OF PRICE AND WAGE RIGIDITY

INTRODUCTION

Previous chapters assumed that prices and wages are fully flexible. This chapter shifts gears and considers **nominal rigidities**—the lack of flexibility in the price level or the nominal wage rate—that form the basis of the **Keynesian model** of business cycle fluctuations. Keynesian theory emphasizes the role of these rigidities in causing recessions and the need for monetary and fiscal policy to combat them.

We begin with some evidence on price and wage rigidities in the U.S. economy. Next, we introduce nominal rigidities into our life-cycle model. Specifically, we use the two central elements of chapter 7—the price level equation (based on the equality of money demand and supply) and the transition equation—to show how nominal rigidities can restrict output and employment. Finally, we consider the roles of monetary and fiscal policies in restoring the full-employment level of output.

As we'll show, monetary policy works through the price level equation. Fiscal policy enters through the transition equation. Graphing these two relationships produces the famous Keynesian IS-LM diagram showing how the level and composition of output are influenced by monetary and fiscal policies. The IS-LM diagram indicates the level of *aggregate demand*: how much output will be purchased, given the price level and monetary and fiscal policy. Combining this with a characterization of *aggregate supply*—how much output will be produced, given the price level—lets us determine output and price levels for situations in which the output price level itself is not completely rigid, notably the case of nominal wage rigidity. We do this in a second famous Keynesian diagram: the so-called *aggregate demand–aggregate supply diagram*.

This chapter's central questions include:

- What are wage and price rigidities, and why do they arise?

- How can wage or price rigidities restrict output and employment?

Nominal rigidity
The sluggish adjustment, especially downward adjustment, of a price or nominal wage rate

Keynesian model
A macroeconomic model that emphasizes the role of market imperfections (especially price and wage rigidities) in causing recessions and the role of economic policy in combating recessions

- How can monetary and fiscal policy overcome nominal rigidities?

- How do monetary and fiscal policies affect the short-run composition of output?

- What are the relative strengths of monetary and fiscal policy in combating recessions?

PRICE AND WAGE ADJUSTMENT PROCESS

So far we've viewed prices and wages as mechanisms for clearing markets, always adjusting to equate supply and demand. But price or wage adjustment is not always fluid. Prices for commodities or inputs may change less often or by smaller amounts than simple economic theory suggests. Such rigidity, more accurately called *price stickiness* because prices do eventually adjust, arises in various commodity and input markets. Let's review the assumption of full price adjustment and then consider price rigidity.

FULLY FLEXIBLE PRICES
Many markets closely follow the flexible-price paradigm. For example, the interest rate on U.S. Treasury bills is determined continuously in world financial markets, which match the global supply and demand for these securities. The prices of gold and wheat also fluctuate constantly to clear their respective markets. Each of these markets satisfies the requirements for perfect competition: many sellers, many buyers, homogeneous commodities (e.g., one ounce of gold is indistinguishable from any other), and adequate information on the part of buyers and sellers about the current price. In such markets there are strong forces driving prices to adjust. If the price is too low (i.e., the quantity demanded exceeds the quantity supplied), prospective buyers will bid up the price, knowing that for a bit more than the current price, they can satisfy their demand. If it is too high (i.e., the quantity supplied exceeds the quantity demanded), suppliers will cut their prices, because accepting a bit less will bring them all the demand they want.

PRICE AND WAGE RIGIDITY
In less competitive markets, the forces generating price adjustment may be weaker. A seller may be less eager to cut her price if she must advertise the price cut extensively to gain customers, or if she expects relatively few customers to shift from other producers. She may also be reluctant to cut her price if doing so may be interpreted as a signal of inferior product quality or if she is unaware of the prices other producers are charging.

In labor markets, too, the relationship between suppliers (workers) and demanders (firms) often precludes rapid wage adjustment. Collective bargaining between labor unions and employers is a case in point. Such bargaining typically determines wages only once every three years. This doesn't mean wages are fixed in nominal terms for a three-year period; what it means is that the pattern of nominal wage growth is predetermined and does not respond to changes in market conditions during the contract period. For example, a contract might call for annual increases of 4 percent in its second and third years, regardless of ensuing changes in economic conditions, including the inflation rate.

Some rigidities are actually introduced by government legislation or regulation. One important example is the legally mandated minimum wage. The government periodically adjusts the minimum wage with the intention of maintaining the income of minimum-wage workers at some reasonable standard of living. For example, President Clinton signed legislation in 1996 raising the U.S. federal minimum wage from $4.25 to $5.15 per hour.

CASE STUDY
U.S. MAGAZINE PRICES

In one study of price adjustment, economist Stephen Cecchetti examined the prices charged for a sample of 38 magazines over the period from 1953 to 1979 and found substantial price stickiness.[1] Considerable inflation in the general price level—enough to reduce the real magazine price (its price relative to the general price level) by as much as one-quarter—typically occurred between any two changes in the price of any particular magazine.

During the low-inflation period of 1953–1965, magazine prices changed on average only once every 7.5 years. As the annual inflation rate rose from 1965 through 1979, magazine price changes became more frequent, occurring once every 3.25 years. Still, these findings suggest that magazine producers respond to changes in their costs (as represented by the general price level) only after a considerable lag.

CASE STUDY
THE WAGE ADJUSTMENT PROCESS

In the real world, there is not a single wage rate but many wage rates, varying among workers according to their skills, education, experience, profession, and other qualifications. We might expect the average wage rate to rise at the rate of inflation, but there is no reason that all wages should rise at precisely this rate. After all, the demands for different types of workers change from year to year. For example, during a period of reductions in defense spending, the earnings of aircraft factory workers are likely to fall relative to those of other workers. If there is zero inflation, we'd expect to see some fraction of workers taking pay cuts. Even with a small, positive rate of

1 Stephen G. Cecchetti, "The Frequency of Price Adjustment: A Study of Newsstand Prices of Magazines, 1953–79," Journal of Econometrics 31 (April 1986): 255–274.

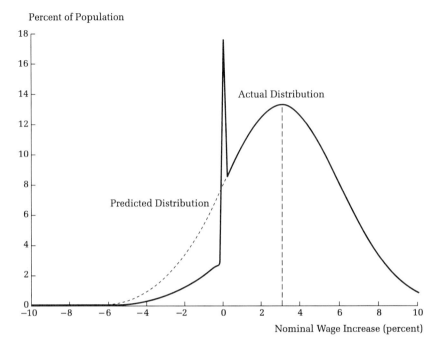

Percent of Population

FIGURE 8.1 DISTRIBUTION OF NOMINAL WAGE GROWTH

In a given year, we should expect to observe a distribution of nominal wage rate changes centered around an average value (here 3 percent). Actually, though, there are far fewer nominal wage reductions than this theory predicts, with many individuals (roughly 9.4 percent of all wage earners) receiving no change in wages instead of a nominal wage reduction. This is evidence that wage rate changes face downward rigidity at zero.

Source: Shulamit Kahn, ''Evidence of Nominal Wage Stickiness from Microdata'' (Boston University, 1995).

inflation, the changes in some wage rates should be negative. In reality, though, relatively few workers experience cuts in their nominal wages from one year to the next, although many receive a nominal wage increase of exactly zero; they are paid the same wage as the year before.

Boston University economist Shulamit Kahn plotted the distribution of wage rate changes among individuals with the same employer in successive years.[2] Absent wage rigidity, we should observe a symmetric distribution of nominal wage rate changes centered around the average increase. This corresponds to the dotted curve in Figure 8.1 (in which the average wage increase equals 3 percent). But Kahn found that there were far fewer wage declines than projected, with many workers for whom a negative wage change was projected piling up at a nominal wage change of zero. This provides evidence of *downward* rigidity in the wage adjustment process. Downward nominal rigidity means that a wage or price may not fall enough to increase the quantity (in this case, of labor) demanded and clear labor or product markets. For the typical year during the period studied, 1970 through 1988, Kahn found that approximately 9.4 percent of wage earners were affected by this rigidity, receiving a nominal wage

2 Shulamit Kahn, ''Evidence of Nominal Wage Stickiness from Microdata'' (Boston University, 1995).

change of zero instead of a nominal wage reduction. In contrast, she found very little nominal rigidity in the compensation of salaried employees.

PRICE RIGIDITY AND THE KEYNESIAN MODEL

These cases of commodity and input price rigidity are examples of *nominal rigidities* —stickiness in the level of a particular price. They may be contrasted with **real rigidities**—the stickiness of one price *relative* to another. For example, if the minimum wage were expressed in real rather than nominal terms—not as $5.15 per hour, but as 5.15 1998 dollars per hour—the rigidity would apply to the wage rate relative to the price level. Although we will discuss this distinction further in chapter 9, traditional Keynesian analysis has emphasized the role of nominal rigidities.

Moreover, because the Keynesian approach views recessions as manifestations of weak demand, the model focuses particularly on downward nominal rigidity, like that observed in the U.S. labor market. If market forces call for a rise in an employee's wage, this rigidity will have no impact. If conditions dictate a nominal wage reduction, though, some workers whose wages cannot be reduced may lose their jobs.

Analyzing the general impact of downward wage and price rigidities provides an important introduction to the Keynesian perspective, one on which we will build in subsequent chapters in comparing recent approaches to understanding business cycle fluctuations.

DEVELOPING THE KEYNESIAN APPROACH

Keynesians have traditionally traced recessions and their accompanying unemployment to incomplete short-run price or wage adjustment. In the longer run, they assume that prices and wages fully adjust to clear input and product markets. Hence, understanding the Keynesian approach requires us to focus on short-run behavior. In terms of the life-cycle model, this means concentrating on the immediate effects of wage and price rigidities in the current period while maintaining the assumption that such rigidities do not apply in subsequent periods as the economy's transition unfolds. Because most of our analysis refers to a single period, time subscripts will generally not be necessary. For simplicity, we will once again use the version of the life-cycle model in which only the older generation consumes. Our analysis begins with the case in which the price level is rigid. Complete price rigidity may be an extreme assumption, but studying this initial case will prove helpful when we turn to the case of nominal wage rigidity, in which output prices are flexible.

DERIVING THE IS-LM FRAMEWORK

The Keynesian model can be described with the same two relationships used in chapter 7 to trace the evolution of the monetary economy. The only difference here

Real rigidity
The stickiness or sluggish adjustment of one price relative to another, such as the nominal wage relative to the general price level

will be the assumption that prices do not freely adjust. The first key relationship is the price equation based on the equality of money supply and money demand.

Recall the model of money demand in which the young generation carries a certain fraction, γ, of its wages into old age in the form of money balances. The amount of money demanded by the younger generation equals γ times the wage rate, w, times the number of young people, N. Setting this total demand for money equal to the real money supply, M/P, and solving for P yields the expression for the price level, $P = M/\gamma Nw$. We can use this expression to relate the price level to output by using the fact that the wage, w, equals labor's share of income, $(1 - \beta)$, times output per young person, y:

$$P = \frac{M}{\gamma N(1 - \beta)y}.$$

The second fundamental equation from chapter 7 is the transition equation for the economy's capital-labor ratio. We write it here as a relationship between the next period's capital-labor ratio, k_{+1}, and the current period's output per worker, y, simply by using the production function to replace Ak^β by y:

$k_{+1} = (1 - \gamma)(1 - \beta)y - f.$

As before, f is the sum of government debt purchases and net tax payments per young person.

Let's recall how we used these two equations in chapter 7 to trace out the evolution of output, capital, and the price level over time. Starting with the current period's capital-labor ratio, k, we determine the current period's output per young person, y, based on the Cobb-Douglas production function, $y = Ak^\beta$. Inserting this value of output in the price level equation gives a solution for the current period's price level, P. Substituting the solution for y into the transition equation gives us next period's capital-labor ratio, k_{+1}, which then forms the basis for solving for next period's output and price level in the same way.

Now suppose the price level is downwardly rigid and that the value of the price level obtained in this manner is below the minimum price level, say $\bar{P}$, that can exist in the current period. Then, our solution for P is infeasible. But if we substitute the lowest feasible price level $\bar{P}$ on the left-hand side of the price level equation, something on the right-hand side of the equation must also change in order for the equality to be preserved—that is, for the real quantities of money demanded and supplied to remain equal. As we'll see shortly, it is output that falls below the level achieved with flexible prices, raising the right-hand side of the equation to the point that it equals the left-hand side.

To analyze how price rigidity (and later, wage rigidity) affects output, it's useful to rewrite the two key equations in terms of the level of output, Y, rather than output per worker, y. This avoids any ambiguity that might be caused by the fact that, with unemployment, the number of workers and the number of young persons need not be the same. Also, because it is now the level of output, rather than the price level, that we need to determine, we divide the equation based on the equality of money demand and supply by the fixed price level, $\bar{P}$, and multiply by Y to express the equation in terms of output rather than the price level. The resulting equation, commonly called the **LM curve**, is[3]

$$Y = \frac{M}{\gamma[r_{+1}](1 - \beta)\bar{P}}.$$

Note that we have written this expression to indicate explicitly that the share of wages allocated to money balances, γ, depends on the next period's real interest rate, r_{+1}. Although much of chapter 7 focused on the special case in which γ is fixed, we also indicated there that this share normally declines as the opportunity cost of holding money (rather than capital)—the nominal interest rate in the next period, i_{+1}—rises. For simplicity, we will assume in this chapter that the expected inflation rate is zero, so that the nominal interest rate i_{+1} equals the real interest rate r_{+1}.

The second fundamental equation is based on the transition equation. Because we'll be interested in the impact of policy on the interest rate as well as on output, we combine the transition equation with the expression relating next period's real interest rate to the capital-labor ratio, $r_{+1} = A\beta k_{+1}^{\beta-1}$. This gives us an equation relating the next period's interest rate to current output, called the **IS curve**,[4] which we write for convenience as an expression for current output, Y, in terms of the next period's interest rate, r_{+1}:

$$Y = \frac{F + \phi[r_{+1}]}{(1 - \beta)(1 - \gamma[r_{+1}])},$$

where F equals total government receipts and ϕ is a term that declines as r_{+1} increases.[5]

Let's take a close look at the LM and IS equations. The LM curve is simply a relationship between the level of output, Y, and next period's interest rate, r_{+1}. Why? Because the parameter β is a fixed number, the nominal money supply is set at M, and the price level is rigid at $\bar{P}$. The IS curve is also a relationship between Y and r_{+1}. Why? Because in the IS equation, β is a fixed parameter. So long as the government fiscal policy maintains F at a given level, the IS curve simply relates Y and r_{+1}.

Since the LM and IS equations represent two equations in two unknowns, we can solve them to determine the current level of output, Y, and the next period's interest rate, r_{+1}. We can also see the channels through which monetary and fiscal policy may be used to influence the values of Y and r_{+1}, to help overcome the impact of the price rigidity on output. Changes in the nominal money supply M alter the LM curve, whereas changes in fiscal policy—as represented by government absorption of resources from the young, F—alter the IS curve.

Let's look at each of these curves separately before combining them to determine output and the interest rate.

LM curve
A curve showing all combinations of current output and next period's interest rate at which the quantity of money demanded equals the money supply

IS curve
A curve showing all combinations of current output and next period's interest rate consistent with the economy's transition equation, given a fixed value of the fiscal variable, F

3 To remember what this curve represents, note that the L and M stand for liquidity preference (money demand) and money supply.

4 The I and S stand for the investment and saving the young do.

5 Its exact form is $\phi = N(\beta A)^{1/(1-\beta)} r_{+1}^{-1/(1-\beta)}$. This expression for the IS curve is derived in the following manner. First, we substitute the expression for k_{+1} in terms of y (from the transition equation) into the expression for r_{+1} in terms of k_{+1}, to obtain an expression relating r_{+1} to y; then, in this expression, we substitute Y/N for y and F/N for f; finally, we solve the resulting expression for Y in terms of r_{+1}.

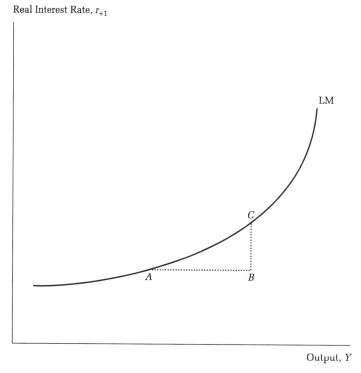

FIGURE 8.2 LM CURVE
The LM curve plots combinations of income, Y, and the interest rate, r_{+1}, at which money supply equals money demand, given a fixed price level, $\bar{P}$. The curve slopes upward because a higher level of income increases the quantity of money demanded. To reestablish equality with the fixed money supply, there must be an increase in the interest rate, which causes an offsetting decrease in the quantity of money demanded.

LM CURVE

The LM curve plots combinations of income, Y, and the real interest rate, r_{+1}, at which money supply equals money demand, given a fixed price level, $\bar{P}$. According to the expression for the LM curve, a higher interest rate, and hence a lower value of γ, implies a higher level of output, Y. Figure 8.2 graphs the LM curve.

The logic behind the positive slope of the LM curve is straightforward and relates to the fact that the quantity of money demanded increases with income but falls with the interest rate. Suppose we were at a particular point on the curve, such as A, with the money market in equilibrium. An increase in income would disturb that equilibrium by raising the quantity of money demanded above the fixed real money supply $M/\bar{P}$ (at point B). In order to reduce money demand and reestablish equilibrium, γ (the share of income devoted to holding money) must fall, and this requires a rise in the interest rate (at point C).

The position of the LM curve depends on the value the government chooses for the nominal money stock, M. As we'll see, monetary policy operates by shifting the LM curve.

Real Interest Rate, r_{+1}

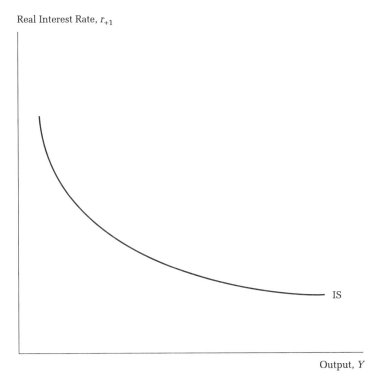

Output, Y

FIGURE 8.3 IS CURVE
The IS curve plots combinations of output, Y, and the real interest rate, r_{+1}, that satisfy the economy's transition equation. The curve slopes downward because a higher rate of current output means higher income for each young person. The higher the income of the young, the more capital they purchase and bring into the next period. The more capital they accumulate, the lower the return to capital needed to get firms to demand the capital being supplied. So the higher the output this period, the lower the interest rate next period.

IS CURVE

The IS curve represents an inverse relationship between the current level of output and the next period's interest rate. Because ϕ and γ each falls as r_{+1} rises, an increase in r_{+1} lowers the numerator and raises the denominator of the expression for Y, with both of these effects lowering the resulting value of Y. This relationship is depicted by the curve shown in Figure 8.3. Why should higher current output require a lower interest rate in the next period? Here's the logic. The more output produced in this period, the more income each young person will earn. The higher the income of the young, the more capital they purchase and bring into the next period. The more capital is accumulated, the higher the next period's capital-labor ratio will be and the lower the return to capital—the real interest rate—that will be needed to get firms to demand all the capital being supplied. Thus, the higher the output this period, the lower the interest rate next period.

Note that the position of the IS curve depends on the level of F, the resources the government takes from each young person. We consider the impact of a change in F below, when discussing fiscal policy.

OUTPUT DETERMINATION WITH RIGID PRICES

The IS curve indicates the combinations of the current period's income and the next period's interest rate that are consistent with the transition equation. The LM curve tells us the combinations of the current period's income and the next period's interest rate at which money supply equals money demand. We use these two curves to solve for Y and r_{+1}. The solution is given by their point of intersection, such as point A in Figure 8.4, where income is Y^0 and the interest rate is r^0. Point A lies on the LM curve, so the quantity of money demanded based on interest rate r^0 and income Y^0 equals the quantity of money supplied, $M/\bar{P}$. Because point A also lies on the IS curve, the same interest rate and level of income, r^0 and Y^0, are consistent with the transition equation relating current income and next period's capital stock and interest rate.

When the price level is "too high" (above the one that would prevail under flexible prices), the level of output is "too low." In Figure 8.4, this situation is represented by the fact that Y^0 lies below the value of output determined by the Cobb-Douglas production function with the full utilization of labor and capital, labeled Y^f. We refer to this higher level of output as the economy's **potential** or **full employment output** level.

Is there a price level for which the IS-LM solution for output equals Y^f? There is. Note that the position of the LM curve depends on the price level. Suppose the price level were fixed at a value lower than $\bar{P}$. This would mean a larger real stock of money. For any given interest rate, the equation for the LM curve indicates that income would be higher. As a result, the LM curve would lie to the right of the original one. Since the position of the LM curve depends on the price level, we can imagine lower and lower values of the price level shifting the LM curve out until, at a price level $\hat{P}$, the IS curve and the LM curve labeled LM' in Figure 8.4 intersect at Y^f, with an interest rate r^1. This solution is simply the one we would have obtained had prices been flexible.[6] In other words, we can reinterpret our previous flexible price analysis in terms of the IS-LM framework. The gap between Y^0 and Y^f results from downward price rigidity.

AGGREGATE DEMAND AND UNEMPLOYMENT

To see why the output level at which IS and LM intersect lies below the full-employment level Y^f, let's consider what would happen if firms did produce Y^f. In particular, let's ask whether all of this output would be purchased by households and the government.

Purchases by households equal investment by the young plus consumption by the old. The young invest all of their income, except for that which they pay to the

---

Potential (full employment) output

The economy's level of output when all available inputs are fully employed

---

6 If—contrary to our assumption—$\hat{P}$ actually exceeded $\bar{P}$, then the downward price rigidity would not be binding. That is, the price level $\hat{P}$ would be feasible, and at this price level the level of output Y^f would be produced. In this case, the LM curve drawn for $P = \bar{P}$ would intersect the IS curve to the right of Y^f at an infeasible level of output. The highest level of output possible would be Y^f, which would be sustained by the price level $\hat{P}$.

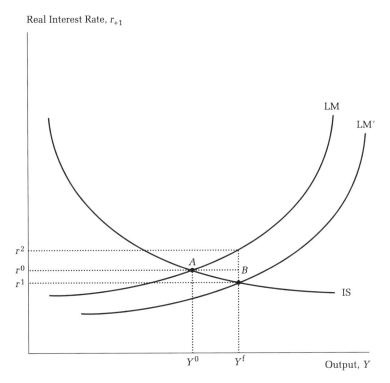

Real Interest Rate, r_{+1}

Output, Y

FIGURE 8.4 EQUILIBRIUM WITH RIGID PRICES
The IS and LM curves represent two relationships between current income and next period's interest rate. The point where the two curves intersect represents the unique combination of Y and r_{+1} that satisfies both relationships. At such an intersection, the money market is in equilibrium (since the point lies on the LM curve) and the transition equation is satisfied (since it lies on the IS curve). Notice that the level of output determined at this intersection (e.g., Y^0) lies below the full employment level (Y^f). Because the rigid price level is "too high," the level of output is "too low." If the price level could fall, the LM curve could shift right to intersect the IS curve at full employment output.

government or choose to hold as money balances (that is, $(1 - \gamma)(1 - \beta)Y^f - F$). In addition to consuming their capital holdings, the old consume all of their income, except that which they pay to the government, plus all of the proceeds from disposing of their money balances. Because their net payments to the government equal what the government purchases, G, minus what the government takes in from the young, F, the old must pay $G - F$ to the government. Thus, their consumption equals $K + \beta Y^f + M/\bar{P} - (G - F)$. Since the old already own the capital stock K, their purchases of output are reflected in the last three terms of this expression. Adding together capital purchases by the young, consumption purchases by the old, and government purchases, G, we see that total purchases would equal $Y^f + M/\bar{P} - \gamma(1 - \beta)Y^f$.

But note that the last two terms in this expression equal the supply of money less the quantity of money demanded by the young *at the full employment level of output.* Hence, total purchases will equal Y^f if and only if the demand for and supply of money are equal (that is, if the difference between the last two terms equals zero) at this level of output. But we know $\bar{P}$ is too high for this to happen. As we see from Figure 8.4, the interest rate determined by the IS curve at Y^f—r^1—lies below that on the LM curve—r^2. Thus, if the interest rate is consistent with the amount of capital being accumulated (that is, if it lies on the IS curve), the demand for money exceeds its supply. This excess demand for money translates into an excess supply of output: purchases will fall short of full employment production by the extent to which money demand exceeds money supply. Macroeconomists refer to this situation as a lack of *aggregate demand* for output, because total purchases fall short of the level of output at Y^f.

Normally we would expect producers who are unable to sell all their output to cut their prices. Indeed, a sufficient reduction in the price level would raise the level of real money balances and increase purchases enough to sustain the full employment level of output. But with rigid prices, this can't occur. Being unable to sell all they can produce, firms have little choice but to reduce production to the equilibrium level Y^0.[7]

If firms produce output below their capacity—Y^0 rather than Y^f—they will require fewer workers to produce this output. How many workers will they hire? It is not entirely evident, since as output declines, there is not only excess labor but also excess capital available. Perhaps the most straightforward assumption is that firms maintain the same ratio of capital to labor, reducing both employment and the utilization of capital at the same rate.[8] If the number of workers needed to produce the level of output Y^0 equals L^0, then we refer to those $N - L^0$ workers without jobs as experiencing *involuntary* (or *Keynesian*) *unemployment*. They would be willing to work at the going wage (and, indeed, at any wage, since labor supply is assumed to be independent of the wage) but are unable to do so. We will discuss the distinction between this and other types of unemployment later, when we consider the case of wage rigidity.

INFLUENCING OUTPUT: THE ROLE OF MONETARY AND FISCAL POLICY

In the Keynesian model, downward price rigidity may cause output to lie below its full employment level. How can monetary and fiscal policy be used to address this problem? We'll consider each in turn.

MONETARY POLICY

The logic behind monetary policy is straightforward. The lack of aggregate demand comes from too high a price level, making the real money stock, and thus the consumption purchases of the old, too low to sustain the full employment level of output. But the real money stock equals the ratio of the nominal money stock to the price level. Even if the price level cannot fall, the real money stock can still be raised (and with it, aggregate demand) through an increase in the nominal money stock.

7 How did the price level get too high in the first place? As one example, take a price level that was consistent with full employment when initially established but became too high after a leftward shift in the IS or LM curve and hence in their point of intersection.

8 Recall from chapter 4 that during recessions, capacity utilization falls along with employment.

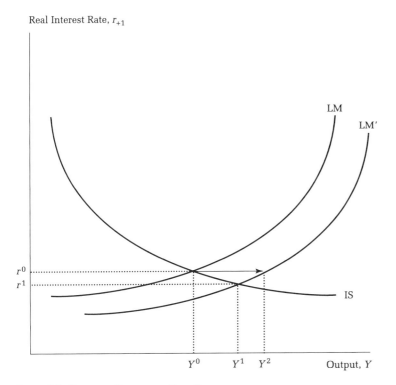

Real Interest Rate, r_{+1}

FIGURE 8.5 MONETARY POLICY WITH RIGID PRICES
When the price level is downwardly rigid, changes in the nominal money supply are not neutral. An increase in the money supply shifts the LM curve to the right, leading to an increase in income from Y^0 to Y^1 and a reduction in the interest rate from r^0 to r^1. The initial increase in M raises consumption by the old, which initiates a chain of further increases in output, consumption, and investment.

How can this be done? As we saw in chapter 7, the government may increase the nominal money supply in several ways. Perhaps the simplest way is to make transfers to the old in proportion to the money they already hold. This policy is neutral in the absence of Keynesian rigidities; as we found in chapter 7, doubling the money supply would lead to an immediate doubling of the price level, with no change in consumption by the old or saving by the young.

But in the present context, this same change will not be neutral. It will increase output and employment by shifting the LM curve to the right. For example, suppose the nominal money supply is increased by ΔM, from M to $M + \Delta M$. From the expression for the LM curve, we can see that the new value of Y corresponding to any particular value of r_{+1} will be higher, as depicted by the rightward shift from LM to LM' in Figure 8.5. This makes sense, because the higher real stock of money can meet the increase in money demand that occurs as income rises. The figure also indicates that the new LM curve intersects the IS curve at a higher level of output, Y^1, and a lower interest rate, r^1, than at the original equilibrium (Y^0, r^0).

To see why equilibrium output increases, let's consider what happens when the old receive a transfer from the government in the form of newly printed money. The old wish to consume all the resources at their disposal. With the additional money and the same price level, they will have more purchasing power and seek to consume more. In a full employment situation, as we have already learned, their attempt to increase consumption would simply lead to an increase in the price level, fully offsetting their initial increase in purchasing power. However, with the price level fixed at $\bar{P}$, the economy has unemployed resources, and firms can increase output. Initially, consumption and output will rise by the full increase in the real money stock given to the elderly, $\Delta M / \bar{P}$.

As time passes, output will increase by even more than this initial increase in the real money stock. The first-stage increase in output of $\Delta M / \bar{P}$ raises the income of both the young (through higher employment) and the old (more of whose capital comes into use). The increased income of the old raises their consumption and output still further. The increased income of the young raises their acquisition of real assets, which increases investment and output. In turn, these increases in output contribute to additional increases in the income of the old and the young, and more output increases in the form of consumption and investment. This chain of increases in output that multiplies the initial impact of policy is referred to as a *multiplier* process. How much will output ultimately increase? If the interest rate did not fall, output would increase by $\Delta M / \gamma(1 - \beta)\bar{P}$—the distance of the rightward shift in the LM curve[9]—to Y^2. In this case, the **multiplier** of a change in the money stock—the dollar change in output for each dollar change in the real money supply M/P—would be $1/\gamma(1 - \beta)$. Because both γ and $(1 - \beta)$ are less than 1, this multiplier exceeds one.[10]

As output and investment increase, so does the capital stock in the following period. This is reflected by the negative slope of the IS curve. As output increases, the interest rate facing the young must fall. They respond by shifting more of their wages into money and less into the purchase of output for investment. This moderation of the increase in demand for investment goods means a smaller increase in aggregate demand and thus output. As a result of the interest sensitivity of money demand, output increases from Y^0 only to Y^1, rather than Y^2.

FISCAL POLICY

As we've seen, monetary policy overcomes the lack of aggregate demand resulting from a shortage of real money balances. It does so by increasing the nominal and thus real money balances of the elderly, leading them to increase their consumption purchases. Fiscal policy attacks the problem from a different direction, accomplishing a net increase in output by driving up the interest rate and encouraging the young to demand less money and more capital.

To see this, let's consider the impact of an increase in government purchases paid for with payments from the young through taxes or bond purchases—through an increase in F, say ΔF, that equals the increase in government purchases, ΔG. The increase in government purchases directly raises aggregate demand by ΔG. Taking ΔF

Multiplier
The ratio of a change in output to the change in the policy variable that causes it

9 We can verify that the curve shifts by this amount by solving the LM curve expression for Y, given r, when the money supply equals M and M + ΔM, respectively.

10 We can see this increase in output as the sum of output increases arising from an infinite sequence of rounds. In the first round, the consumption spending of the old increases output by ΔM/P̄. In the second round, given the constant income shares of labor and capital, the income of the young increases by their share of the extra output, (1 − β)ΔM/P̄, and their extra spending on investment (rather than on additional money balances) equals (1 − γ)(1 − β)ΔM/P̄. The income of the old in the second round increases by βΔM/P̄, all of which they consume. Hence, additional purchases for investment and consumption in the second round lead to more total output of (1 − γ)(1 − β)ΔM/P̄ + βΔM/P̄, or [1 − (1 − γ)β]ΔM/P̄. Following this pattern, we'll find the additional increase in output to be [1 − (1 − γ)β]²ΔM/P̄ in the third round, and so on, for a total increase of ΔM/γ(1 − β)P̄.

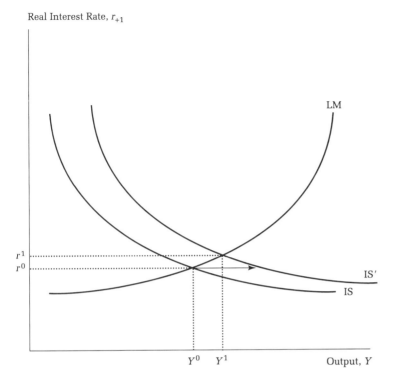

FIGURE 8.6 FISCAL POLICY WITH RIGID PRICES
An increase in F, the resources the government takes from the young, leads to a rightward shift of the IS curve, resulting in higher output and a higher interest rate. By absorbing more of young people's income, the government leaves less that can be used to purchase capital for production in the next period. That raises the interest rate, reducing the demand for money. To reestablish equilibrium, income must rise so that the quantity of money demanded once again equals the fixed money supply.

away from the young reduces their aggregate demand, namely, for investment goods. As we'll see, though, the increase in aggregate demand by the government exceeds the reduction in aggregate demand by the young. Let's begin by considering how the IS curve is affected by fiscal policy.

Fiscal policy influences the position of the IS curve through the term F on the right-hand side of the expression relating Y to r_{+1}. As the expression indicates, an increase in F increases the value of Y associated with any given value of r_{+1}—representing a rightward shift in the IS curve. The logic is that by absorbing more of the income of the young, the government leaves less that can be used to purchase new capital for production in the next period; the less capital, the higher the interest rate. Put another way, to obtain the same level of capital, and the same interest rate, a higher level of income is necessary. This rightward shift of the IS curve is shown in Figure 8.6. The formula for the IS curve indicates that if F increases by ΔF, then the IS curve shifts to the right by the distance $\Delta F/(1 - \beta)(1 - \gamma)$.

Figure 8.6 also indicates that, given the position of the LM curve, such a shift in the IS curve causes equilibrium output to increase to Y^1 and the interest rate to increase to r^1. Why does output rise? The key is the increase in the interest rate, because it reduces the amount of money demanded by the young. Without a reduction in the quantity of money demanded, the increase in F (with the proceeds spent on government purchases) could not in itself induce a change in output or employment. Suppose that the quantity of money demanded did not change. Then, as a result of the increase in government purchases paid for by the young, the younger generation would have to reduce its own purchases of capital by the same amount—also ΔG—given to the government. Thus, there would be no increase in aggregate demand and output; the increase in government purchases would come entirely from funds that otherwise would have been used for private investment. This displacement process, known as *crowding out*, would be complete.

However, with the demand for money sensitive to the interest rate, this initial crowding out of investment leads to less capital accumulation and, hence, a higher interest rate, which in turn induces a reduction in money demand, leaving the young with more funds to invest in capital. Though investment still declines, there is incomplete crowding out, and output increases. In other words, the government's increase in spending is less than fully offset by the decline in spending by the young. As in the case of monetary policy, this initial increase in output will lead to further increases, as the increased incomes of young and old lead to additional increases in investment and consumption, until the new equilibrium output level, Y^1, is reached.[11] Indeed, were there no crowding out (that is, if the LM curve were horizontal and the interest rate did not rise), this process of successive increases in output would lead to a total increase in output (equal to the rightward shift in the IS curve) of $\Delta G/ (1 - \gamma)(1 - \beta)$, with a multiplier once again greater than 1.

Although the interest sensitivity of money demand works against monetary policy, it makes fiscal policy effective. Fiscal policy works because, as it drives up the interest rate and crowds out investment, the quantity of money demanded also falls. This means that investment purchases by the young fall by less than government spending increases—that is, total aggregate demand and, therefore, output increases.

11 Even though there is additional investment, it never fully reaches its original level. If it did, next period's interest rate would not rise.

12 Although Table 8.1 focuses on macroeconomic differences in the short run, there are long-run differences as well. In particular, an expansionary fiscal policy that reduces investment will reduce the nation's future productive capacity, and hence its future output. An expansionary monetary policy that increases investment will have the opposite impact in the future, increasing productive capacity.

Measuring Policy Effectiveness

Table 8.1 summarizes the impact of monetary and fiscal policy on important macroeconomic variables. Although the two policies have similar effects on employment, output, and consumption, they have different effects on investment and the interest rate.[12]

In our model, a key to the relative effectiveness of monetary and fiscal policy is the degree to which the demand for money is sensitive to the interest rate. As we noted above, expansionary monetary policy is hindered by the interest sensitivity of money demand, whereas expansionary fiscal policy depends on the interest sensitivity of money demand in order for crowding out not to be complete. We should expect that as

TABLE 8.1 IMPACT OF MONETARY AND FISCAL POLICY WITH RIGID PRICES: A SUMMARY

Variable	Monetary Policy (increase in M)	Fiscal Policy (increase in F)
Output (Y)	Increases	Increases
Employment (L)	Increases	Increases
Consumption (C)	Increases	Increases
Investment (I)	Increases	Decreases
Interest rate, next period (r_{+1})	Decreases	Increases

the demand for money becomes more interest sensitive, monetary policy becomes less effective at increasing output, and fiscal policy more effective.

The degree to which the demand for money is sensitive to the interest rate is an empirical question, about which there is considerable debate. The belief that the demand for money is relatively insensitive to the interest rate is an important component of a school of thought known as **monetarism**. Monetarists believe that changes in the money supply play a central role in determining output.

NATIONAL SAVING AND THE PARADOX OF THRIFT

Earlier chapters showed how changes in national saving can affect the future level of output by changing current investment and capital accumulation. In the IS-LM model, changes in saving may also influence the current level of output. In particular, a decline in saving may raise current output.

Expansionary fiscal policy provides one example. The rightward shift in the IS curve (in Figure 8.6) is caused by the government's taking resources from savers—the young—and consuming those resources (spending them on government consumption). In this policy the initial decline in national saving (at the level of output Y^0) equals ΔF, the amount taken from the saving of the young and used to increase current government consumption. Ultimately, as output is raised, saving and investment by the young rebound so that the net decline in national saving is smaller than the initial one. Still, the policy ends up reducing national saving as it stimulates output.

Just as a reduction in national saving can increase current output, an increase in national saving can reduce current output. This increase in saving could result from a reversal of the fiscal policy just considered or from a change in private saving behavior. In this chapter, we have considered a simplified model of household behavior in which individuals do not consume when young. But in our more general model, a decline in the share of resources consumed by the young, α, would have the same

Monetarism
A school of thought that emphasizes the effect of changes in the money supply on economic activity

impact on the IS curve as a reduction in F, causing the curve to shift to the left. At any given level of income it would lead to more saving and investment and, hence, to a higher capital stock in the next period and a lower interest rate. However, with inflexible prices, this shift also lowers aggregate demand and causes an immediate decline in current output. Indeed, as discussed in chapter 11, economists view an increase in the propensity to save as a possible explanation for the onset of the Great Depression of the 1930s.

As current output declines, the initial increase in saving is partially offset by the reduction in saving and investment by the young caused by the decline in their income. Hence, saving increases by less—perhaps far less—than the initial rise in saving. Thus, in the Keynesian model, an initial attempt to increase saving may not increase saving by very much, whereas it may at the same time reduce current output, perhaps by a lot. This phenomenon—attempts to increase saving not succeeding very well—was described by Keynes as the **paradox of thrift**.

Paradox of thrift
Attempts to increase saving may not succeed very well because the initial increase in saving reduces income, which makes the ultimate rise in saving smaller than the initial increase

Case Study
Financing Social Security

In the period during and immediately after the Great Depression, Keynesian unemployment was a highly significant concern. Many policymakers advocated financing the new U.S. Social Security system on a pay-as-you-go basis, under which the payroll taxes of workers are paid immediately to contemporaneous elderly as benefit payments. Others wanted to fund the system by investing workers' payroll taxes in a trust fund that would earn interest and be used to pay the workers' own benefits when they retired.

Compared with the pay-as-you-go option, funding Social Security means greater national saving.[13] But in a Keynesian context, it also means a downward shift in the IS curve and a reduction in current output and employment. In an economy emerging from the Great Depression, the concern about current economic conditions led the majority of policymakers to opt for the pay-as-you-go method of financing Social Security, a financing mechanism that has now lasted for six decades.

NOMINAL WAGE RIGIDITY

We now turn from price rigidity to nominal wage rigidity. With the nominal wage fixed, variations in the price level can cause the real wage to change and, with it, the level of labor demand by firms and, potentially, the levels of employment and output.

With one adjustment, we can also apply the IS-LM analysis to the case of rigid nominal wages. This adjustment involves the fact that now, as output changes, the price level changes as well. Because the LM curve depends on the price level, we must keep track of additional shifts in this curve caused by price level changes. We'll begin with a look at the labor market, to see how output and the price level are related when the nominal wage is fixed.

NOMINAL WAGE RIGIDITY AND UNEMPLOYMENT

Recall chapter 3's analysis of how wages and employment are determined. At any given time, competitive firms demand labor up to the point where the marginal product of labor equals the real wage. The labor demand schedule is labeled D in Figure 8.7, which graphs labor, L, against the real wage, w.[14] The real wage itself equals the nominal wage, W, divided by the price level, P. In our basic model, labor supply is fixed (it doesn't depend on the real wage), so the labor supply schedule S in Figure 8.7 is simply a vertical line at $L = N$. Combining these two curves yields the familiar determination of employment at N and a real wage rate of w^e.

As long as the real wage is w^e, there will be no unemployment. But suppose the real wage is higher. For example, suppose labor market rigidity prevents the nominal wage from falling below a certain value, say $\overline{W}$. Then, since the real wage equals the nominal wage divided by the price level, the smallest real wage that can be paid when the price level is P is $\overline{W}/P$. Stated differently, this constraint will not allow a real wage as low as w^e unless the price level is at least as high as $\hat{P} = \overline{W}/w^e$.

Figure 8.7 shows the impact of nominal wage rigidity on employment. If the price level is P^0 (lower than $\hat{P}$) and the nominal wage is fixed at $\overline{W}$, then the prevailing

13 As we saw in chapter 6, when government uses its revenue to purchase capital rather than goods and services for current consumption, this capital is added to that acquired by the private sector to determine the economy's overall level of capital.

14 We saw this curve in a somewhat different form in Figure 3.2, which plotted the real wage offered by firms versus the capital-labor ratio, k. Since the capital stock is given in the current period, increases in k are associated with decreases in employment. Hence, the positive relationship between w and k shown in the earlier figure translates into the negative relationship between w and employment shown here.

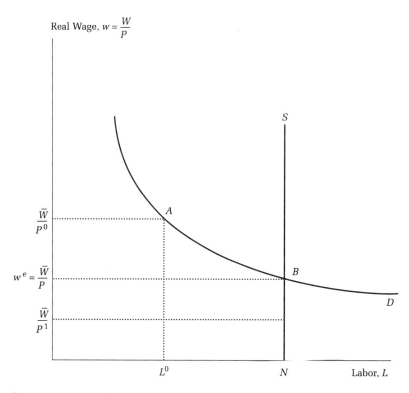

Real Wage, $w = \dfrac{W}{P}$

FIGURE 8.7 NOMINAL WAGE RIGIDITY AND UNEMPLOYMENT

In the absence of wage rigidities, the real wage is determined by the interaction of labor supply (S) and demand (D); N employees are hired at a real wage of w^e. However, if the nominal wage cannot fall below $\overline{W}$, unemployment may result. Unless the price level is at least as high as $\hat{P} = \overline{W}/w^e$, the real wage will be above w^e and employment will be determined along the labor demand schedule. For example, at price level P^0 ($<\hat{P}$), the real wage is above w^e and firms find it profitable to hire only L^0 workers. Unless the price level rises and drives down the real wage, $N - L^0$ workers will suffer involuntary unemployment.

Involuntary unemployment
A situation in which an individual is unable to find work at the going wage

15 How does this labor market outcome compare to the outcome in the case of rigid prices? When downward price rigidity causes output to lie below Y^f, say at the level of output that requires L^0 workers, firms simply will not hire additional workers at any wage. Their labor demand curve ceases to apply; they no longer base hiring decisions on a comparison of the marginal product of labor (indicated by the height of their labor demand curve) and the real wage, because they cannot sell the extra output that additional labor would produce.

real wage, $\overline{W}/P^0$, is above w^e. At this higher real wage, firms find it profitable to hire fewer workers—L^0 instead of N. With the supply of workers exceeding the demand, all demand is satisfied and the remaining excess supply of labor goes unused. Firms are still hiring workers to the point where the marginal product of labor equals the real wage—at point A in the figure—but the labor market does not clear.[15]

The surplus workers, numbering $N - L^0$, suffer from **involuntary unemployment**: they are willing to work at the going wage but can't find work. Involuntary unemployment is a very specific concept. It applies only to those who are willing to work at the wage rate actually being paid to others with comparable skills. It does not apply, for example, to the low-skilled individual who is willing to work only for a high wage rate, nor does it apply to the worker in a declining industry who chooses not to work when the industry's lower marginal product of labor dictates a reduced wage rate. Each of these workers wishes to be employed *under certain circumstances*, but not at a wage rate currently being paid to others with comparable skills. If workers can find work at wage rates being paid to others with comparable skills but choose not to accept such jobs, they are said to experience **voluntary unemployment**.

The distinction between voluntary and involuntary unemployment relates not to the welfare of the unemployed—voluntarily unemployed workers needn't be particularly happy being unemployed—but to the reasons for their unemployment and, ultimately, to the question of how government should react. As we will see in chapter 10, the social costs of recession are higher, and the case for government intervention more compelling, if unemployment is involuntary.

Let's return to Figure 8.7. If the price level were high enough, say at P^1, the corresponding real wage compatible with the downwardly rigid nominal wage, $\overline{W}/P^1$, would be below w^e. At this low real wage, labor demand would exceed labor supply. The scarcity of labor would cause the nominal wage to rise to the level $w^e P^1$, at which point the real wage would equal its market-clearing value, w^e, and employment would equal N, as shown at point B in the figure. The nominal wage constraint would have no impact, since it prevents the nominal wage from falling below $\overline{W}$ but not from rising above it, and there would be no unemployment.

AGGREGATE SUPPLY CURVE

We can summarize this impact of wage rigidity on output by graphing the various combinations of output and the price level that are compatible with the nominal wage constraint $\overline{W}$. The resulting curve, shown in Figure 8.8, is called the economy's **aggregate supply curve**. By analogy to the supply curve of an individual market, it indicates the level of output that the production sector of the economy as whole will supply at each particular price level. The points A and B in Figure 8.8 correspond to the points with the same labels in Figure 8.7. As shown, the aggregate supply curve is vertical above the price level $\hat{P}$, because above that level—at point B, for example—the wage rigidity is not binding and the economy produces its full employment level of output Y^f. Absent wage rigidity, the aggregate supply curve would simply be a vertical line at Y^f, because any price level would be compatible with full employment and a market-clearing real wage.

How is this curve affected by the level of a rigid nominal wage? For a higher fixed nominal wage, any given price level will translate into a higher real wage as well. In this case, the critical price level above which there is no involuntary unemployment rises; each price level below this critical level will now be associated with a lower level of employment and output and a higher level of unemployment, as indicated in Figure 8.8 by the curve AS'.

MONETARY AND FISCAL POLICY IN THE RIGID NOMINAL-WAGE REGIME

In contrast to the case of price rigidity, under nominal wage rigidity, expansionary monetary and fiscal policy will increase the price level as well as output. The effect will be to dampen the expansionary effects of both types of policies.

Voluntary unemployment
A situation in which an individual chooses not to accept work at a wage rate being paid to others with comparable skills

Aggregate supply curve
A curve representing all possible combinations of the price level and the level of output that are consistent with labor market equilibrium

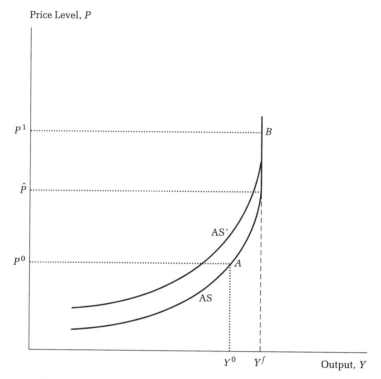

FIGURE 8.8 AGGREGATE SUPPLY CURVE
The aggregate supply curve shows various combinations of the price level and output that are consistent with a particular nominal wage rigidity. The curve AS indicates that for any price level below $\hat{P}$, output will fall below its full employment level Y^f as a result of a binding nominal wage. An increase in the rigid nominal wage shifts the aggregate supply curve up, from AS to AS'.

To understand why the price level increases, consider a particular expansionary policy: a transfer of money to the elderly. As before, a money supply increase raises the elderly's purchasing power and increases their demand for goods and services. Now, though, as they begin spending their money, the excess demand will lead producers to increase their prices (since only the nominal wage is rigid). As prices rise, suppliers' real labor costs decline, allowing them to hire more workers to meet the extra demand. (In the fixed-price regime, no such price increase was needed, since excessively high nominal wages weren't the source of the problem.) Although output increases, it increases by less than in the case of fixed prices, because the initial increase in consumption, equal to the rise in the real money stock M/P, is reduced in magnitude by the rise in P.

It is clear, then, that the impact of an increase in the money supply, although still positive, will be smaller than in the case of rigid prices, since some of the stimulus will be absorbed by increases in the price level. The same intuition suggests that fiscal

*"I may have something rather outside your field.
Would you consider indentured servitude?"*

policy will be weakened too. An increase in output due to a fiscal stimulus will also raise the price level, for the same reason that a money-induced output expansion does. This will lower the real money stock and have the same impact on output as a direct reduction in the money supply.

The effects of these differences on monetary and fiscal policy multipliers are shown in Figures 8.9 and 8.10, respectively. Figure 8.9 compares the effect of a money supply increase in the rigid price and rigid wage regimes. In the former case, the LM curve shifts to LM'. In the latter, the LM curve initially shifts to LM', but the induced price rise then reduces the real money stock and causes the curve to shift back to LM''. The smaller net shift in the LM curve means a smaller rise in output and a smaller fall in the interest rate.

With fiscal policy, an increase in F causes IS to shift to IS', as illustrated in Figure 8.10. As we've seen, with rigid prices, that is the end of the story. However, in the rigid wage case, the price-induced shift in the LM curve to LM' makes fiscal policy less effective at increasing output, as the interest rate increases by more than when the price level is rigid.

Thus, by permitting some price increase in response to expansionary monetary or fiscal policy, nominal wage rigidity represents a middle ground between the price rigidity case and the full employment case, in which real output cannot increase at all in the short run and price increases absorb the full impact of policy changes.

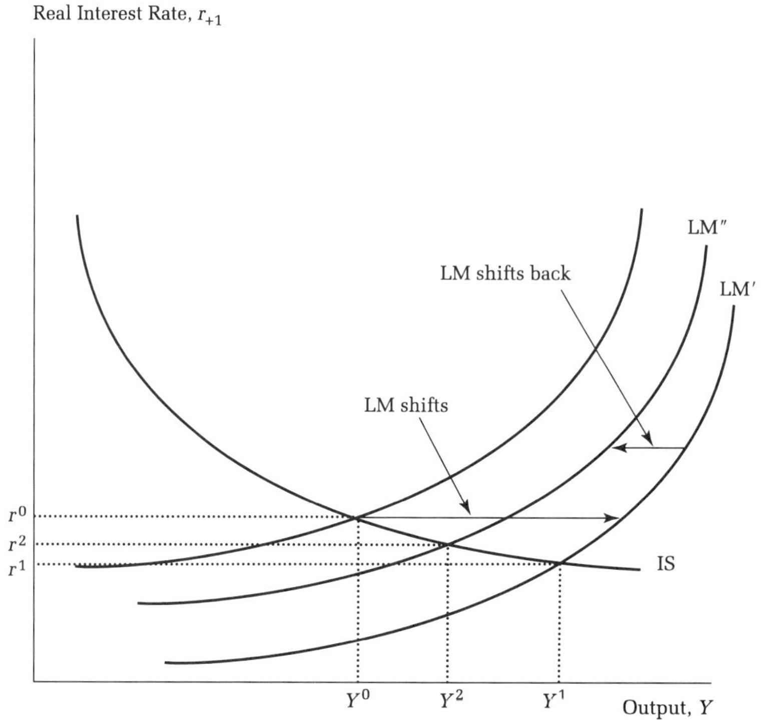

Real Interest Rate, r_{+1}

FIGURE 8.9 MONETARY POLICY WITH RIGID NOMINAL WAGES
With a rigid price level, an increase in the nominal money supply shifts the *LM* curve to *LM'*. Output increases from Y^0 to Y^1 and the interest rate falls (from r^0 to r^1). In a rigid wage regime, the same increase in the nominal money stock leads to the same initial shift of LM to LM'. However, the resulting increase in the price level reduces the real money stock and causes LM to shift back to LM''. The net result is a smaller increase in output (from Y^0 to Y^2) and a smaller decrease in the interest rate (from r^0 to r^2).

AGGREGATE DEMAND CURVE

How much of the stimulus will go toward price increases, and how much toward output increases? We can answer this question by using the aggregate supply curve introduced in Figure 8.8 along with an **aggregate demand curve**, which traces the level of output at each particular price level that corresponds to the intersection of the IS and LM curves.

For any given price level, the level of the nominal money supply, M, determines the position of the LM curve. The level of fiscal stimulus, F, determines the position of the IS curve. These curves intersect at the output level at which the level of aggregate demand equals output. This is one particular combination of price level and output consistent with the equality of aggregate demand and output.

Because the position of the LM curve depends on the real money supply, M/P, a drop in the price level shifts it outward, leading to a higher level of output; a rise in the price level shifts the LM curve inward, leading to a lower level of output. If we plot, for

Aggregate demand curve
A curve representing the level of aggregate demand, as determined by the intersection of IS and LM curves, for all possible values of the price level

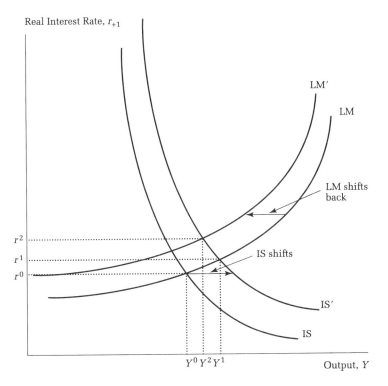

FIGURE 8.10 FISCAL POLICY WITH RIGID NOMINAL WAGES

With a rigid price level, an increase in F shifts the IS curve to IS'. Output increases from Y^0 to Y^1, and the interest rate increases from r^0 to r^1. In a rigid wage regime, the same increase in F leads to the same shift of IS. In this case, however, as output rises, so does the price level. The resulting decrease in the real money supply shifts the LM curve inward to LM'. The net result is a smaller increase in output (from Y^0 to Y^2) and a larger increase in the interest rate (from r^0 to r^2).

different values of the price level, the level of output at which the IS and LM curves intersect, we get the aggregate demand curve. The intersection of this curve, labeled AD in Figure 8.11, and the aggregate supply curve AS indicates the equilibrium level of output and the price level.

Now consider what happens to the aggregate demand curve if we increase the nominal money supply. For any given price level, this shifts the LM curve to the right, increasing the level of output at which the IS and LM curves intersect. Because the same is true for every other price level, the level of aggregate demand corresponding to each price level rises. This implies a rightward shift of the aggregate demand curve, as shown by the curve labeled AD' in Figure 8.11. An increase in F has a similar impact on the aggregate demand curve: it shifts the IS curve to the right and, for any given price level, increases the level of output at which the IS and LM curves intersect.

Thus, the rightward movement of the aggregate demand curve represents the increase in output that would be forthcoming if the price level remained fixed, as in the

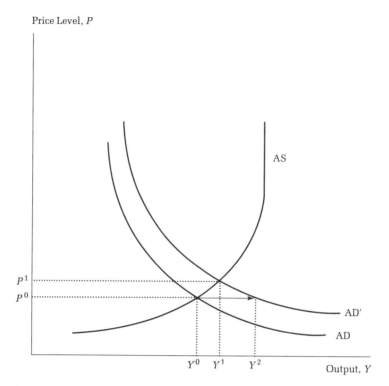

FIGURE 8.11 AGGREGATE DEMAND CURVE AND IMPACT OF POLICY
Together, the aggregate demand and aggregate supply curves determine the price level and the level of output. An expansionary monetary or fiscal policy shifts the aggregate demand curve to the right, from AD to AD′. If the price level did not rise, output would increase to Y^2. However, as dictated by the upward-sloping aggregate supply curve AS, both output and the price level increase.

rigid price case. However, because the aggregate supply curve is upward sloping in the rigid nominal wage case, part of the shift in the aggregate demand curve is reflected in a higher price level, as output rises only to Y^1 rather than Y^2.[16] The distance from Y^0 to Y^2 corresponds to the initial shift of the LM curve in Figure 8.9 or the IS curve in Figure 8.10. The reduction in output back to Y^1 corresponds to the backward shift in the LM curve in either of these two figures that comes from a rise in the price level.

16 In the rigid price case, the aggregate supply curve is a backward L: horizontal at the rigid price level, $\bar{P}$, for any level of output below Y^f, because rightward shifts in the aggregate demand curve affect only output, not the price level; but still vertical at Y^f, because output cannot rise more and prices are only rigid downward.

CHAPTER SUMMARY

1. Short-run nominal price and wage rigidities lower current output and generate involuntary unemployment, a situation in which some workers are unable to find work at the going wage.

2. The Keynesian model uses two key relationships: the equality of money demand and supply (the LM curve) and the transition equation that determines next period's capital stock and rate of interest (a reformulation of which is the IS curve). The IS and LM curves jointly determine the prevailing level of output and the interest rate.

3. Increases in the money supply shift the LM curve downward, and increases in government absorption (increases in F) shift the IS curve upward. Both shifts lead to higher aggregate demand and output, but through different channels. Increasing the money supply leads to a reduction in the next period's interest rate and an increase in current investment. Increasing F, by contrast, increases government purchases while crowding out current investment.

4. We measure and describe the impact of monetary and fiscal policy using policy multipliers. These multipliers indicate by how much output increases following a one-unit increase in the real money supply or absorption by the government of a unit of resources from the young. Either type of policy may have an impact on output many times larger than the initial change in the policy variable itself. The relative strengths of monetary and fiscal policy depend on the interest sensitivity of the demand for money; the more sensitive that money demand is, the stronger is fiscal policy and the weaker is monetary policy.

5. In the presence of nominal rigidities, a rise in national saving, brought about by a decrease in either household or government consumption, leads to a reduction in aggregate demand and, therefore, current output. The decline in current output moderates the initial increase in national saving. This phenomenon is known as the *paradox of thrift*.

6. We can use the aggregate supply–aggregate demand framework to determine the impact of a fiscal or monetary stimulus on prices and output in the rigid-nominal-wage regime.

CHAPTER 9

UNDERSTANDING RECESSIONS

INTRODUCTION

What causes recessions, and how they can be avoided? These are two of the most important, but least settled, questions in macroeconomics. Economists have strikingly different theories of recessions and expansions, none of which fits all the facts. Nevertheless, each provides important insights into the forces that may precipitate booms and busts. Take the Keynesian and real business cycle models. The former model blames recessions on nominal price and wage rigidities. The latter blames them on technology shocks.

This chapter studies these models at greater depth and introduces other prominent theories of recessions. One is the so-called *misperception theory*. According to this theory, households and firms think rationally about the state of the economy (they form what economists call *rational expectations*), but formulate their labor supply and production decisions with imperfect information about the various shocks, policy and otherwise, hitting the economy. The mistakes that result cause output to fluctuate.

Another explanation of recessions is the *sectoral shift model*. Here, shifts in the composition of the goods and services produced by different sectors of the economy are associated with temporary declines in output and increases in unemployment. Why? Because workers laid off from contracting industries need time to find jobs in expanding ones.

The misperception, real business cycle, and sectoral shift explanations share the assumption that prices and wages are fully flexible. In that respect, they differ from both the traditional Keynesian model and more recent models of nominal rigidities proposed by the *New Keynesians*. New Keynesians go beyond traditional Keynesians in seeking to understand the sources of price and wage rigidity. They stress three sources of rigidity: long-term nominal wage and price contracts, simple inertia, and monopolistic price setting by firms with market power. Each of these sources can cause, or at least contribute to, recession.

The New Keynesians have also developed an explanation of recession—termed *coordination failure*—that doesn't hinge on nominal rigidities but does represent another way that markets may perform badly. Their coordination models stress that the economy is more than the sum of its parts and that it needs synchronized (co-ordinated) action by individual households and firms to sustain a high level of output and employment. The potential for such failures is closely connected with the state of business and consumer confidence—what Keynes called *animal spirits*.

The *political business cycle theory* is our final explanation of upturns and downturns. According to this theory, politicians use monetary and fiscal policies to expand the economy prior to an election and then to restrain it.

Our discussion begins with the *Phillips curve*, named after British economist A. W. Phillips, which relates the annual inflation rate to the annual unemployment rate. During the 1950s and 1960s, there was a strong inverse relationship between the two rates in the United States: a prediction of the traditional Keynesian model. But this relationship evaporated after 1969, when the Phillips curve appeared to start shifting. The empirical instability of the Phillips curve provides a natural entree into the critique of the traditional Keynesian model by rational expectations economists and their proffered microbased alternative—the misperception theory.

Microbased models of macrophenomena are *neoclassical models*. The mis-perception, real business cycle, and sectoral shift models are all neoclassical models, and we'll discuss the latter two after examining the misperception theory. Finally, we'll turn to the New Keynesian and political business cycle explanations of recessions.

Here are some of the key questions we'll address:

- What are the principal theories of recessions?

- Are the different theories mutually compatible?

- Are recessions necessarily a sign of market failure?

- What are the policy implications of the different theories?

- What's the evidence for and against particular theories of recessions?

THE 1950–1969 PHILLIPS CURVE AND THE KEYNESIAN MODEL

The relationship between inflation and unemployment in the United States has framed much of the postwar debate about the cause of recession. Figure 9.1 plots U.S. inflation and unemployment rates for the period 1950 through 1969. Most data points satisfy

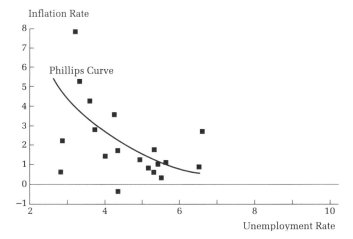

FIGURE 9.1 U.S. PHILLIPS CURVE, 1950–1969
This figure plots combinations of U.S. inflation and unemployment rates for the period 1950–1969. On the average, when the inflation rate was high, the unemployment rate was low, and vice versa. This generally inverse relationship is summarized by the downwardly sloping Phillips curve. Originally it was interpreted as representing a stable trade-off between inflation and unemployment.

the following property: when the inflation rate is low, the unemployment rate is high, and when the inflation rate is high, the unemployment rate is low. We summarize this generally inverse relationship with a simple curve—the **Phillips curve**—which lies closest to the data points in the diagram.

The negative slope of this Phillips curve suggested the possibility of an inflation-unemployment policy trade-off in which the government could permanently lower unemployment by raising the inflation rate. Such a trade-off is consistent with the Keynesian model presented in the previous chapter.

To see why, assume that nominal wage rigidity is the reason that the aggregate supply and aggregate demand curves of Figure 9.2 intersect at point A, which involves a level of output, Y^0, below full employment. Now suppose that workers through, say, their unions, raise their nominal wage each period in line with the preceding period's inflation rate. If inflation last period was 5 percent, the workers set their nominal wage 5 percent higher this period, and so forth.

In Figure 9.2, the economy is initially at point A (the intersection of the aggregate demand curve, AD, and the aggregate supply curve AS) having experienced, we'll assume, 5 percent inflation and a 7 percent unemployment rate in the previous period. This point is recorded as point D in the Phillips curve drawn in Figure 9.3. Since there was 5 percent inflation last period, workers raise their nominal wages this period by 5 percent, which shifts the aggregate supply curve to AS'. If the government increases the money supply this period by 5 percent, the aggregate demand curve shifts to AD', leaving the economy at point B in Figure 9.2. There is no change in equilibrium output because there is no change in either the real money supply or the real wage, which

Phillips curve
A curve fit to observed combinations of the inflation and the employment rates

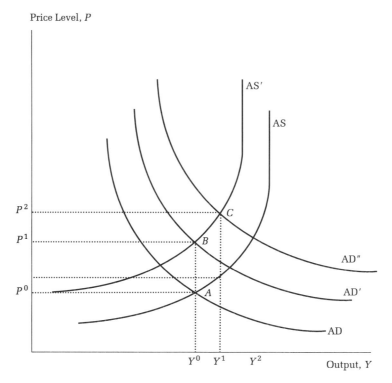

FIGURE 9.2 OUTPUT DETERMINATION IN THE KEYNESIAN MODEL
Together, the aggregate demand and aggregate suply surves determine the price level and the level of output. If workers raise their nominal wages by the same percentage as the government raises the money supply, the aggregate supply and demand curves will shift by the same percentage, leaving output and unemployment unchanged. This is illustrated by the movement from point A to point B. If, on the other hand, the money supply is increased by a larger percentage than is the nominal wage, the aggregate demand curve will shift out relative to the aggregate supply curve, leading to more output and lower unemployment. This is illustrated by the movement from point A to point C.

determine the levels of aggregate demand and aggregate supply, respectively. This new intersection at B in Figure 9.2 corresponds to the original point on the Phillips curve, point D in Figure 9.3.

Suppose instead that the government now increases the money supply by more than 5 percent, leading the aggregate demand curve to shift to AD″ and to equilibrium at point C. In this case, the inflation rate will exceed 5 percent and the unemployment rate will be less than 7 percent, as the real wage falls and employers increase production. Specifically, suppose the movement from point A to point C entails a 10 percent inflation rate and a reduction in the unemployment rate to 4 percent. Then this period's Phillips curve observation is point E in Figure 9.3 rather than point D.

The economy will remain at point E on the Phillips curve next period and in subsequent periods if the government increases the money supply each period by precisely 10 percent, in line with workers' ongoing myopic adjustment of their nominal wages; workers will raise their nominal wages by 10 percent each period, the gov-

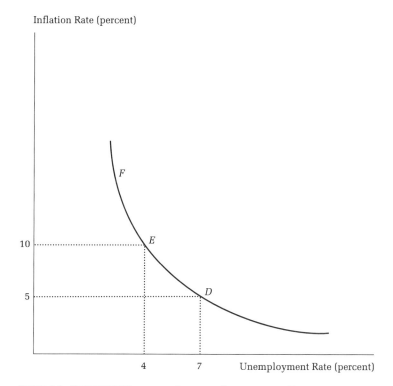

Inflation Rate (percent)

FIGURE 9.3 KEYNESIANS' PERMANENT INFLATION-UNEMPLOYMENT TRADE-OFF
If workers raise their nominal wage demands each period in the light of the previous period's inflation rate, the government can lower the unemployment rate by increasing the inflation rate.

ernment will increase the money supply by 10 percent each period, and the price level will rise by 10 percent each period, leaving the workers' real wage unchanged, as well as the economy's output, employment, and unemployment. In terms of Figure 9.2, aggregate demand and supply curves will shift upward each period by the same percentage.

The movement from point D to point E in Figure 9.3 is thus the result of the government's increasing the money supply for one period by a greater percentage than it did in the previous period and exploiting the workers' myopic adjustment of their nominal wages to inflation to lower their real wages. Keynesian economists, thinking through this scenario, also pointed out that if the government could move the economy from D to E on the Phillips curve, it could use the same trick to move it from E to, say, F—simply increasing the money supply in one period by more than it had the previous period and relying on workers' myopia and their apparent disregard for their real wage. To the Keynesians, then, the Phillips curve offered the possibility of permanently lowering unemployment, albeit at the cost of a permanently higher rate of inflation.

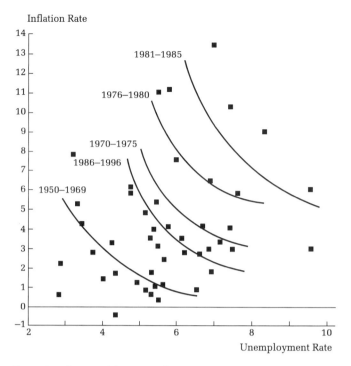

FIGURE 9.4 SHIFTING U.S. PHILLIPS CURVE, 1950–1960

The U.S. Phillips curve for the period 1950–1996 does a poor job of explaining the unemployment and inflation data for the entire period. In fact, all the data for the period 1970–1996 lie northeast of the original Phillips curve, indicating higher inflation for any given level of unemployment. "The" Phillips curve has shifted dramatically over time. For example, a 6 percent unemployment rate was associated with a roughly 1 percent inflation rate during the period 1950–1969, but with a roughly 8 percent inflation rate from 1976–1980.

SHIFTING PHILLIPS CURVE

The 1960s were heady times for Keynesian economists. They had empirical support for a stable Phillips curve, a theoretical explanation for its stability, and the policy-makers' ears. All the policymakers needed to do was to tell the Keynesians which combination of inflation and unemployment they most preferred, and the Keynesians would come up with a monetary and fiscal policy package to deliver it by shifting the aggregate demand curve by just the right amount.

Unfortunately, things weren't that simple. As economists continued to collect data on U.S. inflation and unemployment, they noticed that many of the points were landing far afield of the 1950–1969 Phillips curve. These new data undermined the idea of a stable inflation-unemployment trade-off. Figure 9.4 makes this clear. It plots inflation and unemployment rates for the period 1950 through 1996. It also reproduces Figure 9.1's Phillips curve for the period 1950 through 1969. Note how poorly the Phillips curve for the earlier period fits the data over the entire period.

Figure 9.4 also fits Phillips curves to the inflation and unemployment data for five other periods: 1970–1975, 1976–1980, 1981–1985, and 1986–1996. What emerges is a picture of the Phillips curve's shifting over time. For example, during the period 1950–1969, a 6 percent unemployment rate would have been associated with an inflation rate of about 1 percent, whereas in the period 1976–1980, a 6 percent unemployment rate was associated with an inflation rate of roughly 8 percent.

NATURAL RATE HYPOTHESIS

The earliest explanations of a shifting Phillips curve were provided by Nobel laureate Milton Friedman and Edmund Phelps of Columbia University. They argued that workers were rational economic actors and, as such, were interested in their real wage rather than their nominal wage. "Yes," Friedman and Phelps said, "the government can *temporarily* get workers to accept a lower real wage by setting price inflation above nominal wage inflation. But once workers realize their real wage has declined, they will adjust their nominal wage demands to restore their former real wage levels."

In terms of Figure 9.2, Friedman and Phelps conceded that the government could temporarily move the economy from point A to point C by inflating by more than workers expected. But, they argued, the economy wouldn't stay at the level of output and unemployment associated with point C. Having experienced a decline in their real wage, workers would *temporarily* set their nominal wage demands in *excess* of the expected level of inflation, in order to catch up. This means that the aggregate supply curve would shift upward through time by a greater percentage than would the aggregate demand curve, until the two curves again intersected at the initial level of output, Y^0 (and unemployment).

Friedman and Phelps further pointed out that during the transition back to the original level of unemployment, the Phillips curve would appear to shift. Figure 9.5 makes this clear. It reproduces Figure 9.3's Phillips curve but adds a second higher Phillips curve. The Friedman-Phelps argument is that the government could temporarily move the economy from point D to point E by setting inflation at higher values than expected, but that once workers caught on, they would restore their real wages, moving the economy back to the original level of unemployment, but leaving it with a higher level of inflation as indicated by point G in the diagram. Once workers got used to this higher level of inflation, the government could try to fool them again, by producing an even higher level of inflation; that is, the government could work off the higher Phillips curve in Figure 9.5, but only temporarily. Eventually workers would set their nominal wages high enough to restore their real wage, making the Phillips curve shift upward yet again. *In the long run, Friedman and Phelps argued that there was no inflation and unemployment trade-off.* Indeed, they claimed that the long-run Phillips curve was, as depicted in Figure 9.5, vertical at a rate of unemployment they dubbed the **natural rate of unemployment**.

Natural rate of unemployment
The unemployment rate that occurs when expected inflation equals actual inflation

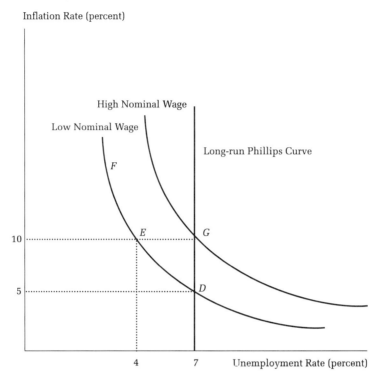

FIGURE 9.5 A SHIFTING PHILLIPS CURVE NULLIFIES THE INFLATION-UNEMPLOYMENT TRADE-OFF
According to Friedman and Phelps, the position of the Phillips curve depends on the level of nominal wages, which ultimately depends on the expected inflation rate. Their natural rate hypothesis undermined the notion of a stable unemployment-inflation trade-off. The government may try to use monetary policy to move the Phillips curve from point *D* to point *E*, thus lowering the unemployment rate. Workers, however, will realize that the higher money supply means higher price levels and lower real wages. To compensate, they demand higher nominal wages. This shifts the Phillips curve upward to the one labeled "High Nominal Wage." As a result, the unemployment rate stays at 7 percent, but the inflation rate rises to 10 percent.

IS THE NATURAL RATE OF UNEMPLOYMENT POSITIVE?

In our model, if the real wage workers demand in the long run corresponds to the real wage required to sustain full employment, the natural rate of unemployment equals zero. Alternatively, if the real wage demanded by workers is higher than the full employment real wage, the natural rate is positive. A natural rate of unemployment of zero is possible in our model, but is it feasible in the real world? The answer is no. In the real world, achieving an unemployment rate that is literally zero is impossible because (1) there are always unemployed workers searching for new jobs as well as new workers searching for their first jobs and (2) searching for a job takes time. Economists use the term **frictional unemployment** to refer to the amount of unemployment arising purely as a result of job changes and first-time job acquisitions. In the real world, then, the natural rate of unemployment reflects frictional unemployment plus the un-

Frictional unemployment
Unemployment arising solely as a result of job changes or first-time job acquisitions

employment that arises if the real wage is set above its market-clearing level. It also incorporates voluntary unemployment.

THE PHILLIPS CURVE AND THE TRADITIONAL KEYNESIAN MODEL: A SUMMARY

To summarize, the traditional Keynesian model with wage rigidity links recessions to excessively high real wages. If workers care about their nominal rather than their real wages, then government monetary or fiscal policy can be used to raise the price level, lower the real wage, and achieve full employment. Friedman and Phelps challenged this view. They pointed out that workers care about their real wages and set their nominal wage demands based on their anticipation of inflation. Although workers might be fooled in the short run about the actual level of inflation, eventually they would realize their real wage had declined and adjust their nominal wage demands accordingly. As a result, monetary or fiscal policies would not, in the long run, reduce either the real wage or unemployment. Rather, such policies would simply leave the economy with a higher rate of inflation.

THE SHORT-RUN TRADE-OFF VERSUS RATIONAL EXPECTATIONS

By the early 1970s most economists had acknowledged that there was no long-run inflation-unemployment trade-off, but most still argued that there was a short-run trade-off. "True," they said, "workers might eventually adjust their nominal wage demands in the light of inflation, but in the short run, the government need only produce more inflation than workers expect in order to lower the real wage." According to these economists, the government could, at least in the short run, shift the AD curve without causing a fully offsetting shift in the AS curve, and thereby lower unemployment.

This view—that the government could temporarily fool workers into accepting lower real wages—reflected economists' assumption that people form their expectations of future inflation based on simple extrapolations of past inflation without regard to the likely policy of the government. The **rational expectations** revolution of the mid-1970s, led by University of Chicago economists Robert Lucas and Thomas Sargent, questioned this view.

Lucas, the 1995 Nobel laureate in economics, and Sargent argued two things: first, that theories of the macroeconomy should be derived from the microeconomic behavior of individual households and firms and, second, that the rationality assumption, applied routinely in microeconomics to explain the utility maximization of households and the profit maximization of firms, also applies to the formation of expectations.

Rational expectations
A forecast of an economic variable based on the rational processing of all available information

"Which came first, the wage boost or the price hike?"

From The Wall Street Journal, *by permission of Cartoon Features Syndicate.*

Rational workers, Lucas and Sargent pointed out, would not form their expectation of future inflation based simply on some arbitrary extrapolation of past inflation. Rather, they would consider all features of the economy that influence the future inflation rate, including the government's likely monetary and fiscal policy decisions. Thus, Lucas and Sargent questioned the ability of the government to fool workers systematically. In effect, they argued that if the government is planning to fool the workers, the workers will realize what the government is up to and set their nominal wage demands in anticipation of the government's attempt to fool them.

In denying that the government could fool workers into accepting a lower real wage, Lucas and Sargent weren't claiming that workers had perfect knowledge of the government's actions or that workers couldn't be surprised by those actions. What they were saying is that workers would not systematically be surprised by government policy, since the workers would think through what surprises the government was trying to cook up.

Lucas and Sargent acknowledged the empirical evidence supporting at least a short-run Phillips curve. However, they argued that the empirical short-run Phillips curve could be explained as the outcome of shocks to the economy, including policy shocks, that were unanticipated not only by workers and the public generally but also by policymakers. On the other hand, any policy change that was planned, and thus anticipated by policymakers, would be taken into account by workers in setting their nominal wage demands. Therefore, only those policy shocks that were unanticipated by policymakers would move the economy away from its natural unemployment rate.

There are many reasons that policymakers as well as the general public may be unable to forecast future policy decisions perfectly. First, policies are generally not made by a single individual, and predicting the outcome of group decisions is not always easy. Second, most policies require time to be approved and implemented, and the amount of time required for approval and implementation is not necessarily known in advance. Third, the potency of a particular policy may vary over time in ways that policymakers cannot perfectly predict. Fourth, particular policy decisions may depend on contemporaneous economic events that are not fully predictable.

MISPERCEPTION THEORY

The rational expectations economists developed their **misperception theory** to spell out precisely how unexpected policy shocks would affect the economy. These models departed from the traditional Keynesian view in three respects: they (1) emphasized the role of rational expectations, (2) assumed that nominal prices and wages were fully flexible, and (3) stressed that either firms or households or both may have less-than-perfect information about the economy, including the government's monetary and fiscal policies.

The misperception models show how the mistakes that firms or households make in predicting the true state of the economy, including economic policy, can lead to observed increases (decreases) in inflation that are associated with decreases (increases) in unemployment. To build some intuition, consider the example of a group of workers trying to decide how much to work. Assume they know the nominal wage they can earn, but not the precise value of the general price level. This means, of course, that they also don't know the precise value of their real wage.

Because they lack full information, those workers have an inference problem. Suppose they are offered a high nominal wage. What are they to make of it? The high nominal wage might reflect an unobserved increase in the money supply that has raised all prices as well as nominal wages. In this case, the high nominal wage might not reflect a high real wage; indeed, depending on the size of the increase in the price level, the high nominal wage might really correspond to a low real wage. On the other hand, the high nominal wage being offered might reflect an increased demand for their services. In this case, the higher nominal wage would represent a higher real wage; in other words, the rise in their nominal wage would not be associated with a rise in the general price level.

The strategy that workers will follow is to supply more labor when their nominal wage is high, but not as much as they would supply if they knew for sure that the price level hadn't risen. Conversely, when their nominal wage is low, workers will supply

Misperception theory
A macroeconomic model in which workers or employers misperceive the state of the economy and, as a consequence, increase or decrease their labor supply or demand

less labor, but not as little as they would supply if they knew for sure that the price level hadn't fallen.

The outcome of this strategy is that the economy will exhibit a short-run Phillips curve. To see this, consider what happens if there is an unexpected increase in the money supply. This will drive up nominal prices and wages (both of which are flexible in the misperception model). More workers will choose to work, and those who choose to work will work for more hours. Why? Because, in the short run, they observe the nominal wage but not the price level and are thus mistakenly led to believe that their real wage has risen. Note that the data of the economy will record both a higher value of inflation and a decrease in unemployment; we'll have a movement along a short-run Phillips curve.

The government, observing this short-run inflation and unemployment relationship, might be tempted to try to exploit it by systematically increasing the money supply over time. But such a policy would lead only to an upward shift in the short-run Phillips curve. The reason is that workers, being rational, will adjust upward their expectations of how much the government is systematically increasing the money supply each period.

ILLUSTRATING A MISPERCEPTION MODEL WITH A LABOR SUPPLY AND DEMAND DIAGRAM

Figure 9.6 illustrates many of these points using a modified version of the labor supply and demand diagram introduced in Chapter 8. There are two modifications to the diagram. First, we graph the nominal wage, W, rather than the real wage, W/P, on the vertical axis. And second, we assume that the supply of labor depends, in a positive way, on the level of the real wage workers believe they are receiving.

In the diagram, $D(W/P)$ stands for the demand for labor, which depends on the real wage firms believe they are paying, and $S(W/P)$ stands for the supply of labor, which depends on the real wage workers believe they are receiving. Suppose the price level has been at P^0 for a long time. Then, in the initial equilibrium at point A, the nominal wage is W^0, and both the actual and perceived price levels equal P^0. Firms and workers correctly perceive that they are paying and receiving a real wage of W^0/P^0. As indicated, the initial equilibrium level of employment is L^0.

Now consider an unexpected increase in the money supply that raises the price level from P^0 to P^1. If firms correctly perceive this increase in the price level, their labor demand curve shifts outward to $D(W/P^1)$. That's because a given value of the nominal wage now corresponds to a lower real wage, and firms demand more labor, the lower the real wage. If the workers also correctly perceive the price increase, their labor supply curve will shift to $S(W/P^1)$. The reason in this case is that a given nominal wage now corresponds to a lower real wage, and workers supply less labor, the lower the real wage.

To understand the new equilibrium at point B, consider a value, W^1, of the nominal wage that keeps the real wage W^1/P^1 equal to its initial value W^0/P^0. At this value of the nominal wage, the amount of labor demanded and the amount supplied

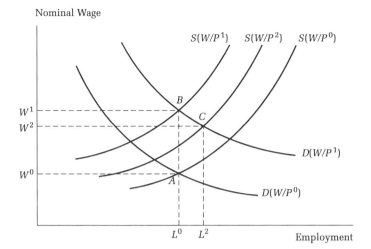

Nominal Wage

FIGURE 9.6 MISPERCEPTION THEORY'S EXPLANATION OF EMPLOYMENT INCREASES IN RESPONSE TO A MONETARY EXPANSION

At point A the nominal wage is W^0 and employment is L^0. In addition, the actual and perceived price level equals P^0. Firms and workers correctly perceive that they are paying and receiving a real wage of W^0/P^0. If an unexpected increase in the money supply raises the price level to P^1 and firms realize this, labor demand shifts to $D(W/P^1)$. If workers misperceive the extent of the price increase and believe it is only P^2 (a smaller value than P^1), the labor supply curve shifts to $S(W/P^2)$ and employment increases from L^0 to L^2. Once workers correctly perceive the price level, their labor supply shifts to $S(W/P^1)$ and employment returns to L^0.

both equal L^0. This observation is confirmed by the original demand and supply curves evaluated at the same real wage: W^0/P^0. Hence, as diagrammed, the new demand and supply curves both go through, and therefore intersect at the point (W^1, L^0). We conclude then that if both firms and workers correctly perceive the percentage increase in the price level, the nominal wage will rise by the same percentage, leaving employment unchanged at L^0.

Next suppose that firms correctly perceive that the price level has risen to P^1 but that workers believe it has only risen to P^2, a value less than P^1. In this case, the labor demand curve is $D(W/P^1)$ and the labor supply curve is $S(W/P^2)$. Equilibrium employment will rise to L^2 at point C, and the nominal wage will rise to W^2. Since W^2 is less than W^1, the actual real wage, W^2/P^1, will be lower than in the initial equilibrium, explaining why firms end up hiring more labor. Because workers misperceive the price level, they end up supplying more labor (L^2 rather than L^0) at a lower (actual) real wage (W^2/P^1 rather than W^1/P^1).

Once workers correctly perceive that the price level is P^1 and not P^2, their labor supply curve will shift to $S(W/P^1)$ and employment will return to L^0. Hence, we have the makings of a short-run Phillips curve: temporary increases in employment (reductions in unemployment) associated with higher prices (and inflation given the previous period's price level).

CASE STUDY
INTERNATIONAL COMPARISONS OF THE INFLATION-UNEMPLOYMENT TRADE-OFF

If the misperception theory is correct, short-run Phillips curves should be steeper in countries with sizable variation in their rates of monetary growth and, thus, their inflation rates. The steeper the short-run Phillips curve is, the less sensitive unemployment will be to a given change in the inflation rate. In countries with considerable variation in inflation, changes in nominal variables, such as nominal wages, are more likely to reflect changes in the underlying price level than changes in relative demands and supplies for the services of particular workers or the products of particular firms. Hence, in such countries, a given change in nominal variables arising from a given change in inflation is less likely to be misconstrued as a change in real prices or wages and therefore is less likely to lower unemployment.

Robert Lucas examined this proposition using data on 18 countries for the years 1952 through 1967.[1] Lucas studied output rather than unemployment, and he found striking evidence that the short-run output-inflation trade-off depended on the degree of a country's inflation variability. Compare, for example, Lucas's findings for the United States and Argentina. Of the 18 countries in his sample, the United States exhibited the least variability in inflation and Argentina the most. Argentina's inflation rate between 1952 and 1967 was 285 times more variable than was the U.S. inflation rate. As Lucas predicted, the response of real output to a given percentage increase in the money supply (as represented by nominal income) was much larger in the United States than in Argentina. Indeed, the output response in the United States was nine times larger than in Argentina.

CRITIQUING THE MISPERCEPTION THEORY

The misperception theory was in vogue for much of the 1970s, but by the end of the decade, many economists began to ask how much of the blame for recessions and credit for expansions could really be attributed to mistaken beliefs about the state of the economy, including the state of economic policy. Critics of the theory pointed out how easily firms and workers could educate themselves about economic conditions and government policies by listening to the business news on radio and television, reading the financial pages of newspapers, or checking government reports. The availability of information about the general price level, which plays a central role in many misperception models, is a case in point. In the United States, the Bureau of Labor Statistics (BLS) issues monthly values of consumer and producer price indexes that are now available on the BLS price index hot line and over the Internet.

The misperception theorists' response to this critique is that their models, particularly those featuring imperfect information about the price level, are simply heuristic devices. They refer to a broad array of information about the state of the economy about which individual households and firms have little precise knowledge. True,

1 See Robert E. Lucas, Jr. "Some International Evidence on Output-Inflation Tradeoffs," American Economic Review 63 (June 1973): 326–334.

they'd say, there are a lot of data available on the economy, but these data tend to be highly aggregated, are often reported with a considerable lag, and are frequently revised. Furthermore, firms and households make a host of long-term investments, ranging from building new factories to relocating to take new jobs, based on their forecasts of economic conditions many years in the future. No economic reports available at the time these investment decisions are made will tell them precisely what the future will bring. Although rational firms and households will form their best estimates of the future economic conditions, they aren't clairvoyant. Hence, the possibility exists that large segments of the economy will over- or underexpand as a result of misperceiving the current state of the economy, or at least its future state. To the extent that labor supply is variable, this over- or underexpansion will cause employment fluctuations.

REAL BUSINESS CYCLE THEORY

Whether the criticisms of the misperception theory and the traditional Keynesian model were fully justified is an open question. In any case, in the early 1980s, Edward Prescott of the University of Minnesota, Finn Kydland of Carnegie-Mellon University, and other prominent economists began to forge a new approach to understanding business cycles: the *real business cycle theory*, introduced in chapter 4. Their models are essentially elaborate versions of our life-cycle model with flexible prices and wages and variable labor supply.

The central question posed by the real business cycle theory is how much economic fluctuation can be explained simply by shocks arising in a neoclassical model with neither price or nominal wage rigidities nor imperfect information. The shocks envisaged by the theory include changes in firms' production technologies, changes in households' preferences about when and what to consume, and changes in government policy. They also include exogenous changes in the economy's capital stock, labor force, and natural resources resulting from wars, natural catastrophes, pestilence, and so forth. Finally, they include changes in international conditions that alter the terms at which the domestic economy can trade its output for foreign output. Good examples of such changes in the terms of trade are increases in oil prices that have occurred periodically as a result of Middle East wars and other disturbances and the cartelization of the oil market by the Organization of Petroleum Exporting Countries (OPEC).

Most real business cycle research has focused on supply-side shocks, primarily shocks to the economy's production function. We illustrated a particular type of supply-side shock in chapter 4 when we considered the dynamic effects of a temporary increase in the Cobb-Douglas technology coefficient, A. We saw that even a technological improvement that lasts only one period can affect the course of the economy over many periods because it alters the time path of saving and capital accumulation.

Table 9.1 Illustrating a Real Business Cycle

Period	A_t	k_t	Y_t	w_t	r_t	S_t	C_t
0	9	5.987	1540	10.8	.771	−60	1599
1	10	5.389	1657	11.6	.923	41	1616
2	11	5.801	1864	13.0	.946	72	1792
3	9	6.524	1580	11.1	.726	−99	1679
4	10	5.529	1670	11.7	.906	32	1639
5	11	5.846	1868	13.1	.959	69	1799
6	9	6.539	1581	11.1	.725	−101	1681
7	10	5.533	1671	11.7	.906	31	1639
8	11	5.847	1868	13.1	.959	69	1799
9	9	6.539	1581	11.1	.725	−101	1681
10	10	5.533	1671	11.7	.906	31	1639
11	11	5.847	1868	13.1	.959	69	1799
12	9	6.540	1581	11.1	.725	−101	1681

Assumptions: $k_0 = 5.987$; $\alpha = .5$; $\beta = .3$; $N = 100$; $k_{t+1} = A_t(1 - \alpha)(1 - \beta)k_t^{\beta}$

Illustrating a Real Business Cycle

Let's consider how our simple two-period life-cycle model reacts to a recurring pattern of low, medium, and high values of the technology coefficient, A. For this exercise we'll use the chapter 3 version of the model, which has no money and no fiscal policy but does include consumption when young and when old. We'll assume that β (capital's income share) equals .3 and that α (the share of wages spent on consumption when young) equals .5. Our simulation will begin at time 0 when A equals 9. At time 1, A will equal 10, and at time 2, it will equal 11. Then the cycle of values will commence again, with A equaling 9 at time 3, and so on.

Our capital-labor transition equation is $k_{t+1} = A_t(1 - \alpha)(1 - \beta)k_t^{\beta}$, or, after inserting the assumed values of α and β, $k_{t+1} = .35\, A_t k_t^{.3}$. Table 9.1 traces the time paths of the economy's capital-labor ratio, output, the real wage, the real interest rate, aggregate saving, and aggregate consumption. The table assumes a capital-labor ratio of 5.987 at time 0. This is the steady-state capital-labor ratio that would prevail if A remained constant at 10.

The technology shocks produce a cycle in each of the economy's macrovariables. In the long run, the cycle is regular since each variable eventually repeats itself every three years. For example, in the long run, the economy's output cycles from 1,581, to 1,671, to 1,868, and then back to 1,581, and so forth. The average of 1,581, 1,671, and 1,868 is 1,707, so in the long run, the economy fluctuates around a stable value of output equal to 1,707.

The induced cycle in saving is particularly noteworthy. When technology is at its lowest value, the economy dissaves. For example, in the long run, when A equals 9, the level of this dissaving is −101, which is −7.4 percent of output. In contrast, when technology is at its intermediate and high values, the economy saves. The long-run positive saving is 31 when A equals 10 and 69 when A equals 11. These values are, respectively, 1.8 percent and 3.7 percent of the contemporaneous long-run levels of output.

The pattern of disinvesting (since saving equals investment) when times are bad and investing when times are good makes the capital-labor ratio lower in good times but higher in bad times than would otherwise be the case. These changes in the capital-labor ratio dampen somewhat the impact on output of the changes in technology. For example, in the long run, each time A_t falls from 11 to 9—an 18 percent decline—output drops from 1,868 to 1,581, which is only a 15 percent decline. In addition to dampening output fluctuations, the volatile pattern of saving serves to stabilize consumption. There is a 9 percent difference between the largest and smallest levels of aggregate consumption over the cycle (1,639 and 1,799, respectively), compared to the 15 percent difference in the largest and smallest values of output.

GENERATING DIFFERENT BUSINESS CYCLES BY VARYING THE ASSUMED PATH OF A

A perfectly regular business cycle, like the long-run cycle of Table 9.1, is not something we observe in the data. But if we make alternative assumptions about the way A varies through time, we can produce virtually any time path of output we want. For example, we could add some random variation to the cycle in A. This would produce nonregular business cycles. In addition, we could add to this random cycle in A an underlying time trend, so that A would cycle around a trend rather than around some stable value. If we were to assume a large enough trend relative to the amplitude of the cycle in A, we could ensure that the value of A_t would never fall below A_{t-1}, that is, that the change in technology between $t-1$ and t was never negative. Why might we want to rule out an absolute decline in the level of technology? Well, if we view the technology coefficient A as reflecting the state of knowledge, we may not want to assume that knowledge can disappear.

HOW DO REAL BUSINESS CYCLE MODELS EXPLAIN UNEMPLOYMENT?

Real business cycle models explain unemployment as the voluntary decision of workers to reduce their labor supply in response to temporary declines in their real wage. In the simple model used to produce Table 9.1 we omitted leisure from the Cobb-Douglas utility function and simply assumed that young people work full time regardless of the wage they receive. But it is easy to extend the model to include leisure when young, as well as leisure when old, in the utility function. If we do, the amount that each person works when young and when old will depend on the real wage when young and the real wage when old. In particular, the higher the ratio of the real wage when young to the real wage when old, the higher will be the ratio of labor supplied when young to labor supplied when old. This propensity to supply more labor during periods when the real wage is relatively high—called **intertemporal substitution**—is how real business cycle theorists explain unemployment during

Intertemporal substitution
The propensity to supply more labor during periods when the real wage is relatively high and less during periods when the real wage is relatively low

TABLE 9.2 COMPARING THE PREDICTIONS OF THE KYDLAND-PRESCOTT REAL BUSINESS CYCLE MODEL WITH THE U.S. DATA

	Standard Deviation		Correlation of Real GNP	
	Of Actual Data	Of Predicted Data	With Actual Data	With Predicted Data
Real GNP	1.8	1.8	1.0	1.0
Consumption	NA	.5	NA	0.8
Services	.6	NA	0.7	NA
Nondurables	1.2	NA	0.8	NA
Investment	5.3	5.5	0.9	0.9
Inventories	1.7	2.2	0.5	0.6
Total Hours	1.7	1.2	0.8	0.9
Worked Productivity (GNP per hour)	1.0	0.7	0.3	0.9

Source: Edward C. Prescott, "Theory Ahead of Business Cycle Measurement," *Quarterly Review*, Federal Reserve Bank of Minneapolis (Fall 1986): 9–33.

Note: All variables are measured as percentage deviations from trend. NA: Not available.

recessions. Their argument is simply that during recessions real wages are depressed because of adverse productivity shocks, and workers respond to these temporary reductions in their real wages by reducing their labor supply. Unemployment, then, arises from the voluntary choice of the unemployed not to work. Given this, there is no need for government policy intervention.

HOW WELL DO REAL BUSINESS CYCLE MODELS EXPLAIN THE BUSINESS CYCLE?

Real business cycle economists test their models by assuming the values of particular parameters and specifying the way they believe real shocks evolve. (In the context of our model, this means assuming values of α and β and a process for how A changes through time.) They then simulate their models and compare the simulated data with actual data. Table 9.2 shows how the predictions of the Kydland-Prescott real business cycle model compare with actual data on the U.S. economy. The table shows the actual variability, over time, of real GNP and five other macrovariables, as well as the actual correlation, over time, of real GNP with these other variables.[2] It also shows the variability of these variables as well as their correlation with real GNP as predicted by the Kydland-Prescott model. The predictions accord fairly well with the actual data.

CRITIQUING THE REAL BUSINESS CYCLE MODEL

Notwithstanding these and similar findings, the theory of real business cycles can be criticized on several grounds. First, since it is hard to measure certain types of real shocks (such as the annual rate of technological advance in computer software), it is

2 *Variability is measured here by the standard deviation of the variable in question. A standard deviation is a measure of how much a variable (e.g., the annual growth of GNP) varies, on average, from its mean value (e.g., the average annual growth rate of GNP). The correlation coefficients in Table 9.2 measure the extent to which two variables vary over time in the same manner. Correlation coefficients range from −1 to +1, −1 meaning that when one variable rises by a given percentage, the other always falls by the same percentage, and +1 meaning that if one variable rises by a given percentage, the other does as well. A correlation coefficient of zero means that the two variables are unrelated.*

hard to know when, or even if, they are occurring. Second, since many real shocks are not readily observable, one can "explain" any change in output as the result of some unobserved real shock. Third, it is hard to believe that the massive and sustained unemployment during the Great Depression and during similar sharp downturns in the economy can really be explained as a voluntary decision by workers to take more leisure in anticipation of working harder as soon as things turned around. Fourth, the labor supply of individual workers does not appear to be sufficiently responsive to intertemporal wage differences—differences in wages across time—to explain the bulk of variation in the use of labor over the business cycle.[3] Fifth, if shocks are technological in nature, they are likely both to be industry specific and to average out in the aggregate economy.

Real business cycle theorists have responses to each of these criticisms. First, they point out that some real shocks, such as those due to natural disasters and changes in the international terms of trade, are observable. Second, even if it is hard to measure the precise state of technology, we certainly know that technological breakthroughs occur and that many are very important; so there are shocks to technology, even if we can't measure precisely their size and frequency. Third, although one could "explain" all macroeconomic fluctuations by assuming enough shocks of the right form, the question is whether one can explain a good deal of the variation over time in macrovariables based on a limited and plausible set of shocks. Fourth, much of the blame for the Great Depression may be placed on the banking panics of the early 1930s, the attendant failure of large numbers of banks, the collapse of credit, and the subsequent closing of many businesses. This episode could well be viewed as a type of aggregate productivity shock leading to very low real wages. Fifth, the reason that workers don't alter their hours of work in response to changes in their real wages as much as the simple real business cycle models predict is that, given the fixed costs of searching for and hiring workers, their employers find it more profitable to require their workers to work full time. In this case, firms will lay off some of their workers in downturns rather than permit those they don't lay off to work less than full time. These layoffs explain the unemployment we see in recessions. Sixth, although there are undoubtedly industry-specific shocks, they may be correlated and thereby produce an aggregate shock. For example, it is hard to think of an industry that didn't experience a positive technology shock with the advent of computers.

CASE STUDY
OIL PRICE SHOCKS AND RECESSIONS

Oil and oil-based products represent our major sources of energy. They enter as direct or indirect inputs into the production of virtually every good and service. Accordingly, we expect the performance of the economy to be particularly sensitive to changes in the price of oil. Real business cycle theorists point to periodic sharp increases in the price of oil as a clear-cut example of supply-side shocks.

3 See, for example, Joseph G. Altonji, "Intertemporal Substitution in Labor Supply: Evidence from Micro Data," Journal of Political Economy 94, pt. 2 (June 1986): 176–215.

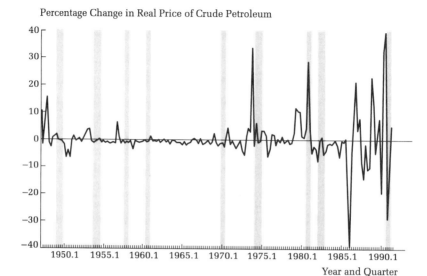

Percentage Change in Real Price of Crude Petroleum

FIGURE 9.7 OIL PRICE SHOCKS AND POSTWAR RECESSIONS, 1947–1991
This figure plots quarterly percentage changes in the real price of crude petroleum for the years 1947–1991, with recession periods shaded. Eight of the nine recessions were immediately preceded by, or coincident with, abrupt increases in oil prices. According to real business cycle theorists, these price increases are tantamount to reductions in the technology parameter, A. Reductions in A lower the marginal product of labor and, consequently, the real wage that firms are willing to pay. A lower real wage means workers supply less labor. Hence, output and employment fall. Keynesians argue that employment falls because nominal wage stickiness keeps real wages from falling enough to maintain full employment.

Source: U.S. Department of Commerce.

Since crude oil is an internationally traded good, its price depends on domestic and foreign supplies and demands. When foreign demand rises or foreign supply declines, the price of crude oil rises both at home and abroad. This reflects the *law of one price*, discussed in chapter 13. Such price increases represent an external real shock to the domestic economy.

The postwar period has witnessed several quite significant oil price shocks. Figure 9.7 graphs the quarterly percentage change in the inflation-adjusted real price of crude petroleum for the period from 1947 to 1991. The shading of the figure indicates the nine recessions the United States has experienced since 1947. As the figure shows, four of these recessions either have been directly preceded by or occurred at the same time as abrupt increases of 10 percent or more in the real price of oil. Another four recessions have coincided with or followed shortly after price increases ranging from 4 to 7 percent.

The fact that eight of the last nine U.S. recessions have been associated with oil price rises suggests more than just coincidence. From the perspective of our simple real business cycle model, an oil price rise can be viewed as a reduction in A. The reason is that A captures everything, apart from capital and labor, that determines the production of output. Thus, A includes raw material inputs, such as oil. The higher the price of oil is, the less oil will be used in production and, so, the lower will be the value of A.

Although there is no disputing the fact that sudden rises in oil prices represent real shocks to the economy, we can question the degree to which the recessions associated with these shocks have reflected the factors stressed by real business cycle theorists versus those stressed by Keynesians. Real business cycle proponents would argue as follows: "The temporary decline in the real wage associated with these shocks prompted workers to reduce their labor supply. This labor supply reduction, together with the shock itself, explains the decline in output."

For their part, Keynesians would argue: "The oil price increase meant that nominal wages had to fall to produce the required fall in real wages. Given nominal wage stickiness, this could not be achieved in the short term. As a consequence, firms were forced to lay off enough workers to restore equality between the marginal product of labor and the temporarily rigid real wage."

Who is right? The answer appears to be both. Undoubtedly some workers responded to the decline in their real wages by reducing their labor supply, and others failed to accept cuts in their nominal wages and found themselves laid off. What remains unclear is precisely what share of the unemployment induced by oil price shocks is attributable to each of these two models or, for that matter, to other models such as the sectoral shift model we'll now review.

SECTORAL SHIFT MODEL

Advocates of the **sectoral shift model** also lay claim to the evidence connecting oil price shocks to recessions.[4] Their model attributes recessions to shocks that favor specific industries but hurt others. These shocks require workers to relocate across industries. The process of relocation temporarily raises unemployment and lowers output. The reason is that many of the workers laid off from contracting industries spend time unemployed until they find jobs in expanding industries. Thus, according to sectoral shift theorists, the degree of frictional unemployment in the economy is not fixed. Instead, they claim, variations in the degree of frictional unemployment explain much of the fluctuation in aggregate unemployment.

Sectoral shifts can result from changes in either the pattern of demand for different products or the relative costs of producing different products. An oil price shock is an example of the latter. Since certain goods and services are more energy intensive (use relatively more energy in production) than others, an oil price shock will raise the costs of, and reduce the demands for, energy-intensive goods relative to other products.

Consider the U.S. recession that began in November 1973 and ended in March 1975. As Figure 9.7 shows, this recession coincided with a more than 30 percent

Sectoral shift model
A theory that traces business cycles to shifts of employment and output among industries

4 A seminal empirical study supporting the sectoral shift model is David M. Lilien's "Sectoral Shifts and Cyclical Unemployment," Journal of Political Economy 90, no. 4 (August 1982): 777–793.

Rob Rogers © United Feature Syndicate. Reprinted by permission.

increase in the real price of crude oil, the result of OPEC's decision to curtail oil production and thereby raise the price of oil following the 1973 Yom Kippur War. During
this recession, the share of U.S. employment in energy-intensive durable manufacturing fell by over 9 percent, whereas in other industries, such as retail trade and services,
total employment (as well as the share of employment) actually rose.

Another example of a U.S. recession that may have been caused by sectoral shifts
is the February 1945–October 1946 contraction that occurred as World War II ended.
In the aftermath of the war, the U.S. economy faced the task of shifting quickly from
producing war materials to producing consumer goods. Between 1945 and 1946, defense expenditures fell by a whopping 78 percent! The U.S. economy also had to contend with large numbers of troops returning home from military service. Between 1945
and 1946, over 9 million military personnel (equal in size to almost 17 percent of
the labor force) left active duty. If we view the military as an industry, the dramatic
decline in the demand for troops, like the dramatic decline in the demand for war
materials, represents a shift in the industrial pattern of demand and, consequently,
production.

CRITIQUING THE SECTORAL SHIFT MODEL

Critics of the sectoral shift model admit that exogenous shifts in the industrial pattern
of costs and demand may be important in raising frictional unemployment in isolated
instances, such as in the aftermath of World War II. But they contend that much of the
interindustry shifts in employment may reflect a response to, rather than the cause of,
recessions. Recessions, they argue, lower incomes and reduce the demand for income-
sensitive commodities, such as vacation travel, relative to the demand for income-
insensitive commodities, such as haircuts and doctors' visits. In addition, they point

out, if recessions simply reflected shifts in the composition of demand, we would expect to find that periods of high unemployment—when contracting industries are laying off workers—are also periods in which expanding industries are trying to hire workers. Thus, a high unemployment rate should be coincident with a high **job vacancy rate**, the fraction of jobs in the economy that employers are trying to fill. But the evidence on unemployment and job vacancies is just the opposite: when the unemployment rate is high, the job vacancy rate is low.

Sectoral shift proponents respond that it's hard to think of a cause of recession that hits all industries uniformly. Even if wages or prices are sticky, they are not likely to be equally sticky in all industries. Hence, drawing a clear distinction between recessions due to aggregate shocks (nominal or real) and those due to interindustry variations in shocks (nominal or real) may be impossible. Moreover, the sectoral shifters concede that some unemployment results from purely aggregate shocks; indeed, they view the inverse relationship between unemployment and job vacancies as reflecting this aggregate shock component of the business cycle. But they point out that the unemployment–job vacancy relationship isn't stable over time and contend that changes in this relationship reflect sectoral shifts. Finally, they point out that job mobility rises during recessions.

POLICIES TO DEAL WITH SECTORAL SHIFTS

Assuming the sectoral shift model is at least partly correct, what remedies for recession does it suggest? One possibility is to help workers in declining sectors find jobs in expanding sectors. For the government, the practical problem in providing such assistance is knowing ahead of time which sectors are starting to decline and which are starting to expand. If it takes too long to help workers relocate, the recession will already be over.

Even if the government can intervene quickly, there is the question of whether it should. After all, expanding sectors are free to place ads in local and national newspapers and engage in other types of advertising and recruiting activities in searching for new workers. And displaced workers are free to advertise their availability. If there is no obvious failure in the market for finding workers, should the government intervene? Maybe not. However, as we'll discuss when we consider theories of coordination failures, this type of market, in which parties search for each other, does suffer from a particular type of failure: each party has an incentive to let the other party do the searching.

NEW KEYNESIAN MODELS OF RECESSIONS

Their differences notwithstanding, the misperception, real business cycle, and sectoral shift theories each connect macroeconomic outcomes to microeconomic behavior. As these theories were being developed, the desirability of grounding macroeconomics in

Job vacancy rate
The fraction of available jobs currently unfilled

microeconomics also became apparent to another set of economists, the New Keynesians, many of whom felt that nominal rigidities were at the core of macroeconomic fluctuations. Consequently, they set about developing macromodels based on microeconomic explanations of such rigidities. We now discuss several of these **New Keynesian models**.[5]

LONG-TERM NOMINAL WAGE AND PRICE CONTRACTS

Certain nominal wages and prices are set for extended periods of time by explicit contract. Examples include formal (written) long-term nominal-wage contracts negotiated between labor unions and employers and formal long-term contracts that specify the nominal prices that producers of final products will pay their suppliers of intermediate products and raw materials. In addition, there are implicit wage or price contracts that reflect an informal understanding between the parties concerned about how nominal wages or prices will change over a given period of time.

By establishing contracts, workers and firms limit the amount of time they spend negotiating with one another. Without these formal or informal understandings, negotiating would be endless and very costly. (Imagine workers' negotiating with their employers over each hour's pay.) Long-term contracts also provide mechanisms for the contracting parties to pool their risks. Take the case of a firm that agrees to give its workers a 5 percent pay raise for each of the next three years. In making this agreement, the firm is assuring each worker that she'll receive a 5 percent raise regardless of whether the firm makes large or small profits during the three years.

Wage and price contracts aren't all negotiated simultaneously and aren't equally long. Instead, contracts are **staggered** so that, at any point in time, some are being renegotiated and others are not. Consequently, at any point in time, a fraction of the economy's wages and prices are fixed in nominal terms.

The New Keynesians have modeled the effects of monetary policy shocks in settings of staggered nominal wage or price contracts.[6] In so doing, they assume that workers and firms think rationally about the future when they negotiate their contracts. Thinking rationally about the future includes thinking about how the government's monetary policy will affect the future course of inflation and, thus, the real value of the nominal wages and prices being set in the contract.

The New Keynesians made several points with their staggered contracts models. First, they showed that increases in the money supply that were unanticipated at the time the contracts were made would temporarily raise output and lower unemployment (that is, produce a short-run Phillips curve). Second, they showed that increases in the money supply that were anticipated at the time the contracts were made would have no impact on output or employment because workers and firms would form their contracts in anticipation of the money supply increases. And third, they showed that increases in the money supply that occur while a contract is in force have real effects even though they are fully recognized and, thus, anticipated. These effects die out gradually as contracts expire, rather than instantaneously, as in the misperception

---

New Keynesian models
Macroeconomic models that seek to provide microeconomic explanations of wage and price rigidities and other sources of market failure

Staggered contracts
Contracts with different expiration dates that set the wage rates at various firms

5 For an excellent collection of the leading articles on New Keynesian economics see N. Gregory Mankiw and David Romer, eds., New Keynesian Economics (Cambridge, MA: MIT Press, 1991).

6 The seminal articles in this literature are Stanley Fischer's "Long-Term Contracts, Rational Expectations, and the Optimal Money Supply Rule," Journal of Political Economy 85, no. 1 (February 1977): 191–206, and John B. Taylor's "Aggregate Dynamics and Staggered Contracts," Journal of Political Economy 88, no. 1 (February 1980): 1–23.

model. This third point suggested that the distinction between anticipated and un-anticipated policies needs to be drawn very precisely if it is to have any meaning.

OTHER EXPLANATIONS OF NOMINAL RIGIDITIES

A different group of New Keynesians has sought to explain price and wage stickiness as the consequence of inertia, imperfect competition, or firms' and workers' efforts to avoid the costs of changing nominal prices and wages. Inertia refers simply to an irrational failure to make price and wage adjustments. Imperfect competition refers to the hesitancy of firms with market power to (1) raise their nominal prices for fear that their competition won't follow, leaving them with greatly reduced demand for their products, or (2) lower their nominal prices for fear of setting off a price war. The third explanation of price and wage stickiness—the costs of adjusting nominal prices and wages—is referred to by the shorthand term **menu costs**. The term derives from the frequently used example of restaurants, which have to pay the cost of printing new menus each time they change their nominal prices. Menu costs are generally thought to be small, but still large enough to deter firms and workers from adjusting their prices and wages in response to small changes in the level of aggregate demand.

Regardless of the reasons that firms and workers fail to adjust their nominal prices and wages fully, the consequences for the firms and workers may be minor. Imperfectly competitive firms know that if they set their price a bit too high (relative to the profit-maximizing price), they won't lose all their market. If they set their price a bit too low, they won't lose all their profits. Similarly, groups of workers that have market power in bargaining with their employers (trade unions, for example) realize that if they set their wage a bit too high, they will not all be fired, and that if they set it a bit too low, they will still want to keep working with the firm.

For any particular firm or set of workers, the consequences of failing to adjust nominal prices or wages may be small. However, if enough firms and workers fail to adjust, the consequences for the aggregate economy can be significant. To see why, consider again the *LM* equation under the simplifying assumption that γ is fixed at $\bar{\gamma}$, $M/P = \bar{\gamma}(1 - \beta)Y$. Now suppose that the money supply, M, is decreased by a small amount, say 1 percent, but firms fail to lower their prices by 1 percent. As argued, in the case of monopolistic competition, the loss to individual firms of not adjusting their prices could well be quite small—much less than 1 percent. What happens to total output? According to the *LM* equation, output will fall by a full 1 percent—a nontrivial decrease.

The inertia and menu costs models generate a short-run Phillips curve, but they also suggest that anticipated monetary policy will alter output and employment. For example, in the case of inertia, firms and workers may know that the government is raising the money supply, but they will still fail to adjust their nominal prices and wages—at least in the short run.

Menu costs
The typically small costs incurred by firms in changing the prices they charge

CASE STUDY
DO ANTICIPATED OR UNANTICIPATED MONEY SHOCKS AFFECT U.S. OUTPUT?

Harvard's Robert Barro tested whether deviations of U.S. output growth from its underlying time trend are caused by (1) all changes in the money supply, anticipated or not, as suggested by the traditional Keynesian model, New Keynesian models of menu costs and inertial price and wage setting, and New Keynesian contract models (in the case of anticipations formed within the contract period) or (2) only unanticipated changes in the money supply, as suggested by the misperception model, the New Keynesian price and wage contracts models (in the case of anticipations as of the time of contracting), and other models featuring rational expectations.[7] Barro used a statistical technique to decompose the annual change in the money supply (measured as M1) into two components: the anticipated change in the money supply and the unanticipated change. He then determined which of the two components was causing output to vary from its trend value. Barro's results indicated that only unanticipated changes matter.

Figure 9.8 presents some of Barro's data. It shows three time series for the years 1946 through 1976: the deviation of output growth from its time trend (output shocks), the unanticipated percentage change in the money supply (unexpected money shocks), and the anticipated percentage change in the money supply (expected money shocks). Note the fairly close relationship between output growth and unexpected money shocks. In contrast, there is little relationship between output growth and expected money shocks.

Barro's findings are striking but not definitive. There is nothing sacrosanct about the way he divides money supply changes into anticipated and unanticipated components. Different decompositions produce somewhat different results about the relative importance of anticipated and unanticipated money shocks. In addition, the observed correlation between output shocks and unexpected money supply shocks may reflect a reverse causation, in which unexpected output shocks lead the government to alter the money supply in ways that had not been anticipated. Finally, Barro effectively groups all anticipated changes in the money supply together without regard to whether they occurred before or after prevailing nominal wage and price contracts were made. In so doing, Barro may have biased his test against a finding that anticipated money supply changes matter.

Coordination failure
The failure of economic agents to coordinate their activities in ways that would be mutually beneficial

7 Robert J. Barro, "Unanticipated Money, Output, and the Price Level in the United States," Journal of Political Economy 86, no. 4 (August 1978).

COORDINATION FAILURES

New Keynesians raise other concerns about the functioning of markets besides the potential for nominal rigidities. One of these falls under the heading of **coordination failure**: the failure of individuals or firms to coordinate their activities in ways that would be mutually beneficial. A specific parable helps convey the main issues.

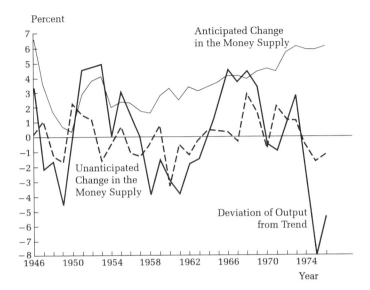

FIGURE 9.8 OUTPUT SHOCKS AND ANTICIPATED AND UNANTICIPATED CHANGES IN THE MONEY SUPPLY
Robert Barro decomposed annual money supply changes into anticipated and unanticipated components to test whether either component caused output to deviate from its trend value. He found a fairly close relationship between output growth and unexpected money but little relationship between output growth and expected money shocks. He interpreted these findings as evidence in favor of the misperception model, New Keynesian wage and price contract models, and other frameworks featuring rational expectations.

Source: R. J. Barro, "Unanticipated Money Output, and the Price Level in the United States," Journal of Political Economy 86, no. 4 (August 1978).

Suppose each firm were to choose its hours of operation without regard to the operating hours of other firms. The result would be some firms' operating from, say, 9 A.M. to 5 P.M., some from 11 A.M. to 7 P.M., others from 1 P.M. to 9 P.M., and so on. This clearly would raise the cost to firms of transacting with one another; any two firms with different hours would be able to contact one another only during their common hours of operation. It would also increase the amount of time people had to spend shopping; those who routinely shop in the morning would have to make a special trip to shop in stores that were open only after noon.

Although the coordination of operating hours is obviously highly important, it is not something the free market necessarily produces. If firms were operating at very different hours, they might all recognize the need to coordinate their hours but not know on which hours to synchronize. Consequently, they might continue to operate at a lower level of economic efficiency and produce less output than if they were able to agree on their hours of operation or if they were compelled by law or persuaded by custom to operate during the same hours.

This example contains two elements common to virtually all models of coordination failures. First, there are external benefits, or *spillover effects*. Specifically, imagine that one firm alters its hours to match those of other firms. The firm that changes its hours provides a benefit to these other firms, since they now can contact this firm more easily and their customers can now shop during the same hours at a larger number of firms. Second, there are **multiple equilibria**. We can have an equilibrium with no coordination of operating hours. Or we can have an equilibrium with perfect coordination, indeed a different equilibrium for each potential common choice of operating hours. There will also be equilibria in between the extremes of no coordination and perfect coordination. For example, a third of all firms might coordinate on one set of hours, another third might coordinate on a second set of hours, and the final third might coordinate on a yet a third set of hours.

Coordination Failures and Recessions

Peter Diamond, an MIT economist, wrote the seminal article on coordination failures in 1982.[8] Diamond's example involves the search costs incurred by firms that are trying to sell products to or buy products from other firms. The more effort the selling firm puts out searching for a buying firm, the less time the buying firm will have to spend searching for the selling firm and vice versa.

If each firm's search effort is positively related to the level of its production, then it will be mutually beneficial for all firms to agree to search more (and thus produce higher levels of output). But if each firm believes other firms are searching (and producing) at low levels, it will not have sufficient incentive to search on its own at a higher level. As a result, the economy may end up at an equilibrium with a low level of production rather than a high one. Moving the economy from such a low-output equilibrium to a high-output equilibrium may not be easy, since it requires changing businesspeople's beliefs about the state of economy.

Illustrating Coordination Failures with Our Model

In our simple two-period life-cycle model, we have not encountered any problems of multiple equilibria. But if we make different assumptions about households' saving behavior and firms' production functions, we can produce more than one transition path for the capital-labor ratio—more than one dynamic equilibrium.

Figure 9.9 shows two alternative transition paths for the capital-labor ratio resulting from two alternative k_{t+1} curves. These two curves could arise if there were two different transition equations relating k_{t+1} to k_t. The two equations might reflect two possible values of the technology coefficient A that could prevail—one high and one low. The high value of A might arise from coordinated actions by firms (e.g., searching harder for each other or setting the same hours); the low value could reflect a failure to coordinate actions. The decision by firms to coordinate at time t would depend on their beliefs about the actions others will take. If each firm believed the others were searching hard, it too would search hard, making A high. If each firm believed the others were not searching hard, it would not search hard, making A small.

Note that starting at time 0 with a capital-labor ratio of k_0, the economy can move along either the lower capital-labor ratio (and lower output) transition path or the

Multiple equilibria
Multiple positions at which the economy can be in equilibrium

8 Peter Diamond, "Aggregate Demand Management in Search Equilibrium," Journal of Political Economy 90 (1982): 881–894.

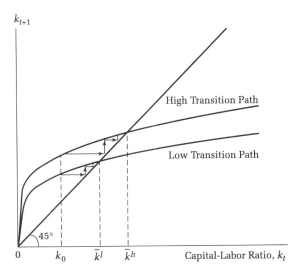

FIGURE 9.9 ILLUSTRATING MULTIPLE EQUILIBRIA IN THE TWO-PERIOD MODEL
With coordination failures, there may be more than one possible transition path for the capital-labor ratio and more than one steady state toward which the economy can converge. For example, a high degree of coordination among firms might imply a high value of the technology parameter, A, and a high transition curve. Poor coordination would mean a low A and a low transition curve. If so, then starting at k_0, the economy might move along the lower path and end up at $\bar{k}^l$ or along the higher path and end up at $\bar{k}^h$.

higher capital-labor ratio (and higher output) transition path. If it takes the low path, the economy ends up with a steady-state capital-labor ratio of $\bar{k}^l$; if it takes the high path, it ends up with a steady-state capital-labor ratio of $\bar{k}^h$. Alternatively, it could oscillate between the two paths over time in response to changes in firms' beliefs about whether other firms are coordinating their behavior (e.g., searching hard for each other or setting the same hours). If beliefs continue to change through time, the economy will never converge to a steady state but rather will fluctuate between high and low levels of output. It will experience recessions and expansions.

CASE STUDY
CONSUMER AND BUSINESS CONFIDENCE AND THE BUSINESS CYCLE

The potential for coordination failures may explain why there is so much interest in indexes of consumer and business confidence. Figure 9.10 shows how one index of consumer confidence has varied since 1960 during periods of booms and busts. The figure shows that consumer confidence is procyclical; it is low during recessions and high during booms. In addition, as mentioned in chapter 4, consumer confidence is a *leading indicator*—a variable that turns down before the economy contracts and turns up before the economy starts to recover.

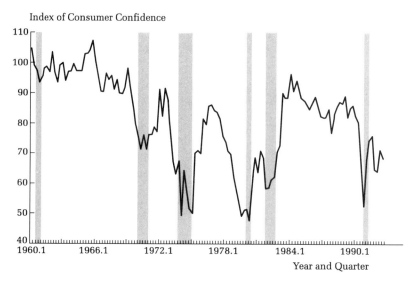

Index of Consumer Confidence

FIGURE 9.10 INDEX OF CONSUMER CONFIDENCE IN RECENT RECESSIONS
Some models of coordination failure suggest that consumer confidence is critical in moving the economy from a low-output equilibrium to a high-output equilibrium. If so, an index of consumer confidence should be a leading indicator of output. This figure plots such an index for the years 1960–1992, with recessions shaded. In fact, confidence turned up before or at the ends of all six recessions.

Source: University of Michigan, Survey Research Center.

Figure 9.10 shows that consumer confidence (technically called *consumer sentiment*) was falling several quarters before the start of each recession between 1960 and 1992. The figure also shows that confidence turned up prior to the ends of recessions that began in 1960, 1980, 1981, and 1990. In the case of the recessions that began in 1969 and 1973, consumer confidence turned up just as the recessions ended. Even these two cases support the view that consumer confidence causes, rather than responds to, economic events. Recessions end when the economy begins to rebound from zero or negative growth, not when it has actually fully recovered in terms of achieving its natural rate of unemployment. If consumer confidence were determined simply by immediate circumstances, we wouldn't expect a recovery of consumer confidence, coming out of a recession, until the economy actually neared its cyclical peak. So the recovery of confidence at the troughs of recessions means that consumers are really looking beyond the immediate state of the economy in forming their expectations and, presumably, their economic plans for the future.

If, as suggested by certain models of coordination failures, consumer confidence is critical to moving the economy from a low-output and employment equilibrium to a high-output and employment equilibrium, we would expect the level of consumer confidence to be a leading indicator for the following reason. In these models, changes in beliefs about the state of the economy signal firms that it is advantageous to contract their production (in the case of a reduction in confidence) or expand their production (in the case of an increase in confidence). Hence, changes in beliefs (consumer confidence) will precede changes in the economy.

Policy Responses to Coordination Failures

What can governments do to prevent coordination failures? Certain coordination problems may be relatively easy to fix. Take the case of firms choosing different operating hours. The government can resolve this problem simply by mandating that all firms open and close at the same times. Other problems, like the failure of firms to search for each other in the marketplace, might be addressed by subsidizing particular activities, like advertising. Finally, public officials can, and often do, attempt to raise consumer confidence through upbeat press conferences and the like. During the Great Depression, President Roosevelt tried to raise confidence by proclaiming, "The only thing we have to fear is fear itself. And in the early 1980s, President Reagan relied on his indefatigable optimism to talk the American economy out of recession. Pep talks may be an effective tool to combat particular coordination failures, but their use requires that governments be able to recognize such failures when they arise.

POLITICAL BUSINESS CYCLES

Our final theory—the theory of **political business cycles**—argues that when the public votes, it places great weight—potentially undue weight—on the current state of the economy.[9] Consequently, politicians will take actions to increase output and employment prior to elections and then undo these actions after the election, creating a business cycle. Political business cycles can be understood in terms of either the traditional Keynesian model or the real business cycle model. In the traditional Keynesian model, politicians, prior to elections, can be viewed as using monetary or fiscal policy to shift the AD curve. Once the election is over, the reversal of these policies (perhaps to curb inflation or lower interest rates) will cause the curve to shift back. In the process, output and employment will first expand and then contract.

In the real business cycle model, politicians can use temporary tax cuts to stimulate additional labor supply before an election and then raise tax rates once the election is over. The labor supplied by a young generation relative to the labor supplied by the same generation when it is old one period later depends on the ratio of wages that can be earned in the two periods. Although we have not discussed labor income taxes, adding such taxes to the model with variable labor supply would lead to the result that the ratio of labor supplied when young to labor supplied when old depends on the ratio of the after-tax wages in the two periods. Hence, if politicians reduce labor income taxes in time t and raise them in time $t + 1$, this will raise the ratio of after-tax wages when young to after-tax wages when old, inducing the young at time t to work

Political business cycle theory
The view that business fluctuations are caused by politicians' trying to stimulate the economy prior to elections and contract the economy afterward

9 One of the first studies of the political business cycle was William Nordhaus, "The Political Business Cycle," Review of Economic Studies 42 (1975): 169–190. More recent studies include Alberto Alesina, "Macroeconomics and Politics," NBER Macroeconomics Annual 3 (1988): 13–52, and Torsten Persson and Guido Tabellini, Macroeconomic Policy, Credibility, and Politics (Cambridge, MA: MIT Press, 1990).

more in time t and less in time $t + 1$. If the election is held at time t, there will be more employment and more output to which the politicians can point in claiming that their governance is good for the economy.

What can be done to prevent politicians from manipulating the economy? A possibility is to insulate fiscal and monetary authorities from the political process to the extent possible. One way to do this is to give these authorities long-term contracts, so their own positions are not threatened by actions that displease the incumbents. As we'll discuss in chapter 14, the U.S. monetary authority—the board of governors of the Federal Reserve System—is structured in just this manner, as are the central banks of Germany, Switzerland, and many other countries. On the fiscal side, the Japanese Ministry of Finance represents one of the few cases in which the top fiscal authorities, through long-term tenure in their jobs, are relatively free of political pressure.

WHAT CAUSES RECESSIONS? A BOTTOM LINE

We've now discussed seven explanations of recessions: the traditional Keynesian theory, the misperception theory, the real business cycle theory, the sectoral shift theory, New Keynesian theories of nominal price and wage rigidities, New Keynesian models of coordination failures, and models of the political business cycle. Table 9.3 summarizes the seven explanations of recessions and their policy prescriptions.

Former president Harry Truman would have seen this large number of explanations as an embarrassment of riches. Truman used to say that he was looking for a one-handed economist, because his economic advisers were always saying "on the one hand this and on the other hand that." Macroeconomists would certainly love to discover the single explanation of, and cure for, recessions. Indeed, the search for *the* explanation has motivated much macroeconomic research, past and present. But why should recessions have a single cause? And why should the set of causes be the same for each recession? There is certainly no theoretical requirement that this be the case.

Instead of all recessions having the same origin, it seems more likely that there are multiple and varied causes of recessions. The seven general theories discussed here have all probably played major and minor roles in the long history of U.S. and foreign business cycles. Once we accept this view, we can better understand why none of the different theories of recessions has been able to fit all the facts. Unfortunately, this view leaves economists with the very difficult task of sorting out the precise importance of particular theories in particular recessions.

Table 9.3 Alternative Explanations of Recessions and Their Policy Implications

Theory	Cause of Recession	Policy Implications
Traditional Keynesian Model	Nominal wage or price rigidities prevent economy from equilibrating at full employment.	Monetary or fiscal policy can be used to expand output.
Misperception Theory	Workers (firms) misconstrue decreases in their nominal wages (prices) arising from unexpected decreases in the money supply as reductions in their real wages (prices); they reduce their supply of (demand for) labor; output falls.	Workers and firms have rational expectations, so only unexpected changes in the money supply have real effects.
Real Business Cycle Theory	Workers voluntarily work less during periods when their real wages are low. Temporarily low real wages reflect negative technology shocks.	Since unemployment is voluntary, there is no economic rationale for policy intervention.
Sectoral Shift Model	Shocks to particular sectors of the economy lead to time-consuming reallocation of inputs across sectors; this reallocation temporarily lowers output.	Government assistance in helping labor and capital relocate may mitigate output loss.
New Keynesian Theories of Wage and Price Rigidities	Explicit or implicit long-term contracts, inertia, imperfect competition, or menu costs explain nominal wage and price rigidities that prevent economy from reaching full employment.	Depending on the source of the nominal rigidity, expected as well as unexpected increases in the money supply can raise output.
New Keynesian Models of Coordination Failures	Failure of firms to coordinate actions (e.g., searching for one another or setting the same operating hours) leads to low output equilibrium.	Government pep talks may help the private sector choose high output equilibrium.
Political Business Cycles	Incumbent politicians expand economy prior to elections; once they are reelected, they contract the economy.	Monetary and fiscal policies are used for short-term political expediency. Independence of fiscal and monetary authorities from politicians can help.

CHAPTER SUMMARY

1. This chapter discussed alternative explanations of economic fluctuations. Much of the discussion was framed in terms of the Phillips curve—the presumed inverse relationship between inflation and unemployment. During the 1950s and 1960s, this relationship seemed fairly stable, and it provided empirical support for the traditional Keynesian model, which stressed the potential for monetary and fiscal policies to raise output and lower unemployment when either nominal wages or prices are sticky.

2. The post-1969 data on inflation and unemployment deviate systematically from the Phillips curve drawn to fit the 1950–1969 data. Milton Friedman and Edmund Phelps explained this outcome in terms of the adjustment of expectations by those setting prices and wages. They argued that over time, nominal wages and prices are set in the light of the expected rate of inflation. As a result, the Phillips curve shifts over time, with each new short-run curve depending on the current state of expectations about inflation. In the long run, the Phillips curve is vertical; there is no long-run trade-off between inflation and unemployment.

3. Friedman's and Phelps's work left open the possibility of a short-run inflation-unemployment trade-off in which the government could try to fool the public by producing more inflation than expected. The rational expectations revolution, led by Robert E. Lucas, Jr., and Thomas Sargent, denied even this means of using monetary policy to lower unemployment. Lucas and Sargent pointed out that a rational public would see through the government's attempts to fool them and would adjust its expectations about inflation accordingly. As a result, anticipated money injections would have no impact on the level of unemployment.

4. The rational expectations school also questioned the traditional Keynesian assumption of nominal rigidities as the underlying factor keeping the economy from attaining full employment. Rather than assume markets were somewhat dysfunctional, rational expectations economists developed the misperception theory, which assumed flexible nominal wages and prices but stressed the lack of complete information on the part of economic agents about the state of the economy, particularly monetary policy and the price level. Their misperception models predicted that only unanticipated injections of money would raise output and lower unemployment. Such unanticipated monetary policy would be unexpected by both the public and the policymakers themselves.

5. Real business cycle theorists developed other flexible wage and price models in which supply-side shocks, such as oil price increases, altered the productive

capacity and output of the economy. These economists explained employment fluctuations in terms of workers' labor supply decisions. During periods of low productivity, wages would be low and workers would choose to take more leisure and therefore work less. The opposite would be true during periods of high productivity and high wages.

6. The aggregate supply-side shocks stressed by the real business cycle models raised the question of whether shocks to particular sectors of the economy might not also be important. The sectoral shift model explains unemployment in terms of the search and relocation time required for workers laid off from sectors experiencing negative shocks to find jobs in sectors experiencing positive shocks.

7. The neoclassical misperception, real business cycle, and sectoral shift models did not convince a number of economists, who continued to question the assumption of flexible prices and wages. A group of these New Keynesian economists developed microeconomic explanations for nominal rigidities. These explanations include formal as well as informal nominal wage and price contracts, inertia, small costs of altering prices and wages (menu costs), and imperfect competition. According to certain versions of these models, both expected as well as unexpected monetary policy may affect the economy.

8. A different set of New Keynesians began to question the performance of markets along other dimensions, particularly the ability of individual households and firms to coordinate their economic actions when such coordination would be mutually beneficial. Despite the collective benefits, individual economic agents may not have sufficient private incentive to produce at the socially desirable level of output. In addition to externalities, coordination failure models feature multiple equilibria: multiple time paths along which the economy might move. According to these models, recessions can be viewed as the economy's moving from a good to a bad equilibrium in which economic agents fail to coordinate their actions.

9. The political business cycle model argues that politicians will use monetary and fiscal policies to stimulate the economy prior to elections. In terms of the traditional Keynesian model with nominal rigidities and nonrational expectations, a politician might argue for printing more money prior to an election but reducing the growth in money after the election to limit the attendant increase in inflation. In terms of the real business cycle model, the method by which politicians can spur the economy is by announcing short-term tax cuts. These tax cuts will lead workers to work more while the tax rate is low, knowing that once the tax rate is raised, they'll work less.

10. Each theory discussed in this chapter provides some insight into the potential causes of recessions and expansions. Although there is evidence in support of each, none fits all the facts perfectly. Economists have tended to look for the definitive model of the business cycle—but there may not be one. Instead, each of the different explanations may play a part in some, if not all, economic fluctuations.

CHAPTER 10

THE NATURE AND COSTS OF UNEMPLOYMENT

INTRODUCTION

The unemployment rate is a key indicator of macroeconomic performance. On average, it has peaked at 7.8 percent and bottomed at 4.6 percent in the past eight U.S. business cycles. Having an unemployment rate of 7.8 rather than 4.6 percent matters. It means an extra 4.3 million unemployed American workers!

Avoiding and mitigating recessions, with their attendant unemployment, is the main objective of *countercyclical* monetary and fiscal policy. But not all recessions are as easily attacked as those envisaged by the simple Keynesian model. Moreover, the social benefits of combating unemployment depend on whether unemployment is involuntary or voluntary. Hence, both the effectiveness and value of countercyclical policy depend largely on the causes of unemployment. Much can be learned about these causes by studying unemployment spells—specifically how they begin, who experiences them, and how long they last.

Our study of unemployment starts with *labor force dynamics*—the movements of individuals into and out of jobs and into and out of the labor force. We'll consider how these dynamics vary over the business cycle and how they square with different theories of unemployment. Next we'll turn to differences in unemployment rates across different demographic groups. This decomposition sheds extra light on the causes and costs of unemployment. Finally, we'll point out that unemployment insurance, although it limits workers' financial losses, may raise the level of unemployment.

The following questions guide our inquiry:

- How does the rate of unemployment vary by age, sex, and race?

- What is Okun's law, and how does it measure the costs of recession?

- What determines the natural rate of unemployment?

- What is the relationship between unemployment and labor turnover—the movement of workers into and out of jobs?

- What is the duration of a typical unemployment spell?

- How does unemployment insurance work? Does it raise the unemployment rate?

LABOR FORCE DYNAMICS

The household survey used to compile official U.S. unemployment statistics classifies individuals into three categories. The first two—*employed* and *unemployed*—comprise the labor force. The third is *out of the labor force*. At the end of 1996, there were 133.9 million adults in the U.S. civilian labor force, of whom 126.7 million were employed and 7.2 million were unemployed. The remaining 66.6 million were out of the labor force. Among those not employed, the distinction between being unemployed and being out of the labor force rests primarily on whether individuals report that they are seeking work.

In some cases, as with full-time students or persons who are seriously ill, the classification "out of the labor force" is straightforward. But in other cases, it's more difficult to tell whether an individual is unemployed or truly out of the labor force. This classification difficulty is evident in the close correlation over time in the unemployment rate and the *labor force participation rate*—the fraction of the population that is in the labor force.

Figure 10.1 shows both rates for the period since 1950. The labor force participation rate has increased since the mid-1960s, from about 59 percent then to around 67 percent now. This trend reflects the increasing participation of women in the labor market that has more than offset the declining rate of male labor force participation. There are also cyclical movements in the labor force participation rate. Indeed, the labor force participation rate has often dropped temporarily when the unemployment rate has risen. This pattern is particularly noticeable during the 1990–1991 recession (point *D* in the figure) but can also be observed just after the troughs of the two recessions at the beginning and middle of the 1970s (points *A* and *B*) and again near the trough of the deep recession of 1981–1982 (point *C*). This negative correlation between the unemployment rate and the labor force participation rate suggests that, for some individuals, the distinction between the two situations is neither precise nor important. These individuals may report that they aren't seeking work and consequently may be classified as out of the labor force when, indeed, they would take a job if one came their way. Alternatively, they may report that they are seeking work, when, in fact, they aren't particularly eager to accept new employment.

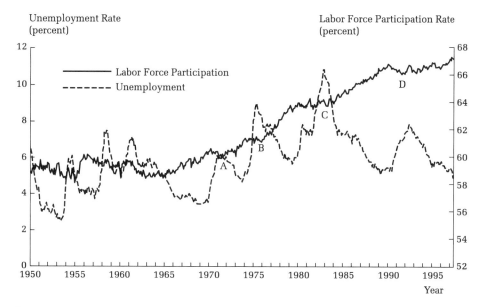

Unemployment Rate
(percent)

Labor Force Participation Rate
(percent)

FIGURE 10.1   UNEMPLOYMENT AND LABOR FORCE PARTICIPATION RATES SINCE 1950
The labor force participation rate measures the fraction of the adult population in the labor force. Since the mid-1960s, the participation rate has increased from about 59 percent to about 67 percent today. Despite its upward trend, the participation rate also varies cyclically, often dropping as the unemployment rate increases. This is evident near the troughs of the two recessions of the 1970s (points *A* and *B*), the deep recession of 1981–1982 (point *C*), and the recession of 1990–1991 (point *D*).

Source: Bureau of Labor Statistics.

NET VERSUS GROSS CHANGES IN WORK STATUS

The swings over time in the labor force participation and unemployment rates shown in Figure 10.1 represent net changes in employment status—the net change in the fraction of the labor force that is unemployed and the net change in the fraction of the overall population participating in the labor market. As net measures, they mask larger *gross flows* into and out of the labor market and into and out of jobs. Even when there is little change in the unemployment rate, many workers lose their jobs, and many others find work. Figure 10.2 illustrates the distinction between gross and net labor force flows.

It is useful to think of three pools of individuals at any point in time: (1) the employed, (2) the unemployed, and (3) those not in the labor force. From period to period (in the case of labor force statistics, we typically measure changes from month to month), each pool's size changes as a result of *net inflows*: the number of individuals entering the state (*inflows*) less the number leaving it (*outflows*). If inflows exceed outflows, net inflows are positive and the category's population increases. If outflows exceed inflows, net inflows are negative and the category's population decreases.

These flows, traced in Figure 10.2, are called labor force *transitions*. Transitions into employment are also called *accessions*; transitions out of employment are called

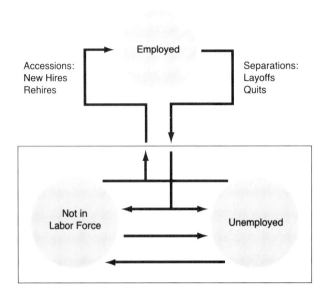

FIGURE 10.2 LABOR MARKET DYNAMICS
From one period to the next, employed workers may lose or leave their jobs (through layoffs or quits) and move to either the "unemployed" or the "not in the labor force" states. Similarly, those who are unemployed or not in the labor force may become "employed" as new hires or rehires. Finally, some individuals may move between unemployment and "not in the labor force."

New hires
Workers hired by a firm for the first time

Rehires
Workers recalled to employment by a firm after being out of work

Layoffs
Involuntary separations from (transitions out of) employment

Quits
Voluntary separations from (transitions out of) employment

1 These statistics are based on Figure 1 of Olivier Jean Blanchard and Peter Diamond, "The Cyclical Behavior of the Gross Flows of U.S. Workers," Brookings Papers on Economic Activity 2 (1990): 85–143.

separations. Accessions are divided into **new hires** and **rehires**, which, as the names indicate, refer respectively to workers hired by a firm for the first time and those recalled to the firm's employ after being out of work. Such recalled workers are returning from **layoffs**, one of the forms of separation. Layoffs are involuntary separations, whereas **quits** are generally voluntarily separations. Workers who quit their jobs or are laid off can become unemployed or leave the labor force, and those who are hired can come either from being unemployed or from being out of the labor force. There are also transitions between the two states of nonemployment—unemployed and not in the labor force—as some individuals without jobs begin looking for work while others stop doing so.

In any given month, employment grows to the extent that accessions exceed separations. *However, even when there is little net employment growth—when accessions and separations roughly offset each other—there is considerable labor force mobility; that is, both accessions and separations are large relative to the number of employed individuals.* For example, between January 1968 and May 1986, the level of employment increased by an average of 0.5 percent per month. This net monthly increase in employment resulted from an average of 3.4 accessions and 2.9 separations per hundred people employed.[1] That is, nearly 3 in every 100 workers were laid off or quit in the average month during the period, and a slightly larger number was hired.

"Brodkin, now that the economy is creating jobs at a faster than expected clip, why don't you go out and find yourself one?"

Both net and gross labor force transitions are important. The net flows indicate the direction of movement of the economy as a whole, and the gross flows indicate the extent of labor force mobility—how likely an individual is to move from one labor force classification to another.

CASE STUDY
SMALL BUSINESS—THE ENGINE OF JOB CREATION?

In supporting their pet business tax cuts, politicians often claim they are trying to help small businesses "grow" the economy because "the majority of new jobs are created by small business." Is small business that important to job creation? The answer depends. If we look only at *gross* job creation—at accessions but not separations or, perhaps, at only firms that add employees but not those that shrink or go bankrupt—then small business does account for a disproportionate amount of job growth. But if we are talking about *net* job creation, the answer is no, because small business also accounts for a disproportionate amount of job destruction. Smaller firms create and destroy a disproportionate share of jobs—they have more *labor turnover*—because, as a group, their performance is quite volatile. Some small firms grow very rapidly, while many others fail and go bankrupt.

For example, during the period 1972–1986 the average net annual decline in manufacturing employment was 2.3 percent among firms with fewer than 100 workers and 1.9 percent among firms with over 1,000 workers.[2] That is, the small firms actually

2 Steven J. Davis and John Haltiwanger, "Gross Job Creation, Gross Job Destruction, and Employment Reallocation," Quarterly Journal of Economics *(August 1992): 819–863.*

shrank faster than the large firms, on average, although the rates of change were quite similar.[3] However, among only those firms whose employment *increased*, the average annual rate of job growth was 14.0 percent for firms with under 100 workers and just 6.0 percent among firms with over 1000 employees. Thus, there was pretty impressive growth for small business—but just among those firms that grew! Overall, this growth was more than offset by very sharp declines among small firms that did not grow.

THE SOURCES AND DURATION OF UNEMPLOYMENT

Three paths lead to unemployment: job loss (being laid off), job leaving (quitting), and entry into the labor force without a job. Figure 10.3 decomposes post-1970 unemployment according to these paths. Clearly, layoff unemployment is the major source of unemployment volatility, rising sharply when the unemployment rate rises. This source of unemployment accounts for only 2 percentage points of the total unemployment rate at expansion peaks and over 6 percentage points at recession troughs. By contrast, the unemployment rate attributable to quits has been quite stable over time at

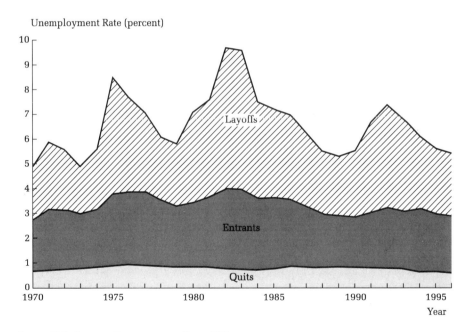

FIGURE 10.3 TYPES OF UNEMPLOYMENT SINCE 1970

A person may become unemployed through job loss (separation by being laid off), entry into the labor force without a job, or job leaving (separation by quitting). This figure shows that the last category has been quite stable since 1970. Unemployment through entrants has been somewhat more variable, rising during recessions. Most of the increase in unemployment during recession is attributable to layoffs, which have varied between 2 and 6 percentage points of unemployment.

Source: Economic Report of the President, *1997.*

3 The fact that both large and small firms shrank reflects the general shift in employment away from manufacturing during this period, a trend we mentioned in chapter 1.

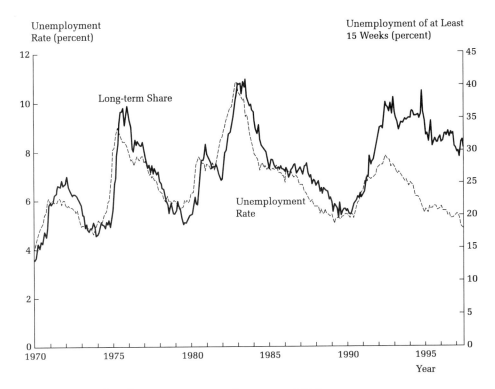

FIGURE 10.4 LONG-TERM UNEMPLOYMENT AND THE UNEMPLOYMENT RATE
Long-term unemployment is defined here as being without a job for at least 15 weeks. When unemployment is high, so is the share of unemployment accounted for by long-term spells.

Source: Bureau of Labor Statistics.

less than 1 percent. Unemployment due to labor force entry, accounting typically for about 2 percentage points of the unemployment rate, is somewhat more variable over the cycle.[4]

The durations of the unemployment spells also change during recessions. They increase. To illustrate, average duration was 12.0 weeks in July 1990, the month of an expansion peak, but rose to 13.5 weeks by April 1991. Figure 10.4 plots the aggregate unemployment rate against the fraction of unemployed workers who have been unemployed for at least 15 weeks—the long-term unemployed. The figure shows a strong correspondence between the two series. When unemployment is high, so is the share of unemployment that is accounted for by long-term spells. *Thus, during recessions, a greater share of unemployment is accounted for by workers who have been laid off, and more unemployment is long term in nature.* Note, though, that the decline in the share of long-term unemployed has been less pronounced during the most recent expansion than in previous ones, a phenomenon that has not yet received much attention.

4 *Unemployment attributable to labor force entry rises slightly in recession not because more people enter the labor force, but because those who do enter remain unemployed for a longer period of time—reflecting the association between the duration and level of unemployment that we are about to consider.*

LABOR FORCE DYNAMICS AND THEORIES OF UNEMPLOYMENT

Chapters 8 and 9 provided different theories of recessions and their attendant unemployment, but there is considerable unemployment even during booms. Hence, we need to explain boom unemployment as well as that arising during busts.

INVOLUNTARY UNEMPLOYMENT

The Keynesian model emphasizes involuntary unemployment—when an individual wants to work but can't find a job at the going wage. The rise in layoffs during recession seems to support the Keynesian view, since layoffs appear to be involuntary ways of becoming unemployed.

But layoffs account for a significant share of unemployment even during good times. Can there be involuntary unemployment when the rate of employment is high? There can be if nominal rigidities are not fully overcome, even during expansions of aggregate demand (outward shifts of the AD curve). As discussed in chapter 9, if the nominal wage rises with the price level to maintain a real wage that exceeds the market-clearing level, then increases in the price level will not eliminate involuntary unemployment. No matter how high the price level goes, if the nominal wage keeps pace, firms won't find it profitable to hire additional workers.

Models of Real Wage Rigidity

Insider-outsider theory
An explanation of labor market behavior that posits that insiders (individuals already employed) negotiate higher real wages for themselves at the expense of outsiders

Efficiency wage theory
The idea that keeping wages high makes workers perform better for fear of losing their jobs

5 See Assar Lindbeck and Dennis J. Snower, The Insider-Outsider Theory of Employment and Unemployment (Cambridge, MA: MIT Press, 1989).

6 See Carl Shapiro and Joseph E. Stiglitz, "Involuntary Unemployment as a Worker Discipline Device," American Economic Review (1984): 433–444.

Who imposes real wage rigidity? The government does in the case of low-skill jobs. How? By periodically adjusting the minimum wage to prevent the real value of the minimum wage from falling when there is ongoing inflation. Labor unions also try to set real wages above market-clearing values in their collective bargaining agreements. Even nonunionized workers may be able to set their real wages above competitive levels. Because of their firm-specific human capital and the costs of hiring and training new workers, workers already employed by firms (*insiders*) have special bargaining power that unemployed workers (*outsiders*) don't have. According to this **insider-outsider theory**, the insiders use this power to secure above-market-clearing real wages.[5]

An alternative theory that also features excessively high real wages places the responsibility for these wages and involuntary unemployment on firms. According to this **efficiency wage theory**, firms set their wage rate above market-clearing levels as a way of eliciting good job performance by workers whose job performance is difficult to monitor.[6] To understand this theory, suppose labor supply is fixed and that the labor market would clear (supply would equal demand) at a wage rate of $10 per hour. Now consider the employment policy of a firm that hires workers to manufacture hand grenades. This is a tricky job requiring lots of care because poorly constructed grenades may explode accidentally. Once hired, each worker chooses whether to work carefully or not, a decision that cannot be observed by the firm. If the worker exercises care, the hand grenades he produces always work as designed. If the worker is careless, the grenades he produces occasionally malfunction, injuring or killing the soldiers transporting them. When such malfunctions occur, the worker who produced the defective grenade is fired.

Even though the firm could hire workers for $10 an hour, it might find it desirable to pay more, say $20 per hour, to give workers a strong incentive to do their job right and not end up being fired. Workers hired at $10 an hour would see little point in being careful; if fired, they could quickly find work elsewhere at the same wage rate in a full employment economy. By contrast, workers receiving, say, $20 an hour would know that if they lost their job they'd likely end up earning $10 an hour. The $20 hourly wage in this example is called an *efficiency wage* because the firm chooses it to elicit more efficient (in this case, more careful) work effort. Paying efficiency wages may be in a firm's own interest, but the practice, if widespread, can produce involuntary unemployment. If all employers choose to pay a wage above the market-clearing $10 per hour, there will be too few jobs to go around. Such involuntary unemployment reinforces the efficiency wages by giving employed workers an additional reason to avoid being fired: the possibility of not finding another job. Hence, to lessen shirking on the job, employers can rely on a combination of higher wages and the prospect of unemployment. As unemployment becomes a more likely consequence of being fired (i.e., as the unemployment rate rises), firms can reduce the wages they pay and still elicit efficient labor effort.

This trade-off is represented in Figure 10.5 by the curve labeled S*—the "no-shirking constraint."[7] At each wage, it indicates the level of employment (and unemployment) needed to provide workers with a strong enough incentive not to shirk; the higher the wage is, the lower the requisite level of unemployment. The intersection of the no-shirking constraint and the labor demand curve, D, is the equilibrium point at which the labor demanded at the going wage leaves just enough workers unemployed to satisfy the no-shirking constraint at that wage. This intersection occurs at a real wage w^1 and a level of unemployment $(N - L^1)$.

The insider-outsider and efficiency wage theories differ in their explanations for involuntary unemployment, but both theories emphasize that such unemployment is not exclusively a temporary, recession-related phenomenon.

CASE STUDY
WAGES IN THE FAST-FOOD INDUSTRY

Economists have identified many examples of companies' paying what appear to be efficiency wages. The case most often cited is Henry Ford's decision early in this century to offer workers $5 a day, far more than the going wage at the time.[8] More recent evidence comes from the fast-food industry.

Individual outlets of McDonald's, Kentucky Fried Chicken, and similar fast-food concerns are owned either directly by the parent company or by a local individual

7 This diagram is presented in Bruce C. Greenwald and Joseph E. Stiglitz, "Financial Market Imperfections and Business Cycles," Quarterly Journal of Economics (February 1993): 77–114.

8 Daniel Raff and Lawrence Summers, "Did Henry Ford Pay Efficiency Wages?" Journal of Labor Economics (1987).

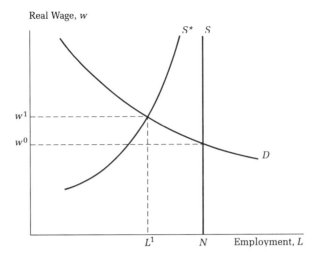

FIGURE 10.5 EFFICIENCY WAGES AND UNEMPLOYMENT

An efficiency wage is a wage set above the rate needed to attract new workers (w^0) as a way of ensuring good perfor-mance. The curve labeled S^* is called a no-shirking constraint. At each wage rate, it indicates the level of employment needed to provide workers with an incentive not to shirk. The intersection of S^* with the labor demand curve, D, determines a wage (w^1) that leaves just enough workers unemployed to satisfy the no-shirking constraint. Involuntary unemployment of $N - L^1$ results.

under a franchise agreement. In the latter case, the parent company exerts control over production methods and policies as a way of ensuring that all the company's outlets, whether franchised or company owned, meet certain standards of uniformity from the customer's perspective. However, wage rates vary from location to location according to local labor market conditions.

Interestingly, the wage rates paid by individual outlets also vary systematically according to the outlet's form of ownership. Alan Krueger of Princeton University found that higher-level employees earned 9 percent more, and full-time crew workers 2 percent more, at company-owned outlets than at franchised outlets.[9] Why? Accord-ing to the efficiency wage theory, firms pay higher wages when it is difficult to monitor work effort. This is precisely the case for the distant owners of company-owned out-lets. These owners find it much more difficult to check on the quality of work effort in their outlets than do owners of a franchise who typically live near the outlet and often work there themselves. The higher wages paid by the distant outlet owner act as a substitute for the extra monitoring that local ownership otherwise would provide.

9 Alan B. Krueger, "Ownership, Agency, and Wages: An Examination of Franchising in the Fast Food Industry," Quarterly Journal of Economics (February 1991): 75–101.

VOLUNTARY UNEMPLOYMENT

In contrast to the Keynesian view, the real business cycle model attributes recessions not to troubled labor markets, but rather to technology shocks that reduce real wages. The drop in the real wage induces some workers to opt for unemployment; they decline to work at the lower real wage. Such voluntary unemployment arises in booms as well. Even in booms, there are those who are able to work but aren't willing to accept employment at wages commensurate with their skills.

How much unemployment is voluntary? A good place to start counting is with job leavers. In contrast to being laid off, quitting is a voluntary act. We might exclude labor force entrants from the ranks of the voluntarily unemployed since those unwilling to work wouldn't enter the labor force.

Viewing unemployment by those who quit as a proxy for voluntary unemployment suggests that voluntary unemployment generally accounts for a certain share of unemployment, but little of the rise in unemployment during recessions (recall Figure 10.3). However, this conclusion may be unwarranted. Some laid-off workers and some new entrants may also be voluntarily unemployed. For example, a laid-off worker may already, during her current unemployment spell, have rejected jobs at the going wage. As another example, a worker offered a wage cut by an employer might refuse to accept it and prompt a layoff, thinking that the going wage in other jobs is higher than it actually is.

In summary, quits appear to represent some but not all voluntary unemployment. Thus, the relative stability of quits over the business cycle does not necessarily mean that voluntary unemployment is equally stable.

MISPERCEPTION UNEMPLOYMENT

The misperception theory says that workers may temporarily reject work if they believe that the nominal wage rate they are being offered corresponds to a lower real wage than it actually does—if they think, that is, that the price level is higher than it actually is. Such misperception unemployment doesn't fit neatly into the voluntary-involuntary categorization. It is voluntary in that workers choose not to work. Yet it also satisfies the definition of involuntary unemployment: workers without jobs would accept work at the nominal wage offered if they knew how high the real wage actually was.

How important is the misperception theory in explaining recessions? Because it presumes that workers voluntarily leave their jobs in search of better wages, it seems contradicted by the relative stability of quits over the business cycle. But there may be additional voluntary unemployment in the layoff category. However, in this case there is an additional piece of damaging evidence. The notion of workers' being "fooled" clearly relates to the short run, until they acquire the correct information on prices. If recessions were caused by lots of workers quitting or accepting layoff because they temporarily thought their wages were too low, we would expect an increase in the share of unemployment accounted for by short-term unemployment—just the opposite of what occurs.

FRICTIONAL UNEMPLOYMENT

Frictional unemployment results from the continual movement of individuals across jobs as the composition of production shifts among industries and regions, as individuals seek better compensation and working conditions, and as older workers retire and younger ones take their places. Also called *search unemployment*, frictional unemployment occurs as workers learn about and search for new jobs. Frictional unemployment can arise initially through a layoff, a quit, or labor force entry and, given the dynamic nature of the U.S. economy, there is little doubt that significant frictional unemployment exists.[10]

Frictional unemployment occurs in part because workers do not have perfect information about alternative jobs and wages. However, there is no presumption of wholesale misinformation on the part of workers. This is not the only difference between frictional and misperception unemployment. The misperception theory explains unemployment fluctuations, whereas frictional unemployment explains why there is always some measured unemployment.

Frictional unemployment shouldn't last long, as individuals move from one job to another or find work after entering the labor force. Hence, it seems that frictional unemployment, though perhaps always present and significant, shouldn't explain the rise of unemployment during recessions, when the duration of unemployment rises. However, this ignores the fact that the degree of labor market stability changes over time. When there is a big shift in activity among productive sectors or regions, we expect more workers to experience frictional unemployment. Futhermore, such major sectoral shifts might also take longer to occur, causing the typical unemployment spell of the frictionally unemployed worker to lengthen. This is the *sectoral shock model* discussed in chapter 9—a model that, particularly for the 1970s, successfully explains cyclical swings in unemployment as resulting from sectoral shifts in industry, measured by the variation in job creation (increases in employment) and job destruction (decreases in employment) across different industries.

SUMMARY

In recessions, the fraction of unemployment accounted for by layoffs and long spells of unemployment increases. This is consistent with the Keynesian view that unemployment is involuntary, but not necessarily inconsistent with theories of voluntary and frictional unemployment. Frictional unemployment explains unemployment even in booms, but so do recent extensions of Keynesian theory, which focus on real wage rigidities. *Hence, unemployment, in good times and bad, has a variety of explanations.*

10 For example, Davis and Haltiwanger, "Gross Job Creation," in their study of manufacturing firms between 1972 and 1986, found that in the average year, growing firms increased their workforce by an average of 9.2 percent whereas shrinking firms reduced their workforce by an average of 11.3 percent.

UNEMPLOYMENT: A DISAGGREGATE VIEW

Studying the labor market behavior of particular population subgroups uncovers patterns not observable in the aggregate. We'll begin by looking at the differences in labor force participation and unemployment according to sex and then consider differences by age, race, and the duration of unemployment spells.

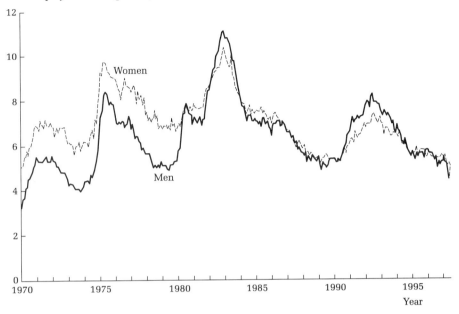

FIGURE 10.6 UNEMPLOYMENT RATES, BY SEX, SINCE 1970

Until the late 1970s, the unemployment rate for women exceeded the rate for men by 1 or 2 percentage points. Since then, the rates have been much closer. This convergence is thought to be related to the increased labor force participation of women.

Source: Bureau of Labor Statistics.

DIFFERENCES BY SEX IN EMPLOYMENT AND UNEMPLOYMENT

The aggregate U.S. labor force participation rate has increased during the past few decades. However, this trend masks differences between men and women. The labor force participation rate among men has declined (from 86 percent in 1950 to 75 percent in 1997), primarily because of a drop in participation among the elderly. By contrast, the labor force participation rate among women has risen sharply over the same period, from 34 percent to 60 percent. Thus, the difference in participation rates between men and women dropped from 52 percentage points in 1950 to 15 percentage points in 1997.

The growing importance of women in the U.S. workforce has been accompanied by a change in their unemployment experience. Figure 10.6 graphs unemployment rates for men and women for the period since 1970. The female unemployment rate exceeded the male rate until the 1980s, typically by 1 or 2 percentage points. Since then, the two rates have been much closer to one another. This is not surprising. As the typical woman's labor force experience has shifted over time from occasional work to career employment, there has been a reduction in the frictional unemployment normally associated with the job search of labor force entrants. Put simply, as women's

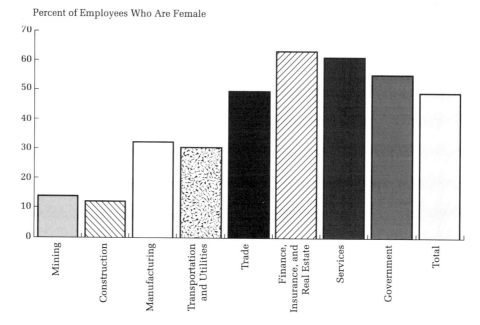

Percent of Employees Who Are Female

FIGURE 10.7 PERCENTAGE OF FEMALE EMPLOYEES, BY INDUSTRY, FEBRUARY 1996
The male unemployment rate is more volatile than the female rate, primarily because women are disproportionately employed in less cyclical industries. The figure shows the relatively small fractions of women employed in such highly cyclical industries as mining, construction, and manufacturing, and the large fractions employed in the more stable service and government sectors.

Source: U.S. Department of Labor, Bureau of Labor Statistics, Employment, Hours, and Earnings in the United States, 1988–96.

labor force participation patterns have become more like men's, so has their unemployment experience.

Although the unemployment rates of women and men are now relatively similar in a typical year, the male rate is more volatile. The reason is that women are disproportionately employed in less cyclical industries. We saw in chapter 4 that heavy industries have much more volatile swings in output than trade and services, in part because the demand for the durable investment goods they produce is so much more volatile than consumption over the cycle. There is similar volatility in these industries' employment levels. As Figure 10.7 shows, women account for a relatively small share of the employment in the more cyclical industries—around 10 percent in mining and construction and 30 percent in manufacturing, as compared to nearly 50 percent in wholesale and retail trade and over 60 percent in services.

UNEMPLOYMENT DISTINCTIONS BY AGE AND RACE

Although male-female unemployment rate differences have narrowed over time, very large differences remain by age and race. Figure 10.8 plots the gaps since 1972 between the overall unemployment rate and (1) the unemployment rate for teenagers between

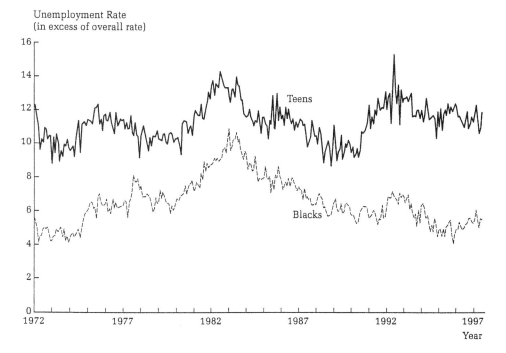

Unemployment Rate
(in excess of overall rate)

FIGURE 10.8 UNEMPLOYMENT RATES, BY AGE AND RACE, SINCE 1972
Over time, there has been a significant gap between the overall unemployment rate and the rates for teenagers and minorities. Further, as the periods of the early 1980s and early 1990s illustrate, the rates for teenagers and nonwhites tend to rise more during recessions than the overall rate does.

Source: Bureau of Labor Statistics.

ages 16 and 19 and (2) that for blacks. Each group had significantly higher unemployment rates over the entire period than did the population as a whole. Those in both categories—black teenagers—experienced truly staggering rates of unemployment. In 1996, 37 percent of black male teenagers were unemployed! Unemployment rates among teenagers and blacks rise more during recessions than the overall rate. For example, each rate rose by 4 percentage points more than the overall rate between early 1980 and late 1982, a period with two recessions.

What explains age and racial differences in the level and volatility of unemployment? For teenagers, the higher level of unemployment is commonly viewed as the result of the higher frictional unemployment associated with labor force entry. Higher frictional unemployment also helps explain the higher level of unemployment among nonwhites. Evidence suggests that a greater share of the unemployment of lower-income workers—and nonwhites, on average, earn less than whites—results from industrial mobility.[11] Similarly, the volatility of the unemployment rate is higher for lower-wage workers as a group, not just for teenagers and nonwhites. This pattern is consistent with the view that unemployment swings arise from increased sectoral

11 *See Chinhui Juhn, Kevin M. Murphy, and Robert H. Topel, "Why Has the Natural Rate of Unemployment Increased over Time?"* Brookings Papers on Economic Activity *22 (1991): 75–126. This paper is also the source for the figures on duration of unemployment spells presented in the next section.*

mobility and frictional unemployment, since groups more prone to frictional unemployment presumably would be more affected by its increase.

SPELLS OF UNEMPLOYMENT: THE LONG AND THE SHORT

At any particular time, the unemployed population includes workers undergoing unemployment spells of different lengths. Some will soon find work (or leave the labor force); others may remain unemployed for a considerable period of time. Any particular unemployment rate could result from different combinations of short-term and long-term unemployment. An annual 5 percent unemployment rate could reflect a different 5 percent of the labor force being unemployed each week (all unemployment spells last one week) or the same 5 percent of the labor force being unemployed for the entire year (all unemployment spells last 52 weeks). These two cases, although they produce the same aggregate unemployment rate, reflect very different patterns of unemployment—from mild and widespread to serious and highly concentrated.

Which of these extremes is more accurate? We saw in Figure 10.4 that the answer varies over the business cycle—the share of long-term unemployment in the total increases during recessions. However long-term unemployment is considerable even during booms. During the expansion years 1987 through 1989, for example, one-tenth of all unemployment resulted from unemployment spells that lasted for an entire year, and nearly half occurred in spells of more than half a year. On the other hand, over one-fifth of all unemployment came in spells of 13 weeks or fewer. Thus, there is no typical unemployment spell. There is considerable long-term unemployment but lots of short-term unemployment as well.

PRIVATE AND SOCIAL COSTS OF UNEMPLOYMENT

What are the costs of unemployment? And to what extent does the government's social insurance safety net cushion unemployment's blows? If social insurance succeeds at its task, then the uneven distribution of unemployment's costs among teenagers, blacks, the long-term unemployed, and certain other groups can be spread over the wider population.

UNEMPLOYMENT AND WELFARE

When considering the costs of unemployment, it is useful to distinguish private costs accruing to those who are unemployed from the social costs accruing to society as a whole. Let's start with a case in which these costs are the same.

One might argue that the cost of unemployment to an individual who does not work equals the wages that he loses during the unemployment spell, whereas the cost to society as a whole is the output that the worker does not produce during the same period. How would these costs compare? In competitive markets, a worker's wage rate equals his marginal product—the additional output his labor produces. Hence, the

Andy Capp reprinted with special permission of King Features Syndicate, Inc.

worker's lost wages would equal society's lost output, and private and social costs of unemployment would be the same. But do lost wages and output provide an accurate measure of the loss to the unemployed and society? The answer is no. They could overstate or understate the true costs, depending on the reasons for and impacts of unemployment.

Does Reduced Output Overstate the Costs of Unemployment?

To see how lost output can overstate the cost of unemployment, consider the case of voluntary unemployment. In Figure 10.9 there are N potential workers who collectively have an upward-sloping labor supply curve, S. The curve indicates the number of workers willing to work at the real wage, w. In equilibrium, only L^0 workers are willing to work at the going wage, w^0. The remaining $N - L^0$ individuals are voluntarily unemployed.

By choosing not to work, an individual forgoes the wages he would have earned. But the individual must gain at least as much by not working; he can't be worse off, or else he wouldn't have opted for unemployment. What form does this gain take? The simplest answer is the value of increased leisure time—the time made available by not being at work. By leisure we don't simply mean sitting around watching television, but the whole range of activities one engages in when not at work, such as repairing one's house or helping to care for other family members. An individual might save money performing these activities himself, rather than working at a low-wage job and hiring someone else to perform the services. We call such activities **home production**.

GDP, we know, is not a perfect measure of national output, and the exclusion of leisure is one important reason why. Even though GDP falls as the result of voluntary unemployment, the concomitant increase in the value of leisure could well exceed the loss in measured GDP. That is, the costs to the worker of voluntary unemployment could well be negative with the increased value of leisure exceeding the lost wages. In terms of Figure 10.9, increasing employment from L^0 to N increases output by the light gray area under the demand curve. This is because the demand curve's height measures the marginal product of each additional worker's labor. In effect, the light gray area is

Home production
Goods and services that an individual produces for himself or herself, rather than purchasing them in a market

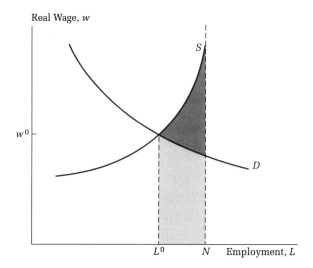

FIGURE 10.9 COST OF VOLUNTARY UNEMPLOYMENT
In equilibrium, the level of employment is determined at the intersection of the labor supply and demand curves—at L^0.
$N - L^0$ individuals are voluntarily unemployed. Each of these individuals forgoes the wages he could have earned but
gains the value of increased leisure time. Increasing employment to N would increase output by the light gray area
under the demand curve—the sum of the marginal products of each $N - L^0$ individuals. However, the lost value of their
leisure would equal the area under the labor supply curve between L^0 and N—the sum of the values each worker places
on his time. On balance, the lost value of leisure would exceed the increased value of output by the dark gray area.

the sum of the marginal products of each of the $N - L^0$ workers. However, the lost value
of these added workers' leisure equals the area under the supply curve between L^0 and
N, because the supply curve measures the value that each of these additional workers
places on her time. On balance, as employment increases from L^0 to N, the lost value of
leisure exceeds the increased value of output by the dark gray area in the figure.

Although the costs of voluntary unemployment may be nonexistent or negative,
involuntary unemployment presents the other extreme. An involuntarily unemployed
person might be willing to work for much less than the going wage and still be unable
to find work. Such a person might gain little from being unemployed—it is not an
outcome of choice. Still, even an involuntarily unemployed worker may place some
value on increased leisure time. This situation is shown in Figure 10.10. Here, the
labor supply and labor demand curves intersect at a real wage w^0 and a level of employment L^0. However, because the market exhibits a downwardly rigid wage, the real
wage is fixed at w^1. As a result, the market produces involuntary unemployment of
$L^0 - L^1$. The output lost as a result equals the value firms would have placed on these
workers' production, equal to the area under the demand curve between L^0 and L^1—
the sum of the shaded areas in the figure. However, these unemployed workers do
place some value on the leisure they gain, equal to the area under the labor supply
curve between L^0 and L^1—the dark gray area. Hence, the net loss to society, although
positive, equals the light gray area—less than the full value of lost output.

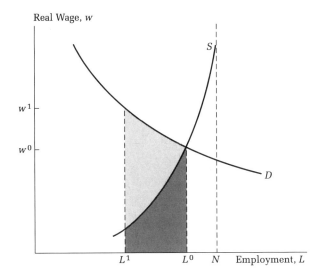

FIGURE 10.10 COST OF INVOLUNTARY UNEMPLOYMENT

The equilibrium wage rate is w^0 and equilibrium employment is L^0. However, because of downward rigidity, the real wage is fixed at w^1. Involuntary unemployment of $L^0 - L^1$ results. The output loss is the area under the demand curve between L^0 and L^1 — the sum of the shaded areas. The unemployed individuals do place some value on the leisure they gain, equal to the dark gray area under the labor supply curve between L^0 and L^1. The net loss to society equals the light gray area, which is less than the value of the lost output.

Thus, *by failing to account for the increased value of leisure and home production that unemployment permits, the loss in GDP overstates unemployment's cost to both the worker and society. The magnitude of this overstatement depends on the share of unemployment that is voluntary and the extent to which involuntarily unemployed workers value the free time that accompanies unemployment.*

Does Reduced Output Understate the Costs of Unemployment?

Individuals might value a short period away from work, but not all unemployment is brief or conveniently timed. For some unemployed workers, enforced, full-time leisure may hold little attraction. Heightened family problems and alcoholism are frequently cited side effects that detract from the value of this "leisure." Also on the list is crime, committed not only out of despair but also as an alternative means of generating income when the legal labor market fails to deliver. Clearly, the social costs of certain crimes are far greater than the value of the output the criminal might have produced if working legally.

The relationship between crime and unemployment is hard to measure because so many crimes go unreported. Still, the two phenomena do appear to be connected. Figure 10.11 plots the U.S. unemployment and crime rates for the period 1960 through 1994. Although the generally upward movement of the crime rate masks the relationship somewhat, we can see quite clearly that the two rates moved together during the

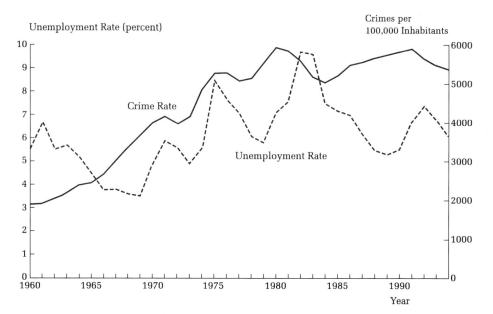

FIGURE 10.11 UNEMPLOYMENT AND CRIME
The relationship between crime and unemployment is complex, but the two phenomena do appear to be connected. The two rates moved together during the recessions of the early and mid-1970s. The crime rate also rose with the onset of the two recessions of the early 1980s and that of the 1990s, although its rise and fall preceded those of the unemployment rate.

Source: Sourcebook of Criminal Justice Statistics, *1995.*

recessions in the early and mid-1970s. The crime rate rose again with the onset of the two recessions of the early 1980s and that of the early 1990s, its rise and fall actually preceding those of the unemployment rate.

Spreading the Burden of Unemployment: Unemployment Insurance

12 Other components of fiscal policy based on income rather than employment status also provide social insurance to the unemployed. These include programs aimed at low-income individuals and families, such as food stamps and Temporary Assistance for Needy Families. Indirectly, the income tax also provides insurance, because the reduction in income arising from unemployment reduces the affected individual's income tax liability as well.

How can the costs borne by the unemployed be lessened? There are two approaches: reducing the costs of unemployment to the individual and society, or, without actually reducing the costs of unemployment, shifting these costs from the unemployed to the general population. The first approach involves reducing the rate of unemployment, by fighting recessions and attempting to reduce the *natural rate* of unemployment that prevails even in good times. The second approach involves social insurance. Although reducing the social costs of unemployment is clearly a desirable objective, realistic policy design must recognize that not all costly unemployment will be eliminated. This is where the safety net of social insurance becomes relevant.

The most important social insurance program used to offset the risks of unemployment is *unemployment insurance (UI)*.[12] Unemployment insurance does not eliminate the costs of unemployment—it does not address society's loss of output—but it does partially shift the costs of unemployment from unemployed workers to the more general population, who pay the taxes needed to finance the payments to the unemployed.

A worker who becomes unemployed in the United States receives benefits based on her prior earnings. The exact rules and benefit levels vary by state, with some federal direction and control. A measure of the generosity of benefits is the *wage replacement rate*—the ratio of weekly benefits to the weekly wages lost by the unemployed workers. As of late 1993, this rate averaged .37, meaning that just over a third of lost wages were replaced by benefits.[13]

Individuals can normally receive benefits for as long as they remain unemployed (until they find a job or leave the labor force), up to a maximum of 26 weeks. During and after recessions, the 26-week limit is typically extended by federal legislation. Still, some workers remain unemployed even after 26 or more weeks and exhaust their benefits. Others not protected are labor force entrants who did not have a job before their unemployment spell began and those in specific occupations (such as in agriculture) that are not covered by the unemployment insurance system. Because of benefit exhaustion and lack of coverage or qualification, many unemployed workers do not receive unemployment compensation. In an average week in 1996, for example, 7.2 million U.S. workers were classified as unemployed, but of these, only 2.7 million received unemployment insurance benefits.

Although unemployment insurance and other social insurance programs, in spreading the burden of unemployment more evenly across the population, clearly act in the right direction, there still remains a considerable disparity in how different families fare during recession. Because they are more susceptible to elevated unemployment when the general unemployment rate rises, members of lower-income groups have their income fall proportionately more during recessions, even when unemployment compensation and low-income social insurance transfer programs are taken into account.[14]

CASE STUDY
DOES UNEMPLOYMENT INSURANCE CAUSE UNEMPLOYMENT?

Both theory and evidence suggest that unemployment insurance itself may cause some of the unemployment it is aimed at cushioning. If unemployment is made less costly to those it directly affects, their incentive to avoid being unemployed is reduced. This reduced incentive may contribute to unemployment in two ways: by making unemployment spells more likely to occur and making them last longer, once they occur.

UI may increase the likelihood of unemployment by lessening workers' initial aversion to employment in highly cyclical industries or in jobs with an elevated prospect of future unemployment. Knowing that the safety net is there, workers may be

13 U.S. Committee on Ways and Means, Overview of Entitlement Programs: 1994 Green Book (Washington, DC: U.S. Government Printing Office, July 15, 1994), p. 275.

14 See Rebecca M. Blank, "Disaggregating the Effect of the Business Cycle on the Distribution of Income," Economica (1989): 141–163.

willing to take greater risks, choosing jobs with higher wages but less certain prospects than they otherwise would. Ultimately, more unemployment will result.

In addition, UI may increase the duration of unemployment spells by making workers who are already unemployed less willing to accept a new job—more likely to impose higher standards in their job search. The reason is straightforward: they will lose their benefits upon accepting a new job, unless those benefits were about to lapse anyway. Corroborating this theory is a study by Lawrence Katz of Harvard University and Bruce Meyer of Northwestern University.[15] Examining the pattern of U.S. unemployment spells, they found that workers receiving unemployment compensation were much more likely to become reemployed around the time of benefit exhaustion, but that no such pattern existed for workers not eligible to receive benefits in the first place. They estimated that a one-week increase in the maximum duration of benefits would increase the average duration of unemployment spells of UI recipients by .16 to .20 week.

BENEFITS OF REDUCING UNEMPLOYMENT: OKUN'S LAW AND THE NATURAL RATE

So far we have emphasized the distinction between the private costs (borne by the worker) and the social costs of unemployment and the distinction between these social costs and a simple measure commonly used to approximate them: the wages and output lost as a direct result of the affected worker's unemployment. However, there are additional factors that make unemployment more costly to society, and reducing it more beneficial, than our previous analysis indicates. First, reductions in unemployment are typically accompanied by other changes in the economy that also lead to increased output. Second, reducing the current rate of unemployment may actually contribute to a subsequent reduction in the natural rate of unemployment, helping to make lower unemployment more sustainable. We consider each of these factors in turn.

OKUN'S LAW

Figure 10.12 plots annual changes in the rate of unemployment against the annual rate of GDP growth in the United States for each year during the period 1960 through 1996. As we would anticipate, there is a negative relationship between the two series, with increases in unemployment being associated with lower growth in GDP. However, compared to our theoretical predictions, the implied effect of unemployment on growth is too powerful. Each percentage point increase in the unemployment rate should be associated with about 0.7 percent lower GDP growth. But the relationship that best fits the data, represented by the straight line in Figure 10.12,[16] indicates a decline in GDP growth nearly three times as large: each percentage point increase in

15 Lawrence F. Katz and Bruce D. Meyer, "The Impact of the Potential Duration of Unemployment Benefits on the Duration of Unemployment," Journal of Public Economics 41 (April 1990): 45–72.

16 This line is derived from the data in the figure using a common technique called ordinary least squares regression, which chooses the straight line that minimizes the sum of squared vertical differences between the line and each observation.

Growth Rate, Real GDP (percent)

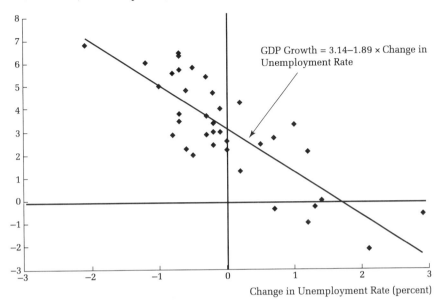

GDP Growth = 3.14–1.89 × Change in
Unemployment Rate

Change in Unemployment Rate (percent)

FIGURE 10.12 GDP GROWTH AND THE UNEMPLOYMENT RATE, 1960–1996
Between 1960 and 1996, there was a negative relationship between annual changes in the GDP growth rate and annual
changes in the unemployment rate. Each percentage point increase in the unemployment rate was associated with a
1.89 percentage point decline in the growth rate of real GDP.

Source: Economic Report of the President, *1997.*

Okun's Law
An empirical relationship
between reductions in the
unemployment rate and
increases in the GDP growth
rate

*17 The expression for Okun's Law
is $(GDP_t - GDP_{t-1})/GDP_{t-1} =
a - b(u_t - u_{t-1})$, where GDP_t is
real GDP in year t and u_t is the
corresponding unemployment
rate. In Figure 10.12, a is
estimated to be 3.14 and b is 1.89,
indicating that real GDP would
grow by just over 3 percent
annually with no change in the
unemployment rate. (Put another
way, a real GDP growth rate of
more than 3 percent would be
required for the unemployment
rate to decline.) Actually, when
Okun first introduced his "law,"
the coefficient b was closer to 3
than 2. Nevertheless, his original
reasoning concerning why the
coefficient exceeds its theoreti-
cally predicted value still applies.
  Okun's Law is sometimes
expressed in a slightly different
way, as a relationship between two
gaps: the percentage gap between
GDP_t and a hypothetical construct
known as potential GDP and the
gap between the unemployment
rate u_t and the natural rate of
unemployment. The distinction
between this and the form used
here is not empirically significant.*

the unemployment rate is associated with a nearly 2 percent (almost three times 0.7)
decline in the growth of output.

This important observation, that output is much more sensitive to the unemployment rate than basic theory would suggest, was first formalized by Arthur
Okun, head of the President's Council of Economic Advisors, during the late 1960s.
The empirical relationship that each percentage point of reduced unemployment is
associated with about 2 percent faster GDP growth is known as **Okun's Law**.[17] The
explanation for GDP's apparent oversensitivity to the unemployment rate lies in the
fact that when unemployment changes, other economic changes also typically occur
that reinforce the direct impact of unemployment on output.

To see how these other factors enter, let's consider the growth accounting
framework derived in chapter 1:

$$\frac{\Delta Y}{Y} = \frac{\Delta A}{A} + \beta \frac{\Delta K}{K} + (1 - \beta)\frac{\Delta L}{L}.$$

This equation says that the growth rate of output ($\Delta Y/Y$) equals the growth rate of the
level of multifactor productivity ($\Delta A/A$) plus β times the growth rate of the capital
stock input ($\Delta K/K$) plus $(1 - \beta)$ times the growth rate of the labor input ($\Delta L/L$).

This equation predicts that for each 1 percent increase in the growth rate of labor input, output will grow by $(1 - \beta)$ percent—about 0.7 percent—more. How does the growth rate of labor input relate to unemployment? A 1 percentage point decrease in the unemployment rate is roughly equivalent to a 1 percent increase in employment.[18] Thus, equating the growth rate of labor input with that of employment, we should expect a decrease in the unemployment rate of 1 percentage point to increase output by about 0.7 percent.

But we can also see from this relationship that two other factors, capital stock growth and technological progress, also affect the growth rate of output. As documented in chapter 1, productivity growth, $\Delta A/A$, also tends to be procyclical. In Chapter 4 we noted that this phenomenon might be attributed to **labor hoarding** during recessions—firms' maintaining excess labor to avoid the hiring and retraining costs associated with new employees. With more labor than necessary to produce the level of output actually produced, the measured level of productivity, based on a comparison of outputs and inputs, falls. Thus, when employment grows rapidly, labor hoarding is reduced and the measured level of technology tends to grow too, reinforcing the impact of the growth of labor input on the growth of output.

The procyclicality of multifactor productivity helps explain Okun's Law, but it is important to recognize that factors other than a decline in the unemployment rate can increase labor input. Let's consider the ways in which labor input may grow.

Although we have not always emphasized the distinction between labor input and employment, an accurate measure of labor input, L, takes account not only of the number of workers employed, say E, but also of the number of hours each worker is employed, say H. The resulting measure is the number of worker-hours, $L = E \times H$. Using the definition of the unemployment rate as the fraction of the labor force, LF, that is not employed, we may write this expression for the labor input as

$$L = H \times LF \times (1 - u),$$

which, in terms of growth rates, may approximately be expressed as[19]

$$\frac{\Delta L}{L} = \frac{\Delta H}{H} + \frac{\Delta LF}{LF} - \Delta u,$$

where $\Delta L/L$, $\Delta H/H$, and $\Delta LF/LF$ are the growth rates of the labor input, hours per worker, and the labor force, and Δu is the change in the unemployment rate from the previous period, $\Delta u_t = u_t - u_{t-1}$. This expression says that, holding the growth rates of the labor force and hours per worker fixed, a 1 percentage point decrease in the unemployment rate will increase the growth rate of labor input by 1 percent. However, as the unemployment rate falls, the other terms on the right-hand side of this expression typically rise.

Hours per worker are procyclical, increasing during expansions and decreasing during recessions. This may be viewed as another manifestation of labor hoarding, with firms choosing to spread the lower work load during recessions more thinly among existing workers instead of reducing the level of employment. Labor force par-

Labor hoarding
A situation in which a firm maintains excess labor in order to avoid hiring and retraining costs

18 That is, if the rate of unemployment goes down by 1 percentage point from, say, 6 percent to 5 percent, this represents an increase in employment from 94 percent to 95 percent of the labor force—roughly a 1 percent increase in employment.

19 We use two approximations here. First (as in chapter 1), the growth rate of any product $a \times b$ equals the growth rate of a plus the growth rate of b; second, the growth rate of $(1 - u_t)$, equal to $[(1 - u_t) - (1 - u_{t-1})]/(1 - u_{t-1})$, is close to $\Delta u_t = u_t - u_{t-1}$ when u_{t-1} is small compared to 1.

ticipation itself is also procyclical; the labor force participation rate rises as the unemployment rate falls. This relationship between nonparticipation and unemployment highlights the lack of a clear distinction between these two labor force states for some workers. For example, individuals who see that the unemployment rate is high may simply not look for a job or may give up looking; they are said to be **discouraged workers**. When the unemployment rate falls, some of these workers typically reenter the labor force.

With both the labor force and hours per worker tending to increase as the unemployment rate declines, a 1 percentage point decline in the unemployment rate is normally associated with a growth rate of labor input in excess of 1 percent, leading to an increase in output growth of more than $(1 - \beta)$ percent. Adding to this the increase in productivity growth that also normally occurs yields the output increase of between 2 and 3 percent predicted by Okun's Law.

What does Okun's Law imply about the social benefits of reducing unemployment? It suggests they are larger than would be implied simply by looking at the change in the unemployment rate, because there are many types of **disguised unemployment** that also decrease when the measured unemployment rate declines. This disguised unemployment occurs in the form of underemployment of employed workers (having them work fewer hours or do less productive work) and understatement of the true number of individuals who are unemployed (through reduced labor force participation).

DETERMINING THE NATURAL RATE OF UNEMPLOYMENT

Despite the potential benefits of reduced unemployment, policies aimed at lowering the unemployment rate face a barrier in the form of the natural rate of unemployment. Is there a role for policy in determining the natural rate of unemployment itself, or is fighting unemployment primarily an activity for recessionary times?

There is, of course, no exact measure of "the" natural rate of unemployment. Unlike the actual unemployment rate, the natural rate is a theoretical construct—the lowest rate of unemployment that the economy can sustain indefinitely, at a stable rate of inflation. However, if we assume that the economy rarely reduces the level of unemployment below its natural rate, we can estimate the natural rate by looking at the rate of unemployment at the height of expansions. Doing so suggests that the natural rate of unemployment in the United States may have increased over time, at least until the late 1980s. As Figure 10.1 showed, the unemployment rate fell as low as 2.5 percent in the 1950s. For several months in the late 1960s, the rate dipped to 3.4 percent. By the early 1970s, economists viewed 4 percent as a reasonable estimate of the natural rate of unemployment, suggesting that the rates below 4 percent during the late 1960s were not sustainable without the increasing inflation. But the unemployment rate has exceeded 4 percent since then, and indeed, exceeded 5 percent for the entire period between December 1973 and April 1997. Economists now generally place the natural rate somewhere between 5 and 6 percent.

Discouraged workers
Individuals who have dropped out of the labor force because of lack of success in finding jobs

Disguised unemployment
Unmeasured unemployment that takes the form of underemployment or reduced participation in the labor force

Why has the natural rate of unemployment risen? The answer does not appear to be demographic shifts. Other explanations are a general increase in frictional unemployment due to sectoral shifts and an increase in voluntary unemployment due to the stagnant real wages of the 1970s and 1980s that were documented in chapter 1's discussion of the productivity slowdown. Each of these explanations finds some support in the data. Neither suggests an obvious role for expansionary monetary or fiscal policy in reducing the natural rate of unemployment.

However, there are other explanations of the natural rate's evolution that provide a clearer role for policy. For example, the insider-outsider theory of involuntary unemployment, discussed above, posits that real wage rigidities are imposed by "insiders" at the highest levels consistent with the maintenance of their own employment. The population of involuntarily unemployed "outsiders" help account for the natural rate of unemployment, but government might be able to change the size of this population. A policy of increasing aggregate demand (shifting the AD curve to the right), thereby increasing the price level, might force down the real wage. The fall in the real wage would induce firms to hire some of the outsiders. After a period of employment, such workers might attain the status of insiders and help keep the real wage down to ensure their own continued employment. This reasoning suggests that the natural rate of unemployment in part may be determined by the actual level of unemployment, that is, that any particular level of unemployment may itself be self-sustaining—an outcome called **hysteresis**.[20]

There are other reasons that the natural rate might be affected by policy. For example, there is some evidence that early employment experience affects the future employability of teenagers. Without sufficient work experience when young, they may fail to gain the skills needed for successful job performance and experience unemployment more frequently when older.[21] Hence, if individuals come of age during a period of very low unemployment, when they are more likely to be employed, they will also experience less unemployment in the future, causing the future natural rate to be lower.

If the natural rate of unemployment itself can be affected by general economic conditions and the actual unemployment rates that prevail, then policies to reduce the measured unemployment rate take on added value. Beyond reducing the temporary gap between the actual unemployment rate and the natural rate, they might contribute to a more permanent lowering of unemployment through a reduction in the natural rate.

Hysteresis
Changes in the natural rate of unemployment in response to changes in the actual unemployment rate

20 See Olivier J. Blanchard and Lawrence H. Summers, "Hysteresis and the European Unemployment Problem," in Stanley Fischer, ed., NBER Macroeconomics Annual 1986 (Cambridge, MA: MIT Press, 1986), pp. 15–78.

21 See, for example, David Ellwood, "Teenage Unemployment: Permanent Scars or Temporary Blemishes?" in Richard Freeman and David Wise eds., The Youth Labor Market Problem: Its Nature, Causes and Consequences (Chicago: University of Chicago Press, 1982).

CASE STUDY
UNEMPLOYMENT IN THE UNITED STATES AND EUROPE

Distinguishing between cyclical swings in unemployment around the natural rate and movement of the natural rate itself is not easy. Figure 10.13 illustrates this. It compares the unemployment rates of the United States and the four leading economies of

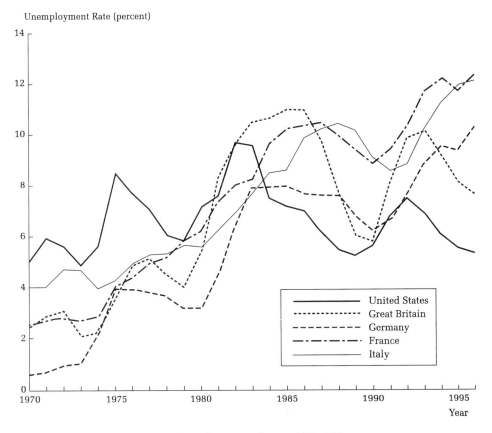

Unemployment Rate (percent)

FIGURE 10.13 UNEMPLOYMENT IN THE UNITED STATES AND EUROPE, 1970–1996
Distinguishing between cyclical swings in the unemployment rate around the natural rate and the movement of the natural rate itself is not easy. Since 1970, the unemployment rates in the major European countries, in contrast to those in the United States, seem to have followed an increasing trend. However, at certain times, for example, the period 1990–1991, the unemployment rates in some European countries—here, Germany and Great Britain—have fallen back to rough equality with the U.S. rate. Has the natural rate risen in Europe, or have the recessions there been more serious and prolonged than in the United States?

Source: OECD, Economic Outlook.

Europe: France, Italy, Germany and Great Britain. Each of these European countries has seen its unemployment rate rise much more rapidly than that of the United States during the past two decades. Until 1981, the U.S. unemployment rate exceeded that of each European country in every year. Since 1984, the pattern has been reversed, with European unemployment rates nearly always higher. It was during the late 1980s, when European rates hovered around 10 percent even as the U.S. rate was falling, that many economists concluded that the natural rate of unemployment in Europe had risen, and sought to explain why. By 1990, though, some European unemployment rates, notably those of Germany and the United Kingdom, had fallen sharply, back roughly to the level of the United States. Did this disprove the theory that the natural rate in these countries exceeded that of the United States? Or did the rise in European unemployment that followed during the early 1990s provide further confirmation of the higher natural rates? This remains an open question.

SUMMING UP: UNEMPLOYMENT AND WHAT TO DO ABOUT IT

Table 10.1 summarizes the major theories discussed in this chapter. In each case, the table notes the explanation for unemployment, evidence that supports the theory, the social costs of unemployment, and the appropriate policy responses. The table's

TABLE 10.1 THEORIES OF UNEMPLOYMENT: CAUSES, EVIDENCE, COSTS, AND POLICY RESPONSES

Type of Unemployment	Cyclical	Long-Term
Involuntary		
Cause	Nominal rigidity	Real rigidity (insider-outsider, efficiency wage)
Evidence	Layoffs rise in recession	Efficiency wage patterns observed
Costs	Lost output in excess of value of leisure	Lost output in excess of value of leisure
Policy	Expansionary policy	Expansionary policy, if natural rate can be influenced (hysteresis)
Voluntary		
Cause	Fluctuations in real wages or value of leisure	Leisure more valuable than output
Evidence	Unemployment is sensitive to the receipt of unemployment compensation	Quits lead to a stable share of unemployment
Costs	None (negative, since being unemployed is a voluntary decision)	None (negative, since being unemployed is a voluntary decision)
Policy	None	None
Frictional		
Cause	Sectoral shifts	Job search and labor turnover
Evidence	Unemployment rate higher during periods of greater industrial transition	Much unemployment comes in short spells
Costs	None (part of normal labor market process)	None (part of normal labor market process)
Policy	None	None

middle column refers to cyclical unemployment—the rise in unemployment during recession. The third column refers to the unemployment experienced even during periods of economic expansion. The only clear case for monetary and fiscal policy intervention occurs when unemployment is involuntary. Even in this case, though, there are further issues—discussed in the next chapter—to consider before taking action.

CHAPTER SUMMARY

1. The U.S. labor market is dynamic, with sizable gross flows among the three labor market states: employed, unemployed, and not in the labor force. The unemployment rate—the fraction of the labor force that is unemployed—follows the business cycle very closely and typically ranges between 5 and 10 percent.

2. Unemployment may arise for many initial reasons, including job loss (layoffs), leaving a job (quits), and entry into the labor force without a job (entrants). It may be of either long or short duration. In the late 1980s, one-fifth of all unemployment occurred in spells of fewer than three months (13 weeks), but nearly half occurred in spells of at least six months.

3. Unemployment may be voluntary, involuntary, or frictional, although it is difficult to determine the precise importance of each of these causes in explaining either the natural rate of unemployment—the economy's lowest sustainable rate of unemployment—or the rise in unemployment that occurs during recessions. Frictional unemployment is not necessarily constant; sectoral shifts appear to help explain the rise in unemployment observed in some recessions. Conversely, involuntary unemployment, an important feature of recessions, may be present even in better times if labor market imperfections take the form of real wage rigidities, as predicted by the insider-outsider and efficiency wage theories.

4. Quit unemployment generally accounts for about 1 percentage point of unemployment in good times and bad, and labor force entry accounts for perhaps another 2 percentage points, but the bulk of the cyclical variation in unemployment comes from layoffs. Although they account for as little as 2 percentage points of unemployment in booms, layoffs lead to as much as 6 percentage points of unemployment during recessions. Unemployment duration varies over the business cycle, too, with the share of unemployment accounted for by long spells closely following the rate of unemployment.

5. Women experience unemployment rates comparable to men's, reflecting the growing similarity of men's and women's roles in the labor force. Teenagers and nonwhites, on the other hand, are much more likely than others to be unemployed and to suffer from additional unemployment in recessions. Although their elevated and volatile unemployment rates may be explained in part by differences in job skills and industries, such explanations do not lessen the seriousness of the unemployment problem.

6. The burden of unemployment may be measured in two ways: the social burden—the loss to society as a whole—and the private burden—the loss to the unemployed worker herself. Lost output and wages represent only an initial estimate of the respective burdens. Some factors (such as increased leisure) reduce both social and private costs; other factors (such as increased crime) increase them. Government policy to reduce the unemployment rate seeks to reduce both private and social costs; social insurance seeks to spread the social costs of unemployment more evenly across the population. The major social insurance program aimed at unemployment, unemployment insurance, cushions the financial losses from unemployment but may also encourage the unemployed to remain so.

7. Programs to reduce the social costs of unemployment depend on lowering the rate of unemployment. Okun's Law indicates the output gains associated with reductions in the unemployment rate. Such gains may be quite large, because reductions in the unemployment rate are accompanied by increased hours per worker, labor force participation, and productivity—all signs that as measured unemployment declines, so does disguised unemployment. Some view reducing unemployment as a problem of recessionary times, but it may also be possible to reduce the natural rate of unemployment itself. Some theories of hysteresis view the natural rate of unemployment as being determined in part by actual rates of unemployment, but because the natural rate itself cannot be observed, such theories are hard to confirm.

CHAPTER 11

COUNTERCYCLICAL POLICY

INTRODUCTION

The costs of recession and their remedies depend on the causes of recession. Take the real business cycle theory, which traces recessions to negative productivity shocks. It says that recessions are unavoidable, that they entail only voluntary unemployment, and that the best policy response is no response. The sectoral shift hypothesis says much the same thing, but connects recessions to shifts in demand among industries and characterizes unemployment as frictional. The traditional Keynesian model, on the other hand, blames recessions on market failures rather than normal economic forces. Its chief culprit is nominal rigidities, its chief concern is involuntary unemployment, and its chief prescription is aggressive use of monetary and fiscal policy.

The plethora of theoretical explanations of and responses to business cycle fluctuations is one of several reasons that *stabilization policy*—government policy aimed at preventing recessions—is tricky business. This chapter's case studies illustrate the difficulty of stabilizing the economy in practice. First, policymakers have to figure out if the country is really experiencing a recession. Next they have to understand what's causing it. Then they have to decide whether it's worth fighting. Finally, they have to act in time.

The Great Depression of the 1930s, the first case study, illustrates each of these problems. The Great Depression was the major economic event of the twentieth century. It deserves and receives careful attention. Once we've examined this economically tragic episode, we turn our attention to policymakers' postwar policy struggles with inflation, oil shocks, and the shifting Phillips curve. To get things rolling, we start the chapter by addressing the following fundamental question: Are recessions are worth fighting? Specifically, will the gains in reduced unemployment from fighting recessions outweigh the likely costs of higher inflation?

Before proceeding, take a glance at this chapter's main queries.

- How do the costs of inflation compare with the costs of unemployment?

- Why is it hard to measure the stance of monetary or fiscal policy?

- Have policymakers succeeded in stabilizing the U.S. economy?

- How long are the lags in implementing policy, and why do they arise?

- How can a lack of credibility compromise policy effectiveness?

- How does uncertainty about the economy influence policy design?

- How can incomes policies augment, or substitute for, monetary and fiscal policy?

ASSESSING THE COSTS AND BENEFITS OF INTERVENTION

The Keynesian model of nominal rigidities tells us that monetary and fiscal policy are each able to restore an economy's output and employment to their full employment levels. When the nominal rigidity takes the form of rigid nominal wages, growth in output will be accompanied by a more rapid rise in prices than would otherwise have occurred. This positive association between output and inflation translates into a negative association between unemployment and inflation—the Phillips curve relationship introduced in chapter 9. The association between the two suggests weighing the benefits of reduced unemployment against the costs of increased inflation.

But the real trade-off between output and inflation is not clear because the Phillips curve has not been stable over time. In the Friedman-Phelps analysis, the economy ultimately returns to a natural rate of unemployment, which suggests only a temporary trade-off of higher inflation for lower unemployment. Eventually nominal wages catch up with the faster growth of prices, driving real wages back up and eliminating any policy-induced gains in employment. In other words, temporary reductions in unemployment come at the expense of permanently higher inflation. The misperceptions theory is even more discouraging, arguing that reductions in unemployment will be temporary and arise only if the inflation results from unpredictable policy actions. On the other hand, some more recent Keynesian theories, such as the insider-outsider theory, suggest that the natural rate of unemployment can itself be influenced by policy. If this is so, the trade-off between inflation and unemployment may be permanent, with higher inflation in the short run reducing the natural rate of unemployment that the economy sustains in the long run.

Thus, a sustained increase in the inflation rate may generate a permanent reduction in the unemployment rate, a temporary one, or none at all, depending on which model best fits the facts. Clearly, a policy that increases the inflation rate is easier to justify in the first case than in the last, but policymakers are often hard-pressed to distinguish among the cases because of confusing evidence and, alas, conflicting assessments by economists.

THE COSTS OF INFLATION

What are the costs of higher inflation? To begin, it's important to distinguish between *anticipated* and *unanticipated* inflation. When the inflation rate is higher than anticipated, significant sums can be redistributed from creditors to debtors, including the government.[1] This occurs because the observed real interest rate equals the nominal interest rate less the actual inflation rate. When the inflation rate is higher than expected, the nominal interest rate agreed to in advance ends up being too low to deliver the real interest rate initially anticipated. Hence, lenders may receive a low or even negative real return. The same logic applies to other nominal contracts, such as private pensions, that are not indexed to the price level. A sudden burst of inflation drives the real value of such pensions below what was anticipated, making recipients worse off and pension providers better off.

Such redistributions from surprise inflation are significant, but they do not represent net costs to society as a whole because the winners' gains roughly balance the losers' losses. Moreover, in the long run, a steady inflation rate will become the anticipated rate. Hence, considering the costs of a permanent increase in the rate of inflation requires considering the costs of anticipated inflation.

THE COSTS OF ANTICIPATED INFLATION

The government raises revenue, called *seigniorage*, by printing money. The effect is the same as if a tax were collected directly from households and businesses; their available resources are reduced because the associated increase in prices reduces the real value of their money holdings. Thus, seigniorage is often referred to as the "inflation tax."

Given the low rates of U.S. inflation in recent years, seigniorage has been very modest—only 1 to 2 percent of the U.S. federal budget. Moreover, the cost of seigniorage to society as a whole is much smaller than the total seigniorage collected. Why? Because the government uses its seigniorage to benefit society by purchasing goods and services, making transfer payments, or reducing other taxes. Economists argue that the net social costs of seigniorage arise only from the distortions associated with its accompanying inflation. *Shoeleather costs* are one example. In holding less money at any given time to avoid the inflation tax, households and firms must visit their banks more often (and wear out their shoes) to obtain the funds needed to conduct transactions. *Menu costs* are another example. As prices rise more rapidly, restaurants and other businesses must change their menus and price lists more often.

How costly are these distortions? Typically, the distortions associated with collecting taxes, which economists call the *excess burden* of taxation, produce social

1 When the inflation rate is lower than anticipated, the transfers go in the opposite direction. As discussed in chapter 7, significant over- and underpredictions are common.

losses equivalent to a small fraction of the tax revenue. But even if the excess burden from seigniorage is as big as the additional seigniorage itself, that is not very big. In mid-1997, the U.S. monetary base was $465 billion. An extra 1 percent tax on this base, associated with a 1 percentage point increase in the inflation rate, would produce about $4.7 billion of revenue annually—about 0.06 percent of GDP. It is doubtful that the associated excess burden would exceed this amount.[2]

Whatever the precise excess burden from seigniorage, the potential loss of perhaps a few billion dollars a year from an extra percentage point of inflation seems very small compared to the associated gains from reducing unemployment. According to Okun's Law, GDP will be roughly 2 percent larger—about $160 billion—for each percentage point reduction in the unemployment rate. Based on the short-run Phillips curve, a 1 percentage point increase in the inflation rate produces, at least temporarily, about a 1/2 percentage point drop in the unemployment rate, which translates into an output gain of about $80 billion.

What Is the Right Comparison?

Accepting higher inflation to reduce unemployment may seem compelling, but there are complicating factors. The gains from reducing unemployment may be overstated and the costs of inflation understated. In addition, the gains may be temporary and the costs permanent.

As discussed in chapter 10, the social loss from unemployment will be overstated by the associated reduction in measured GDP when unemployment is voluntary, and potentially even when it is involuntary. This is because GDP leaves out home production and leisure, which rise when market employment falls. Also, there may be costs of increased inflation that exceed small shoeleather and menu costs. There is some evidence that higher inflation is associated with more uncertainty about the rate of inflation, making risk-averse households worse off.[3] Inflation also interacts with various tax provisions, further distorting the behavior of households and businesses. For example, the government permits firms to deduct depreciation from income in calculating their income tax liabilities. But these deductions are based on the prices originally paid for capital goods, which, with ongoing inflation, may be quite low compared to current prices. As a result, inflation reduces the real value of depreciation deductions and increases the income taxes that firms must pay. This discourages them from investing in capital goods that depreciate rapidly.[4]

More important than these refinements is the question of the permanence of changes in inflation and unemployment. As the natural rate theory suggests, the output gain may be temporary but the inflation increase permanent. An output gain of $80 billion seems large relative to a cost of, say, $5 billion, but a one-time gain of $80 billion is not so large when compared to the total cost of $5 billion a year forever, perhaps growing over time with the size of the economy. Indeed, the present discounted value of the small but permanent costs of higher inflation may outweigh the large but temporary benefits of reduced unemployment.[5]

2 Indeed, since virtually all taxes produce excess burdens, the net excess burden of additional seigniorage may actually be negative. The reason is that printing money to pay the government's bills permits reduction of other taxes and the excess burden from collecting them. As a consequence, some seigniorage may actually be beneficial. See Edmund S. Phelps, "Inflation in the Theory of Public Finance," Swedish Journal of Economics 75 (1973): 67–82, and N. Gregory Mankiw, "The Optimal Collection of Seigniorage," Journal of Monetary Economics 20 (September 1987): 327–341.

3 Laurence Ball and Stephen G. Cecchetti, "Inflation and Uncertainty at Short and Long Horizons," Brookings Papers on Economic Activity 21 (1990): 215–254, provide supporting evidence and discussion of this hypothesis.

4 See Alan J. Auerbach, "Inflation and the Choice of Asset Life," Journal of Political Economy 87 (June 1979): 621–638.

5 For example, if the annual loss from inflation started at $5 billion and grew annually at 1 percent per year, the present value of current and future losses, discounted at an interest rate of 5 percent, would be $125 billion. For an elaboration of this point, see Martin Feldstein, "The Welfare Cost of Permanent Inflation and Optimal Short-Run Economic Policy," Journal of Political Economy 87 (August 1979): 749–768.

SUMMARY

The net benefits of reducing unemployment depend largely on how long the reduction lasts. According to the natural rate theory, deviations from the natural rate of unemployment are temporary. Hence, policies to decrease unemployment have a temporary impact on unemployment and output—*unless they alter the natural rate itself*—but a permanent impact on inflation. The benefits of unemployment-reducing stabilization policy are enhanced if the natural rate itself can be influenced by policy, or if the "temporary" deviations of unemployment from its natural rate persist for a long time. At the other extreme, if predictable policy changes have no impact on unemployment, even in the short run (as the misperceptions theory suggests), then the benefits of inflationary policy are nil.

Having considered the costs and benefits of reducing unemployment, let's look at actual stabilization policies aimed at achieving this goal, starting with those initiated during the Great Depression.

MONETARY AND FISCAL POLICY DURING THE GREAT DEPRESSION

Countercyclical stabilization policy began during the Great Depression of the 1930s. Indeed, its birth was marked by the publication of John Maynard Keynes's *The General Theory of Employment, Interest and Money* in 1936. In this classic work, Keynes argued that government intervention, particularly through expansionary fiscal policy, would help restore full employment.

By the standard of recent U.S. business cycles, the depth and length of the Depression were staggering. At the Depression's 1933 trough, the unemployment rate reached 25 percent—three times greater than the 8 percent rate recorded at the trough of the 1990–1991 recession! Figure 11.1 shows that output declined for the 4 years of the Great Depression, from 1929 to 1933. By comparison, postwar recessions have averaged less than 11 months. During this prolonged decline, real output fell by 27 percent. And despite the resumption of economic growth in 1933, it took another 6 years—and the recovery from *another downturn*, the 1937–1938 recession—for U.S. GDP to grow much beyond its 1929 level. Put another way, an entire decade of economic growth was lost.

It is easy to understand why the Depression led Keynes and others to advocate government intervention. But ideas are not actions. Although the idea of countercyclical policy may have originated during the Depression, there is debate about the extent to which it was practiced and its effectiveness. Indeed, some economists think that monetary policy actually *caused* the Great Depression.

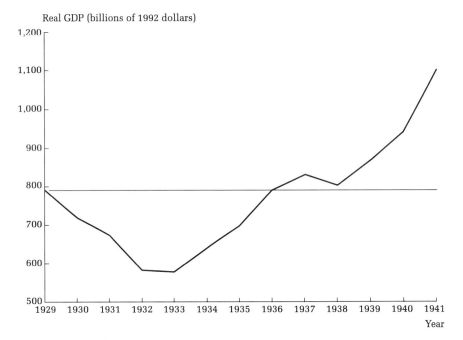

Real GDP (billions of 1992 dollars)

Figure 11.1 Real GDP During the Depression
The depth and length of the Great Depression were staggering. Output declined by 27 percent between 1929 and 1933.
It took another six years — and the recovery from another downturn — for the U.S. economy to grow appreciably beyond
its 1929 output level.

Source: Survey of Current Business, *May 1997.*

Case Study:
Monetary Policy and the Onset of the Depression

In their classic treatise on U.S. monetary history, Milton Friedman and Anna Schwartz
argued that declines in the U.S. money stock in the early 1930s kicked off the Great
Depression.[6] The Friedman-Schwartz argument can be understood by looking at
Figure 11.2, which plots the annual growth rate of real GDP against that of the nominal
money stock during the previous year. The figure shows a clear relationship between
money growth and real output changes. In particular, money supply growth was negative throughout the early 1930s as real output fell.

Did monetary policy cause the Depression? Figure 11.2 seems to support this
hypothesis. But there is more to the story. Consider the IS and LM curves in Figure
11.3. Recall that each curve relates the interest rate to output, based on a fundamental
economic relationship. The IS curve is derived from the transition equation that
relates capital accumulation to income. Its negative slope reflects the fact that higher

6 Milton Friedman and Anna
Jacobson Schwartz, A Monetary
History of the United States,
1867–1960 (Princeton, NJ:
Princeton University Press, 1963),
chap. 7.

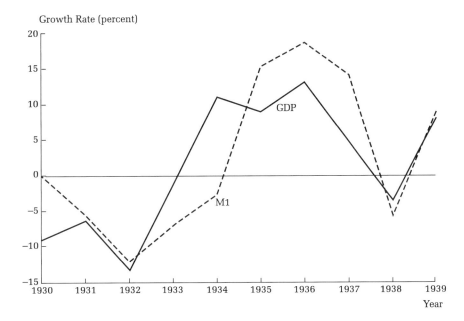

FIGURE 11.2 GROWTH RATES OF REAL GDP AND M1
Annual growth rates of real GDP and the money supply were closely correlated in the 1930s.

Source: GDP: Survey of Current Business, *May 1997*; M1: Milton Friedman and Anna Schwartz, A Monetary History of the United States *(Princeton, NJ: Princeton University Press, 1963).*

income means more saving, more capital, and hence lower interest rates. The LM curve is derived from the condition that money demand equals money supply. Its slope is positive, reflecting the fact that a higher level of income, which raises the demand for money, requires an offsetting higher interest rate to reduce the demand for money and reestablish equilibrium with an unchanged money supply. Given the price level, each LM curve is drawn for a fixed value of the nominal money supply, M, and each IS curve is drawn for a particular value of F, the level of resources government takes from the young.

Within this framework, the Friedman-Schwartz argument is that a drop in the money supply affects output through a leftward shift in the LM curve, to the curve labeled LM' in the diagram. As the equilibrium moves from point A to point B, output falls from Y^0 to Y^1 and the real interest rate rises from r^0 to r^1. In addition, real money balances, M/P, fall. In fact, the initial stages of the Great Depression witnessed all three of these things: a decline in output, a rise in real interest rates, and a decline in real money balances. But the decline in output relative to that of real money balances turned out to be greater than a leftward shift in the LM curve would by itself suggest.

To see this, let's write the formula for the LM curve as $(M/P)/Y = \gamma[r_{+1}](1 - \beta)$. As the interest rate rises and discourages the holding of money, γ falls. Therefore, so does $(M/P)/Y$. Put another way, the velocity of money, $v = PY/M$, rises when the

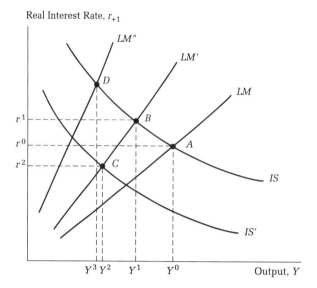

Real Interest Rate, r_{+1}

FIGURE 11.3 CAUSES OF DECLINING OUTPUT
In the IS-LM framework, the Friedman-Schwartz story is that a drop in the money supply affects output through a left-ward shift of the LM curve to LM'. The model predicts that as equilibrium moves from point A to point B, output falls from Y^0 to Y^1, and the interest rate rises from r^0 to r^1. In addition, real money balances fall. In the initial stages of the Great Depression, all three of these events occurred. However, the decline in output relative to the decline in real balances turned out to be greater than this story suggests.

interest rate rises, as households conserve on their holdings of money balances. But as Figure 11.4 shows, velocity didn't rise during the early 1930s; it fell! This casts doubt on the notion that a decline in the money supply, by itself, caused the Depression.

Are there other explanations for the decline in output in the early 1930s that are consistent with a decline in velocity? One such explanation involves a downward shift in the IS curve arising from a sudden drop in consumer spending. In this story, the decline in spending was caused by a loss of confidence after Black Tuesday, October 29, 1929—the day the stock market crashed.[7] As discussed in chapter 8, a drop in the share of income consumed by the young—an increase in their propensity to save—increases next period's capital stock and reduces the prospective interest rate for any given level of output. In other words, it shifts the IS curve downward, lowering output and the interest rate. Given the value of M/P, a lower value of Y means lower velocity.

For a large enough shift in the IS curve, the interest rate may have fallen even as the LM curve also shifted to the left, as shown by the intersection of the IS' and LM' curves at point C in Figure 11.4. This decline in the interest rate would be consistent with an increase in γ and the observed drop in velocity.

This reduced-consumption story seems plausible, because it explains how velocity could have fallen in the face of a contracting money supply. But it encounters a problem in suggesting that the *decline* in velocity should have been caused by a

7 See Peter Temin, Did Monetary Forces Cause the Great Depression? *(New York: Norton, 1976).*

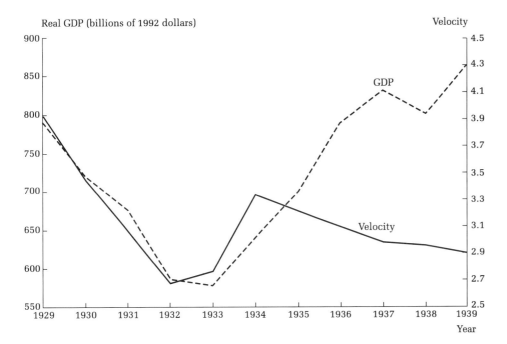

FIGURE 11.4 VELOCITY AND REAL OUTPUT, 1929–1939

In the IS-LM model, a leftward shift of LM caused by a reduction in the money supply should cause the velocity of money to rise as the interest rate rises. However, velocity actually fell during the early 1930s, casting doubt on the notion that a decline in the money supply alone caused the Depression. Further shifts in IS and LM suggested by other theories can help explain what happened.

Source: Survey of Current Business, *May 1997; Friedman and Schwartz,* Monetary History of the United States.

decline in the interest rate. As mentioned, real interest rates rose in the early 1930s. In fact, they were quite high relative to their levels in the years just before and after.[8]

How could the real interest rate have risen at the same time velocity fell? Equivalently, how could γ have risen at the same time that the real interest rate rose? Clearly, γ must have risen in response to some other factor, despite the rise in real interest rates. Such a shift—referred to as an increase in *liquidity preference*—may have resulted from an increase in the perceived riskiness of other assets, such as stocks and bonds.

In terms of our model, an increase in liquidity preference is represented by an increase in the value of γ corresponding to any given interest rate, making money demand higher for any given interest rate and income level and leading to an excess demand for money. With the money supply fixed, equilibrium in the money market can be reestablished only through a fall in income, which means a leftward shift in the LM curve, as shown by the further shift from LM' to LM'' in Figure 11.4. The intersection of this new LM curve and the original IS curve occurs at point D. As the figure shows, this additional shift is consistent with a higher interest rate. Moreover, the

8 For estimates of real interest rates during this period, see Christina Romer, "What Ended the Great Depression?" Journal of Economic History 52 (December 1992): 757–784.

further decline in output from Y^1 to Y^3 translates into a decline in velocity, since the money supply does not change as output falls. A large enough rise in liquidity preference could thus have outweighed the positive impact on velocity of the declining money supply, causing a net decline in velocity as output fell and interest rates rose. As discussed in chapter 14, this explanation may be related to the problems of the banking sector during the Depression.

Once the Depression began, another factor came into play that may also have caused a contractionary shift in the LM curve: deflation. Between 1929 and 1933, the price level *fell* at a 7 percent annual rate. So far, we've made the simplifying assumption in our short-run analysis that the expected inflation rate is zero, and hence the nominal and real interest rates are the same. However, inflation expectations presumably changed after the Depression began and individuals saw the severe deflation that was occurring. It's easy to show that expected deflation shifts the LM curve to the left.[9]

In summary, the Depression occurred against the backdrop of a declining money supply, but contractionary monetary policy per se cannot explain the extent to which output declined. A loss of consumer confidence and a rise in liquidity preference also appear to have played a role, but the relative importance of these factors remains unresolved, notwithstanding more than 50 years of debate.

CASE STUDY
THE SLOW RECOVERY AND THE ROLE OF POLICY

The U.S. economy began to recover in 1933. The NBER places the business cycle trough in March of that year—the same month in which Franklin Roosevelt's inauguration heralded the arrival of the New Deal and a commitment to greater government involvement in the economy. The recovery took a long time. Real output growth was essentially zero between 1929 and 1938, and single-digit unemployment rates did not reappear until 1941, at the beginning of World War II.

One reason the recovery took so long is that the initial decline in output was so great. As Figure 11.2 shows, real output grew very rapidly during the mid-1930s, but from very low levels. Fiscal policy may be another reason. Indeed, it may have helped cause the 1930s' second serious recession, in 1937–1938.

How active was fiscal policy during the New Deal? Answering this question requires a measure of fiscal policy. According to the Keynesian approach, fiscal policy stimulates output by reducing saving. An increase in F, the resources of the young that are borrowed or taxed, reduces the amount of capital accumulation, raising the prospective interest rate for any given level of output—shifting the IS curve upward—and thereby raising the equilibrium level of output.

Unfortunately, we do not have a direct measure of F for the Depression period. Instead, we have the traditional measure of fiscal stimulus, the federal government's budget deficit. For some policy changes, an increase in F would be related to an increase in the deficit, but for others it would not. For example, a debt-financed increase

9 To understand this, recall that the demand for money is sensitive to the nominal interest rate, which equals the real interest rate plus the expected inflation rate. Expected deflation lowers the nominal interest rate below the prospective real interest rate, r_{+1}. This relatively low nominal rate, in turn, increases the demand for money, given any real interest rate and level of income. As in the case of an increase in liquidity preference, the LM curve shifts leftward, reducing output, raising the real interest rate, and lowering velocity.

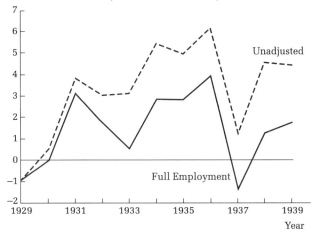

Real Federal Deficit (billions of 1947 dollars)

FIGURE 11.5 FISCAL POLICY DURING THE DEPRESSION
One measure of fiscal stimulus is the federal government's budget deficit. The trend in this variable suggests some expansion during the mid-1930s. But the deficit itself depends on the level of economic activity. A better measure is the full employment budget deficit, an estimate of what the deficit would be at full employment. Based on this measure, fiscal policy does not appear to have been very expansionary between 1933 and 1936.

Source: Brown, "Fiscal Policy in the 'Thirties: A Reappraisal," American Economic Review *46 (December 1956) 857–879.*

in government purchases or transfer payments would increase both F and the deficit, whereas paying for such purchases with taxes on the young would increase F but not the deficit. Thus, although increased budget deficits may signify expansionary fiscal policy, not all expansionary fiscal policies are associated with increases in the budget deficit.

Figure 11.5 presents the federal budget deficit for the years 1929 through 1939, measured in 1947 dollars. Subject to the caveat just discussed, the trend does suggest some fiscal expansion in the mid-1930s, as the deficit rose from around $3 billion in 1933 to between $5 and $6 billion during the years 1934 through 1936. But there is a fundamental problem in interpreting this trend as evidence of intentional fiscal expansion: the deficit itself depends on the level of economic activity, even without a change in policy.

As discussed in chapter 6, government receipts and expenditures tend to vary with the business cycle. Some transfer payments automatically rise when unemployment rises and income falls. Most sources of tax revenue, such as the individual and corporate income taxes, automatically shrink as output declines. Thus, even without a change in spending programs or tax schedules, the deficit will naturally increase during a recession. To the extent that such changes help keep consumption from falling, they reduce the severity of the recession. For this reason, they are referred to as **automatic stabilizers**. Automatic stabilizers help reduce the economy's volatility, but their presence makes it difficult to identify actual changes in fiscal policy.

Automatic stabilizers
Changes in tax revenues and transfer payments that are automatically triggered by changes in national income and that smooth fluctuations in disposable income over the business cycle

To identify fiscal policy changes in the presence of automatic stabilizers, we can ask what the budget deficit would be were the economy at its full employment level of output. With output hypothetically held fixed, the deficit can change only if there is an explicit change in government policy, not through the work of automatic stabilizers. This construct, called the **full employment deficit**, is useful in assessing fiscal policy during the Depression. Indeed, it was actually introduced for this very purpose, and is shown for the period by the solid line in Figure 11.5.[10]

Based on this measure, fiscal policy does not appear to have been particularly expansionary during FDR's first term, from 1933 through 1936. The full employment deficit did not surpass its 1931 level until 1936, and even then it did so by only a small amount. If active policy helped speed the 1933–1937 recovery, it appears to have been through expansionary monetary policy (see Figure 11.2) rather than fiscal policy. Moreover, the full employment deficit reached its lowest level of the decade in 1937. Combined with the contraction of the money supply in that same year, policy can certainly be blamed for the ensuing recession.

In summary, although available measures of fiscal policy during the Depression are imperfect, active fiscal policy doesn't appear to have played an important role in the economic recovery. Monetary policy may have aided the post-1933 expansion, but monetary and fiscal policy both appear to have contributed to the 1937–1938 recession. This episode illuminates not only the problem of gauging policy, but also the difficulty of implementing it successfully. On the other hand, the length of the Depression indicates that the economy will not always revert quickly on its own to the natural rate of unemployment. Hence, although it is difficult to practice, counter-cyclical policy may offer a significant payoff if successful.

Full employment deficit
An estimate of what the government's budget deficit would be if the economy were at the full employment level of output

Policy lag
The time that passes between the need for a policy and when it starts to work; the sum of the inside and outside lags

Inside lag
The time that passes between the need for a policy and its enactment

10 See E. Cary Brown, "Fiscal Policy in the 'Thirties: A Reappraisal," *American Economic Review* 46 (December 1956): 857–879.

THE CHALLENGE OF ACTIVIST POLICY

As our study of the Depression suggests, active use of monetary and fiscal policy can be problematic. Most policies take effect with a time lag, are based on imperfect information about the state of the economy, and may lack credibility in the eyes of the public.

POLICY LAGS

In the Depression, policymakers took four years of sharply falling real output—from 1929 to 1933—to acknowledge the need for fiscal expansion. This example exaggerates typical response lags, but such **policy lags** are inherent in the conduct of stabilization policy. There are two types of lags between the date at which a policy should take effect and the date at which it does take effect. The **inside lag** lasts from the point at which the need for a policy shift arises to the time the policy is finally introduced. One factor contributing to the inside lag is that certain data on economic conditions (such as the level of GDP) become available only after a delay of months and often undergo important revisions thereafter. The **outside lag** extends from when the policies are introduced to when they take effect. Unless economic conditions can be fully anticipated, both lags are inevitable.

CASE STUDY
THE 1992 PRESIDENTIAL ELECTION AND THE RECESSION

Inside lags can affect election outcomes as well as economic policy. The central issue of the 1992 U.S. presidential campaign was the recession that began in July 1990. At the end of October 1992, just a week before the election, preliminary figures on the third-quarter (July through September) economic growth rate became available. This rate, equivalent to 2.7 percent on an annual basis, was fairly high. President Bush used this information to support his claim that the economy was growing strongly. Apparently the voters didn't believe him because he was badly beaten in the 1992 election. But President Bush had been right. Indeed, an important revision in the third-quarter growth estimate came out a month after the election. It showed an even higher growth rate of GNP in the third quarter: 3.9 percent on an annual basis.

The NBER's business cycle dating group didn't make the outgoing president any happier when it announced in December 1992 (a month after the election) that the recession had ended over a year earlier—in March 1991. Since the NBER waited until April 1991 before declaring that the recession began in July 1990, the recession actually ended a month *before* the NBER announced its beginning. The time line in Figure 11.6 illustrates these delays in the dating of the 1990–1991 recession.

The moral of this story is that it may take a long time—perhaps longer than a recession lasts—for economists as well as voters to make an accurate assessment of the economy's economic performance.

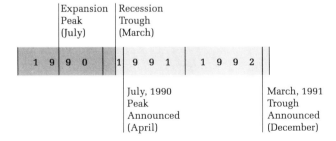

FIGURE 11.6 DATING THE 1990–1991 RECESSION
The 1990–1991 recession ended 1 month before the NBER dated its beginning and 21 months before the NBER dated its end.

Outside lag
The time that passes between the enactment of a policy and when it starts to work

©1992 Luckovich; Atlanta Constitution.

LAGS AND THE DETERMINATION OF POLICY

Even after information becomes available, it takes time to enact a policy. Here, monetary policy has a clear advantage. The Fed can alter monetary policy almost instantaneously. In contrast, changes in fiscal policy (other than automatic stabilizers) require formulation, congressional action, and presidential signature—a process that can take several months or more. Once these inside lags have been overcome, the outside lags take effect. Whatever their multipliers, changes in monetary or fiscal variables do not have an instantaneous impact on the economy.

What causes outside lags? Let's go back to the policy multipliers introduced in chapter 8. We saw there that the multiplier for any monetary or fiscal policy could be thought of as occurring in a series of successive changes. For example, in our basic two-period life-cycle model with rigid prices and involuntary unemployment, a dollar increase in the money supply, given to the old, would initially increase the elderly's consumption, and hence output, by a dollar. This dollar increase in output (and income) would go to suppliers of labor (the young) and capital (the old), leading to increased investment and consumption and another round of increased output and income, and so on. As we saw in our original discussion, similar patterns apply to fiscal policy changes. We did not discuss how long each of these rounds takes, but, in all, it may well take as long as one to two years for most of the multiplier impact to be realized.

How do policy lags affect countercyclical policy design? Recall that the average length of postwar recessions has been less than 11 months. Therefore, the economy can be well into a recession even before its existence is recognized and well out of the recession before policies can be enacted and work. As a result, the scope for countercyclical policy is greatly reduced, even if such policy, instituted at the right time (which might well be before the recession actually began), would be desirable and effective.

IMPERFECT INFORMATION

Closely related to the problem of lags is the problem of information about the state of the economy. Even after information becomes available, it may not be enough for the policymaker to know the right response. Part of the problem here relates to the magnitude and lags of policy multipliers. Not knowing the effect or timing of a policy clearly hinders policy activism.[11] But the uncertainty also relates to the current state of affairs. For example, policymakers may not know why interest rates or inflation might have risen. Along with lags, this uncertainty can hamper policy design.

CASE STUDY
"WHIP INFLATION NOW" AND THE OIL SHOCK

Supply shocks can cause both inflation and Keynesian unemployment, and failure to understand this led to proposals for contractionary fiscal policy during a severe recession.

The 1973–1975 recession was one of the most serious since the 1930s. It lasted 16 months and raised the unemployment rate to 9 percent. As with many other postwar business cycle fluctuations, this recession began with a sharp rise in the price of oil—in this case, due to the 1973 Arab oil embargo. The oil price rise contributed to **stagflation**, the combination of high inflation and poor economic growth. Figure 11.7 shows the quarterly growth rates of real GDP and the GDP deflator for the period 1973 through 1975. The GDP growth rate was most negative in the first quarter of 1975, just one quarter after the one in which prices rose fastest.

Stagflation was something of a mystery at the time, because the prevailing assumption was that increased inflation should be associated with *faster* growth, as represented by a short-run Phillips curve trade-off. Such a short-run trade-off can be realized through a monetary or fiscal expansion in our short-run Keynesian model. Either policy will increase both output and prices if nominal wages are rigid.

To understand stagflation, remember that, just as in the market for a single commodity, higher prices can be caused not only by higher demand but also by lower supply. An oil shock that increases the cost of imported materials is equivalent to a decline in the productivity term A in our production function. This decline will generally cause a reduction in output and an increase in the general price level (not just the price of oil).

To see this, first suppose there is no change in employment. Then, with the same amount of capital and labor, the reduction in A will cause output to fall. With lower output comes a reduction in the demand for money. Given a fixed nominal money supply, equilibrium in the money market requires either that the interest rate fall to

Stagflation
A recession accompanied by high inflation

11 An early and succinct statement of this point was made by William Brainard, "Uncertainty and the Effectiveness of Policy," American Economic Review 57 (May 1967): 411–425.

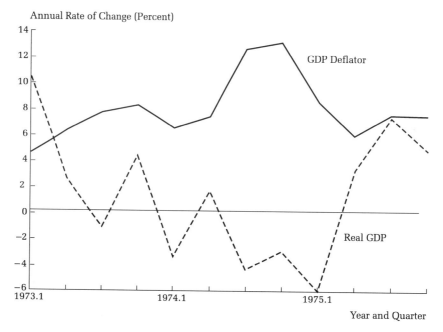

FIGURE 11.7 STAGFLATION, 1973–1975

The 1973–1975 recession was the most serious since the 1930s. It lasted 16 months and raised the unemployment rate to 9 percent. Unlike many earlier recessions, it featured stagflation: high inflation and low economic growth.

Source: National Income and Product Accounts.

increase money demand or that the price level rise to reduce the real money supply. However, as output decreases, saving and capital accumulation decrease too. These decreases raise the prospective interest rate and lower money demand still further. Thus, to reestablish money market equilibrium, the price level—and the inflation rate as well—must be higher than they would have been without the oil shock.

We show this result in Figure 11.8 using the AD-AS framework. If employment is fixed, then the aggregate supply curve is vertical; the level of output produced does not depend on the price level, only on the levels of capital (K), technology (A), and labor. However, as the level of technology A is effectively reduced by the oil shock, this vertical aggregate supply curve shifts to the left, from AS to AS′, leading to lower output and a higher price level.

In addition to the direct reduction in output from lower productivity, there may be an additional reduction caused by a decline in employment. The reduction in productivity also reduces the marginal product of labor—and hence the real wage rate that firms can pay for a given level of employment. Under the real business cycle view, this reduction in the real wage would lead to increased voluntary unemployment, shifting the vertical AS curve even farther to the left as the decline in labor joins the decline in technology in reducing output. Under the Keynesian view, with rigid nom-

Price Level

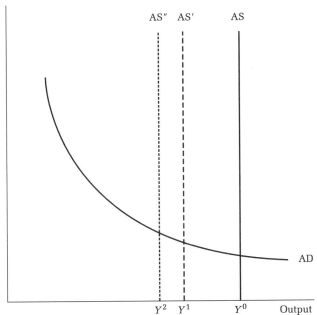

FIGURE 11.8 PRODUCTIVITY SHOCKS, OUTPUT, AND UNEMPLOYMENT
According to the real business cycle model, an oil shock can contribute to a decline in output in two ways. For a given level of employment, it lowers the effective level of technology and hence output, as represented by a shift from AS to AS'. In addition, the associated decline in the real wage may cause an increase in voluntary unemployment, leading to a further decline in output to Y^2. Each decline in output is associated with a higher price level and rate of inflation, leading to stagflation. Under the Keynesian rigid wage model, the employment effect is uncertain, as the decline in productivity lowers labor demand but the reduction in real wages (brought about by an increase in the price level) increases labor demand.

inal wages, the impact on employment is not so clear. On the one hand, the decline in productivity lowers the real wage that firms can afford to pay for any given level of employment. By itself, this effect would reduce employment. But the associated rise in the price level will lower the real wage imposed by the rigid nominal wage, making labor cheaper to the firm and leading to higher employment. Depending on which of these effects dominates, employment could fall or rise.

In any case, there actually was a sharp increase in unemployment—whether voluntary or involuntary—after the oil shock, from under 5 percent to as high as 9 percent of the labor force. According to the official dating, the recession began in November 1973. Figure 11.7 shows that real GDP growth was negative in all but the second quarter of 1974 (when it was barely positive) and very negative—at an annual rate of −6.0 percent—in the first quarter of 1975.

When President Ford took office in August 1974, he initially, sought to introduce *contractionary* fiscal policy, specifically through reduced government purchases, to fight inflation. Using the slogan "Whip Inflation Now" and passing out buttons with the acronym WIN in observation of the goal, he stated, "Inflation is domestic enemy number one."[12] This might have been reasonable had the increased inflation not been due to a supply shock. And, to be fair, there was no strong evidence of recession when Ford took his anti-inflation stance. Though GDP growth had been poor, as of August the unemployment rate had risen only slightly (to 5.5 percent), consistent with the fact that the unemployment rate tends to lag the business cycle.[13] Thus, a combination of uncertainty and lags contributed to policy mistakes. By January, the president had abandoned his WIN campaign and reversed course on fiscal policy. His expansionary fiscal measures were instituted in the spring of 1975—just as the recession ended.

RATIONAL EXPECTATIONS AND THE LUCAS CRITIQUE

Imperfect information about the state of the economy, policy lags, and policy multipliers can frustrate policymakers. But other unstable and unobservable factors can also influence outcomes. One example is consumer confidence. A fiscal policy aimed at stimulating consumption purchases, such as transfers to the elderly financed by taxes on the young, might fail if those receiving the transfers were so worried about economic conditions that they saved the funds received.[14]

Consumer confidence represents households' expectations about the strength of the economy. Other expectations are also important. In chapter 9 outward shifts in the Phillips curve were explained in terms of higher nominal wage demands by workers who base their demands on their expectations of inflation. The higher the expected rate of inflation, the higher will be workers' nominal wage demands and the higher will be the inflation rate needed to achieve any particular level of employment. Hence, in order to determine the rate of growth of the money supply—and the associated inflation rate—needed to achieve a particular unemployment rate, policymakers must know what inflation rate is expected. The higher the expected inflation rate, the higher the required rate of money growth. Using a Phillips curve estimated from an earlier period of, say, low rates of expected inflation will cause policymakers to underpredict the level of inflation needed to achieve any particular level of employment.

Basing policy on a relationship like the Phillips curve, without accounting for the impact of expectations, may lead to serious policy errors. This argument was forcefully enunciated by Nobel laureate Robert Lucas in the 1970s and is now known as the **Lucas critique**.[15] In fact, the Lucas critique goes further, arguing that the policy itself will influence future expectations. Thus, policymakers need to consider not only the current state of expectations but also how their policies may influence these expectations. In Lucas's misperceptions theory, the Phillips curve shifts in response to predictable changes in the money growth rate, eliminating the trade-off between inflation and unemployment.

In other settings, this influence of policy on expectations may actually cause policy to destabilize the economy. One example discussed in Chapter 16 is the *investment tax credit*, a tax subsidy once provided businesses for purchasing new machinery

---

Lucas critique
The idea that policy analysis is mistaken if it does not take into account the way the policy affects expectations and, consequently, economic actions

12 For a lucid account of policy during this period, see Alan S. Blinder, Economic Policy and the Great Stagflation (New York: Academic Press, 1979).

13 Indeed, the unemployment rate actually peaked in May 1975, two months after the recession ended.

14 Although the elderly consume all their resources in our model, we can imagine a more realistic model in which even the elderly would need to save for consumption in their remaining years.

15 See Robert E. Lucas, "Econometric Policy Evaluation: A Critique," in K. Brunner and A. Meltzer, eds., The Phillips Curve and Labor Markets (Amsterdam: North-Holland, 1976) pp. 19–46.

Inflation Rate

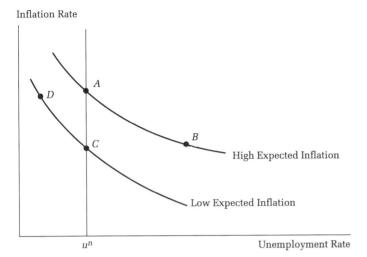

FIGURE 11.9 PROBLEM OF DYNAMIC INCONSISTENCY
If workers expect rapid money growth, they may demand high nominal wages, shifting the Phillips curve upward. Once they have done so, government faces an unpleasant choice. It can pursue the expected policy and achieve the natural rate, but at a high inflation rate (point A). If it attempts to maintain a low inflation rate by keeping money growth unexpectedly low, it risks an elevated unemployment rate, at B. Why isn't the promise of low inflation credible? If government actually prefers point D to point C, it might promise low inflation, then renege. However, if government has this incentive to renege, its promise of low inflation will not be credible in the first place.

and equipment. The credit has often been introduced or increased during recessions in order to encourage more investment. Although this may seem like a reasonable anti-recession policy, it may lead investors at the onset of a recession to defer investment, thereby worsening the recession, until the credit is put in place or increased.

Expectations have a pervasive impact on economic behavior. Yet it is hard to measure them or determine precisely their dependence on policy actions. This poses serious problems for policy designers.

DYNAMIC INCONSISTENCY

The Lucas critique emphasizes that economic relationships depend on households' and firms' expectations about future economic conditions, including future policy actions. Sometimes the government may be hindered in achieving its goals because of the nature of the policy that individuals expect it to enact. For example, if workers expect the government to pursue a policy of very rapid money growth, they may demand high nominal wages, shifting the Phillips curve up. Once they have done so, the government faces the unpleasant choice shown in Figure 11.9. If it pursues the policy workers expect, it may achieve the natural rate of unemployment, but at a high inflation rate—point A in the diagram. If it seeks to maintain a low inflation rate by keeping money growth unexpectedly slow, it risks an elevated unemployment rate, as shown by point B.

"All right, I lied to you. *All* governments lie!"

The solution here seems obvious: announce in advance a policy of slow money growth and low inflation, so that this policy is fully expected, and then follow such a policy, landing the economy at the desirable point, C. But suppose that the government actually prefers point D, with its even lower unemployment rate achieved at a somewhat higher rate of inflation, to point C. Then, having promised low inflation and convinced the workers of it, the government would have every incentive to renege on its promise, letting money and prices grow more rapidly, temporarily forcing real wages down, and attaining the lower rate of unemployment at point D on the lower Phillips curve. However, if the government has this incentive to renege, its promise of low inflation will not be credible in the first place. As a result, high inflation will be expected, and the government faces its unpleasant trade-off. Even though point C is preferable to point A, the government must settle for point A if it is to achieve full employment.

This example illustrates the problem of **dynamic inconsistency**, also called *time inconsistency*. A policy is time inconsistent if the government will wish to revise it once time has passed and actions (in this case, the setting of nominal wages) have been taken by the public. The policy of low money growth is time inconsistent because

Dynamic inconsistency

The problem that arises in any situation in which government has an incentive to revise an announced policy after the public has reacted to it once low nominal wage agreements have been established, the government has the incentive to increase money growth above the promised rate. In other words, the government has the incentive to promise low inflation but not deliver.

The problem of dynamic inconsistency leads to a counterintuitive result: things being made *worse* by the availability of options. If the government had no volition regarding monetary policy—if, once announced, the money growth rate could not be changed—then the lower inflation rate at point C in Figure 11.9 could be achieved. This suggests one possible solution to the problem: the government could give up the opportunity to change policy. For this approach—called a **precommitment strategy**—to work, the government must *really* give up the option of changing policy, not just say that it is doing so.

There are many real-world examples of precommitment strategies involving monetary and fiscal policy. Perhaps the most common is the establishment of an independent central bank to control the money supply, with leaders who believe in maintaining price stability. In the United States, for example, the Federal Reserve sets monetary policy and often follows a path less expansionary than that desired by the president and Congress. More generally, the adoption of simple money supply rules that are easy to adhere to, easy to monitor, and thus, perhaps, more difficult to break—just letting the money supply grow by 3 percent per year, for example—may serve the same purpose.

Along with the inability to time countercyclical policy changes correctly, the problem of dynamic inconsistency represents a second reason to eschew activist policy, favoring an approach of "rules" over one of "discretion." But forsaking activist policy presents costs as well, for it means giving up the opportunity to alter policy even when the benefits may be very clear, as in an unusually serious depression. The government may wish to take steps to strengthen its commitment to maintain a policy while stopping short of surrendering its options entirely.[16]

ADDITIONAL TOOLS TO FIGHT INFLATION: WAGE AND PRICE CONTROLS AND INCOMES POLICIES

The government's ability to control inflation depends not only on its pursuit of a low-inflation policy but on its ability to get firms and workers to adopt wage-setting behavior consistent with this policy. Given the time inconsistency problem, it may be very difficult to bring inflation expectations down, even if the government really does intend to follow a low-inflation program. With a citizenry skeptical of government promises, such a policy may have to be practiced for a considerable period before nominal wage growth moderates. In terms of Figure 11.9, the economy may need to spend a long time at point B before lower inflation expectations and nominal wage settlements shift the Phillips curve down and make point C feasible. This is the nature of the inflation-unemployment trade-off described by the natural rate theory.

Precommitment strategy
Government's deliberate choice to give up the opportunity to change its economic policy

16 Perhaps the best example of how a precommitment device can backfire comes from the movie world. In the cold war–era movie *Dr. Strangelove*, the Russians set up not an independent monetary authority but an independent "doomsday machine" that would automatically destroy the world if U.S. planes attacked. This machine made credible the Russian threat of retaliation (or it would have, had its existence been made public), but it did not improve social welfare when U.S. planes attacked. (Ironically, evidence surfaced in 1993 that Russia actually had developed such a doomsday machine during the 1970s—as in the movie, without warning the United States.) This example helps illustrate why precommitment to rules should not be absolute; why it is better to have Fed chairman Alan Greenspan—a committed inflation fighter, but still a human—controlling the money supply than to have a machine to do so.

To those frustrated by a government's inability to alter expectations, another route suggests itself: induce firms and workers to behave as if they expect low inflation (even though they don't) by making it costly to raise wages and prices. This can be accomplished either by making such increases illegal or by imposing financial penalties on firms that do not play along. The first of these approaches is known as *wage and price controls*. Policies that use the second approach are called **incomes policies**.

Combined with an underlying monetary and fiscal policy consistent with a lower inflation rate, temporary controls and incomes policies appear to offer an improved short-run trade-off between inflation and unemployment. The combined approach can be understood by looking again at Figure 11.9. First, let's review what would happen under a conventional anti-inflation policy.

Suppose the economy is initially at point A, at the natural rate of unemployment, u^n, and a high inflation rate, say 7 percent, and that the government wishes to slow inflation. To do so, it reduces the growth rate of the money supply, from 7 percent to 3 percent. If nominal wage growth dropped to 3 percent immediately, the economy could move directly from point A to point C, with real wages and the real money stock unaffected. But if inflation expectations—and nominal wage growth—remain at 7 percent, this outcome is not possible.

With price inflation of 3 percent and wage growth of 7 percent, real wages will rise, reducing employment. Without a change in inflation expectations, the short-run Phillips curve through point A governs the inflation-unemployment trade-off, causing the economy to move initially toward point B instead of point C. Eventually a period of 3 percent inflation at point B might bring expected inflation down to 3 percent, reducing nominal wage growth and permitting a move back to full employment at point C, at the lower rate of inflation. But suppose that upon changing its monetary policy, the government immediately instituted a policy that prevented nominal wages from growing faster than 3 percent annually. Then, with a 3 percent rate of money growth and price inflation, real wages would remain constant, and point C would be reached immediately. Eventually everyone would expect the 3 percent inflation rate, the short-run Phillips curve would pass through point C, and this point could be maintained without controls.

Incomes policy
Government policy designed to control inflation by penalizing firms that raise prices or wages

17 This problem plagues not just attempts at general price controls but also controls imposed on specific markets. In the United States, ceilings on mortgage interest rates, apartment rents, and gasoline prices aimed at preventing these prices from rising have typically led to shortages and queues.

Controlling the growth of wages and prices in so direct a manner seems simple and straightforward, but the simplicity is deceptive. Except in wartime, U.S. governments have been loath to disturb the market process of wage and price determination so fundamentally. There are two sets of problems with wage and price controls. First, by interfering with the free market, they prevent the natural changes in relative wages and prices that normally occur in a dynamic economy, leading to shortages and surpluses.[17] Second, they can be effective only when combined with an underlying monetary and fiscal policy consistent with the rate of inflation imposed, as clarified in the preceding example. They may be useful as an interim measure to help bring expectations into line with policy, but they don't change the long-run trade-off between inflation and unemployment.

Consider what would happen if, for example, the government imposed wage and price growth of 3 percent *without* slowing the rate of money growth. The real money supply, M/P, would grow, increasing the demand for consumption. But with no change in real wages, employment would stay constant, and so would output. As a result, there would be overall shortages of goods and services, a condition known as *repressed inflation*. Lifting controls under such circumstances would cause a sudden rise in prices, back to their uncontrolled level.

CASE STUDY
NIXON'S WAGE-PRICE FREEZE

On August 15, 1971, President Nixon went on television to announce that he was freezing essentially all wages and prices in the economy at their current levels for a period of 90 days, with a period of controlled growth to follow. He soon established the Cost of Living Council to oversee wage and price growth during this period, which began in November 1971. Wage and price controls lasted until spring 1974, by which time the OPEC oil shock had occurred, complicating the process of controlling prices directly.

The Nixon policy brought down the inflation rate temporarily, hardly surprising given that direct controls were placed on price increases. But it also ushered in a brief period of extremely rapid growth. From the last quarter of 1971 through the first quarter of 1973, the unemployment rate fell from 6 percent to 5 percent, and real GDP grew at an average annual rate of 8.0 percent, a growth rate not sustained for any period of comparable length since. Thereafter, though, as controls were lifted, inflation rose even as growth slowed. Disentangling the effects of the Nixon controls from those of the OPEC shock that occurred in late 1973 is difficult, but economists have generally concluded that the underlying monetary policy followed during the early 1970s was far too expansionary to be consistent with the controls—and that, as the result of repressed inflation, prices rose more rapidly once controls were lifted.[18]

WHAT HAS POLICY ACHIEVED?

No postwar U.S. recession has been remotely as serious as the Great Depression. In fact, recessions have been much shorter since World War II than in the period before the Depression. From this evidence, activist policy appears to have been a success. Nevertheless, some economists attribute the apparently smoother behavior of real GNP and the unemployment rate during the postwar period simply to better data. That is, the sharp up-and-down swings of the pre-Depression era reflect poor measurement rather than the absence of countercyclical policy. Improved measurement cannot

18 *See Blinder,* Economic Policy and the Great Stagflation, *chap. 6.*

"The economy is better under Clinton, but I give all the credit to Greenspan."

Lee Lorenz ©1996 from The New Yorker Collection. All Rights Reserved.

make the Depression disappear. However, comparing the postwar and pre-Depression periods does suggest that activist macroeconomic policies have failed to make the economy *significantly* more stable. This has left many macroeconomists skeptical about the ability of countercyclical policy to stabilize the economy.

CHAPTER SUMMARY

1. Reduced unemployment and increased growth are the major benefits of stabilization policy; increased inflation is the major cost. Given the inflation-unemployment trade-off suggested by short-run Phillips curves and the unemployment-output relationship given by Okun's Law, the gains from reducing unemployment appear to swamp the costs of increasing inflation.

2. According to the natural rate view of unemployment, the short-run Phillips curve is unstable, so unemployment gains will be temporary (unless the natural rate itself is affected) but inflation will be permanently higher. Under the misperceptions theory, the higher inflation caused by expansionary policy occurs without even a temporary reduction in unemployment, eliminating the short-run

trade-off entirely. The attractiveness of activist policy thus depends very much on how long, and by how much, unemployment can be reduced.

3. Countercyclical policy began in the United States during the Great Depression, spurred by Keynes's *General Theory* and the severity of economic circumstances. The Depression's length and depth suggest that there was considerable scope for activist policy. But even during that period, there were signs of the problems that activist policy has encountered in the years since. Contractionary monetary policy may well have deepened and lengthened the Depression in the early 1930s, and both monetary and fiscal policy appear to have contributed to the 1937–1938 recession that further delayed recovery .

4. Fighting recessions requires deft timing. The average postwar recession has lasted just 11 months. Given the policy lags associated with receiving information, acting on it (inside lags), and waiting for policies to have an impact once introduced (outside lags), it is nearly impossible to use policy to fight a recession before the recession is over. The problem is particularly acute for fiscal policy, given the time it takes for fiscal initiatives to be enacted. An exception is the automatic stabilizers, such as reductions in income tax collections and increases in some transfer payments, that take effect without any change in policy.

5. In addition to lags, imperfect information confounds policymakers, who may be unsure of the causes of economic conditions—for example, whether inflation is due to a supply shock—and the timing and size of policy multipliers. One source of instability is the expectations of households and firms. Failing to account for the importance of such expectations and their dependence on policy—the problem targeted by the Lucas critique—can lead policymakers astray.

6. Activism itself can contribute to a lack of credibility that further hampers policy from achieving its objectives. Given the problem of dynamic inconsistency, it is sometimes desirable for policymakers to accept obstacles to the practice of activist policy and adhere more closely to simple rules.

7. Given the time-inconsistency problem, wage and price controls and incomes policies may ease the transition to a lower inflation rate by bringing expectations into line with policy. However, such intervention in wage and price setting distorts relative prices and can work only if the underlying monetary and fiscal policy, in particular the growth rate of money supply, is consistent with the inflation rate imposed. Otherwise repressed inflation will result.

THE INTERNATIONAL ECONOMY

SAVING AND GROWTH IN THE INTERNATIONAL ECONOMY

INTRODUCTION

Virtually all of the world's countries trade with one another. U.S. **exports** (goods and services sold to foreign countries) represent more than 10 percent of its GDP. Since U.S. **imports** (goods and services purchased from foreign countries) are roughly equal in size, international trade, as measured by the sum of exports and imports, is more than a fifth the size of the U.S. economy.

International trade is becoming ever more important as trade barriers and transportation costs fall and the world becomes more closely linked through the Internet and other communication technologies. U.S. trade has roughly doubled as a share of GDP since 1960. As Figure 12.1 shows, U.S. exports accounted for less than 5 percent of GDP in 1960 but 11 percent in 1996. Imports have generally grown more rapidly than exports. Indeed, in the mid-1980s imports exceeded exports by more than 3 percent of GDP. This *trade imbalance* raised concerns about U.S. competitiveness.

The public generally views the *trade deficit* (the excess of imports over exports) as bad for an economy and its workers. But trade deficits can arise in both weak and strong economies and are not, in and of themselves, a cause for concern. Moreover, trade deficits do not necessarily coincide with recessions. Since the mid-1960s, the U.S. *trade surplus* (the excess of exports over imports) has been positive in only three years (1970, 1973, and 1975), all of which included periods of recession.

Why trade deficits sometimes signal strength and other times weakness is addressed in this chapter. As you read, bear these questions in mind:

- What causes trade deficits?

- What are the effects of policies aimed at reducing trade deficits?

- How does international investment lead to the international equalization of real interest rates and real wages?

Exports
Goods and services sold to foreign buyers

Imports
Goods and services purchased from foreign sellers

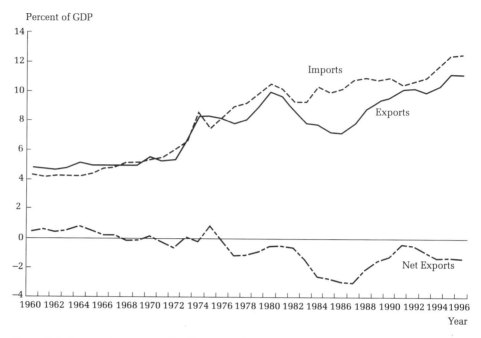

FIGURE 12.1 EXPORTS, IMPORTS, AND NET EXPORTS, 1960–1996

U.S. imports and exports have grown over time as a share of GDP. Because imports have grown faster than exports, the United States has experienced trade deficits—imports that exceed exports—since 1976.

Source: Bureau of Economic Analysis.

- Who gains, and who loses, from international investment?

- How can economic development be accelerated through international investment?

- How are economic disturbances at home transmitted abroad?

Our life-cycle model is ready-made for considering international trade and investment. All we need do is add a second country and permit the two countries to buy output from one another and invest in one another. Before doing so, we review the relationship between international investment and the trade deficit.

INTERNATIONAL INVESTMENT AND THE TRADE DEFICIT

Domestic investment
The increase in the domestic capital stock; it equals national saving minus net foreign investment

Recall that the net amount a country invests abroad, I^f, equals the difference between its saving, S, and its **domestic investment**, I. The reason that $I^f = S - I$ is that a country's saving must be invested somewhere, so the part that isn't invested at home must be invested abroad.

For a country to invest internationally, it must add to the amount of capital it owns abroad. This can happen in one of several ways. Specifically, the country can export capital goods abroad directly, or it can export consumption goods abroad and use the proceeds from these exports to purchase capital goods in the foreign country. Both of these ways of investing more capital abroad involve the country's increasing its exports relative to its imports; both involve increasing its *trade surplus*, $X - M$, or, equivalently, reducing $M - X$, its *trade deficit*. Another way for the country to invest more abroad is to simply use the income, E, that it earns on its existing foreign assets to purchase additional foreign capital.[1]

The point that a country's **net foreign investment** equals its trade surplus plus its net foreign income ($I^f = X - M + E$) is easy to understand when the international economy features only one commodity. Let's say that this commodity is corn, which can either be planted (invested) at home or abroad or eaten (consumed). For a country to plant more corn abroad (to increase its net foreign investment) in a given period, it must physically get more corn abroad over which it has control; in other words, it must add to the quantity of corn it owns abroad. One way to do this is to export more corn during the period than it imports. The other way is to leave abroad the corn it earns in the foreign country in the form of capital income earned on its initial net foreign assets. To summarize,

$$S - I = I^f = X - M + E.$$

As these identities make clear, for a given level of net foreign income, E, reducing the trade deficit (raising $X - M$) requires increasing net foreign investment, I^f. But since I^f equals national saving less domestic investment, reducing the trade deficit requires increasing the difference between national saving and domestic investment. Thus, if a country saves more but chooses not to invest the additional saving at home, its trade deficit will fall. Alternatively, its trade deficit will fall if its saving remains the same but it decides to invest less at home. The size of the trade deficit depends on both saving and domestic investment decisions, which are influenced by quite different factors.

We study a country's saving by considering changes over time in its citizens' ownership of assets. We study its domestic investment by considering changes over time in the domestic capital stock. The difference between a country's ownership of assets and its domestic capital stock equals its net foreign assets. Change over time in a country's net foreign assets is what we mean by net foreign investment. Our strategy for understanding a country's net foreign investment is to examine how its net foreign asset position changes over time. We start by considering the motivating force for investing abroad: earning a higher rate of return on assets.

Net foreign investment
The difference between national saving and domestic investment

1 A third way, ignored in this chapter, is for the country to reduce its net transfers abroad.

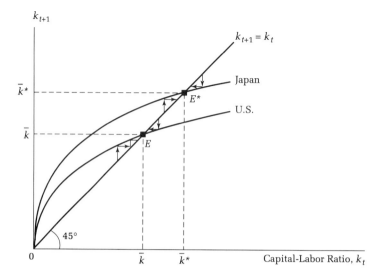

FIGURE 12.2 EQUILIBRIUM IN AUTARKY

In the absence of international trade, each nation's capital-labor ratio is determined by its own transition curve. Because Japan has a higher propensity to save—a lower value of α—its transition curve is higher. Consequently, the Japanese steady-state capital-labor ratio of $\bar{k}^*$ exceeds the U.S. steady-state ratio of $\bar{k}$.

FACTOR PRICE EQUALIZATION

Figure 12.2 graphs the transition curves of two countries, which we'll call the United States and Japan, under the temporary assumption that the countries are in **autarky**—closed to international trade. The Japanese curve lies above the American curve. This reflects our stipulation that the consumption propensity (the α) of young Japanese is lower than that of young Americans. Since the two economies don't trade or invest in one another, they end up in two different steady states. Japan lands at point E^* with a larger steady-state capital-labor ratio than the United States, which lands with at point E. As a result, the Japanese steady-state real wage rate is higher than that of the United States, and its steady-state real interest rate is lower.

Can these factor price differences persist if the two economies become open to international trade and investment? The answer is no. If the real interest rate were higher in the United States, Japanese savers would invest in the United States rather than in Japan. But in moving their capital from Japan to the United States, Japanese savers lower the capital-labor ratio in Japan and raise it in the United States. This, in turn, reduces the real interest rate in the United States and raises it in Japan, with the process continuing until real interest rates are equalized. At this point, Japanese investors (the Japanese elderly in our model) are just as happy to invest in Japan as in the United States. In our open-economy model, real wage rates as well as real interest rates will be equalized. The reason is simple. Since the real interest rate in each country depends on its capital-labor ratio, and since the two countries' real interest rates are equalized, their capital-labor ratios are equalized as well. But since each country's real

Autarky
Economic self-sufficiency in which a nation is closed to international trade

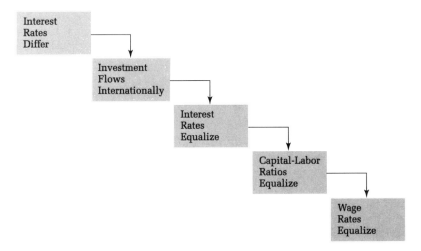

FIGURE 12.3 FACTOR-PRICE EQUALIZATION
With the opening of international trade, cross-country differences in real interest rates trigger international investment flows as capital suppliers seek the highest possible rates of return. These flows eliminate real interest rate disparities by increasing the supply of capital to high-return nations while decreasing it in low-return, capital-exporting nations. Equal real interest rates imply equal capital-labor ratios, and, given identical production technologies, equal real wage rates (for labor of equivalent skills and experience) across countries.

wage also depends on its capital-labor ratio, it follows that each country will have the same real wage.[2] Therefore, cross-border investment serves to equate not only returns to capital—the real interest rates in the two countries—but also returns to labor—the real wage rate in each country. Economists refer to this outcome, depicted in Figure 12.3, as **factor price equalization**.[3]

EVIDENCE ON FACTOR PRICE EQUALIZATION

Does investment flow freely enough among countries to produce factor price equalization? Figure 12.4 shows post-1980 real interest rates on government-issued bonds for the five major Western economies (the United States, Japan, Germany,[4] France, and the United Kingdom), known as the *G-5 countries*.

There is evidence that real interest rates do move together. In 1984, when the U.S. real interest rate equaled 4 percent, all five countries had real interest rates of 4 percent or more. In 1988, four of the five had rates at or below 3 percent, and all five countries had significantly lower rates than in 1984. There are, however, significant differences among the countries in certain years. These differences do not necessarily contradict factor price equalization. According to the Fisher equation, the real interest rate equals the nominal interest rate minus the inflation rate:

$r = i - \pi.$

When investors compare interest rates in different countries, they know only the nominal interest rate. If inflation turns out to be higher than expected in one country,

Factor price equalization
The equalization of real interest and real wage rates across countries

2 This assumes that both countries have the same production function.

3 In multigood international trade models, factor-price equalization can occur without capital flows.

4 The pre-1991 German data are for the former West Germany.

Real Interest Rate (percent)

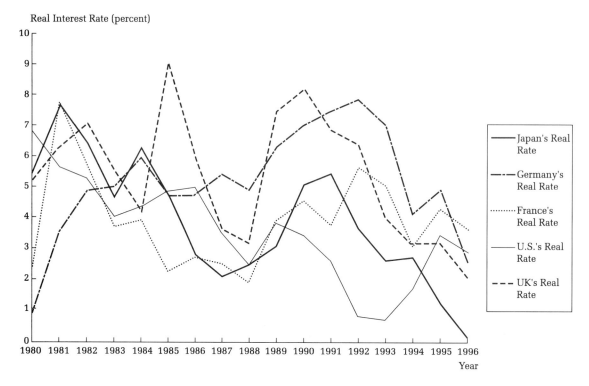

FIGURE 12.4 REAL INTEREST RATES FOR THE G-5 NATIONS, 1980–1996

Over time, real interest rates appear to move together in G-5 countries. In 1984, all five rates clustered between 4 and 6 percent, and in 1988, each of the five rates was significantly lower. However, in some years, such as 1993, there are large disparities among G-5 real interest rates. These differences may reflect errors in forecasting inflation rates.

Source: OECD.

the corresponding real interest rate will be lower. If inflation is lower than expected, the real interest rate will turn out to be higher. Thus, cross-country differences in observed real interest rates could be due to differences in errors in forecasting the inflation rate rather than differences in expected real interest rates.

It is more difficult to test the other implication of factor price equalization theory—that real wages are equalized across countries. There are several reasons for this. First, labor is much more heterogeneous than interest-bearing assets. To compare real wage rates across countries, one must adjust for differences in labor quality, such as education and skill levels. Second, although interest rates are "unit free" (they are simply percentages), real wage rates are not; they are expressed in terms of the currency of the country in which they are earned. As discussed in the next chapter, it is much easier to compare 4.5 percent in the United States to 5.2 percent in the United Kingdom than to compare the purchasing power of $11 an hour in the United States to the purchasing power of 6 pounds sterling an hour in the United Kingdom.

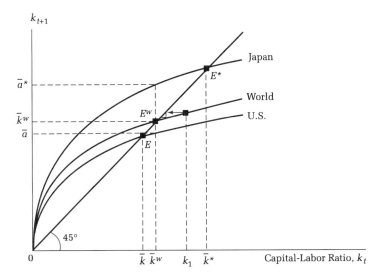

FIGURE 12.5 TWO-COUNTRY EQUILIBRIUM

In autarky, the capital-labor transition curves for Japan and the United State are the curves labeled "Japan" and "U.S." Once trade begins, the evolution of the common, worldwide capital-labor ratio is governed by the world transition curve, a weighted average of the two countries' curves. The steady-state world capital-labor ratio equals $\bar{k}^w$. With international investment, the U.S. and Japanese curves measure assets owned by domestic residents, not the domestic capital stocks. Because the U.S. asset curve lies below the world transition curve, U.S. asset ownership falls short of the U.S. capital stock. Some of that stock is owned by the Japanese.

ANALYZING THE TWO-COUNTRY MODEL

Figure 12.5 starts using our two-country model to understand factor price equalization and its implications for international investment. The figure reproduces the autarkic transition curves for Japan and the United States. Although these curves are useful reference points, they no longer govern capital accumulation when the two countries are open to international trade and investment. If they did, the two countries would have different capital-labor ratios and different factor prices, which contradicts factor price equalization.

So what determines the common capital-labor ratio in both countries, which we call the *world capital-labor ratio*? The answer is the transition curve labeled "World." The equation underlying this curve is derived in the same way we derived the transition curve equation for a closed economy. We start by noting that since the capital-labor ratio is the same in both countries at any point in time, it must also equal the worldwide ratio of capital to labor. But the worldwide ratio of capital to labor simply equals the sum of all the assets accumulated in the two countries, divided by the sum of both of their working populations. That is, in period $t + 1$,

$$k_{t+1} = \frac{Na_{t+1} + Na^*_{t+1}}{N + N^*},$$

where k now stands for the world capital-labor ratio, N still stands for the population of each cohort, a still stands for assets per old person, and * stands for the foreign country. Thus a^*_{t+1} refers to the asset per old person in Japan at time $t + 1$.

For the United States, the accumulation of assets by young people remains the same as before:

$$Na_{t+1} = N(1 - \alpha)w_t.$$

For Japan, we have a corresponding equation describing saving by the young:

$$N^* a^*_{t+1} = N^*(1 - \alpha^*)w_t,$$

where α^* is the fraction of first-period earnings not saved. We do not need a superscript for the real wage rate, w_t; factor price equalization ensures that it is the same in both countries:

$$w_t = (1 - \beta)Ak_t^\beta.$$

WORLDWIDE TRANSITION EQUATION

As indicated, the worldwide capital-labor ratio in period t determines the world real wage rate, which then separately determines the amount of assets the young in each country bring into period $t + 1$. The total of those assets, when divided by the sum of the two countries' populations, gives the next period's capital-labor ratio. Thus, we end up with a transition equation for the world capital-labor ratio:[5]

$$k_{t+1} = (1 - \bar{\alpha})(1 - \beta)Ak_t^\beta,$$

where

$$\bar{\alpha} = \frac{N\alpha + N^* \alpha^*}{N + N^*}.$$

The transition equation for worldwide capital accumulation has the same form as the transition equation for a single economy. In place of a single country's value of α, though, it depends on a weighted average of the values α and α^*, with weights equal to the relative population sizes of the two countries. This is the relationship shown as the intermediate curve in Figure 12.5, labeled "World." At point E^w, the world capital stock reaches a long-run steady state, with a worldwide capital-labor ratio, $\bar{k}^w$ (for "world"), that is larger than the capital-labor ratio prevailing in autarky in the United States, $\bar{k}$, but smaller than the capital-labor ratio prevailing in autarky in Japan, $\bar{k}^*$. As before, if the world capital-labor ratio begins at a value less (greater) than $\bar{k}^w$, capital will accumulate (decumulate) worldwide until it reaches $\bar{k}^w$.

ASSET ACCUMULATION ALONG THE TRANSITION PATH

5 To produce this equation, divide the sum of U.S. assets, $N(1 - \alpha)(1 - \beta)Ak_t^\beta$, plus Japanese assets, $N^*(1 - \alpha^*)(1 - \beta)Ak_t^\beta$, by the total world workforce, $N^* + N$.

Although the curves labeled "Japan" and "U.S." in Figure 12.5 no longer tell us about capital accumulation, when the two economies are open to trade, the two curves do tell the amount of assets per old person. Specifically, for any worldwide capital-labor ratio in period t, k_t, we move vertically to these two curves to determine the level of assets per worker (or per old person) in Japan and the United States in period $t + 1$. Since the capital-labor ratio in period $t + 1$ is given by the middle curve in the diagram, U.S. assets per worker always fall short of U.S. capital per worker, whereas the opposite is true for Japan. The level of assets Americans own abroad—the U.S. **net foreign asset position**—equals the difference between U.S. assets and U.S. domestic capital and is negative. The Japanese net foreign asset position is, on the other hand, positive.

TRACING THE WORLD ECONOMY'S TRANSITION

Now we'll use the two-country model to trace the world economy's transition starting from autarky. Specifically, let's suppose that at time 0, the world economy is in its steady-state autarkic position denoted by points E and E^* in Figure 12.5. Now suppose that during period 0, the Japanese and U.S. governments permit free international investment. What will happen? The answer is that investment will immediately flow from Japan to the United States during period 0 so as to equalize the capital-labor ratios in the two countries at time 1.

This worldwide capital-labor ratio at time 1, k_1, is calculated by dividing total world assets at the beginning of time 1 by the total world labor force.[6] Starting with k_1 we now use the world capital-labor transition curve (labeled "World" in the figure) to trace the transition path of the world's capital-labor ratio to its final steady-state value of $\bar{k}^w$.

During the transition, we can measure each period's capital-labor ratio on the horizontal axis. We can read up to the U.S. and Japanese asset curves to find the respective asset holdings of the two countries in that period. Doing so, we observe that in each period, Japanese assets per young person exceed its capital per young person, whereas the opposite is true for the United States. Hence, during the transition as well as in the final steady state, Japan has positive net foreign assets and the United States has negative net foreign assets.

NET FOREIGN INVESTMENT DURING THE TRANSITION

U.S. net foreign investment during any two periods equals the change in U.S. net foreign assets between the periods. Thus,

$$I_t^f = K_{t+1}^f - K_t^f,$$

where K^f stands for net foreign assets.

Let's first think about I_0^f, net foreign investment during period 0. Since the world economy is in autarky in period 0, we know that K_0^f equals zero. We also know that K_1^f is negative. U.S. assets at time 1 are less than the U.S. capital stock at time 1. That means U.S. net foreign investment at time 0, when the transition begins, is negative; the United States imports capital from abroad. Next, consider I_t^f when t is large enough so the economy has reached its steady state. In the steady state, the U.S. net foreign asset position does not change from one period to the next, so K_{t+1}^f equals K_t^f, and net foreign investment is zero. Thus, we've learned that during the transition from autarky, U.S. net foreign investment starts out negative and ultimately becomes zero.

Net foreign asset position
The difference between a nation's worldwide ownership of assets and its domestic capital stock

6 One can show mathematically that k_1 always lies to the right of the steady-state world capital-labor ratio.

THE TRADE BALANCE DURING THE TRANSITION

Now that we know about the qualitative pattern of U.S. net foreign investment during the transition, let's use this knowledge to understand how the trade balance evolves. Recall that net foreign investment equals the sum of the trade balance plus net foreign income. But since net foreign income simply equals the real interest rate at time t multiplied by U.S. net foreign assets, we can write

$$I_t^f = X_t - M_t + r_t K_t^f.$$

Let's use this expression to think about the trade deficit at time 0. First, we know that K_0^f equals zero and that I_0^f is negative. Hence, it follows that $X_0 - M_0$ is negative; the United States runs a trade deficit at time 0. Next, consider the U.S. trade deficit in the long-run steady state. We know that in the steady state, I_t^f equals zero. We also know that K_t^f is negative because the transition curve lies above the U.S. asset curve. Consequently, we can infer from the above formula that in the long run, $X_t - M_t$ is positive; in other words, in the long run, the United States runs a trade surplus.

Thus, the U.S. trade balance starts off negative and ultimately becomes positive. What explains this pattern? The answer is that at the beginning of the transition, the United States runs a trade deficit in order to import additional capital from abroad. But in the long run, it runs a trade surplus as the Japanese repatriate back to Japan the capital income on their U.S. investments.

A TRANSITION ARISING FROM A DECLINE IN THE U.S. PROPENSITY TO SAVE

To continue building your intuition and understanding of international investment and the trade balance, examine Figure 12.6 and Table 12.1, which consider a transition from a different steady state in which the United States and Japan initially have the same propensity to save. In terms of Figure 12.6, both countries initially have the same asset accumulation curve—the one labeled "Japan." Then, even with the opportunity for world trade, there is no net trade or foreign investment; input prices are already equal.

In Figure 12.6, the initial capital-labor ratio is $\bar{k}^*$. That value (given in the first line of Table 12.1) for year 0 is 8.71. It is based on the parameter values $A = 10, \beta = .3$, and $\alpha = .35$. Each country's saving and investment are initially zero, as are net foreign investment by the United States in Japan (i^f) and net Japanese assets owned by the United States (k^f)—the lowercase letters indicating that each is expressed relative to the number of people per generation. Thus, net exports from the United States (nx) also equal zero.

Suppose that during period 1, the desire for consumption when young, as represented by α, rises permanently in the United States above the value that continues to prevail in Japan. In Figure 12.6, the increase in α causes a downward shift in the asset accumulation curve, to the one labeled "U.S." As a result of the reduced U.S. asset demand, the world economy's transition is now governed by the middle curve, labeled "World," and has a capital-labor ratio less than k^* entering period 2—as determined by the height of the initial point labeled 1 on the middle curve.

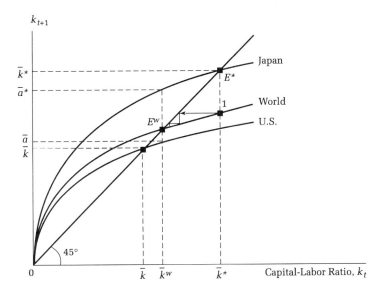

FIGURE 12.6 INCREASE IN U.S. CONSUMPTION

Initially, the United States and Japan have the same propensity to save and so share a common asset curve—the one marked "Japan." There is no net trade or foreign investment. If the desire for consumption when young then rises permanently in the United States, the country's asset accumulation curve rotates downward to the one marked "U.S." From that point on, the world economy's transition is governed by the middle "World" curve. Ultimately, the world capital-labor ratio converges to $\bar{k}^w$.

TABLE 12.1 TRANSITION ARISING FROM INCREASED U.S. CONSUMPTION

	U.S.			Japan						
Period k	c_y	c_o	s	c_y^*	c_o^*	s^*	i	i^f	k^f	nx
0	8.71	4.69	14.45	0.00	4.69	14.45	0.00	0.00	0.00	0.00	0.00
1	8.71	6.70	14.45	−2.01	4.69	14.45	0.00	−1.34	−0.67	0.00	−0.67
2	7.37	6.37	11.67	−0.33	4.46	15.17	−0.43	−0.36	0.03	−0.67	0.53
3	7.01	6.28	11.26	−0.10	4.39	14.64	−0.12	−0.10	0.01	−0.64	0.50
4	6.91	6.25	11.15	−0.03	4.37	14.49	−0.04	−0.03	0.00	−0.63	0.49
5	6.87	6.24	11.11	−0.01	4.37	14.45	−0.01	−0.01	0.00	−0.62	0.49
6	6.86	6.24	11.10	0.00	4.37	14.43	0.00	0.00	0.00	−0.62	0.49
⋮	⋮	⋮	⋮	⋮	⋮	⋮	⋮	⋮	⋮	⋮	⋮
∞	6.86	6.24	11.10	0.00	4.37	14.43	0.00	0.00	0.00	−0.62	0.49

Assumptions regarding production: $\beta = .3$; $A = 10$. Assumptions regarding preferences in the U.S.: $\alpha = 5$, $N = 200$; in Japan: $\alpha^* = .35$, $N^* = 100$

Ultimately, the world capital-labor ratio will converge to a value of 6.86 at E^w. Figure 12.6 shows that in the steady state, the U.S. capital stock exceeds U.S.-owned assets (since $\bar{k}^w > \bar{a}$), so $\bar{k}^f$ is negative, as indicated in the last row of Table 12.1. As we have already noted, even though each country's domestic investment must be zero in the steady state (for k is not changing), the U.S. trade balance must be positive and precisely equal to the real interest payments on the Japanese-owned capital in the United States.

However, the United States must first import the Japanese capital. This initial capital importation occurs in period 1, when U.S. preferences change. The increased preference for first-period consumption in the United States increases actual first-period consumption. Rather than consuming 4.69 units each (0.35 times their real wages), young people in period 1 consume 6.70 units per person—half of their real wages. Since the behavior of the elderly does not change (they consume all their income plus their assets), U.S. saving declines by the same amount: $6.70 - 4.69 = 2.01$ units per each young person.

In a closed economy, U.S. investment would fully reflect this decline and produce a higher real interest rate in the United States than in Japan. But in an open economy, factor price equalization brings enough Japanese investment into the United States to keep the U.S. real interest rate from rising above the Japanese rate. Net U.S. foreign investment equals $-.67$ units per worker in period 1, reflecting the investment from Japan.[7]

As the summary in Appendix 12A of our two-country model makes clear, we can solve for all variables during the transition in each successive period in a systematic way. Given the world's initial capital-labor ratio, we can determine the worldwide real wage rate. Consumption by each young person is this real wage rate multiplied by the appropriate value of α. Consumption by the young in period 2 is smaller than in period 1 because of the lower real wage rate following the decline in the world capital-labor ratio. Consumption by the elderly equals domestic assets multiplied by 1 plus the real interest rate. We calculate the real interest rate, like the real wage rate, using the world capital-labor ratio.

The level of assets equals the previous period's saving by the young. National saving in each country is the difference between its national income and the combined consumption by its young and old. World investment is the sum of the two countries' saving and is divided between the countries in a way that maintains equal capital-labor ratios. Each country's net foreign asset position equals its domestically owned assets minus its domestic capital stock. Finally, its trade balance equals its net foreign investment less its net foreign income.

Returning to the question of how the trade balance evolves over time, recall the model's prediction that a decline in the U.S. propensity to save leads it to run a trade deficit initially, but ultimately a trade surplus. Table 12.1 shows that the turnaround in the trade balance occurs in period 2. In period 2, the United States runs a trade surplus, reflecting the real interest on the Japanese-owned U.S. capital stock that is flowing back to Japan.

7 The decline in Japanese investment per worker is twice the Japanese foreign investment per U.S. worker because the United States is assumed to have twice the population of Japan.

CASE STUDY
U.S. TRADE DEFICITS AND SAVING IN THE 1980s

Is Table 12.1 consistent with the U.S. experience as its national saving declined in the 1980s? Could that decline have reflected a decreased propensity to save? Initially, the decline in U.S. saving was almost fully reflected in the trade deficit; domestic investment fell little relative to GDP. Toward the late 1980s, though, the gap between U.S. saving and investment narrowed, as the trade balance improved. This is precisely the pattern the model predicts will result from a decreased propensity to save—initially, a significant part of the decline in saving is absorbed by a decline in net exports. Later, net exports recover.

EFFECTS OF TRADE POLICY

The increased foreign ownership of the U.S. capital stock associated with past U.S. trade deficits has caused considerable concern in some circles. Nationalists may be concerned about gross foreign ownership of U.S. capital, while macroeconomists worry about the trend in the U.S. net foreign asset position.

In recent years, foreign-owned assets in the United States have grown more rapidly than U.S.-owned assets abroad. Figure 12.7 shows the trends in these two series since 1978. In 1987, Americans crossed the line from owning more abroad than foreigners own in the United States to owning less abroad than foreigners own here. By 1996, foreigners owned $5.1 trillion—about one-sixth—of all U.S. capital. This sum exceeded U.S. holdings of foreign assets by over $800 billion.

Americans would certainly be better off if they were wealthy enough to own all the capital in the United States, but this is not a feasible alternative. It is possible to restrict foreign ownership of U.S. capital, but not if the United States wants to maintain its domestic capital stock at its present level. As we now show, eliminating foreign ownership would cause a decline in the U.S. standard of living.

THE COSTS OF RESTRICTING FOREIGN INVESTMENT

Consider Figure 12.6 again and assume that the world economy is initially in its steady state at point E^w. What would happen if the U.S. Congress decided in period 1 to outlaw foreign ownership of American-based capital? The answer is that the United States would find that its capital-labor ratio was no longer being determined by the curve labeled "World" but instead by the lower curve labeled "U.S."

Starting from the worldwide capital-labor ratio $\bar{k}^w$ in period 1, the United States would have a capital-labor ratio of just $\bar{a}$ in period 2. Even this lower capital-labor ratio would be unsustainable. Starting with this period 2 capital-labor ratio on the horizontal

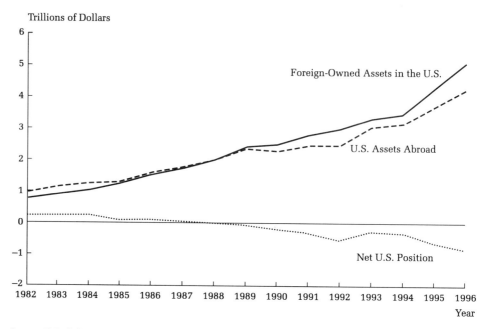

FIGURE 12.7 U.S. NET FOREIGN ASSET POSITION, 1982–1996
In recent years, foreign asset holding in the United States has grown faster than U.S. asset holding abroad, leading to a negative U.S. net foreign asset position.

Source: Survey of Current Business, *July 1997.*

axis in the figure, we obtain a still lower value for the period 3 capital-labor ratio based on the U.S. curve.

As each successive U.S. generation saved less than the previous generation, the capital stock would fall over time to a lower steady-state value, bringing the United States to point E, with capital and assets per worker equal to $\bar{k}$. By requiring all its domestic capital to be domestically owned, the United States would lose not only the capital that had initially been owned by foreigners—dropping from $\bar{k}^w$ to $\bar{a}$—but would suffer a decrease in its own national wealth, from $\bar{a}$ to $\bar{k}$.

What would be the welfare effects of closing the United States to international trade? To begin, the initial elderly Americans are made better off. Having already locked in their real wages in period 1, the initial elderly benefit from the higher real interest rates that accompany a lower capital-labor ratio. Thus, they get the best of both worlds: a high capital-labor ratio when working (and hence a high real wage) and a lower capital-labor ratio when retired (and hence a higher real interest rate).

The initial young and all subsequent American generations are in a different boat. They all experience lower real wages during their work spans because the Japanese no longer invest any of their capital in the United States. Although they earn higher real returns on their saving, on balance they are worse off.

For the Japanese, the pattern of factor price and welfare changes is the reverse. According to Figure 12.6, Japan's capital-labor ratio increases from $\bar{k}^w$ to $\bar{k}^*$. This means lower real interest rates in Japan and higher real wages. Although this capital deepening makes the initial elderly Japanese worse off, initial young and all newborn Japanese benefit from the resulting higher real wage.

Thus, there are winners and losers among generations within each country. In one sense, though, the world as a whole is worse off because the winners' gains are smaller than the losers' losses. Put another way, trade expands the size of the social pie to be divided among different individuals. We refer to this expansion of the social pie as the **gains from trade**. Restricting trade reduces the size of this pie because it makes capital less productive. When the United States closes its borders, all Japanese capital must be invested in Japan, where it earns a lower rate of return than it would in the United States.

RECOVERING FROM A WAR WITH AND WITHOUT FOREIGN INVESTMENT

How does foreign investment assist a country in recovering from a war that has destroyed much of its capital stock? Or, for that matter, how might it assist Eastern European and other developing countries that historically have been cut off from international trade and find themselves with low levels of capital per worker?

Figure 12.8 answers these question. It compares the recovery of a country ("Japan") from a decimated capital stock with and without foreign investment from

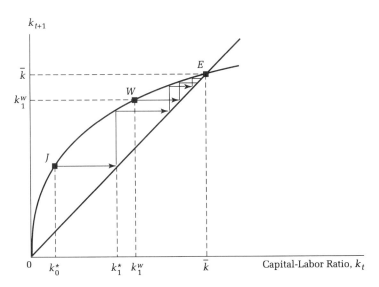

FIGURE 12.8 RECOVERY FROM WAR: CLOSED VERSUS OPEN ECONOMY
If Japan is closed to foreign trade after the war, its period 1 capital-labor ratio is k_1^*, and its transition follows the arrows emanating from point J. However, if Japan imports capital from the United States, its period 1 capital-labor ratio is k_1^w, and its transition follows the arrows emanating from point W, which entails a much faster economic recovery.

Gains from trade
The improvement in economic well-being resulting from specialization and exchange

a second country ("U.S."). To keep things simple, we assume the United States has the same saving propensity as Japan but suffers no loss of capital. We also assume the initial U.S. capital-labor ratio equals its steady-state value $\bar{k}$.

The figure presents two alternative transition paths beginning in period 1, each based on Japan's period 0 capital-labor ratio of k_0^*. For the closed economy case, we simply move vertically from this capital stock to point J to locate the period 1 capital-labor ratio Japan is capable of generating through its own saving, k_1^*. Then we follow the usual transition process from this capital-labor ratio to $\bar{k}$, at point E.

For the open economy case, we combine Japan's assets in period 1 with those generated by the United States, to achieve a worldwide capital-labor ratio that equals k_1^w. The worldwide transition—for the United States as well as for Japan—then proceeds to point E from point W, thus beginning at a much higher capital-labor ratio than the closed economy process.

Table 12.2 gives a numerical comparison of these transitions, with $\alpha = \alpha^* = .5$. (The closed economy case repeats the simulation given in Table 3.1.) In each case, Japan saves 2.45 units per young person in period 0 because of its very low initial capital-labor ratio. Even with this high level of saving, though, Japan still has lower assets per worker than the United States—3.95 versus 5.99—at the beginning of period 1. If the Japanese economy is closed, this gap in assets per worker translates into a continuing gap between the capital-labor ratios of the two countries. In the open economy case, however, U.S. residents invest enough of their saving in Japan during period 0 that the capital-labor ratios, and hence real interest rates, in the two nations are equalized in period 1. This means 1.36 units of capital per Japanese worker must be imported from the United States. This number appears as Japan's trade deficit in period 0.

In the open economy scenario, once Japan has the same capital-labor ratio as the United States at the beginning of period 1, it has the same productive potential. Each country has the same output per young person in period 1. The young in period 1 have the same real wages and the same consumption per capita in each country. The old generations of period 1 do differ in their consumption, however, because part of the Japanese capital stock is owned by U.S. citizens. Each old person consumes her assets plus the real interest on these assets. The real interest rate is the same worldwide, but U.S. assets per old person include the capital shipped to Japan in period 0. Hence, consumption by the elderly in the United States exceeds that of their counterparts in Japan. In order to consume their foreign-owned assets plus accrued real interest, the U.S. elderly must bring all of this back from Japan; Japan runs a trade surplus big enough to reduce foreign ownership of its capital stock to zero.

In subsequent periods of the open economy transition, the two countries grow together back to the steady-state capital-labor ratio, but there is no further foreign investment or capital ownership. Since the young behave identically in the two countries, asset accumulation per capita, and hence the next period's capital per worker, is equal without international investment.

As the simulation shows, access to the world capital market speeds the developing country's ability to recover its prewar living standards. Whereas just over half

TABLE 12.2 TRANSITION FOLLOWING A WAR: CLOSED VERSUS OPEN ECONOMIES

Period	k	y	c_y	c_o	s	i	i^f	k^f	nx
Japan, Closed									
0	1.50	11.29	3.95	4.89	2.45	2.45	0.00	0.00	0.00
1	3.95	15.10	5.29	8.48	1.33	1.33	0.00	0.00	0.00
2	5.29	16.48	5.77	10.23	0.48	0.48	0.00	0.00	0.00
3	5.77	16.29	5.92	10.84	0.15	0.15	0.00	0.00	0.00
4	5.92	17.05	5.97	11.04	0.05	0.05	0.00	0.00	0.00
5	5.97	17.09	5.98	11.09	0.01	0.01	0.00	0.00	0.00
6	5.98	17.10	5.99	11.11	0.00	0.00	0.00	0.00	0.00
⋮	⋮	⋮	⋮	⋮	⋮	⋮	⋮	⋮	⋮
∞	5.99	15.54	5.99	11.12	0.00	0.00	0.00	0.00	0.00
Japan, Open									
0	1.50	11.29	3.95	4.89	2.45	3.81	−1.36	0.00	−1.36
1	5.31	16.50	5.78	7.64	1.82	0.47	1.36	−1.36	2.62
2	5.78	16.92	5.92	10.85	0.15	0.15	0.00	0.00	0.00
3	5.92	17.05	5.97	11.04	0.05	0.05	0.00	0.00	0.00
4	5.97	17.09	5.98	11.10	0.01	0.01	0.00	0.00	0.00
5	5.98	17.10	5.99	11.11	0.00	0.00	0.00	0.00	0.00
6	5.99	17.11	5.99	11.12	0.00	0.00	0.00	0.00	0.00
⋮	⋮	⋮	⋮	⋮	⋮	⋮	⋮	⋮	⋮
∞	5.99	15.54	5.99	11.12	0.00	0.00	0.00	0.00	0.00
U.S., Open									
0	5.99	17.11	5.99	11.12	0.00	−0.68	0.68	0.00	0.68
1	5.31	16.50	5.78	11.57	−0.21	0.47	−0.68	0.68	−1.31
2	5.78	16.92	5.92	10.85	0.15	0.15	0.00	0.00	0.00
3	5.92	17.05	5.97	11.04	0.05	0.05	0.00	0.00	0.00
4	5.97	17.09	5.98	11.10	0.01	0.01	0.00	0.00	0.00
5	5.98	17.10	5.99	11.11	0.00	0.00	0.00	0.00	0.00
6	5.99	17.11	5.99	11.12	0.00	0.00	0.00	0.00	0.00
⋮	⋮	⋮	⋮	⋮	⋮	⋮	⋮	⋮	⋮
∞	5.99	15.54	5.99	11.12	0.00	0.00	0.00	0.00	0.00

Assumptions: $\alpha = \alpha^* = .5$; $N = 200$; $N^* = 100$

the gap in the capital-labor ratio is erased during the first period (about 30 years) if Japan's economy is closed, 85 percent of the gap is eliminated with the aid of imported capital.

CASE STUDY
JAPAN AFTER WORLD WAR II

According to our model, a country recovering from the wartime destruction of its capital should run a trade deficit for a time in order to import foreign-owned capital. That's followed by a trade surplus to reverse the pattern of foreign ownership, followed by balanced trade. Did Japan experience this pattern after World War II? Yes. Figure 12.9 shows that Japan ran trade deficits during all but one year in the 1960s and 1970s. Since then, it has run trade surpluses, reaching over 4 percent of GDP in the mid-1980s. But in recent years these surpluses have declined to almost zero.

Given this recent moderation of Japan's trade surpluses, why do they still receive so much attention in the U.S. popular press? One reason is that Japan has continued to

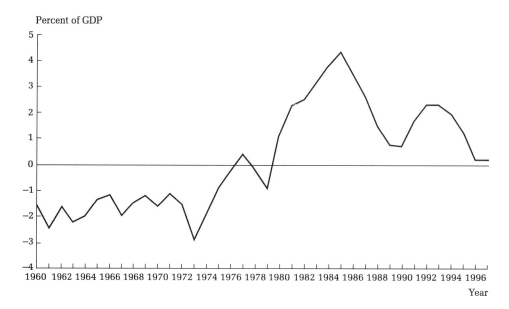

FIGURE 12.9 JAPAN'S TRADE BALANCE, 1960–1997
According to our model, an open economy recovering from wartime destruction of its capital stock should run a trade deficit for a time in order to import capital. Later, it should experience a trade surplus, followed by balanced trade. The Japanese experience since 1960 follows this pattern. During the 1960s and 1970s, Japan's trade balance was negative in every year but one. Since then, Japan has run trade surpluses, totaling, in the mid-1980s more than 4 percent of GDP. But in recent years, Japan's trade surplus has declined almost to zero.

Source: OECD, National Accounts.

run large trade surpluses with the United States, even as the U.S. trade deficit has fallen. In 1992, for example, Japan's $36.8 billion trade surplus with the United States accounted for more than all of the U.S. trade deficit. In other words, the United States ran a trade surplus with the rest of the world. At the same time, Japan has run trade deficits with other regions, notably the oil-producing countries from which it imports fuel.

This distinction between a bilateral (between two countries) trade balance and a country's overall trade balance with the rest of the world does not arise in our two-country model, where the rest of the world is just one country. As the case of U.S.-Japan trade shows, however, the distinction is important in the real world, in which many countries trade simultaneously. In this context, our two-country model really tells us about a country's overall trade balance, not about its bilateral trade balances with particular countries. The latter will be determined by the types of goods and services different that countries produce and is more a question of international trade theory than macroeconomics.

CASE STUDY
U.S. Industrialization in the Nineteenth Century

Like Japan recovering from World War II, the United States in the nineteenth century had access to the latest technology but a relative scarcity of capital due, in part, to its high rate of immigration. As our model predicts, the United States imported capital for a time before reversing the pattern of foreign ownership. Figure 12.10 shows net foreign investment relative to GNP for successive five-year periods between 1868 and 1931. It indicates that net foreign ownership of the U.S. capital stock rose for most of the period until 1896 but fell thereafter.

For the United States in the last century, Japan in the 1950s, and Eastern Europe today, trade deficits have signified not weakness but recovery from weakness. The trade surpluses Japan ran in the 1980s coincided with the arrival of prosperity and the ability to repay foreign borrowing. As in the example based on a decline in a country's propensity to save (see Table 12.1), there is a pattern of trade deficits followed by trade surpluses. However, the implications for national welfare of a postwar transition are quite different from those in which trade deficits arise from increased consumption, not increased investment. In that case, trade deficits coincide with a reduction in national output. In the case of a postwar transition, the opposite is true. Yet in each case, the opportunity to import capital improves the welfare of the importing country relative to its position without international trade and investment.

FISCAL POLICY IN THE OPEN ECONOMY

Adding fiscal policy to our two-country model is easy. We just need to recall that the amount that each government takes from its young workers in taxes or borrowing,

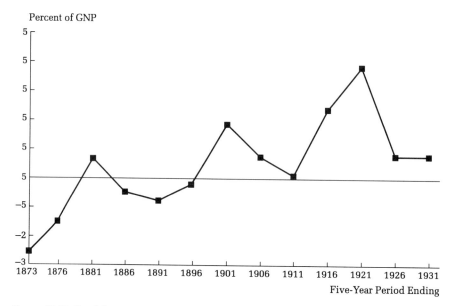

FIGURE 12.10 NET U.S. INTERNATIONAL INVESTMENT, PERCENTAGE OF GNP, 1873–1931

During the nineteenth century, the growing U.S. economy experienced a relative scarcity of capital. As our model predicts and the figure shows, it imported capital from abroad. After the turn of the century, the trade balance shifted into surplus.

Source: Historical Statistics of the United States, *Part 1.*

which we denote by f, reduces the amount of capital assets they bring into their old age. For example, the total amount of assets accumulated by domestic young workers at $t + 1$ is

$$Na_{t+1} = N(1 - \alpha)w_t - f.$$

Using this expression and its counterpart (with $*$s) for the foreign country, the formula for the world's capital-labor ratio becomes

$$k_{t+1} = (1 - \bar{\alpha})(1 - \beta)Ak_t^\beta - \bar{f},$$

where

$$\bar{f} = \frac{Nf + N^*f^*}{N + N^*}.$$

This is the same transition equation we had before, except we are now subtracting $\bar{f}$, which is the weighted average of the values of f at home and abroad. The presence of these fiscal variables in the asset accumulation and world capital-labor ratio equations shifts the corresponding curves downward. To see this, consider again Figure 12.6. Assume initially that the United States and Japan have the same saving behavior and no fiscal policy. In this case, their asset accumulation curves as well as the world capital-labor transition curve will correspond to the curve labeled "Japan." Next suppose the United States taxes young people to pay for government consumption or to make transfers to the elderly. The result is that its f becomes positive. This shifts the U.S. asset accumulation curve down to a curve similar to that labeled "U.S."[8] and the world capital-labor transition curve down to the curve labeled "World." The resulting transition path of the world's capital-labor ratio, its effect on factor prices, and the welfare of different generations in Japan and the United States is the same that would arise had the U.S. asset accumulation curve shifted due to an increase in the U.S. propensity to consume. The lesson is that in an open economy setting, domestic fiscal policy has international ramifications. This is one reason that developed economies spend a considerable amount of time discussing and coordinating their fiscal actions.

A second lesson to be learned about fiscal policy in the international arena is that a country's relative size is critical for determining whether its fiscal policy will have much of an impact on anything except its own asset accumulation. Look again at the formula for $\bar{f}$. Now suppose that you live in the home country and that the home country is tiny relative to the foreign country. This means that N is tiny relative to N^*. Consequently, any change your country makes to its f will have a negligible affect on $\bar{f}$, and thus on the world's capital-labor ratio. It follows that your fiscal policy is completely ineffective in altering macroeconomic conditions in your own country. Instead, your country's macroconditions will reflect your large trading partners' saving behavior and fiscal policies. As we'll see in the next chapter, small, open economies are also unable to use fiscal policy to offset short-run Keynesian nominal rigidities.

CHAPTER SUMMARY

1. International trade is of growing importance to the U.S. economy. Since 1960, U.S. imports and exports have roughly doubled as a share of GDP.

2. Net foreign investment is the difference between national saving and domestic investment. It also equals the trade surplus (the difference between exports and imports) plus net foreign income earned abroad.

3. When investment can flow from one country to another, it will do so as long as real rates of return to capital differ. Investment flows drive these rates together. This process of factor price equalization leads not only to equal real interest rates, but also to equal real wage rates for comparably skilled and educated workers. It also determines how much investment takes place in each country. The level of each country's domestic investment, together with its level of national saving, determines its net foreign investment and, given its net foreign income, its trade surplus.

8 Because the curve shifts downward at all points, it does not intersect the origin, as the curve labeled "U.S." does. However, this difference is not significant here.

4. A higher trade deficits means that national saving has fallen relative to domestic investment. Trade deficits induced by an absolute reduction in national saving are associated with a decline in a nation's standard of living. Trying, in this case, to erase the rise in the trade deficit by preventing foreigners from investing in one's country means less domestic investment and an even lower living standard. Trade deficits resulting from increased investment, such as those that incurred during Japan's recovery from World War II and the U.S. industrial expansion of the nineteenth century, signify growth, not economic decline.

5. A trade deficit need not be bad, and a trade surplus need not be good. A country importing capital from abroad to offset a decline in its saving rate must eventually run trade surpluses to pay real interest to the foreigners who own these assets. The trade surplus thus represents the GDP the country does not have available for its own use.

6. An open economy's fiscal policy influences not only its own asset accumulation, but also worldwide capital accumulation and factor prices. The impact of a country's fiscal policy on its domestic capital stock and world factor prices depends on its relative size. Small, open economies are not able to use fiscal policy to affect these variables. Instead, these variables are dictated to them by the saving and fiscal policies of their large foreign trading partners.

APPENDIX 12A
TRACING THE PATH OF THE WORLD ECONOMY

1. Wages and interest rates are based on the world capital-labor ratio:

$$w_t = (1 - \beta)ak_t^{\beta} \quad r_t = \beta A k_t^{(\beta-1)}.$$

2. Domestic assets per old person equal last period's saving by the young:

$$a_t = (1 - \alpha)w_{t-1}.$$

3. Calculate consumption by the young and old:

$$c_{yt} = \alpha w_t \quad c_{ot} = a_t(1 + r_t).$$

4. National saving equals national income less consumption:

$$S_t = Nw_t + r_tNa_t - Nc_{yt} - Nc_{ot}.$$

5. The world capital stock evolves according to:

$$k_{t+1} = (1 - \bar{\alpha})(1 - \beta)Ak_t^{\beta}.$$

6. Domestic investment is the change in domestic capital; net foreign investment is the difference between national saving and domestic investment:

$$I_t = Nk_{t+1} - Nk_t \quad I_t^f = S_t - I_t.$$

7. Net foreign assets equal domestic assets less domestic capital; net exports equal net foreign investment less net foreign capital income:

$$K_t^f = Na_t - Nk_t \quad X_t - M_t = I_t^f - r_t K_t^f.$$

MONEY, EXCHANGE RATES, AND POLICY IN THE OPEN ECONOMY

INTRODUCTION

How are nominal variables determined in the international economy? What sets the **exchange rate**—the rate at which one country's money is traded for another? What are the open economy impacts of monetary, fiscal, and exchange-rate policies?

To address these questions, we give each country in our two-country model its own money. The revised model exhibits the same real-side behavior, including investment by one country in the other. But now the purchase of foreign goods or assets by domestic residents requires foreign money. In demanding foreign money, domestic residents offer their own money in exchange, thus producing a foreign exchange market.

The importance of this market to the economy depends on the presence or absence of nominal rigidities. We cover both of these bases, but start with the assumption of fully flexible prices and wages and then consider nominal wage rigidity.

Here are the chapter's critical queries:

- How do flexible and fixed exchange rate regimes differ?

- What is the U.S. postwar experience with exchange rate regimes?

- How does the *law of one price* connect prices of traded goods through the exchange rate?

- What is the difference between nominal and real exchange rates?

- How are exchange rate and monetary policies related?

- When will monetary policy in one country affect nominal variables in another?

Exchange rate
The rate at which one country's currency is traded for another's

- Does openness alter the relative efficacy of monetary and fiscal policies?

- How do nominal rigidities affect the choice of exchange rate regimes?

UNDERSTANDING EXCHANGE RATES

An exchange rate tells how many units of one type of money are needed to buy a unit of another. Exchange rates are generally quoted as the number of units of foreign currency per unit of domestic currency. For example, Americans quote the exchange rate between French francs and dollars as francs per dollar, whereas the French quote it as dollars per franc. The franc-dollar exchange rate on September 19, 1997, illustrates these two ways of quoting the same exchange rate. Americans that day quoted the rate as 5.98 (5.98 francs per dollar); the French quoted the rate as .17 (17 cents per franc). (Notice that one rate is the reciprocal of the other.) Regardless of how the rate is quoted, on September 19, 1997, it took almost 6 francs to buy $1.00 or, equivalently, about 17 cents to buy 1 franc.

Foreign exchange markets are global and operate around the clock. Exchange rates set in these markets are continually changing in response to changes in supply and demand. Increases in exchange rates are called **appreciations**; decreases are called **depreciations**. Thus, if the franc-dollar exchange rate, as quoted by Americans, rises from 6 to, say, 10, we say that the dollar has appreciated relative to the franc because it takes more francs (10 rather than 6) to purchase $1.00. Alternatively, we say that the franc has depreciated relative to the dollar since it takes fewer dollars, .10, rather than .17, to buy a franc.

Exchange rates can be either **flexible** or **fixed**. Flexible exchange rates, also called *floating* rates, are determined by the exchange market, free of government intervention. Fixed exchange rates are exchange rates whose values are fixed by the government at particular levels. When a government raises its fixed exchange rate to a higher value (meaning more foreign currency per unit of domestic currency), we call this a *revaluation*; when it lowers its fixed rate (meaning less foreign currency per unit of domestic currency), we call this a *devaluation*.

Governments can fix their exchange rates in different ways. One way is to buy or sell their own currency in the foreign exchange market, thereby ensuring that demand and supply for their currency equilibrate at the exchange rate they want to set. Another way is to legally forbid their citizens from exchanging domestic for foreign currency at other than the officially designated rate. As with any other form of government price fixing, if the exchange rate is not set at the market-clearing level, supply will not equal demand at the official rate. Consequently, there will be an excess supply of the money that is overvalued, at the official exchange rate, and an excess demand for the money that is undervalued, at the official rate.

Appreciation
An increase in a country's exchange rate due to an increase in demand for that country's currency or a decrease in its supply

Depreciation
A decrease in a country's exchange rate due to a decrease in demand for the country's currency or an increase in its supply

Flexible exchange rates
An exchange rate determined by the forces of supply and demand without government intervention

Fixed exchange rates
An exchange rate determined by government intervention in the foreign exchange market or by government decree

Governments with legally determined, rather than market-determined, exchange rates deal with this disequilibrium by restricting the amount of foreign currency they allow their citizens to purchase with domestic currency. This gives rise to illegal *black markets* in foreign exchange, in which the public swaps its domestic currency for foreign currency at a rate foreigners find more attractive than the official rate. Officially determined exchange rates and black markets operating side by side are a common feature of many developing economies.

CASE STUDY
POSTWAR U.S. EXCHANGE RATE REGIMES

The United States has had considerable experience with both fixed and flexible exchange rate regimes. In the postwar period, the U.S. government maintained fixed exchange rates with France, Germany, Great Britain, and most other Western European countries until the early 1970s. This system of fixed rates required government intervention in the foreign exchange market and, as we'll see, close international coordination of monetary policy. But this coordination broke down, in large part because the United States wanted to expand its money supply more rapidly than did the other countries. As a result, the fixed rate regime gave way to a flexible rate regime, in which the U.S. dollar floats (fluctuates freely) in relation to the currencies of Western Europe, as well as those of most other countries, including Japan.

When the United States moved to flexible rates with its Western European trading partners, these countries, with the temporary exception of Great Britain, chose to maintain fixed exchange rates with one another in what is called the *European exchange rate mechanism* (ERM). Figure 13.1 illustrates this point. It tracks the franc-dollar, the mark-dollar, and the mark-franc exchange rates over the period 1951 through 1996. Note that the mark-dollar exchange rate was fixed at around 4 marks per dollar between 1951 and 1970. The franc-dollar exchange was fixed at 3.5 francs per dollar from 1951 through 1956. Between 1957 and 1958 the franc was devalued to 4.9 francs per dollar. This franc-dollar exchange rate prevailed until 1969, when the French and U.S. governments stopped pegging the franc-dollar exchange rate, leaving the franc to float against the dollar.

Since 1970 the mark-dollar and franc-dollar exchange rates have fluctuated considerably. For example, in 1975, the U.S.-French exchange rate stood at only 4.3 francs per dollar. A decade later, the franc stood at 8.9 francs per dollar. Between 1970 and 1996 the fluctuations in the franc-dollar exchange rate mirrored those in the mark-dollar exchange rate because the French and Germans were pegging the franc-mark rate.

As Figure 13.1 indicates, apart from an occasional discrete devaluation of the franc in relation to the mark, the French and German exchange authorities were very successful between 1951 and 1992 in stabilizing the franc-mark exchange rate—until 1993. In the summer of that year, several European currencies, including the French

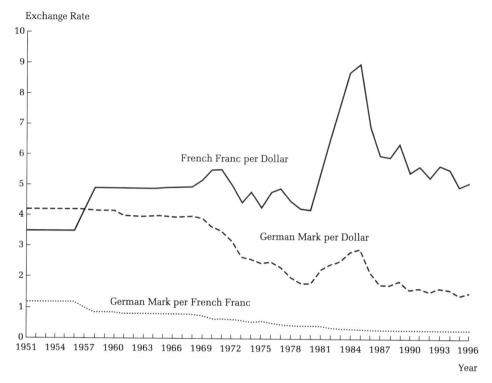

FIGURE 13.1 U.S. NOMINAL EXCHANGE RATES, 1951–1996
Before 1974 the United States maintained fixed exchange rates with Germany and France. Since then, both rates have fluctuated considerably. Although the United States moved to flexible exchange rates, most Western European nations maintained fixed rates with one another.

Source: Economic Report of the President, *1997.*

franc and the Italian lira, were devalued against the German mark. This marked the end of the old ERM. In its place a new ERM was erected, which permitted currencies to float by as much as 15 percent on either side of specified central rates before governments would intervene to stabilize their values.

CASE STUDY
FIXED EXCHANGE RATES UNDER THE GOLD STANDARD

Two countries can fix their exchange rate by agreeing on a set rate at which they will exchange each other's money. Alternatively, they can set a rate of exchange between a given commodity and their own money (e.g., dollars per bar of gold). Countries that peg the value of a particular commodity in terms of their money are said to be on a *commodity standard.* When two countries peg their monies to the same commodity, they indirectly fix the exchange rate between their two monies.

Suppose the United States pegs the dollar at $20.00 per barrel of oil, and Britain pegs the pound at £15.00 per barrel. The pound-dollar exchange rate in this case will be £15.00/$20.00, or 0.75 pound per dollar. Any other rate would present an arbitrage opportunity—an opportunity to buy low and sell high. For example, if the exchange rate were 1 pound per dollar rather than 0.75 pound per dollar, anyone with 15 pounds could purchase a barrel of oil in England, sell it for $20.00 in the United States, and convert the $20.00 into 20 pounds, for a quick profit of 5 pounds.

The use of a commodity standard to fix the exchange rate has historical precedent. The United States and most European countries pegged their monies to gold throughout most of the last century and a good part of this century. Whenever the exchange rate between two countries on the **gold standard** moved even slightly away from the rate determined by comparing their prices of gold, arbitrageurs responded by purchasing gold in one country and shipping it for sale to the other. The gold standard, together with rough seas, explains why there are so many boats laden with gold lying at the bottom of the Atlantic Ocean.

THE LAW OF ONE PRICE AND REAL VERSUS NOMINAL EXCHANGE RATES

The **law of one price** is the proposition that, ignoring shipping costs, commodity taxes, and tariffs, traded goods should cost the same in all locations, within a particular country or in different countries. The law of one price is dictated by competition. If the same commodity can be purchased at location A for less than at location B, purchasers will seek to buy the commodity at A rather than B. This will drive up the price at location A and drive down the price at location B until, in equilibrium, the two prices are identical.

In the international context, the law of one price dictates that, apart from shipping fees, commodity taxes, and tariffs, traded goods should cost the same whether they are purchased at home or abroad. Thus, if a bushel of wheat costs $3 in the United States, it should take only $3 worth of francs to buy a bushel of wheat in France. If the price of a bushel of wheat in France is 15 francs, an American wheat dealer should be able to swap her $3 for just enough French francs—15—to purchase the wheat in France; that is, the exchange rate should be 5 francs per dollar. If the exchange rate were not equal to 5 francs per dollar, it would be cheaper to buy wheat in one country than in the other. Such a disequilibrium could be corrected by changes in the dollar price of U.S. wheat, changes in the franc price of French wheat, or a realignment (an increase or a decrease) of the franc-dollar exchange rate.

Gold standard
An arrangement in which the currencies of most countries are convertible into gold at a fixed rate

Law of one price
The proposition that identical goods should have the same real cost everywhere they are traded

CASE STUDY
PURCHASING POWER PARITY AND INTERNATIONAL BIG MAC PRICES

Another way to describe the law of one price in the international context is to say that a given amount of money, say dollars, should have the same power to purchase traded goods (again ignoring shipping fees, commodity taxes, and tariffs), whether those traded goods are purchased at home or abroad. This is why economists refer to the law of one price in the international context as **purchasing power parity**. For goods that are exchanged in well-developed international markets, such as oil, purchasing power parity can readily be verified. We simply check that the price paid by one country for oil delivered to its ports is the same as that paid by other countries, after converting the foreign payment into domestic currency and adjusting for differences in shipping costs.

For other goods, determining whether purchasing power parity holds, or should hold, is not so easy. Take McDonald's Big Mac hamburger. McDonald's sells Big Macs around the world. Many ingredients used to produce Big Macs are imported, and, for that reason, we might think the price of Big Macs would be the same throughout the world after converting local prices into dollars via the exchange rate. On the other hand, some of the inputs used in producing Big Macs, such as the electricity used to light the store, are nontraded. Since the dollar price of such nontraded inputs will not necessarily be the same internationally, there is no reason to believe purchasing power parity will hold with respect to Big Macs. Even if all inputs into Big Macs were imported, it would still be a challenge to test for purchasing power parity based on Big Macs because of the need to adjust for shipping costs and tax differences across countries.

We shouldn't, on a priori grounds, expect purchasing power parity to hold perfectly with respect to the Big Mac. Still, it's interesting to know the extent to which it fails. The article from *The Economist* (box 13.1) tells us. It presents the dollar prices of Big Macs prevailing in 32 different countries on April 12, 1997. The table also reports the local currency price of the Big Macs as well as the exchange rates used to convert these prices into dollars. On this particular day, a Big Mac in the United States cost $2.42. But around the world, the price ranged from $4.02 in Switzerland to $1.16 in China—a huge difference. For Taiwan, Argentina, and Japan, the dollar prices of Big Macs were quite close to that in the United States. Hence, measured in Big Macs, the purchasing power of a dollar was almost equal on that day in all four of these countries.

Purchasing power parity
The proposition that a unit of a country's currency should be able to purchase the same quantity of goods and services at home or, after being converted into foreign currency, abroad

REAL VERSUS NOMINAL EXCHANGE RATES

The ratio of the dollar price of Big Macs in the United States to that in Russia on April 12, 1997, was 1.26, indicating that Big Macs cost 26 percent more in the United States on that day than in Russia. What if we now form such a relative price ratio, not for a particular good or service, but for a representative basket of goods and services produced in the home and foreign countries? Doing so produces the **real exchange rate**. The real exchange rate, also known as the *terms of trade*, measures the relative cost of purchasing domestic versus foreign goods and services.

Let e^R stand for the real exchange rate and e stand for the actual or, as economists call it, the **nominal exchange rate**. Then, the real exchange rate is

$$e^R = \frac{\text{Domestic price level in domestic currency}}{\text{Foreign price level in domestic currency}} = \frac{P}{P^*/e},$$

where P stands for the domestic price level and P^* stands for the foreign price level. Thus, if the United States is the home country, the domestic price level is the amount of dollars needed to purchase a specific basket of goods in the United States. If Spain is the foreign country, the foreign price level is the amount of Spanish pesetas it would take to purchase this same basket of goods in Spain. By dividing the Spanish price level by the nominal exchange rate, we express, in dollars, the cost of purchasing the basket of goods in Spain. This dollar cost of the basket in Spain is divided into the dollar cost of the basket in the United States to arrive at the real exchange rate.

There is no requirement that increases in the nominal exchange rate be associated with increases in the real exchange rate. To see this, first write the real exchange rate as the product of the nominal exchange rate and the ratio of the domestic to the foreign price levels: $e^R = e(P/P^*)$. Now observe that if increases in e are associated with equal proportionate decreases in P/P^*, e^R will be unchanged.

If purchasing power parity held for all goods and services in the basket, then the dollar cost of the basket in Spain would equal the dollar cost of the basket in the United States; the real exchange rate would equal 1 and be constant over time. Purchasing power parity holds reasonably well for many traded goods (e.g., oil and wheat), but not very well for nontraded goods. In countries like the United States, in which nontraded goods constitute a large share of GDP, there is no reason to expect the real exchange rate to remain constant through time.

Figure 13.2 shows changes over time in indexes of the Japanese yen–U.S. dollar real and nominal exchange rates. Both indexes have base values of 100 for March 1973. Note that the short-run fluctuations in the nominal exchange rate produce similar short-run fluctuations in the real exchange rate, but the longer-run movements of the two curves are quite different. Consider, for example, the period January 1974 through January 1976. Over this two-year period, the dollar depreciated in real terms in relation to the yen by 6 percent (the real exchange rate fell), whereas it appreciated in nominal terms by 1 percent (the nominal exchange rate rose). In Figure 13.2, this is apparent in the growing gap between the nominal and real exchange rate lines. The explanation for this difference in the movements of the real and nominal exchange rates is that the ratio of the Japanese price level to the U.S. price level rose by about 7 percent over the period.

Real exchange rate
The ratio of the price of a fixed basket of goods and services in the domestic economy to the price, in domestic currency, of the same basket in a foreign country

Nominal exchange rate
The number of units of a foreign country's currency that can be purchased with one unit of the home country's currency

Box 13.1

Big MacCurrencies

Can hamburgers provide hot tips about exchange rates?

Is the world's exchange-rate system on the brink of collapse? Just like the old gold standard and the fixed rates of the Bretton Woods system, another international currency benchmark could be doomed: the hamburger standard. For more than a decade, *The Economist*'s Big Mac index has provided a delectable guide to whether currencies are at their "correct" level. But news in February that McDonald's was about to slash the American price of its Big Mac by 65% sent shivers through financial markets. Would this blatant competitive devaluation reduce the hamburger standard to ashes?

It certainly threatened to leave us in a pickle. The Big Mac index is based upon the theory of purchasing-power parity (PPP)—the notion that a dollar should buy the same amount in all countries. In the long run, argue PPP fans, currencies should move towards the rate which equalises the prices of an identical basket of goods in each country. Our "basket" is a McDonald's Big Mac, which is now produced in over 100 countries. The Big Mac PPP is the exchange rate that would leave hamburgers costing the same in America as abroad. Comparing actual exchange rates with PPP provides one indication of whether a currency is under- or over-valued.

Massive discounting in America by McDonald's would distort our PPP calculations. But financial markets have been given a reprieve: the discounts do not yet affect the Big Mac. So our annual burgernomics-fest can be served.

The first column in the table shows local-currency prices of a Big Mac; the second converts them into dollars. The average American price (including tax) is $2.42. China is the place for bargain hunters: a Beijing Big Mac costs only $1.16. At the other extreme, Big Mac fans pay a beefy $4.02 in Switzerland. In other words, the yuan is the most undervalued currency (by 52%), the Swiss franc the most overvalued (by 66%).

The third column calculates Big Mac PPPS. For example, dividing the German price by the American one gives a dollar PPP of DM 2.02. The actual rate on April 7th was DM1.71, implying that the D-mark is 18% overvalued against the dollar. But over the past two years the dollar has risen nearer to its PPP against most currencies. The yen is now close to its PPP of ¥121. Two years ago the Big Mac index suggested that it was 100% overvalued against the dollar.

Some critics find these conclusions hard to swallow. Yes, we admit it, the Big Mac is not a perfect measure. Price differences may be distorted by trade barriers on beef, sales taxes, or large variations in the cost of non-traded inputs such as rents. All the same, the index tends to come up with PPP estimates that are similar to those based on more sophisticated methods.

Moreover, research by Robert Cumby, an economist at Georgetown ↗

University, suggests that a currency's deviation from Big Mac PPP can be a useful predictor of exchange rates. Over the past year, the Big Mac index has correctly predicted the direction of exchange-rate movements for eight of 12 currencies of large industrial economies. Of the seven currencies which changed by more than 10%, the Big Mac standard got the direction right in six cases. Better than some highly-paid currency forecasters. Investors who turned up their noses at the Big Mac index should now be feeling cheesed off.

THE HAMBURGER STANDARD

	BIG MAC PRICES		IMPLIED PPP* OF THE DOLLAR	ACTUAL $ EXCHANGE RATE 7/4/97	LOCAL CURRENCY UNDER(−)/ OVER(+) VALUATION,[†] %
	IN LOCAL CURRENCY	IN DOLLARS			
UNITED STATES[‡]	$2.42	2.42	–	–	–
ARGENTINA	PESO2.50	2.50	1.03	1.00	+3
AUSTRALIA	A$2.50	1.94	1.03	1.29	−20
AUSTRIA	SCH34.00	2.82	14.0	12.0	+17
BELGIUM	BFR109	3.09	45.0	35.3	+28
BRAZIL	REAL2.97	2.81	1.23	1.06	+16
BRITAIN	£1.81	2.95	1.34††	1.63††	+22
CANADA	C$2.88	2.07	1.19	1.39	−14
CHILE	PESO1,200	2.88	496	417	+19
CHINA	YUAN9.70	1.16	4.01	8.33	−52
CZECH REPUBLIC	CKR53.0	1.81	21.9	29.2	−25
DENMARK	DKR25.75	3.95	10.6	6.52	+63
FRANCE	FFR17.5	3.04	7.23	5.76	+26
GERMANY	DM4.90	2.86	2.02	1.71	+18
HONG KONG	HK$9.90	1.28	4.09	7.75	−47
HUNGARY	FORINT271	1.52	112	178	−37
ISRAEL	SHEKEL11.5	3.40	4.75	3.38	+40
ITALY	LIRE4,600	2.73	1,901	1,683	+13
JAPAN	¥294	2.34	121	126	−3
MALAYSIA	M$3.87	1.55	1.60	2.50	−36
MEXICO	PESO14.9	1.89	6.16	7.90	−22
NETHERLANDS	FL5.45	2.83	2.25	1.92	+17
NEW ZEALAND	NZ$3.25	2.24	1.34	1.45	−7
POLAND	ZLOTY4.30	1.39	1.78	3.10	−43
RUSSIA	ROUBLE11,000	1.92	4,545	5,739	−21
SINGAPORE	S$3.00	2.08	1.24	1.44	−14
SOUTH AFRICA	RAND7.80	1.76	3.22	4.43	−27
SOUTH KOREA	WON2,300	2.57	950	894	+6
SPAIN	PTA375	2.60	155	144	+7
SWEDEN	SKR26.0	3.37	10.7	7.72	+39
SWITZERLAND	SFR5.90	4.02	2.44	1.47	+66
TAIWAN	NT$68.0	2.47	28.1	27.6	+2
THAILAND	BAHT46.7	1.79	19.3	26.1	−26

* PURCHASING-POWER PARITY; LOCAL PRICE DIVIDED BY PRICE IN THE UNITED STATES.
† AGAINST DOLLAR
‡ AVERAGE OF NEW YORK, CHICAGO, SAN FRANCISCO AND ATLANTA
†† DOLLARS PER POUND
SOURCE: MCDONALD'S

Indexes of Nominal and Real Yen/Dollar Exchange Rates

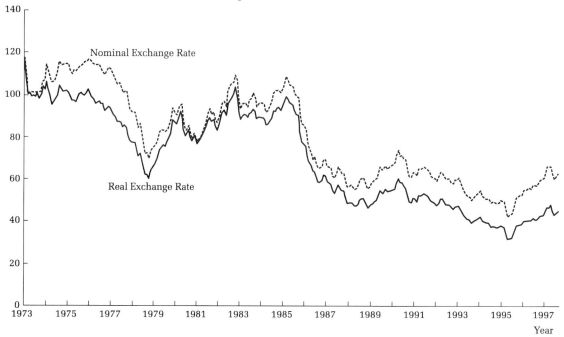

Figure 13.2 Indexes of U.S. Monthly Nominal and Real Exchange Rates with Japan, January 1973– August 1997
Short-run fluctuations in the nominal exchange rate are associated with similar fluctuations in the real exchange rate. The longer-run movements of the two rates are quite different. This is apparent in the growing gap between the nominal and real exchange rate lines between, say, January 1974 and January 1976.

Source: Federal Reserve Board.

ADDING ANOTHER COUNTRY TO OUR MODEL WITH MONEY

This section first discusses the nominal side of our two-country international economy, including the determination of the nominal exchange rate. We then examine the real side of the economy. Finally, we combine these analyses and describe how to solve for all the real and nominal variables in the economy. We'll assume that wages as well as prices are fully flexible, until we reach the last part of this chapter, which considers nominal wage rigidities. We'll see there how such rigidities alter our conclusions about fiscal, monetary, and exchange rate policies in the open economy.

RELATING THE NOMINAL EXCHANGE RATE TO FOREIGN AND DOMESTIC PRICE LEVELS

In adding another country to our model of chapter 7, which includes money, we'll keep things simple by assuming that each country produces the same good and that there are no shipping fees, commodity taxes, tariffs, or other costs involved in one country's sale of this good to the other. Given these assumptions and a competitive international market for the single good, the law of one price dictates that the foreign price of the good, expressed in terms of domestic currency, is the same as the domestic price. Another way to say this is that the real exchange rate—the ratio of the price of the domestic good relative to the price of the foreign good measured in domestic currency—equals 1 in our model.

What does a real exchange rate equal to 1 mean for the relationship between the nominal exchange rate and the price levels of the two countries? The answer can be seen by setting the real exchange rate, e^R, equal to 1 in the expression $e^R = e(P/P^*)$. Doing so and rearranging terms produces the following simple formula:

$$e = \frac{P^*}{P}.$$

According to this formula, the nominal exchange rate is just the ratio of the foreign price level to the domestic price level. If the foreign currency is, say, francs, and the domestic currency is dollars, this formula indicates that the nominal exchange rate equals the number of francs per unit of the good divided by the number of dollars per unit. Canceling the "per unit of the good" from the numerator and denominator of this verbal equation leaves the exchange rate equaling what it is supposed to equal: the number of francs per dollar.

Since the nominal exchange rate equals the ratio of the foreign to the domestic price level, an increase in this ratio will lead to an appreciation, and a decrease to a depreciation, of the nominal exchange rate. Thus, if the foreign price level rises more rapidly than the domestic price level, the ratio of the foreign to the domestic price level will rise and the nominal exchange rate will appreciate. Alternatively, if the foreign price level rises less rapidly than the domestic price level, the foreign to domestic price ratio will fall, and the exchange rate will depreciate. A third possibility is that foreign and domestic prices change at the same rate; the inflation rates at home and abroad are equal. In this case, the foreign to domestic price ratio will not change, and neither will the exchange rate. We can summarize the relationship between the nominal exchange rate and the foreign and domestic inflation rates with the following equation, which can be derived, as an approximation, from the above equation for two successive periods:

$$\frac{e_{t+1} - e_t}{e_t} = \pi^*_{t+1} - \pi_{t+1},$$

where π^*_t and π_t are the foreign and domestic inflation rates, respectively. In words, this equation says that, over a given period of time, the percentage increase in the nominal exchange rate equals the contemporaneous difference between the foreign and domestic inflation rates.

Figure 13.3 examines how well this equation explains post-1975 movements of three U.S. exchange rates: the U.S. dollar–German mark rate, the U.S. dollar–Japanese

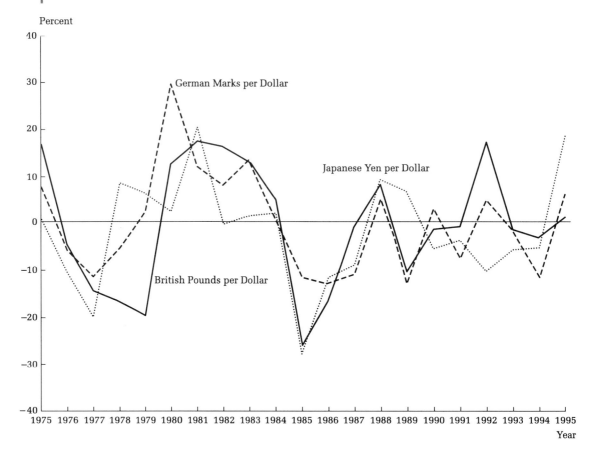

FIGURE 13.3 PERCENTAGE CHANGE IN FOREIGN-U.S. EXCHANGE RATES LESS DIFFERENCE BETWEEN FOREIGN AND U.S. INFLATION RATES
The percentage increase in the nominal exchange rate over a given period of time should equal the contemporaneous difference between the foreign and domestic inflation rates. This relationship does appear to hold over long periods. The three plots differ from zero in most years, but each straddles the horizontal line at zero.

Source: OECD; Economic Report of the President, 1997.

yen rate, and the U.S. dollar–British pound rate. For each year, it plots the annual percentage changes in these three exchange rates (the left-hand side of the above equation) minus the difference between each foreign country's inflation rate and the U.S. inflation rate (the right-hand side of the equation). If the equation held perfectly, all the points on these three plots would equal zero and would fall on the horizontal line emanating from point 0 on the vertical axis. The three plots clearly differ from zero in most years, but each of the plots straddles the horizontal line marked 0. Hence, the above relationship appears to hold over long periods of time.

RELATING THE EXCHANGE RATE TO THE MONEY SUPPLIES OF EACH COUNTRY

As we know, equating the supply of and demand for money produces an equation relating the price level to the money supply. For the home country, this equation is $P = M/\gamma wN$, where M stands for the money supply, γ is the money demand preference parameter (which depends, in general, on the nominal interest rate), w is the domestic wage, and N is the size of each cohort. An equivalent expression relates the price level in the foreign country to the foreign country's money supply: $P^* = M^*/\gamma^* w^* N^*$.

To keep things simple we'll assume that both γ and γ^* are constants and equal to each other. We also know from the previous chapter that international capital mobility leads to the same capital-labor ratio in each country, and thus the same real wages. Hence, w equals w^*. The ratio P^*/P can then be written as

$$\frac{P^*}{P} = \frac{M^*/N^*}{M/N}.$$

The intuition here is straightforward. The money demands of young people in the two countries are identical, so differences between the two countries with respect to their price levels can arise only because of differences in the supply of money per young person (or per capita, since multiplying both N^* and N by 2 leaves the equation unchanged). As the formula indicates, if the money supply per young person is twice as large in the foreign country as it is in the home country, the foreign price level will be double the domestic price level.

We've now made two points with our model. First, the exchange rate equals the foreign-domestic price ratio. Second, the foreign-domestic price ratio equals the foreign-domestic ratio of money supply per young person. Eliminating the foreign-domestic price ratio from these two equations generates:

$$e = \frac{M^*/N^*}{M/N}.$$

In words, the exchange rate equals the ratio of the foreign money supply per young person to the domestic money supply per young person. It tells us that if the foreign money supply increases (decreases) relative to the domestic money supply, the exchange rate will appreciate (depreciate). Intuitively, if the foreign country increases its stock of money per young person relatively more than does the home country, the foreign currency will become relatively abundant, and more of the foreign country's currency will have to be surrendered to obtain one unit of the home country's currency.

ADDING THE REAL SIDE TO THE MODEL

Now that we know how the nominal exchange rate is determined, we turn to the real side of our international economy. Because capital is internationally mobile, it will flow between the two countries until the real interest rate and capital-labor ratio, on which it depends, are the same in both places. The equalization of capital-labor ratios in the two countries also means that real wages, which depend on the capital-labor ratio, are equalized.

Recall that the total world capital stock at a point in time is simply the sum of the capital assets owned by the elderly at home and abroad. In this chapter, we'll assume that individuals do not consume when young but do demand money. Consequently, the amount of assets the domestic young of time t bring into their old age (time $t + 1$) is $N[(1 - \gamma)w_t - f]$, where f continues to refer to payments by each young person to the government for taxes or the purchase of government bonds. The corresponding formula for the assets of young people in the foreign country is $N^*[(1 - \gamma)w_t - f^*]$.

Forming the ratio of total world assets to the total world labor force $(N + N^*)$ and using the fact that the wage equals the marginal product of labor, we can write the transition equation for the world's capital-labor ratio as

$$k_{t+1} = A(1 - \gamma)(1 - \beta)k_t^\beta - \bar{f},$$

where

$$\bar{f} = \frac{Nf + N^*f^*}{N + N^*}.$$

Recall that $\bar{f}$ is the population-weighted averages of payments collected by home and foreign governments from their respective young workers each period.

Also recall that a country's fiscal policy influences the world's capital-labor ratio and, thus, its own capital-labor ratio (since they are the same) only to the extent that it alters $\bar{f}$, the worldwide average stance of fiscal policy. If the home country is very small relative to the foreign country (e.g., Bermuda versus the United States), N will be very small relative to N^*, so that an increase in f will have a trivial effect on $\bar{f}$. Thus, *fiscal policy in a small, open economy will be ineffective in altering the country's capital-labor ratio, its real wage, or its real interest rate.*

DETERMINING ALL REAL AND NOMINAL VARIABLES

Given the initial world capital-labor ratio as well as $\bar{f}$, it's straightforward to solve for the entire transition path of the world's capital-labor ratio and for all other future real variables. The calculation of nominal variables is also straightforward. The nominal exchange rate is determined by the ratio of the two countries' money supplies per young person, which, for the moment, we assume are fixed. Given these money supplies, we can solve for the nominal exchange rate. Second, given each country's money supply, we can solve for each country's price level at each point in time using the formulas for the domestic and foreign price levels.

MANAGING THE EXCHANGE RATE

Our formula linking the exchange rate to the ratio of money supplies per young person, $e = (M^*/N^*)/(M/N)$, discloses two important things about the relationship between exchange rate and monetary policies. First, these policies are not independent. A country can control either its money supply or its exchange rate, but not both. If a country unilaterally changes its monetary policy, this will change its exchange rate. Alternatively, if a country unilaterally tries to fix its exchange rate at a value different from the ratio of the two money supplies, its own money supply will have to adjust—by enough to bring the ratio of the two money supplies per worker in line with the level fixed for the exchange rate.

Second, the formula tells us that countries share the same exchange rate and thus must coordinate their exchange rate policies. Suppose the home country wants the exchange rate to appreciate. It can try to produce an appreciation by decreasing its money supply. But if the foreign country wants to keep the exchange rate unchanged, it can follow suit by decreasing its own money supply, by an equal percentage. The net result will be the same ratio of the two countries' money supplies and the same exchange rate.

DISTINGUISHING FLEXIBLE AND FIXED EXCHANGE RATE REGIMES

Our formula connecting the nominal exchange rate to the ratio of money supplies can also help us think about the difference between flexible and fixed exchange rates. In a flexible exchange rate regime, the governments set their money supplies and let their exchange rates freely adjust according to the resulting ratio of the two money supplies. In a fixed exchange rate regime, one of the two countries, with the acquiescence of the other, sets the exchange rate and permits its money supply to adjust to the level required to satisfy our formula. Thus, in a flexible exchange rate regime, the government maintains direct control of its money supply and loses direct control of its exchange rate, whereas the opposite occurs in a fixed exchange rate regime.

Although the variable under direct government control differs in the two regimes, the equation relating the nominal exchange rate to the ratio of money supplies holds in both regimes. Hence, one might ask whether it really matters if a country chooses a flexible or fixed exchange rate regime. The answer is that, assuming freely flexible prices and wages, it may not matter. According to our model, if countries with flexible exchange rates can freely adjust their money supplies, they can do so to produce the same real economic outcomes as would arise under a fixed exchange rate regime. Conversely, if countries with fixed exchange rates can freely change the value at which their exchange rate is fixed, they can replicate any real outcomes that would arise in a flexible exchange rate regime.

ILLUSTRATING MONETARY POLICY IN A FLEXIBLE EXCHANGE RATE REGIME

To demonstrate the potential equivalence of flexible and fixed exchange rate regimes, we'll now show how a simple monetary policy can be conducted equally well in a flexible or a fixed exchange rate regime. Under this policy, the home country prints 10 percent more money each period to finance transfer payments to its elderly. To keep matters simple, we'll assume the foreign country keeps its money supply fixed. In a closed economy, this policy raises the price level by 10 percent each period but has no real effects.[1] Each period the elderly end up paying for the transfers they receive through an implicit tax: the decline in the real value of their money balances resulting from the induced price rise.

In our open economy, the same situation holds. The home country's printing of money to make transfers to its elderly leaves them with more nominal money holdings but the same real money balances after taking account of the induced increase in prices. As in the closed economy case, the policy has no impact on the saving of the domestic young, nor does it alter the saving of the foreign young. Hence, it leaves unchanged the total capital accumulation of the young each period and, thus, the world's capital-labor transition equation. In sum, as in the closed economy model, this monetary policy in the open economy is neutral. It raises domestic prices each period but leaves the real side of the domestic and the foreign economies the same.

The policy does, however, alter the nominal exchange rate. Each period the relative value of the home country's money—the exchange rate—depreciates by 10 percent. We can see this either by considering the formula $e_t = (M_t^*/N^*)/(M_t/N)$ and noting that under the policy we're considering, the ratio of the foreign to the domestic money supply per young worker falls by 10 percent each period. Alternatively, we can refer to our formula that relates the percentage change in the exchange rate (from one period to the next) to the difference between the foreign and domestic inflation rates. In this case, the difference between these inflation rates is minus 10 percent, meaning that the nominal exchange rate falls by 10 percent each period.

As an example, take the case in which $N = N^*$, and suppose that the foreign and domestic money supplies are both 100 at time 0. The exchange rate will equal 1.000. At that point, the domestic government begins to raise its money supply each period by 10 percent. In period 1 the domestic money supply will be set at 110.0. In period 2 it will be 121.0. In period 3 it will be 133.1, and so forth. What will be the values of the exchange rate in these periods? The answer, found by forming the ratio of the money supplies, is .909 in period 1, .826 in period 2, .751 in period 3, and so forth, with the exchange rate falling by 10 percent each period.

What happens to the foreign price level as a result of the domestic country's monetary policy? Nothing! The nominal exchange rate fully adjusts to insulate the foreign country from the domestic country's change in its money supply. As a result, this policy produces no changes in any domestic real variables, no changes in any variables (except the nominal exchange rate) in the foreign country, but a 10 percent depreciation of the domestic currency each period as well as a 10 percent domestic inflation.

ILLUSTRATING EXCHANGE RATE POLICY IN A FIXED EXCHANGE RATE REGIME

The monetary policy just described can also be conducted in a fixed exchange rate regime. Intuitively, since $e_t = (M_t^*/N^*)/(M_t/N)$, the government can set e_t and let M_t adjust to that value (i.e., set its money supply indirectly), rather than setting the value of M_t directly and letting e_t adjust (as in the case of a flexible exchange rate regime). In a fixed exchange rate regime, governments set their exchange rates by intervening in the foreign exchange market by either selling or buying their own currency. In conducting the above-described policy, the domestic government needs to intervene in the foreign exchange market to produce a lower exchange rate each period. In terms of our numerical example, the domestic government needs to fix its exchange rate at .909 in period 1, at .826 in period 2, at .751 in period 3, and so on—the same values to which the exchange rate equilibrates in the flexible exchange regime.

Let's call the domestic money *dollars* and the foreign money *francs*, and continue to assume that the foreign government keeps its money supply fixed. To produce a 10 percent depreciation of the dollar each period, the domestic government must print additional dollars each period and sell these dollars for francs on the foreign exchange market. This raises the total supply of dollars being offered in exchange for francs and leads to an increase in the number of dollars needed to purchase one franc—that is, a depreciation of the dollar. For example, to set the exchange rate in period 1 at .909, the domestic government needs to print dollars and spend them—on francs in the foreign exchange market—until the market exchange rate settles at .909 franc per dollar or, equivalently, 1.1 dollars per franc. The fact that the government continues to print and sell dollars until its targeted exchange rate is met is why we say that the change in the domestic money supply under this policy is endogenous.

To complete our analysis of this exchange rate intervention, we need to clarify what the domestic government does with the francs it purchases on the foreign exchange market. One possibility—the one we'll consider here—is to give them to the domestic elderly as a transfer payment.[2] Of course, the domestic elderly are interested in getting dollars to spend on their final period consumption. Accordingly, they will turn around and exchange these francs for dollars on the foreign exchange market.

The net result of these transactions is that the domestic elderly will purchase back from the foreign exchange market the dollars just sold there by their government. In other words, rather than hand over directly to its domestic elderly the additional dollars it prints, as occurs in the flexible exchange rate scenario, the domestic government does so indirectly by (1) printing dollars, (2) trading these dollars for francs on the exchange market, (3) giving those francs to its elderly, and (4) letting its elderly purchase the dollars just printed by the government. In both the flexible and the fixed exchange rate regimes, the result is the same: the domestic elderly end up with 10 percent more dollars but are no better off because of the induced 10 percent rise in the domestic price level. In addition, the nominal exchange rate depreciates by 10 percent.

DO FLEXIBLE AND FIXED EXCHANGE RATE REGIMES REALLY DIFFER?

We've just shown that, absent price or wage rigidities, a particular type of monetary policy can be conducted equally well in both flexible and fixed exchange rate regimes. This is not an isolated example. On the contrary, *absent nominal rigidities, any monetary (or, for that matter, fiscal) policy conducted in a flexible exchange regime can also be conducted in a fixed exchange regime and vice versa—if there are no*

2 The domestic government need not make transfer payments to its elderly residents in foreign currency. Instead, it can purchase foreign assets with the francs, sell the foreign assets for dollars, and transfer these dollars to its elderly.

restrictions in the flexible exchange regime on the government's management of its money supply and if there are no restrictions in the fixed exchange regime on the government's management of its exchange rate. These are two big ifs. Under flexible exchange rate regimes, the government may have less latitude to adjust its money supply than is needed to keep its exchange rate either fixed or on a specifically targeted path. Similarly, under fixed exchange rates, a country may have less latitude to adjust its exchange rate than is needed to keep its money supply either fixed or changing in a desired manner.

In switching from one regime to another, governments often take political positions that restrict their repeating the policies they conducted in the former regime. Thus, in our example of a flexible exchange rate regime with an ongoing 10 percent inflation, the price stabilization might come about after the government switches to a fixed exchange rate regime and publicly announces that it will keep the exchange rate perfectly fixed. As we know from our formula relating the exchange rate to the ratio of foreign to domestic price levels, if the foreign price level is fixed and the exchange rate is fixed, the domestic price level will be fixed as well.

Of course, such price stabilization policy could also be conducted in a flexible exchange rate regime by having the government adjust its money supply to keep the price level fixed. But it may be easier for the government to convince the public that it is actively trying to stabilize prices if it fixes the exchange rate than if it announces it is using monetary policy to stabilize prices. In the former case, the government can point to a concrete achievement of its policy: a fixed exchange rate. In contrast, if the government says it is choosing a path of money supply to stabilize prices, the public has to decide whether the changes in the money supply chosen by the government really are those needed to keep prices from rising. Recall that the price level formula contains money demand factors as well as the money supply. If the public isn't sure how these money demand factors are changing through time, it won't know for sure whether the government is really choosing the money supply appropriate to eliminate inflation. Of course, the public can observe inflation directly, but inflation is usually reported with a time lag. In addition, the government can always claim that it missed its inflation target because of unexpected changes in the demand for money.

CASE STUDY
STABILIZING THE ARGENTINE PESO

Argentina's economic history redounds with episodes of high inflation followed by short-lived attempts to control the growth of its money supply. One such episode occurred in 1979 when the Argentine inflation rate was running at 150 percent per year. The Argentine finance minister, Martinez de Hoz, announced that the government would manage the dollar-peso exchange rate so that its value would depreciate over time according to a set schedule laid out in a *tablita*. In terms of our formula,

$e_t = (M_t^*/N^*)/M_t/N)$, the *tablita*'s requirement that it fall more slowly than in the past meant that M_t would rise at a slower rate than previously. The *tablita* policy was reasonably successful, at least in terms of controlling inflation. By the end of 1980, the Argentine inflation rate was running at well below 100 percent per year.

ARGUMENTS FOR AND AGAINST FLEXIBLE AND FIXED EXCHANGE RATES

The discussion suggests that the choice between fixed and flexible exchange rate regimes may have more to do with the issue of political commitment (keeping politicians time consistent) than with any meaningful economic distinctions. But there are additional arguments for and against the two regimes. Transactions costs make fixed exchange rates relatively more attractive, whereas the loss of independence in conducting monetary policy, the need for coordination between monetary and exchange authorities, and the possibility of running out of international reserves make flexible exchange rates relatively more attractive. After discussing these issues, we'll add nominal wage rigidity to our model and show how this alters the comparison of exchange rate regimes.

TRANSACTIONS COSTS AND FLEXIBLE EXCHANGE RATES

Flexible exchange rates raise the costs of transacting in foreign currencies. With constantly fluctuating rates, international traders must continually check the values of these rates to assess the profitability of their international transactions. The burden of keeping abreast of the latest values of exchange rates and the paperwork involved in exchanging currencies is particularly great in the case of international transactions involving a large number of countries. Thinking about trade among the 50 states of the United States can help illuminate this point. The 50 states can be viewed as participating in a fixed exchange rate regime. The only difference between this fixed exchange rate regime and the one between, say, the United States and Western Europe in the 1950s and 1960s is that each of the 50 states uses the same form of money: dollars.

Imagine the cost of conducting trade within the United States if each state had its own money whose relative values fluctuated continually. A supermarket in Boston considering purchasing apples from Washington State, California, New York, or Ohio would have to ascertain the value of each of these states' exchange rates with Massachusetts in order to convert each of the four local apple prices into amounts of Massachusetts money. Extrapolating this example to the myriad interstate transactions conducted in the United States, you quickly get a sense of the additional transactions costs arising from flexible exchange rates.

INDEPENDENCE IN THE OPERATION OF MONETARY POLICY

One argument against fixed rates is the potential loss in flexibility in conducting monetary policy. We say "potential" because, as we showed above, if a country has enough leeway in setting its exchange rate, it can adjust that rate over time to produce the same changes in its money supply that would occur under fixed rates. But in actual practice, nations adopting fixed rate regimes have been quite reluctant to alter their exchange rates.

Figure 13.1 makes this clear. It shows that during the 1950s and 1960s, when the German mark and French franc were pegged to the dollar, there was very little movement in either the mark-dollar or franc-dollar exchange rates except for a few occasions when either the mark or the franc was revalued against the dollar. In adhering for long periods of time to an essentially rigid exchange rate with the dollar, Germany and France, in effect, agreed to follow the course of monetary policy being conducted by the United States. These countries' willingness to adopt the same monetary policy as the United States lasted until the early 1970s, when the United States began increasing its money supply at a faster rate. At this point Germany and France realized that to maintain the same exchange rate with the United States, they would also have to increase the growth rate of their money supplies and that this would spell higher inflation for them, just as it spelled higher inflation for the United States. Neither Germany nor France was willing to tolerate higher inflation, so they elected to steer their own course of monetary policy within the ERM and let their exchange rates float against the dollar.

In opting to run independent monetary policies, Germany and France not only were able to choose their own inflation rates but also were able to decide for themselves how much real resources (via seigniorage and the like) they wanted to extract from the private sector through monetary policy. They were also able to use monetary policy to offset recessions caused or exacerbated by Keynesian short-run nominal rigidities.

The original ERM, which lasted from 1974 through 1993, allowed Germany and France to conduct monetary policy independent of the United States, but it did not permit Germany and France to conduct monetary policy independent of each other. In the summer of 1993 France's desire to conduct a more expansionary monetary policy than that being pursued by Germany led to the devaluation of the franc relative to the mark and to a new, much looser ERM.

MAINTAINING A FIXED EXCHANGE RATE WITH LIMITED INTERNATIONAL RESERVES

Yet another concern with fixed exchange rates is that the exchange rate authorities may not have sufficient resources with which to intervene on the foreign exchange market and fix the exchange rate at the level they desire. Suppose, for example, the Irish government wants to revalue its currency, the punt, in relation to the dollar. To do so, it needs to sell dollars and buy punts. But where will it get the dollars that it needs to sell in exchange for punts? The first possible source is its **international reserves**—its holdings of foreign financial assets (e.g., U.S. Treasury bonds). It will sell these assets for dollars and use the dollars to purchase punts. By selling reserves for dollars, the exchange authorities reduce the number of dollars in circulation, but in selling these dollars for punts, they restore the dollars back into circulation. The net result of these transactions is equivalent to directly selling foreign reserves for punts. This approach reduces the supply of punts held by the public, raises the ratio of the U.S. to Irish money supplies and, as our formula for the exchange rate indicates, raises the value of the punt in relation to the dollar.

Now what happens if the Irish exchange authorities run out of foreign reserves before they have moved the exchange rate to the degree they intended? Well, with the agreement of the rest of the government, they could sell other types of government assets for punts (or, if you like, for dollars and then spend the dollars on punts). If there are no other government assets available to sell, the exchange authorities could tax the public and purchase assets with the tax proceeds. But the rest of the government may balk at this proposition, putting an end to the attempt to fix the exchange rate at the desired level. This potential for the government to give up trying to peg the exchange rate at a particular value (so to speak, to punt) does not arise in our model because the model does not consider the specific institutional framework of the government.

To be evenhanded in evaluating the two exchange regimes, we need to point out that in a flexible exchange rate regime, the Irish government may encounter the same sort of difficulty in reducing its money supply. In a flexible regime, the counterpart of the above policy is for the Irish government to reduce the money supply by increasing taxes on the elderly. As we showed in chapter 7, this policy doesn't affect the welfare of the Irish elderly because what they lose in taxes, they gain in an increase in the real value of their remaining money balances associated with the decline in the price level. This point notwithstanding, the political fallout from raising taxes may preclude conducting such a monetary policy.

Speculation against Fixed Exchange Rate Regimes

One of the concerns about fixed exchange rates is that they are subject to speculative attacks. In a typical attack, speculators come to believe the government will not be able to maintain the current rate and will have to devalue. In terms of our example, speculators might come to believe that once the Irish government's foreign reserves are exhausted, it will simply devalue the punt. If the punt is currently pegged at 0.7 punt per dollar but is expected to be devalued in the near future to, say, 0.8 punt per dollar, a speculator can expect to make, in short order, a 0.1 punt profit on each dollar she buys from the government. Each dollar obtained by selling 0.7 punt prior to the devaluation can be exchanged for 0.8 punt after the devaluation. Notice that anyone holding punts prior to the devaluation can speculate against the punt by selling them for dollars. Hence, if enough people come to expect a devaluation, the Irish government will find itself forced to purchase huge quantities of punts or devalue.

International reserves
A government's holdings of assets denominated in foreign currencies

THE OPEN ECONOMY MODEL WITH NOMINAL WAGE RIGIDITY

Our strategy for adding nominal wage rigidity to our open economy model is simply to modify our IS-LM framework to take into account the economy's openness.[3] Once we've done this, we'll be in a position to consider how this nominal rigidity influences the choice of exchange regimes. In what follows we drop time subscripts.

IS CURVE IN THE OPEN ECONOMY

The key modification to our IS-LM framework concerns the IS curve, which relates a country's interest rate next period to its income and fiscal policy this period. The logic of the IS curve for a closed economy is simple: a country's income and fiscal policy in this period affect the young people's saving in this period and, thus, its capital stock next period, on which next period's interest rate depends.

In an open economy, however, the interest rate is no longer determined by the saving of the domestic young, but rather by the saving of the young at home and abroad—that is, by worldwide capital accumulation. Consequently, a country's own income and fiscal policies this period influence the interest rate next period only to the extent that they alter world saving and, thus, next period's world capital stock.

The following equation, which relates the world's capital stock next period to this period's domestic and foreign income and fiscal policies, makes this clear:

$$K_{+1} = (1 - \gamma)(Y + Y^*) - (F + F^*).$$

If we add to this formula the fact that $r_{+1} = A[K_{+1}/(N + N^*)]^{\beta - 1}$, we have everything we need to form the open economy IS curve. That is, since domestic income, Y, affects the world capital stock, K_{+1}, and the world capital stock determines the interest rate, r_{+1}, we have a relationship between domestic income and the interest rate.[4]

How does the open economy IS curve compare with the closed economy curve in which Y^* and F^* are set equal to zero? As shown in Figure 13.4, it's flatter. To understand why, consider point A, which lies on both the closed and open economy IS curves. Now consider the change in domestic income needed to lower the interest rate from r^0 to r^1. In the closed economy case, income must rise from Y^0 to Y^1, as depicted by the movement from point A to point B. In the open economy case, this same increase in domestic income produces the same absolute increase in capital next period, but a smaller increase in next period's world capital-labor ratio, since we divide the world capital stock by $N + N^*$, rather than just N. Consequently, an increase in domestic income of only $Y^1 - Y^0$ would not suffice to lower the interest rate (which depends on the world capital-labor ratio) from r^0 to r^1. Rather, a bigger increase, $Y^2 - Y^1$, is needed. Thus, the open economy IS curve runs through points A and C.

Note that the smaller an economy is relative to the world economy, the flatter will be its IS curve. It's also true that the smaller the size of the economy, the less effective will be its fiscal policy as a tool for combating nominal rigidities. In terms of

[3] What results is essentially the Mundell-Fleming model, originally developed by Robert Mundell of Columbia University and Marcus Fleming of the International Monetary Fund.

[4] Our analysis here takes foreign output, Y^*, and foreign fiscal policy, F^*, as given.

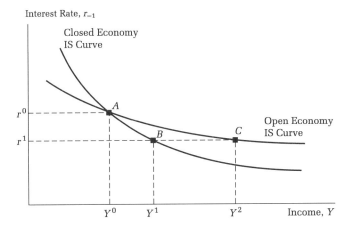

FIGURE 13.4 OPEN ECONOMY IS CURVE
In the open economy, the interest rate is determined by the world capital-labor ratio, which small economies are unable to influence very much. The smaller an economy is relative to the world economy, the flatter its IS curve will be.

the IS curve, this means that the upward shift of the IS curve will be smaller, the smaller the size of the economy.

For a small, open economy—one too small to affect the world's capital stock materially or its overall fiscal policy—the IS curve is a horizontal line whose height is set by next period's exogenous interest rate and whose position doesn't change in response to changes in its fiscal policy. Since it no longer shifts the IS curve, fiscal policy in a small, open economy is completely impotent as a means of overcoming short-run nominal rigidities.

On the other hand, a flat IS curve makes monetary policy more effective. Figure 13.5 shows that a given rightward shift of the LM curve will produce a bigger increase in output and employment if the IS curve is flat than if it slopes downward. The reason is that with a downward-sloping IS curve, the interest rate would fall. That would raise the demand for money and would mean that income need not rise by as much (as with a flat IS curve) to reestablish money market equilibrium with the larger money supply.

To summarize, *although small, open economies facing nominal wage rigidity can't rely on fiscal policy, they can expect their monetary policy to be more effective than that of a large, open economy*, since their IS curve is flat. But, as we've discussed, the choice of exchange regime affects the ability to conduct independent monetary policy. Let's examine this choice for a small, open economy.

POLICIES IN SMALL, OPEN ECONOMIES WITH RIGID NOMINAL WAGES

While thinking about monetary policy and exchange regimes in the context of rigid nominal wages, bear in mind three points about the price level. First, firms will increase their employment and output only if the real wage they face falls—if, that is, the price level rises (given that the nominal wage is fixed). Second, since the price level

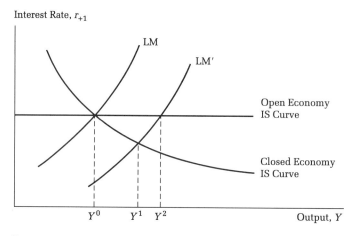

FIGURE 13.5 WHY MONETARY POLICY IS MORE EFFECTIVE IN AN OPEN ECONOMY
For a small, open economy, the IS curve is effectively horizontal. This makes fiscal policy completely ineffective, but makes monetary policy more effective. For a given shift in LM, there is a larger increase in output than with a downward-sloping IS curve.

enters the LM curve, an increase in M will produce an initial rightward shift of the LM curve, as well as a partially offsetting leftward shift in the LM curve, because it will raise the price level. Third, the law of one price dictates that $eP = P^*$. So any changes in P must be consistent with this relationship.[5]

Now let's turn to the case of a flexible exchange rate. In this case, our analysis of the operation of monetary policy is identical to that in chapter 8, except that the IS curve is now a flat line. A rise in the money supply shifts the LM curve rightward, but causes the price level to rise (and the real wage to fall), producing a less than fully offsetting leftward shift in the LM curve. As shown in Figure 13.6, the net impact of the monetary expansion is a rise in output and employment. With a flexible exchange rate, any change in P leads to a change in e to satisfy $eP = P^*$. So the law of one price places no restriction on the movement of the price level.

Next consider our small, open economy with rigid nominal wages but an exchange rate fixed at $\bar{e}$. In this case the law of one price fixes the price level P at the value $P^*/\bar{e}$. Since both the price level and the nominal wage are fixed, the real wage is fixed as well, meaning that employment and output will also be fixed. Hence, *in a small, open economy with a fixed exchange rate, neither fiscal nor monetary policy will be able to raise output and employment.*

Let's examine this conclusion in terms of the IS-LM diagram. Suppose the government tries to expand the money supply to raise employment and output. In Figure 13.6, which assumed a flexible exchange rate, we saw that this policy would be effective in shifting the LM curve rightward. With a fixed exchange rate, however, the LM curve ends up where it started; there is no net shift in the curve. The reason is that with a fixed exchange rate, the government loses control of the money supply. As

5 *In what follows, we take P^* as given.*

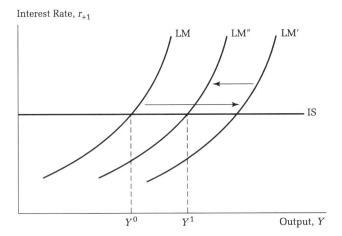

Interest Rate, r_{+1}

Output, Y

FIGURE 13.6 MONETARY EXPANSION IN A SMALL, OPEN ECONOMY
With a flexible exchange rate and a flat IS curve, a rise in the money supply shifts the LM curve to LM'. That causes the price level to rise, producing a less than fully offsetting leftward shift to LM". The net impact is a rise in output from Y^0 to Y^1 and a corresponding increase in employment.

it tries to expand the money supply, it finds that its exchange rate is depreciating. In order to keep this from happening, it has to purchase back from the foreign exchange market all the money it injects into the economy. Hence, the initial rightward shift of the LM curve arising from the expansion of the money supply is completely reversed by the leftward shift arising from the contraction in the money supply needed to maintain the fixed exchange rate.

AN ARGUMENT FOR FIXED EXCHANGE RATES: MITIGATING OUTPUT FLUCTUATIONS

If, as we've said, monetary policy can work only if the exchange rate is flexible, can any case be made for fixed rates in the context of rigid nominal wages? The answer is yes. Suppose that liquidity preference, which in our model refers to the demand for money function, $\gamma[\ ]$, is highly volatile, shifting the LM curve leftward or rightward for a given monetary policy. In a flexible exchange rate regime, this volatility translates into a highly volatile output level. It also translates into a highly volatile exchange rate, because the exchange rate depends on the price level ($e = P^*/P$), and the price level depends on the level of γ.

With flexible exchange rates, the government can use monetary policy to offset those output declines emanating from sporadic leftward shifts in the LM curve. But what if it doesn't, perhaps because of a delay in recognizing the need for intervention? Then, as shown in Figure 13.7, when the LM curve shifts leftward, there will be less output and employment than under a fixed exchange rate.

To see why a fixed exchange rate regime stabilizes output, recall that with a fixed exchange rate, the money supply automatically adjusts to keep the domestic price

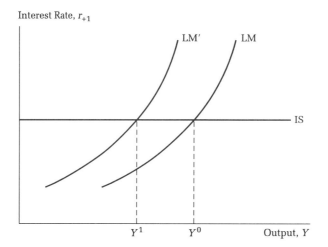

FIGURE 13.7 IMPACT OF AN INCREASE IN LIQUIDITY PREFERENCE
Increases in the demand for money function, $\gamma[\ ]$, shift LM to the left, leading to less output and employment and a lower price level. With flexible exchange rates, the government can offset this shift by increasing the money supply. But it may fail to do so. With a fixed exchange rate, the government is obliged to increase the money supply and restore the original position of the LM curve in order to prevent the exchange rate from appreciating.

level fixed at $P^*/\bar{e}$. An increase in the demand for money brought about by an increase in the value of γ at each interest rate, which shifts the LM curve leftward, will induce a fall in the price level. Other things equal, this fall in the price level means an exchange rate appreciation as well as a higher real wage. To keep this from happening, the exchange authorities end up selling more of the home country's money in the foreign exchange market, thereby raising the money supply and shifting the LM curve rightward. The rightward shift will fully offset the initial leftward shift, leaving the economy at the same level of output and employment. The reason is that with the exchange rate fixed, P will remain fixed at $P^*/\bar{e}$, so the real wage will remain at its initial value.

We conclude that a fixed exchange regime will stabilize the economy in response to shocks to its money demand. If the economy is initially at full employment, using a fixed exchange rate to make sure it stays there seems like a good idea. On the other hand, if the economy is not initially at full employment, the government will have to abandon its fixed exchange rate if it wants to use monetary policy to expand output and employment.

CASE STUDY
EUROPEAN MONETARY INTEGRATION

In 1999 most major Western European economies are scheduled to adopt a single currency called the *euro*. The major exception is Great Britain, which is likely to keep the pound sterling as its currency. Germany, France, Italy, and the other adopters of the euro will forfeit the right to conduct their own monetary policy. Instead, the supply of euros will be determined by a new European central bank situated in Brussels, the capital of the EC. The seigniorage raised by this bank will be distributed back to member countries.

Part of the impetus for a single European currency is political, reflecting the belief that a single currency and monetary policy will contribute to the goal of a "United States of Europe"—a single European nation with a single set of domestic and foreign policies. Apart from political motivations, there are economic arguments for a single currency. Chief among them are the reduction in transactions costs of inter-European commerce associated with trading in so many different currencies and the elimination of economic fallout from currency instability (modeled in this chapter as arising from fluctuations in the money demand function). The strongest economic argument against a single currency is that member countries will lose an important policy instrument, their own monetary policies, for combating recessions and financing government programs.

CHAPTER SUMMARY

1. This chapter adds money to our two-country model. The result is an open economy model with an important new variable, the nominal exchange rate. The nominal exchange rate indicates how many units of foreign money it takes to buy one unit of domestic money.

2. Nominal exchange rates determined by private market forces are described as floating, or flexible, exchange rates. Nominal exchange rates that are either legally set by governments or established through government intervention in the foreign exchange market are called fixed exchange rates.

3. A fixed exchange rate set by law gives rise to a black market if it differs from the rate at which supply of and demand for a country's money are equal. In most of today's fixed exchange rate regimes, governments directly exchange their money for that of other countries in the foreign exchange market. In the last century and part of this century, countries established fixed exchange rates by fixing the amount of their monies that would be exchanged for gold.

4. Regardless of how the nominal exchange rate is determined, it can be used to compare the prices of goods and services in one country with those in another, where both foreign and domestic prices are measured in the same currency.

Forming such a relative price ratio for a comprehensive basket of goods and services produces the real exchange rate. If all goods were traded and there were no shipping costs, commodity taxes, or tariffs—the world of our model—the real exchange rate would be unity. This is a reflection of the law of one price, which states that, apart from these factors, the price of a good or service cannot be higher at one location than at another.

5. Because the real exchange rate in our model is unity, the nominal exchange rate equals the ratio of the foreign to the domestic price level. Consequently, changes over time in the nominal exchange rate reflect differences in countries' inflation rates. Since the ratio of the foreign to the domestic price level depends on the ratio of the foreign to the domestic money supply, exchange rate policies and monetary policies are linked. Specifically, a country can set either its money supply or its exchange rate, but not both. In flexible exchange rate regimes, countries set their money supplies and allow their nominal exchange rates to equilibrate endogenously. In fixed exchange rate regimes, countries set their nominal exchange rates and let their money supplies adjust to whatever level is needed to sustain the rate being fixed.

6. Even though the same monetary policy can, in principal, be run in either regime, the switch from one monetary policy to another may, for political and credibility reasons, be associated with a change in exchange rate regimes. Indeed, switching from flexible to fixed exchange rates is a common feature of price stabilization policies. By rigidly controlling their exchange rates, governments indirectly slow the growth rate of their money supplies and thereby lower the rate of inflation.

7. Besides helping some countries control their inflation rates, fixed exchange rates can reduce the information and other costs associated with transacting in multiple currencies whose relative values are continually changing. Against the advantages of fixed exchange rates must be piled several disadvantages. First, since countries share their exchange rates, they need, in fixed rate regimes, to coordinate their exchange rate policies. Second, this coordination may entail one country's effectively adopting the monetary policy of the other, thus forgoing the option of independently altering its money supply. A third concern is the potential problem of running out of international reserves amid a speculative attack on the exchange rate.

8. The final part of this chapter added nominal wage rigidity to the two-country model. The resulting open economy IS-LM model differs from the closed economy model because the IS curve is flatter. Indeed, in the case of a small, open economy, the IS curve is a horizontal line, unaffected by domestic fiscal policy. This impotence of fiscal policy in a small, open economy leaves monetary policy

as the means by which such an economy can combat nominal rigidities. A horizontal IS curve also makes monetary policy more effective.

9. In the case of nominal wage rigidity, monetary expansion will expand output and employment, assuming the exchange rate is flexible. If it is fixed, the exchange authorities will end up purchasing back on the foreign exchange market all the additional money that has been created. The net impact will be no expansion in the money supply and no change in output. This automatic stabilization of the level of output in a fixed exchange regime is an attractive way to deal with output volatility brought about by sporadic shifts in the money demand function.

PART FIVE

ENRICHING THE MODEL

THE BANKING SYSTEM, THE FEDERAL RESERVE, AND THE MONEY SUPPLY

INTRODUCTION

This chapter describes how the banking system operates and how central banks control their countries' money supplies. The U.S. central bank is the **Federal Reserve System**—the Fed. We discussed the Fed briefly in chapter 7, and we'll examine it here in some detail. We begin by pointing out that a bank is a type of *financial intermediary*—a business that helps households and firms conduct financial transactions with one another, including borrowing and investing. We then enumerate the different types of financial intermediaries and indicate, in general terms, how they fit into our model.

With this background, we will study banks as a special type of financial intermediary—one that offers households and firms a highly liquid way of investing. The word "demand" in demand deposits (checking accounts) reflects the fact that funds deposited in a bank can be accessed (demanded) at a moment's notice simply by writing a check. The liquidity of demand deposits, as well as their other money-like properties, explains their inclusion, along with currency, traveler's checks, and other checkable deposits, in **M1**, the principal definition of money. Demand deposits as well as the other components of M1 are also included in the government's broader definitions of money, M2 and M3. These three definitions of money are referred to as the government's **monetary aggregates**.

Another feature that makes banks such special financial intermediaries is their ability to increase the total volume of demand deposits and thus expand the M1, M2, and M3 money supplies. Banks do this by lending to borrowers a portion of the funds that have been deposited with them. A good part of these re-lent funds ends up back in banks as additional demand deposits. As we'll see, the extent of this deposit expansion by the banks depends on the fraction of their deposits they do not lend out, but rather hold as *reserves* against the possibility that the funds deposited with them will be withdrawn.

Federal Reserve System
The central bank and monetary authority of the United States; known as "the Fed"

M1
A measure of the money supply consisting of currency and coin held by the nonbank public, checkable deposits, and traveler's checks

Monetary aggregates
Measures of the economy's money supply

The Federal Reserve's **reserve requirements** specify the minimum fractions of their deposits that banks must hold as reserves. Through these requirements, the Federal Reserve influences the extent to which initial deposits in the banking system are expanded (or multiplied) through bank lending in determining total deposits. Since deposits constitute well over half of both M1 and the other monetary aggregates, the Federal Reserve's reserve requirements influence the size of these aggregates.

The Federal Reserve has another method, more direct, of controlling the money supply. It determines the basic amount of money the government injects into the economy—the *monetary base*. Each one dollar increase in the monetary base can lead to more than a one dollar increase in M1, depending on how much of that dollar increase is held in currency and how much is deposited in banks and other depository institutions, setting off the deposit expansion process.

The ratio of M1 to the monetary base is called the *M1 money multiplier*. It indicates by how much M1 rises as a result of each one dollar increase in the monetary base. After discussing the private banking system, we will take a close look at the determinants of the M1 money multiplier. Next we'll consider the two basic methods the Federal Reserve uses to increase the monetary base: *open market operations* and *discount window lending*. We'll also discuss how the Fed's reserve requirements influence the sizes of money multipliers.

Although it directly controls the monetary base, the Federal Reserve has only indirect control of the money multipliers and therefore only indirect control of the monetary aggregates. This raises the question of how well it can exercise that control, the next subject considered in this chapter. Specifically, we'll examine the divergent paths taken by different monetary aggregates in the postwar period. We'll also consider how much of the variability in the monetary aggregates is due to variability in money multipliers. Finally, we'll consider the Federal Reserve's failure to control M1 during the Great Depression.

Beyond the question of how well the government can control the monetary aggregates is the question of whether it *should* try to control them. Nobel laureate Milton Friedman and other economists believe the government should target the growth of a particular monetary aggregate. Other economists believe the Fed should adjust the monetary aggregates to target the level of interest rates. We'll consider this debate as well as the episode in the late 1970s in which the Federal Reserve sought to target the growth of M1. Finally, we'll consider the possibility that the money supply is endogenous—that the government's control of the money supply is a response to, rather than a cause of, changes in the economy.

The next-to-last section of this chapter is also concerned with monetary control. It discusses banking panics—episodes that have severely tested the Fed's ability to control M1 and other broad monetary aggregates. It also considers the role of *deposit insurance* in preventing bank panics. This section provides the occasion to review the near-collapse of the U.S. banking system during the Great Depression as well as the savings and loan crisis of the 1980s.

Reserve requirements
The legally required minimum level of reserves a bank must maintain, as a fraction of its deposits

The final section will, as always, sum up what we've discussed, including the answers to the following questions:

- What are financial intermediaries?

- How do banks affect the money supply?

- What factors determine the size of the money multiplier?

- How does the Federal Reserve attempt to control the money supply?

- How effective is the Federal Reserve in controlling different monetary aggregates?

- What causes bank panics, and what can the government do to prevent them?

- What problems are caused by deposit insurance?

UNDERSTANDING FINANCIAL INTERMEDIARIES

Financial intermediaries match suppliers of funds with demanders of funds, but in an indirect way. Consider a bank that makes a loan to a local business. The funds the bank uses to make the business loan are, in part, those supplied to it by its depositors. The bank acts as a go-between in helping its depositors lend money to that firm. A second example is an investment bank that helps a start-up company sell shares of stock to the public. By selling stock, the company seeks to obtain (demands) the funds needed to finance its business operations. In buying the stock, the public is supplying the funds to meet this demand. By bringing the seller (supplier of) and purchasers of (demanders for) the stock together, the investment bank is intermediating between the two.

Matching suppliers of funds with demanders is just one service that financial intermediaries provide. They also reduce the transactions costs of buying or selling financial assets. A mutual fund can combine the savings of a large number of small investors and make bulk purchases of a diversified set of financial securities. A savings and loan association (S&L) can combine small deposits of individual savers to provide mortgages to home buyers who might otherwise need to spend a great deal of time borrowing small sums of money from a large number of friends, relatives, and others.

Financial intermediaries also economize on the costs of acquiring information. Consider a stockbroker who invests time and money to learn the value of a particular company. The broker can share this information at no additional cost with all his clients, advising them in the process whether to buy or sell the company's stock. The

Financial intermediary
An institution that serves as a go-between, accepting funds from savers and lending those funds to consumers and investors

alternative—having each of the broker's clients collect this same information—would result in much higher information costs.

Advanced economies have a broad array of financial intermediaries, including commercial banks, investment banks, savings and loan associations, credit agencies, credit unions, finance companies, mutual funds, pension funds, money market mutual funds, insurance brokers, real estate brokers, stockbrokers, and bond traders. These businesses help households and firms obtain loans and other types of financing, invest their savings, economize on their cash balances, diversify the risk of their investments, and acquire insurance. The financial services sector is of growing importance to the U.S. economy. In 1959 this sector accounted for 13.6 percent of U.S. GDP. By 1994 its share of GDP had grown to 18.4 percent.

FINANCIAL INTERMEDIARIES AND OUR MODEL

In our model so far we've ignored financial intermediation. In effect, we've assumed that each generation can invest its savings with the model's firms and incur no costs in doing so. Adding such costs to our model would produce a demand by each generation for the services of financial intermediaries to reduce transactions costs, obtain information, and diversify investment risk. *Risk diversification* refers to the simple idea that you shouldn't put all your investment eggs in the same basket.

BALANCE SHEETS OF FINANCIAL INTERMEDIARIES

We can summarize the activities of a financial intermediary in terms of a *balance sheet* that lists its assets and debts. The IOUs received by an intermediary in exchange for loans it makes or the financial assets it purchases enter its balance sheets as assets. They indicate amounts owed to the financial intermediary by borrowers or by firms in which the intermediary has invested. The IOUs issued by the financial intermediary in exchange for the funds placed with it enter the intermediary's balance sheets as liabilities.

Every financial intermediary needs an initial sum of money to begin operation. This *owners' equity* is provided by the owners of the intermediary, and some of it is used to purchase the office space, computers, and furniture needed to get the operation going. The rest is kept in the form of money for use in initiating lending. Owners' equity counts as another liability, since it is ultimately owed to the owners of the intermediary. On the other hand, the office buildings and other physical capital, as well as any financial assets acquired, are counted as assets. The amount of liabilities of a financial intermediary always equals the amount of its assets. That's because every dollar received by an intermediary is counted as a liability, and every dollar lent or otherwise invested by an intermediary is counted as an asset.

LIABILITIES OF FINANCIAL INTERMEDIARIES AND U.S. MONETARY AGGREGATES

Demand deposits are the most liquid liabilities of financial intermediaries. But they are not the only liabilities included in some definitions of money. Savings accounts, time deposits, and money market mutual fund shares are reasonably liquid and, consequently, are counted in the broader definitions of money called **M2** and **M3**.[1] M2 primarily adds savings accounts, small time deposits, and money market mutual funds to M1.[2] M3 primarily adds large time deposits to M2.[3] Figure 14.1 shows the relative sizes of M1, M2, and M3 in 1997, as well as their components. In that year, M1 was just over one-fourth the size of M2 and about one-fifth the size of M3.

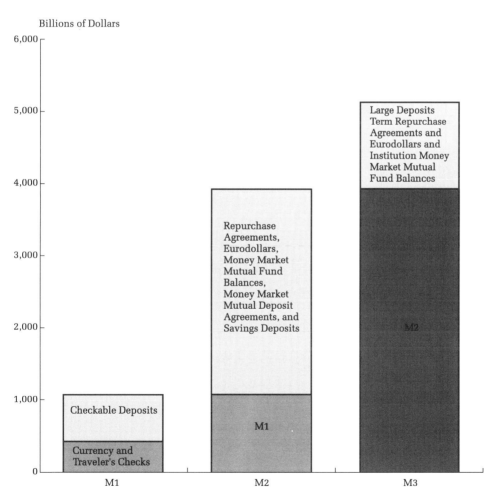

M2
A monetary aggregate consisting of M1 plus savings deposits, small time deposits, and money market mutual funds balances

M3
A monetary aggregate consisting of M2 plus large time deposits and negotiable certificates of deposit

1 Checks can be written on a money market mutual fund, but they typically must exceed a certain minimum amount.

2 M2 also includes saving certificates, overnight repurchase agreements (essentially, interest-bearing checking accounts of businesses), and Eurodollar deposits (dollar deposits in European banks).

3 M3 also includes term repurchase agreements, term Eurodollar deposits, and money market mutual fund shares owned by institutions.

FIGURE 14.1 SIZE AND COMPOSITION OF U.S. MONETARY AGGREGATES, 1997
In June 1997, M1 was just over one-fourth the size of M2 and about one-fifth the size of M3.

Source: Board of Governors, Federal Reserve System.

BANKS AS SPECIAL FINANCIAL INTERMEDIARIES

Most of this chapter studies those functions of financial intermediaries that involve creation of checkable deposits. To keep our terminology simple, we refer to these intermediaries as "banks." But our definition really includes any institution that accepts deposits and allows its depositors to write checks on those balances. Commercial banks, savings and loans, mutual savings banks, and credit unions all qualify under this definition. Their demand deposits and other checkable deposits are counted as part of the M1 money supply, and each of these financial intermediaries is capable of "creating money."

BANKS AS REPOSITORIES OF MONEY AND ISSUERS OF LIQUID LIABILITIES

Banks provide the standard services of financial intermediaries, including matching suppliers and demanders of funds, reducing the transactions costs of investing and borrowing, and acquiring information about the profitability of particular investments. But banks also play a special role as depositories for the money held by individuals and firms. Indeed, the earliest banks were temporary repositories used by people worried about having their money stolen.

Negotiable checks, which are IOUs of banks that can be exchanged for goods and services, trace their origins to the Middle Ages. It was awkward for depositors to withdraw their money each time they wanted to make a purchase, so banks permitted depositors to use a written claim on money they held in the bank. This precursor to the modern-day bank check could then be presented by the recipient to the bank in exchange for the indicated sum of money. Negotiable checks, then and now, reduce the necessity for frequent trips to the bank and also reduce the likelihood of having money stolen while shopping.

BANK RESERVES AND THE EXPANSION OF DEMAND DEPOSITS

The earliest banks simply stored all of their depositors' money for as long as those depositors desired. But it didn't take long for astute bank managers to notice that they were continuously holding large amounts of money in their vaults. Not all depositors withdrew their money at the same time. Also, as ongoing businesses, banks were constantly receiving new deposits of money that offset any old deposits that were withdrawn. The banks soon realized they could lend or invest at least some of the monies deposited with them and still be able to cover periodic withdrawals by their depositors.

Funds that banks keep in reserve to cover withdrawals are called **bank reserves**. These reserves play a key role in determining the expansion of demand deposits and the money supply. To see this, let's take the case of the hypothetical, First National Bank of Lake Wobegon, Minnesota. First National is established by a group of investors who contribute $1,000 of owners' equity to set up the bank. In its first act of business, First National Bank lends the $1,000 to Dewey, Cheatham, and Howe, a local law firm. The loan is an asset of the bank. At this stage of First National's financial dealings its balance sheet looks like this:

Bank reserves
Funds held in reserve by banks against the possibility that deposits will be withdrawn

First National Bank Balance Sheet

Assets		Liabilities	
Type	Amount	Type	Amount
Loans	$1,000	Owners' equity	$1,000
Total assets	**$1,000**	**Total liabilities**	**$1,000**

In the balance sheet, the $1,000 of owners' equity is a liability of the bank since it represents a claim by the owners on the bank's assets.

Now suppose Dewey, Cheatham, and Howe decides to hold the $1,000 it borrows in the form of a checking account balance at First National Bank. Also suppose the bank adds these funds to its reserves, which previously were zero. In this case the bank's balance sheet becomes:

First National Bank Balance Sheet

Assets		Liabilities	
Type	Amount	Type	Amount
Reserves	$1,000	Deposits	$1,000
Loans	1,000	Owners' equity	1,000
Total assets	**$2,000**	**Total liabilities**	**$2,000**

Although owners' equity isn't changed by Dewey, Cheatham, and Howe's decision to keep its money in First National Bank, both the bank's liabilities and its assets rise by $1,000. The $1,000 increase in liabilities reflects the $1,000 checking account balance of Dewey, Cheatham, and Howe, and the $1,000 increase in assets reflects the bank's increased reserves. Since checking account balances are part of M1, this transaction has increased the economy's money supply by $1,000.

So far the initial $1,000 placed in First National Bank by its founders has led to the creation of an equal amount of demand deposits. But what if the bank is required to hold, say, only 20 percent of the funds deposited with it as reserves? In that case, it will find itself holding $800 in **excess reserves**—reserves in excess of those required to cover the risk of a withdrawal of deposits. Realizing it has $800 in excess reserves, First National Bank lends $800 to Specific Motors Corporation, which also deposits the funds back in First National Bank. Now the balance sheet is:

First National Bank Balance Sheet

Assets		Liabilities	
Type	Amount	Type	Amount
Reserves	$1,000	Deposits	$1,800
Loans	1,800	Owners' equity	1,000
Total assets	**$2,800**	**Total liabilities**	**$2,800**

Excess reserves
Reserves held by depository institutions over and above the legally required minimum level

We can see that the $1,000 originally put in the bank has supported the creation of $1,800 in demand deposits, which are part of M1. The $1,000 of reserves is now made up of $360 (20 percent of $1,800) in required reserves and $640 of excess reserves. Because the bank still has excess reserves, it can make additional loans and create additional demand deposits. If this process continues, with First National always lending out its excess reserves, where will it end up? The answer is given in the following balance sheet:

First National Bank Balance Sheet

Assets		Liabilities	
Type	Amount	Type	Amount
Reserves	$1,000	Deposits	$5,000
Loans	5,000	Owners' equity	1,000
Total assets	**$6,000**	**Total liabilities**	**$6,000**

According to this balance sheet, the original $1,000 contributed to the bank has led to the creation of $5,000 worth of demand deposits. At this point, First National's $1,000 of reserves equals its required reserves: 20 percent of its $5,000 demand deposits. Its excess reserves are zero, so we say the bank is "loaned up." Thus, the process of deposit creation continues until the reserves on the volume of demand deposits created just equal the amount of money injected into the bank: $1,000.

In this example, we assumed that any funds lent by First National Bank were always deposited right back into that bank. So the amount of demand deposits created by the banking system as a whole is the same as the amount created by this individual bank: $5,000. More realistically, suppose the funds lent by First National Bank are deposited in other banks that also keep 20 percent of their deposits as reserves and lend out all their excess reserves. It turns out that the result is the same. The $1,000 initially injected into the banking system will lead to creation of $5,000 of demand deposits (which, again, are M1 money). It really makes no difference in which bank the deposits are held. All that matters is the total amount of demand deposits created. These transactions illustrate the so-called money multiplier, whose formula we'll now derive.

THE MONEY MULTIPLIER AND THE MONETARY BASE

The banking system multiplies the amount of money put into banks through the process of deposit creation. Suppose for a moment that there were no currency. In that case, all money injected into the economy by the government—which we call the **monetary base**—would be deposited in banks and end up being held as reserves against deposits created by the banking system. The M1 money supply would include only demand deposits, and we would have the following formula relating M1 to the monetary base, *MB*:

Monetary base
The sum of bank reserves and currency held by the public

$$M1 = \frac{1}{rd}\ MB.$$

In this equation *rd* stands for the *reserve-deposit ratio*—the amount of reserves per dollar of demand deposits. If we multiply both sides of the equation by *rd*, we find that all of the monetary base ends up being held as reserves against the demand deposits (equal here to M1) created by the banking system. In this case, in which all the monetary base is deposited in banks, the **M1 money multiplier** is $1/rd$. It indicates by how much the monetary base is expanded, through the process of deposit creation, to determine total demand deposits and, thus, M1. For example, if *rd* equals .2, indicating that banks keep reserves equal to 20 percent of their deposits, the money multiplier equals 1/.2, or 5, and M1 equals five times the monetary base.

In reality, of course, not all the monetary base is held as reserves against demand deposits. Some is held by the public as cash (currency), and some is held as reserves against time and other types of deposits. Obviously the monetary base must be held somewhere. So, if it's not being held by individuals and firms as cash, then it must be sitting as reserves in commercial banks, in savings and loans, or in other depository institutions. Thus, we can write

Monetary base = Currency + reserves.

In June 1997, the U.S. monetary base was \$461 billion, of which \$414 billion was held as currency and the rest as reserves.

Since the U.S. monetary base is not all held as bank reserves, we have to modify our formula relating M1 to the monetary base. Let's start by noting that M1 equals currency plus demand deposits and letting *cd* stand for the public's desired ratio of currency to demand deposits.[4] Then,

M1 = Currency + demand deposits = $(cd + 1) \times$ demand deposits.

Now the monetary base, MB, equals currency plus bank reserves. But bank reserves equal *rd* times demand deposits. Hence,

MB = Currency + reserves = $(cd + rd) \times$ demand deposits.

Dividing the equation for M1 by the equation for MB, we have

$$M1 \text{ money multiplier} = \frac{M1}{MB} = \frac{cd + 1}{cd + rd}.$$

We see that the M1 money multiplier depends on two things: the public's desired ratio of currency to demand deposits, *cd*, and the reserve deposit ratio, *rd*.

How big is the M1 money multiplier? Well, in June 1997, *cd* equaled .64 and *rd* equaled .07, so the multiplier was 2.31. Figure 14.2 shows that there has been a steady decline in the M1 money multiplier since 1959. In 1959 the multiplier stood at 3.4— nearly 50 percent larger than its value in 1997. The decline in the money multiplier reflects a rise in *cd* from .26 to .64 that offset a decline in *rd* from .11 to .07.

To this point, we have focused on the M1 money multiplier, but the analogous money multipliers for the M2 and M3 monetary aggregates have also changed over

M1 money multiplier
The ratio of the M1 monetary aggregate to the monetary base

4 In this formula, demand deposits include all noncurrency components of M1.

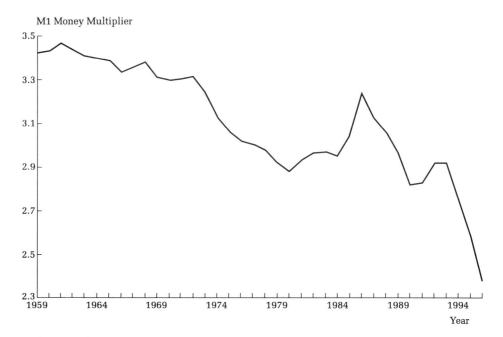

Figure 14.2 U.S. M1 Money Multiplier since 1959
The M1 money multiplier has declined substantially since 1959.

Source: Economic Report of the President, *1997.*

time. As we'll see, the variability of all three money multipliers has affected the Fed's ability to control the growth of the money supply, however defined. But before we discuss how well the Federal Reserve has been able to control these aggregates, let's review the origins and functions of the Federal Reserve and its monetary control mechanisms.

THE FEDERAL RESERVE AND THE CONDUCT OF MONETARY POLICY

The Federal Reserve System was established in 1913 in the aftermath of the banking panic of 1907. It replaced the National Banking System, a set of federally chartered national banks created during the Civil War. The National Banking System did provide the country with a fairly uniform currency, but it had no governing body to direct member banks to adjust the money supply to prevailing economic conditions.

The Federal Reserve's main purpose was "to furnish an elastic currency" in order to "safeguard the country from the possible results of financial panic or stringency" and to ensure that "there will be no ... wide fluctuations of interest rates from season

"Personally, I liked this roller coaster a lot better before the Federal Reserve Board got hold of it."

to season."[5] Its secondary purposes were to provide a clearinghouse for checks, maintain the country's position in the international gold standard, and reduce interregional interest rate differentials. Since its founding, the functions of the Federal Reserve have been expanded. They now include regulating the banking system and intervening in the foreign exchange market.

STRUCTURE AND GOVERNANCE OF THE FEDERAL RESERVE SYSTEM

The Federal Reserve System encompasses 12 regional Federal Reserve banks, one in each Federal Reserve district.[6] All federally chartered banks belong to the Federal Reserve System, and state-chartered banks may join if they wish. Before 1980 a bank's membership in the system brought certain privileges and responsibilities, but in 1980 Congress extended these privileges and responsibilities to nonmember banks as well. The most important privileges are access to check-clearing services and being able to borrow from the Fed, a topic we'll discuss shortly.

Member banks must satisfy the Fed's reserve requirements. Banks can hold their reserves as cash in their vaults or deposit them in a regional Federal Reserve bank. Reserves deposited with the Fed earn no interest. From the banks' point of view, this inability to earn interest on required reserves represents an extra cost of doing business.

The Federal Reserve is headquartered in Washington, D.C. There, its governing body, the Board of Governors, meets to determine Federal Reserve policy. The seven governors are chosen by the president to serve staggered 14-year terms. The president also selects one of the seven governors to preside for a four-year term as chairman of the board. The long terms of appointment of the governors and the chairman were established to help insulate the Fed from political pressures. Given the ease with which

5 The first quotation is from the Federal Reserve charter. The latter two are from Parker H. Willis, The Federal Reserve: A Study of the Banking System of the United States *(New York: Doubleday, Page, 1915).*

6 The Federal Reserve banks are located in New York, Boston, Philadelphia, Richmond, Atlanta, St. Louis, Cleveland, Chicago, Kansas City, Dallas, Minneapolis, and San Francisco. Their locations have not changed since the founding of the Fed, which helps explain their geographical distribution (two banks in Missouri and just one in California, for example).

governments can print money and the political goodwill money can buy, preserving the independence of a country's central bank can be vitally important. Independent central banks are able to limit the growth rate of the money supply, thereby limiting the rate of inflation and avoiding the problem of time-inconsistent monetary policy discussed in chapter 11.[7] Germany and Switzerland are cases in point. Their central banks are among the most independent in the world and have presided over lower inflation rates than in virtually any other developed country.

MECHANISMS OF MONETARY CONTROL

The Fed employs three methods to control the money supply: engaging in open market operations, making loans to banks through its discount window, and setting reserve requirements. In an **open market operation** the Fed increases the monetary base by printing money and using it to purchase U.S. Treasury bonds held by the public.[8] This base money finds its way into banks and triggers the deposit expansion process. **Discount window lending** also increases the monetary base. In this case, the Fed prints money to make loans to individual banks. Since M1 and the other money aggregates are related, via their money multipliers, to the monetary base, increases in the monetary base produced by open market operations or discount window lending increase the size of monetary aggregates. In contrast, changing reserve requirements leaves the monetary base unaffected, but alters the size of monetary aggregates by influencing the reserve deposit ratios entering the money multipliers. Let's consider each of the three money control mechanisms in turn.

OPEN MARKET OPERATIONS

Every month or two, the Fed's board of governors meets with the president of the Federal Reserve Bank of New York and a rotating set of four of the presidents of the other regional Federal Reserve banks. This larger assembly, called the *Federal Open Market Committee* (FOMC), issues directives to the bond-trading desk of the Federal Reserve Bank of New York concerning the type and quantity of open market operations it should engage in. If the FOMC wants to increase the money supply via an open market operation, it will direct the desk to buy Treasury bonds on the bond market. In purchasing the bonds, the desk gives the bond seller, say Salomon Brothers, a check written on the Federal Reserve. Salomon Brothers deposits the check in its bank, which, in turn, presents it to the Federal Reserve for payment. The Federal Reserve makes payment by crediting Salomon's bank with additional bank reserves equal to the amount of the check. As a result of this transaction, the Fed ends up holding additional Treasury bonds, and Salomon ends up with a larger demand deposit. Salomon's bank, assuming it was fully loaned up prior to the transaction, finds itself holding excess reserves. This triggers the process of deposit creation.

The opposite set of transactions arises if the FOMC orders the trading desk to sell Treasury bonds. In this case, the trading desk will hand over Treasury bonds in exchange for a check from Salomon Brothers. The Fed will then clear the check with Salomon's bank by reducing that bank's reserves in the amount of the check. If

Open market operation
The purchase or sale of government securities by the Federal Reserve in order to change the money supply

Discount window lending
Loans made by the Fed to banks, thereby increasing the monetary base

7 See Alberto Alesina and Lawrence H. Summers, "Central Bank Independence and Macroeconomic Performance: Some Comparative Evidence," Journal of Money, Credit, and Banking *25 (May 1993): 151–162.*

8 The term "printing money" is used here to refer to the Fed's creation of money rather than the actual printing of currency. When the Fed makes a purchase, it simply writes a check on itself. The bank that ultimately receives the check will present it to the Fed and be credited with an increase in its reserve account. In other words, the Fed ultimately makes its purchases by creating what is essentially a larger checking account for the bank that demands payment of the Fed's check. Currency is actually printed by the Bureau of Engraving and Printing, part of the U.S. Treasury.

Salomon's bank was fully loaded up, it will find itself with insufficient reserves and begin reducing its loans. This leads to a contraction of demand deposits that is just the opposite of the expansion of demand deposits.

USING OPEN MARKET OPERATIONS TO FINANCE GOVERNMENT EXPENDITURES

Although the route is somewhat circuitous, the open market operations play a critical role in the government's printing of money, some of which may be used to finance its expenditures. We first discussed monetary finance of government expenditures in chapter 7, where we assumed that the governmental authority that purchases goods and services and makes transfer payments is also authorized to print the money needed to cover such expenditures. In reality, two different agencies, the Treasury and the Federal Reserve, must act jointly in order for a government expenditure to be financed by money creation.

To see how this works, suppose the government wants to purchase a new airplane (*Air Force 2*) from the Boeing Company for the vice president and finance it by printing money. The transactions, diagrammed in Figure 14.3, proceed as follows. First, the Treasury sells bonds to the public to obtain the money to purchase the plane. Second, the Federal Reserve "monetizes" this government borrowing by printing money and using it to buy back from the public the bonds just purchased from the Treasury. The bottom line is that the vice president ends up with a new plane paid for by freshly printed money. The Treasury and the Federal Reserve go through the act of selling bonds to and buying bonds from the public. But in the end, the Treasury is just handing the Federal Reserve some of its bonds in exchange for money, which it then uses to buy the plane.

LENDING THROUGH THE DISCOUNT WINDOW

Open market operations involve the Fed's exchanging money for a financial security— a U.S. Treasury bond. The Fed's lending through its discount window involves quite similar transactions. As before, the Fed swaps money for a financial security, in this case, an IOU from a bank. Banks that borrow through the discount window receive their borrowed funds in the form of increases in their reserve accounts at the Fed.

Why do banks occasionally need to borrow funds? Usually it is because they find themselves with too few reserves to meet their reserve requirements. To see how this may happen, consider again the balance sheet of First National Bank when it is fully loaned up, with $1,000 of reserves, which equal 20 percent of its $5,000 in deposits:

First National Bank Balance Sheet

Assets		Liabilities	
Type	Amount	Type	Amount
Reserves	$1,000	Deposits	$5,000
Loans	5,000	Owners' equity	1,000
Total assets	**$6,000**	**Total liabilities**	**$6,000**

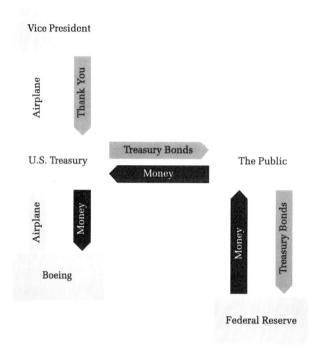

FIGURE 14.3 TRANSACTIONS ASSOCIATED WITH PRINTING MONEY TO BUY AIR FORCE 2
The government wishes to purchase *Air Force* 2 and finance it by printing money. First, the Treasury sells bonds to the public to obtain the money needed to purchase the plane. The Fed then "monetizes" this borrowing by printing money and using it to buy back from the public the bonds just purchased from the Treasury. This is equivalent to the Treasury's handing the Fed some of its bonds in exchange for the money it uses to buy the plane.

Starting from this position, suppose that Dewey, Cheatham, and Howe withdraws its $1,000 deposit by writing a check to make a $1,000 purchase. If First National Bank can't call back or sell off $1,000 of its loans, it will be forced to use its $1,000 of reserves to pay this check. Its balance sheet will then look like this:

First National Bank Balance Sheet

Assets		Liabilities	
Type	Amount	Type	Amount
Reserves	$ 0	Deposits	$4,000
Loans	5,000	Owners' equity	1,000
Total assets	**$5,000**	**Total liabilities**	**$5,000**

The bank now finds itself with zero reserves. Since its deposits equal $4,000 and it needs to keep its reserves equal to 20 percent of its deposits, it must come up with $800 in additional reserves. One possibility is to borrow the $800 from either the Fed or other banks that may have excess reserves. The market for the interbank borrowing of excess reserves is called the *federal funds market*, and the interest rate charged there is called the **federal funds rate**.

Once First National Bank borrows the $800, its balance sheet becomes:

First National Bank Balance Sheet

Assets		Liabilities	
Type	Amount	Type	Amount
Reserves	$ 800	Deposits	$4,000
Loans	5,000	Borrowings	800
		Owners' equity	1,000
Total assets	**$5,800**	**Total liabilities**	**$5,800**

The $800 the bank borrows shows up in this balance sheet as an additional liability, as well as an additional reserve asset.

The ability to borrow from the Fed is particularly important for banks experiencing unexpectedly large withdrawals of deposits. In such circumstances, banks may find they can't borrow as much as they'd like in the federal funds market, at least not at the going federal funds rate. In this circumstance they may be forced to turn to the Fed, the so-called *lender of last resort*, and borrow funds through the discount window.

There is a key difference between an open market purchase of bonds and providing loans through the discount window. In the former case, the Fed initiates the increase in the monetary base and, thus, the money supply. In the latter case, the borrowing bank initiates the increase. If banks were free to borrow as much and as often as they wished through the discount window, the money supply would be completely dependent on their decisions. But the Fed doesn't allow such unlimited borrowing. On the contrary, it decides how much to lend on a bank-by-bank basis. The more a particular bank borrows, the more likely it is the Fed will prohibit further borrowing, so banks think twice about borrowing from the discount window. They don't want to jeopardize their ability to borrow at future dates when their need may be greater.

The Fed also influences the amount borrowed by adjusting the rate of interest it charges on its loans—the **discount rate**. As Figure 14.4 indicates, since the Federal funds market was established in 1955, the Fed has set the discount rate both above and below the federal funds rate. The lower the Fed sets the discount rate compared to the prevailing federal funds rate, the more it encourages borrowing through its window rather than through the federal funds market. Hence, in setting its discount rate the Fed can indirectly control the expansion of the monetary base arising from borrowing through the discount window.

RESERVE REQUIREMENTS

According to our formula for the M1 money multiplier, $(cd + 1)/(cd + rd)$, a fall in the reserve requirement, rd, holding base constant, will produce an increase in M1. As previously mentioned, the Federal Reserve determines the minimum amount of reserves banks must hold. Currently the Fed subjects all depository institutions—

Federal funds rate
The interest rate prevailing in the federal funds market for day-to-day lending and borrowing of reserves among financial institutions

Discount rate
The interest rate charged by the Federal Reserve on its loans to banks

commercial banks, savings and loan associations, mutual savings banks, and credit unions—to the same reserve requirements on their checkable deposits. As of 1994, there were no reserves required on a depository institution's first $4.0 million. Required reserves equaled 3 percent of all deposits between $4.0 million and $51.9 million, and 10 percent of all deposits over $51.9. Although these dollar limits change annually to reflect the growth of the banking system, changes in the percentage reserve requirements themselves are infrequent. But when the requirements do change, they can change significantly. For example, in April 1992 the Fed reduced what was a top rate of 12 percent to the present 10 percent figure.

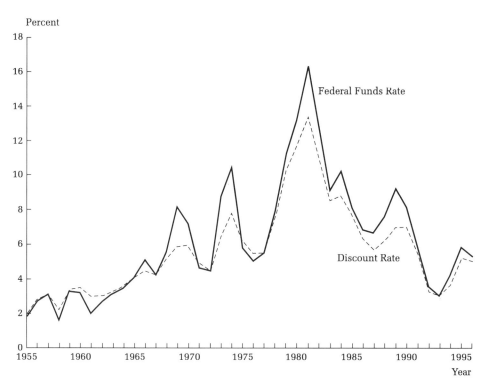

FIGURE 14.4 FEDERAL RESERVE DISCOUNT RATE AND THE FEDERAL FUNDS RATE, 1955–1996
The Fed influences the amount banks borrow by setting the discount rate—the rate it charges on loans. The lower it sets the discount rate relative to the federal funds rate, the more it encourages borrowing through the discount window rather than through the federal funds market. By adjusting the discount rate, the Fed indirectly controls the expansion of the monetary base.

Source: Economic Report of the President, *1997.*

HOW WELL DOES THE FED CONTROL THE MONEY SUPPLY?

Earlier chapters discussed how changes in the money supply can have important effects on macroeconomic performance. This section examines the Fed's ability to use the instruments just discussed to control the money supply. We begin by asking which of the three monetary aggregates, M1, M2, or M3, the Fed should try to control. As we'll see, the answer is not obvious.

DIVERGENT PATHS OF THE MONETARY AGGREGATES

If M1, M2, and M3 always grew at the same rate, the choice among the three aggregates would be unimportant. But the three aggregates have grown at quite different rates over time, and so it's difficult to assess the stance of monetary policy. Figure 14.5

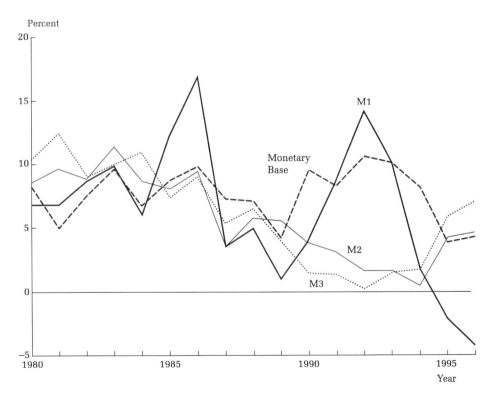

FIGURE 14.5   GROWTH RATES OF U.S. MONETARY AGGREGATES, 1980–1996

In any given year, the growth rates of monetary aggregates can be different. In 1982, M1 growth accelerated, but M2 and M3 growth decelerated. In 1995 and again in 1996, M1 decelerated, but M2 and M3 growth accelerated. Such differences make it hard to gauge the stance of monetary policy.

Source: Economic Report of the President, *1997.*

highlights this point. It compares the annual growth rates of the monetary aggregates and the monetary base over the years 1980 through 1996. Although the curves follow roughly the same pattern, in any given year the growth rates of the aggregates can be considerably different.

In the recession year 1982, for example, M1 growth accelerated, reaching 8.7 percent, compared with 6.8 percent for 1981. In contrast, growth of both M2 and M3 decelerated. M2 growth in 1982 was 8.8 percent, down from 9.7 percent in the previous year; 1982 M3 growth was 9.0 percent, down from 12.5 percent in the previous year. The years 1995 and 1996 saw precisely the opposite pattern, with M1 growth decelerating while growth in M2 and M3 picked up. What should we make of these facts? If we take M1 as our definition of the money supply, we have to conclude that during 1982, when the economy was in recession, monetary policy was expansionary, while in 1995 and 1996, during a strong economic expansion, monetary policy was contractionary. On the other hand, if we take M2 or M3 as our definition, we conclude that monetary policy was contractionary in 1982 but expansionary in 1995 and 1996.

One answer to this conundrum, which is less than fully satisfying, is that there is no single best measure of the money supply. Rather, there is a range of items—coins, currency, demand deposits, savings and money market accounts, and others—all of which have money-like properties and all of which must be considered to gain a complete understanding of the state of monetary affairs. According to this line of argument, the Fed should simultaneously consider each of its different measures of money, with the degree of attention paid to particular measures depending on prevailing economic circumstances. The problem with such ad hoc assessments is that the Fed may end up placing too much emphasis on certain monetary aggregates and not enough on others. Consequently, it may inadvertently pursue expansionary monetary policy by increasing the monetary base, lowering its discount rate, or lowering reserve requirements, when a contractionary policy is called for, or vice versa.

UNDERSTANDING THE VARIABILITY OF THE MONETARY AGGREGATES

Figure 14.5 also shows that the monetary aggregates have not maintained a stable relationship over time to the monetary base, because annual growth rates of the aggregates and the base have differed. Another way to say this is that the money multipliers of the different aggregates have varied through time.

How significant are such fluctuations in the money multipliers? The question is important because we've seen that the Fed can control the size of the monetary base directly but can influence the size of money multipliers only indirectly. The Fed can determine exactly how much it wants to increase the monetary base by deciding how much to spend on the purchase of Treasury bonds and how much to lend through its discount window. In contrast, the elements entering the money multipliers are largely determined by the private sector.

To understand this, recall that the formula for the M1 money multiplier depends on two parameters: the ratio of currency to demand deposits, *cd*, and the reserve deposit ratio, *rd*. The Fed has no direct control over *cd*. Instead, the public decides how

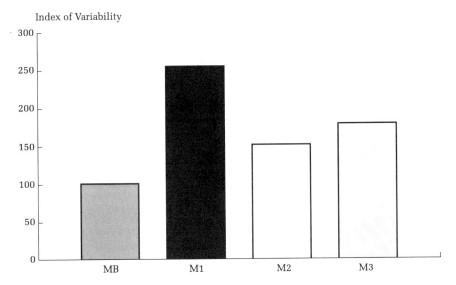

FIGURE 14.6 **VARIABILITY OF GROWTH RATES OF U.S. MONETARY AGGREGATES AND THE MONETARY BASE, 1980–1996**

The variability in the growth of the three monetary aggregates has exceeded that of the monetary base (MB) by a wide margin. Consequently, many of the changes in the aggregates have been due to changes in the money multipliers rather than to changes in the base.

to divide its money between cash and demand deposits. The Fed can set a floor under the reserve deposit ratio through its reserve requirements, but the banking system is free to set a reserve deposit ratio above the Fed's reserve requirement by choosing to hold excess reserves. In addition, a large fraction of nonbank checkable deposits entering M1 is not subject to reserve requirements.

Figure 14.6 compares the variability of annual growth rates of M1, M2, and M3 over the years 1980 through 1996 with the variability of growth in the monetary base.[9] It shows that the variability of growth in each of the three monetary aggregates exceeds that of the monetary base by a wide margin. For example, variability of M1 growth is over twice as large as variability in monetary base growth. Clearly, then, a large portion of the changes in the monetary aggregates are due not to changes in the monetary base, over which the government has direct control, but rather to changes in money multipliers, over which the government has only indirect control.

CASE STUDY

MONETARY CONTROL DURING THE GREAT DEPRESSION

In their famous book, *A Monetary History of the United States*, economists Milton Friedman and Anna Schwartz laid much of the blame for the severity and length of the

9 The figure's index of variability equals 100 times the standard deviation of the growth rate of MB, M1, M2, or M3 divided by the standard deviation of the growth rate of MB.

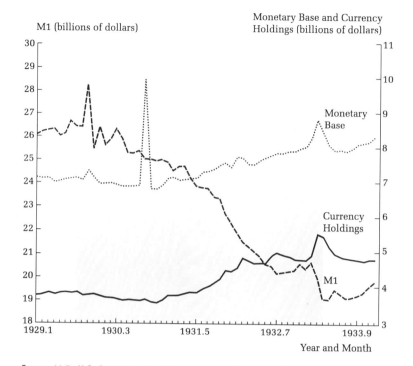

FIGURE 14.7 U.S. CURRENCY HOLDINGS, MONETARY BASE, AND M1, JANUARY 1929–DECEMBER 1933
Did the Fed cause M1 to decline during the Great Depression? Not directly, since it increased the monetary base by 18 percent between August 1929 and March 1933. Nevertheless, M1 declined by 28 percent during the period as the money multiplier fell from 3.7 to 2.3. This reflected, in part, a substantial increase in the ratio of currency to demand deposits.

Source: Million Friedman and Anna Schwartz, A Monetary History of the United States, 1867–1960 *(Princeton, NJ: Princeton University Press, 1963).*

Great Depression on the Federal Reserve's monetary policy. There was a significant decline in M1 in the early 1930s and again in 1937. Both declines were followed in quick succession by sharp drops in U.S. output. These comovements of M1 and output during the Great Depression raise two questions. First, did the decline in M1 cause output to decline? Second, did the Fed cause M1 to decline?

We addressed the first question in chapter 11, where we pointed out that the decline in M1 by itself seems insufficient to explain the severity of the drop in output. To answer the second question, we must recognize that the Fed did not directly attempt to reduce M1. In fact, as shown in Figure 14.7, the Fed increased the monetary base by 18 percent between August 1929 and March 1933 (the beginning and the end of the first recession of the Great Depression) and by 8 percent between May 1937 and June 1938 (the beginning and the end of the second recession). Despite these increases in the base, M1 declined by 28 percent between August 1929 and March 1933 and 5 percent between May 1937 and June 1938. The reason is that the M1 money multiplier declined dramatically during both periods. In August 1929 the M1 money multiplier was 3.7. By March 1933 it was 2.3. In May 1937 the multiplier again equaled 2.3, but it fell to 2.0 by June 1938.

Both declines in the M1 multiplier were due to increases in cd, the public's desired ratio of currency to demand deposits, as well as in rd, the fraction of deposits held by the banking system as reserves. The increases in cd and rd reflect a natural reaction to the events of the day. Since one of every three banks failed during the Great Depression, it is not surprising that the public became wary of depositing funds in banks and other depository institutions and shifted toward holding currency. Nor is it surprising that banks became cautious about having low levels of reserves and took steps to raise their reserve deposit ratios.

Figure 14.7 also shows what happened to the currency holdings of the public and to M1 during the period 1929 through 1933. Since the difference between M1 and currency is essentially the amount of demand deposits, the figure documents a substantial increase in the ratio of currency to demand deposits.

Given the evidence in Figure 14.7, are Friedman and Schwartz right in indicting the Fed for causing the Great Depression? There are two points of view. On the one hand, the Fed did nothing directly to reduce M1 and actually took steps to raise it by increasing the monetary base.[10] On the other hand, the Fed should have recognized that the M1 money multiplier was falling and increased the monetary base much more dramatically than it did. Both arguments have merit, but most economists—as well as officials now running the Federal Reserve—appear to accept the Friedman and Schwartz dictum that the Federal Reserve should take whatever steps are necessary to preclude precipitous declines in M1 and other monetary aggregates, whatever the causes of such declines.

SHOULD THE FED TARGET THE GROWTH OF MONETARY AGGREGATES OR INTEREST RATES?

In conducting monetary policy, the Fed usually either targets the growth of some monetary aggregate or else tries to control some other economic variable, such as the interest rate, that is related to the level of economic activity.[11] Which strategy is better? The answer to the question depends partly on what sorts of changes the economy is experiencing and partly on what information policymakers have available.

To see this, consider the short-run Keynesian IS-LM model for the case in which prices are downwardly rigid. Assume that Fed policymakers can observe the interest rate immediately by looking at financial market transactions, but they learn the level of output only with a lag. Let's examine two cases. In the first, the economy experiences *nominal shocks*—unanticipated fluctuations in the LM curve due to shifts in the money demand function, $\gamma[r]$. In the second, it experiences *real shocks*—unanticipated fluctuations in the IS curve due, for example, to changes in the expected productivity of investment.

10 Part of the increase in the monetary base was automatic. At the time, the United States was still on the gold standard, and in the early 1930s it experienced an inflow of gold from abroad, which it was obligated to purchase with dollars. Another reason to question the Fed's efforts in the early 1930s in increasing the monetary base is that the Fed kept its discount rate fairly high.

11 A seminal paper on this issue is William Poole's "Optimal Choice of Monetary Policy Instruments in a Simple Stochastic Macro Model," Quarterly Journal of Economics 84 (May 1970): 197–216.

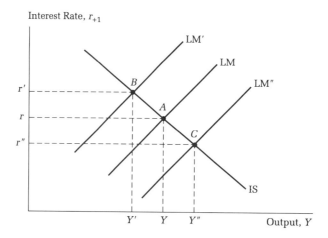

FIGURE 14.8 MONEY SUPPLY TARGETING IN THE FACE OF NOMINAL SHOCKS
An unfavorable nominal shock shifts the LM curve leftward to LM′, whereas a favorable shock shifts it rightward to LM″.
In both cases, policymakers see the interest rate move away from its original level. To maintain its interest rate target,
the Fed responds to a rise (fall) in the interest rate by increasing (decreasing) the money supply. In so doing, it restores
LM to its original position.

Consider Figure 14.8, in which the IS and LM curves initially intersect at point A with output level Y. An unfavorable nominal shock would cause the LM curve to shift leftward to LM′; a favorable shock would move it rightward to LM″. In either case, policymakers see the interest rate move away from its original level of r. If the Fed is trying to maintain an interest rate target of r, it would respond to an increase in r by printing more money and to a decrease in r by reducing the money supply. In both cases the effect is to shift the LM curve back to the right, restoring it to its original position. Regardless of the nature of the nominal shock, the Fed's policy maintains the level of output and interest rate that originally prevailed at point A.

What if the Fed were targeting the money supply? That amounts to accepting any shift in the LM curve, since the Fed's only means of moving that curve is to change the money supply. If the LM curve shifts to the left, Fed policy is to leave it there. In effect, it accepts the higher interest rate and lower level of output. If LM shifts rightward, money supply targeting results in a lower interest rate and more output. We conclude that money supply targeting in the face of nominal shocks leads to fluctuations in interest rates (between $r′$ and $r″$) and output (between $Y′$ and $Y″$), whereas interest rate targeting does not.

What if the economy experiences real shocks? This situation is depicted in Figure 14.9. Starting from point A, suppose an unfavorable real shock shifts the IS curve inward to IS′. Again, the Fed cannot immediately observe the level of output but does see the interest fall from r to $r′$ (point B). If it is pursuing an interest rate target, the Fed will reduce the money supply, thus shifting the LM curve leftward to LM′ (point C). This restores the interest rate and, although the Fed doesn't know it, reduces output to

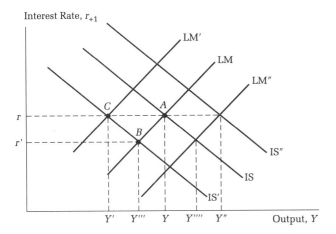

FIGURE 14.9 INTEREST RATE TARGETING IN THE FACE OF REAL SHOCKS
Starting at point *A*, an unfavorable real shock shifts the IS curve inward to IS′. The Fed sees the interest rate fall from *r* to *r*′ at point *B*. If it is targeting the interest rate, the Fed reduces the money supply, shifting the LM curve to LM′ and producing an equilibrium at point *C*. This restores the interest rate but reduces output to *Y*′. Interest rate targeting amplifies real shocks. If the Fed targets the money supply, it does nothing when IS shifts down.

Y'. The opposite would be true if a favorable real shock shifted the IS curve outward. Thus, interest rate targeting under real shocks exaggerates fluctuations in output.

If the Fed is targeting the money supply, it does nothing. Holding the money supply constant means holding the original LM curve constant. After an unfavorable real shock (downward shift of IS), this means accepting the lower interest rate and, in effect, allowing output to fall. For a favorable shock, it means accepting a higher interest rate and level of output. But note that the fluctuations in output are smaller with a money supply target. With interest rate targeting, output fluctuates between Y' and Y''. With a money supply target, the fluctuations are only from Y''' to Y''''.

To summarize, in a Keynesian setting in which the interest rate is immediately observable but output is not, targeting the interest rate is appropriate if the economy is experiencing nominal shocks (which shift the LM curve, reflecting changes in money demand). On the other hand, if the economy is experiencing real shocks (which shift the IS curve, reflecting changes in saving and investment), targeting the money supply will dampen the fluctuations in the interest rate and output.

CASE STUDY
PAUL VOLCKER'S EXPERIMENT IN MONEY SUPPLY TARGETING

In August 1979 Paul Volcker became Federal Reserve chairman. His mandate was to lower an inflation rate that had reached double digits. In October Volcker announced that the Fed would no longer use its monetary control instruments (open market

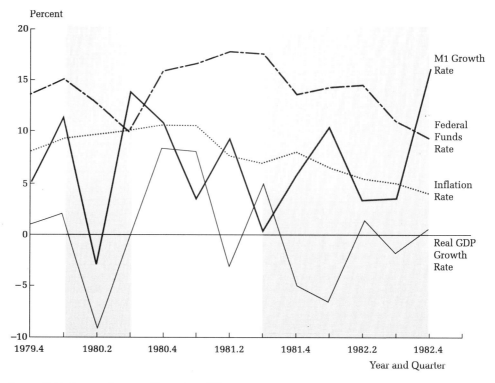

FIGURE 14.10 GROWTH RATES OF M1 AND REAL GDP, THE INFLATION RATE, AND THE FEDERAL FUNDS RATE, OCTOBER 1979–OCTOBER 1982

In October 1979, Paul Volcker announced M1 growth rate targets of 4.5 to 7 percent for 1980, 6 to 8.5 percent for 1981, and 2.5 to 5.5 percent for 1982. The evidence shows that the Fed missed each of these targets. In addition, M1 growth varied widely from quarter to quarter.

Sources: Economic Report of the President, *1981–1983; National Income and Product Accounts.*

purchases, discount lending, and reserve requirements) to target the federal funds rate but rather would target the growth of the monetary aggregates much more closely. The Fed even announced a set of target ranges for the annual growth of M1. In 1980, 1981, and 1982, for example, the M1 growth target ranges were set at 4.5 to 7.0 percent, 6.0 to 8.5 percent, and 2.5 to 5.5 percent, respectively.

Figure 14.10 shows the growth rate of M1, the federal funds rate, the inflation rate, and the growth rate of output during the Volcker experiment, between October 1979 and October 1982. First notice that the Fed repeatedly missed its M1 growth target over this period. Over the 13 quarters of the period, the M1 growth rate, measured at an annual rate, ranged from a low of −3 percent to a high of 16 percent. In addition to permitting M1 growth to vary widely from quarter to quarter, the Fed failed to keep the annual growth of M1 within its target ranges in 1980, 1981, or 1982. The annual M1 growth rates in those years were 7.5 percent, 5.1 percent, and 8.8 percent, respectively.

The Volcker experiment cannot be viewed as successful targeting of monetary growth. However, Volcker's willingness to let interest rates rise, if necessary, to lower inflation, did lead to dramatically higher interest rates. In the first six months of the experiment, the federal funds rate rose by 5 percentage points, to over 15 percent. Other short-term interest rates rose by similar amounts. This increase in interest rates was largely responsible for the recession that began in January 1980 and lasted through July 1980. As Figure 14.10 indicates, this recession was insufficient to wring inflation out of the economy; inflation was still running at 11 percent in the fall of 1980. In the winter of 1981 Volcker again temporarily reduced the growth rate of money, raising the federal funds rate to nearly 18 percent. These extraordinarily high interest rates culminated in the recession of 1981–1982, during which output fell more sharply than at any other time since the Great Depression. The recession's only saving grace was that it brought inflation down below 5 percent.

Two lessons can be drawn from the Volcker experiment. First, targeting money supply growth, come what may, is easier said than done. The Fed could have hit its targeted growth rates of M1 between 1979 and 1982 but chose not to, apparently because it felt the need to respond to events as they unfolded. These events included a larger-than-expected response of interest rates to the Fed's change in policy, President Carter's credit controls imposed in March 1980, substantial increases in oil prices at the end of 1979 and again in early 1981, and, finally, the period's two recessions. In terms of Figure 14.8, we can think of the first three of these events as producing a leftward shift of the LM curve that raised interest rates and made setting money supply growth targets quite difficult.[12]

The second lesson is that it takes more than words to convince financial markets that inflation is coming down. Recall that the nominal interest rate is the sum of the real interest rate and the expected inflation rate. In declaring war on inflation, Volcker may have hoped that the inflation premium embedded in nominal interest rates would fall, thereby lowering nominal rates. Evidently that did not occur until the two recessions actually put a damper on price increases.

Endogenous monetary policy
A monetary policy that merely accommodates whatever price level the public believes will arise

THE ENDOGENEITY OF THE MONEY SUPPLY

A final question is whether the Fed actually sets its monetary policies independently or whether it merely accommodates whatever price level the public chooses to believe will arise. This possibility of **endogenous monetary policy** can be understood through our IS-LM diagram. Figure 14.11 shows one possible short-run equilibrium in which the IS and LM curves intersect at the full-employment level of output, Y^f. The money supply and price level underlying this LM curve are M and P, respectively. The figure also shows another short-run equilibrium, based on the same value of the money supply, M, but a higher price level, P'. Output in this short-run equilibrium is Y', which is less than the full employment level.

While the Fed is pursuing its monetary policy, private sector decision makers are formulating their estimates of future inflation rates. Suppose the private sector, for

12 Volcker's October 1979 announcement produced major concern about a credit crunch. As described in chapter 15, such concern can be viewed as raising the demand for money and thus shifting the LM curve to the left. The imposition of credit controls added to concern about a credit crunch, further shifting the LM curve to the left. Finally, the rise in oil prices in a setting in which other prices were growing at rather inflexible rates meant a higher price level, which also shifted the LM curve to the left.

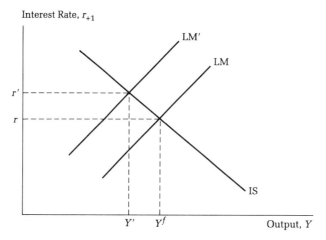

FIGURE 14.11 IS MONETARY POLICY ENDOGENOUS?
With price level P and money supply M, IS and LM intersect to determine full employment output, Y^f . If the public comes to believe the price level will be $P' > P$, the LM curve shifts to LM' and the resulting equilibrium output level is $Y' < Y^f$ The Fed can accommodate that higher price level by increasing the money supply, restoring the LM curve to its original position and ensuring full employment, but at the cost of an increase in prices. Or it can keep the money supply fixed at M and generate unemployment. If the Fed accommodates the higher prices, the private sector is really determining monetary policy by forcing the Fed to adapt to the price level it chooses.

whatever reason, believes the price level will be P' rather than P. Prices are set, wages are negotiated, and the price level ends up at P'. The central bank now faces a dilemma. It can accommodate the higher price level P' by increasing the money supply to M', so that M' exceeds M by the same percentage as P' exceeds P. If it does so, it will restore the LM curve to its initial position and ensure full employment, but at the cost of an increase in prices. Alternatively, it can keep the money supply fixed at M and generate unemployment. This unemployment will put downward pressure on prices, leading, over time, to a lower price level, P, and restoring full employment. The trade-off for the central bank is between maintaining full employment, but accepting a rise in prices, and accepting some temporary unemployment with no long-term rise in prices.

If it does accommodate, the central bank still remains free to claim that it is determining the price level through its monetary policy, even though the reality is quite different. It is really the private sector that determines monetary policy by forcing the central bank to adapt the money supply to the price level the private sector chooses.

BANK RUNS AND DEPOSIT INSURANCE

In choosing to hold less than 100 percent of the money deposited with it in reserve, any bank leaves itself open to the risk of a bank run, in which depositors, suddenly and en masse, seek to withdraw their deposits. The bank's assets are the ultimate

TABLE 14.1 JULY 16, 1997, BALANCE SHEET OF U.S. COMMERCIAL BANKS (BILLIONS OF DOLLARS)

Assets

Total assets	*4,612.2*
Cash assets, including reserves	246.4
U.S. government securities	722.1
Other securities	306.2
Commercial and industrial loans	821.3
Real estate loans	1,184.8
Consumer loans	519.2
Interbank loans	194.3
Other loans and leases	395.0
Other assets	222.9

Liabilities

Total liabilities	*4,612.2*
Transaction (Checkable) deposits	693.4
Nontransaction deposits	2,300.4
Borrowings	727.2
Other liabilities	499.2
Owners' equity	392.0

Source: Board of Governors, Federal Reserve System

security underlying its deposits, so it's not surprising that many runs on banks were precipitated by fears that banks were insolvent—that their assets were less than their liabilities (excluding owners' equity). Banks can respond to a run by trying to retrieve the funds they have lent or invested, but liquidating loans and other assets takes time. Depending on the economic circumstances of their creditors, banks may be unable to retrieve all the funds they have lent out or otherwise invested. Finally, banks may be unable to borrow from other banks, financial intermediaries, or the government to stave off a run on their deposits. The simple reason is that these potential lenders cannot be sure that they'll be repaid.

Banks could try to avoid bank runs by holding 100 percent reserves. They could also make their liabilities less liquid by requiring a waiting period before returning their depositors' money. But either option would reduce bank profits. Indeed, the second option—reducing the liquidity of bank liabilities—would eliminate the special service provided by banks: enabling depositors to have ready access to their money by writing negotiable checks.

The difference between the liquidity of banks' liabilities and their assets is illustrated in Table 14.1, which shows the composition of U.S. commercial bank assets and liabilities as July 1997. A total of 65 percent of commercial bank liabilities listed in the table consisted of deposits, all of which can be withdrawn from banks quite quickly. Owners of demand (transaction) deposits can withdraw their funds at any time from the bank, and owners of saving and time (nontransaction) deposits can withdraw their funds over a very short period of time (although early withdrawal may entail a loss of interest). The other liabilities of banks—primarily bank borrowing and owners' equity—are much less liquid.

On the asset side of the commercial banks' balance sheet, the most liquid bank assets are cash assets (including reserves and banks' vault cash) and securities. Together, these assets constitute just 28 percent of total commercial bank assets. Their remaining assets, such as loans to commercial and industrial, real estate, and consumer borrowers, are fairly illiquid.

Thus, we can conclude that the liabilities of U.S. commercial banks are much more liquid than are their assets. In the absence of deposit insurance, which we discuss below, U.S. commercial banks would be highly vulnerable to bank runs.

CASE STUDY

THE BANKING PANIC OF THE GREAT DEPRESSION AND THE ESTABLISHMENT OF DEPOSIT INSURANCE

Of the periodic banking panics experienced throughout U.S. history, the panic of the early 1930s was by far the most severe.[13] From the end of 1930 through March 1933, one of every three U.S. banks failed or was taken over by a competitor. There were actually three separate crises during this period. The first began in October 1930, a year after the stock market crashed. It was touched off by the failure of a relatively small number of banks in the Midwest and South. A second panic began in March and continued through the end of 1931. It was brought on by the continuing decline in real output at home, news of major bank closings in Europe, and Britain's decision in September 1931 to abandon the gold standard. In the fall of 1932 as well as the winter of 1933, bank failures in the Midwest and West touched off yet a third round of panic. Almost 2,000 banks nationwide were forced to close. As in the previous runs, the public attempted to convert deposits into currency. In the first two months of 1933 alone, currency held by the public rose by 16 percent.

Deposit insurance
A government program that insures bank deposits against the possibility of bank failure

13 Chapter 7 of Milton Friedman and Anna Schwartz's A Monetary History of the United States (Princeton, NJ: Princeton University Press, 1963), presents an excellent description of the banking crisis of the early 1930s.

On March 6, 1933, President Franklin D. Roosevelt ordered U.S. banks closed for a week—a suspension of banking operations without precedent in the nation's history. During this "bank holiday," depositors were unable to withdraw their funds. Roosevelt's action put a temporary lid on bank failures, but it didn't bring them to an end. Another 2,000 or so banks chose to go out of business rather than reopen after the bank holiday.

What ultimately eliminated banking panics was the establishment of the Federal Deposit Insurance Corporation (FDIC). Starting on January 1, 1934, the FDIC provided **deposit insurance** to all member banks of the Federal Reserve as well as to nonmember banks that applied for and were approved for this insurance. If an insured bank failed, the FDIC would cover deposits up to $2,500. This amount has been increased over time. Currently the FDIC insures deposits up to $100,000. In order to cover losses on deposits from troubled banks, the FDIC charges all its enrolled banks insurance premiums that vary with the amount of deposits the bank has at risk.

Deposit insurance was an instant success. By early 1934, most commercial banks, accounting for virtually all bank deposits, had signed up for FDIC insurance. The protection afforded by the government's deposit insurance dramatically reduced runs on banks as well as the number of bank failures. In 1934 there were only 61 bank failures, compared with 4,000 in 1933.

PROBLEMS CAUSED BY DEPOSIT INSURANCE AND THE NEED FOR BANK REGULATION

Notwithstanding its success in eliminating bank runs, deposit insurance, like other forms of insurance, produces a problem called *moral hazard*—the tendency of those covered by insurance to take less care to avoid the risk of a loss. For example, insured car owners may be less likely to lock their cars and garage them in safe places; home owners with fire insurance may be less likely to check their smoke detectors. In the case of deposit insurance, bank managers may take unwarranted risks in investing their institutions' assets. They realize that if their potentially high-stakes gambles pay off, their banks will earn large profits. On the other hand, if the gambles fail, and they end up with too little money to cover their deposits, their depositors will be paid by the FDIC. Investment losses that are passed to the FDIC are ultimately paid for by the general public, through either higher service fees charged by banks to cover their insurance premium payments to the FDIC or in general taxes, when the FDIC's insurance premiums are insufficient to cover its insurance payments.

To prevent the managers of banks and other federally insured depository institutions from gambling at the expense of the general public, the government employs three methods of regulating the investment strategies of these financial intermediaries. The first are laws stipulating the kinds of investments these intermediaries can and cannot make. For example, the Glass-Steagall Act of 1933 prohibits commercial banks from investing in stocks.

The second regulatory device is *capital requirements*, which stipulate that owners' equity must exceed a certain fraction of the bank's total assets. When owners' equity is small, the owners of the bank have little to lose if the bank fails. By specifying minimum levels of owners' equity, the government seeks to ensure that the bank's owners have a personal stake in the outcome of their investments. Currently, capital requirements range from 3 to 6 percent of assets, depending on the bank's financial condition.

A third regulatory mechanism is periodic examination of the investments of banks and other insured depository institutions. Three regulatory bodies oversee the investments of federally chartered banks: the Comptroller of the Currency, the FDIC, and the Federal Reserve. Examiners from these agencies make frequent unscheduled visits to banks in order to check their books, review the quality of their loans, and make sure they are meeting their capital requirements. These federal regulators can raise banks' capital requirements, force banks to sell off assets they view as too risky, and replace bank managers.

Case Study
The S&L Crisis

In 1934 the federal government established the Federal Saving and Loan Insurance Corporation (FSLIC) to insure the savings accounts and time deposits of savings and loans (S&Ls) and mutual savings banks. The federal government also established the Federal Home Loan Bank Board (FHLBB) to regulate the S&Ls. The FHLBB had great success until the 1980s, when a combination of policy changes, external events, regulatory failures, and moral hazard led to the fiasco known as the S&L crisis.

In 1980 federal legislation deregulated the investments of the S&Ls. Previously S&Ls had been forced to invest the funds deposited with them almost exclusively in home mortgages. Now they were permitted to invest the bulk of their funds in other types of assets, including commercial real estate, consumer loans, and commercial loans. They were even allowed to invest up to 10 percent of their assets in financial securities such as common stock, government and standard corporate bonds, and high-risk corporate bonds. The new legislation raised the size of FSLIC-insured deposits from $40,000 to $100,000 and eliminated a government-imposed ceiling, *Regulation Q*, on the interest rate that banks and S&Ls could pay depositors.

With the lifting of Regulation Q, the S&Ls were forced to pay the high short-term interest rates prevailing in the early 1980s. At the same time, most of their investments were still tied up in home mortgages, a large portion of which had been issued at low interest rates. The resulting squeeze on profits led many S&L managers to pursue higher-yielding, if riskier, investment strategies. Many of these new investments, as well as many of the S&Ls' previous investments, proved highly unprofitable, because of both the sharp national recession of 1981–1982 and the collapse of real estate prices in Texas and elsewhere.

By the mid-1980s almost half of the S&Ls in the country were technically insolvent. Their owners' equity was negative, because their liabilities (apart from owners' equity) exceeded their assets. The Bush administration and Congress did not wish to admit publicly that FSLIC needed about $25 billion in tax revenues to cover the insured deposits of these insolvent S&Ls, so they put off dealing with the problem. While regulators dallied, the crisis worsened. By 1990 the losses of the S&Ls had grown to a staggering $200 billion. Finally, the federal government took action. It eliminated the FHLBB and the FSLIC and set up a new institution, the *Resolution Trust Corporation*, to manage and resolve the outstanding claims of the insolvent S&Ls. It also transferred to the FDIC the responsibility for regulating the S&Ls and insuring their deposits.

CHAPTER SUMMARY

1. This chapter discussed the banking system, the Federal Reserve, and money supply determination. It began by describing the role of financial intermediaries in the economy. Financial intermediaries bring together suppliers and demanders of funds, reduce transactions and information acquisition costs, and help savers diversify the risk of their investments.

2. Banks are a special type of financial intermediary that provide suppliers of funds with very liquid demand deposits that can be accessed simply by writing a check. Because demand deposits are so liquid, they are included, along with currency and traveler's checks, in the U.S. government's principal definition of money, M1. The government's other two definitions of money, M2 and M3, incorporate M1, but also include time deposits and other fairly liquid liabilities of financial intermediaries.

3. In lending out a portion of the funds deposited with them, banks are able to multiply the size of their demand deposits. They can do so because funds lent by one bank are generally redeposited in some other bank. The total amount of demand deposits created through the banks' deposit expansion process depends on the fraction of their deposits that banks hold as reserves.

4. The Federal Reserve also plays a role in determining the size of the money supply. The Fed determines the size of the monetary base—the basic amount of money injected by the government into the economy. A portion of the monetary base is held by the public as currency, but the rest is held as reserves by banks and other depository institutions, providing the basis for the deposit expansion process.

5. The amount of M1 created for each dollar of monetary base is called the M1 money multiplier. Similar multipliers can be defined for M2 and M3. The size of the M1 money multiplier depends on the public's desired ratio of currency to demand deposits and the reserve deposit ratio. The Federal Reserve directly influences the reserve deposit ratio through its reserve requirements, which establish a minimum value for this ratio. Banks are free to hold reserves in excess of the Fed's reserve requirement.

6. Every few months, the Federal Open Market Committee decides how much to change the monetary base through open market operations. Open market operations involve the purchase or sale by the Fed of U.S. Treasury bonds. To increase the monetary base, the Fed purchases bonds using newly printed money, thereby injecting money into the economy. If it wants to decrease the base, the Fed sells bonds for money.

7. The Fed may also alter the size of the monetary base by lending through its discount window. Discount window lending is similar to an open market purchase. The Fed prints money to purchase an IOU, but a bank IOU rather than a Treasury bond. The interest rate the Fed charges is called the discount rate. Banks borrow from the Fed and from each other when they need extra money to meet their reserve requirements.

8. The Fed has complete control over changes in the monetary base but only indirect control over the M1, M2, and M3 money multipliers. These multipliers are not stable over time, and their variability accounts for much of the variability of the monetary aggregates. In fact, the three multipliers do not ordinarily change at the same rate or even in the same direction. This greatly complicates the Fed's problem of monetary control and raises the question of which monetary aggregate the Fed should target.

9. Even if the Fed knew which aggregate was "the" money supply and even if it could completely control that aggregate, there would remain the question of how to conduct monetary policy. Some economists argue that the Fed should target the money supply; others argue that the Fed should target interest rates. Using our IS-LM framework, we showed that targeting the interest rate is appropriate for an economy experiencing nominal shocks, whereas targeting the money supply is better if the economy is experiencing real shocks.

10. Congress established deposit insurance in 1933 after repeated bank panics. Deposit insurance has proved quite successful in strengthening public faith in financial institutions. However, deposit insurance has its own problems. Chief among them is the problem of moral hazard: the tendency of bank managers to make excessively risky investments, knowing that much of the risk is covered by deposit insurance. In the United States, banking legislation, capital requirements, and bank examinations are used by the government to combat this moral hazard problem. These regulatory mechanisms were less than successful during the S&L crisis of the 1980s.

CHAPTER 15

SAVING BEHAVIOR AND CREDIT MARKETS

INTRODUCTION

Saving plays a critical role in determining an economy's current and future performance. To explain fully this important variable, we discuss two alternative motives for saving beyond saving for retirement: *precautionary saving* (saving against unforeseen contingencies) and saving for bequests and other private intergenerational transfers. We'll also consider the desire and ability of households to dissave—to consume more than their current income. Dissaving often requires borrowing against future income. Since borrowing is facilitated by credit markets, our discussion of dissaving leads us to examine these markets: how they work, how they affect capital accumulation, and how they can break down, especially during recessions.

We begin by cataloging the economic risks households face and describing how households factor these risks into their saving decisions. Then we extend our two-period model to consider a simple case of income uncertainty. Our second topic is saving and bequests. We first show how to adapt our model to account for bequests and other private intergenerational transfers. Next, we describe the importance of private intergenerational transfers to aggregate U.S. wealth accumulation. We then contrast intended and unintended bequests. Our third topic is credit markets—specifically, how they fit into our model and how imperfections in these markets can alter the availability of credit and the level of national saving.

Here are some key questions:

- What economic uncertainties do individuals face that motivate their saving?

- How does insurance pool economic risks and reduce precautionary saving?

- How do bequests fit into our two-period model?

- How important are private intergenerational transfers to U.S. wealth accumulation?

- What is Ricardian equivalence, and how can it be tested?

- How can we add credit markets to our model?

- How do credit markets affect the economy's saving?

- What explains credit market imperfections?

PRECAUTIONARY SAVING

Life is full of economic risks and uncertainties. Most workers don't know whether they'll be employed in future years, let alone precisely what their real wages will be. Retirees don't know what return they'll receive on their savings or whether they'll live long enough to spend the assets that took years to accumulate. The healthy don't know how long they'll remain well, or what it will cost if they become ill. Parents don't know what it will cost to send their children to college, or even if their children will choose to go to college. The list goes on and on.

As overwhelming as these risks and uncertainties may be, households are not likely to ignore them when deciding how much to save. Economic theory argues that households instead make their saving decisions by considering each possible future economic circumstance, as well as the likelihood of that circumstance's occurring. In evaluating their different possible economic futures, households are likely to exhibit *risk aversion*. That is, they weigh bad outcomes, such as the unexpected loss of $1,000, more heavily than good outcomes, such as the unexpected receipt of $1,000. One way risk-averse households seek to limit their economic setbacks is by increasing their current saving. Such **precautionary saving** (saving induced by uncertainty) provides households with additional assets they can draw on in an emergency.

IMPACT OF UNCERTAINTY ON SAVING AND CAPITAL FORMATION: AN EXAMPLE

Chapter 2 studied the behavior of Franco. As a typical young person born at time t, Franco's income is w_t in his first period of life. He must decide how much to consume and how much to save for his old age. Given the opportunity to invest any income he saves at an interest rate of r_{t+1}, Franco faces the budget constraint illustrated in Figure 15.1. Each point along this constraint represents an affordable combination of first- and second-period consumption.

Given this budget constraint, Franco uses his utility function to evaluate each possible consumption combination and then choose the combination that gives him the largest amount of utility, or satisfaction. The best combination is the one on the highest attainable indifference curve. This combination is shown as point E, where an

Precautionary saving
Saving aimed at building up assets to protect against unforeseen contingencies

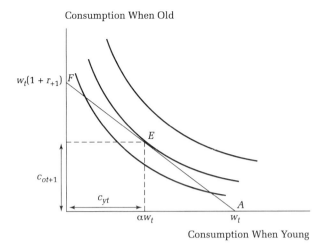

Consumption When Old

$w_t(1 + r_{+1})$

F

E

c_{ot+1}

c_{yt}

αw_t

w_t

A

Consumption When Young

FIGURE 15.1 FRANCO'S BUDGET CONSTRAINT WITH CERTAIN SECOND-PERIOD INCOME
Franco uses his utility function to evaluate each possible consumption combination along budget constraint FA. He chooses the one at E. He consumes αw_t when young, saves and invests $(1 - \alpha)w_t$ and consumes $(1 - \alpha)w_t(1 + r_{t+1})$ when old.

indifference curve is just tangent to (just touches) his budget constraint. Franco consumes αw_t when young, saves and invests $(1 - \alpha)w_t$, and consumes $(1 - \alpha)w_t(1 + r_{t+1})$ when old.

Now suppose Franco's second-period income is uncertain. At the end of his old age, Franco faces a fifty-fifty chance of either receiving or losing an amount of income equal to x. The present value of x is v: $v = x/(1 + r_{t+1})$. If Franco is lucky, his old-age income and consumption will be higher than they are under certainty; but if he is unlucky, both will be smaller. Figure 15.2 shows how these two outcomes affect Franco's lifetime budget constraint. The constraint labeled "Good State" shows Franco's consumption opportunities if he is lucky and receives an extra x in old age. The one labeled "Bad State" shows his opportunities if he is unlucky and loses x in old age. Faced with this uncertainty, what will Franco do? Because he's risk averse, we expect him to be more concerned with the downside risk—the possibility of losing x—than with the upside potential of gaining x. Suppose Franco is so risk averse that he considers only the worst-case scenario. To be on the safe side, he determines which combination along the bad state budget constraint gives him the most satisfaction. That combination is shown at point D, where an indifference curve is tangent to the low budget constraint.

Franco decides to consume a fraction, α, of $w_t - v$, which is the present value of his lifetime income in the worst-case scenario. Franco's saving when young will equal his (certain) income when young, w_t, less this amount of consumption; it will equal $(1 - \alpha)w_t + \alpha v$. By comparing points D and E, we can see how uncertainty about his

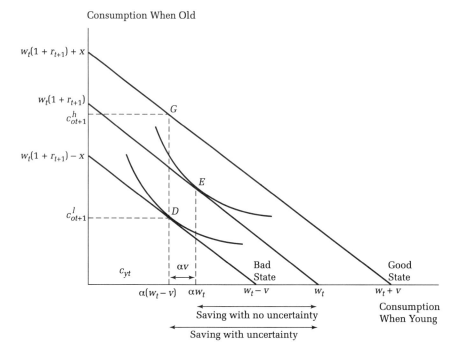

Consumption When Old

FIGURE 15.2 FRANCO'S PRECAUTIONARY SAVING

At the end of his old age, Franco faces a fifty–fifty chance of either receiving or losing x, with present value v. The "Good State" budget constraint shows his consumption opportunities if he receives x; the "Bad State" constraint shows what happens if he loses x. If Franco is very risk averse, he considers only the bad state and chooses point D along the lower constraint. He consumes $\alpha(w_t - v)$ when young and saves $(1 - \alpha)w_t + \alpha v$. The extra, precautionary saving (αv) is his response to this uncertainty.

1 Franco's consumption during his old age will be determined by which budget constraint actually materializes. If he is unlucky, his second-period consumption will be c^l_{ot+1}, the value determined by point D along the low-budget constraint. However, if he is lucky, his consumption will be c^h_{ot+1}, determined at point G along the high-budget constraint.

future income leads Franco to save αv more than if x were zero and he were certain what his future income would be. This extra precautionary saving is Franco's response to uncertainty.[1]

Let's now think about the aggregate effect of precautionary saving. As a result of income uncertainty, Franco (and everyone else in his generation) will save more. This raises capital accumulation. To see this, recall that the amount of capital per worker in period $t + 1$ is just the amount of saving per worker in period t. Therefore, the formula for the capital-labor transition equation with income uncertainty is $k_{t+1} = (1 - \alpha)w_t + \alpha v$; in the absence of uncertainty the formula is $k_{t+1} = (1 - \alpha)w_t$.

Figure 15.3 graphs the two capital-labor transition curves. In the absence of uncertainty about second-period income, the economy's capital-labor ratio would converge to $\bar{k}$, determined by the intersection of the lower transition curve with the 45-degree line. With uncertainty, the transition curve will be αv higher, and its intersection with the 45-degree line will determine a higher steady-state capital-labor ratio, $\bar{k}'$.

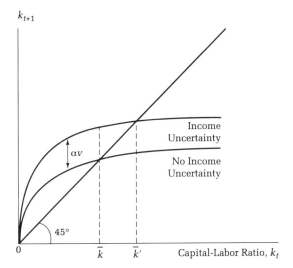

FIGURE 15.3 INCOME UNCERTAINTY AND THE CAPITAL-LABOR TRANSITION CURVE
As a result of income uncertainty, each generation will save more than if income were certain. This raises capital accumulation and shifts the transition curve upward. The steady-state capital-labor ratio will be higher — $\bar{k}'$ rather than $\bar{k}$.

PRIVATE INSURANCE AND ITS IMPACT ON CAPITAL FORMATION

Although income uncertainty is good for capital formation, it comes at the expense of everyone's worrying about suffering a decline in living standard in old age. Individuals naturally try to avoid this risk by purchasing insurance. Insurance provides a mechanism for transferring windfalls from the lucky to the unlucky members of each generation. Specifically, suppose there is an equal number of winners and losers in each generation. Insurance would effectively lead each winner to hand his winning (of x) to a loser.[2]

In this example, aggregate winnings equal aggregate losses, so there is no *aggregate uncertainty* and insurance will leave everyone in exactly the same position as if there were no uncertainty. Thus, with insurance, everyone ends up on the middle constraint in Figure 15.2. Since the insurance fully offsets the uncertainty about future income, there is no need for precautionary saving, and the relevant transition curve is the lower one in Figure 15.3.

The elimination of uncertainty and its associated precautionary saving through insurance hinges critically on the absence of aggregate uncertainty. To see this, consider what happens if we assume that all members of each generation end up either winners or losers. In this case, there is no way for the winners to pool their winnings with the losers. When one member of a generation wins, everyone else in her generation wins, and when one member loses, everyone else loses. Such aggregate income uncertainty precludes the establishment of a private insurance market. It also leaves the economy operating on the higher transition curve in Figure 15.3.

2 Here's how the insurance might operate: Franco would purchase a policy that would cost him x in premium payments to be paid at the end of his old age. The policy would promise to pay him nothing if he is lucky but $2x$ if he is unlucky. If Franco is lucky, his receipt of x at the end of his old age will just cover his premium payment. If he is unlucky, his loss of x plus his premium payment of x will be offset by his insurance payoff of $2x$.

GOVERNMENT'S PROVISION OF SOCIAL INSURANCE

To supplement private insurance, governments maintain an array of **social insurance** programs that mitigate the economic risks we face and thereby influence our precautionary saving. Governments may do this out of a paternalistic concern that some individuals will underinsure on their own or because private insurance markets either don't exist or function poorly. Take our original example of uncertain old-age income in which there is no aggregate uncertainty and suppose private insurance companies are unable to verify whether a particular individual is lucky. If so, a private insurance market cannot exist because anyone who was insured would have an incentive to lie and claim that she had been unlucky and had lost x.

Fraud is just one of the problems private insurance companies face. Another is *moral hazard*—the propensity of those covered by insurance to take less care to avoid the risks against which they are insured. A third problem is *adverse selection*—the fact that individuals with higher risks of an insurable loss have a greater incentive to purchase insurance than those with lower risks. If high-risk individuals cannot be distinguished from low-risk individuals, insurance companies have to worry about getting saddled with a pool of particularly high-risk policy holders.

These problems confronting private insurers explain why certain forms of insurance (e.g., insuring future labor earnings) are either unavailable or are so expensive that most people remain uninsured. In response to particular insurance market failures, many governments provide the insurance directly. Governments, through their tax and other records, have certain informational advantages over private insurance companies. In addition, they can force everyone to purchase insurance and so avoid adverse selection. Finally, governments do not necessarily need to break even. They can operate their insurance programs at a loss that ends up being absorbed by taxpayers.

This last point is particularly relevant when we consider the government's response to aggregate uncertainty. Such uncertainty may preclude pooling of risks within a generation, but the government can use its intergenerational tax and transfer policies to pool risks across generations. As an example, consider a government decision to lower taxes during a recession and raise them many years in the future in order to satisfy its intertemporal budget constraint. In taking these steps, the government benefits current generations, who are suffering the effects of the recession, at the expense of future generations. In other words, the government pools risks among current and future generations. Such intergenerational risk sharing is beyond the scope of private insurance markets because future generations can't buy insurance policies before they're born.

TYPES OF GOVERNMENT INSURANCE

Social insurance
Government programs designed to insulate individuals partially from economic misfortune

Government insurance may be extensive. In the United States, the federal government insures workers against unemployment and disability through unemployment compensation and social security disability insurance. It insures citizens against falling into poverty through welfare programs. It provides life insurance through social security survivor benefits, health insurance to the elderly through Medicare, and life span insurance (which we'll discuss momentarily) through social security retirement benefits and other annuities. Even so, providing insurance is not the only function of these social insurance programs. They also serve systematically to transfer funds across and within different generations independent of issues of economic risk. They are components of U.S. *intergenerational* and *intragenerational redistribution policy*.

Governments also use their tax systems to provide insurance and redistribute funds within and across generations. Consider the *progressive income taxation* that occurs in most countries. A progressive tax places a proportionately larger tax burden on those with larger incomes. As a result, it makes the distribution of after-tax income more equal than the distribution of before-tax income. This redistribution benefits those with permanently low incomes. It also helps those with temporarily low incomes resulting from loss of a job or ill health. Thus, progressive income taxation plays two roles: it systematically redistributes income from the rich to the poor and helps provide insurance by taking proportionately more from those whose incomes are unexpectedly high and proportionately less from those whose incomes are unexpectedly low.

HOW IMPORTANT IS PRECAUTIONARY SAVING?

Measuring precautionary saving is an exceedingly difficult task. Precautionary saving depends on economic risks that are hard to quantify and on the availability of government and private insurance. In the case of government insurance, discerning precisely the amount of insurance provided by complex tax and transfer provisions is no easy task. For private insurance, we must consider informal insurance arrangements as well as the formal sale of insurance contracts by insurance companies. The reason is that friends and relatives can also provide one another with insurance. They do so by standing ready to assist each other financially and in other ways in the event of economic reverses. Since the scope of such informal or implicit insurance arrangements is hard to quantify, it's difficult to know for sure what uninsured risks any particular saver faces.

In the absence of hard facts, economists have developed elaborate computer simulation models to help them understand how precautionary saving may be related to different possible levels of uninsured risk.[3] These studies show that precautionary saving can be substantial, but also quite sensitive to the type and amount of insurance available to savers.

SAVING AND BEQUESTS

An important form of precautionary saving is saving for the eventuality that we live longer than we expect. Such saving gives rise to *unintended bequests*—people's dying

3 See, for example, R. Glenn Hubbard, Jonathan Skinner, and Stephen P. Zeldes, "Precautionary Saving and Social Insurance," Journal of Political Economy *103* (April 1995): 360–399.

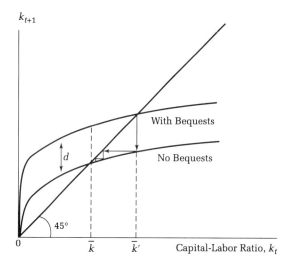

FIGURE 15.4 BEQUESTS AND THE CAPITAL-LABOR TRANSITION CURVE
The larger the level of bequests and other transfers each young person receives at time t, the higher the transition curve will be at time $t + 1$. A higher curve means a higher steady-state capital-labor ratio.

and leaving behind assets they had hoped to live long enough to consume. Before considering unintended as well as intended bequests, let's clarify how bequests and other intergenerational transfers alter capital accumulation. Let's also consider the importance of private intergenerational transfers to U.S. wealth accumulation.

IMPACT OF BEQUESTS ON CAPITAL ACCUMULATION

Modifying our capital-labor transition equation to incorporate bequests and other intergenerational transfers is easy. Let d_t stand for the bequests, gifts, and other transfers received by each young person at time t. Then each young person will have d_t plus her wages, w_t, less her payments to the government for taxes and bond purchases, f_t, out of which to save for old age. Let's take the simple case that the young do not consume (α, the propensity to consume when young, is zero). In this case, $k_{t+1} = w_t - f_t + d_t$. Replacing w_t by the formula for the marginal product of labor yields the following version of the transition equation:

$$k_{t+1} = A(1 - \beta)k_t^{\beta} - f_t + d_t.$$

Note that the larger d_t is (the amount generation t inherits and the amount generation $t - 1$ bequeaths or gives as gifts), the larger the capital-labor ratio at time $t + 1$ will be. Figure 15.4 shows, for the case in which f_t and d_t are constant, that intergenerational transfers shift the transition curve upward and raise the capital-labor ratio.

CASE STUDY
PRIVATE INTERGENERATIONAL TRANSFERS AND TOTAL U.S. WEALTH

Are private intergenerational transfers a significant part of total wealth accumulation? Answering this question is harder than it might seem because many intergenerational transfers are not reported. Laurence Kotlikoff and Lawrence H. Summers took a different measurement approach.[4] They noted that if intergenerational transfers were insignificant, then each living cohort's total wealth holdings should be related to the difference between its labor income, net of government taxes and transfers, and its consumption expenditures. In contrast, if cohorts had received significant transfers, their wealth would exceed the amount saved out of their posttax labor earnings, and the difference would be due to intergenerational transfers.

To understand the Kotlikoff-Summers methodology in terms of our model, consider the elderly's accumulated wealth at time t. Each old person's assets can be written as $a_t = w_{t-1} - c_{yt-1} - f_{t-1} + d_{t-1}$, where we allow the possibility of consumption when young. Kotlikoff and Summers's procedure was to estimate the size of d_{t-1}, called *transfer wealth*, by subtracting the calculated value of $w_{t-1} - c_{yt-1} - f_{t-1}$, called *life-cycle wealth*, from total wealth, a_t.

To their surprise, Kotlikoff and Summers found that life-cycle wealth represented only about a fifth of total U.S. wealth in 1974, with the other four-fifths traceable to transfer wealth. However, the share of transfer wealth was closer to one-half once they took into account that the past consumption of cohorts alive in 1974 would have been smaller (and their life-cycle wealth larger) in the absence of intergenerational transfers.

Although these findings have not been universally accepted, almost all economists agree that bequests are important enough to U.S. wealth accumulation to merit careful study.[5] Kotlikoff and Summers also pointed out that bequests are not necessarily incompatible with life-cycle saving behavior. That's because funds saved for retirement may be bequeathed by people who die before they have a chance to consume them.

4 Laurence J. Kotlikoff and Lawrence H. Summers, "The Role of Intergenerational Transfers in Aggregate Capital Formation," Journal of Political Economy *89, no. 4 (August 1981): 706–732.*

5 For a debate on the Kotlikoff-Summers study, see Franco Modigliani's "The Role of Intergenerational Transfers and Life Cycle Saving in the Accumulation of Wealth" and Laurence J. Kotlikoff, "Intergenerational Transfers and Savings," Journal of Economic Perspectives *2, no. 2 (Spring 1988): 15–40 and 41–58.*

LIFE SPAN UNCERTAINTY, ANNUITIES, AND UNINTENDED BEQUESTS

Life span uncertainty is a particularly pressing problem for the elderly, who face a significant chance of dying each year. Their problem, apart from death itself, is knowing how quickly to spend their accumulated assets. If they spend too fast and live longer than expected, they risk a significant drop in living standards. On the other hand, if they spend too slowly, they risk dying with a lot of unconsumed assets, thereby leaving unintended bequests. This second option, consuming assets at a slow rate, is the safe bet that risk-averse individuals will choose. In so doing they will save more, or at least dissave less. In effect, life span uncertainty gives rise to precautionary saving.

Death is unavoidable, but there is a way to hedge the economic risks of not knowing when you will die. The way is to use **annuities**, a financial security that pays a stream of income to its owner as long as the owner lives. To understand how an annuities market works, let's add to our two-period model the assumption that half the members of each generation die before they engage in second-period consumption. Let's further assume that no one knows who will die early.

Now suppose that all members of each generation agree to place all of their saving when young into a collective investment pool. The funds placed in this pool, plus interest income, are to be paid out at the end of the next period to members of the generation lucky enough to survive. In handing over their saving, members of each generation would be buying an annuity—a claim to income in their old age conditional on their survival.

Establishment of an annuity market allows the survivors to consume all the funds their generation saved when young. Consequently, it eliminates the unintended bequests that generation would otherwise have made. If the annuity market is first established for generation t, then no subsequent generation will receive an inheritance from its parents. By eliminating the need for precautionary saving, the annuity market eliminates a source of wealth accumulation for those later generations. The effect, depicted in Figure 15.4, is a downward shift in the capital-labor transition curve. The transition to the new, lower steady-state capital-labor ratio, $\bar{k}$, is shown by the arrows.

Annuity
An income stream that continues until the recipient dies

6 See Alan J. Auerbach, Laurence J. Kotlikoff, and David Weil, "The Increasing Annuitization of the Elderly—Estimates and Implications for Intergenerational Transfers, Inequality, and National Saving," National Bureau of Economic Research Working Paper No. 4182, 1992, revised April 1993.

7 This would not be true if elderly households purchased additional life insurance to offset their increased degree of annuitization. But the evidence on life insurance actually goes the other way. Between 1960 and 1990, life insurance declined relative to the size of the elderly's total remaining lifetime resources.

CASE STUDY
THE INCREASING ANNUITIZATION OF THE ELDERLY IN THE UNITED STATES

Chapter 2 pointed out that the U.S. national saving rate has fallen dramatically since the 1950s and 1960s. Part of the explanation may lie in the increased share of the remaining lifetime resources of America's elderly that has been annuitized. Annuitized wealth is nonbequeathable. It is the sum of the elderly's human wealth (the present value of their future labor earnings) plus their pension wealth (the present value of their social security and private pension benefits). Nonannuitized wealth is bequeathable and equals the elderly's net wealth (the difference between their financial and real assets and their liabilities).

Figure 15.5 is based on a study we did with Brown University's David Weil.[6] It shows that annuitized resources represented only about one-third of the elderly's resources in 1962, but almost half in 1983. Since annuitized resources are not bequeathable, this increase in annuitization has implications for the amount of unintended bequests.[7] All told, the increased annuitization appears to be responsible for reducing the annual flow of bequests in the United States by about one-third. Since every dollar not bequeathed by the elderly is a dollar that the elderly as a group consume, the increased annuitization has also meant more consumption by the elderly and less national saving.

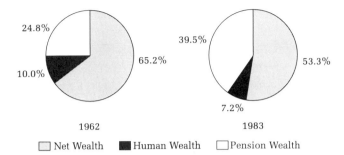

24.8%

65.2%

10.0%

39.5%

53.3%

7.2%

1962

1983

☐ Net Wealth   ■ Human Wealth   ☐ Pension Wealth

FIGURE 15.5 ANNUITIZED AND NONANNUITIZED RESOURCES OF THE U.S. ELDERLY, 1962 AND 1983
One reason the U.S. national saving rate has fallen may be the increased fraction of the elderly's assets held in non-bequeathable form. In 1962, annuitized resources represented about one-third of the elderly's total resources. By 1983, they represented almost one-half.

Source: A. Auerbach, L. Kotlikoff, and D. Weil, ''The Increasing Annuitization of the Elderly—Estimates and Implications for Intergenerational Transfers, Inequality, and National Saving,'' NBER Working Paper No. 4182, 1992, revised April 1993.

INTENTIONAL BEQUESTS AND GIFTS

Unintended bequests represent a substantial portion of total private intergenerational transfers. However, it appears that many bequests and all *intervivos gifts*—gifts made between the living—are intentional. Intervivos gifts take many forms. When parents pay their children's college tuition, give them automobiles, provide them with low-interest loans to buy a house, or give them a share of the family business, they are providing intervivos gifts. Among the very wealthy, large transfers of money or financial securities are common forms of gift giving.

Individuals who purchase life insurance desire to leave a bequest. Those elderly who engage in significant saving also appear to be doing so in order to leave a bequest. For the superwealthy, who would find it almost impossible to consume all their wealth, there is no question that the bulk of the bequests they make are fully anticipated and intended.

How can we add the desire to make intergenerational transfers to our life-cycle model? Gary Becker, Nobel laureate in economics and University of Chicago professor, and Robert Barro of Harvard University have provided one answer.[8] They pointed out how parents' altruistic concern for their children may be modeled by assuming that parents obtain utility from the utility attained by their children. In other words, the utility of individuals born at time t, u_t, depends not only on c_{yt} and c_{ot+1}, but also on u_{t+1}, the utility enjoyed by their children. u_{t+1} itself depends on the consumption when young and old enjoyed by children born at time $t + 1$. Therefore, parents care not only about their own consumption when young and old but also about their children's consumption when young and old.

Barro took the analysis one step further. He pointed out that if every generation is intergenerationally altruistic, the children born at time $t + 1$ will care about the utility of *their* children—those born at time $t + 2$. Consequently, the generation born at

8 *See Gary Becker,* A Treatise on the Family *(Cambridge, MA: Harvard University Press, 1981), and Robert Barro, "Are Government Bonds Net Wealth?"* Journal of Political Economy *82 (November–December 1974): 1095–1117.*

time *t* will care not only about its children's consumption but also about its grand-children's consumption. Continuing with this reasoning, Barro concluded that those born at time *t* will care about the consumption by *all* their descendants into the infinite future. For this reason, economists refer to the life-cycle utility function, aug-mented to include altruistic concern for children, as the *infinite horizon utility func-tion*. Maximizing this utility function produces a plan for how much each member of the altruistically linked dynasty will consume when he is alive and how much he will intentionally transfer to his children as either a gift (while he is living) or a bequest (after his death).

INTERGENERATIONAL ALTRUISM AND RICARDIAN EQUIVALENCE

Becker and Barro pointed out that altruistically linked generations will pool their incomes in deciding how much each of them should consume and, for that matter, how much they collectively should leave to their descendants. Barro showed that this income sharing has strong implications for the effectiveness of government inter-generational redistribution policies.

To understand Barro's argument, consider the case of Stan and his son, Rudi, with whom Stan is altruistically linked. Stan has a higher lifetime income than Rudi does and decides to transfer $10,000 to Rudi. Now the government comes along, takes $5,000 from Rudi, and gives it to Stan as part of its policy of taxing the young to make social security transfer payments to the old. How will Stan respond? According to Barro, Stan will return the $5,000 to Rudi as a gift or bequest. Stan will offset the gov-ernment's intergenerational transfer with his own private intergenerational transfer. In so doing, he will produce **Ricardian equivalence**.[9] David Ricardo was a famous nineteenth-century British economist who first raised the possibility that private transfers may nullify the effects of government intergenerational transfers.

Stan realizes that the government's policy has not changed his and Rudi's col-lective income. Unless he hands back the $5,000 to Rudi, Stan will not succeed in his utility-maximizing objective of raising Rudi's consumption by a total of $10,000. Indeed, Ricardian equivalence will hold whether the government redistributes from Rudi to Stan or from Stan to Rudi. To see this, consider Stan's reaction to a govern-ment policy that redistributes $5,000 from himself to Rudi. Stan will reduce his own private transfer from $10,000 to $5,000 because he realizes that the government has already transferred $5,000 of his income to Rudi.

Here is the point of the example: If altruistic linkages across generations are strong enough, they will give rise to private sector transfers that fully offset the government's intergenerational redistribution. This is true for all government inter-generational redistribution policies, including those associated with increases in the government's official debt (which "pay-as-you-go" Social Security transfers are not). It is also true for redistribution across generations that are not alive at the same time. If the government uses its fiscal policies to redistribute $5,000 to Stan from Rudi's child, Greg, Stan will transfer the $5,000 to Rudi, who will then transfer the funds to Greg.

Ricardian equivalence
The proposition that private intergenerational transfers neutralize government intergenerational transfers

9 *"Equivalence" refers to the fact that in the presence of inter-generational altruism, taxing future generations is equivalent to taxing current generations.*

If Ricardian equivalence holds, then intergenerational redistribution will not alter private sector consumption or national saving. We can see this by using our transition formula for the capital-labor ratio. Take the simple case in which individuals consume only when old. As we mentioned above, the transition equation is then $k_{t+1} = w_t - f_t + d_t$. Now consider a government policy of taxing the young at time t to finance transfer payments to the old at time t. This policy raises f_t. If d_t remains unchanged, k_{t+1} will be reduced. However, Ricardian equivalence predicts that the old at time t, who, after all, are the parents of the young at time t, will simply transfer back to the young the funds the government gives them. The result is an increase in d_t that exactly equals the increase in f_t, leaving k_{t+1} unchanged.

CASE STUDY
ARE U.S. EXTENDED FAMILIES ALTRUISTICALLY LINKED?

If altruistically linked extended family members really do pool their incomes in deciding how much each should consume, then the amount any particular member consumes will depend on the total income of the extended family, not on that person's share of the total. In our example, this means that Stan's share of his plus Rudi's total consumption should not depend on Stan's share of their total income. Another way to state this is that the ratio of Stan's consumption to Rudi's should not depend on the ratio of Stan's income to Rudi's.

Northwestern University economist Joseph Altonji, Columbia University economist Fumio Hayashi, and Laurence Kotlikoff used U.S. data to study whether the ratio of parents' consumption to that of their adult children depends on the ratio of parents' income to their children's.[10] They found strong evidence that relative incomes do influence the relative consumption levels of extended family members. In fact, their findings suggest that extended family members have essentially no economic interdependence when it comes to deciding how much to consume and save. Thus, although the Barro-Becker altruism model may describe particular extended families, it doesn't do a good job of explaining how most U.S. extended families behave. Ricardian equivalence doesn't seem to hold in the United States.

MODELING CREDIT MARKETS

We've seen how uncertainty and bequests can raise a country's saving. Next, let's explore how credit markets can reduce saving by expanding consumption opportunities. We add credit markets to our two-period life-cycle model by assuming that in each generation, there are two types of individuals: borrowers, B, and lenders, L. Borrower types wish to borrow from the lender types. To produce this result, we assume B types

10 See Joseph G. Altonji, Fumio Hayashi, and Laurence J. Kotlikoff, "Is the Extended Family Altruistically Linked? Direct Tests Using Micro Data," American Economic Review 82, no. 5 (December 1992): 1177–1198.

can work only when old and wish to consume only when young; L types work only when young and wish to consume only when old. These assumptions are summarized in the following table:

	Type L	Type B
When young	Works	Consumes
When old	Consumes	Works

As the table shows, there is a mismatch between when the B and L types receive their income and when they wish to do their consumption. Let's consider how they can resolve this mismatch.

THE DEMAND FOR CREDIT

To consume when young, B types will have to borrow against their old-age labor income. Let's assume that Bs can find lenders willing to make them loans at the prevailing interest rate. In this case, the amount each B borrows when young is the amount she consumes when young. Hence, her assets at time $t + 1$, a_{t+1}, will be negative (she'll be in debt) and will equal minus her consumption when young. Thus,

$$a_{t+1} = -c_{yt}.$$

When our type B individual is old, she'll use her old-age labor earnings, w_{t+1}, to repay her debt as well as the interest owed on it:

$$w_{t+1} = -a_{t+1}(1 + r_{t+1}).$$

Combining these two equations gives us the lifetime budget constraint facing type B individuals:

$$c_{yt} = \frac{w_{t+1}}{1 + r_{t+1}}.$$

As always, the budget constraint indicates that the present value of consumption expenditures equals the present value of labor income. Compare this lifetime budget constraint and the one introduced in Chapter 2 (p. 38). Note that old-age consumption does not appear on the left-hand side here. Also, the present value of earnings when old, rather than earnings when young, appears on the right-hand side. Figure 15.6 graphs this budget constraint. The intersection of the constraint with the vertical axis indicates second-period labor earnings. Its intersection with the horizontal axis shows the present value of this income, which also equals consumption when young.

Because each B wants to borrow the present value of her old age labor earnings, the total demand for loans each period equals this desired amount of borrowing times the number of type Bs. Recall that there are N individuals in each generation. Of these, we'll assume that the fraction m are type Bs and the remainder $(1 - m)$ are type Ls. Thus, the total credit demanded at time t is N times m times $(w_{t+1}/1 + r_{t+1})$.

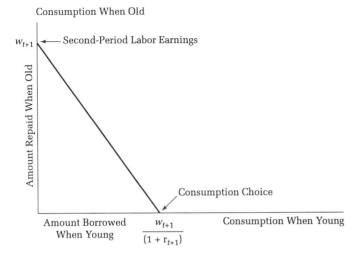

FIGURE 15.6 BUDGET CONSTRAINT OF A TYPE B INDIVIDUAL
Type B individuals work when old and consume when young; they are borrowers during their first period of life. Since the Bs earn w_{t+1} when old, they can borrow and consume a maximum of $w_{t+1}/(1 + r_{t+1})$ when young.

THE SUPPLY OF CREDIT

Who will supply credit (make loans) to young B types at time t? It will not be the elderly of time t. They will all be dead at time $t + 1$ when the young B borrowers are in a position to repay their loans. Therefore, it must be those L types who are young at time t. We'll assume for the moment that the Ls are sure that any funds they lend to their B contemporaries will be repaid at the same interest rate available by investing in capital. In that case, the young L types will be indifferent between making loans to Bs and investing in capital.

There are N times $(1 - m)$ lenders in each generation, and each saves her entire wages, w_t. Therefore, the total savings of the L types at time t is N times $(1 - m)$ times w_t. As long as those total savings exceed the amount the B types wish to borrow, the Ls can fully satisfy the demand for credit and still have funds left to invest in capital.

CAPITAL ACCUMULATION IN THE PRESENCE OF BORROWING

As the previous sentence indicates, the amount of capital brought into period $t + 1$ by the generation born in period t equals the total savings of the young Ls less the amount of those savings they lend to the young Bs. Hence, our formula for the capital-labor ratio at time $t + 1$ is

$$k_{t+1} = (1 - m)w_t - m\,\frac{w_{t+1}}{1 + r_{t+1}}.$$

To understand this formula better, multiply both sides of this equation by the total workforce N.[11] Then the left-hand side of the equation is the absolute amount of

11 The workforce equals N because at any point in time there are N times m old Bs working alongside N times (1 − m) young Ls, and Nm + N(1 − m) = N.

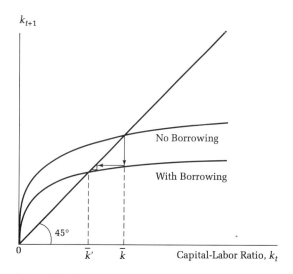

FIGURE 15.7 BORROWING AND THE CAPITAL-LABOR TRANSITION CURVE
If m is the fraction of borrowers in each generation, then an increase in m raises total borrowing and reduces capital formation. Here, the transition curve marked "No Borrowing" corresponds to $m = 0$. As m increases, less is saved, and the transition curve rotates downward.

capital at time $t + 1$ and the right-hand side is just the total savings of the L types minus the total amount of loans they provide to the B types.

If m equals zero (there are no B types in each generation), the formula reduces to $k_{t+1} = w_t$. This is our standard expression for the capital-labor ratio at $t + 1$ in the case that α, the propensity to consume when young, equals zero. When m is a positive fraction, the formula indicates that there is less capital per worker at the beginning of time $t + 1$ than if m equals zero.

To derive the capital-labor transition equation from this equation, we need only replace the wage and interest rates with the appropriate formulas for the marginal products of labor or capital. For example, we replace r_{t+1} by the formula for the marginal product of capital at time $t + 1$. Unfortunately, this substitution leads to a messy nonlinear relationship between k_t and k_{t+1} in which k_{t+1} shows up on both sides of the equation. Nonetheless, we can still use the equation to determine the value of k_{t+1} given a value of k_t.[12] In addition, the transition diagram implied by this equation has the same general shape as in the absence of borrowing.

Figure 15.7 makes this point. It graphs the capital-labor transition equation for both cases: when there is no borrowing (m is zero) and when there is borrowing (when m is greater than zero). Note that the curve with borrowing lies below the one without borrowing. This reflects the fact that as more of the young generation's saving is channeled into lending, that generation invests less in capital. An increase in the proportion of borrowers in a generation (an increase in m) rotates the transition curve downward and leads to a lower steady-state capital-labor ratio.

12 Given the value of k_t, the value of k_{t+1} that satisfies the equation can be found by trying different values of k_{t+1} until we find one that makes the right-hand side of the equation equal to the left-hand side.

CREDIT MARKET IMPERFECTIONS

So far, we've assumed that the *B* types always repay their loans. To see the importance of this assumption, let's now check the other extreme. Suppose the *B*s are given loans when young and choose not to work when old. With no wage income, they default on their loans. This could happen if the legal system permitted personal bankruptcy and could not be used to compel the *B*s to work in their old age. Under these rather extreme assumptions, the credit market will collapse. The *L* types, knowing they face default on any loans they make, won't make any. As a result, the *B* types will face a **credit constraint** (a restriction on credit); they'll be unable to borrow (to obtain credit) and consume when young. Clearly, if there were some way to compel the *B* types to work when old to repay their borrowing, they would be better off.

This credit market imperfection cannot be cured by raising the interest rate charged on loans. Since they have no intention of repaying, the *B*s will agree to any interest rate, no matter how high, and still default in their old age.[13] Regardless of what interest rate lenders charge, the effective interest rate they actually receive is zero once they take default into account.

The inability of some people to borrow at prevailing interest rates is not simply a theoretical possibility. On the contrary, real-world lenders routinely turn down loan applications from borrowers they deem to be poor risks. Even borrowers who are generally viewed as creditworthy may find themselves unable to borrow during economic downturns, when lenders realize the likelihood of loan default has risen.

WHY BORROWING RATES MAY EXCEED LENDING RATES

If *B*s never repay their loans, a complete collapse of the credit market is guaranteed. A more realistic assumption is that some *B* types are trustworthy and will repay their loans. Others, who cannot be distinguished in advance, are untrustworthy and will default on their loans. If the proportion of trustworthy borrowers is sufficiently high, lenders may be willing to make loans, but only at an interest rate that factors in the likelihood of default. For example, if the *lending rate*—the real rate of interest lenders can earn by investing in capital or other nonloan assets—is 10 percent and the likely default loss is 5 percent of each dollar loaned out, lenders might charge borrowers 15 percent. They would require 10 percent to cover their opportunity cost (investing in real capital) and an additional 5 percent to cover the risk of default. If lenders pool their loans through financial intermediaries that deal with large numbers of borrowers, each lender can safely expect to lose only 5 percent of his funds through default. Hence, by altering our assumption about the likelihood of default, we can generate an outcome that is also quite commonplace in the real world: the *borrowing rate* of interest exceeds the lending rate.

Interestingly, the real losers here are the trustworthy borrowers. The bad risks can borrow at 15 percent, default on their loans, and consume for free when young. However, the good risks (who do repay their loans) must pay a higher interest rate on the funds they borrow. Furthermore, since they will be forced to use more of their

Credit constraint
A restriction on the availability of credit

13 *The potential inability of interest rates to equate the supply of credit to its demand was pointed out in Joseph Stiglitz and Andrew Weiss's seminal article,* "Credit Rationing in Markets with Imperfect Information," American Economic Review *71 (June 1981): 393–410.*

Rob Rogers © United Feature Syndicate. Reprinted by permission.

old-age earnings to repay interest, the amount of principal they can borrow when young is reduced.

To illustrate the excess of borrowing rates over lending rates, compare the mortgage interest rate charged new home buyers, assuming the mortgage is paid off in ten years, with the interest rate on 10-year U.S. Treasury bonds. The mortgage rate has exceeded the Treasury bond rate in each year since 1963, which is the first year of available data. Over the entire period, the mortgage rate averaged 9.1 percent, whereas the Treasury bond rate averaged 7.8 percent.[14]

CASE STUDY
CREDIT LIBERALIZATION AND THE DECLINE IN NORWEGIAN SAVING

So far we've talked only about the market determination of credit conditions. Government policy can also influence credit availability and thus the position of the capital-labor transition curve. The Norwegian government's highly restrictive *interest rate ceilings* and **credit controls** are a case in point. Before 1984, the government's interest rate ceilings limited the rate of return that financial intermediaries could pay to depositors and other suppliers of funds. Naturally, this limited the amount of funds that such suppliers made available to these financial intermediaries. In addition, the government's credit controls directly restricted the amounts that financial intermediaries could lend.

In 1984 the Norwegian government deregulated its financial markets, including its credit markets. The result was a dramatic surge in borrowing by young and middle-aged Norwegians to purchase consumer durables and homes, as well as nondurable consumption goods and services. In the housing market, so much pent-up demand was re-

Credit controls
Imposed limits on the amount of funds that financial intermediaries may lend

14 Part of the differences can be attributed to the transactions costs banks incur in attracting mortgagees, checking their credit references, and issuing them the mortgages.

leased that urban housing prices rose by almost 80 percent between 1984 and 1987. Since the existing housing stock was owned primarily by older Norwegians, this tremendous windfall gain permitted them to join the country's consumption spending spree.

Not surprisingly, Norwegian saving plunged. In 1984 the Norwegian private saving rate stood at 9.5 percent.[15] By 1986 it was actually negative 1.8 percent! Norway is not an isolated example. Denmark, Sweden, Finland, and Italy also deregulated their credit markets in the 1980s, and all experienced sharp reductions in their saving rates.[16]

CASE STUDY
ARE U.S. CITIZENS CREDIT CONSTRAINED?

Although the United States is a wealthy country, not all citizens are wealthy. The distribution of wealth holdings is highly skewed. The richest 1 percent of U.S. households own over one-third of all U.S. household net wealth. The poorest 20 percent of households own less than 1 percent of wealth.[17] In addition, much of the wealth that low- and middle-income households own is in the form of housing and cannot be easily liquidated to spend on consumption. Roughly one-quarter of U.S. households appear to have few, if any, liquid financial assets.[18]

Low financial wealth holdings of some U.S. households raises the possibility of widespread liquidity constraints but doesn't prove they exist. As a result, economists have sought other ways to identify credit constraints. A study by Johns Hopkins economist Christopher Carroll and Harvard economist Lawrence Summers shows that age-consumption profiles tend to parallel quite closely the age-disposable income profiles.[19] This seems to suggest credit constraints. But the fact that consumption tracks disposable income may simply reflect households' uncertainty about what their future earnings will be. When earnings are uncertain, we would also expect age-consumption profiles to track age-disposable income profiles as households adjust their consumption spending upward or downward in response to their actual realized incomes.

Another study, by David Wilcox, an economist with the Federal Reserve, shows that social security recipients wait until they actually receive their annual social security benefit cost-of-living increases before spending them, even though the benefit increases are announced six months in advance.[20] Although this also suggests credit-constrained consumption, there are counterarguments. First, most social security beneficiaries have sufficient liquid assets to pay for an increase in consumption at the time they first learn about the rise in their future benefits. They simply choose not to do so. Second, some recipients may not know about the pending increase in benefits. Third, recipients spend most of the increase on durables. Since purchasing durables constitutes a form of saving rather than immediate consumption, we can read Wilcox's evidence as indicating that the timing of the government's net taxation has little, if any, effect on the timing of consumption. That is precisely the prediction of the non-credit-constrained life-cycle model.

15 The private savings rate is defined as (1) national saving less the government deficit divided by (2) GDP less net taxes.

16 See Olli-Pekka Lehmussaari, "Deregulation and Consumption: Saving Dynamics in the Nordic Countries," International Monetary Fund Staff Papers 37(1) (March 1990): 71–94; and Luigi Guiso, Tullio Jappelli, and Daniele Terlizzse, "Saving and Capital Market Imperfections: The Italian Experience," Scandinavian Journal of Economics 94, no. 2 (1992): 197–213.

17 See Arthur B. Kennickell and R. Louise Woodburn, "Estimation of Household Net Worth Using Model-Based and Design-Based Weights: Evidence from the 1989 Survey of Consumer Finances," mimeo, Board of Governors of the Federal Reserve System (April 1992).

18 See Peter A. Diamond and Jerry A. Hausman, "Individual Retirement and Saving Behavior," Journal of Public Economics 23 (February–March 1984): 81–114.

19 Christopher D. Carroll and Lawrence H. Summers, "Consumption Growth Parallels Income Growth: Some New Evidence," in B. Douglas Bernheim and John B. Shoven, eds., National Saving and Economic Performance (Chicago: University of Chicago Press, 1991), pp. 305–348.

20 See David W. Wilcox, "Social Security Benefits, Consumption Expenditure, and the Life Cycle Hypothesis," Journal of Political Economy 97, no. 2 (April 1989): 288–304.

More sophisticated studies than those just mentioned have been designed to test for credit constraints in the context of income uncertainty.[21] These studies indicate that about one in five U.S. households is credit constrained, but their findings are far from definitive for a variety of reasons. The bottom line is that economists do not yet have a precise understanding of the extent and importance of credit constraints in the United States.

Chapter Summary

1. In addition to saving for retirement, people save against economic uncertainties and save to make bequests and gifts. This chapter explored these saving motives. It also considered the potential for young people to dissave by borrowing against their future income.

2. Adding uncertain second-period income to our model generates precautionary saving, which leads to an upward shift in the capital-labor ratio transition curve and more capital accumulation over time. Private insurance may reduce or eliminate the need for precautionary saving and, as a result, shift the capital-labor ratio transition curve downward.

3. Governments also provide insurance and thereby influence the amount of precautionary saving. They do so through social insurance programs and through progressive taxation.

4. Although no one knows for sure the contribution of precautionary saving to total saving, simulation studies suggest that precautionary saving can be substantial depending on the type of uncertainty and the availability of insurance.

5. Like precautionary saving, intentional saving for bequests and gifts shifts the capital-labor transition curve upward. This leads to a higher long-run level of capital per worker. The transition curve will also be higher as a result of unintended bequests. Unintended bequests are those left by individuals who die before consuming all the accumulated assets they did not plan to bequeath.

6. Research on U.S. bequests and other private intergenerational transfers suggests that, intended or not, such transfers have played a significant role in explaining total U.S. wealth accumulation. This role appears to be diminishing as more of the resources of the elderly become annuitized.

21 See, for example, Robert E. Hall, "Stochastic Implications of the Life Cycle–Permanent Income Hypothesis: Theory and Evidence," Journal of Political Economy 86 (December 1978): 971–987; Robert E. Hall and Frederic S. Mishkin, "The Sensitivity of Consumption to Transitory Income: Estimates from Panel Data on Households," Econometrica 50, no. 2 (1982): 461–481; Fumio Hayashi, "The Effects of Liquidity Constraints on Consumption: A Cross-Sectional Analysis," Quarterly Journal of Economics 100 (February 1985): 183–206; and Stephen P. Zeldes, "Consumption and Liquidity Constraints: An Empirical Investigation," Journal of Political Economy 97 (1989): 305–346.

7. If private intergenerational transfers arise as the result of altruistic links between parents and children, Ricardian equivalence will hold. Ricardian equivalence is the proposition that private intergenerational redistribution will offset government redistribution, dollar for dollar. Particular extended families may exhibit altruistic linkages, but as a group, U.S. citizens apparently do not. Hence, Ricardian equivalence does not appear to hold for the economy as a whole.

8. Borrowing and credit markets arise in our two-period model if, in each generation, there are those who want to borrow and those who want to lend. By making loans to their contemporaries, young lenders reduce the amount of their saving used to invest in capital. This extension of credit shifts the capital-labor transition curve downward and depresses the economy's capital accumulation.

9. The availability of credit hinges on the knowledge lenders have about the creditworthiness of borrowers. It also depends on the legal institutions available to enforce repayment. These factors can influence the spread between borrowing and lending rates. In the United States a segment of society appears to be credit constrained.

CHAPTER 16

FINANCIAL MARKETS AND THE INVESTMENT DECISION

INTRODUCTION

Investment is the purchase of capital goods used in producing output. In an average year, it accounts for only 15 percent of U.S. GDP. However, macroeconomists spend much more than 15 percent of their time studying investment because of its importance to the economy. Investment, also referred to as *capital accumulation*, affects the growth rates of output and labor productivity and thus helps determine the economy's long-run performance. But investment is highly volatile and also greatly affects the economy's short-run behavior. It often fluctuates more than household consumption, which accounts for about two-thirds of GDP. To reduce these fluctuations, governments often use monetary and fiscal policy to stabilize the level of investment.

This chapter studies firms' investment decisions in more detail: how they choose which capital goods to buy, how they *finance* (obtain the funds needed for) their investments, and how they react to government investment incentives. The chapter also considers shifts over time in the composition of the aggregate capital stock and the macroeconomic implications of these shifts.

The **user cost of capital** plays a key role in firms' investment decisions because it measures the annual cost of using the capital a firm is thinking of buying. This variable depends on a variety of factors, including the firm's technology, its expectations, and its access to credit markets. But it also depends on government policy and, as such, provides a key channel through which the government influences the amount and type of investment in the economy.

Our study of investment begins with postwar changes in its composition. But before moving on, take a look at this chapter's key questions:

- How and why has the composition of investment changed over time?

- How do tax policies influence the user cost of capital and investment?

User cost of capital
The total cost to a firm of using a unit of capital for one period

TABLE 16.1 PRIVATE INVESTMENT IN THE UNITED STATES, 1996 (BILLIONS OF DOLLARS)

Gross private domestic investment	1,117.0	
Inventory investment	15.4	
Fixed investment	1,101.5	
Nonresidential structures		213.4
Nonresidential equipment		791.1
Residential structures		310.5

Source: National Income and Product Accounts.

- How has the financing of U.S. investment changed in recent years?

- How do credit constraints affect the level and stability of investment?

- Why are certain types of investment more volatile than others?

ANATOMY OF POSTWAR U.S. INVESTMENT

In 1996 U.S. gross investment totaled $1,117.0 billion and accounted for 14.7 percent of GDP.[1] Table 16.1 breaks down this investment into fixed investment—the purchase of durable goods (those lasting more than a year) that are used to produce output—and *inventory investment*—the purchase of goods that the firm will process or is holding for sale. Think of the assembly line used to manufacture automobiles. Fixed capital (the machines along the line) and labor are used to add value to inventories that enter as raw materials (steel, glass, and so forth) and leave as finished goods. The addition of robots and other machines used along the assembly line is counted as fixed investment. Increases in the stock of raw materials held ready for production, the work in process along the assembly line, or finished cars awaiting shipment all represent inventory investment.

Inventories may include durable goods, but the distinction is that the durable goods held in inventory are themselves the subject of the production process. When General Motors adds a finished automobile to a lot awaiting shipment, that constitutes inventory investment. However, if the same car is immediately purchased by a limousine service to be used to provide limousine rides, it is considered as fixed investment.[2]

Inventory investment is typically a very small component of investment. For example, it equaled just $15.4 billion in 1996, out of $1.1 trillion in total investment. Most private investment is fixed investment, which includes both nonresidential investment (also called *business fixed investment*) and residential investment: construction of houses, apartment buildings, condominiums, and so forth. In 1996, business

1 Recall that gross investment equals the amount of capital purchased, whereas net investment equals the change in the capital stock. Net investment equals gross investment minus the depreciation of existing capital.

2 This distinction between inventory and fixed investment may exist even within a single company. For example, a retail electronics store may purchase a personal computer it intends to resell. This is considered inventory investment, because the store's production process is the retail distribution of computers. At the same time, the store may purchase a computer for its own use, to manage its accounts and billing. This is considered fixed investment, because this computer is not being marketed by the firm.

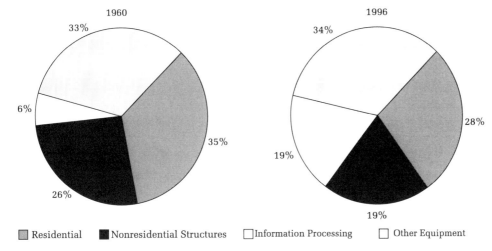

FIGURE 16.1 COMPONENTS OF FIXED INVESTMENT, 1960 AND 1996

Between 1960 and 1996, investment in housing and nonresidential structures fell as a share of fixed investment. By contrast, investment in information processing equipment grew from 6 percent of the total in 1960 to 19 percent in 1996.

Source: National Income and Product Accounts.

fixed investment accounted for nearly three-fourths of all fixed investment. Almost three-fourths of this nonresidential investment was purchases of *producers' durable equipment*—machinery, trucks, tractors, tools, computers—rather than the construction of factories, office buildings, and other nonresidential structures.

Figure 16.1 compares the composition of U.S. fixed investment in 1996 with that in 1960, separating information processing equipment from all other equipment. Note that residential construction has fallen as a share of total fixed investment in recent decades. This drop is at least partly attributable to the slowdown in household formation—a prime determinant of new housing construction—that followed the postwar baby boom.[3] The share of investment in nonresidential structures also fell over the period. Together, nonresidential and residential construction fell from 61 percent of fixed investment in 1960 to 47 percent in 1996.

The most striking change from 1960 to 1996, though, is in the share of investment accounted for by information processing equipment, including computers. From just 6 percent of fixed investment in 1960, investment in information processing equipment expanded to 19 percent of the total by 1996. Investment is thus increasingly typified by lawyers buying computers and investment bankers buying mobile telephones and less by steel companies building blast furnaces, automobile companies installing assembly lines, and home builders developing large tracts of starter homes for new families.

3 See N. Gregory Mankiw and David N. Weil, "The Baby Boom, the Baby Bust, and the Housing Market," Regional Science and Urban Economics *19 (May 1989): 235–258.*

THE INCENTIVE TO INVEST

In our life-cycle model, the economy's capital stock in a particular period equals the capital brought into old age by that period's older generation. The period's net investment equals the increase in the capital stock over the previous period. At the beginning of their old age, the elderly may invest their capital in their own firms or supply their capital to other firms that pay the market rental rate for capital—the real interest rate.

In the real world, most nonresidential investment and a portion of residential investment is undertaken by businesses. To finance this investment, businesses obtain funds from households with the assistance of financial intermediaries. We'll discuss shortly why the method of obtaining funds may matter. Initially, though, we'll assume that regardless of how a firm obtains funds, it must offer the market rate of return.

USER COST OF CAPITAL

Imagine that a firm is considering the purchase of a unit of capital to use for one period. (The same general approach applies to multiperiod decisions as well.) For each dollar it obtains from households, directly or through financial intermediaries, it must repay the dollar of principal plus interest in the following period. Part of this repayment will consist of the capital itself or the funds raised by selling the capital to a third party.

How much must the firm earn in order to repay principal plus interest? Let's first review our earlier analysis of this problem, from chapter 3. With the dollar of capital still in hand one period later, the firm needs to earn the real rate of interest, r, on its investment in order to have the $1 + r$ dollars to repay. Hence, the investment's return—its *marginal product*—must be at least as high as the interest rate, r. Firms acquire capital as long as it is profitable to do so. That is, they acquire it to the point where the marginal product of capital, *MPK*, equals r:

$$MPK = r.$$

In this case, we may think of r as the price that the firm pays in order to use one dollar of capital for one period; r is the *user cost of capital*.

Accounting for Depreciation

The formula for the user cost of capital needs to be modified in the presence of depreciation. As a tangible asset, capital will depreciate in the period between its purchase and its sale one period later. Let's assume it has lost a fraction δ of its value, and is now worth just $(1 - \delta)$ per dollar originally invested. Then, for each dollar of capital originally purchased, the firm will have $(1 - \delta)$ dollars of capital, but it must repay a total of $(1 + r)$ dollars. Hence, the capital itself must yield a return of at least $(r + \delta)$. The firm will invest in capital to the point where its marginal product just equals this value:

$MPK = r + \delta.$

This revised expression (the right hand-side of the above formula) is referred to as the *user cost of capital*, because it indicates the full cost to the firm of using capital in production. In the previous instance, the user cost of capital was simply the interest rate. However, the physical investment's loss of value imposes another cost, depreciation, that must be made up by a higher rate of return.

The User Cost: A Numerical Example

A numerical example illustrates how to calculate the user cost of capital. Suppose a company is considering whether to purchase a computer for $2,000. Once purchased, the computer will depreciate and lose 35 percent of its value after one year, at which time the firm must pay the suppliers of funds 6 percent interest, along with principal, or $2,120. Selling the computer would raise only $1,300 (.65 times $2,000), so the firm needs to earn an additional $820—41 (6 + 35) percent of the initial purchase price to break even.

CORPORATE INCOME TAX, USER COST OF CAPITAL, AND INVESTMENT

Monetary and fiscal policies can affect the interest rate and the amount of capital in the economy. The impact on the interest rate represents one way that government policy influences the user cost of capital, for all types of investment. However, through specific tax provisions, the government also influences the composition of the capital stock. The impact of such tax provisions can be determined by considering how they affect the user cost of particular types of capital. This section considers the most important of these tax provisions, the corporate income tax.

CORPORATE INCOME TAX

Most U.S. nonresidential investment is undertaken by corporations. Businesses choose the corporate form of organization for a variety of legal and financial reasons, but being a corporation has tax consequences as well. The income a corporation earns for its owners its *stockholders* is subject to the **corporate income tax**.

The corporate income tax adds a third term to the user cost of capital. For each dollar of interest the corporation pays to its suppliers of funds, it must also remit a certain amount to the government. This tax component, say τ per dollar of capital, increases the user cost to

$MPK = r + \delta + \tau.$

The term τ accounts for the share of a firm's earnings after depreciation that must be paid in taxes. Thus, it increases with the corporate tax rate.

Corporate income tax
A tax on corporate profits

To see how this works, take the numerical example introduced earlier with a value of τ equal to 3 percent. With a 6 percent interest rate and a 35 percent depreciation rate, it is now no longer sufficient to earn a rate of return of 41 percent on the investment. If the firm did earn 41 percent, it would have to pay some of this to the government in taxes, leaving it with less than it would need to cover interest and depreciation. The user cost formula tells us that to cover these costs and taxes as well, the marginal product of capital would have to be $6 + 35 + 3 = 44$ percent.

How does the corporate income tax affect the economy's capital stock? Let's start by assuming that the tax applies to all types of capital, and then ask how our answer is affected by the fact that the corporate tax does not apply to all types of investment.

Relating Changes in the User Cost to Changes in Investment

We have just observed that for a given interest rate, a rise in the corporate tax raises the user cost of capital. Now let's consider, graphically and algebraically, how this tax affects the economy's capital stock and investment. To do so, remember that the capital stock and the interest rate are jointly determined by the demand for capital by firms and the supply of capital by households, so that the interest rate itself may change in response to the corporate tax.

The demand for capital by firms is governed by the production function and the user cost of capital just derived. For any given interest rate, introducing a corporate tax raises the user cost, thereby requiring a higher marginal product of capital. This leads each firm to demand less capital at any interest rate. The drop in demand for capital for the economy as a whole may be calculated by equating the marginal product of capital to the user cost of capital. For period $t + 1$, this yields

$$A\beta k_{t+1}^{\beta-1} = r_{t+1} + \delta + \tau,$$

which, as we vary r_{t+1}, traces out a demand curve for capital relating the capital-labor ratio to the interest rate. Figure 16.2 shows two such demand curves. The first, labeled D, corresponds to the case where $\tau = 0$. The second, labeled D', corresponds to a positive value of τ. It lies a distance τ below curve D because if r_{t+1} falls by exactly τ as the tax is introduced, the user cost doesn't change, and neither does the quantity of capital demanded.

Now let's consider supply conditions. Recall how the supply of capital by households is determined when there is no first-period consumption ($\alpha = 0$). In this case, the next period's capital stock (per young person) equals

$$k_{t+1} = (1 - \gamma)(1 - \beta)y_t - f_t,$$

where $1 - \beta$ is the share of income going to labor, γ is the share of labor income put into money holdings (rather than capital), and f_t is the sum of taxes paid and government bonds purchased by each young person. In words, on a per worker basis, the total amount of capital in the economy equals the amount the young save, net of the amount they choose to hold as money and the amount they give to the government.

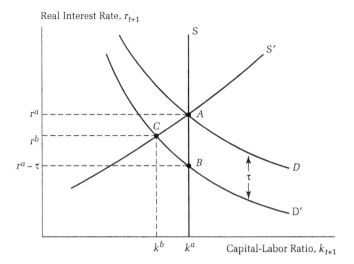

FIGURE 16.2 CAPITAL STOCK DETERMINATION: THE CORPORATE TAX
A corporate income tax shifts the demand for capital curve downward from D to D'. If the supply of capital is independent of the interest rate, the tax merely lowers the interest rate from r^a to $r^a - \tau$, with no change in the capital-labor
ratio. If the supply of capital does depend on the interest rate, the tax lowers both the interest rate (to r^b) and the
capital-labor ratio.

This expression gives us a supply curve for k_{t+1}. Unlike the demand curve, the
supply curve is not shifted by the imposition of a corporate tax, which has no direct
impact on f_t, the payments to the government by the young, who own no capital. Log-
ically, then, introducing a corporate tax can alter the overall amount of capital only if
the quantity supplied depends on the interest rate, as shown by the upward sloping
supply curve labeled S′ in Figure 16.2. Otherwise, with the vertical supply curve, S,
the corporate tax shifts the demand curve downward, reducing the interest rate from r^a
at point A to $r^a - \tau$ at point B, but leaving the capital-labor ratio unchanged at k^a.

Could the supply of capital depend on the interest rate? There are three reasons
that it might. First, a reduction in the interest rate will increase γ if the demand for
money is interest sensitive. Second, the quantity of capital supplied may fall along
with r_{t+1} if young households save less as a result. In the above supply equation for
k_{t+1}, α is fixed at zero and young households consume none of their income. In our
more general model with $\alpha > 0$, an increase in α reduces the supply of capital. The
value of α may be increased by a reduction in the after-tax interest rate households
receive. Third, we have ignored the possibility of international capital flows. A decline
in the domestic rate of return may cause savers to invest abroad, thereby reducing the
domestic supply of capital.

If the supply of capital is interest sensitive, a corporate tax will discourage
overall saving. With a positively sloped supply curve, such as S′ in Figure 16.2, a tax
that shifts the demand curve downward lowers both the interest rate and the quantity
of capital per worker, as shown at point C.

EFFECTS OF SECTOR-SPECIFIC TAXATION

Let's return to the fact that the corporate tax does not affect all types of investment equally. Nonresidential investment (mostly undertaken by corporations) is generally subject to a tax, whereas residential investment (mostly undertaken by households) is not. Hence, for a given interest rate, only the corporate cost of capital will rise in response to a rise in the corporate income tax. This will reduce the quantity of capital demanded by corporations for any given interest rate. Because the demand curve for noncorporate capital is not affected, overall (corporate plus noncorporate) demand also falls at each interest rate. Once again, if the supply of capital is fixed, the interest rate must fall in order to stimulate demand back to its original level. Now, though, as the interest rate falls, the user cost of noncorporate capital will fall. The demand for capital, and hence investment, by the noncorporate sector will rise. Even if the supply curve for capital is not completely vertical, the initial reduction in demand will still lead to some reduction in the interest rate, as shown in Figure 16.2, and hence some increase in the quantity of noncorporate capital demanded.

In summary, whether the overall capital stock declines will depend on whether the supply of capital falls with a decline in the interest rate. But regardless of what happens to the overall capital stock, the corporate tax will cause a change in the capital stock's composition, driving capital out of the corporate sector and into other sectors not subject to that tax. The same logic applies to other tax measures that affect the user cost of capital, some of which we now consider.

TAX POLICY AND CAPITAL'S USER COST IN PRACTICE

Often the government seeks to influence the level and composition of investment by offering **investment incentives**—provisions that reduce a firm's taxes according to the amount of investment it undertakes. One of the most common investment incentives is the **investment tax credit**, which gives each investor a tax rebate equal to some fraction of the cost of newly purchased capital. A 7 percent investment tax credit was first introduced by President Kennedy in 1962. In the decades since, the credit has been temporarily suspended (in 1966), repealed (in 1969), reinstated (in 1971), increased to 10 percent (in 1974), and repealed again (in 1986).

Another investment incentive is **accelerated depreciation** allowances. The corporate income tax permits deductions for depreciation, called depreciation allowances. An accelerated depreciation program increases the deductions investors are permitted to take. The higher the firm's deductions, the lower its taxes.

Investment incentives affect the user cost of capital by reducing the taxes the firm must pay for each unit of capital it buys. This lowers the value of the tax component, τ, in the user cost formula, thereby lowering the user cost itself. Thus, the value of τ depends not only on the corporate tax rate, but also on the generosity of investment incentives. A low value of τ can be consistent with a high corporate tax rate if

Investment incentives
Tax subsidies designed to encourage particular types of investment spending

Investment tax credit
A provision in the tax code that gives an investor a tax rebate equal to some fraction of the cost of newly purchased capital

Accelerated depreciation
A provision in the tax code that increases the present value of deductions for depreciation by allowing firms to take the deductions soon after investment is undertaken

investment incentives are generous enough. Indeed, in the early 1980s, the value of τ for corporate investment in equipment was actually negative, despite a high corporate tax, because of the combined impact of accelerated depreciation and the investment tax credit.[4]

What purpose is served by simultaneously having tax provisions that raise and lower the corporate user cost of capital? There are two answers. First, the corporate income tax is levied on the income from all types of corporate capital, whereas investment incentives typically apply only to some types of corporate investment. For example, the investment tax credit has typically applied to purchases of machinery and equipment but not inventories or structures.

Second, the generational consequences of the policies differ. A corporate tax introduced in period t immediately lowers the income of the elderly in period t; an investment incentive introduced in period t offers a reduction in taxes only for those undertaking investment: the young in period t and future generations. Used in concert, then, the corporate income tax and the investment tax credit provide a way of increasing taxes on those currently holding assets in our model, the elderly, without necessarily altering the user cost of capital. Put another way, the government can preserve a tax on asset holders while lowering the user cost of capital if it uses investment incentives rather than reducing the corporate tax rate. This advantage of investment incentives is sometimes expressed in terms of their having a greater bang for the buck than cuts in the corporate tax rate, entailing a smaller loss in tax revenue to produce a given reduction in the user cost of capital.

CASE STUDY
HOUSING INVESTMENT IN THE 1980S

How significant have user cost of capital changes been in influencing the composition of investment? Changes in the tax treatment of housing in the 1980s offer a natural experiment. Over the years, many factors, such as the decline in the rate of household formation, have contributed to the reduced share of residential construction in total investment that was pictured in Figure 16.1. However, these factors determining the overall demand for housing have less impact on the type of housing built.

Housing construction includes both single-family houses and multifamily dwellings. The former, which account for the majority of residential construction, are primarily owned by their occupants, hence the term *owner-occupied housing*. Some multifamily housing units, condominiums, and cooperatives are also owner occupied, but rental units dominate this category. Thus, we can think of single-family houses as primarily owner occupied and multifamily housing as primarily rented.

The identity of a residence's owner matters because the tax system provides a significant benefit to owner occupation. Capital income in the United States, including the rental income from housing, is subject to the income tax, but the income from owner-occupied housing—the imputed rent discussed in chapter 5—is not. An

4 See Alan J. Auerbach, *"Corporate Taxation in the United States,"* Brookings Papers on Economic Activity *14 (1983): 451–505.*

income tax raises the user cost and reduces the quantity of capital demanded at any given interest rate, so this distinction makes the user cost of owning a house lower than the user cost of investing in a house that will be rented to others. However, the extent of the gap in user costs between owned and rented housing has changed over time, with two major changes occurring in the 1980s.

In 1981, accelerated depreciation allowances were introduced for investments in rental housing. They lowered the user cost of capital for rental housing and made it a relatively more attractive investment than owner-occupied housing, which was unaffected by this provision. In 1986, the accelerated depreciation provisions of 1981 were reversed, and other rules that were changed acted to increase the user cost of capital still further for rental housing. As Figure 16.3 shows, these two tax changes

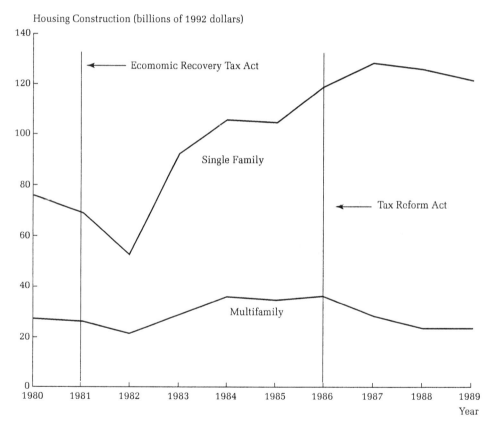

FIGURE 16.3 HOUSING CONSTRUCTION IN THE 1980S
Changes in accelerated depreciation allowances affected the patterns of housing investment during the 1980s. Allowances were increased for rental housing in 1981 and helped stabilize multifamily housing investment during the recession of 1982. Those provisions were reversed in 1986, and investment in multifamily housing fell despite a generally good economic climate.

Source: National Income and Product Accounts.

affected the pattern of housing investment during the 1980s. In the recession year of 1982, investment in single-family housing dropped sharply, whereas newly favored multifamily housing investment declined only slightly. In 1987, on the other hand, despite the generally good economic climate and the increase in single-family housing construction, multifamily housing construction fell. In short, the very different patterns observed in 1982 and 1987 are exactly what the user cost theory would predict.

A NOTE ON EXPECTATIONS

The user cost of capital indicates the rate of return that a firm's new investments must earn to break even, under any single set of tax rules. Matters become more complicated when the tax system changes over time. Anticipated future changes in tax policy can themselves influence current investment.

Take the investment tax credit, which has been altered several times since it was introduced in the United States in 1962. Often, changes in the credit were anticipated by investors even though they had not been announced in advance. In some cases, though, the impending changes were even built into law.

How do anticipated changes in the investment tax credit affect investment? An investment tax credit in itself reduces the user cost of capital and encourages investment. Knowledge that it will apply only temporarily provides a further spur to investment, as firms try to squeeze investment that they might have undertaken over the succeeding few years into the period when the credit applies. This makes the temporary investment tax credit an even more powerful tool for influencing investment in the short run than a permanent investment tax credit.[5]

A temporary tax credit has its costs too. Suppose the government alters the investment tax credit frequently. Firms anticipating that the government will introduce or increase the investment tax credit may delay some of their investment in order to have it qualify for the credit. This delay may be particularly severe at the onset of recessions, if firms anticipate that the government will introduce the investment tax credit as an antirecession device, as it often has. As a result, the temporary tax credit and other investment incentives may actually contribute to the instability of investment.

CORPORATE FINANCIAL POLICY

When a firm determines how much to invest, it must also decide on its *financial policy*—how to obtain the funds to pay for its investment. A firm's financial policy, and the constraints that it faces in setting such policy, may affect its cost of capital and therefore its level of investment.

Ultimately, any funds the firm obtains for investment must be provided by households that save. But financial intermediaries often play a role in bringing

5 Thus, if investment tax credits are usually temporary, they will be associated with larger swings in investment than if they were expected to be of more permanent duration. This illustrates the main point of the Lucas critique of stabilization policy that we discussed in chapter 11: we cannot know how policy will affect behavior unless we know what expectations are and how these expectations are influenced by the policy itself.

savers and investors together. Some funds come through loans from banks. Additional amounts are raised with the help of stockbrokers and investment bankers who sell the firm's *securities*—financial assets representing claims on the assets of the business—to savers in exchange for the funds. These securities can take the form of *stock*—each share of which represents ownership of a small part of the business—or *bonds*—essentially loans made by the household to the business. Stocks and bonds can be held directly by individual investors, or indirectly through *mutual funds*, which pool the securities of several firms. A firm's *debt* equals the sum of its bonds and bank loans; its *equity* equals the amount of stock outstanding. A key decision for the firm is determining the composition of its *capital structure*—how much of its investment to finance with debt and how much with equity.

DEBT-EQUITY DECISION

Equity ownership nominally provides a shareholder with voting power over a firm's management decisions. In practice, this power is so dispersed that the typical shareholder is essentially just a supplier of funds like a lender and should expect to receive the same rate of return from the firm, whether it comes in the form of interest or dividends. But if the firm must offer the same rate of return to suppliers of equity and debt, it is logical to ask whether it matters how firms obtain their funds. Indeed, one of the classic results in the field of financial economics, known as the **Modigliani-Miller theorem**, says that under certain conditions, the debt-equity choice is irrelevant precisely because neither firms nor those who supply funds care about the label given to the transaction between them.[6] Households or banks should require the same rate of return, regardless of whether the return comes in the form of interest payments or dividends. Given this requirement, choosing one method of finance instead of another offers firms no advantage or disadvantage in terms of their user cost of capital.

The Modigliani-Miller theorem is significant, but the conditions on which it is based are rarely satisfied. In particular, there are tax advantages to using debt finance, and there are reasons that debt finance may be disadvantageous or simply not feasible. As a result, corporate financial structure may have an important impact on the cost of capital and the investment behavior of individual firms as well as the economy's overall performance.

DEBT AND TAXES

A corporate income tax raises the user cost of capital because the corporation must pay a tax in addition to the return paid to its shareholders. However, the corporate income tax does not apply to the capital income earned by the corporation that it pays out in interest payments. That is, interest payments, like allowances for depreciation, are deducted from the income on which the corporation must pay tax.

The deductibility of interest reduces the tax component, τ, in the user cost formula presented earlier. Why, then, don't corporations rely solely on debt finance? There are several reasons. First, debt finance restricts the firm's flexibility, because by law interest payments are tax deductible only if they are fixed. Thus, during bad

---

Modigliani-Miller theorem
The proposition that the value of a firm is the same whether it is financed by debt or by equity

6 *The theorem takes its name from its two authors, Nobel laureates Franco Modigliani of MIT and Merton Miller of the University of Chicago.*

economic times, when its earnings may be low, an equity-financed corporation may reduce the dividend payments it makes. A debt-financed corporation can't do so. If required interest payments cannot be met, the debt-financed corporation may default on its debt and be forced into bankruptcy.

A second reason that firms may not rely on debt finance is that they may be subject to *credit rationing*. Financial markets operate poorly when information about the borrower is lacking. Untested firms may find lenders unwilling to commit funds or willing to lend only at very high interest rates. These firms may achieve a lower user cost of capital by relying on the funds they already have on hand, despite the tax benefits of debt finance. Rather than paying their current earnings out to existing shareholders as dividends, the firms can use these *retained earnings* to finance new investment. Such a strategy, called **internal finance**, increases the firm's equity.

Because of bankruptcy risk, credit rationing, and other factors, firms do rely heavily on equity finance despite the tax advantages of borrowing. However, there are major differences in financial structure across firms and, for the same firm, over the business cycle. In addition, financing patterns have changed over time.

CASE STUDY
INTEREST RATE SPREADS AND THE BUSINESS CYCLE

Interest rates faced by borrowers generally exceed those promised to lenders, reflecting the uncertainty about borrowers' prospects for repayment. Because lenders cannot perfectly separate bad credit risks from good, they must charge even some credit-worthy firms a higher interest rate. The greater the uncertainty, or the lower the average quality of firms, the higher the rate is that lenders must charge. Based on this logic, we would expect borrowing rates to vary among firms according to their perceived prospects, with firms classified as bad risks, or those whose prospects are unknown, facing higher borrowing rates, even if they are actually creditworthy.

One indicator of this variation in borrowing rates is the interest rate gap between bonds issued by blue chip companies and those issued by companies with less well-known prospects. The greater the gap called the *yield spread* between these two types of bonds, the less attractive debt finance will be for the riskier enterprises.

Figure 16.4 graphs the yield spread on corporate bonds since 1970. The spread is measured by the difference between the interest rate offered on bonds given an AAA rating (the safest) by Moody's Investors Service and those given a BAA rating (a much lower one). Yield spreads move with the business cycle, rising during recessions, as the prospects of riskier companies become more suspect. This is another reason that investment is sensitive to business cycle conditions: debt finance becomes less accessible to riskier companies.

The yield spread was highest in the 1980s, presumably reflecting the sharp increase in borrowing that occurred in that decade.

Internal finance
A firm's strategy of retaining its current earnings to finance new investment

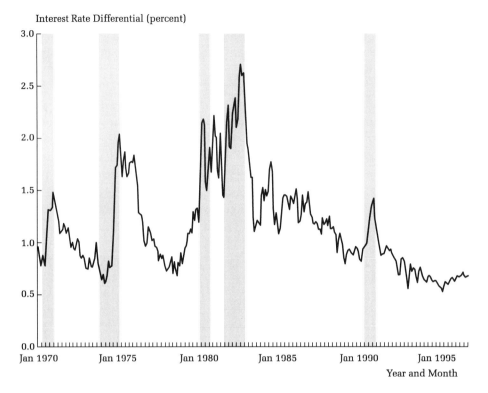

Interest Rate Differential (percent)

FIGURE 16.4 BOND YIELD SPREAD, 1970–1996

Borrowing rates vary among firms based on their perceived riskiness. One indicator of this variation is the interest rate gap between bonds issued by blue chip firms and those issued by less well-known firms. The yield spread moves with the business cycle, rising during recessions as riskier firms become more suspect.

Source: Economic Report of the President, *1997.*

CASE STUDY
CORPORATE BORROWING IN THE 1980S

The corporate income tax and the tax incentive for corporate borrowing date to 1909, but it was only in the 1980s that corporations began relying heavily on debt finance. Figure 16.5 shows the trend in the ratio of debt to capital (or assets) of the U.S. non-financial corporate sector since 1980. From 1980 to 1992, the ratio rose from 22.2 percent to 34.6 percent. During this period, the aggregate corporate capital stock actually fell in real (1992 dollars) terms—by $581 billion—even though real corporate debt rose by $963 billion. That is, in the aggregate, none of the debt raised during the period was actually needed to buy new capital. Instead, it went to redeem equity from shareholders, as corporations replaced equity with debt. Some of the replacement of debt for equity occurred as companies borrowed to repurchase their own stock. In other cases

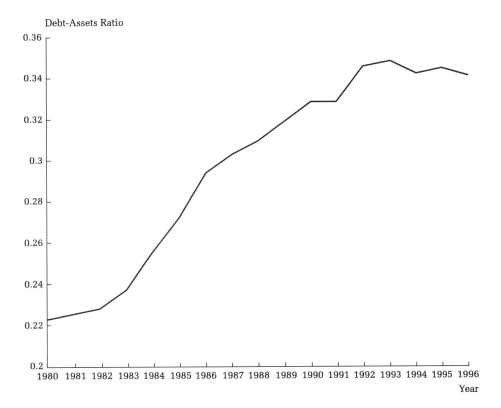

Debt-Assets Ratio

FIGURE 16.5 U.S. CORPORATE FINANCE SINCE 1980
In the 1980s, corporations began relying more heavily on debt finance than in the past. The ratio of debt to assets grew dramatically.

Source: Board of Governors, Federal Reserve System.

the equity disappeared through *leveraged buyouts*—transactions in which one company borrowed funds to purchase the equity of another company.

There are many theories as to why corporate borrowing increased, but it is difficult to find one that is entirely convincing. The tax advantage to borrowing existed before. Had the risks of bankruptcy suddenly fallen, we should have observed a decline in bankruptcies and business failures during this period and a drop in the yield spread between safe and risky firms. However, the yield spread rose in the 1980s. Furthermore, the rate of business failures actually rose sharply in the 1980s, reaching unprecedented postwar levels even during the long economic expansion that began in late 1982 and carried into 1990. This evidence does not support the hypothesis that reduced risk led to more borrowing, but seems merely to demonstrate that additional borrowing makes firms more likely to fail.

Should the heightened risk of business failure concern us? Some economists argue that higher levels of corporate debt increase the potential severity of recessions, because small initial reductions in income may set off a wave of business failures and further reductions in output and employment. However, the short and relatively mild recession of 1990–1991 does not seem to have borne out this concern. In any event, as data from the mid-1990s suggest, the surge in borrowing seems to have subsided, at least for the moment.

CASE STUDY
CREDIT CONSTRAINTS IN THE UNITED STATES AND JAPAN

Credit rationing limits the extent to which some firms can borrow. Such firms must rely on internal funds to finance their investment. This not only increases the share of equity in their financial structure but may also raise the volatility of their investment. A credit-constrained firm's investment is determined by its own current earnings, not the economy-wide level of income. And, as Figure 16.6 shows, corporate profits are far more volatile than income, as measured by GDP.

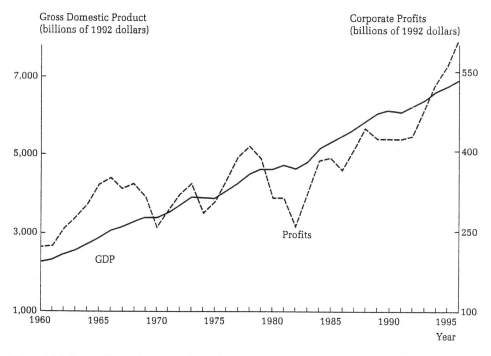

FIGURE 16.6 OUTPUT VERSUS PROFITS, 1960–1996
Credit rationing can make investment more volatile since a credit-constrained firm's investment is determined by its own earnings, not by aggregate income. Corporate profits are far more volatile than income, measured by GDP.

Source: National Income and Product Accounts.

What types of firms are credit constrained? The answer, at least in the United States, is small firms.[7] That's because smaller firms are often younger firms with less of a track record to show prospective lenders. In Japan, size isn't a central determinant of whether a firm relies on internal finance. The critical factor there seems to be the lack of affiliation with a *keiretsu*, a group of industrial firms tied together by their relationship to a main bank. Many firms in Japan, large and small, belong to such groups, centered around some of the world's largest banks.[8] Firms outside the groups must issue corporate debt and rely on various bank lenders for loans, much as U.S. companies do. Within the groups, however, firms obtain a considerable share of their debt through loans from a single bank, and even the smaller firms do not appear to experience credit rationing.

The *keiretsu* increases credit availability in two ways. First, it encourages the gathering and transmission of information about each member company's management and prospects. Second, it coordinates responses to financial distress. A U.S. bankruptcy might involve a protracted court proceeding pitting several different classes of lenders against one another. A member of a Japanese group, on the other hand, has one major lender well informed about the firm's problems and prospects. This improves the chances of reaching an agreement regarding the changes necessary for renewed success.[9]

The prevalence of industrial group membership in Japan, and the associated freedom from credit rationing, helps explain why Japanese firms, on average, have used a higher ratio of debt to equity finance than their U.S. counterparts.[10] Given the tax advantages to borrowing (similar in Japan to those in the United States), this higher debt-equity ratio may itself have led to a lower Japanese user cost of capital and contributed to Japan's higher rate of investment.

UNDERSTANDING INVESTMENT DYNAMICS

Investment is more volatile than total output. This fact has several complementary explanations. The accelerator theory shows that investment is related to changes in output, which vary more than the level of output itself. Credit rationing may become more severe during recessions. Firms dependent on internal funds will experience large swings in investment simply because of the volatility of corporate profits. In addition, changes in tax policy may actually destabilize investment. These factors explain the volatility of investment, regardless of type. However, other factors explain why certain types of investment are particularly volatile.

Figure 16.7 graphs the three types of nonresidential investment (structures, equipment, and inventories) for the period since 1960. For each type of investment, the graph shows real investment in each year as a share of real GDP. Aside from the general trend in business fixed investment away from structures and toward

7 See Steven M. Fazzari, R. Glenn Hubbard, and Bruce C. Petersen, "Financing Constraints and Corporate Investment," Brookings Papers on Economic Activity *19 (1988): 141–195.*

8 See Takeo Hoshi, Anil Kashyap, and David Scharfstein, "Corporate Structure, Liquidity, and Investment: Evidence from Japanese Industrial Groups," Quarterly Journal of Economics *106 (February 1991): 33–60.*

9 *Ibid. cites the case of Mazda, the large Japanese automobile manufacturer, which encountered serious financial problems in the 1970s. A member of the Sumitomo group, Mazda emerged from financial trouble under the leadership of one of the Sumitomo bank's managing directors.*

10 Albert Ando and Alan J. Auerbach, "The Cost of Capital in the United States and Japan," Journal of Japanese and International Economies *2 (1988): 134–158, found that Japanese debt-asset ratios were roughly double those in the United States until the 1980s.*

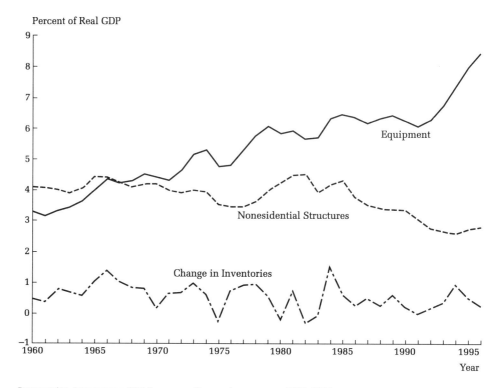

Percent of Real GDP

FIGURE 16.7 INVESTMENT-GDP RATIOS, BY TYPE OF INVESTMENT, 1960–1996
Of the various types of investment, inventory investment is the most volatile and structures investment the least. Fluctuations are also influenced by tax policies. Structures investment peaked in 1982, just after the introduction of enhanced depreciation provisions.

Source: National Income and Product Accounts.

equipment, the figure shows evidence of the impact of tax policies on investment. For example, structures investment reached its highest value in 1982, the year after accelerated depreciation was greatly enhanced.

Figure 16.7 also exhibits the differing volatility of the types of investment. One measure of volatility is the range in year-to-year changes in the investment-GDP ratio. By this measure, inventory investment is by far the most volatile, with the annual changes in its ratio to GDP ranging between -1.0 and $+1.6$ percent. The range of values for equipment investment ($-.5$ percent to $+.6$ percent) suggests slightly more volatility than those for structures investment ($-.6$ percent to $+.4$ percent). The volatility of inventory investment means that, despite its small share of investment in a typical year, it accounts for a significant share of the swings in investment over the business cycle.

The different cyclical behavior of inventories and other types of investment may be explained by technical factors that influence firms' responses to changes in user cost. By its nature, fixed investment in equipment and structures is subject to constraints on how fast and by how much firms can invest in response to changes in the amount of capital they wish to have. Economists characterize these constraints in terms of **irreversibility**—the difficulty in disposing of capital goods once they have been purchased—and **adjustment lags**—the delays firms encounter in altering their investment plans.

IRREVERSIBILITY

In our two-period life-cycle model, we may think of the existing capital stock as being consumed by the old at the end of each period, with new capital being accumulated by the young. Because these two acts are separate, it is entirely feasible for the young to accumulate less capital than the old generation consumes. In the actual economy, this represents an accurate description of inventory investment. Inventories are continually being turned over, as the existing stock of goods held in inventory is used up and replaced. Even if the number of shirts held in a retailer's inventory is the same at the end of a year as at the beginning, they are not the same shirts. Hence, there is no reason that the business cannot reduce its shirt inventory. If it wishes to do so, it simply does not replace every shirt it sells from inventory.

Unlike inventories, fixed capital goods are not used up each year. Under normal circumstances, this distinction is not important. In our model, rather than consuming their capital goods directly, the old could sell their capital to the young, who would purchase less new capital and provide the old with the funds necessary to finance their consumption. But this means that the capital stock the young carry into the next period must be at least as large as that being sold by the old. Put another way, gross investment—the amount of new capital purchased—cannot be negative. We characterize this restriction by saying that fixed investment is *irreversible*.

Irreversibility doesn't mean that net fixed investment must be positive. Recall that net investment, $K_{t+1} - K_t$, equals gross investment, I_t, less depreciation, D_t. If gross investment is small enough, net investment will be negative. In fact, net fixed investment in the United States has been negative at times, during both the Depression and World War II, when government absorption of funds (represented in our model by a high value of F_t) *crowded out* private investment.

How, then, does irreversibility help explain why net investment is usually positive? In an economy experiencing shifts in production among several sectors, irreversibility may constrain some sectors without affecting others. Even in a declining economy, some industries' output may rise, and with it their demand for capital. Since each type of gross investment is subject to its own irreversibility constraint, the types of capital in increased demand (say, computers) will experience positive gross investment even as there is zero gross investment in other types of capital (for example, coal furnaces in North Dakota). Thus, gross investment will be positive in the aggregate, even during recessions, making it more likely that net investment will be positive too.

What types of fixed investment would be most subject to the irreversibility constraint? Aside from those used in declining industries, we normally expect long-lived capital goods, particularly structures, to be most susceptible. Capital goods that

Irreversibility
The difficulty of reversing an investment once it has been initiated

Adjustment lag
A delay in the response that brings investment to its desired level

depreciate rapidly (like trucks or computers) can experience quite negative *net* investment while gross investment is still positive. This helps explain why, even during booms in which investment as a whole is strong, certain types of investment may not be.

CASE STUDY
THE EMPTY OFFICE BUILDINGS

According to Figure 16.7 investment in nonresidential structures was weak in the boom years of the late 1980s. Rather than looking at conditions that prevailed during this period for an explanation, many economists blame the strong investment in structures that occurred during the early 1980s.

Legislative changes in 1981 provided investment incentives in the form of accelerated depreciation. The incentives applied not only to multifamily rental housing, which we have already considered, but also to business fixed investment. In the case of commercial office buildings, the interaction of accelerated depreciation with other tax provisions transformed such investments into *tax shelters*—investments that provided wealthy individuals with large tax deductions against their other income. This possibility for tax shelters sparked a boom in the construction of commercial buildings. But as Figure 16.8 shows, the building was excessive. The vacancy rate of office space grew throughout the early 1980s, as more and more office space became available.

The Tax Reform Act of 1986 eliminated not only accelerated depreciation but also the other provisions that gave rise to tax shelter opportunities. This reform raised the user cost of capital for nonresidential structures, making investors less interested in owning such structures. But the scores of modern office buildings that had been accumulated in the early 1980s, with the expectation that beneficial tax provisions would be maintained, did not disappear; their construction was irreversible. This excess capacity inhibited additional commercial building as the rest of the economy boomed. Despite several years of reduced construction activity, the vacancy rate in 1989 remained well above its level of the early 1980s. Then it began to rise again, as the recession of 1990–1991 took its toll on the demand for office space.

ADJUSTMENT LAGS

Even when irreversibility is not an issue, firms are still constrained in how fast they can respond to changing investment incentives. It is relatively simple to purchase more computers or stock more shirts in inventory as income rises. However, building an extra factory, office building, or nuclear power plant takes time, generally years, to complete. We refer to the delayed response in bringing investment to its desired level as an *adjustment lag*.

Adjustment lags exist because it is difficult to make large changes in the capital stock immediately. In economic terms, rapid capital stock adjustment is costly. Very

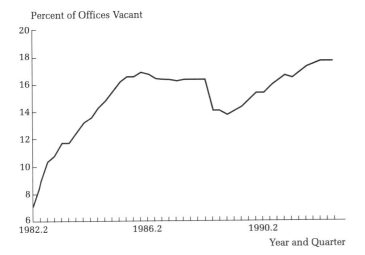

Percent of Offices Vacant

Year and Quarter

FIGURE 16.8 OFFICE VACANCY RATES IN U.S. DOWNTOWNS, APRIL 1982–OCTOBER 1992

The investment incentives of the early 1980s led to increased commercial construction and a rise in office vacancy rates. This excess capacity remained in place even after the Tax Reform Act of 1986 discouraged holding of such property. Even with a sharp drop in new construction in the late 1980s, vacancy rates remained high and the need for new investment remained low.

Source: Coldwell Banker Commercial.

rapid adjustment may be possible but too expensive to justify under normal economic circumstances. For example, it might be possible to build a new factory in a year, rather than two, by hiring more construction workers and paying them overtime wages to work longer hours, but this would increase production costs. Unless having the building completed a year earlier increases the firm's earnings sufficiently, it will not elect the faster, costlier production schedule.

With production lags, firms will not instantaneously equate the marginal product of capital to the user cost of capital. Instead, they will only gradually adjust their capital stock in the direction dictated by the user cost. Adjustment costs make the investment process more complicated to explain, but they also give rise to a model, called *Tobin's q-theory* of investment, that helps us describe this process.

CASE STUDY

INVESTMENT AND THE STOCK MARKET: TOBIN'S *q*-THEORY

How can we predict the pattern of investment in the presence of adjustment costs? Nobel laureate James Tobin of Yale University reasoned that as investment booms confront the costs of adjustment, the full unit cost of acquiring and installing capital, which he called *q*, should be higher.[11] Testing **Tobin's q-theory** requires a measure of *q*, which includes all the costs of overtime, retraining, work disruptions, and so forth

Tobin's *q*-theory
The proposition that the rate of investment depends on the ratio of the market value of capital to its replacement cost

11 James Tobin, "A General Equilibrium Approach to Monetary Theory," Journal of Money, Credit, and Banking *1 (February 1969): 15–29.*

FIGURE 16.9 INVESTMENT AND THE VALUE OF U.S. NONFINANCIAL CORPORATIONS, 1987–1996
According to the q-theory, investment booms should be accompanied by rises in the stock market. The data offer only mixed support for this. While investment has generally followed the stock market since 1990, it was stronger in the late 1980s than the stock market would have predicted.

Source: Board of Governors, Federal Reserve System.

associated with the construction and absorption of new plant and equipment. Fumio Hayashi of Columbia University had an insight about how to arrive at such a measure.[12] Whenever investment becomes more expensive for a firm to undertake, the comparable capital goods the firm already has in place will rise in value, because having them available saves the firm from incurring the costs of new investment. We may be able to discern changes in the value of a firm's physical assets by looking at changes in what people are willing to pay for the firm—its value in the stock market.

Simply put, this interpretation of Tobin's q-theory says that investment booms should be accompanied by rises in the stock market, other things being equal. It also has the important implication that firms, seeking a signal from financial markets regarding how much they should invest, need only look at the performance of their company's stock. If their stock is highly valued, they should increase their investment.

Figure 16.9 puts this theory to the test, plotting real net investment by the U.S. corporate sector (excluding farms and financial businesses) against a measure of Tobin's q: the aggregate value of these corporations' debt plus equity, divided by their

12 Fumio Hayashi, "Tobin's Marginal q and Average q: A Neoclassical Interpretation," *Econometrica* 50 (January 1982): 213–224.

assets. The figure offers only mixed support for the q-theory. During the period beginning in 1990, the stock market and investment moved together fairly well. However, during the late 1980s, investment performance was better than the stock market would have indicated.

What can we conclude from this evidence? Perhaps the q-theory does not explain changes in investment behavior. Alternatively, the theory may apply, but stock market value may not be a very accurate measure of the value of the firm's capital stock. Indeed, the question of whether the stock market tracks the underlying value of corporate assets—whether it reflects "market fundamentals"—is a controversial one in the field of financial economics.

Many economists accept the central hypothesis underlying empirical tests of the q-theory: that the stock market accurately reflects the value of the firm. This **efficient markets hypothesis** says that at any given time, the stock market value of a firm represents the value of that firm's underlying assets, based on all information currently available. But others question whether such a hypothesis is plausible, arguing that daily movements in the stock market are far too large to be justified by changes in the underlying value of corporate assets. Perhaps the best evidence here is the stock market crash of October 1987, when the market lost roughly one-fifth of its value in a single day. Was there an underlying 20 percent reduction in the value of corporate assets that just happened to come to the light that day? Few economists think so. Not surprisingly, then, corporate investment showed little response to the stock market crash. Hence, although costs of adjustment may be important and the q-theory itself may be valid, the stock market may not provide a very good indicator of q or of how much firms should invest.

CHAPTER SUMMARY

1. This chapter described how businesses determine their investment, how this investment is financed, and how it's influenced by government policy.

2. The composition of U.S. investment has changed over time, reflecting both the changing economy and government policy. Computers and information processing equipment now account for about one-fifth of all gross investment in the United States. As the population has aged and the rate of family formation has declined, housing construction has receded in importance. However, housing investment has been buoyed by the favorable tax treatment accorded owner-occupied housing.

3. Nonresidential investment frequently has been the focus of changes in the corporate tax and in investment incentives, notably the investment tax credit and

Efficient markets hypothesis
The proposition that the stock market value of a firm reflects the true value of that firm's underlying assets based on all available information

accelerated depreciation. The effects of these provisions are summarized by the user cost of capital, which indicates the marginal product of capital the investing firm must earn in order to cover all the costs of using capital in production.

4. Changes in taxation can affect aggregate investment only to the extent that they alter aggregate saving. However, tax provisions that affect only some types of investment also influence the composition of investment. The frequency with which some tax provisions have been changed highlights the importance of investor expectations and the potential of policy to be destabilizing.

5. Although they are equal in the aggregate, investment and saving are typically distinct acts undertaken by different parties. Directly or through the banking system, households supply funds to the businesses that actually undertake investment. Through its financial policy, each firm makes several decisions regarding how to obtain the funds it needs for investment, including the appropriate mix of debt and equity and the extent to which it will rely on internal finance.

6. Although the Modigliani-Miller theorem cautions that financial policy is relevant only to the extent that there are underlying differences among methods of finance, such differences are indeed present. The corporate tax system provides a tax benefit for the use of debt finance that lowers the user cost of capital for debt-financed investment. This benefit must be weighed against the reduced flexibility that fixed interest payments impose on the firm.

7. Riskier firms may be credit constrained, able to borrow only at very high interest rates, and thus forced to depend on internal finance. Dependence on internal finance influences not only the level of a firm's investment but also the investment's cyclical volatility.

8. The volatility of investment also depends on technological factors, the irreversibility of fixed investment, and lags in the investment process that help to explain why inventory investment exhibits much wider swings than fixed investment. With these technological constraints on investment, firms cannot follow the simple rule of equating instantaneously the marginal product of capital to its user cost.

9. Tobin's q-theory of investment suggests that firms facing adjustment costs can take movements in their stock prices as indicators of how much to invest. This is a useful approach only if a firm's stock price reflects the underlying value of that firm's assets, as dictated by the efficient markets hypothesis, the accuracy of which remains hotly disputed.

Index

Accelerated depreciation, 440–443
Accelerator, 107
Accessions (employment), 267–269
Accumulating capital. *See* Investment
Activist policy, 295–319
    challenges, 306–315
    exchange rates, 360–365
    questionability, 317–318
Actual real interest rates, 134
AD curve, 224–226. *See also* Aggregate demand
Adjustment
    for inflation, 127
    lags, 451–453
    prices and wages, 202–205
Adverse selection, 416
African Americans in labor force, 279
Age. *See* Generations
Aggregate demand, 201, 224–226
    demand-supply diagram, 201
        stagflation, 310
    overcoming lack of (*see* Fiscal policy)
    Phillips curve and, 231–232
    unemployment and, 210–212
Aggregate supply, 201, 221–223
    demand-supply diagram, 201
        stagflation, 310
    Phillips curve and, 231–232
Aggregate uncertainty, 415–416
Altonji, Joseph, 423
Altruism, 422–423
Ando, Albert, 29
Animal spirits, 230
Annuities, 420–422
Anticipated inflation, costs, 297–298
Appreciations, 348
Argentina
    peso of (case study), 364–365
    Phillips curve of (case study), 242
AS curve, 221–223. *See also* Aggregate supply
Asset accumulation, 330. *See also* Investment
    decline in saving and (case studies), 46–48, 155–156,
        332–335
Assets, 31
ATMs (automatic teller machines), 178
Autarky, 326
Automatic stabilizers, 305

Balance sheets, 382, 384–386
Banks
    ATMs (automatic teller machines), 178
    bank notes, 175
    bank runs, 175, 404–408
        Great Depression (case study), 406
    borrowing funds from Fed, 391–393
    deposit insurance, 404–408
    as financial intermediaries, 384–386
    regulating, 407
    reserves, 384–386, 393–394
Barro, Robert, 421
Barter system, 171
Base year, 125, 129
Becker, Gary, 421
Beliefs in money, 173–176
Bequests, 417–423
Big Mac prices, international (case study), 352, 354–355
Bills of exchange, 175
Bismarck, 158–162
Black markets in foreign exchange, 349
Black Plague (case study), 70–73
Blacks in labor force, 279
BLS price index, 242
Bonds (for deficit finance), 156–158, 444
    for G-5 countries, 327–329
    indexed, 135
    surprise inflation and, 194–195
    U.S. Treasury bonds, 391–393
    yield spread, 445
Borrowing, 55, 156–158. *See also* Bonds
    corporate, in 1980s (case study), 446–448
    credit cards, 178
    credit markets, 423–430
    Federal Reserve discount window, 391–393
    lending rates and, 427
    taxes and, 444–445
Budget
    budget constraints
        generational differences, 67
        indifference curves, 44
        intertemporal budget constraint, 142, 144–145
        lifetime budget constraint, 37–39
        money and, 179–181
        transitions in generational policy, 153
        uncertainty on saving and capital formation, 412–415

Budget (cont.)
budget deficit, 128, 142
unexpected inflation and, 194–195
generational accounting, 141, 146–150, 157
economic transitions and, 153–155
United States (case study), 147–150
Bureau of Labor Statistics (BLS), 242
Bush, George, 307
Business confidence, 257–259, 302, 312
beliefs in money, 173–176
fixed exchange rates, 367
Business cycles, 85–88
anatomy of, 90–94
consumer and business confidence, 257–259, 302, 312
interest rate spreads and, 445
international correlation, 99–100
political business cycle theory, 230, 259
questioning cyclic pattern, 102–104
real business cycle theory, 85, 104–109, 243–249, 261
unemployment and, 245
seasonal adjustments, 101
turning points, 93–94
volatility, 86–90
major industry and, 91
World War II (case study), 89
Business fixed investment, 434
Business structures, 8

California, recession in (case study), 92–93
Capacity utilization, 98
Capital, 6
accumulating (see Investment)
age transition and, 50
capacity utilization, 98
Cobb-Douglas production function, 6–8
demand, 57–59
diminishing returns, 8, 16
embodied/disembodied productivity changes, 12
government formation, 163–164
government-owned, consumption of, 121–122
human capital, 31, 56
importing, 334
labor and (see Capital-labor ratio)
marginal product/cost, 57–58
measuring, 8–10
quality, 12, 21
structures, 54–56, 444
supply, 34–36
user cost, 433, 436
corporate income tax, 437–439
tax policy, 440–443
Capital deepening, 19
Capital income, 33
housing investment and, 441–443
Capital-labor ratio. See also Cobb-Douglas production function
bequests and, 418

Black Plague and (case study), 70–73
demand for money and, 183–188
deriving IS-LM diagram, 206
diminishing returns, 8, 16
interest rates and, 58
modeling growth (see Economic growth)
post-WWII Japan and Germany (case study), 68–70
restricting foreign investment, 335–337
tracking, 74–78
transition path, 73–78
uncertainty on saving, 412–415
United States vs. Japan, 326–329
worldwide, 329–335
Capital requirements, 407
Capital stock, 65
ownership, 31
war and (case study), 68–70
Carroll, Christopher, 429
Carter, Jimmy, 403
Case studies
altruism across extended families, 423
annuitization (U.S.), 420
Argentine peso, 364–365
Black Plague, 70–73
budget deficits (U.S.), 143–144
business cycle volatility and WWII, 89
California's recession, 92–93
consumer and business confidence, 257–259
corporate borrowing (1980s), 446–448
currency of India, 176
decline in U.S. saving, 46–48, 155–156, 332–335
deflation, U.S. (1865–1879), 187
empty office buildings, 452
European monetary integration, 372–373
exchange rates (U.S.), 349
fast-food industry wages, 273
financing social security (U.S.), 218–219
generational accounts (U.S.), 147–150
German hyperinflation, 182
government investment (U.S.), 163–164
Great Depression
deposit insurance, 406
monetary control, 399–401
monetary policy, 300–306
growth (U.S.), sources of, 14–16
housing investment, 441–443
interest rates and business cycles, 445
intergenerational transfers and U.S. wealth, 419
lotteries, 40
magazine prices, 203
money shocks and U.S. output, 254
money supply targeted by Fed, 401–403
monies (U.S.), 174–176
Norwegian saving, 428
oil price shocks, 247–249, 309–312
ownership of U.S. private capital stock, 31–32

Phillips curves, comparing internationally, 242
post-WWII capital deepening (case study), 68–70
Presidential election (U.S., 1992), recession and, 307
privatizing social security, 161–162
productivity growth, 12–13
real GDP measurement biases, 130–131
sales tax, 115–116
S&L crisis (1980s), 408
small business and job creation, 269
stock market and investment, 453–455
trade deficit since 1980 (U.S.), 123
trade surplus and saving (U.S.), 335
UI as cause of unemployment, 285
unemployment, U.S. and Europe, 290–292
unexpected inflation (U.S.), 195
wage adjustment process, 203–205
wages and prices freeze (1971), 317
worldwide demographic transition, 48–50
Chain weighting, 130
Checking accounts. *See* Demand deposits
Child-parent relationships. *See* Generations
China, 25
Civil War (U.S.), monies and, 175
Clinton, Bill, 203
Closed economies, 46
Closed economy, recovering from wars, 337–341
Cobb, Charles, 7
Cobb-Douglas production function, 6–8
    intensive form, 16
    marginal products and, 57
    money, 181–183
Collective bargaining, 202–203
Commodity standards, 350–351
Commodity substitution, 127
Compound interest, 40
Confidence, 302, 312
    beliefs in money, 173–176
    business cycle and, 257–259
    fixed exchange rates, 367
Constant returns to scale, 8
Constraints, credit, 427–430
Consumer confidence, 257–259, 302, 312
    fixed exchange rates, 367
Consumer durables, 7
Consumer Price Index (CPI), 125–131
Consumption, 34, 62. *See also* Capital; Expenditures; Saving
    credit-constrained (case study), 429
    deciding to save, 41–45
    decline in U.S. saving (case studies), 46–48, 155–156, 332–335
    demand for money and, 181–183
    distortionary fiscal policy, 165
    generational differences, 67
    government, financing, 152
    government-owned capital goods, 121–122
    investment vs., 119–120
    lifetime budget constraint, 37–39

printing money for, 188–192
    smoothing, 107
    technology shocks and, 107
    volatility, 98–99
Continentals, 175
Contractionary fiscal policy, 311–312
Contracts on wages/prices, 252
Convergence of economy, 64–66
Coordination failures, 230, 254–259, 261
Corporate borrowing in 1980s (case study), 446–448
Corporate financial policy, 443–449
Corporate income tax, 437–439
Corporate profits, 57, 115
Cost of Living Council, 317
Costs
    financial intermediaries and transactions, 381
    foreign currency transactions, 365
    government intervention, 296–299
    unemployment, 280–286
Countercyclical stabilization policy, 295–319
    costs and benefits, 296–299
    exchange rates, 360–365
    during Great Depression, 299–306
CPI (Consumer Price Index), 125–131
    biases in and reform, 127–129
Credit
    constraints/controls, 427–430, 448–449
    demand, 424
    markets for, 423–430
    rationing, 445
Credit cards, 178
Crime as unemployment, 283
Crowding out, 123, 216, 451
Currency. *See* Money
Currency substitution, 174
Current Population Study, 95

Day care, 135
de Hoz, Martinez, 364
Death, bequests at, 417, 419–421
Debt, 444
    debt-equity decision, 444
    taxes and, 444–445
    unexpected inflation and, 194–195
Deficits. *See also* Borrowing
    budget deficits, 128, 142
        unexpected inflation and, 194–195
        United States (case study), 143–144
    financing, 156–158 (*see also* Borrowing)
    full employment deficit, 306
    trade deficit, 122–124, 323
        foreign investment, 324–329
        Japan after WWII (case study), 340
        national saving and, 122
        United States (since 1980), 123
        worldwide transition, 332

Deflation, 180
    in United States, 186–188
Deflator, GDP, 131, 169
Demand
    credit, 424
    labor and capital, 56–59 (*see also* Capital-labor ratio; Labor)
        interest and wage rates, 59
    money, 181–183, 206
        inflation and, 193
        interest rate sensitivity, 216–217
        LM curve for (*see* LM curve)
        transition equation, 183–188
Demand deposits, 169, 384–386
Demographic transition in age, 48–50
Deposit insurance, 404–408
    establishment of (case study), 406
    moral hazard of, and regulation, 407
Depreciation, 348
    accelerated, 440
    NDP (net domestic product), 117–118
    user cost of capital, 436
Devaluations, 348
Developed/developing countries, 24–26
Diamond, Peter, 256
Diminishing returns, 8, 16
Disability insurance. *See* Social security
Discount rate, 393–394
Discount window (Fed.), 391–393
Discounting, 40
Discouraged workers, 289
Disembodied productivity, 12
Disguised unemployment, 289
Disposable income, 118. *See also* Income
Dissaving. *See* Saving
Distorted markets, 136
Distortionary fiscal policy, 165
Diversifying risk, 382
Dividends, 55, 118
Dollars. *See* Money
Domestic investment, 47, 324–325
Domestic net worth, 31
Domestic price levels, 356–358
Domestic product. *See* GDP
Douglas, Paul, 7
Downward nominal rigidity, 204
Durable goods, 120–121
Duration
    business cycles, 86
    unemployment, 270–271, 280, 285
Dynamic input supplies, 34–37
Dynamic (time) inconsistency, 313–315

Economic fluctuations, 86–90
    anatomy of, 90–94
    explaining, 98–104
    fiscal policy and, 150–156

    fixed exchange rates, 371–372
    monetary aggregates and multipliers, 396 (*see also* Multipliers)
    questioning cyclic pattern, 102–104
    real business cycle theory, 85, 104–109, 243–249, 261
    seasonal adjustments on, 101
    supply-side shocks and, 243–249
Economic growth, 4, 13–16
    developing vs. developed countries, 24–26
    endogenous growth, 26, 79–80
    fluctuations (*see* Economic fluctuations)
    generational differences, 66–77
    growth accounting, 14–16
    modeling, 60–62
    monetary aggregates and, 395–403
    policy and (*see* Policy)
    population growth, 49–50
    of price level, 186–188
    social security and, 158
    speed of, 64
    technology (*see* Technology)
    tracking (numerical example), 62–64
    transition equation (*see* Transition equation/path)
    unemployment rate and, 286–289
    U.S. slowdown/performance, 18–24
Economic models, xvii
    endogenous growth models, 26, 79–80
    Keynesian model, 201
        developing, 205–210 (*see also* Keynesian model)
    life-cycle model (*see* Life-cycle model)
    modeling growth, 60–62
    money, 179–183 (*see also* Money)
    New Keynesians (*see* New Keynesians)
    population and technological change, 78–80
    random walk theory, 103
    recessions
        New Keynesian models, 251–259, 261
        political business cycles, 259, 261
        real business cycle theory, 85, 104–109, 243–249, 261
        sectoral shift model, 249–251, 261
    social security, 159–161
    theories of unemployment, 272–276
    two-country model, 329–335
Economic policy. *See* Policy
Economic theories, evaluating, xviii
Economy
    changes in time, 64
    imperfect information, 309–312
    industrial vs. service, 20
    international (*see* Open economies)
    misperception theory, 229–230, 239–243, 261
        unemployment under, 275
    multiple equilibria, 256
    steady state, 65–66, 78–80
    underground (unreported), 136
Efficiency wage theory, 272–273
Efficient markets hypothesis, 455

Elderly, 35. *See also* Generations
    annuities, 420–422
    increasing money of (*see* Fiscal policy)
    life span uncertainty, 419
    printing money for, 188–190
Embodied productivity, 12
Employment. *See also* Labor (labor force); Unemployment
    age and race distinctions, 278–280
    aggregate demand and, 210–212
    costs of unemployment, 280–286
    definitions for employed, unemployed, 96
    frictional, 236, 275–276, 290
        unfixed (nonconstant), 249–251
    full employment deficit, 306
    full employment output, 210–212
    gender differences, 277
    hoarding labor, 97, 288
    hours worked, 96
    human capital, 31, 56
    increasing, benefits of, 286–292
    inflation and (*see* Phillips curve)
    job vacancy rate, 251
    misperception theory and, 240–241, 275
    nature of unemployment, 265–294
    nominal wage rigidity and, 219–221
    nonmarket activities, 135–136
    participation rate, 96, 266
    real business cycles (*see* Real business cycle theory)
    small businesses (case study), 269
    theories of unemployment, 272–276
    transitions into/out of, 267–269
    UI (unemployment insurance), 284–286
        as cause of unemployment (case study), 285
    unemployment rate, 94–98
    wage adjustment process (case study), 203–205
Employment-population ratio, 10
Empty office buildings (case study), 452
Endogenous growth, 26, 79–80
Endogenous monetary supply, 403–404
England. *See* United Kingdom
Environment damage, 136
Epidemics (plagues)
    capital-labor ratio and, 70–73
    transition path diagrams, 76
Equilibrium, 53
    steady state, 65–66, 78–80
    wage and interest rates, 59
Equipment, 8
Equity, 55
    debt-equity decision, 444
    leveraged buyouts, 447
ERM (exchange rate mechanism), 349, 366
Europe
    exchange rates (case study), 349
    monetary integration (case study), 372–373
    unemployment in (case study), 290–292

Excess burden on taxation, 297–298
Excess reserves, 385
Exchange rates, 347–351
    under commodity standards, 350–351
    ERM (exchange rate mechanism), 349
    flexible vs. fixed, 348, 361, 363–367
    managing, 360–365
    money supply and, 359
    output fluctuations, 371–372
    price levels and, 356–358
    real vs. nominal, 352–353
Expansions, economic, 4, 85–88
Expectations of tax policy changes, 443
Expected real interest rates, 134
Expenditures, government, 142–144. *See also* Consumption
    capital formation, 163–164
    financing, 152, 391
    nonindexed, 195
    valuing, 135–136
Experiments to evaluate theories, xviii
Exponents, 82–83
Exports/imports, 323
    capital imports, 334
    trade balance (*see* Trade deficit; Trade surplus)
Extended families and altruism (case studies), 423

Factor incomes method, 113
Factor price equalization, 326–329
    two-country model, 329–335
Fast-food industry wages (case study), 273
FDIC (Federal Deposit Insurance Corporation), 406
    bank regulation, 407
Federal funds rate, 393–394
Federal Home Loan Bank Board (FHLBB), 408
Federal Reserve System (Fed), 98, 175, 379–380
    choosing targets, 399–403
    controlling money supply, 395–404
    discount window (Treasury bonds), 391–393
    M1–M3 aggregates (*see* Monetary aggregates)
    monetary policy, 388–394
Female-male comparison. *See* Gender differences
Fertility rate, U.S., 48–50
FHLBB (Federal Home Loan Bank Board), 408
Fiat money, 175
Final goods and services, 112
Final sales method, 113
Financial assets, 31
Financial intermediaries, 379, 381–383
    banks as, 384–386 (*see also* Banks)
    deposit insurance, 404–408
    liabilities, 382–383
        bank runs, 404–408
    transaction costs, 381
Financial liability, 31
Financial policy, 443–449
Financial securities, 391–393, 420–422, 444

Financing social security (case study), 218–219
Firms, 54–56
First Bank of the United States, 175
First-period saving, 45
Fiscal policy, 141–167, 214–216. *See also* Activist policy;
        Policy
    contractionary, 311–312
    dealing with sectoral shifts, 251
    deficit finance, 156–158 (*see also* Borrowing)
    distortionary, 165
    economic transitions and, 150–156
    generational accounting, 141, 146–150, 157
        economic transitions and, 153–155
        United States (case study), 147–150
    Great Depression, 299–306
    information-unemployment trade-off, 231
    intertemporal budget constraint, 142, 144–145, 153
    measuring effectiveness, 216–217
    monetary policy and, 170–171
    natural rate of unemployment and, 290
    open economies, 341–343
    politics and, 259–260
    printing money, 188–192 (*see also* Money supply)
    rational expectations theory, 237–239
    social security (*see* Social security)
    speed of enacting, 308
    taxes (*see* Taxes)
    value-added tax, 115–116
    wage rigidity and, 221–224
Fisher, Irving, 132
Fisher equation, 132
Fixed exchange rates, 348, 361
    commodity standards, 350–351
    limited international reserves, 366–367
    monetary policy, 362–364, 370
    monetary policy independence, 366
    output fluctuations, 371–372
    speculations against, 367
    switching to flexible rates, 364
Flexibility, price, 202–205
Flexible exchange rates, 348, 361
    monetary policy, 361, 363, 370
    output fluctuations, 371–372
    switching to fixed rates, 364
    transaction costs, 365
Flow variables, 10
Fluctuations. *See* Economic fluctuations
Ford, Gerald, 311–312
Ford, Henry, 273
Foreign investment, 47, 122–124, 331
    recovering from wars, 337–341
    restriction costs, 335–337
    trade deficit and, 324–329
Foreign price levels, 356–358
Foreshadowing business cycles, 93–94
Formation of capital. *See* Investment

France
    bond interest rates, 327–329
    European monetary integration (case study), 372–373
    exchange rates (case study), 349
    independent monetary policy, 366
Frequency of business cycles, 86
Frictional unemployment, 236, 275–276, 290
    unfixed (nonconstant), 249–251
Friedman, Milton, 235, 300, 399
Full employment deficit, 306
Full employment output, 210–212
Fully flexible prices, 202–205

G-5 countries, 327
Gains from trade, 337
GDP (gross domestic product), 3
    components, 119–122
    deflator (normal vs. real GDP), 131, 169
    developing vs. developed countries, 24–26
    fluctuations in, 86–90
    increases in (*see* Economic growth)
    measuring, 112–116, 135–137
    per capita, 5
    real GDP, 129–131
    seasonal adjustments on, 101
    unemployment rate vs., 286–289
    U.S. slowdown in growth, 18–22
    voluntary unemployment and, 281
Gender differences
    employment, 277–278
    generational accounting (U.S.), 147–150
    labor force and unemployment, 277
General equilibrium, 53
General Motors, 54
Generational accounting, 141, 146–150
    deficit finance vs., 157
    economic transitions and, 153–155
    social security (*see* Social security)
    United States (case study), 147–150
Generational policy. *See* Fiscal policy
Generations
    differences between
        budget constraints, 67
        consumption, 67
        demand for money, 181–182
        employment status, 278–280
        growth and, 66–77
        input supply and, 34–37
        lifetime budget constraint, 37–39
        MRS and, 43
        social security (*see* Social security)
        worldwide demographic transition, 48–50
    intergenerational altruism, 422–423
    intergenerational transfers (bequests), 417–423
    intragenerational transfers, 165
        social security benefits, 162

life span uncertainty, 419
pooling risks across, 416
printing money for elderly/young, 188–192
redistribution policy among, 417
Germany
age transition in, 48–50
bond interest rates, 327–329
European monetary integration (case study), 372–373
exchange rates (case study), 349
hyperinflation in, 173–174, 182
independent monetary policy, 366
post-WWII capital deepening (case study), 68–70
GIBC (government intertemporal budget constraint), 142, 144–145
transitions in generational policy, 153
Gifts, 421
Glass-Steagall Act of 1993, 407
GNP (gross national product), 116
Gold standard, 176–177
fixed exchange rates, 350–351
Goods. *See also* Services
barter system, 171
commodity substitution, 127
distortionary fiscal policy, 165
durable, 120–121
exports/imports, XPOST
government-owned, consumption of, 121–122
government purchase, 163–164
home production, 281
illegal, GDP and, 136
international imports/exports, 323
law of one price, 351–356
new and improved, 128
price adjustment, 202–205
purchasing power parity, 352–353
value added, 113–115
Government
aggregate uncertainty and, 416
attempting to fool workers, 237–239
capital formation (investment), 163–164
capital goods of, consuming, 121–122
consumption, printing money for, 190–191
deficit finance, 156–158 (*see also* Borrowing)
deficits (*see* Deficits)
expenditures, 142–144
financing, 152, 391
nonindexed, 195
valuing, 135–136
international reserves, 366–367
intertemporal budget constraint, 142, 144–145
transitions in generational policy, 153
intervention, costs/benefits, 296–299
invention (*see* Policy)
involuntary unemployment and, 221
nonindexed taxation and spending, 195
policy (*see* Policy)
precommitment strategy, 315

printing money (*see* Money supply)
regulation, 22 (*see also* Policy)
banks, 407
prices/wages, 203
social insurance, 284–285, 416
taxes (*see* Taxes)
transfer payments (*see* Transfer payments)
Government insurance, 416–417
Great Britain. *See* United Kingdom
Great Depression, 295
establishing deposit insurance (case study), 406
monetary control during, 399–401
policy during, 299–306
Greenbacks, 175
Gross domestic product. *See* GDP
Gross investment, 9
Gross national product (GNP), 116
Gross work status changes, 267–269
Growth, 4
economic (*see* Economic growth)
endogenous growth, 26, 79–80
inflation (*see* Inflation)
population, 49–50
productivity growth (case study), 12–13
technology, 14

Hamburger prices, international (case study), 352, 354–355
Happiness level (utility functions), 41–45
Hayashi, Fumio, 423, 454
Health insurance for elderly. *See* Social security
Hiring, 268
Hoarding labor, 97, 288
"Holey money," 176
Home production, 281
Hours worked, 96. *See also* Labor (labor force)
Households
generational accounting, 141, 146–150, 157
economic transitions and, 153–155
intragenerational transfers, 165
social security benefits, 162
personal income, 118
price changes for (*see* CPI)
survey of, 95
Housing, 8, 120
Housing investment (case study), 441–443
Human capital, 31, 56
Hyperinflation, 173–174
in Germany (case study), 182
Hysteresis, 290

Illegal sales and GDP, 136
Imperfect competition, 253
Imperfect information, 309–312
Imports/exports, 323
capital imports, 334
trade balance (*see* Trade deficit; Trade surplus)

Imputed rent, 120
Incentives
 distortionary fiscal policy, 165
 investment, 436
 saving propensities, 41–45, 77
Income
 capital income, 33
 disposable, 118
 incomes policy, 316–317
 intragenerational transfers, 165
  social security benefits, 162
 national accounting, 111
 national identity, 111, 122–124
 NI (national income), 117–118
 nonmarket activities, 135–136
 personal, 118
 progressive income taxation, 417
 proprietors', 115
 relationship with output, 112
 rental, 115
 unreported, 136
 wage adjustment process (case study), 203–205
Income taxes, 118, 147–149. See also Taxes
 corporate income tax, 437–439
 distortionary fiscal policy, 165
 nonindexed, 195
 political business cycles, 259, 261
Independent monetary policy, 366
Index of leading indicators, 93–94
Indexed bonds, 135
Indexing taxes for inflation, 195
India, currency of (case study), 176
Indifference curves, 42–45
Indirect taxes, 117
Industrialization of United States (case study), 341
Industry
 coordination failures, 254–259, 261
 economy of, 20
 fast-food, wages in (case study), 273
 frictional unemployment, 236, 275–276, 290
  unfixed (nonconstant), 249–251
 major, business cycle volatility, 91
 output fluctuations, 98–99
 responses to shocks, 249–251, 261
 sectoral differences (see Sectoral differences)
 small businesses (case study), 269
Inertia, 253
Infinite horizon utility function, 422
Inflation, 125–127, 131
 adjusting money amounts for, 127
 costs, 297
 employment and (see Phillips curve)
 hyperinflation, 173–174, 182
 money supply and, 192–195
 permanence of changes in, 298
 present value discounting, 29

 repressed, 317
 unexpected, government debt and, 194–195
 United States, 186–188
 wage and price controls, incomes policies, 315–317
Inflation premium, 132
"Inflation tax." See Seigniorage
Inflows, labor force, 267–269
Information, money demand and, 193
Inputs, 3
 profit maximization, 56–59
 relationship with output, 112
 supplies of, 30–32
  dynamic, 34–37
 units, 8
Inside lags, 306–309
Insider-outside theory, 272
Institution of money, 173–176
Insurance
 deposit insurance, 404–408
 government insurance, 416–417
 life insurance, 421
 private, capital formation and, 415
 provided by social security (see Social security)
 social insurance, 284–285, 416
 unemployment insurance (UI), 284–286
Integration (monetary) of Europe (case study), 372–373
Intentional bequests, 421
Interest payments as tax deductions, 444–445
Interest rates
 capital-labor ratio and, 58
 ceilings, 428
 compound interest, 40
 consumption and, 38
 equilibrium values, 59
 Fed's choosing to target, 399–403
 fully flexible, 202–205
 G-5 countries, 327–329
 inflation and, 193
 IS curve for (see IS curve)
 money demand sensitivity, 216–217
 money velocity and, 178, 303
 present value, 40
 profit maximization and, 57–59
 real vs. nominal, 132–135
 social security funds and, 160
 yield spread and business cycle, 445
Intergenerational altruism, 422–423
Intergenerational transfers (bequests), 417–423
Intermediate goods and services, 113–115
Internal finance, 445
International
 contemporaneous economic fluctuations, 99–100
 economies (see Open economies)
 investment (see Foreign investment)
 McDonald's Big Mac prices (case study), 352, 354–355
 Phillips curves, comparing, 242

reserves, limited, 366–367
trade policy, 335–343
unemployment comparisons (case study), 290–292
Intertemporal budget constraint, 142, 144–145
privatizing social security, 162
transitions in generational policy, 153
Intertemporal substitution, 245
Intervention, government. *See* Government; Policy
Intervivos gifts, 421
Intragenerational transfers, 165
redistribution policy, 417
social security benefits, 162
Inventories, 7, 8
Inventory investment, 434
Investment, foreign. *See* Foreign investment
Investment (capital accumulation), 9, 19
accelerator, 107
adjustment lags, 451–453
of banks, federal observation, 407–408
bequests (intergenerational transfers), 418–419
borrowing and, 425–426
consumption vs., 119–120
decline in U.S. saving (case studies), 46–48, 155–156, 332–335
deficit finance and, 157–158
domestic, 47
dynamics of, 449–455
financial policy, 443–449
foreign (*see* Foreign investment; Open economies)
government consumption and, 152–153
housing investment (case study), 441–443
incentives for, 436, 440
irreversibility, 451
misperception theory and, 243
in monetary economy, 183–188
national, 30, 45–48
government consumption and, 152–153
paradox of thrift, 217–219
steady state, 66
net foreign investment, 122–124
in open economies, 330
present values, 39–41
private insurance and, 415
S&L crisis (case study), 408
technology shocks and, 107
Tobin's q-theory, 453–455
uncertainty on saving (example), 412–415
U.S. government (case study), 163–164
user cost of capital, 438–439
volatility, 98–99
Investment tax credits, 312–313, 440, 443
Involuntary unemployment, 212, 220, 272–274
costs, 282–283
IOUs, 175, 382
Irreversibility of investment, 451
IS curve, 207, 209
aggregate demand curve, 224–226

aggregate supply curve, 221–223
endogeneity of money supply, 403–404
Great Depression, 300–304
influencing with fiscal policy, 215–216
open economies, 368–369
IS-LM diagram, 201, 205–210
aggregate demand curve, 224–226
aggregate supply curve, 221–223
endogeneity of money supply, 403–404
Great Depression, 300–304
influencing with policy, 212–217
monetary policy, open economies, 370
open economy model, 368–369
Issuing bonds. *See* Bonds

Japan
after World War II (case study), 340
age transition in, 48–50
bond interest rates, 327–329
credit constraints, 448–449
exchange rate indexes, 353, 356
open economy transition curve, 326–329
post-WWII capital deepening (case study), 68–70
Job vacancy rate, 251
Jorgenson, Dale, 15

K*eiretsu*, 449
Keynes, John Maynard, 299
Keynesian (involuntary) unemployment, 212, 220, 272–274
Keynesian model, 201. *See also* New Keynesians
developing, 205–210
misperception theory vs., 239
political business cycles, 259, 261
price rigidity and, 205
recessions, 229–235, 261
Kotlikoff, Laurence, 419, 423
Kuznets, Simon, 89
Kydland, Finn, 243
Kydland-Prescott real business cycle model, 246

Labor (labor force), 21. *See also* Employment; Unemployment
age and race distinctions, 278–280
age transition and, 50
capital and (*see* Capital-labor ratio)
Cobb-Douglas production function, 6–8
intensive form, 16
marginal products and, 57
money, 181–183
costs of unemployment, 280–286
definition of labor force, 96
diminishing returns, 8, 16
dynamics, 265–271
theories of unemployment, 272–276
epidemics (plagues) and, 70–73
gender differences, 277
labor hoarding, 97, 288

Labor (cont.)
    labor income, 115n
    labor productivity, 16–22
        slowdown in United States, 18–22
        workers' compensation, 17
    life-cycle model and, 48–50
    marginal product/cost, 17, 57–58
    measuring labor, 8–10
    misperception theory, 240–241, 275
    modeling growth (*see* Economic growth)
    Okun's law, 286–289
    participation rate, 96, 266
    quality of labor, 12, 21
    small businesses (case study), 269
    supply, 35–36
    taxes on (*see* Income taxes; Taxes)
    transitions in, 267–269
    turnover in, 269
    wage adjustment process (case study), 203–205
    work status changes, 267–269
    workers' compensation, 17
Land, 8
Laspeyres index, 129
Law of one price, 248, 351–356
Laws
    crime/punishment as unemployment, 283
    illegal goods and services, GDP and, 136
Layoffs, 268, 270
Leading indicators, 93–94
Lender of last resort, 393–394
Lending rates, 427
Leveraged buyouts, 447
Liabilities of financial intermediaries, 382–383
    bank runs and, 404–408
Life-cycle model, xvi–xviii, 29
    coordination failures, 256
    credit markets, 423–430
    developing Keynesian model, 205–210 (*see also* Keynesian model)
    economic fluctuations, 86–90
        anatomy of, 90–94
        explaining, 98–104
        questioning cyclic pattern, 102–104
        real business cycle theory, 85, 104–109, 243–249, 261
        seasonal adjustments on, 101
    intergenerational transfers, 421
    investment irreversibility, 451
    money, 179–183 (*see also* Money)
    New Keynesian models, 251–259, 261
    political business cycles, 259, 261
    population and technological change, 78–80
    sectoral shift model, 249–251, 261
    social security, 159–161
    technological improvement and, 244
    two-period, 32–34
Life-cycle wealth, 419
Life insurance, 421

Life span uncertainty, 419
Lifetime budget constraint, 37–39
    generational differences, 67
    indifference curves, 44
    money and, 179–181
    uncertainty on saving and capital formation, 412–415
Liquid liabilities, 382–383
    banks and, 384
    banks runs and, 404–408
Liquidity, 172
Liquidity preference, 303
Livingston Survey of business leaders' inflation expectation, 195
LM curve, 207–208
    aggregate demand curve, 224–226
    aggregate supply curve, 221–223
    endogeneity of money supply, 403–404
    Great Depression, 300–304
    influencing with monetary policy, 213
Loans. *See* Borrowing
Long-run (steady state), 65–66
Lotteries (case study), 40
Lucas, Robert, 237, 242, 312
Lucas critique, 312

M1 monetary aggregate, 169, 379, 383
    during Great Depression (case study), 399–401
    growth rates and variability, 395–403
    multipliers (*see* Multipliers)
    reserve requirement and, 393–394
    targeted by Fed (1979–1982), 402–403
    velocity, 178
M2, M3 monetary aggregates, 169, 383
    growth rates and variability, 395–403
Macroeconomics models. *See* Economic models
Macroeconomics questions, xv
Maddison, Angus, 15
Magazine prices (case study), 203
Male-female comparison. *See* Gender differences
Marginal cost of capital, 57
Marginal cost of labor, 57
Marginal product, 436
    of capital, 57
    of labor, 17, 57
Marginal rate of substitution (MRS), 43
Maximizing profits, 56–59
McDonald's Big Mac prices (case study), 352, 354–355
Means of payment, 172
Measuring output, 111–137
    GDP (gross domestic products), 112–116, 135–137
    inflation, 125–127, 131
    real GDP, biases (case study), 130–131
    real interest rate, 133–135
    relationships among measures, 116–119
Measuring policy effectiveness, 216–217
Media of exchange, 172
Medicare. *See* Social security

Menu costs, 253, 297

Microeconomics vs. macroeconomics, xv

Minimum wage regulation, 203

Misperception theory, 229–230, 239–243, 261
  unemployment under, 275

Models for economic behavior. *See* Economic models

Modigliani, Franco, 29

Modigliani-Miller theorem, 444

Monetarism, 217

Monetary aggregates, 169, 379, 383
  divergent paths, 395
  Fed's choosing to target, 399–403
  variability, 396

Monetary base, 193, 380, 386–388

Monetary policy, 170, 212–214. *See also* Activist policy; Policy
  credit availability, 428
  European monetary integration (case study), 372–373
  exchange rates, 347–351
  Federal Reserve System and, 388–394 (*see also* Federal Reserve System)
  fiscal policy and, 170–171
  flexible vs. fixed exchange rates, 360–365, 370
  Great Depression (case studies), 299–306, 399–401
  independence of, 366
  information-unemployment trade-off, 231
  international reserves and, 366–367
  long-term wage and price contracts, 252
  measuring effectiveness, 216–217
  not changing when possible, 315
  open economy with wage rigidity, 369–371
  politics and, 259–260
  printing money (*see* Money supply)
  rational expectations theory, 237–239
  speed of enacting, 308
  wage rigidity and, 221–224

Money
  adjusting for inflation, 127
  classical view, 177–179
  commodity standards, 350–351
  currency substitution, 174
  defining, 171–176
  demand, 181–183, 206
    inflation and, 193
    interest rate sensitivity, 216–217
    transition equation, 183–188
  deposit insurance, 404–408
  economic models and, 179–183
  exchange rates, 347–351
  Fed and (*see* Federal Reserve System)
  German hyperinflation (case study), 182
  gold standard, 176–177
    fixed exchange rates, 350–351
  LM curve for (*see* LM curve)
  measures (*see* Monetary aggregates)
  multipliers (*see* Multipliers)
  neutrality, 170, 188

present value discounting, 29

printing (*see* Money supply; Seigniorage)

real value, 173–176

repositories, banks as, 384

shocks, affecting U.S. output (case study), 254

United States (case study), 174–176

velocity of, Great Depression, 301–303

volatility of, automatic stabilizers, 305

Money supply, 177
  banks as repositories, 384
  controlled by Fed, 395–404
  demand for money and, 184–187
  endogeneity, 403–404
  exchange rates and, 359
  financial intermediaries, 381–386
  inflation and, 192–195
  influencing output with, 212–214
  international reserves, 366–367
  LM curve for (*see* LM curve)
  misperception theory and, 240
  Phillips curve and, 231–233
  seigniorage (printing money), 193
    costs, 297–298
    for elderly/young, 188–192
    European monetary integration (case study), 373
  staggered contract models and, 252
  targeted by Fed, 400–403

Monitoring over time
  capital-labor ratio, 74–77
  saving propensities, 77
  transition path (numerical example), 62–64

Moral hazards, 407, 416

MRS (marginal rate of substitution), 43

Multifactor productivity, 7, 12–13
  embodied vs. disembodied, 12

Multiple equilibria, 256

Multipliers, 214, 308, 380, 387
  fluctuations in, 396
  during Great Depression (case study), 399–401

National
  currency (U.S.) production, 175 (*see also* Money supply)
  gross national product (GNP), 116
  income identity, 122–124
  saving/investment, 45–48 (*see also* Deficits)
    deficit finance and, 157–158
    government consumption and, 152–153
    paradox of thrift, 217–219
    rate of, after WWII (case study), 155–156
    steady state, 66
    trade deficit and, 122–124

National Bureau of Economic Research. *See* NBER

National income accounting, 111

National income identity, 111, 113

National income (NI), 117–118

National saving/investment, 30

Natural experiments, xviii
Natural rate of unemployment, 235–237
    determining, 289–290
NBER (National Bureau of Economic Research), 86
    1990–1991 recession, U.S. (case study), 307
NDP (net domestic product), 117
Neoclassical models, 230
Net domestic product (NDP), 117
Net foreign asset position, 331
Net foreign investment, 122–124, 325, 331
Net national debt, 143
Net national saving rate, 155
Net of accumulated depreciation, 9
Net work status changes, 267–269
Neutrality of money, 170, 188
New Deal, policy during, 304–306
New goods, CPI and, 128
New hires, 268
New Keynesians, 229–230
    coordination failures, 254–259
Newly industrialized countries (NICs), 25–26
NI (national income), 117–118
NICs (newly industrialized countries), 25–26
Nixon, Richard, 317
No-shirking constant, 273
Nominal exchange rates, 352–353
    monetary policy and, 362
    price levels and, 356–358
Nominal GDP, 129–131. See also GDP
    real GDP vs., 131
Nominal interest rates, 132–135
    inflation and, 193
Nominal rigidities, 201, 205. See also Rigidities
Nominal shocks, Fed's targets and, 399–401
Nominal wage rate, 132
Nominal wage rigidity, 219–226
    open economy model, 368–373
    policy and, 221–224
    unemployment and, 219–221
Nominal wages, long-term contracts, 252
Nonannuitized wealth, 420
Nondurable goods, 120–121
Nonindexed taxation and spending, 195
Nonmarket activities, 135–136
Norway, saving and (case study), 428

OECD (Organization for Economic Cooperation and Development), 22
Oil shocks (case studies), 247–249
    industry-specific responses to, 249
    "Whip Inflation Now" campaign (case study), 309–312
Okun, Arthur, 287
Okun's law, 286–289
Old Age & Survivors' Insurance. See Social security
Onset of Great Depression, 300–304
Open economies, 47, 323–345
    exchange rates, 347–351

    nominal, and price levels, 356–358
        real, 359–360
    fiscal policy, 341–343
    investment and trade deficit/surplus, 324–329
    law of one price, 351–356
    nominal wage rigidity, 368–373
    recovering from wars, 337–341
    two-country model, 329–335
Operating hours, coordinating, 255
Outflows, labor force, 267–269
Output/production
    business cycles and, 98–99
    consumption (see Consumption)
    developing vs. developed countries, 24–26
    diminishing returns, 8, 16
    fluctuations, fixed exchange rates and, 371–372
    growth (see Growth)
    influencing with policy, 212–217 (see also Fiscal policy; Monetary policy)
    interest rates and (see IS curve)
    investment (see Investment)
    labor and capital vs. (see Cobb-Douglas production function)
    labor productivity, 16–22
    measuring, 111–137
        GDP (gross domestic product), 112–116, 135–137
        inflation, 125–127, 131
        real interest rate, 133–135
        relationships among measures, 116–119
    money shocks and (case study), 254
    populations vs. (see GDP)
    potential full employment output, 210–212
    price rigidity and, 206, 210–212
    profit maximization, 56–59
    random walk theory, 103
    reduced from unemployment, 281–284
    relationship with inputs, 112
    saving (see Saving)
    seasonal cycles, 101
    units of, 8
    volatility, investment and consumption vs., 107
Outside lags, 307–309
Overtime hours worked, 96
Owner-occupied housing, 441
Owner's equity, 382
Owning capital, 30–32

Paasche index, 129
Paradox of thrift, 217–219
Parent-child relationships. See Generations
Path of transition. See Transition equation/path
Pay-as-you-go financing, 158–162
Payroll taxes, 147–149. See also Taxes
Per capita GDP, 5
    developing vs. developed countries, 24–26
Perfect competition, 58
Permanence of inflation/unemployment changes, 298

Personal income, 118
Phelps, Edmund, 235
Phillips, A. W., 230
Phillips curve, 229–235
    comparing internationally (case study), 242
    long-run (natural rate), 235–237
    unsteady (shifting), 234–235
Plagues (epidemics)
    capital-labor ratio and, 70–73
    transition path diagrams, 76
Policy
    coordination failures and, 259
    corporate financial policy, 443–449
    credit availability, 428
    dynamic (time) inconsistency, 313–315
    fiscal (see Fiscal policy)
    Great Depression, 299–306
    incomes policy, 316–317
    influence of expectations, 312–313
    information-unemployment trade-off, 231
    intra-, intergenerational redistribution policy, 417
    minimum wage regulation, 203
    monetary (see Monetary policy)
    multipliers (see Multipliers)
    not changing when possible, 315
    policy lags, 306–309
    politics and, 259–260
    rational expectations theory, 237–239
    sectoral shifts and fluctuations, 90, 251
    speed of enacting, 308
    stabilization/activist policy, 295–319
        challenges, 306–315
        exchange rates, 360–365
        questionability, 317–318
    tax policy, 440–443 (see also Taxes)
    trade policy, 335–343
Political business cycle theory, 230, 259, 261
Pollution, 136
Population, 78–79
    epidemics (plagues), 70–73
    growth, 49–50
    surveying unemployment, 95–96
Potential full employment output, 210–212
Powers (exponents), 82–83
PPP (purchasing power parity), 352–353
Precautionary saving, 412–417
Precommitment strategy, 315
Predicting business cycles, 93–94
Premium, inflation, 132
Prescott, Edward, 243
Present value, 39–41
Present value discounting, 29
Price controls, 316–317
Price index, 125–131
    availability, 242
Price levels, 125–131

adjustment, 202–205
determining over time, 184–187
law of one price, 351–356
long-term contracts, 252
money neutrality and, 188
nominal exchange rates and, 356–358
open economy with wage rigidity, 369–371
policy with wage rigidity and, 221–224
Price rigidity/stickiness, 201, 210–216. See also Rigidities, price
    New Keynesian explanations for, 253
    output determination, 210–212
    paradox of thrift, 217–219
    relative, 205
Printing money. See Money supply; Seigniorage
Private
    capital, private vs. governmental, 163
    costs of unemployment, 280–286
    insurance, capital formation and, 415
    social security (case study), 161–162
Procyclical behavior, 97
Producers' durable equipment, 435
Production. See Output/production
Productivity, 7, 12–13. See also Economic growth; Growth; Output/production
    developing vs. developed countries, 24–26
    embodied vs. disembodied, 12
    labor productivity, 16–22
Profits, 115
    maximizing, 56–59
    zero-profit condition, 58
Progressive income taxation, 195, 417
Propensities, saving. See Saving, propensity toward
Proprietors' income, 115
Punishment, unemployment as, 283
Purchasing power parity, 352–353
Pure profit, 57

Quality
    capital (see Capital, quality)
    goods, 128
    labor (see Labor, quality)
    life, 41–45, 136
Quantity equation, 177
    German hyperinflation (case study), 182
Quantity indexes, 129–131
Quantity theory of money, 177
Quits (from labor force), 268, 270
    measuring voluntary unemployment, 275

Race distinctions in labor force, 278–280
Random walk theory, 103
Rates. See Growth
Rational expectations, 229, 237–239, 312
    misperception theory, 239–243, 261, 275
Rationing credit. See Credit
R&D (research and development), 21

Reagan, Ronald, 92
Real assets, 31
Real business cycle theory, 85, 104–109, 243–249, 261
    consumer and business confidence, 257–259
    political business cycles, 259, 261
    recessions, 229
    unemployment and, 245
Real exchange rates, 352–353, 359–360
Real GDP, 3, 129–131. *See also* GDP
    measurement biases (case study), 130–131
    nominal GDP vs., 131
Real interest rates, 132–135
Real rigidities, 205
Real shocks, Fed's targets and, 399–401
Real stock of money, 177
Real value of money, 173–176
Real wages. *See also* Wages
    price level and, 184–186
    rigidity, models of, 272–273
Recessions, 4, 85–88, 229–264
    California (case study), 92–93
    causes of (summary), 260–261
    coordination failures and, 256
    Great Depression (*see* Great Depression)
    index of leading indicators, 93–94
    labor hoarding, 97, 288
    misperception theory, 239–243, 261, 275
    natural rate hypothesis, 235–237
    New Keynesian models, 251–259, 261
    oil price shocks (case study), 247–249, 309–312
    Phillips curve, 229–235, 229–237
    political business cycles, 259, 261
    Presidential election (U.S., 1992) (case study), 307
    rational expectations, 229–237, 237–239
    real business cycle theory, 85, 104–109, 243–249, 261
    sectoral changes vs., 90
    sectoral shift model, 249–251, 261
    unemployment duration, 271
    unemployment insurance, 285
    unemployment rate, 94
Recovering from wars, 337–341
Recovery from Great Depression, 300–304
Redistribution, intergenerational, 165
Reforming the CPI, 128
Regional economic fluctuations, 90
Regulating banks, 407
Regulation, government, 22
Regulation Q, 408
Rehires, 268
Rent and rental income, 115, 120
Repressed inflation, 317
Research and development (R&D), 21
Reserves
    bank reserves, 384–386
        requirements for, 380, 393–394
    bank runs, 404–408

international reserves, 366–367
reserve-deposit ratio, 387
Resolution Trust Corporation, 408
Restricting foreign investment, 335–337
Retained earnings, 118, 445
Revaluations, 348
Revenues, government, 142–143
Ricardian equivalence, 162, 422
Ricardo, David, 422
Rigidities, 201–205
    New Keynesian explanations for, 253
    output and, 206
    prices, 210–216
        magazine prices (case study), 203
        nominal vs. real, 205
        output determination, 210–212
        paradox of thrift, 217–219
        policy influencing output, 212–217
    wages, 219–226
        adjustment process (case study), 203–205
        models of, 272–273
        open economy model, 368–373
        policy, 221–224
        unemployment and, 219–221
Risks
    diversifying with financial intermediaries, 382
    insurance against (*see* Insurance)
    moral hazards, 407, 416
    precautionary saving against, 412–417
    risk aversion, 412
Robert, Cumby, 354
Romer, Christina, 89
Roosevelt, Franklin D., 406

Salary. *See* Wages
Sales, illegal, GDP and, 136
Sales taxes, 115
    distortionary fiscal policy, 165
Sargent, Thomas, 237
Saving, 19, 32, 34
    bequests (intergenerational transfers), 417–423
    credit markets, 423–430
    distortionary fiscal policy, 165
    epidemics (plagues) and, 72
    foreign investment and, 324–329
    national, 30, 45–48
        deficit finance and, 157–158
        government consumption and, 152–153
        paradox of thrift, 217–219
        steady state, 66
        trade deficit and, 122–124
    Norwegian (case study), 428
    post–WWII Japan and Germany, 69
    precautionary saving, 412–417
    present values, 39–41
    propensity toward, 41–45, 77

savings and loan crisis (case study), 408
United States (case studies)
decline in, 46–48, 155–156, 332–335
trade surplus and, 335
Schwartz, Anna, 300, 399
Seasonal cycles, 101
Sectoral differences
economic fluctuations and, 90
frictional unemployment, 236, 275–276, 290
unfixed (nonconstant), 249–251
output fluctuations, 98–99
responses to shocks, 249–251, 261
small businesses and job creation (case study), 269
taxation, 440
Sectoral shift model, 229
Securities. *See* Financial securities
Seigniorage, 193
costs, 297–298
European monetary integration (case study), 373
Self-propelled change. *See* Endogenous growth
Sentiment, consumer. *See* Confidence
Separations (employment), 268–269
Services. *See also* Goods
barter system, 171
distortionary fiscal policy, 165
durable goods and, 121
economy of, 20
exports/imports, XPOST
from government-owned capital goods, 121–122
home production, 281
housing, 120
illegal, GDP and, 136
international imports/exports, 323
price adjustment, 202–205
value added, 113–115
Sex comparisons. *See* Gender differences
Shifting Phillips curve, 234–235
natural rate hypothesis, 235–237
Shocks
explaining fluctuations by, 243–249
Fed's targets and, 399–401
industry-specific responses to, 249–251, 261
money, U.S. output and (case study), 254
oil prices (case studies), 247–249, 309–312
technology, 104–109 (*see also* Technology)
Shoeleather costs, 297
S&L crisis in 1980s (case study), 408
Small businesses (case study), 269
Social costs of unemployment, 280–286
Social insurance, 284–285, 416. *See also* Insurance
Social security, 149, 158–162
credit-constrained consumption, 429
financing (case study), 218–219
printing money for benefits, 188–190
privatizing in U.S. (case study), 161–162
Ricardian equivalence proposition, 162

Solow, Robert, 14
Solow residual, 14
Speculation against fixed exchange rates, 367
Speed of enacting policy, 308
Spending, government. *See* Expenditures, government
Spillover effects, 255–256
international, 99–100
Stabilization policy, 295–319
challenges, 306–315
costs and benefits, 296–299
exchange rates, 360–365
during Great Depression, 299–306
questionability, 317–318
Stagflation, 309–312
Staggered contracts, 252
State lotteries (case study), 40
Steady state, 65–66
population and technology, 78–80
Stickiness, 201. *See also* Rigidities
New Keynesian explanations for, 253
relative, 205
Stock of money, 177
Stock variables, 10
Stocks, 55, 444
commercial banks and, 407
corporate income tax, 437–439
Tobin's *q*-theory, 453–455
Summers, Lawrence H., 419, 429
Supply
credit, 425
inputs, 30–32
dynamic, 34–37
labor, 48–50 (*see also* Labor [labor force])
money (*see* Money supply)
shocks
economic fluctuations and, 243–249
industry-specific responses to, 249–251, 261
oil prices (case studies), 247–249, 309–312
supply-side economics, 166
Surplus in open economies. *See* Trade surplus
Surprise inflation, 194–195

Tablita policy, Argentina (case study), 364–365
Tax policy, 440–443
Tax Reform Act (1986), 452
Taxes, 142
automatic stabilizers, 305
corporate income tax, 437–439
debt and, 444–445
distortionary fiscal policy, 165
excess burden on taxation, 297–298
financing government consumption, 152
generational accounting, 146–150, 157
economic transitions and, 153–155
income taxes, 118
indirect taxes, 117

Taxes (cont.)
  "inflation tax" (*see* Seigniorage)
  intertemporal budget constraint, 142, 144–145, 153
  investment tax credits, 312–313, 440, 443
  on money (*see* Monetary policy)
  nonindexed, 195
  political business cycles, 259, 261
  progressive income taxation, 417
  sales tax, 115
  sector-specific, 440
  social security (*see* Social security)
  unreported income, 136
  value-added tax, 115–116
Technology, 78–80
  consumption and investment and, 107
  of economics, 3
  growth, 14, 79–80
  real business cycles, 244
  seasonal cycles, 101
  shocks, 104–109
Teenagers, employment, 278–289
Temporary tax credits, 443
Terms of trade, 353
Theories, economic, xviii
Thrift, paradox of, 217–219
Time (dynamic) inconsistency, 313–315
Tobin, James, 453
Tobin's *q*-theory of investment, 453–455
Total U.S. wealth, 419
Trabant, 136
Tracking
  capital-labor ratio, 74–77
  saving propensities, 77
  transition path (numerical example), 62–64
Trade deficit, 122–124, 323
  Japan after WWII (case study), 340
  national saving and, 122
  United States (since 1980), 123
  worldwide transition, 332
Trade imbalance, 323
Trade policy, 335–343
Trade surplus, 123, 323
  Japan after WWII (case study), 340
  U.S. saving and (case study), 335
  during worldwide transition, 332
Transaction costs
  financial intermediaries and, 381
  foreign currencies, 365
Transfer payments, 118, 142
  automatic stabilizers, 305
  generational accounting, 146–150, 157
    economic transitions and, 153–155
  intragenerational transfers, 165
    social security benefits, 162
  printing money for, 188–192 (*see also* Money supply)
  social security, 158–162

Transfer wealth, 419
Transition equation/path, 60–62, 73–78
  bonds (deficit finance) and, 157
  demand for money and, 183–188
  deriving IS-LM diagram, 206
  determining steady state, 65–66
  fiscal policy and, 150–156
  open economies, 326–329
  recovering from wars, 337–341
  saving differences, 77
  tracking capital-labor ratio, 74–77
  tracking (numerical example), 62–64
  uncertainty on saving, 412–415
  worldwide, 330–331
Transitions, labor force, 267–269
Treasury bonds, 391–393
Truman, Harry, 260
Turning points in business cycles, 93–94
Turnover taxes, 116
Two-country model, fiscal policy, 341–343
Two-period life-cycle model, 32–34. *See also* Life-cycle model
  coordination failures, 256
  credit markets, 423–430
  developing Keynesian model, 205–210
  investment irreversibility, 451
  New Keynesian models, 251–259, 261
  population and technological change, 78–80
  real business cycle theory, 85, 104–109, 243–249, 261

UI (unemployment insurance), 284–286
  as cause of unemployment (case study), 285
Uncertainty and saving, 412–415
Underground economy, 136
Unemployment, 94–98, 265–294, 276–280. *See also* Employment; Labor
  age and race distinctions, 278–280
  aggregate demand and, 210–212
  costs, 280–286
  definition, 95
  disguised, 289
  Europe vs. United States (case study), 290–292
  frictional, 275–276, 290
    unfixed (nonconstant), 249–251
  full employment deficit, 306
  gender differences, 277
  inflation and (*see* Phillips curve)
  involuntary (Keynesian), 20, 212, 272–274
    costs, 282–283
  job vacancy rate, 251
  labor hoarding, 97, 288
  natural rate, 235–237, 289–290
  nominal wage rigidity and, 219–221
  Okun's law, 286–289
  permanence of changes in, 298
  real business cycles, 245
  reduced output from, 281–284

reducing, benefits of, 286–292
sources and duration, 270–271, 280
theories of, 272–276
UI (unemployment insurance), 284–286
 as cause of unemployment (case study), 285
voluntary, 221, 274
 costs, 281–282
Unexpected inflation, 194–195
Unintended bequests, 417, 419–421
United Kingdom
bond interest rates, 327–329
exchange rates (case study), 349
United States
age transition in, 48–50
annuitization in (case study), 420
bond interest rates, 327–329
budget deficits (case study), 143–144
commercial bank assets (1997), 405–406
credit constraints, 429, 448–449
decline in saving (case studies), 46–48, 155–156, 332–335
deflation in, 186–188
different monies in, 174–176
economic fluctuations (1854–1990), 86–88
exchange rate indexes, 353, 356
exchange rates (case study), 349
gender differences in labor force, 277–278
generational accounts (case study), 147–150
GNP vs. GDP, 116
government investment (case study), 163–164
Great Depression (*see* Great Depression)
industrialization in 1800s (case study), 341
investment, postwar, 434–435
Kydland-Prescott real business cycle model, 246
labor force participation rate, 266
labor productivity slowdown, 18–22
M1 money multiplier, 387–388
magazine prices (case study), 203
monetary base of (1997), 387
money shocks and output (case study), 254
number of firms, 54
oil price shocks (case studies), 248, 309–312
open economy transition curve, 326–329
Phillips curve, 229–230, 234–235, 242
Presidential election (1992), recession and (case study), 307
private capital stock ownership (case study), 31–32
relatively weak growth performance, 22–24
restricting foreign investment, 335–337
social security system, 159 (*see also* Social security)
 financing (case study), 218–219
 privatizing (case study), 161–162
sources of growth (case study), 14–16
total wealth, 419
trade deficit (since 1980), 123
trade surplus and saving (cast study), 335
unemployment in, Europe vs. (case study), 290–292

unemployment insurance, 285
wages and prices freeze (case study), 317
Units of account, 172
Unreported income, 136
U.S. Treasury bonds, 391–393
User cost of capital, 433, 436
corporate income tax, 437–439
tax policy, 440–443
Utility functions, 41–45
Utils (as unit of utility), 41

Value added, 113–115
Value-added method, 113–115
Value-added tax, 115–116
Variability of monetary aggregates, 396
Variables
flow vs. stock variables, 10
procyclical behavior, 97
steady state, 65–66, 78–80
Velocity of money, 177–179
Great Depression, 301–303
Volatility
business cycles, 86–90
 major industry and, 91
 World War II and (case study), 89
consumption smoothing, 107
employment (*see* Unemployment)
investment, 449–455
money, automatic stabilizers, 305
sectoral outputs, 98–99
Volcker, Paul, 401–403
Voluntary unemployment, 221, 274
costs, 281–282
unemployment insurance and (case study), 285

Wages (workers' compensation), 17
adjustment, 202–205
consumption and, 38
controls on, 316–317
costs of unemployment, 280–286
efficiency wage theory, 272–273
epidemics (plagues) and, 70–73
equilibrium values, 59
fast-food industry (case study), 273
human capital, 56
long-term contracts, 252
nominal rate, 132
nonmarket activities, 135–136
price level and, 184–186
replacement rate, 285
rigidity, 219–226
 models, 272–273
 New Keynesian explanations for, 253
 open economy model, 368–373

Wages (cont.)
      policy and, 221–224
      unemployment and, 219–221
  taxes on (*see* Income taxes; Taxes)
Wars
  capital stock and (case study), 68–70
  foreign investment after, 337–341
  transition path diagrams, 76
Weil, David, 420
Weiss, Andrew, 13
Welfare, 280–284, 336
''Whip Inflation Now'' campaign (case study), 309–312
Wilcox, David, 429
Women. *See* Gender differences
Work status changes, 267–269
Workers' compensation. *See* Wages
Working. *See* Labor (labor force)
World capital-labor ratio, 329–335
World War II
  budget deficits after (U.S.), 143–144
  business cycle volatility (case study), 89
  investment after (U.S.), 434–435
  Japan after (case study), 340
  Japanese and German capital deepening after (case study), 68–70
  production shift following, 250
  saving decline after (U.S.), 155–156
Worldwide demographic transition, 48–50
Worldwide transition equation/path, 330–331

Yield spread, 445
Youth. *See also* Generations
  printing money for, 191–192

Zero-profit condition, 58

U.S. FINANCIAL MARKET DATA; EXCHANGE RATES

Year	M1	M2	M3	Monetary Base	3-Month U.S. Treasury Bill Rate	10-Year U.S. Bond Rate	Mark/Dollar	Yen/Dollar
	(billions of dollars)				%		Exchange Rate	
1959	140.0	297.8	299.7	40,880	3.40	4.33		
1960	140.7	312.4	315.2	40,997	2.92	4.12		
1961	145.2	335.5	340.8	41,853	2.37	3.88		
1962	147.8	362.7	371.3	42,957	2.77	3.95		
1963	153.3	393.2	405.9	45,003	3.15	4.00		
1964	160.3	424.7	442.4	47,161	3.54	4.19		
1965	167.8	459.2	482.1	49,620	3.95	4.28		
1966	172.0	480.2	505.4	51,565	4.88	4.92		
1967	183.3	524.8	557.9	54,579	4.32	5.07		
1968	197.4	566.8	607.2	58,357	5.33	5.65		
1969	203.9	587.9	615.9	61,569	6.67	6.67		
1970	214.4	626.5	677.1	65,013	6.45	7.35		
1971	228.3	710.2	776.0	69,108	4.34	6.16		
1972	249.2	802.3	886.0	75,167	4.07	6.21	3.1886	303.13
1973	262.8	855.5	985.0	81,073	7.04	6.84	2.6715	271.31
1974	274.2	902.4	1,070.0	87,535	7.88	7.56	2.5868	291.84
1975	287.4	1,017.0	1,172.0	93,887	5.83	7.99	2.4614	296.78
1976	306.3	1,152.7	1,312.0	101,515	4.98	7.61	2.5185	296.45
1977	331.2	1,271.5	1,472.5	110,324	5.26	7.42	2.3236	268.62
1978	358.4	1,368.0	1,646.8	120,445	7.22	8.41	2.0097	210.39
1979	382.9	1,475.7	1,806.6	131,143	10.04	9.44	1.8343	219.02
1980	408.9	1,601.1	1,992.2	142,004	11.50	11.46	1.8175	226.63
1981	436.8	1,756.2	2,240.9	149,021	14.02	13.91	2.2632	220.63
1982	474.6	1,910.8	2,442.3	160,127	10.68	13.00	2.4281	249.06
1983	521.2	2,127.7	2,684.8	175,467	8.63	11.10	2.5539	237.55
1984	552.2	2,312.2	2,979.8	187,333	9.58	12.44	2.8455	237.46
1985	619.9	2,497.6	3,198.3	203,609	7.48	10.62	2.9420	238.47
1986	724.4	2,733.9	3,486.4	223,651	5.98	7.68	2.1705	168.35
1987	749.7	2,832.7	3,672.5	239,799	5.82	8.39	1.7981	144.60
1988	787.0	2,996.3	3,912.9	256,905	6.69	8.85	1.7570	128.17
1989	794.2	3,160.9	4,065.9	267,625	8.12	8.49	1.8808	138.07
1990	825.8	3,279.5	4,125.9	293,190	7.51	8.55	1.6166	145.00
1991	897.3	3,379.6	4,180.4	317,403	5.42	7.86	1.6610	134.59
1992	1,025.0	3,434.0	4,190.4	351,347	3.45	7.01	1.5618	126.78
1993	1,129.8	3,486.6	4,254.4	386,880	3.02	5.87	1.6545	111.08
1994	1,150.7	3,502.1	4,327.3	418,484	4.29	7.09	1.6216	102.18
1995	1,129.0	3,655.0	4,592.5	434,523	5.51	6.57	1.4321	93.96
1996	1,081.1	3,821.8	4,920.5	452,669	5.02	6.44	1.5049	108.78
1997	1,068.7	4,019.3	5,333.0	481,230	5.07	6.35	1.7348	121.06

	U.S. PRICE INDICES				U.S. LABOR FORCE AND PRODUCTIVITY DATA				
	GDP Deflator		**Consumer Price Index**						**Index of**
	Index #	% Change	Index #	% Change	**Civilian Population**	**Labor Force**	**Employment**	**Unemployment Rate**	**Output per Hour**
Year	*(1992 = 100)*		*(1982–84 = 100)*		*(thousands of persons)*			*(%)*	*(1992 = 100)*
1959	22.95	1.0	29.1		115,329	68,369	64,630	5.5	50.5
1960	23.27	1.4	29.6	1.4	117,245	69,628	65,778	5.5	51.4
1961	23.54	1.2	29.9	.7	118,771	70,459	65,746	6.7	53.2
1962	23.84	1.3	30.2	1.3	120,153	70,614	66,702	5.5	55.7
1963	24.12	1.2	30.6	1.6	122,416	71,833	67,762	5.7	57.9
1964	24.48	1.5	31.0	1.0	124,485	73,091	69,305	5.2	60.5
1965	24.96	2.0	31.5	1.9	126,513	74,455	71,088	4.5	62.7
1966	25.67	2.8	32.4	3.5	128,058	75,770	72,895	3.8	65.2
1967	26.49	3.2	33.4	3.0	129,874	77,347	74,732	3.8	66.6
1968	27.64	4.4	34.8	4.7	132,028	78,737	75,920	3.6	68.9
1969	28.94	4.7	36.7	6.2	134,335	80,734	77,902	3.5	69.2
1970	30.48	5.3	38.8	5.6	137,085	82,771	78,678	4.9	70.5
1971	32.06	5.2	40.5	3.3	140,216	84,382	79,367	5.9	73.6
1972	33.42	4.2	41.8	3.4	144,126	87,034	82,153	5.6	76.0
1973	35.30	5.6	44.4	8.7	147,096	89,429	85,064	4.9	78.4
1974	38.47	9.0	49.3	12.3	150,120	91,949	86,794	5.6	77.1
1975	42.09	9.4	53.8	6.9	153,153	93,775	85,846	8.5	79.8
1976	44.55	5.8	56.9	4.9	156,150	96,158	88,752	7.7	82.5
1977	47.43	6.5	60.6	6.7	159,033	99,009	92,017	7.1	83.9
1978	50.89	7.3	65.2	9.0	161,910	102,251	96,048	6.1	84.9
1979	55.23	8.5	72.6	13.3	164,863	104,962	98,824	5.8	84.5
1980	60.33	9.2	82.4	12.5	167,745	106,940	99,303	7.1	84.2
1981	66.01	9.4	90.9	8.9	170,130	108,670	100,397	7.6	85.7
1982	70.17	6.3	96.5	3.8	172,271	110,204	99,526	9.7	85.3
1983	73.16	4.3	99.6	3.8	174,215	111,550	100,834	9.6	88.0
1984	75.92	3.8	103.9	3.9	176,383	113,544	105,005	7.5	90.2
1985	78.53	3.4	107.6	3.8	178,206	115,461	107,150	7.2	91.7
1986	80.58	2.6	109.6	1.1	180,587	117,834	109,597	7.0	94.0
1987	83.06	3.1	113.6	4.4	182,753	119,865	112,440	6.2	94.0
1988	86.09	3.7	118.3	4.4	184,613	121,669	114,968	5.5	94.6
1989	89.72	4.2	124.0	4.6	186,393	123,869	117,342	5.3	95.4
1990	93.60	4.3	130.7	6.1	189,164	125,840	118,793	5.6	96.1
1991	97.32	4.0	136.2	3.1	190,925	126,346	117,718	6.8	96.7
1992	100.00	2.8	140.3	2.9	192,805	128,105	118,492	7.5	100.0
1993	102.64	2.6	144.5	2.7	194,838	129,200	120,259	6.9	100.2
1994	105.09	2.4	148.2	2.7	196,814	131,056	123,060	6.1	100.6
1995	107.76	2.5	152.4	2.5	198,584	132,304	124,900	5.6	100.5
1996	110.21	2.3	156.9	3.3	200,591	133,943	126,708	5.4	102.0
1997	112.40	2.0	160.5	1.7	203,133	136,297	129,558	4.9	103.7